In Litigation

In Litigation

Do the "Haves" Still Come Out Ahead?

Edited by HERBERT M. KRITZER
and SUSAN S. SILBEY

Stanford Law and Politics
An imprint of Stanford University Press
Stanford, California
2003

The editors would like to acknowledge the generous assistance of the Institute for Legal Studies, University of Wisconsin–Madison.

Stanford University Press
Stanford, California

Some chapters of this book were originally published in the *Law & Society Review*. They are reprinted by permission of the Law and Society Association.

Library of Congress Cataloging-in-Publication Data

In litigation : do the "haves" still come out ahead? / edited by Herbert M. Kritzer and Susan S. Silbey.
    p.   cm.
    Includes bibliographical references and index.
    ISBN 0-8047-4733-4 (alk. paper).—ISBN 0-8047-4734-2 (pbk. : alk paper)
    1. Justice, Administration—Social aspects—United States.   2. Actions and defenses—Social aspects—United States.   3. Galanter, Marc, 1931–
I. Kritzer, Herbert M., 1947–   II. Silbey, Susan S.
KF8700.I6 2003
340'.115'0973—dc21   2002154092

Printed in the United States of America on acid-free, archival-quality paper.

Original printing 2003

The last figure below indicates the year of this printing:
12   11   10   09   08   07   06   05   04   03

Designed and typeset at Stanford University Press in 10.5/12 Bembo

Contents

Figures and Tables

Figures

Tables

PART ONE

Beginning with the Theory

1

Introduction

IN 1970 MARC GALANTER, then a visiting fellow in the Program in Law and Modernization at Yale Law School, began writing the paper that was to become "Why the 'Haves' Come Out Ahead." He kept adding to it, elaborating the argument and incorporating examples that friends offered. The paper circulated for several years without finding a willing publisher. It had become somewhat long for a social science journal and not quite the stuff of conventional law reviews. It was "rejected by all the leading law reviews and a couple of political science journals as well" (Galanter 1983:24).[1] A decade after its eventual publication, Galanter happened to encounter one of the student law review editors who had rejected the paper and who had since established a reputation as a prominent scholar. He told Galanter "appreciatively how he assigned this paper to his students every year. He was disbelieving when [Galanter] reminded him that as articles editor of a renowned law review, he had rejected it. Most law review rejections are quite cursory, but [to Galanter] this one was memorable because it gave reasons: the paper was 'fascinating and well written' but controverted 'what we can observe' about the legal system, in which 'have nots' 'increasingly come to look to courts for the protection and articulation of their goals'" (Galanter 1999, 1115n2).

In 1973, Galanter had become the editor of the *Law & Society Review* and had moved to the Law School at the State University of New York at Buffalo. During his second year as editor, following the advice of Richard "Red" Schwartz, who was dean of the Law School at Buffalo (and one of the founders of the Law and Society Association), Galanter took the courageous step of publishing this paper, which had still not found a publishing home. He invited Bliss Cartwright and Robert Kidder to edit a special symposium on litigation and dispute processing for the *Review*. Although

Galanter later recalled that he would have "preferred the paper to have appeared independently of [his] editorship," the issue turned out to be path-breaking, spurring several decades of exciting and important research. "Why the 'Haves' Come Out Ahead: Speculations on the Limits of Legal Change" appeared in volume 9, number 1, of the fall 1974 *Law & Society Review.*

As it turned out, the *Law & Society Review* was the appropriate home for the paper because the essay constituted a theoretically-based synthesis of the results of the accumulating body of empirical research on law that the *Review* had been publishing since its inauguration eight years earlier. Since its publication, "Why the 'Haves' Come Out Ahead" has achieved uncontested canonical stature within the broad range of college and university courses in law and social science.[2] It has been cited more often than any other piece of socio-legal research and is listed among the most well cited law review articles of all time.[3]

Offered as much to provoke further discussion and analysis as to produce definite conclusions, "Why the 'Haves' Come Out Ahead" pushed socio-legal scholarship a step closer toward the scientific ambitions of its European forebears. Defining legal experience in terms of the structural characteristics of the parties, Galanter showed how "the basic architecture of the legal system creates and limits the possibilities of using the system for redistributive change." Dividing litigant parties into "one shotters" and "repeat players," Galanter identified a fundamental and apparently predictive variable (litigant experience) for analyzing all sorts of encounters, from citizen's interpretations of events as injurious to interactions with police or litigants in appeals courts.

A one shotter is a person, business, or organizational entity that deals with the legal system infrequently. The one shotter's claim is too large (relative to the person's or group's organizational size and resources) or too small (relative to the cost of remedies) to be managed routinely and rationally, but a one shotter's interest in winning a particular case is very high.

A repeat player, on the other hand, has had, and anticipates having, repeated litigation. Repeat players usually have low stakes in the outcome of any particular case and have the resources to pursue long-term interests. They can anticipate legal problems and can often structure transactions and compile a record to justify their actions. They develop expertise and have access to specialists who are skilled in dealing with particular types of cases or issues. They enjoy economies of scale and encounter low start-up costs for any particular case. For example, an automobile manufacturer may anticipate challenges to a particular part or system and thus develop legal strategies and invest in research to defend itself. Legal strategies can be modified and developed from one case, or group of cases, to the next. Repeat players can also benefit from informal relations with (and "educate") institutional incumbents such as judges, hearing examiners, and court clerks. The credibility and legitimacy that flow from repeated contacts may help to sustain a repeat player's claims.

Repeat players may not settle a particular case when a one shotter would do so. If a repeat player gives in too easily in one case, it may affect the demands made in the next case. Yet they can play the odds and maximize gain over a series of cases even while suffering heavy losses in some. Seldom will one case be critically important. As a result, repeat players consider questions of precedent over the long run and are able to "play for rules." Repeat players may settle (often with low visibility) cases where they expect unfavorable verdicts or rule outcomes. They can trade symbolic defeats for tangible gains. One shotters, by definition, are necessarily more interested in immediate outcomes.

Galanter also examines litigation configurations. One shotters may sue one shotters. Often such cases are between parties who have some ongoing relationship and who are disputing over some indivisible good. Cost barriers will ration access to the legal system in many of these cases. Repeat players may also sue each other, although the sanctions of long-term continuing relations (which they wish to maintain) tend to minimize such cases. Mediation, arbitration, and settlement may be better options. When repeat players are contesting issues of principle, however, some authoritative resolution may be necessary, and the risks or costs of defeat may have to be endured. Likewise, governmental units may find it difficult to settle high-visibility cases because of the unfavorable publicity likely to be generated. Of course, there are also disputes between repeat players who have no relationship to protect.

Perhaps the remaining two litigation patterns in Galanter's matrix are more interesting. Repeat players may sue one shotters. Sometimes these cases take the form of stereotyped mass processing, bearing little resemblance to full-dress, adversarial litigation. Creditors seek default judgments, attachment of wages, property title confirmations, and so on. Traffic violations are processed routinely. Only a bare few are contested. A court in such cases serves more as an administrative office registering previously determined (or highly predictable) outcomes rather than as either an adjudicator or a locus for bargaining in the shadow of the law. Criminal prosecutions and administrative sanctions also fall into this category. Plea bargains and some settlements have to be approved by a judge, but the outcome is essentially determined elsewhere. The great bulk of litigation falls into this category. No particular case raises major public policy or legal concerns. Taken together, such cases reflect the increasingly bureaucratic attributes of a mass society set within an ideology of liberalism.

Finally, one shotters may sue repeat players. The one shotter may seek outside help to create leverage against an entity or organization with much greater power and resources. For example, a consumer is displeased with repairs to an automobile; an employee seeks redress from adverse working conditions or disputes a job termination; a tenant seeks to compel a landlord to make repairs to a dwelling. In such cases, according to Galanter, the advantages of repeat players are maximized. Although some one shotters do win such lawsuits (especially when they are supported by a third party that is itself a repeat player, such as the Equal Employment Opportunity Commission [EEOC], a tenants' union, or an environmental group or agency), the configuration of the parties and their disparate resources suggest that repeat players will prevail in a large majority of these cases.

Specific features of American legal institutions increase the advantages of repeat players. Claims-handling institutions are largely passive and reactive; the plaintiff or moving party must mobilize them and overcome cost barriers to access and resolution. Some of these barriers can be reduced by devices such as fee shifting and contingent fee arrangements, but burdens still remain. The American adversarial system assumes—because no policies or practices exist to challenge the fact—that the parties are endowed equally with economic resources, investigative opportunities, and legal skills, but that is rarely the case. Moreover, most U.S. legal institutions are also overloaded with cases, further advantaging those with resources. Overload often leads to delay, which is time consuming and discounts the value—or likelihood—of recovery. A litigant must have the resources to keep the case alive. Overload also induces institutional actors to place a high value on clearing dockets, discouraging full-dress adjudication in favor of bargaining and negotiation, settlements, routine processing, and diversion, which are also more likely to favor repeat players. Finally, crowded dockets encourage judges, administrators, and legislators to adopt restrictive rules to discourage litigation.

Although Galanter's empirical focus is on the configuration of power and advantage in litigation, and although he provides an analysis of systematic structural disadvantage, the "Haves" article does not assert a class or power elite analysis (although it is often wrongly claimed to offer just such an analysis). Galanter does not say that members of the dominant class, or organizations with great wealth, always win in litigation. Rather, he focuses on the consequences of organization and system that create structural advantages for repeat players. Moreover, he identifies the ways one shotters without power may be able to gain many of the advantages of a repeat player if they can engage the support of repeat players: organizations or lawyers who regularly handle similar cases. Contingent fees, punitive damages, specialization, and participation in networks of those who regularly handle cases of a particular type may all help one shotters acquire some of the advantages possessed by repeat players.

Currently, much that is called "tort reform," part of a political campaign to limit individual access to the courts, seeks to undermine just those structural devices that allow individuals to hire lawyers who can supply the advantages of repeat playership. The "Haves" paper was written in a different age, in an era of enthusiastic liberal reform rather than conservative reaction. Courts and legislatures were expanding individual rights. Legislatures funded legal services programs. Civil rights and consumer protection statutes provided recompense for lawyer's fees in successful litigations. Law was thought to be a prime catalyst for social change. Galanter was supported by the generous funding of the Program in Law and Modernization at Yale Law School, an emblem of this energizing belief in the power of law to transform the world. This was before the ascent of law and economics, before the emergence of critical legal studies and its progeny, before the movement for alternative dispute resolution, before the attacks on civil rights and social change became organizationally consolidated. It was an age of hopefulness that saw the triumph of the civil rights movement, the proliferation of public interest law, and many experiments in creating greater access to justice. It was the high point of legal services for the poor, the time of the California Rural Legal Assistance and Nader's Raiders. Women had just arrived in the nation's law schools in large numbers. Although establishment lawyers found the ferment worrisome, it was a heady time for those who ardently wished to transform law from an instrument of oppression into a tool of liberation.

"Why the 'Haves' Come Out Ahead" challenged (analytically, rather than politically) the triumphalism of progressive legal scholars. In effect, Galanter attempted to show that, "examined from the bottom up, the United States displayed in a subtle form many of the contradictions that rendered grand programs of reform largely symbolic in their results. Of course, the symbolic role of law was not unfamiliar to law and society scholars" (Galanter, 1999:1115; cf. Gusfield 1963; Edelman 1964). But the social transformations of the 1960s had sought much more than new icons; progressives had sought and achieved redistributive changes in at least some aspects of American law and society. Thus, although Galanter ends on an optimistic note by considering how legal reform could expand the advantages of repeat playing to individuals—so that they could vindicate their rights, the fundamental message was not at all in keeping with the optimism of the times. It was a wake-up call to those who would turn to law for social change.

Times change. Since 1974, movements seeking less government, fewer entitlements, increased personal responsibility, and a reduction in the regulation of wealth and property in favor of greater reliance on the market have been ascendant and successful. Rabid individualism, if not individual rights liberalism, has been the stronger ideology, although challenged by pockets of civic republicanism and similar communitarian perspectives. In the 1960s and early 1970s, there may have been an overemphasis on a "rights strategy" and the efficacy of rights to secure social change. Yet despite its limits, a structure of rights is often a necessary component of change in modern societies with democratic aspirations. Since the 1980s, however, in the United States, these rights, and judicial protection for them, have been steadily eroded by a spate of Supreme Court decisions. Rights are effectively limited; many have been "deconstitutionalized," a more conservative federal judiciary is less aggressive in protecting them, and the Court has placed important new limits on Congress's authority even to legislate in support of rights. Thus, litigation now increasingly offers rights only at a discount, if they are obtainable at all. Moreover, the rhetoric of rights has been picked up by the political Right and has been advanced as a justification for policies reflecting conservative causes; for example, free speech now appears to trump separation of church and state. The result is that where up until the time Galanter wrote "Why the 'Haves' Come Out Ahead" litigation seemed to constitute a liberal strategy for social progress, today conservatives actively engage the legal system to further a very different agenda (Epstein 1985; Den Dulk 2001; Heinz et al. 2002; Southworth 2002; Bisharat 2002).

Anticipating the twenty-fifth anniversary of the publication of "Why the 'Haves' Come Out Ahead," the Institute for Legal Studies at the University of Wisconsin—where Galanter has been teaching, collecting lawyer jokes, and writing these many years—organized a retrospective both to celebrate the paper's fertility and to assess its predictive capacity and prescience. A committee of Joel Grossman, Herbert Kritzer, and Stewart Macaulay selected from among a host of proposed papers the participants in a two-day conference held at the Law School at Wisconsin, May 1–2, 1998. The following summer, the *Law & Society Review* put out a call for papers on the original "Haves" paper. A special issue was published in 1999 (vol. 33, no. 4).[4] The essays in this volume are a selection of those presented at the conference or published in the *Law & Society Review*, plus several new chapters specifically prepared for this volume.

Following this introduction, this volume includes the original paper essentially as it appeared in the *Law & Society Review*.[5] Part two of this volume tests Galanter's hypotheses. Songer, Sheehan, and Haire provide evidence from U.S. Courts of Appeals from 1925 to 1988 that confirms the "Haves" hypotheses, showing that repeat players with considerable organizational strength—the canonical "haves"—are much more likely to win than one-shot litigants, even after controls are introduced for the ideological makeup of the court. Moreover, the advantage in appellate litigation enjoyed by repeat player "haves" is remarkably consistent over time; in particular, the U.S. government—the consummate repeat player—has compiled an impressive record in these courts by dominating opposing litigants over the sixty-four-year period of analysis.

In chapter 4, Harris also provides evidence in support of the "Haves" hypotheses, showing how one shotters can achieve some of the benefits of repeat players. Harris describes the efforts of one group of public interest lawyers—those working in legal services agencies dedicated to law reform—to influence the implementation of redistributive programs for a particular group of "have nots": homeless families or those on the brink of losing their housing. Harris argues that by skillfully combining adversarial legal tactics with collaboration, poverty lawyers can transform judicial decisions into "symbolic resources" to leverage the implementation of redistributive remedies. When the reform lawyers have the authority to participate in the process of administrative rule-making during the implementation process, they can reshape the norms and organizational infrastructures within state agencies. Under these conditions, public interest lawyers can act as repeat players on behalf of the "have nots" during the implementation of judicially imposed remedies. In chapter 5, Kinsey and Stalans examine the role of cultural capital as a mediating variable affecting the parties' capacities in front-line law enforcement encounters. They argue that tax practitioners level the playing field by disrupting social influence and deference processes that would favor repeat players.

Albiston's analysis in chapter 6 elaborates Galanter's model by showing how party capacity works to shape outcomes and doctrinal development through the settlement process as well as through litigation. She argues that repeat players influence the development of law by settling cases they are likely to lose and litigating cases they are likely to win. Although individuals may successfully mobilize the law to gain benefits in their disputes, that success often removes their experiences from the judicial determination of rights, limiting law's capacity to produce social change. This paradox of losing by winning separates the dispute resolution function of courts from their lawmaking function and raises questions about the legitimacy of law.

Chapters 7 and 8 look cross-culturally, finding limited support for the "Haves" hypotheses in Israel and Russia. Dotan shows that in litigation before the Israeli High Court of Justice, the "haves" enjoyed only limited advantage over "have nots" in litigation outcomes. He also found that when "have nots" were represented by legal counsel, the "haves" did not come out ahead. He suggests that the ideological propensities of judges and considerations of institutional autonomy can ameliorate, to some extent, the inherent inferiority of "have nots" in litigation. Dotan also found that the mechanisms that worked in favor of "have nots" operated not only in litigation that reached final judicial disposition but also when the litigation was disposed through out-of-court settlements. Hendley, Murrell, and Ryterman adapt the repeat player concept to the Russian context. Using data from 328 enterprises, they examine whether the concept of the Russian Repeat Players (RRPs) explains the use of protocols of disagreement, petitioning to freeze assets, contractual repayment, and litigation activity. It turns out that RRPs are very different from Galanter's repeat players, generally exhibiting less aggression and innovativeness but suing other RRPs frequently. Examination of factors other than "RRPness" suggests that the presence of lawyers per se is important in determining law-related activity, a result not necessarily expected in Russia.

Part three collects essays that expand Galanter's model with additional theoretical resources. Ewick and Silbey describe the radically different, even contradictory images of law, how it works, and how it ought to work as expressed in ordinary citizens' stories of law. People routinely articulate that the law is not about justice but is rather fixed to advantage the wealthy, big, complex organizations and the usual repeat players: the criminals. This ideological penetration is not complete, however; citizens also describe law as embodying the highest ideals of justice and fairness. In short, the law appears to people as both sacred and profane, God and gimmick, interested and disinterested, here and not here. The multiple and contradictory meanings of legality, Ewick and Silbey argue, protect law from—rather than expose it to—radical critique. Knowing that "the 'haves' come out ahead" operates ideologically to define and sustain legality as a durable and powerful social institution.

Chapter 10 looks inside organizations, the archetypal repeat players in the legal system. Galanter's account, however, devoted relatively little attention to the distinctive legal capacities of organizations as organizations. This chapter extends Galanter's analysis by considering the ability of large bureaucratic organizations to "internalize" legal rules, structure, personnel, and activities. Specifically, Edelman and Suchman posit that the relationship between law and organizations has undergone four interrelated shifts in recent years: (1) the legalization of organization governance; (2) the expansion of private dispute resolution; (3) the rise of in-house counsel; and (4) the reemergence of private policing. These processes interact with one another to transform the large bureaucratic organization from being merely a repeat player in the public legal system to being a full-fledged private legal system in its own right. Although "have not" groups may gain some short-run advantages from the introduction of citizenship norms into the workplace, the organizational annexation of law subtly skews the balance between democratic and bureaucratic tendencies in society as a whole, generally adding to the power and control of dominant elites.

Chapter 11 takes a new look, synthesizing the extensive body of research on party capability. A key finding of that literature is the importance of governments as parties to litigation. Kritzer argues that advantage may not lie so much with "haves" as with governments. Although the evidence presented in previous chapters and elsewhere suggests that parties with more resources have a distinct advantage in litigation, an even greater advantage accrues to governments as parties rather than to individuals or businesses. Moreover, Kritzer argues, the advantage is not merely a consequence of greater resources but derives from government's rule-making authority, with which it can "stack the deck" in its favor, and because, despite formal independence, courts are part of the government. The final chapter by Glenn provides an overall review and assessment of the wide range of research that has been generated by the observation that the "haves" come out ahead, including the fullest possible bibliography to date.

The essays collected in this volume contribute to our quest for understanding the social and political dynamics of the law. They do suggest to us, however, two issues for continuing exploration. First, it appears that, far more than was the case in 1974, government matters. Not only are governments increasingly participants in major litigation, but governmental politics and actions shape the litigation process against which the rituals of the law are played out. If, as we show here, governments are not merely another brand of "official" repeat player, Galanter's configuration of parties needs to reflect this important distinction with a more nuanced and dynamic analysis of relative advantage. Second, and as important, we arrive at a tangle of questions about the relationship between our growing knowledge about the legal world, public perceptions of that world, and the way people act in, through, and with law. Does our knowledge affect the workings of the legal system? Does the effective functioning of legal institutions require the support of myths about the law's moral grandeur? How much cynical knowledge can the public—or scholars—absorb? What does it mean when the "haves" try to convince the "have nots" that the system is unfair and not working well?

Notes

This preface was prepared by editing texts from *Law & Society Review* volume 33, no. 4, (1999), originally authored by Susan Silbey, Herbert Kritzer, Joel Grossman, Stewart Macaulay, and Marc Galanter.

1. In declining the paper, the editor of *Law & Society Review* had "diplomatically said the paper was too long to consider" (Galanter 1983).

2. John Paul Ryan, of the Division for Public Education of the American Bar Association, maintains a library of syllabi for hundreds of law-related courses taught in colleges and universities.

3. The Social Science Citation Index (SSCI) has named it "a citation classic." SSCI lists over 630 citations to the article. A Westlaw search in 2002 of law review publications yielded 584 citations. There is hardly a text or reader in the field that

does not reprint, summarize, or cite it. In "Most Cited Law Review Articles Revisited," Shapiro (1996) calls it a "blockbuster," ranking it thirteenth among the most frequently cited articles in legal scholarship. In their humorous critique of this citation data, Balkin and Levinson describe the Galanter essay's status among the most well cited law review articles as a remarkable Cinderella story because Galanter does not carry the "triple threat" social capital that increases the probabilities of being among the most well cited law review authors. (The "triple threat" is created by scholars who studied at Harvard, Yale, or Chicago; teach at one of these schools; and publish in their law reviews.) Galanter is a single threat, having gone to Chicago; he does have two articles on the list, nonetheless. More important, this story evokes Cinderella because the topic of Galanter's work—the structure of the American legal profession and the litigation system—is not a "hot" topic within the legal academy that might explain citation without high institutional prestige.

4. Actually, the issue did not appear until 2000, although it is dated 1999.

5. We have included a number of minor corrections that Galanter identified for a previous republication of the paper.

References

Bisharat, George E. (2002) "The Pacific Legal Foundation: Lean, Mean, Right Wing Machine." Paper presented at the meeting of Law and Society Association, Vancouver, British Columbia, May 30–June 1.

Den Dulk, Kevin (2001) "Prophets in Caesar's Courts: The Role of Ideas in Catholic and Evangelical Rights Advocacy." Ph.D. dissertation, Department of Political Science, University of Wisconsin–Madison, Chapter 5.

Edelman, Murray (1964) *The Symbolic Uses of Politics*. Urbana: University of Illinois Press.

——— (1971) *Politics as Symbolic Action*. Chicago: Markham Publishing.

Epstein, Lee (1985) *Conservatives in Court*. Knoxville: University of Tennessee Press.

Galanter, Marc (1983) "This Week's Citation Classic." 15 (52) *Current Contents* 24.

——— (1999) 33(4) "Farther Along." *Law & Society Review* 1113–1124.

Gusfield, Joseph (1963) *Symbolic Crusade*. Urbana: University of Illinois Press.

Heinz, John P., Anthony Paik, and Ann Southworth (2002) "Lawyers for Conservative Causes: Clients, Ideology, and Social Distance." Northwestern University Institute for Policy Research Working Paper, no. WP-02-23.

Shapiro, Fred R. (1996) "Most Cited Law Review Articles Revisited." 71 *Chicago Kent Law Review* 751.

Southworth, Ann (2002) "Motivation and Political Commitment in Lawyering for Conservative Causes." Paper presented at the meeting of Law and Society Association, Vancouver, British Columbia, May 30–June 1.

2

Why the "Haves" Come Out Ahead

Speculations on the Limits of Legal Change

THIS ESSAY attempts to discern some of the general features of a legal system like the American by drawing on (and rearranging) commonplaces and less than systematic gleanings from the literature. The speculative and tentative nature of the assertions here will be apparent and is acknowledged here wholesale to spare myself and the reader repeated disclaimers.

I would like to try to put forward some conjectures about the way in which the basic architecture of the legal system creates and limits the possibilities of using the system as a means of redistributive (that is, systemically equalizing) change. Our question, specifically, is, under what conditions can litigation[1] be redistributive, taking litigation in the broadest sense of the presentation of claims to be decided by courts (or court-like agencies) and the whole penumbra of threats, feints, and so forth, surrounding such presentation.

For purposes of this analysis, let us think of the legal system as comprised of these elements:

A body of authoritative normative learning—for short, *RULES*

A set of institutional facilities within which the normative learning is applied to specific cases—for short, *COURTS*

A body of persons with specialized skill in the above—for short, *LAWYERS*

Persons or groups with claims they might make to the courts in reference to the rules, etc.—for short, *PARTIES*

Let us also make the following assumptions about the society and the legal system:

It is a society in which actors with different amounts of wealth and power are constantly in competitive or partially cooperative relationships in which they have opposing interests.

This society has a legal system in which a wide range of disputes and conflicts are settled by court-like agencies which purport to apply pre-existing general norms impartially (that is, unaffected by the identity of the parties).

The rules and the procedures of these institutions are complex: wherever possible disputing units employ specialized intermediaries in dealing with them.

The rules applied by the courts are in part worked out in the process of adjudication (courts devise interstitial rules, combine diverse rules, and apply old rules to new situations). There is a living tradition of such rule-work and a system of communication such that the outcomes in some of the adjudicated cases affect the outcome in classes of future adjudicated cases.

Resources on the institutional side are insufficient for timely full-dress adjudication in every case, so that parties are permitted or even encouraged to forgo bringing cases and to "settle" cases,—that is, to bargain to a mutually acceptable outcome.

There are several levels of agencies, with "higher" agencies announcing (making, interpreting) rules and other "lower" agencies assigned the responsibility of enforcing (implementing, applying) these rules. (Although there is some overlap of function in both theory and practice, I shall treat them as distinct and refer to them as "peak" and "field level" agencies.)

Not all the rules propounded by "peak" agencies are effective at the "field level," due to imperfections in communication, shortages of resources, skill, understanding, commitment and so forth. (Effectiveness at the field level will be referred to as "penetration."[2])

I. A Typology of Parties

Most analyses of the legal system start at the rules end and work down through institutional facilities to see what effect the rules have on the parties. I would like to reverse that procedure and look through the other end of the telescope. Let's think about the different kinds of parties and the effect these differences might have on the way the system works.

Because of differences in their size, differences in the state of the law, and differences in their resources, some of the actors in the society have many occasions to utilize the courts (in the broad sense) to make (or defend) claims; others do so only rarely. We might divide our actors into those claimants who have only occasional recourse to the courts (one-shotters or OS) and repeat players (RP) who are engaged in many similar litigations over time.[3] The spouse in a divorce case, the auto-injury claimant, the criminal accused are OSs; the insurance company, the prosecutor, the finance company are RPs. Obviously this is an oversimplification; there are intermediate cases such as the professional criminal.[4] So we ought to think of OS–RP as a continuum rather than as a dichotomous pair. Typically, the RP is a larger unit and the stakes in any given case are smaller (relative to total worth). OSs are usually smaller units and the stakes represented by the tangible outcome of the case may be high relative to total worth, as in the case of the injury victim or the criminal accused. Or, the OS may suffer from the opposite problem: his claims may be so small and unmanageable (the shortweighted consumer or the holder of performing rights) that the cost of enforcing them outruns any promise of benefit. See Finklestein (1954:284–86).

Let us refine our notion of the RP into an "ideal type" if you will—a unit which has had and anticipates repeated litigation, which has low stakes in the outcome of any one case, and which has the resources to pursue its long-run interests.[5] (This does not include every real-world repeat player; that most common repeat player, the alcoholic derelict, enjoys a few of the advantages that may accrue to the RP [see below]. His resources are too few to bargain in the short run or take heed of the long run.[6]) An OS, on the other hand, is a unit whose claims are too large (relative to his size) or too small (relative to the cost of remedies) to be managed routinely and rationally.

We would expect an RP to play the litigation game differently from an OS. Let us consider some of his advantages:

1. RPs, having done it before, have advance intelligence; they are able to struc-ture the next transaction and build a record. It is the RP who writes the form contract, requires the security deposit, and the like.

2. RPs develop expertise and have ready access to specialists.[7] They enjoy economies of scale and have low start-up costs for any case.[8]

3. RPs have opportunities to develop facilitative informal relations with insti-tutional incumbents.[9]

4. The RP must establish and maintain credibility as a combatant. His interest in his "bargaining reputation" serves as a resource to establish "commitment" to his bargaining positions. With no bargaining reputation to maintain, the OS has more difficulty in convincingly committing himself in bargaining.[10]

5. RPs can play the odds.[11] The larger the matter at issue looms for OS, the more likely he is to adopt a minimax strategy (minimize the probability of maximum loss). Assuming that the stakes are relatively smaller for RPs, they can adopt strategies calculated to maximize gain over a long series of cases, even where this involves the risk of maximum loss[12] in some cases.[13]

6. RPs can play for rules as well as immediate gains. First, it pays an RP to ex-pend resources in influencing the making of the relevant rules by such meth-ods as lobbying.[14] (And his accumulated expertise enables him to do this per-suasively.)

7. RPs can also play for rules in litigation itself, whereas an OS is unlikely to. That is, there is a difference in what they regard as a favorable outcome. Be-cause his stakes in the immediate outcome are high and because by definition OS is unconcerned with the outcome of similar litigation in the future, OS

will have little interest in that element of the outcome which might influence the disposition of the decision-maker next time around. For the RP, on the other hand, anything that will favorably influence the outcomes of future cases is a worthwhile result. The larger the stake for any player and the lower the probability of repeat play, the less likely that he will be concerned with the rules which govern future cases of the same kind. Consider two parents contesting the custody of their only child, the prizefighter vs. the IRS for tax arrears, the convict facing the death penalty. On the other hand, the player with small stakes in the present case and the prospect of a series of similar cases (the IRS, the adoption agency, the prosecutor) may be more interested in the state of the law.

Thus, if we analyze the outcomes of a case into a tangible component and a rule component,[15] we may expect that in case 1, OS will attempt to maximize tangible gain. But if RP is interested in maximizing his tangible gain in a series of cases 1 . . . n, he may be willing to trade off tangible gain in any one case for rule gain (or to minimize rule loss).[16] We assumed that the institutional facilities for litigation were overloaded and settlements were prevalent. We would then expect RPs to "settle" cases where they expected unfavorable rule outcomes.[17] Since they expect to litigate again, RPs can select to adjudicate (or appeal) those cases which they regard as most likely to produce favorable rules.[18] On the other hand, OSs should be willing to trade off the possibility of making "good law" for tangible gain. Thus, we would expect the body of "precedent" cases—that is, cases capable of influencing the outcome of future cases—to be relatively skewed toward those favorable to RP.[19]

Of course it is not suggested that the strategic configuration of the parties is the sole or major determinant of rule-development. Rule-development is shaped by a relatively autonomous learned tradition, by the impingement of intellectual currents from outside, by the preferences and prudences of the decision-makers. But courts are passive and these factors operate only when the process is triggered by parties. The point here is merely to note the superior opportunities of the RP to trigger promising cases and prevent the triggering of unpromising ones. It is not incompatible with a course of rule-development favoring OSs (or, as indicated below, with OSs failing to get the benefit of those favorable new rules).

In stipulating that RPs can play for rules, I do not mean to imply that RPs pursue rule-gain as such. If we recall that not all rules penetrate (i.e., become effectively applied at the field level) we come to some additional advantages of RPs.

RPs, by virtue of experience and expertise, are more likely to be able to discern which rules are likely to "penetrate" and which are likely to remain merely symbolic commitments. RPs may be able to concentrate their resources on rule-changes that are likely to make a tangible difference. They can trade off symbolic defeats for tangible gains.

Since penetration depends in part on the resources of the parties (knowledge, attentiveness, expert services, money), RPs are more likely to be able to invest the matching resources necessary to secure the penetration of rules favorable to them.

It is not suggested that RPs are to be equated with "haves" (in terms of power, wealth and status) or OSs with "have-nots." In the American setting most RPs are larger, richer and more powerful than are most OSs, so these categories overlap, but there are obvious exceptions. RPs may be "have nots" (alcoholic derelicts) or may act as champions of "have nots" (as government does from time to time); OSs such as criminal defendants may be wealthy. What this analysis does is to define a position of advantage in the configuration of contending parties and indicate how those with other advantages tend to occupy this position of advantage and to have their other advantages reinforced and augmented thereby.[20] This position of advantage is one of the ways in which a legal system formally neutral as between "haves" and "have nots" may perpetuate and augment the advantages of the former.[21]

DIGRESSION ON LITIGATION-MINDEDNESS

We have postulated that OSs will be relatively indifferent to the rule-outcomes of particular cases. But one might expect the absolute level of interest in rule-outcomes to vary in different populations: in some there may be widespread and intense concern with securing vindication according to official rules that overshadows interest in the tangible outcomes of disputes; in others rule outcomes may be a matter of relative indifference when compared to tangible outcomes. The level and distribution of such "rule mindedness" may affect the relative strategic position of OSs and RPs. For example, the more rule minded a population, the less we would expect an RP advantage in managing settlement policy.

But such rule mindedness or appetite for official vindication should be distinguished from both (1) readiness to resort to official remedy systems in the first place and (2) high valuation of official rules as symbolic objects. Quite apart from relative concern with rule-outcomes, we might expect populations to differ in their estimates of the propriety and gratification of litigating in the first place.[22] Such attitudes may affect the strategic situation of the parties. For example, the greater the distaste for litigation in a population, the greater the barriers to OSs pressing or defending claims, and the greater the RP advantages, assuming that such sentiments would affect OSs, who are likely to be individuals, more than RPs, who are likely to be organizations.[23] It cannot be assumed that the observed variations in readiness to resort to official tribunals is directly reflective of a "rights consciousness" or appetite for vindication in terms of authoritative norms.[24] Consider the assertion that the low rate of litigation in Japan flows from an undeveloped "sense of justiciable rights" with the implication that the higher rate in the United States flows from such rights-consciousness.[25] But the high rate of settlements and the low rate of appeals in the United States suggest it should not be regarded as having a population with great interest in securing moral victories through official vindication.[26] Mayhew (1973:14, Table I) reports a survey in which a sample of Detroit area residents were asked how they had wanted to see their "most serious problem" settled. Only a tiny minority (0% of landlord-tenant problems; 2% of neighborhood problems; 4% of expensive purchase problems; 9% of public organization problems; 31% of discrimination problems) reported that they sought "justice" or vindication of their legal rights: "most answered that they sought resolution of their problems in some more or less expedient way."

Paradoxically, low valuation of rule-outcomes in particular cases may co-exist with high valuation of rules as symbolic objects. Edelman (1967: chap. 2) distinguishes between remote, diffuse, unorganized publics, for whom rules are a source of symbolic gratification and organized, attentive publics directly concerned with the tangible results of their application. Public appetite for symbolic gratification by the promulgation of rules does not imply a corresponding private appetite for official vindication in terms of rules in particular cases. Attentive RPs on the other hand may be more inclined to regard rules instrumentally as assets rather than as sources of symbolic gratification.

We may think of litigation as typically involving various combinations of OSs and RPs. We can then construct a matrix such as Figure 2.1 and fill in the boxes with some well-known if only approximate American examples. (We ignore for the moment that the terms OS and RP represent ends of a continuum, rather than a dichotomous pair.)

On the basis of our incomplete and unsystematic examples, let us conjecture a bit about the content of these boxes:

Box I: OS vs. OS

The most numerous occupants of this box are divorces and insanity hearings. Most (over 90 per cent of divorces, for example) are uncontested.[27] A large portion of these are really pseudo-litigation, that is, a settlement is worked out between the parties and ratified in the guise of adjudication. When we get real litigation in Box I, it is often between parties who have some intimate tie with one another, fighting over some unsharable good, often with overtones of "spite" and "irrationality." Courts are resorted to where an ongoing relationship is ruptured; they have little to do with the

INITIATOR, CLAIMANT

	One-Shotter	Repeat Player
DEFENDANT		
One-Shotter	I. OS vs OS Parent v. Parent (Custody) Spouse v. Spouse (Divorce) Family v. Family Member (Insanity Commitment) Family v. Family (Inheritance) Neighbor v. Neighbor Partner v. Partner	II. RP vs OS Prosecutor v. Accused Finance Co. v. Debtor Landlord v. Tenant I.R.S. v. Taxpayer Condemnor v. Property Owner
Repeat Player	III. OS vs RP Welfare Client v. Agency Auto Dealer v. Manufacturer Injury Victim v. Insurance Company Tenant v. Landlord Bankrupt Consumer v. Creditors Defamed v. Publisher	IV. RP vs RP Union v. Company Movie Distributor v. Censorship Board Developer v. Suburban Municipality Purchaser v. Supplier Regulatory Agency v. Firms of Regulated Industry

FIGURE 2.1   A taxonomy of litigation by strategic configuration of parties.

routine patterning of activity. The law is invoked *ad hoc* and instrumentally by the parties. There may be a strong interest in vindication, but neither party is likely to have much interest in the long-term state of the law (of, for instance, custody or nuisance). There are few appeals, few test cases, little expenditure of resources on rule-development. Legal doctrine is likely to remain remote from everyday practice and from popular attitudes.[28]

Box II: RP vs. OS

The great bulk of litigation is found in this box—indeed every really numerous kind except personal injury cases, insanity hearings, and divorces. The law is used for routine processing of claims by parties for whom the making of such claims is a regular business activity.[29] Often the cases here take the form of stereotyped mass processing with little of the individuated attention of full-dress adjudication. Even greater numbers of cases are settled "informally" with settlement keyed to possible litigation outcome (discounted by risk, cost, delay).

The state of the law is of interest to the RP, though not to the OS defendants. Insofar as the law is favorable to the RP it is "followed" closely in practice[30] (subject to discount for RP's transaction costs).[31] Transactions are built to fit the rules by creditors, police, draft boards and other RPs.[32] Rules favoring OSs may be less readily applicable, since OSs do not ordinarily plan the underlying transaction, or less meticulously observed in practice, since

OSs are unlikely to be as ready or able as RPs to invest in insuring their penetration to the field level.[33]

Box III: OS vs. RP

All of these are rather infrequent types except for personal injury cases which are distinctive in that free entry to the arena is provided by the contingent fee.[34] In auto injury claims, litigation is routinized and settlement is closely geared to possible litigation outcome. Outside the personal injury area, litigation in Box III is not routine. It usually represents the attempt of some OS to invoke outside help to create leverage on an organization with which he has been having dealings but is now at the point of divorce (for example, the discharged employee or the cancelled franchisee).[35] The OS claimant generally has little interest in the state of the law; the RP defendant, however, is greatly interested.

Box IV: RP vs. RP

Let us consider the general case first and then several special cases. We might expect that there would be little litigation in Box IV, because to the extent that two RPs play with each other repeatedly,[36] the expectation of continued mutually beneficial interaction would give rise to informal bilateral controls.[37] This seems borne out by studies of dealings among businessmen[38] and in labor relations. Official agencies are invoked by unions trying to get established and by management trying to prevent them from getting established, more rarely in dealings between bargaining partners.[39] Units with mutually beneficial relations do not adjust their differences in courts. Where they rely on third parties in dispute-resolution, it is likely to take a form (such as arbitration or a domestic tribunal) detached from official sanctions and applying domestic rather than official rules.

However, there are several special cases. First, there are those RPs who seek not furtherance of tangible interests, but vindication of fundamental cultural commitments. An example would be the organizations which sponsor much church-state litigation.[40] Where RPs are contending about value differences (who is right) rather than interest conflicts (who gets what) there is less tendency to settle and less basis for developing a private system of dispute settlement.[41]

Second, government is a special kind of RP. Informal controls depend upon the ultimate sanction of withdrawal and refusal to continue beneficial relations.[42] To the extent that withdrawal of future association is not possible in dealing with government, the scope of informal controls is correspondingly limited. The development of informal relations between regulatory agencies and regulated firms is well known. And the regulated may have sanctions other than withdrawal which they can apply; for instance, they may threaten political opposition. But the more inclusive the unit of government, the less effective the withdrawal sanction and the greater the likelihood that a party will attempt to invoke outside allies by litigation even while sustaining the ongoing relationship. This applies also to monopolies, units which share the government's relative immunity to withdrawal sanctions.[43] RPs in monopolistic relationships will occasionally invoke formal controls to show prowess, to give credibility to threats, and to provide satisfactions for other audiences. Thus we would expect litigation by and against government to be more frequent than in other RP vs. RP situations. There is a second reason for expecting more litigation when government is a party. That is, that the notion of "gain" (policy as well as monetary) is often more contingent and problematic for governmental units than for other parties, such as businesses or organized interest groups. In some cases courts may, by proffering authoritative interpretations of public policy, redefine an agency's notion of gain. Hence government parties may be more willing to externalize decisions to the courts. And opponents may have more incentive to litigate against government in the hope of securing a shift in its goals.

A somewhat different kind of special case is present where plaintiff and defendant are both RPs but do not deal with each other repeatedly (two insurance companies, for example). In the government/monopoly case, the parties were so inextricably bound together that the force of informal controls was limited; here they are not sufficiently bound to each other to give informal controls their bite; there is nothing to withdraw from! The large one-time deal that falls through, the marginal enterprise—these are staple sources of litigation.

Where there is litigation in the RP vs. RP situation, we might expect that there would be heavy expenditure on rule-development, many appeals, and rapid and elaborate development of the doctrinal law. Since the parties can invest to secure implementation of favorable rules, we would expect practice to be closely articulated to the resulting rules.

On the basis of these preliminary guesses, we can sketch a general profile of litigation and the factors associated with it. The great bulk of litigation is found in Box II; much less in Box III. Most of the litigation in these boxes is mass routine processing of disputes between parties who are strangers (not in mutually beneficial continuing relations) or divorced,[44] and between whom there is a disparity in size. One party is a bureaucratically organized "professional" (in the sense of doing it for a living) who enjoys strategic advantages. Informal controls between the parties are tenuous or ineffective; their relationship is likely to be established and defined by official rules; in litigation, these rules are discounted by transaction costs and manipulated selectively to the advantage of the parties. On the other hand, in Boxes I and IV, we have more infrequent but more individualized litigation between parties of the same general magnitude, among whom there are or were contin-uing multi-stranded relationships with attendant informal controls. Litiga-tion appears when the relationship loses its future value; when its "monop-olistic" character deprives informal controls of sufficient leverage and the parties invoke outside allies to modify it; and when the parties seek to vin-dicate conflicting values.

II. Lawyers

What happens when we introduce lawyers? Parties who have lawyers do better.[45] Lawyers are themselves RPs. Does their presence equalize the par-ties, dispelling the advantage of the RP client? Or does the existence of lawyers amplify the advantage of the RP client? We might assume that RPs (tending to be larger units) who can buy legal services more steadily, in larger quantities, in bulk (by retainer) and at higher rates, would get services of better quality. They would have better information (especially where re-strictions on information about legal services are present).[46] Not only would the RP get more talent to begin with, but he would on the whole get greater continuity, better record-keeping, more anticipatory or preventive work, more experience and specialized skill in pertinent areas, and more control over counsel.

One might expect that just how much the legal services factor would ac-centuate the RP advantage would be related to the way in which the pro-fession was organized. The more members of the profession were identified with their clients (i.e., the less they were held aloof from clients by their loy-alty to courts or an autonomous guild) the more the imbalance would be accentuated.[47] The more close and enduring the lawyer-client relationship, the more the primary loyalty of lawyers is to clients rather than to courts or guild, the more telling the advantages of accumulated expertise and guidance in overall strategy.[48]

What about the specialization of the bar? Might we not expect the exis-tence of specialization to offset RP advantages by providing OS with a spe-cialist who in pursuit of his own career goals would be interested in out-comes that would be advantageous to a whole class of OSs? Does the specialist become the functional equivalent of the RP? We may divide spe-cialists into (1) those specialized by field of law (patent, divorce, etc.), (2) those specialized by the kind of party represented (for example, house coun-sel), and (3) those specialized by both field of law and "side" or party (per-sonal injury plaintiff, criminal defense, labor). Divorce lawyers do not spe-cialize in husbands or wives,[49] nor real-estate lawyers in buyers or sellers. But labor lawyers and tax lawyers and stockholders-derivative-suit lawyers do specialize not only in the field of law but in representing one side. Such spe-

CLIENT	Specialized by Party	LAWYER Specialized by Field and Party	Specialized by Field
Repeat Player	"House Counsel" or General Counsel for Bank, Insurance Co., etc. Corporation Counsel for Government Unit	Prosecutor Personal Injury Defendant Staff Counsel for NAACP Tax Labor/Management Collections	Patent
One-Shotter	"Poverty Lawyers" Legal Aid	Criminal Defense Personal Injury Plaintiff	Bankruptcy Divorce

FIGURE 2.2 A typology of legal specialists.

cialists may represent RPs or OSs. Figure 2.2 provides some well-known examples of different kinds of specialists.

Most specializations cater to the needs of particular kinds of RPs. Those specialists who service OSs have some distinctive features:

First, they tend to make up the "lower echelons" of the legal profession. Compared to the lawyers who provide services to RPs, lawyers in these specialties tend to be drawn from lower socio-economic origins, to have attended local, proprietary or part-time law schools, to practice alone rather than in large firms, and to possess low prestige within the profession.[50] (Of course the correlation is far from perfect; some lawyers who represent OSs do not have these characteristics and some representing RPs do. However, on the whole the difference in professional standing is massive.)

Second, specialists who service OSs tend to have problems of mobilizing a clientele (because of the low state of information among OSs) and encounter "ethical" barriers imposed by the profession which forbid solicitation, advertising, referral fees, advances to clients, and so forth.[51]

Third, the episodic and isolated nature of the relationship with particular OS clients tends to elicit a stereotyped and uncreative brand of legal services. Carlin and Howard (1965:385) observe that:

The quality of service rendered poorer clients is . . . affected by the non-repeating character of the matters they typically bring to lawyers (such as divorce, criminal, personal injury): this combined with the small fees encourages a mass processing of cases. As a result, only a limited amount of time and interest is usually expended on any one case—there is little or no incentive to treat it except as an isolated piece of legal business. Moreover, there is ordinarily no desire to go much beyond the case as the client presents it, and such cases are only accepted when there is a clear-cut cause of action; i.e., when they fit into convenient legal categories and promise a fairly certain return.

Fourth, while they are themselves RPs, these specialists have problems in developing optimizing strategies. What might be good strategy for an insurance company lawyer or prosecutor—trading off some cases for gains on others—is branded as unethical when done by a criminal defense or personal injury plaintiff lawyer.[52] It is not permissible for him to play his series of OSs as if they constituted a single RP.[53]

Conversely, the demands of routine and orderly handling of a whole series of OSs may constrain the lawyer from maximizing advantage for any individual OS. Rosenthal (1970:172) shows that "for all but the largest [personal injury] claims an attorney loses money by thoroughly preparing a case and not settling it early."

For the lawyer who services OSs, with his transient clientele, his permanent "client" is the forum, the opposite party, or the intermediary who supplies clients. Consider, for example, the dependence of the criminal defense lawyer on maintaining cooperative relations with the various members of the "criminal court community."[54] Similarly, Carlin notes that among metropolitan individual practitioners whose clientele consists of OSs, there is a deformation of loyalty toward the intermediary.

In the case of those lawyers specializing in personal injury, local tax, collections, criminal, and to some extent divorce work, the relationship with the client . . . is generally mediated by a broker or business supplier who may be either another lawyer or a layman. In these fields of practice the lawyer is principally concerned with pleasing the broker or winning his approval, more so than he is with satisfying the individual client. The source of business generally counts for more than the client, especially where the client is unlikely to return or to send in other clients. The client is then expendable: he can be exploited to the full. Under these conditions, when a lawyer receives a client . . . he has not so much gained a client as a piece of business, and his attitude is often that of handling a particular piece of merchandise or of developing a volume of a certain kind of merchandise. (Carlin 1962:161–62)[55]

The existence of a specialized bar on the OS side should overcome the gap in expertise, allow some economies of scale, provide for bargaining commitment and personal familiarity. But this is short of overcoming the fundamental strategic advantages of RPs—their capacity to structure the transaction, play the odds, and influence rule-development and enforcement policy.

Specialized lawyers may, by virtue of their identification with parties, become lobbyists, moral entrepreneurs, proponents of reforms on the parties' behalf. But lawyers have a cross-cutting interest in preserving complexity and mystique so that client contact with this area of law is rendered problematic.[56] Lawyers should not be expected to be proponents of reforms which are optimum from the point of view of the clients taken alone. Rather, we would expect them to seek to optimize the clients' position without diminishing that of lawyers. Therefore, specialized lawyers have an interest in a framework which keeps recovery (or whatever) problematic at the same time that they favor changes which improve their clients' position within this framework. (Consider the lobbying efforts of personal injury plaintiffs and defense lawyers.) Considerations of interest are likely to be fused with ideological commitments: the lawyers' preference for complex and finely-tuned bodies of rules, for adversary proceedings, for individualized case-by-case decision-making.[57] Just as the culture of the client population affects strategic position, so does the professional culture of the lawyers.

III. Institutional Facilities

We see then that the strategic advantages of the RP may be augmented by advantages in the distribution of legal services. Both are related to the advantages conferred by the basic features of the institutional facilities for the handling of claims: passivity and overload.

These institutions are passive, first, in the sense that Black refers to as "reactive"—they must be mobilized by the claimant—giving advantage to the claimant with information, ability to surmount cost barriers, and skill to navigate restrictive procedural requirements.[58] They are passive in a further sense that once in the door the burden is on each party to proceed with his case.[59] The presiding official acts as umpire, while the development of the case, collection of evidence and presentation of proof are left to the initiative and resources of the parties.[60] Parties are treated as if they were equally endowed with economic resources, investigative opportunities and legal skills (Cf. Homberger [1971:641]). Where, as is usually the case, they are not, the broader the delegation to the parties, the greater the advantage conferred on the wealthier,[61] more experienced and better organized party.[62]

The advantages conferred by institutional passivity are accentuated by the chronic overload which typically characterizes these institutions.[63] Typically there are far more claims than there are institutional resources for full-dress adjudication of each. In several ways overload creates pressures on claimants to settle rather than to adjudicate:

(a) by causing delay (thereby discounting the value of recovery);

(b) by raising costs (of keeping the case alive);

(c) by inducing institutional incumbents to place a high value on clearing dockets, discouraging full-dress adjudication in favor of bargaining, stereotyping and routine processing;[64]

(d) by inducing the forum to adopt restrictive rules to discourage litigation.[65]

Thus, overload increases the cost and risk of adjudicating and shields existing rules from challenge, diminishing opportunities for rule-change.[66] This
tends to favor the beneficiaries of existing rules.

Second, by increasing the difficulty of challenging going practice, overload also benefits those who reap advantage from the neglect (or systematic
violation) of rules which favor their adversaries.

Third, overload tends to protect the possessor—the party who has the
money or goods—against the claimant.[67] For the most part, this amounts to
favoring RPs over OSs, since RPs typically can structure transactions to put
themselves in the possessor position.[68]

Finally, the overload situation means that there are more commitments in
the formal system than there are resources to honor them—more rights and
rules "on the books" than can be vindicated or enforced. There are, then,
questions of priorities in the allocation of resources. We would expect
judges, police, administrators and other managers of limited institutional facilities to be responsive to the more organized, attentive and influential of
their constituents.[69] Again, these tend to be RPs.

Thus, overloaded and passive institutional facilities provide the setting in
which the RP advantages in strategic position and legal services can have full
play.[70]

IV. Rules[71]

We assume here that rules tend to favor older, culturally dominant interests.[72]
This is not meant to imply that the rules are explicitly designed to favor
these interests,[73] but rather that those groups which have become dominant
have successfully articulated their operations to pre-existing rules.[74] To the
extent that rules are evenhanded or favor the "have nots," the limited resources for their implementation will be allocated, I have argued, so as to
give greater effect to those rules which protect and promote the tangible interests of organized and influential groups. Furthermore, the requirements of
due process, with their barriers or protections against precipitate action, naturally tend to protect the possessor or holder against the claimant.[75] Finally,
the rules are sufficiently complex[76] and problematic (or capable of being
problematic if sufficient resources are expended to make them so) that differences in the quantity and quality of legal services will affect capacity to
derive advantages from the rules.[77]

Thus, we arrive at Figure 2.3 which summarizes why the "haves" tend to
come out ahead. It points to layers of advantages enjoyed by different (but

	Advantages	Enjoyed by
Parties	Ability to structure transaction Specialized expertise, economies of scale Long-term strategy Ability to play for rules Bargaining credibility Ability to invest in penetration	Repeat players (large, professional[*])
Legal services	Skill, specialization, continuity	Organized, professional,[*] wealthy
Institutional facilities	Passivity Cost and delay barriers Favorable priorities	Wealthy, experienced, organized Holders, possessors Beneficiaries of existing rules Organized, attentive
Rules	Favorable rules Due process barriers	Older, culturally dominant Holders, possessors

[*]In the simple sense of "doing it for a living."

FIGURE 2.3 Why the "haves" tend to come out ahead.

largely overlapping) classes of "haves"—advantages which interlock, reinforcing and shielding one another.

V. Alternatives to the Official System

We have been discussing resort to the official system to put forward (or defend against) claims. Actually, resort to this system by claimants (or initiators) is one of several alternatives. Our analysis should consider the relationship of the characteristics of the total official litigation system to its use *vis-à-vis* the alternatives. These include at least the following:

(1) Inaction—"lumping it," not making a claim or complaint. This is done all the time by "claimants" who lack information or access[78] or who knowingly decide gain is too low, cost too high (including psychic cost of litigating where such activity is repugnant). Costs are raised by lack of information or skill, and also include risk. Inaction is also familiar on the part of official complainers (police, agencies, prosecutors) who have incomplete information about violations, limited resources, policies about *de minimus*, schedules of priorities, and so forth.[79]

(2) "Exit"—withdrawal from a situation or relationship by moving, resigning, severing relations, finding new partners, etc. This is of course a very common expedient in many kinds of trouble. Like "lumping it," it is an alternative to invocation of any kind of remedy system—although its presence as a sanction

may be important to the working of other remedies.[80] The use of "exit" options depends on the availability of alternative opportunities or partners (and information about them), the costs of withdrawal, transfer, relocation, development of new relationships, the pull of loyalty to previous arrangements—and on the availability and cost of other remedies.[81]

(3) Resort to some unofficial control system—we are familiar with many instances in which disputes are handled outside the official litigation system. Here we should distinguish (a) those dispute-settlement systems which are normatively and institutionally appended to the official system (such as settlement of auto-injuries, handling of bad checks) from (b) those settlement systems which are relatively independent in norms and sanctions (such as businessmen settling disputes *inter se*, religious groups, gangs).

What we might call the "appended" settlement systems merge imperceptibly into the official litigation system. We might sort them out by the extent to which the official intervention approaches the adjudicatory mode. We find a continuum from situations where parties settle among themselves with an eye to the official rules and sanctions, through situations where official intervention is invoked, to those in which settlement is supervised and/or imposed by officials, to full-dress adjudication (see Figure 2.4). All along this line the sanction is supplied by the official system (though not always in the manner prescribed in the "higher law")[82] and the norms or rules applied are a version of the official rules, although discounted for transaction costs and distorted by their selective use for the purposes of the parties. From these "appended" systems of discounted and privatized official justice, we should distinguish those informal systems of "private justice" which invoke other norms and other sanctions. Such systems of dispute-settlement are typical among people in continuing interaction such as an organized group, a trade, or a university.[83] In sorting out the various types according to the extent and the mode of intervention of third parties, we can distinguish two dimensions: the first is the degree to which the applicable norms are formally articulated, elaborated, and exposed, that is the increasingly organized character of the norms. The second represents the degree to which initiative and binding authority are accorded to the third party, that is, the increasingly organized character of the sanctions. Some conjectures about the character of some of the common types of private systems are presented in Figure 2.5.

Our distinction between "appended" and "private" remedy systems should not be taken as a sharp dichotomy but as pointing to a continuum along which we might range the various remedy systems.[84] There is a clear distinction between appended systems like automobile injury or bad check settlements and private systems like the internal regulation of the Mafia (Cressey, 1969: Chaps. VIII, IX; Ianni, 1972), or the Chinese community.[85]

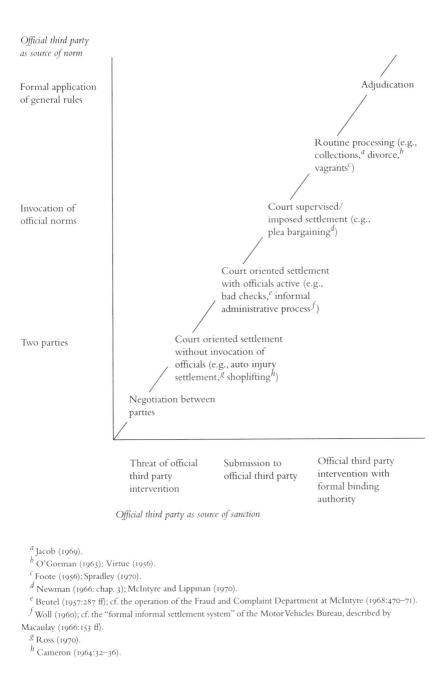

Official third party as source of norm

Formal application of general rules

Invocation of official norms

Two parties

Adjudication

Routine processing (e.g., collections,[a] divorce,[b] vagrants[c])

Court supervised/ imposed settlement (e.g., plea bargaining[d])

Court oriented settlement with officials active (e.g., bad checks,[e] informal administrative process[f])

Court oriented settlement without invocation of officials (e.g., auto injury settlement,[g] shoplifting[h])

Negotiation between parties

Threat of official third party intervention

Submission to official third party

Official third party intervention with formal binding authority

Official third party as source of sanction

[a] Jacob (1969).

[b] O'Gorman (1963); Virtue (1956).

[c] Foote (1956); Spradley (1970).

[d] Newman (1966: chap. 3); McIntyre and Lippman (1970).

[e] Beutel (1957:287 ff); cf. the operation of the Fraud and Complaint Department at McIntyre (1968:470–71).

[f] Woll (1960); cf. the "formal informal settlement system" of the Motor Vehicles Bureau, described by Macaulay (1966:153 ff).

[g] Ross (1970).

[h] Cameron (1964:32–36).

FIGURE 2.4 "Appended" dispute-settlement systems.

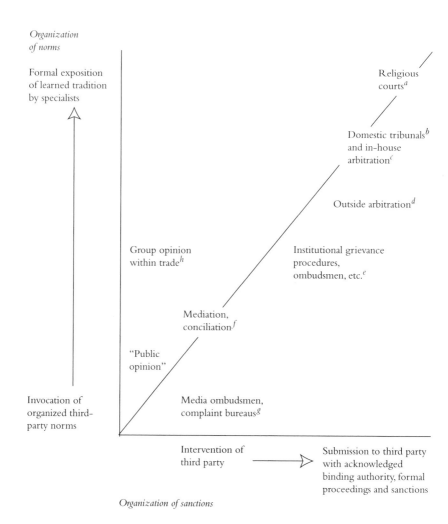

*Organization
of norms*

Formal exposition
of learned tradition
by specialists

Religious
courts[a]

Domestic tribunals[b]
and in-house
arbitration[c]

Outside arbitration[d]

Group opinion
within trade[h]

Institutional grievance
procedures,
ombudsmen, etc.[e]

Mediation,
conciliation[f]

"Public
opinion"

Invocation of
organized third-
party norms

Media ombudsmen,
complaint bureaus[g]

Intervention of
third party

Submission to third party
with acknowledged
binding authority, formal
proceedings and sanctions

Organization of sanctions

[a] Columbia J. of Law and Social Problems (1970, 1971); Shriver (1966); Ford (1970:457–79).
[b] E.g., The International Air Transport Association (Gollan 1970); professional sports leagues and associations (Goldpaper 1971).
[c] Mentschikoff (1961:859).
[d] Bonn (1972); Mentschikoff (1961:856–57).
[e] Gellhorn, 1966; Anderson (1969: chaps IV, V).
[f] E.g., labor-management (Simkin 1971: chap. 3); MacCallum (1967).
[g] E.g., newspaper "action-line" columns, Better Business Bureaus.
[h] Macaulay (1963:63–64); Leif (1970a:29 ff).

FIGURE 2.5 "Private" remedy systems.

REMEDY SYSTEMS

Official		Appended		Private			
Adjudica-tion	Routine processing	Struc-turally interstitial (officials partici-pating)	Oriented to official	Articu-lated to official	Indepen-dent		Oppositional
	Collec-tions, divorce	Plea bar-gaining, bad check recovery	Auto injury settlement	Business-men	Churches, Chinese commu-nity	Gangs	Mafia, revolu-tionaries

EXAMPLES

FIGURE 2.6 A scale of remedy systems from official to private.

The internal regulatory aspects of universities, churches and groups of businessmen lie somewhere in between.[86] It is as if we could visualize a scale stretching from the official remedy system through ones oriented to it through relatively independent systems based on similar values to independent systems based on disparate values (see Figure 2.6).[87]

Presumably it is not accidental that some human encounters are regulated frequently and influentially by the official and its appended systems while others seem to generate controls that make resort to the official and its appended systems rare. Which human encounters are we likely to find regulated at the "official" end of our scale and which at the "private" end? It is submitted that location on our scale varies with factors that we might sum up by calling them the "density" of the relationship. That is, the more inclusive in life-space and temporal span a relationship between parties,[88] the less likely it is that those parties will resort to the official system[89] and more likely that the relationship will be regulated by some independent "private" system.[90] This seems plausible because we would expect inclusive and enduring relationships to create the possibility of effective sanctions;[91] and we would expect participants in such relationships to share a value consensus[92] which provided standards for conduct and legitimized such sanctions in case of deviance.

EXAMPLES

The prevalence of private systems does not necessarily imply that they embody values or norms which are competing or opposed to those of the official system. Our analysis does not impute the plurality of remedy systems to cultural differences as such. It implies that the official system is utilized when there is a disparity between social structure and cultural norm. It is used, that is, where interaction and vulnerability create encounters and relationships which do not generate shared norms (they may be insufficiently shared or insufficiently specific) and/or do not give rise to group structures which permit sanctioning these norms.[93]

Figure 2.7 sketches out such relationships of varying density and suggests the location of various official and private remedy systems.

It restates our surmise of a close association between the density of relationships and remoteness from the official system.[94] We may surmise further that on the whole the official and appended systems flourish in connection with the disputes between parties of disparate size which give rise to the litigation in Boxes II and III of Figure 2.1. Private remedy systems, on the other hand, are more likely to handle disputes between parties of comparable size.[95] The litigation in Boxes I and IV of Figure 2.1, then, seems to represent in large measure the breakdown (or inhibited development) of private remedy systems. Indeed, the distribution of litigation generally forms a mirror image of the presence of private remedy systems. But the mirror is, for the various reasons discussed here, a distorting one.

From the vantage point of the "higher law" what we have called the official system may be visualized as the "upper" lawyers of a massive "legal"[96] iceberg, something like this:

Adjudication

Litigation

Appended Settlement Systems

Private Settlement Systems

Exit Remedies/Self-Help

Inaction ("lumping it")

The uneven and irregular layers are distinct although they merge imperceptibly into one another.[97] As we proceed to discuss possible reforms of the official system, we will want to consider the kind of impact they will have on the whole iceberg.

We will look at some of the connections and flows between layers mainly from the point of view of the construction of the iceberg itself, but aware that flows and connections are also influenced by atmospheric (cultural) factors such as appetite for vindication, psychic cost of litigation, lawyers' culture and the like.

VI. Strategies for Reform

Our categorization of four layers of advantage (Figure 2.3) suggests a typology of strategies for "reform" (taken here to mean equalization-conferring

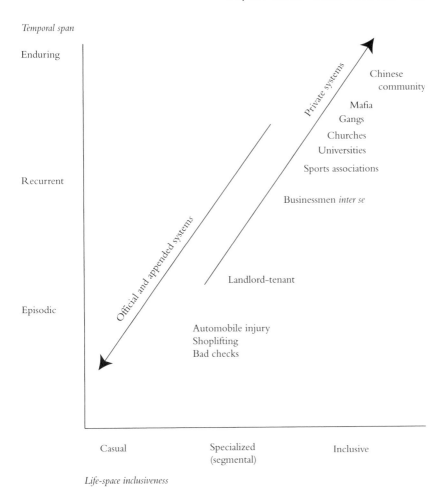

FIGURE 2.7 Relationship between density of social relationships and type of remedy system.

relative advantage on those who did not enjoy it before). We then come to four types of equalizing reform:

(1) rule-change

(2) improvement in institutional facilities

(3) improvement of legal services in quantity and quality

(4) improvement of strategic position of "have not" parties

I shall attempt to sketch some of the possible ramifications of change on each of these levels for other parts of the litigation system and then discuss the relationship between changes in the litigation system and the rest of our legal iceberg. Of course such reforms need not be enacted singly, but may occur in various combinations. However, for our purposes we shall only discuss, first, each type taken in isolation and then, all taken together.

RULE-CHANGE

Obtaining favorable rule-changes is an expensive process. The various kinds of "have nots" (Figure 2.3) have fewer resources to accomplish changes through legislation or administrative policy-making. The advantages of the organized, professional, wealthy and attentive in these forums are well-known. Litigation, on the other hand, has a flavor of equality. The parties are "equal before the law" and the rules of the game do not permit them to deploy all of their resources in the conflict, but require that they proceed within the limiting forms of the trial. Thus, litigation is a particularly tempting arena to "have nots," including those seeking rule-change.[98] Those who seek change through the courts tend to represent relatively isolated interests, unable to carry the day in more political forums.[99]

Litigation may not, however, be a ready source of rule-change for "have nots." Complexity, the need for high inputs of legal services and cost barriers (heightened by overloaded institutional facilities) make challenge of rules expensive. OS claimants, with high stakes in the tangible outcome, are unlikely to try to obtain rule-changes. By definition, a test case—litigation deliberately designed to procure rule-change—is an unthinkable undertaking for an OS. There are some departures from our ideal type: OSs who place a high value on vindication by official rules or whose peculiar strategic situation makes it in their interest to pursue rule victories.[100] But generally the test-case involves some organization which approximates an RP.[101]

The architecture of courts severely limits the scale and scope of changes they can introduce in the rules. Tradition and ideology limit the kinds of matters that come before them; not patterns of practice but individual instances, not "problems" but cases framed by the parties and strained through requirements of standing, case or controversy, jurisdiction, and so forth. Tradition and ideology also limit the kind of decision they can give. Thus, common law courts for example, give an all-or-none,[102] once-and-for-all[103] decision which must be justified in terms of a limited (though flexible) corpus of rules and techniques.[104] By tradition, courts cannot address problems by devising new regulatory or administrative machinery (and have no taxing and spending powers to support it); courts are limited to solutions compatible with the existing institutional framework.[105] Thus, even the most favorably inclined court may not be able to make those rule-changes most useful to a class of "have nots."

Rule-change may make use of the courts more attractive to "have nots." Apart from increasing the possibility of favorable outcomes, it may stimulate organization, rally and encourage litigants. It may directly redistribute symbolic rewards to "have nots" (or their champions). But tangible rewards do not always follow symbolic ones. Indeed, provision of symbolic rewards to "have nots" (or crucial groups of their supporters) may decrease capacity and drive to secure redistribution of tangible benefits.[106]

Rule-changes secured from courts or other peak agencies do not penetrate automatically and costlessly to other levels of the system, as attested by the growing literature on impact.[107] This may be especially true of rule-change secured by adjudication, for several reasons:

(1) Courts are not equipped to assess systematically the impact or penetration problem. Courts typically have no facilities for surveillance, monitoring, or securing systematic enforcement of their decrees. The task of monitoring is left to the parties.[108]

(2) The built-in limits on applicability due to the piecemeal character of adjudication. Thus a Mobilization for Youth lawyer reflects:

. . . What is the ultimate value of winning a test case? In many ways a result cannot be clearcut . . . if the present welfare-residency laws are invalidated, it is quite possible that some other kind of welfare-residency law will spring up in their place. It is not very difficult to come up with a policy that is a little different, stated in different words, but which seeks to achieve the same basic objective. The results of test cases are not generally self-executing. . . . It is not enough to have a law invalidated or a policy declared void if the agency in question can come up with some variant of that policy, not very different in substance but sufficiently different to remove it from the effects of the court order. (Rothwax 1969:143).[109]

(3) The artificial equalizing of parties in adjudication by insulation from the full play of political pressures—the "equality" of the parties, the exclusion of "irrelevant" material, the "independence" of judges—means that judicial outcomes are more likely to be at variance with the existing constellation of political forces than decisions arrived at in forums lacking such insulation. But resources that cannot be employed in the judicial process can reassert themselves at the implementation stage, especially where institutional overload requires another round of decision making (what resources will be deployed to implement which rules) and/or private expenditures to secure implementation. Even where "have nots" secure favorable changes at the rule level, they may not have the resources to secure the penetration of these rules.[110] The impotence of rule-change, whatever its source, is particularly pronounced when there is reliance on unsophisticated OSs to utilize favorable new rules.[111]

Where rule-change promulgated at the peak of the system does have an impact on other levels, we should not assume any isomorphism. The effect on institutional facilities and the strategic position of the parties may be far different than we would predict from the rule-change. Thus, Randall's study of movie censorship shows that liberalization of the rules did not make censorship boards more circumspect; instead, many closed down and the old game between censorship boards and distributors was replaced by a new and rougher game between exhibitors and local government-private group coalitions.[112]

INCREASE IN INSTITUTIONAL FACILITIES

Imagine an increase in institutional facilities for processing claims such that there is timely full-dress adjudication of every claim put forward—no queue, no delay, no stereotyping. Decrease in delay would lower costs for claimants, taking away this advantage of possessor-defendants. Those relieved of the necessity of discounting recovery for delay would have more to spend on legal services. To the extent that settlement had been induced by delay (rather than insuring against the risk of unacceptable loss), claimants would be inclined to litigate more and settle less. More litigation without stereotyping would mean more contests, including more contesting of rules and more rule-change. As discounts diminished, neither side could use settlement policy to prevent rule-loss. Such reforms would for the most part benefit OS claimants, but they would also improve the position of those RP claimants not already in the possessor position, such as the prosecutor where the accused is free on bail.

This assumes no change in the *kind* of institutional facilities. We have merely assumed a greater quantitative availability of courts of the relatively passive variety typical of (at least) "common law" systems in which the case is "tried by the parties before the court. . . . " (Homberger, 1970:31). One may imagine institutions with augmented authority to solicit and supervise litigation, conduct investigations, secure, assemble and present proof; which enjoyed greater flexibility in devising outcomes (such as compromise or mediation); and finally which had available staff for monitoring compliance with their decrees.[113] Greater institutional "activism" might be expected to reduce advantages of party expertise and of differences in the quality and quantity of legal services. Enhanced capacity for securing compliance might be expected to reduce advantages flowing from differences in ability to invest in enforcement. It is hardly necessary to point out that such reforms could be expected to encounter not only resistance from the beneficiaries of the present passive institutional style, but also massive ideological opposition from legal professionals whose fundamental sense of legal propriety would be violated.[114]

INCREASE IN LEGAL SERVICES

The reform envisaged here is an increase in quantity and quality of legal services to "have nots" (including greater availability of information about these services).[115] Presumably this would lower costs, remove the expertise advantage, produce more litigation with more favorable outcomes for "have nots," perhaps with more appeals and more rule challenges, more new rules in their favor. (Public defender, legal aid, judicare, and pre-payment plans approximate this in various fashions.) To the extent that OSs would still have to discount for delay and risk, their gains would be limited (and increase in litigation might mean even more delay). Under certain conditions, increased legal services might use institutional overload as leverage on behalf of "have nots." Our Mobilization for Youth attorney observes:

. . . if the Welfare Department buys out an individual case, we are precluded from getting a principle of law changed, but if we give them one thousand cases to buy out, that law has been effectively changed whether or not the law as written is changed. The practice is changed; the administration is changed; the attitude to the client is changed. The value of a heavy case load is that it allows you to populate the legal process. It allows you to apply remitting pressure on the agency you are dealing with. It creates a force that has to be dealt with, that has to be considered in terms of the decisions that are going to be made prospectively. It means that you are not somebody who will be gone tomorrow, not an isolated case, but a force in the community that will remain once this particular case has been decided.

As a result . . . we have been able, for the first time to participate along with welfare recipients . . . in a rule-making process itself. . . . (Rothwax, 1969:140–41).

The increase in quantity of legal services was accompanied here by increased coordination and organization on the "have not" side, which brings us to our fourth level of reform.

REORGANIZATION OF PARTIES

The reform envisaged here is the organization of "have not" parties (whose position approximates OS) into coherent groups that have the ability to act in a coordinated fashion, play long-run strategies, benefit from high-grade legal services, and so forth.

One can imagine various ways in which OSs might be aggregated into RPs. They include (1) the membership association–bargaining agent (trade unions, tenant unions); (2) the assignee-manager of fragmentary rights (performing rights associations like ASCAP); (3) the interest group-sponsor (NAACP, ACLU, environmental action groups).[116] All of these forms involve upgrading capacities for managing claims by gathering and utilizing information, achieving continuity and persistence, employing expertise, exercising bargaining skill and so forth. These advantages are combined with enhancement of the OS party's strategic position either by aggregating claims that are too small relative to the cost of remedies (consumers, breathers of polluted air, owners of performing rights); or by reducing claims to manageable size by collective action to dispel or share unacceptable risks (tenants, migrant workers).[117] A weaker form of organization would be (4) a clearing-house which established a communication network among OSs. This would lower the costs of information and give RPs a stake in the effect OSs could have on their reputation. A minimal instance of this is represented by the "media ombudsman"—the "action line" type of newspaper column. Finally, there is governmentalization—utilizing the criminal law or the administrative process to make it the responsibility of a public officer to press claims that would be unmanageable in the hands of private grievants.[118]

An organized group is not only better able to secure favorable rule-changes, in courts and elsewhere, but is better able to see that good rules are implemented.[119] It can expend resources on surveillance, monitoring, threats, or litigation that would be uneconomic for an OS. Such new units would in effect be RPs.[120] Their encounters with opposing RPs would move into Box IV of Figure 2.1. Neither would enjoy the strategic advantages of RPs over OSs. One possible result, as we have noted in our discussion of the RP v. RP situation, is delegalization, that is, a movement away from the official system to a private system of dispute-settlement; another would be more intense use of the official system.

Many aspects of "public interest law" can be seen as approximations of this reform. (1) The class action is a device to raise the stakes for an RP, reducing his strategic position to that of an OS by making the stakes more than he can afford to play the odds on,[121] while moving the claimants into a position in which they enjoy the RP advantages without having to undergo the outlay for organizing. (2) Similarly, the "community organizing" aspect of public interest law can be seen as an effort to create a unit (tenants, consumers) which can play the RP game. (3) Such a change in strategic position creates the possibility of a test-case strategy for getting rule-change.[122] Thus "public interest law" can be thought of as a combination of community organizing, class action and test-case strategies, along with increase in legal services.[123]

VII. Reform and the Rest of the Iceberg

The reforms of the official litigation system that we have imagined would, taken together, provide rules more favorable to the "have nots." Redress according to the official rules, undiscounted by delay, strategic disability, disparities of legal services and so forth could be obtained whenever either party found it to his advantage. How might we expect such a utopian upgrading of the official machinery to affect the rest of our legal iceberg?

We would expect more use of the official system. Those who opted for inaction because of information or cost barriers and those who "settled" at discount rates in one of the "appended" systems would in many instances find it to their advantage to use the official system. The appended systems, insofar as they are built on the costs of resort to the official system, would either be abandoned or the outcomes produced would move to approximate closely those produced by adjudication.[124]

On the other hand, our reforms would, by organizing OSs, create many situations in which *both* parties were organized to pursue their long-run interest in the litigation arena. In effect, many of the situations which occupied Boxes II and III of Figure 2.1 (RP v. OS, OS v. RP)—the great staple sources of litigation—would now be moved to Box IV (RP v. RP). We observed earlier that RPs who anticipate continued dealings with one another tend to rely on informal bilateral controls. We might expect then that the official system would be abandoned in favor of private systems of dispute-settlement.[125]

Thus we would expect our reforms to produce a dual movement: the official and its appended systems would be "legalized"[126] while the proliferation of private systems would "de-legalize" many relationships. Which relationships would we expect to move which way? As a first approximation, we might expect that the less "inclusive" relationships currently handled by litigation or in the appended systems would undergo legalization, while relationships at the more inclusive end of the scales (Figure 2.7) would be privatized. Relationships among strangers (casual, episodic, non-recurrent) would be legalized: more dense (recurrent, inclusive) relationships between parties would be candidates for the development of private systems.

Our earlier analysis suggests that the pattern might be more complex. First, for various reasons a class of OSs may be relatively incapable of being organized. Its size, relative to the size and distribution of potential benefits, may require disproportionately large inputs of coordination and organization.[127] Its shared interest may be insufficiently respectable to be publicly acknowledged (for instance, shoplifters, homosexuals until very recently). Or recurrent OS roles may be staffed by shifting population for whom the sides of the transaction are interchangeable.[128] (For instance, home buyers and sellers, negligent motorists and accident victims.)[129] Even where OSs are organizable, we recall that not all RP v. RP encounters lead to the development of private remedy systems. There are RPs engaged in value conflict; there are those relationships with a governmental or other monopoly aspect in which informal controls may falter; and finally there are those RPs whose encounters with one another are nonrecurring. In all of these we might expect legalization rather than privatization.

Whichever way the movement in any given instance, our reforms would entail changes in the distribution of power. RPs would no longer be able to wield their strategic advantages to invoke selectively the enforcement of favorable rules while securing large discounts (or complete shielding by cost and overload) where the rules favored their OS opponents.

Delegalization (by the proliferation of private remedy and bargaining systems) would permit many relationships to be regulated by norms and understandings that departed from the official rules. Such parochial remedy systems would be insulated from the impingement of the official rules by the commitment of the parties to their continuing relationship. Thus, delegalization would entail a kind of pluralism and decentralization. On the other hand, the "legalization" of the official and appended systems would amount to the collapse of species of pluralism and decentralization that are endemic in the kind of (unreformed) legal system we have postulated. The current prevalence of appended and private remedy systems reflects the inefficiency, cumbersomeness and costliness of using the official system. This inefficient, cumbersome and costly character is a source and shield of a kind of decentralization and pluralism. It permits a selective application of the "higher law" in a way that gives effect at the operative level to parochial norms and concerns which are not fully recognized in the "higher law" (such as the right to exclude low status neighbors,[130] or police dominance in encounters with citizens[131]). If the insulation afforded by the costs of getting the "higher law" to prevail were eroded, many relationships would suddenly be exposed to the "higher law" rather than its parochial counterparts. We might expect this to generate new pressures for explicit recognition of these "subterranean" values or for explicit decentralization.

These conjectures about the shape that a "reformed" legal system might take suggest that we take another look at our unreformed system, with its pervasive disparity between authoritative norms and everyday operations. A modern legal system of the type we postulated is characterized structurally by institutional unity and culturally by normative universalism. The power to make, apply and change law is reserved to organs of the public, arranged in unified hierarchic relations, committed to uniform application of universalistic norms.

There is, for example, in American law (that is, in the higher reaches of the system where the learned tradition is propounded) an unrelenting stress on the virtues of uniformity and universality and a pervasive distaste for particularism, compromise and discretion.[132] Yet the cultural attachment to universalism is wedded to and perhaps even intensifies diversity and particularism at the operative level.[133]

The unreformed features of the legal system then appear as a device for maintaining the partial dissociation of everyday practice from these authoritative institutional and normative commitments. Structurally (by cost and institutional overload) and culturally (by ambiguity and normative overload) the unreformed system effects a massive covert delegation from the most authoritative rule-makers to field level officials (and their constituencies) responsive to other norms and priorities than are contained in the "higher law."[134] By their selective application of rules in a context of parochial understandings and priorities, these field level legal communities produce regulatory outcomes which could not be predicted by examination of the authoritative "higher law."[135]

Thus its unreformed character articulates the legal system to the discontinuities of culture and social structure; it provides a way of accommodating cultural heterogeneity and social diversity while propounding universalism and unity; of accommodating vast concentrations of private power while upholding the supremacy of public authority; of accommodating inequality in fact while establishing equality at law; of facilitating action by great collective combines while celebrating individualism. Thus "unreform"—that is, ambiguity and overload of rules, overloaded and inefficient institutional facilities, disparities in the supply of legal services, and disparities in the strategic position of parties—is the foundation of the "dualism"[136] of the legal system. It permits unification and universalism at the symbolic level and diversity and particularism at the operating level.[137]

VIII. Implications for Reform: The Role of Lawyers

We have discussed the way in which the architecture of the legal system tends to confer interlocking advantages on overlapping groups whom we have called the "haves." To what extent might reforms of the legal system dispel these advantages? Reforms will always be less total than the utopian ones envisioned above. Reformers will have limited resources to deploy and they will always be faced with the necessity of choosing which uses of those resources are most productive of equalizing change. What does our analysis suggest about strategies and priorities?

Our analysis suggests that change at the level of substantive rules is not likely in itself to be determinative of redistributive outcomes. Rule-change is in itself likely to have little effect because the system is so constructed that changes in the rules can be filtered out unless accompanied by changes at other levels. In a setting of overloaded institutional facilities, inadequate costly legal services, and unorganized parties, beneficiaries may lack the resources to secure implementation; or an RP may restructure the transaction to escape the thrust of the new rule. (Leff, 1970b; Rothwax, 1969:143; Cf. Grossman, 1970.) Favorable rules are not necessarily (and possibly not typically) in short supply to "have nots"; certainly less so than any of the other resources needed to play the litigation game.[138] Programs of equalizing reform which focus on rule-change can be readily absorbed without any change in power relations. The system has the capacity to change a great deal at the level of rules without corresponding changes in everyday patterns of practice[139] or distribution of tangible advantages. (See, for example, Lipsky, 1970: chap. 4, 5.) Indeed rule-change may become a symbolic substitute for redistribution of advantages. (See Edelman, 1967:40.)

The low potency of substantive rule-change is especially the case with rule-changes procured from courts. That courts can sometimes be induced to propound rule-changes that legislatures would not make points to the limitations as well as the possibilities of court-produced change. With their relative insulation from retaliation by antagonistic interests, courts may more easily propound new rules which depart from prevailing power relations. But such rules require even greater inputs of other resources to secure effective implementation. And courts have less capacity than other rule-makers to create institutional facilities and re-allocate resources to secure implementation of new rules. Litigation then is unlikely to shape decisively the distribution of power in society. It may serve to secure or solidify symbolic commitments. It is vital tactically in securing temporary advantage or protection, providing leverage for organization and articulation of interests and conferring (or withholding) the mantle of legitimacy.[140] The more divided the other holders of power, the greater the redistributive potential of this symbolic/tactical role. (Dahl, 1958:294.)

Our analysis suggests that breaking the interlocked advantages of the "haves" requires attention not only to the level of rules, but also to institutional facilities, legal services and organization of parties. It suggests that litigating and lobbying have to be complemented by interest organizing, provisions of services and invention of new forms of institutional facilities.[141]

The thrust of our analysis is that changes at the level of parties are most likely to generate changes at other levels. If rules are the most abundant resource for reformers, parties capable of pursuing long-range strategies are the rarest. The presence of such parties can generate effective demand for high grade legal services—continuous, expert, and oriented to the long run—and pressure for institutional reforms and favorable rules. This suggests that we can roughly surmise the relative strategic priority of various rule-changes. Rule-changes which relate directly to the strategic position of the parties by facilitating organization, increasing the supply of legal services (where these in turn provide a focus for articulating and organizing common interests) and increasing the costs of opponents—for instance authorization of class action suits, award of attorneys fees and costs, award of provisional remedies—these are the most powerful fulcrum for change.[142] The intensity of the opposition to class action legislation and autonomous reform-oriented legal services[143] such as California Rural Legal Assistance indicates the "haves" own estimation of the relative strategic impact of the several levels.[144]

The contribution of the lawyer to redistributive social change, then, depends upon the organization and culture of the legal profession. We have surmised that court-produced substantive rule-change is unlikely in itself to be a determinative element in producing tangible redistribution of benefits. The leverage provided by litigation depends on its strategic combination with inputs at other levels. The question then is whether the organization of the profession permits lawyers to develop and employ skills at these other levels. The more that lawyers view themselves exclusively as courtroom advocates, the less their willingness to undertake new tasks and form enduring alliances with clients and operate in forums other than courts, the less likely they are to serve as agents of redistributive change. Paradoxically, those legal professions most open to accentuating the advantages of the "haves" (by allowing themselves to be "captured" by recurrent clients) may be most able to become (or have room for, more likely) agents of change, precisely because they provide more license for identification with clients and their "causes" and have a less strict definition of what are properly professional activities.[145]

Notes

Originally published in *Law & Society Review* 9(1): 95–160 (1974); reprinted (with corrections) in R. Cotterrell (Ed.) *Law and Society* (Aldershot: Dartmouth, 1994), pp. 165–230. This essay grew out of a presentation to Robert Stevens's Seminar on the Legal Profession and Social Change at Yale Law School in the autumn of 1970, while the author was Senior Fellow in the School's Law and Modernization Program. It has gathered bulk and I hope substance in the course of a succession of presentations and revisions. It has accumulated a correspondingly heavy burden of obligation to my colleagues and students. I would like to acknowledge the helpful comments of Richard Abel, James Atleson, Guido Calabresi, Kenneth Davidson, Vernon Dibble, William L. F. Felstiner, Lawrence M. Friedman, Marjorie Girth, Paul Goldstein, Mark Haller, Stephen Halpern, Charles M. Hardin, Adolf Homberger, Geoffrey Hazard, Quintin Johnstone, Patrick L. Kelley, David Kirp, Arthur Leff, Stuart Nagel, Philippe Nonet, Saul Touster, David M. Trubek and Stephen Wasby on earlier drafts, and to confer on them the usual dispensation.

The development of this essay was linked in many places to a contemporaneous project on the Deployment Process in the Implementation of Legal Policy supported by the National Science Foundation. I am grateful to the Foundation for affording me the opportunity to pursue several lines of inquiry touched on here. The Foundation bears no responsibility for the views set forth here.

An earlier version was issued as a working paper of the Law and Modernization Program: yet another version of the first part is contained in the proceedings (edited by Lawrence Friedman and Manfred Rehbinder) of the Conference on the Sociology of the Judicial Process, held at Bielefeld, West Germany, in September, 1973.

1. "Litigation" is used here to refer to the pressing of claims oriented to official rules, either by actually invoking official machinery or threatening to do so. Adjudication refers to full-dress individualized and formal application of rules by officials in a particular litigation.

2. Cf. Friedman (1969:43) who defines penetration as "the number of actors and spheres of action that a particular rule . . . actually reaches."

3. The discussion here focuses on litigation, but I believe an analogous analysis might be applied to the regulatory and rule-making phases of legal process. OSs and RPs may be found in regulatory and legislative as well as adjudicative settings. The point is nicely epitomized by the observation of one women's movement lobbyist:

> By coming back week after week . . . we tell them not only that we're here, but that we're here to stay. We're not here to scare anybody. . . . The most threatening thing I can say is that we'll be back. *New York Times*, Jan. 29, 1974, p. 34, col. 7–8.

For an interesting example of this distinction in the regulatory arena, see Lobenthal's (1970:20 ff) description of the regulation of parking near a pier, contrasting the "permanent" shipping company and longshoreman interests with the OS pier visitors, showing how regulation gravitates to the accommodation of the former. This is, of course, akin to the "capture by the regulated" that attends (or afflicts) a variety of administrative agencies. See, e.g., Bernstein (1955); Edelman (1967).

4. Even the taxpayer and the welfare client are not pure OSs, since there is next year's tax bill and next month's welfare check. Our concept of OS conceals the difference between pure OSs—persons such as the accident victim who get in the situation only once—and those who are in a continuing series of transactions (welfare clients or taxpayers) but whose resources permit at most a single crack at litigation.

5. Of course a Repeat Player need not engage in adjudication (or even in litigation). The term includes a party who makes or resists claims which may occupy any sector of the entire range of dispute processing mechanisms discussed in section V below. Perhaps the most successful RPs are those whose antagonists opt for resignation.

6. On the "processing" of these parties and their limited strategic options, see Foote (1956); Spradley (1970: Chap. 6).

7. Ironically, RPs may enjoy access to competent paraprofessional help that is unavailable to OSs. Thus the insurance company can, by employing adjusters, obtain competent and experienced help in routine negotiations without having to resort to expensive professionally qualified personnel. See Ross (1970:25) on the importance of the insurance adjuster in automobile injury settlements.

8. An intriguing example of an RP reaping advantage from a combination of large scale operations and knowledgeability is provided by Skolnick's (1966:174 ff) account of professional burglars' ability to trade clearances for leniency.

9. See, for example, Jacob's (1969:100) description of creditor colonization of small claims courts:

> . . . the neutrality of the judicial process was substantially compromised by the routine relationships which developed between representatives of frequent users

of garnishment and the clerk of the court. The clerk scheduled cases so that one or two of the heavy users appeared each day. This enabled the clerk to equalize the work flow of his office. It also consolidated the cases of large creditors and made it unnecessary for them to come to court every day. It appeared that these heavy users and the clerk got to know each other quite well in the course of several months. Although I observed no other evidence of favoritism toward these creditors, it was apparent that the clerk tended to be more receptive toward the version of the conflict told by the creditor than disclosed by the debtor, simply because one was told by a man he knew and the other by a stranger.

The opportunity for regular participants to establish relations of trust and reciprocity with courts is not confined to these lowly precincts. Scigliano (1971:183–84) observes that:

> The Government's success in the Supreme Court seems to owe something . . . to the credit which the Solicitor General's Office has built up with the Court . . . in the first place, by helping the Court manage its great and growing burden of casework. . . . He holds to a trickle what could be a deluge of Government appeals. . . . In the second place by ensuring that the Government's legal work is competently done. So much so that when the Justices or their clerks want to extract the key issues in a complicated case quickly, they turn, according to common reports, to the Government's brief.
>
> [Third.] The Solicitor General gains further credits . . . by his demonstrations of impartiality and independence from the executive branch.

10. See Ross (1970:156 ff); Schelling (1963:22 ff., 41). An offsetting advantage enjoyed by some OSs deserves mention. Since he does not anticipate continued dealings with his opponent, an OS can do his damnedest without fear of reprisal next time around or on other issues. (The advantages of those who enjoy the luxury of singlemindedness are evidenced by some notorious examples in the legislative arena, for instance, the success of prohibitionists and of the gun lobby.) Thus there may be a bargaining advantage to the OS who (a) has resources to damage his opponent; (b) is convincingly able to threaten to use them. An OS can burn up his capital, but he has to convince the other side he is really likely to do so. Thus an image of irrationality may be a bargaining advantage. See Ross (1970:170n.); Schelling (1963:17). An OS may be able to sustain such an image in a way that an RP cannot. But cf. Leff (1970a:18) on the role of "spite" in collections and the externalization to specialists of "irrational" vengeance.

11. Ross (1970:214) notes that in dealing with the injury claimant, the insurance adjuster enjoys the advantage of "relative indifference to the uncertainty of litigation . . . the insurance company as a whole in defending large numbers of claims is unaffected by the uncertainty with respect to any one claim. . . . from the claimant's viewpoint [litigation] involves a gamble that may be totally lost. By taking many such gambles in litigating large numbers of cases the insurance company is able to regard the choice between the certainty and the gamble with indifference."

12. That is, not the whole of RPs' worth, but the whole matter at issue in a single claim.

13. Cf. the overpayment of small claims and underpayment of large claims in automobile injury cases. Franklin, Chanin and Mark (1961); Conard et al. (1964). If small claim overpayment can be thought of as the product of the transaction costs of the defendants (and, as Ross [1970:207] shows, organizational pressures to close cases), the large claim underpayment represents the discount for delay and risk on the part of the claimant. (Conard et al. 1964:197–99.)

14. Olson's analysis (1965:36-52 127–28) suggests that their relatively small number should enhance the capacity of RPs for coordinated action to further common interests. See note 127.

15. This can be done only where institutions are simultaneously engaged in rule-making and dispute settling. The rule-making function, however, need not be avowed; all that is required is that the outcome in Case 1 influence the outcome in Case 2 in a way that RP can predict.

16. This is not to imply that rule loss or gain is the main determinant of settlement policy. First, the RP must litigate selectively. He can't fight every case. Second, rules are themselves the subject of dispute relatively rarely. Only a small fraction of litigation involves some disagreement between the parties as to what the rules are or ought to be. Dibble (1973).

In addition, the very scale that bestows on RPs strategic advantages in settlement policy exposes them to deviations from their goals. Most RPs are organizations and operate through individual incumbents of particular roles (house counsel, claims adjuster, assistant prosecutor) who are subject to pressures which may lead them to deviate from the optimization of institutional goals. Thus Ross (1970:220–21) notes that insurance companies litigate large cases where, although settlement would be "rational" from the overall viewpoint of the company, it would create unacceptable career risk to incumbents. Newman (1966:72) makes a similar observation about prosecutors' offices. He finds that even where the probability of conviction is slim "in cases involving a serious offense which has received a good deal of publicity . . . a prosecutor may prefer to try the case and have the charge reduction or acquittal decision made by the judge or jury."

17. The assumption here is that "settlement" does not have precedent value. Insofar as claimants or their lawyers form a community which shares such information, this factor is diminished—as it is, for example, in automobile injury litigation where, I am told, settlements have a kind of precedent value.

18. Thus the Solicitor General sanctions appeal to the Supreme Court in one-tenth of the appealable defeats of the Government, while its opponents appeal nearly half of their appealable defeats. Scigliano points out that the Government is more selective because:

> In the first place, lower-court defeats usually mean much less to the United States than they do to other parties. In the second place, the government has, as private litigants do not, an independent source of restraint upon the desire to litigate further (1971:169).

Appellants tend to be winners in the Supreme Court—about two-thirds of cases are decided in their favor. The United States government wins about 70% of the appeals it brings.

What sets the government apart from other litigants is that it wins a much higher percentage of cases in which it is the appellee (56% in 1964–66). (1971:178)

Scigliano assigns as reasons for the government's success in the Supreme Court not only the "government's agreement with the court on doctrinal position" but the "expertise of the Solicitor General's Office" and "the credit which the Solicitor General has developed with the Court." (1971:182.)

More generally, as Rothstein (1974:501) observes:

> The large volume litigant is able to achieve the most favorable forum; emphasize different issues in different courts; take advantage of difference in procedure among courts at the state and federal level; drop or compromise unpromising cases without fear of heavy financial loss; stall some cases and push others; and create rule conflicts in lower courts to encourage assumption of jurisdiction in higher courts. Cf. Hazard (1965:68).

19. Macaulay (1966:99–101) in his study of relations between the automobile manufacturers and their dealers recounts that the manufacturers:

> . . . had an interest in having the [Good Faith Act] construed to provide standards for their field men's conduct. Moreover they had resources to devote to the battle. The amount of money involved might be major to a canceled dealer, but few, if any cases involved a risk of significant liability to the manufacturers even if the dealer won. Thus the manufacturers could afford to fight as long as necessary to get favorable interpretations to set guidelines for the future. While dealers' attorneys might have to work on a contingent fee, the manufacturers already had their own large and competent legal staffs and could afford to hire trial and appellate specialists. . . . an attorney on a contingent fee can afford to invest only so much time in a particular case. Since the manufacturers were interested in guidelines for the future, they could afford to invest, for example, $40,000 worth of attorneys' time in a case they could have settled for $10,000. Moreover, there was the factor of experience. A dealer's attorney usually started without any background in arguing a case under the Good Faith Act. On the other hand, a manufacturer's legal staff became expert in arguing such a case as it faced a series of these suits. It could polish its basic brief in case after case and even influence the company's business practices—such as record keeping—so that it would be ready for any suit.
>
> . . . While individual dealers decide whether or not to file a complaint, the manufacturer, as any fairly wealthy defendant facing a series of related cases, could control the kinds of cases coming before the courts in which the Good Faith Act could be construed. It could defend and bring appeals in those cases where the facts are unfavorable to the dealer, and it could settle any where the facts favor the dealer. Since individual dealers were more interested in money than establishing precedents . . . the manufacturers in this way were free to control the cases the court would see.
>
> The net effect . . . was to prompt a sequence of cases favorable to the manufacturers.

20. Of course, even within the constraints of their strategic position, parties may

fare better or worse according to their several capacities to mobilize and utilize legal resources. Nonet (1969: Chap. IV) refers to this as "legal competence"—that is, the capacity for optimal use of the legal process to pursue one's interests, a capacity which includes information, access, judgment, psychic readiness and so forth.

An interesting example of the effects of such competence is provided by Rosenthal (1970: Chap. 2) who notes the superior results obtained by "active" personal injury plaintiffs. ("Active" clients are defined as those who express special wants to their attorneys, make follow-up demands for attention, marshall information to aid the lawyer, seek quality medical attention, seek a second legal opinion, and bargain about the fee.) He finds such "active" clients drawn disproportionately from those of higher social status (which presumably provides both the confidence and experience to conduct themselves in this active manner).

The thrust of the argument here is that the distribution of capacity to use the law beneficially cannot be attributed solely or primarily to personal characteristics of parties. The personal qualities that make up competence are themselves systematically related to social structure, both to general systems of stratification and to the degree of specialization of the parties. The emphasis here differs somewhat from that of Nonet, who makes competence central and for whom, for example, organization is one means of enhancing competence. This analysis views personal competence as operating marginally within the framework of the parties' relations to each other and to the litigation process. It is submitted that this reversal permits us to account for systematic differentials of competence and for the differences in the structure of opportunities which face various kinds of parties when personal competence is held constant.

21. The tendency for formal equality to be compatible with domination has been noted by Weber (1954:188–91) and Ehrlich (1936:238), who noted "The more the rich and the poor are dealt with according to the same legal propositions, the more the advantage of the rich is increased."

22. Cf. Hahm (1969); Kawashima (1963) for descriptions of cultural settings in which litigation carries high psychic costs. (For the coexistence of anti-litigation attitudes with high rates of litigation, see Kidder [1971].) For a population with a greater propensity to litigate consider the following account (*New York Times*, Oct. 16, 1966) of contemporary Yugoslavia:

> Yugoslavs often complain of a personality characteristic in their neighbors that they call *inat*, which translates roughly as "spite." . . . One finds countless examples of it chronicled in the press. . . . the case of two neighbors in the village of Pomoravije who had been suing each other for 30 years over insults began when one "gave a dirty look" to the other's pet dog.
>
> Last year the second district court in Belgrade was presented with 9000 suits over alleged slanders and insults. Often the cases involve tenants crowded in apartment buildings. In one building in the Street of the October Revolution tenants began 53 suits against each other. Other cases of "spite" suits . . . included "a bent fence, a nasty look." Business enterprises are not immune and one court is handling a complaint of the Zastava Company of Knic over a debt of 10 dinars (less than 1 cent).

In the countryside spite also appears in such petty forms as a brother who sued his sister because she gathered fruit fallen from a tree he regarded as his own.

. . . Dr. Mirko Barjakterevic, professor of ethnology at Belgrade University . . . remarked that few languages had as many expressions for and about spite as Serbian and that at every turn one hears phrases like, "I'm going to teach him a lesson," and "I don't want to be made a fool of."

Consider, too, Frake's ("Litigation in Lipay: A Study in Subanum Law" quoted in Nader [1965:21]) account of the prominence of litigation among the Lipay of the Philippines:

A large share, if not the majority, of legal cases deal with offenses so minor that only the fertile imagination of a Subanum legal authority can magnify them into a serious threat to some person or to society in general. . . . A festivity without litigation is almost as unthinkable as one without drink. If no subject for prosecution immediately presents itself, sooner or later, as the brew relaxes the tongues and actions, someone will make a slip.

In some respects a Lipay trial is more comparable to an American poker game than to our legal proceedings. It is a contest of skill, in this case of verbal skill, accompanied by social merry-making, in which the loser pays a forfeit. He pays for much the same reason we pay a poker debt: so he can play the game again. Even if he does not have the legal authority's ability to deal a verbalized "hand," he can participate as a defendant, plaintiff, kibitzer, singer, and drinker. No one is left out of the range of activities associated with litigation.

Litigation nevertheless has far greater significance in Lipay than this poker-game analogy implies. For it is more than recreation. Litigation together with the rights and duties it generates, so pervades Lipay life that one could not consistently refuse to pay fines and remain a functioning member of society. Along with drinking, feasting, and ceremonializing, litigation provides patterned means of interaction linking the independent nuclear families of Lipay into a social unit, even though there are no formal group ties of comparable extent. The importance of litigation as a social activity makes understandable its prevalence among the peaceful and, by our standards, "law-abiding" residents of Lipay.

23. Generally, sentiments against litigation are less likely to affect organizations precisely because the division of labor within organizations means that litigation will be handled impersonally by specialists who do not have to conduct other relations with the opposing party (as customers, etc.). See Jacob (1969:78 ff) on the separation of collection from merchandising tasks as one of the determinants of creditors' readiness to avail of litigation remedies. And cf. the suggestion (note 16 above) that in complex organizations resort to litigation may be a way to externalize decisions that no one within the organization wants to assume responsibility for.

24. Cf. Zeisel, Kalven & Buchholz (1959: Chap. 20). On the possibility of explaining differences in patterns of litigation by structural rather than cultural factors, see Kidder's (1971: Chap. IX) comparison of Indian and American litigation.

25. Henderson (1968:488) suggests that in Japan, unlike America,

. . . popular sentiment for justiciable rights is still largely absent. And, if dispute settlement is the context from which much of the growth, social meaning and political usefulness of justiciable rights derive—and American experience suggests it is—then the traditional tendency of the Japanese to rely on sublegal conciliatory techniques becomes a key obstacle in the path toward the rule-of-law envisioned by the new constitution.

He notes that

In both traditional and modern Japan, conciliation of one sort or another has been and still is effective in settling the vast majority of disputes arising in the gradually changing social context.

Finding that Californians resorted to litigation about 23 times as often as Japanese, he concludes (1968:453) that traditional conciliation is employed to settle most "disputes that would go to court in a country with a developed sense of justiciable right."

Henderson (1968:454) seems to imply that "in modern society [people] must comport themselves according to reasonable and enforceable principles rather than haggling, negotiating and jockeying about to adjust personal relationships to fit an ever-shifting power balance among individuals."

Cf. Rabinowitz (1968: Part III) for a "cultural" explanation for the relative unimportance of law in Japanese society. (Non-ego-developed personality, non-rational approach to action, extreme specificity of norms with high degree of contextual differentiation.)

26. For an instructive example of response to a claimant who wants vindication rather than a tidy settlement, see Katz (1969:1492):

When I reported my client's instructions not to negotiate settlement at the pre-trial conference, the judge appointed an impartial psychiatrist to examine Mr. Lin.

27. For descriptions of divorce litigation, see Virtue (1956); O'Gorman (1963); Marshall and May (1932).

28. For an estimate of the discrepancy between the law and popular attitudes in a "Box I" area, see Cohen, Robson and Bates (1958).

29. Available quantitative data on the configuration of parties to litigation will be explored in a sequel to this essay. For the moment let me just say that the speculations here fit handily with the available findings. For example, Wanner (1974; 1975), analyzing a sample of 7,900 civil cases in three cities, found that business and governmental units are plaintiffs in almost six out of ten cases; and that they win more, settle less and lose less than individual plaintiffs. Individuals, on the other hand, are defendants in two-thirds of all cases and they win less and lose more than do government or business units. A similar preponderance of business and governmental plaintiffs and individual defendants is reported in virtually all of the many studies of small claims courts. E.g., Pagter et al. (1964) in their study of a metropolitan California small claims court find that individuals made up just over a third of the plaintiffs and over 85% of defendants. A later survey of four small-town California small claims courts (Moulton 1969:1660) found that only 16% of plaintiffs were individuals—but over 93% of defendants.

30. The analysis here assumes that, when called upon, judges apply rules routinely

and relentlessly to RPs and OSs alike. In the event, litigation often involves some admixture of individuation, kadi-justice, fireside equities, sentimentality in favor of the "little guy." (For a comparison of two small claims courts in one of which the admixture is stronger, see Yngvesson [1965]). It also involves some offsetting impurities in favor of frequent users. See note 9 above and note 59 below.

31. Cf. Friedman (1967:806) on the zone of "reciprocal immunities" between, for example, landlord and tenant afforded by the cost of enforcing their rights. The foregoing suggests that these immunities may be reciprocal, but they are not necessarily symmetrical. That is, they may differ in magnitude according to the strategic position of the parties. Cf. Vaughan's (1968:210) description of the "differential dependence" between landlord and low-income tenant. He regards this as reflecting the greater immediacy and constancy of the tenant's need for housing, the landlord's "exercise of privilege in the most elemental routines of the relationship," greater knowledge, and the fact that the landlord, unlike the tenant, does not have all his eggs in one basket (i.e., he is, in our terms, an RP).

> Whereas each tenant is dependent upon one landlord, the landlord typically diffuses his dependency among many tenants. As a result, the owner can rather easily retain an independent position in each relationship.

A similar asymmetry typically attends relations between employer and employee, franchiser and franchisee, insurer and insured, etc.

32. See note 74 below. Cf. Skolnick's (1966:212ff) description of police adjustment to the exclusionary rule.

33. Similarly, even OSs who have procured favorable judgments may experience difficulty at the execution stage. Even where the stakes loom large for OSs, they may be too small to enlist unsubsidized professional help in implementation. A recent survey of consumers who "won" in New York City's Small Claims Court found that almost a third were unable to collect. Marshalls either flatly refused to accept such judgments for collection or "conveyed an impression that, even if they did take a small claims case, they would regard it as an annoyance and would not put much work into it." *New York Times*, Sept. 19, 1971. A subsequent survey (Community Service Society 1974:16) of 195 successful individual plaintiffs in two Manhattan Small Claims Courts revealed that "only 50% of persons who received *judgments* were able to collect these through their own efforts or through use of sheriffs and marshals." (Plaintiffs who received settlements were more successful, collecting in 82% of the cases.) Cf. the finding of Hollingsworth et al. (1973: Table 16) that of winning small claims plaintiffs in Hamilton County only 31% of individuals and unrepresented proprietorships collected half or more of the judgment amount; the corresponding figure for corporations and represented proprietorships was 55%.

34. Perhaps high volume litigation in Box III is particularly susceptible to transformation into relatively unproblematic administrative processing when RPs discover that it is to their advantage and can secure a shift with some gains (or at least no losses) to OSs. Cf. the shift from tort to workman's compensation in the industrial accident area (Friedman and Ladinsky [1967]) and the contemporary shift to no-fault plans in the automobile injury area.

35. Summers (1960:252) reports that

more than 3/4 of the reported cases in which individuals have sought legal protection of their rights under a collective agreement have arisen out of disciplinary discharge.

The association of litigation with "divorce" is clear in Macaulay (1963, 1969) and other discussions of commercial dealings (Bonn 1972b:573 ff). Consumer bankruptcy, another of the more numerous species of litigation in Box III, might be thought of as representing the attempt of the OS to effectuate a "divorce."

36. For example, Babcock (1969:52–54) observes that what gives the suburb its greatest leverage on any one issue is the builder's need to have repeated contact with the regulatory powers of the suburb on various issues.

37. The anticipated beneficial relations need not be with the identical party but may be with other parties with whom that party is in communication. RPs are more likely to participate in a network of communication which cheaply and rapidly disseminates information about the behavior of others in regard to claims and to have an interest and capacity for acquiring and storing that information. In this way RPs can cheaply and effectively affect the business reputation of adversaries and thus their future relations with relevant others. Leff (1970a:26 ff); Macaulay (1963:64).

38. Why is contract doctrine not central to business exchanges?

Briefly put, private, between-the-parties sanctions usually exist, work and do not involve the costs of using contract law either in litigation or as a ploy in negotiations. . . . most importantly, there are relatively few one-shot, but significant, deals. A businessman usually cares about his reputation. He wants to do business again with the man he is dealing with and with others. Friedman and Macaulay (1967:805).

39. Aspin (1966:2) reports that 70 to 75% of all complaints to the NLRB about the unfair labor practices of companies are under the single section [8(a)(3)] which makes it an unfair labor practice for employers to interfere with union organizing. These make up about half of *all* complaints of unfair labor practices.

40. In his description of the organizational participants in church-state litigation, Morgan (1968: chap. 2) points out the difference in approach between value-committed "separationist purists" and their interest-committed "public schoolmen" allies. The latter tend to visualize the game as non-zero-sum and can conceive of advantages in alliances with their parochial-school adversaries. (1968:58n).

41. Cf. Aubert's (1963:27 ff) distinction between conflict careers based upon conflicts of interest and those arising from conflicts of value.

42. This analysis is illuminated by Hirschman's distinction between two modes of remedial action by customers or members disappointed with the performance of organizations: (1) exit (that is, withdrawal of custom or membership); and (2) voice ("attempts at changing the practices and policies and outputs of the firm from which one buys or the organizations to which one belongs") [1970:30]. Hirschman attempts to discern the conditions under which each will be employed and will be effective in restoring performance. He suggests that the role of voice increases as the opportunities for exit decline, but that the possibility of exit increases the effectiveness of the voice mechanism (1970:34, 83). Our analysis suggests that it is useful to distinguish those instances of voice which are "internal," that is, confined to expres-

sion to the other party, and those which are external, that is, seek the intervention of third parties. This corresponds roughly to the distinction between two-party and three-party dispute settlement. We might then restate the assertion to suggest that internal voice is effective where there is a plausible threat of sanction (including exit and external voice).

43. The potency of the monopolistic character of ties in promoting resort to third parties is suggested by the estimate that in the Soviet Union approximately one million contract disputes were arbitrated annually in the early 1960's (Loeber, 1965:128, 133). Cf. Scott's (1965:63–64) suggestion that restricted mobility (defined in terms of job change) is associated with the presence of formal appeal systems in business organizations.

44. That is, the relationship may never have existed, it may have "failed" in that it is no longer mutually beneficial, or the parties may be "divorced." On the incompatibility of litigation with ongoing relations between parties, consider the case of the lawyer employed by a brokerage house who brought suit against his employer in order to challenge New York State's law requiring fingerprinting of employees in the securities industry.

> They told me, "Don, you've done a serious thing: you've sued your employer." And then they handed me [severance pay] checks. They knew I had to sue them. Without making the employer a defendant, it's absolutely impossible to get a determination in court. It was not a matter of my suing them for being bad guys or anything like that and they knew it.
>
> . . . the biggest stumbling block is that I'm virtually blacklisted on Wall Street.

His application for unemployment compensation was rejected on the ground that he had quit his employment without good cause, having provoked his dismissal by refusing to be fingerprinted. *New York Times*, March 2, 1970. It appears that, in the American setting at any rate, litigation is not only incompatible with the maintenance of continuing relationships, but with their subsequent restoration. On the rarity of successful reinstatement of employees ordered reinstated by the NLRB, see Aspin (1966). Bonn (1972a:262) finds this pattern even among users of arbitration, which is supposedly less lethal to continuing relations than litigation. He found that in 78 cases of arbitration in textiles, "business relations were resumed in only fourteen." Cf. Golding's (1969:90) observation that jural forms of dispute-settlement are most appropriate where parties are not involved in a continuing relationship. But the association of litigation with strangers is not invariate. See the Yugoslav and Lipay examples in note 22 above. Cf. the Indian pattern described by Kidder (1971) and by Morrison (1974:39) who recounts that his North Indian villagers "commented scornfully that GR [a chronic litigant] would even take a complete stranger to law—proof that his energies were misdirected."

45. For example, Ross (1970:193) finds that automobile injury claimants represented by attorneys recover more frequently than unrepresented claimants; that among those who recover, represented claimants recover significantly more than do unrepresented claimants with comparable cases. Claimants represented by firms recovered considerably more than claimants represented by solo practitioners; those represented by negligence specialists recovered more than those represented by firm

attorneys. Similarly, Mosier and Soble (1973:35 ff) find that represented tenants fare better in eviction cases than do unrepresented ones. The advantages of having a lawyer in criminal cases are well-known. See, for instance, Nagel (1973).

46. As it happens, the information barriers vary in their restrictiveness. The American Bar Association's Code of Professional Responsibility

> permits advertising directed at corporations, banks, insurance companies, and those who work in the upper echelons of such institutions . . . [while proscribing] most forms of dissemination of information which would reach people of "moderate means" and apprise them of their legal rights and how they can find competent and affordable legal assistants to vindicate those rights. (Burnley 1973:77).

On the disparate effect of these restrictions, cf. note 51.

47. The tension between the lawyer's loyalties to the legal system and to his client has been celebrated by Parsons (1954:381 ff) and Horsky (1952: chap. 3). But note how this same deflection of loyalty from the client is deplored by Blumberg (1967) and others. The difference in evaluation seems to depend on whether the opposing pull is to the autonomous legal tradition, as Parsons (1954) and Horsky (1952) have it, or to the maintenance of mutually beneficial interaction with a particular local institution whose workings embody some admixture of the "higher law" (see note 82 below) with parochial understandings, institutional maintenance needs, etc.

48. Although this is not the place to elaborate it, let me sketch the model that underlies this assertion. (For a somewhat fuller account, see International Legal Center, 1973:4ff.) Let us visualize a series of scales along which legal professions might be ranged:

	A	B
1. Basis of Recruitment	Restricted	Wide
2. Barriers to Entry	High	Low
3. Division of Labor		
a. Coordination	Low	High
b. Specialization	Low	High
4. Range of Services and Functions	Narrow	Wide
5. Enduring Relationships to Client	Low	High
6. Range of Institutional Settings	Narrow	Wide
7. Identification with Clients	Low	High
8. Identification with Authorities	High	Low
9. Guild Control	Tight	Loose
10. Ideology	Legalistic	Problem-solving

It is suggested that the characteristics at the A and B ends of the scale tend to go together, so that we can think of the A and B clusters as means of describing types of bodies of legal professionals, for example, the American legal profession (Hurst 1950; Horsky 1952: Pt. V.; Carlin 1962, 1966; Handler 1967; Smigel 1969) would be a B type, compared to British barristers (Abel-Smith and Stevens 1967) and French *avocats* (Le Paulle 1950); Indian lawyers (Galanter 1968–69), an intermediate case. It is suggested that some characteristics of Type B professions tend to accentuate or amplify the strategic advantages of RP parties. Consideration of, for instance, the British bar, should warn us against concluding that Type B professions are necessarily more conservative in function than Type A. See text, at note 145.

49. Which is not to deny the possibility that such "side" specialization might emerge. One can imagine "women's liberation" divorce lawyers—and anti-alimony ones—devoted to rule-development that would favor one set of OSs.

50. On stratification within the American legal profession see Ladinsky (1963); Lortie (1959); Carlin (1966). But cf. Handler (1967).

51. See Reichstein (1965); *Northwestern University Law Review* (1953). On the differential impact of the "Canons of Ethics" on large law firms and those lawyers who represent OSs, see Carlin (1966); Shuchman (1968); Christianson (1970:136).

52. " . . . the canons of ethics would prevent an attorney for a [one-shotter] . . . from trying to influence his client to drop a case that would create a bad precedent for other clients with similar cases. On the other hand, the canons of ethics do not prevent an attorney from advising a corporation that some of its cases should not be pursued to prevent setting a bad precedent for its other cases." (Rothstein 1974:502).

53. Ross (1970:82) observes the possibility of conflict between client and

> the negligence specialist, who negotiates on a repeated basis with the same insurance companies. [H]is goal of maximizing the return from any given case may conflict with the goal of maximizing returns from the total series of cases he represents.

For a catalog of other potential conflicts in the relationship between specialists and OS clients, see O'Connell (1971:46−47).

54. Blumberg (1967a:47) observes

> [defense] counsel, whether privately retained or of the legal aid variety, have close and continuing relations with the prosecuting office and the court itself. Indeed, lines of communication, influence and contact with those offices, as well as with the other subsidiary divisions of the office of the clerk and the probation division and with the press are essential to the practice of criminal law. Accused persons come and go in the court system, but the structure and its personnel remain to carry on their respective careers, occupational, and organizational enterprises. . . . The accused's lawyer has far greater professional, economic, intellectual, and other ties to the various elements of the court system than to his own client.

Cf. Skolnick (1967); Battle (1971). On the interdependence of prosecutor and public defender, see Sudnow (1965:265, 273).

55. On the "stranger" relationship between accident victim client and lawyer, see Sudnow (1965:265, 273).

56. Cf. Consumer Council (1970:19). In connection with the lawyer's attachment to (or at least appreciation of) the problematic character of the law, consider the following legend, carried at the end of a public service column presented by the Illinois State Bar Association and run in a neighborhood newspaper:

> No person should ever apply or interpret any law without consulting his attorney. Even a slight difference in the facts may change the result under the law. (*Woodlawn Booster*, July 31, 1963)

Where claims become insufficiently problematic they may drop out of the legal sphere entirely (such as social security). In high-volume and repetitive tasks which admit of economies of scale and can be rendered relatively unproblematic, lawyers may be replaced by entrepreneurs—title companies, bank trust departments—serving OSs on a mass basis (or even serving RPs, as do collection agencies). Cf. Johnstone and Hopson (1967:158 ff).

57. Stumpf et al. (1971:60) suggest that professional responses to OEO legal services programs require explanation on ideological ("the highly individualized, case-by-case approach . . . as a prime article of faith") as well as pecuniary grounds. On the components of legalism as an ideology, see Shklar (1964:1–19). Of course this professional culture is not uniform but contains various subcultures. Brill's (1973) observations of OEO poverty lawyers suggest that crucial aspects of professional ideology (e.g., the emphasis on courts, rules and adjudication) are equally pronounced among lawyers who seek far-reaching change through the law.

58. Black (1973:141) observes the departures from the passive or "reactive" stance of legal institutions tend to be skewed along class lines:

. . . governments disproportionately adopt proactive systems of legal mobilization when a social control problem primarily involves the bottom of the social-class system. The common forms of legal misconduct in which upper status citizens indulge, such as breach of contract and warranty, civil negligence, and various forms of trust violation and corruption, are usually left to the gentler hand of a reactive mobilization process.

59. The passivity of courts may be uneven. Cf. Mosier and Soble's (1973:63) description of a Detroit landlord-tenant court:

If a tenant was unrepresented, the judge ordinarily did not question the landlord regarding his claims, nor did the judge explain defenses to the tenant. The most common explanation given a tenant was that the law permitted him only ten days to move and thus the judge's hands were tied. In addition, judges often asked tenants for receipts for rent paid and corroboration of landlord-breach claims. In contrast, the court supplied complaint and notice forms to the landlords and clerks at the court helped them to fill out the forms if necessary. In addition, the in-court observers noticed during the beginning of the study that the court would not dismiss a nonappearing landlord's case until completion of the docket call, which took approximately forty-five minutes (while the tenant sat and waited), but extended no similar courtesy to tardy tenants. However, once the surprised observers questioned the court personnel about the practice, it was changed; thereafter, tenants had thirty minutes after the call within which to appear.

The disparities in help given to landlords and tenants and the treatment of the late landlords and tenants are an indication of the perhaps inevitable bias of the court toward the landlord. Most of the judges and court personnel have a middle-class background and they have become familiar with many landlords and attorneys appearing regularly in the court. The court had years of experience as a vehicle for rent collection and eviction where no defenses could be raised. The judges and clerks repeatedly hear about tenants who fail to pay rent or did damage to the premises, while they probably never have the opportunity to observe the actual condition of the housing that the landlords are renting.

60. Homberger (1970:30–31). For a description of more "active" courts see Kaplan et al. (1958:1221 ff); Homberger (1970). Our description is of courts of the relatively passive variety typical of "common law" systems, but should not be taken as implying that "civil law" systems are ordinarily or typically different in practice. Cf. Merryman (1969:124). The far end of a scale of institutional "activism" might be represented by institutions like the Soviet Procuracy (Berman 1963:238 ff). And, of course, even among common law courts passivity is relative and variable. Courts vary in the extent to which they exercise initiative for the purpose of developing a branch of the law (the "Lord Mansfield Syndrome"—see Lowry 1973) or actively protecting some class of vulnerable parties.

61. As Rothstein (1974:506) sums it up, counsel fees and

> [c]ourt costs, witness fees (especially for experts), investigation costs, court reporters fees, discovery costs, transcript costs, and the cost of any bond needed to secure opponents' damages, all make litigation an expensive task, thereby giving the advantage to those with large financial resources.

62. A further set of institutional limitations should be mentioned here: limitations on the scope of matters that courts hear; the kind of relief that they can give; and on their capacity for systematic enforcement are discussed below. (pp. 136 ff).

63. On the limited supply of institutional facilities, consider Saari's (1967) estimate that in the early 1960's total governmental expenditures for civil and criminal justice in the United States ran about four to five billion dollars annually. (Of this, about 60% went for police and prosecution, about 20% for corrections, and 20% for courts.) This amounted to about 2.5% of direct expenditures of American governments. In 1965–66 expenditures for the judiciary represented $1/17$ of 1% of the total federal budget; $6/10$ of 1% of state budgets; something less than 6% of county and 3% of city budgets.

64. The substitution of bargaining for adjudication need not be regarded as reflecting institutional deficiency. Even in criminal cases it may seem providential:

> It is elementary, historically and statistically, that systems of courts—the number of judges, prosecutors and courtrooms—have been based on the premise that approximately 90 percent of all [criminal] defendants will plead guilty, leaving only 10 percent, more or less, to be tried. The consequences of what might seem on its face a small percentage change in the rate of guilty pleas can be tremendous. . . . in Washington, D.C. . . . the guilty plea rate dropped to 65 percent . . . [T]welve judges out of fifteen in active service were assigned to the criminal calendar and could barely keep up. . . . [T]o have this occur in the National Capital, which ought to be a model for the nation and show place for the world, was little short of disaster (Burger, 1970:931).

65. On institutional coping with overload, see Friedman (1967:798 ff).

66. Cf. Foote (1956:645) on the rarity of appeal in vagrancy cases. Powell and Rohan (1968:177–78) observe that the ordinary week-to-week or month-to-month rental agreement

is tremendously important sociologically in that occupancy thereunder conditions the home life of a very substantial fraction of the population. On the other hand, the financial smallness of the involved rights results in a great dearth of reported decisions from the courts concerning them. Their legal consequences are chiefly fixed in the "over the counter" mass handling of "landlord and tenant" cases of the local courts. So this type of estate, judged sociologically is of great importance, but judged on the basis of its jurisprudential content is almost negligible.

67. In the criminal process, too, the "possessor" (i.e., of defendant's mobility) enjoys great advantages. On the higher likelihood of conviction and of severe sentencing of those detained before trial, see Rankin (1964) and Wald (1964). Engle (1971) finds that among those convicted pre-trial status explains more of the variation in sentencing severity than any of 23 other factors tested.

68. See Leff (1970a:22) on the tendency of RP creditors to put themselves in the possessor position, shifting the costs of "due process" to the OS debtor. There are, however, instances where OSs may use overload to advantage: for instance, the accused out on bail may benefit from delay. Cf. Engle's (1971) observation of the "weakening effect of time on the prosecutor's position." Rioters or rent-strikers may threaten to demand jury trials, but the effectiveness of this tactic depends on a degree of coordination that effectuates a change of scale.

69. For example, the court studied by Zeisel et al. (1959:7) "had chosen to concentrate all of its delay in the personal injury jury calendar and to keep its other law calendars up to date, granting blanket preferment to all commercial cases . . . and to all non-jury personal injury cases." (Recovery in the latter was about 20% lower than jury awards in comparable cases [1959:119].)

70. This analysis has not made separate mention of corruption, that is, the sale by incumbents of system outcomes divergent from those prescribed by authoritative norms. Insofar as such activities are analytically distinguishable from favorable priorities and "benign neglect" it should be noted that, since such enterprise on any considerable scale is confined to the organized, professional and wealthy, this provides yet another layer of advantage to some classes of "haves."

71. I would like to emphasize that the term "rules" is used here as shorthand for all the authoritative normative learning. It is unnecessary for the purpose at hand to take a position on the question of whether all of that learning consists of rules or whether principles, policies, values, and standards are best understood as fundamentally different. It is enough for our purposes to note that this learning is sufficiently complex that the result in many cases is problematic and unknowable in advance.

72. Even assuming that every instance of formulating rules represented a "fair" compromise among "have" and "have not" interests, we should expect the stock of rules existing at any given time to be skewed toward those which favor "haves." The argument (cf. Kennedy 1973:384–85) goes like this: At the time of its formulation, each rule represents a current consensus about a just outcome as among competing interests. Over time the consensus changes, so that many rules are out of line with current understandings of fairness. Rule-makers (legislative, administrative and judicial) can attend to only some of all the possible readjustments. Which ones they will

attend to depends in large measure on the initiative of those affected in raising the issue and mobilizing support to obtain a declaration of the more favorable current consensus. "Haves" (wealthy, professional, repeat players) enjoy a superior ability to elicit such declarations (cf. p. 100 ff); they are thus likely to enjoy the timely benefits of shifts of social consensus in their favor. OSs, on the other hand, will often find it difficult to secure timely changes in the rules to conform to a new consensus more favorable to them. Thus RPs will be the beneficiaries of the time-lag between crystallized rules and current consensus. Thus, even with the most favorable assumptions about rule-making itself, the mere fact that rules accrue through time, and that it requires expenditure of resources to overcome the lag of rules behind current consensus, provides RPs with a relatively more favorable set of rules than the current consensus would provide.

73. This is sometimes the case: consider, for instance, the rules of landlord-tenant. Ohlhausen (1936) suggests that rules as to the availability of provisional remedies display a pronounced pattern of favoring claims of types likely to be brought by the "well to do" over claims of types brought by the impecunious.

74. Thus the modern credit seller-lender team have built their operation upon the destruction of the purchaser's defenses by the holder in due course doctrine originally developed for the entirely different purpose of insuring the circulation of commercial paper. See Rosenthal (1971:377ff). Shuchman (1971:761–62) points out how in consumer bankruptcies:

> Consumer creditors have adjusted their practices so that sufficient proof will be conveniently available for most consumer loans to be excepted from discharge under section 17a(2). They have made wide use of renewals, resetting, and new loans to pay off old loans, with the result that the consumers' entire debt will often be nondischargeable. Section 17a(2) constitutes, in effect, an enabling act—a skeletal outline that the consumer creditor can fill in to create nondischargeable debts—that operated to defeat the consumer's right to the benefits of a discharge in bankruptcy.

Similarly, Shuchman (1969) shows how RP auto dealers and financial institutions have developed patterns for resale of repossessed automobiles that meet statutory resale requirements but which permit subsequent profitable second sale and in addition produce substantial deficiency claims. More generally, recall the often-noted adaptive power of regulated industry which manages, in Hamilton's (1957: chap. 2) terms, to convert "regulations into liberties" and "controls into sanctions."

75. For some examples of possessor-defendants exploiting the full panoply of procedural devices to raise the cost to claimants, see Schrag (1969); Macaulay (1966:98). Large (1972) shows how the doctrines of standing, jurisdiction and other procedural hurdles, effectively obstruct application of favorable substantive law in environmental litigation. Facing these rules in serial array, the environmentalists win many skirmishes but few battles.

76. Cf. the observation of Tullock (1971:48–49) that complexity and detail—the "maze" quality of legal rules—in itself confers advantages on "people of above average intelligence, with literary and scholarly interests"—and by extension on those who can develop expertise or employ professional assistance.

77. For an example of the potency of a combination of complexity and expertise in frustrating recovery, see Laufer (1970). Of course, the advantage may derive not from the outcome, but from the complexity, expense and uncertainty of the litigation process itself. Borkin (1950) shows how, in a setting of economic competition among units of disparate size and resources, patent litigation may be used as a tactic of economic struggle. Cf. Hamilton (1957:75–76).

78. On the contours of "inaction," see Levine and Preston (1970); Mayhew and Riess (1969); Ennis (1967); Republic Research, Inc. (1970); Hallauer (1972).

79. See Rabin (1972), and Miller (1969) (prosecutors); Lafave (1965) and Black (1971) (police); and generally, Davis (1969). Courts are not the only institutions in the legal system which are chronically overloaded. Typically, agencies with enforcement responsibilities have many more authoritative commitments than resources to carry them out. Thus "selective enforcement" is typical and pervasive; the policies that underlie the selection lie, for the most part, beyond the "higher law." On the interaction between enforcement and rule-development, see Gifford (1971).

80. On exit or withdrawal as a sanction, see note 42 and text there. For an attempt to explore propensities to choose among resignation, exit, and voice in response to neighborhood problems, see Orbell and Uno (1972). "Exit" would seem to include much of what goes under the rubric of "self-help." Other common forms of self-help, such as taking possession of property, usually represent a salvage operation in the wake of exit by the other party. Yet other forms, such as force, are probably closer to the dispute settlement systems discussed below.

81. There are, of course, some cases (such as divorce or bankruptcy) in which exit can be accomplished only by securing official certification or permission: that is, it is necessary to resort to an official remedy system in order to effectuate exit.

82. This term is used to refer to the law as a body of authoritative learning (rules, doctrines, principles), as opposed to the parochial embodiments of this higher law, as admixed with local understandings, priorities, and the like.

83. "Private" dispute settlement may entail mainly bargaining or negotiation between the parties (dyadic) or may involve the invocation of some third party in the decision-making position. It is hypothesized that parties whose rules in a transaction or relationship are complementaries (husband-wife, purchaser-supplier, landlord-tenant) will tend to rely on dyadic processes in which group norms enter without specialized apparatus for announcing or enforcing norms. Precisely because of the mutual dependence of the parties, a capacity to sanction is built into the relationship. On the other hand, parties who stand in a parallel position in a set of transactions, such as airlines or stockbrokers *inter se*, tend to develop remedy systems with norm exposition and sanction application by third parties. Again, this is because the parties have little capacity to sanction the deviant directly. This hypothesis may be regarded as a reformulation of Schwartz's (1954) proposition that formal controls appear where informal controls are ineffective and explains this finding of resort to formal controls on an Israeli moshav (cooperative settlement) but not in a kibbutz (collective settlement). In this instance, the interdependence of the kibbutzniks made informal controls effective, while the "independent" moshav members needed formal controls. This echos Durkheim's (1964) notion of different legal controls corresponding to conditions of organic and mechanical solidarity. A corollary to this is

suggested by re-analysis of Mentschikoff's (1961) survey of trade association proclivity to engage in arbitration. Her data indicate that the likelihood of arbitration is strongly associated with the fungibility of goods (her categories are raw, soft and hard goods). Presumably dealings in more unique hard goods entail enduring purchaser-supplier relations which equip the parties with sanctions for dyadic dispute-settlement sanctions which are absent among dealers in fungible goods. Among the latter, sanctions take the form of exclusion from the circle of traders, and it is an organized third party (the trade association) that can best provide this kind of sanction.

84. The distinction is not intended to ignore the overlap and linkage that may exist between "appended" and "private" systems. See, for example, Macaulay's (1966:151 ff) description of the intricate interweaving of official, appended and private systems in the regulation of manufacturer-dealer relations; Randall's (1968: chap. 8) account of the relation between official and industry censorship; Aker's (1968:470) observation of the interpenetration of professional associations and state regulatory boards.

85. On internal regulation in Chinese communities in the United States, see Doo (1973); Light (1972, chap. 5, especially 89–94); Grace (1970).

86. Cf. Mentschikoff's (1961) discussion of various species of commercial arbitration. She distinguishes casual arbitrations conducted by the American Arbitration Association which emphasize general legal norms and standards and where the "ultimate sanction . . . is the rendering of judgment on the award by a court. . . . " (1961:858) from arbitration within

> self-contained trade groups [where] the norms and standards of the group itself
> are being brought to bear by the arbitrators (1961:857)

and the ultimate sanction is an intra-group disciplinary proceeding.

87. The dotted extension of the scale in Figure 2.6 is meant to indicate the possibility of private systems which are not only structurally independent of the official system but in which the shared values comprise an oppositional culture. Presumably this would fit, for example, internal dispute settlement among organized and committed criminals and revolutionaries. Closer to the official might be the subcultures of delinquent gangs. Although they have been characterized as deviant sub-cultures, Matza (1964: chap. 2, esp. 59 ff) argues that in fact the norms of these groups are but variant readings of the official legal culture. Such variant readings may be present elsewhere on the scale; for instance, businessmen may not recognize any divergence of their notion of obligatory business conduct from the law of contract.

88. Since dealings between settlement specialists such as personal injury and defense lawyers may be more recurrent and inclusive than the dealings between parties themselves, one might expect that wherever specialist intermediaries are used, the remedy-system would tend to shift toward the private end of our spectrum. Cf. Skolnick (1967:69) on the "regression to cooperation" in the "criminal court community."

89. Not only is the transient and simplex relationship more likely to be subjected to official regulation, it is apparently more amenable to formal legal control. See, for example, the greater success of anti-discrimination statutes in public accommodation than in housing and in housing than in employment (success here defined merely as

a satisfactory outcome for the particular complainant). See Lockard (1968:91, 122, 138). Mayhew (1968:245 ff; 278 ff) provides an interesting demonstration of the greater impact of official norms in housing than in employment transactions in spite of the greater evaluative resistance to desegregation in the latter.

90. The capacity of continuing or "on-going" relationships to generate effective informal control has been often noted (Macaulay 1963:63–64; Yngvesson 1973). It is not temporal duration *per se* that provides the possibility of control, but the serial or incremental character of the relationship, which provides multiple choice points at which parties can seek and induce adjustment of the relationship. The mortgagor-mortgagee relationship is an enduring one, but one in which there is heavy reliance on official regulation, precisely because the frame is fixed and the parties cannot withdraw or modify it. Contrast landlord-tenant, husband-wife or purchaser-supplier, in which recurrent inputs of cooperative activity are required, the withholding of which gives the parties leverage to secure adjustment. Schelling (1963:41) suggests a basis for this in game theory: threats intended to deter a given act can be delivered with more credibility if they are capable of being decomposed into a number of consecutive smaller threats.

91. Conversely, the official system will tend to be used where such sanctions are unavailable, that is, where the claimee has no hope of any stream of benefits from future relations with the claimant (or those whose future relation with claimee will be influenced by his response to the claim). Hence the association of litigation with the aftermath of "divorce" (marital, commercial or organizational) or the absence of any "marriage" to begin with (e.g., auto injury, criminal). That is, government is the remedy agent of last resort and will be used in situations where one party has a loss and the other party has no expectation of any future benefit from the relationship.

92. This does not imply that the values of the participants are completely independent of and distinct from the officially authoritative ones. More common are what we have referred to (note 87 above) as "variant readings" in which elements of authoritative tradition are re-ordered in the light of parochial understandings and priorities. For example, the understanding of criminal procedure by the police (Skolnick [1966:219 ff.]) or of air pollution laws by health departments (Goldstein and Ford [1971:20 ff.]). Thus the variant legal cultures of various legal communities at the field or operating level can exist with little awareness of principled divergence from the higher law.

93. This comports with Bohannan's (1965:34 ff) notion that law comprises a secondary level of social control in which norms are re-institutionalized in specialized legal institutions. But where Bohannan implies a constant relationship beween the primary institutionalization of norms and their reinstitutionalization in specialized legal institutions, the emphasis here is on the difference in the extent to which relational settings can generate self-corrective remedy systems. Thus it suggests that the legal level is brought into play where the original institutionalization of norms is incomplete, either in the norms or the institutionalization.

Bohannan elaborates his analysis by suggesting (1965:37 ff) that the legal realm can be visualized as comprising various regions of which the "Municipal systems of the sort studied by most jurists deal with a single legal culture within a unicentric power system." (In such a system, differences between institutional practice and legal prescription are matters of phase or lag.) Divergences from unity (cultural, political, or both) define other regions of the legal realm: respectively, colonial law, law in stateless societies and international law.

The analysis here suggests that "municipal systems" themselves may be patchworks in which normative consensus and effective unity of power converge only imperfectly. Thus we might expect a single legal system to include phenomena corresponding to other regions of his schema of the legal realm. The divergence of the "law on the books" and the "law in action" would not then be ascribable solely to lag or "phase" (1965:37) but rather would give expression to the discontinuity between culture and social structure.

94. The association postulated here seems to have support in connection with a number of distinct aspects of legal process:

  Presence of legal controls: Schwartz (1954) may be read as asserting that relational density (and the consequent effectiveness of informal controls) is inversely related to the presence of legal controls (defined in terms of the presence of sanction specialists).

  Invocation (mobilization) of official controls: Black (1971:1097) finds that readiness to invoke police and insistence of complainants on arrest is associated with "relational distance" between the parties. Cf. Kawashima's (1963:45) observation that in Japan, where litigation was rare between parties to an enduring relationship regulated by shared ideals of harmony, resort to officials was common where such ties were absent, as in cases of inter-village and insurer-debtor disputes.

  Elaboration of authoritative doctrine: Derrett (1959:54) suggests that the degree of elaboration of authoritative learned doctrine in classical Hindu law is related to the likelihood that the forums applying such doctrine would be invoked, which is in turn dependent on the absence of domestic controls.

95. There are, of course, exceptions, such as the automobile manufacturers' administration of warranty claims described by Whitford (1968) or those same manufacturers' internal dealer relations tribunals described by Macaulay (1966).

96. The iceberg is not properly a legal one, hence the quotation marks. That is, I do not mean to impute any characteristics that might define the "legal" (officials, coercive sanctions, specialists, general rules) to all the instances in the iceberg. It is an iceberg of potential claims or disputes and the extent to which any sector of it is legalized is problematic. Cf. Abel (1974).

97. Contrast the more symmetrical "great pyramid of legal order" envisioned by Hart and Sacks (1958:312). Where the Hart and Sacks pyramid portrays private and official decision-making as successive moments of an integrated normative and institutional order, the present "iceberg" model suggests that the existence of disparate systems of settling disputes is a reflection of cultural and structural discontinuities.

98. Hazard (1970:246–47) suggests that the attractions of the courts include that they are open as of right, receptive to arguments based on principle and offer the advocate a forum in which he bears no responsibility for the consequences of having his argument prevail.

99. Dolbeare (1967:63). Owen (1971:68, 142) reports the parallel finding that in two Georgia counties "opinion leaders and influentials seldom use the court, except

for economic retrieval." Cf. Howard's (1969:346) observation that " . . . adjudication is preeminently a method for individuals, small groups and minorities who lack access to or sufficient strength within the political arena to mobilize a favorable change in legislative coalitions."

100. There are situations in which no settlement is acceptable to the OS. The most common case, perhaps, is that of the prisoner seeking post-conviction remedies. He has "infinite" costless time and nothing further to lose. Other situations may be imagined in which an OS stands only to gain by a test case and has the resources to expend on it. Consider, for example, the physician charged with ten counts of illegal abortion. Pleading guilty to one count if the state dropped the others and agreeing to a suspended sentence would still entail the loss of his license. Every year of delay is worth money, win or lose: the benefits of delay are greater than the costs of continued litigation.

When the price of alternatives becomes unacceptably high, we may find OSs swimming upstream against a clear rule and strategic disadvantage. (Cf. the explosion of selective service cases in the 1960's.) Such a process may be facilitated by, for example, the free entry afforded by the contingent fee. See Friedman and Ladinsky's (1967) description of the erosion of the fellow servant rule under the steady pounding of litigation by injured workmen with no place else to turn and free entry.

101. See Vose (1967) on the test-case strategy of the NAACP in the restrictive covenant area. By selecting clients to forward an interest (rather than serving the clients) the NAACP made itself an RP with corresponding strategic advantages over the opposite parties (neighborhood associations). The degree of such organizational support of interest groups in litigation affecting municipal powers is described in Vose (1966); but Dolbeare (1967:40), in his study of litigation over public policy issues in a suburban county, found a total absence of interest-group sponsorship and participation in cases at the trial court level. Vose (1972:332) concludes a historical review by observing that:

> Most constitutional cases before the Supreme Court . . . are sponsored or supported by an identifiable voluntary association . . . [This] has been markedly true for decades.

But Hakman (1966, 1969) found management of Supreme Court litigation by organized groups pursuing coherent long-range strategies to be relatively rare. But see Casper (1970) who contends that civil liberties and civil rights litigation in the Supreme Court is increasingly conducted by lawyers who are "group advocates" (that is, have a long-term commitment to a group with whose aims they identify) or "civil libertarians" (that is, have an impersonal commitment to the vindication of broad principles) rather than advocates. He suggests that the former types of representation lead to the posing of broader issues for decision.

102. Although judicial decisions do often embody or ratify compromises agreed upon by the parties, it is precisely at the level of rule promulgation that such splitting the difference is seen as illegitimate. On the ideological pressures limiting the role of compromise in judicial decision see Coons (1964).

103. Cf. Kalven (1958:165). There are, of course, exceptions, such as alimony, to this "once and for all" feature.

104. Hazard (1970:248−50) points out that courts are not well-equipped to address problems by devising systematic legal generalization. They are confined to the facts and theories presented by the parties in specific cases; after deciding the case before them, they lose their power to act; they have little opportunity to elicit commentary until after the event; and generally they can extend but not initiate legal principles. They have limited and rapidly diminishing legitimacy as devisers of new policy. Nor can courts do very much to stimulate and maintain political support for new rules.

105. See generally Friedman (1967:esp. 821); Hazard (1970:248−50). The limits of judicial competence are by no means insurmountable. Courts do administer bankrupt railroads, recalcitrant school districts, offending election boards. But clearly the amount of such affirmative administrative re-ordering that courts can undertake is limited by physical resources as well as by limitations on legitimacy.

106. See Lipsky (1970:176 ff) for an example of the way in which provision of symbolic rewards to more influential reference publics effectively substituted for the tangible reforms demanded by rent-strikers. More generally, Edelman (1967: chap. 2) argues that it is precisely unorganized and diffuse publics that tend to receive symbolic rewards, while organized professional ones reap tangible rewards.

107. For a useful summary of this literature, see Wasby (1970). Some broad generalizations about the conditions conducive to penetration may be found in Grossman (1970:545 ff); Levine (1970:599 ff).

108. Cf. Howard's (1969:365 ff) discussion of the relative ineffectualness of adjudication in voter registration and school integration (as opposed to subsequent legislative/administrative action) as flowing from judicial reliance on party initiative.

109. An analogous conclusion in the consumer protection field is reached by Leff (1970b:356). ("One cannot think of a more expensive and frustrating course than to seek to regulate goods or 'contract' quality through repeated law-suits against inventive 'wrongdoers.'") Leff's critique of Murray's (1969) faith in good rules to secure change in the consumer marketplace parallels Handler's (1966) critique of Reich's (1964a, 1964b) prescription of judicial review to secure change in welfare administration. Cf. Black's (1973:137) observation that institutions which are primarily reactive, requiring mobilization by citizens, tend to deal with specific instances rather than general patterns and, as a consequence, have little preventive capacity.

110. Consider for example the relative absence of litigation about schoolroom religious practices clearly in violation of the Supreme Court's rules, as reported by Dolbeare and Hammond (1971). In this case RPs who were able to secure rule-victories were unable or unwilling to invest resources to secure the implementation of the new rules.

111. See, for example, Mosier and Soble's (1973:61−64) study of the Detroit Landlord-Tenant Court, where even after the enactment of new tenant defenses (landlord breach, retaliation), landlords obtained all they sought in 97% of cases. The new defenses were raised in only 3% of all cases (13% of the 20% that were contested) although, the authors conclude, "many defendants doubtless had valid landlord-breach defenses."

112. Randall (1968: chap. 7). Cf. Macaulay's (1966:156) finding that the most im-

portant impact of the new rules was to provide leverage for the operation of informal and private procedures in which dealers enjoyed greater bargaining power in their negotiations with manufacturers.

113. Some administrative agencies approximate this kind of "activist" posture. Cf. Nonet's (1969:79) description of the California Industrial Accident Commission:

> When the IAC in its early days assumed the responsibility of notifying the injured worker of his rights, of filing his application for him, of guiding him in all procedural steps, when its medical bureau checked the accuracy of his medical record and its referees conducted his case at the hearing, the injured employee was able to obtain his benefits at almost no cost and with minimal demands on his intelligence and capacities.

In the American setting, at least, such institutional activism seems unstable; over time institutions tend to approximate the more passive court model. See Nonet (1969: chaps. 6–7) and generally Bernstein (1955: chap. 7) on the "judicialization" of administrative agencies.

114. Perhaps the expansive political role of the judiciary and the law in American society is acceptable precisely because the former is so passive and the latter so malleable to private goals. Cf. Selznick's (1969:225 ff) discussion of the "privatization" and "voluntarization" of legal regulation in the United States.

115. This would, of course, require the relaxation of barriers on information flow now imposed under the rubric of "professional ethics." See notes 46 and 51 above.

116. For some examples of OSs organizing and managing claims collectively see Davis and Schwartz (1967) and various pieces in Burghardt (1972) (tenant unions); McPherson (1972) (Contract Buyers League); Shover (1966) (Farmers Holiday Association—mortgagors); Finklestein (1954) (ASCAP—performing rights); Vose (1967) (NAACP); Macaulay (1966) (automobile dealers).

117. A similar enhancement of prowess in handling claims may sometimes be provided commercially, as by collection agencies. Nonet (1969:71) observes that insurance coverage may serve as a form of organization:

> When the employer buys insurance [against workman's compensation claims], he not only secures financial coverage for his losses, but he also purchases a claims adjustment service and the legal defense he may need. Only the largest employers can adequately develop such services on their own. . . . Others find in their carrier a specialized claims administration they would otherwise be unable to avail themselves of . . . to the employer, insurance constitutes much more than a way of spreading individual risks over a large group. One of its major functions is to pool the resources of possibly weak and isolated employers so as to provide them with effective means of self-help and legal defense.

118. On criminalization as a mode of aggregating claims, see Friedman (1973:258). This is typically a weak form of organization, for several reasons. First, there is so much law that officials typically have more to do than they have resources to do it with, so they tend to wait for complaints and to treat them as individual grievances. For example, the Fraud and Complaint Bureau described by McIntyre (1968) or the anti-discrimination commission described by Mayhew (1968). Cf. Selznick's (1969:225) observations on a general "tendency to turn enforcement agen-

cies into passive recipients of privately initiated complaints. . . . The focus is more on settling disputes than on affirmative action aimed at realizing public goals." Second, enforcers have a pronounced tendency not to employ litigation against established and respectable institutions. Consider, for instance, the patterns of air pollution enforcement described by Goldstein and Ford (1971) or the Department of Justice position that the penal provisions of the Refuse Act should be brought to bear only on infrequent or accidental polluters, while chronic ones should be handled by more conciliatory and protracted administrative procedures. (1 Env. Rptr. Cur. Dev. no. 12 at 288 [1970]). Compare the reaction of Arizona's Attorney General to the litigation initiated by the overzealous chief of his Consumer Protection Division, who had recently started an investigation of hospital pricing policies.

> I found out much to my shock and chagrin that anybody who is anybody serves on a hospital board of directors and their reaction to our hospital injury was one of defense and protection.
>
> My policy concerning lawsuits . . . is that we don't sue anybody except in the kind of emergency situation that would involve [a business] leaving town or sequestering money or records. . . . I can't conceive any reason why hospitals in this state are going to make me sue them. (*New York Times*, 1973).

119. On the greater strategic thrust of group-sponsored complaints in the area of discrimination, see Mayhew (1968:168–73).

120. Paradoxically, perhaps, the organization of OSs into a unit which can function as an RP entails the possibility of internal disputes with distinctions between OSs and RPs reappearing. On the re-emergence of these disparities in strategic position within, for example, unions, see Atleson (1967:485 ff) (finding it doubtful that Title I of the LMRDA affords significant protection to "single individuals"). Cf. Summers (1960); Atleson (1971) on the poor position of individual workers *vis-à-vis* unions in arbitration proceedings.

121. As an outspoken opponent of class actions puts it:

> When a firm with assets of, say, a billion dollars is sued in a class action with a class of several million and a potential liability of, say, $2 billion, it faces the possibility of destruction. . . . The potential exposure in broad class actions frequently exceeds the net worth of the defendants, and corporate management naturally tends to seek insurance against whatever slight chance of success plaintiffs may have (Simon, 1972:289–90).

He then cites "eminent plaintiffs' counsel" to the effect that:

> I have seen nothing so conducive to settlement of complex litigation as the establishment by the court of a class . . . whereas, if there were no class, it would not be disposed of by settlement.

122. The array of devices for securing judicial determination of broad patterns of behavior also includes the "public interest action" in which a plaintiff is permitted to vindicate rights vested in the general public (typically by challenging exercises of government power). (Homberger, 1974). Unlike the class action, plaintiff does not purport to represent a class of particular individuals (with all the procedural difficulties of that posture) and unlike the classic test case he is not confined to his own

grievance, but is regarded as qualified by virtue of his own injury to represent the interests of the general public.

123. However, there may be tensions among these commitments. Wexler (1970), arguing for the primacy of "organizing" (including training in lay advocacy) in legal practice which aims to help the poor, points to the seductive pull of professional notions of the proper roles and concerns of the lawyer. Cf. Brill's (1973) portrayal of lawyers' professional and personal commitment to "class action" cases (in which the author apparently includes all "test cases") as undercutting their avowed commitment to facilitate community organization. On the inherent limits of "organizing" strategies, see note 127.

124. That is, the "reciprocal immunities" (Friedman 1967:806) built on transaction costs of remedies would be narrowed and would be of the same magnitude for each party.

125. This is in Boxes II and III of Figure 2.1, where both parties are now RPs. But presumably in some of the litigation formerly in Box I, one side is capable of organization but the other is not, so new instances of strategic disparity might emerge. We would expect these to remain in the official system.

126. That is, in which the field level application of the official rules has moved closer to the authoritative "higher law" (see note 82).

127. Olson (1965) argues that capacity for coordinated action to further common interests decreases with the size of the group: " . . . relatively small groups will frequently be able voluntarily to organize and act in support of their common interests, and some large groups normally will not be able to do so" (1965:127). Where smaller groups can act in their common interest, larger ones are likely to be capable of so acting only when they can obtain some coercive power over members or are supplied with some additional selective incentives to induce the contribution of the needed inputs of organizational activity. (On the reliance of organizations on these selective incentives, see Salisbury [1969] and Clark and Wilson [1961].) Such selective incentives may be present in the form of services provided by a group already organized for some other purpose. Thus many interests may gain the benefits of organization only to the extent that those sharing them overlap with those with a more organizable interest (consider, for instance, the prominence of labor unions as lobbyists for consumer interests).

128. Cf. Fuller's (1969:23) observation that the notion of duty is most understandable and acceptable in a society in which relationships are sufficiently fluid and symmetrical so that duties "must in theory and practice be reversible."

129. Curiously these relationships have the character which Rawls (1958:98) postulates as a condition under which parties will agree to be bound by "just" rules; that is, no one knows in advance the position he will occupy in the proposed "practice." The analysis here assumes that while high turnover and unpredictable interchange of roles may approximate this condition in some cases, one of the pervasive and important characteristics of much human arranging is that the participants have a pretty good idea of which role in the arrangement they will play. Rawls (1971:136 ff) suggests that one consequence of this "veil of ignorance" (" . . . no one knows his place in society, his class position or social status; nor does he know his fortune in the distribution of natural assets and abilities, his intelligence and strength and the like") is

that "the parties have no basis for bargaining in the usual sense" and concludes that without such restriction "we would not be able to work out any definite theory of justice at all." "If knowledge of particulars is allowed, then the outcome is biased by arbitrary contingencies." If we posit knowledge of particulars as endemic, we may surmise that a "definite theory of justice" will play at most a minor role in explaining the legal process.

130. On exclusion of undesirable neighbors, see Babcock (1969); of undesirable sojourners, see the banishment policy described in Foote (1956).

131. See the anguished discovery (Seymour 1974:9) of this by a former United States Attorney in his encounter with local justice:

> When the police officer had finished his testimony and left the stand, I moved to dismiss the case as a matter of law, pointing out that the facts were exactly the same as in the case cited in the annotation to the statute. I asked the judge to please look at the statute and read the case under it. Instead he looked me straight in the eye and announced, "Motion denied."

132. It seems hardly necessary to adduce examples of this pervasive distaste of particularism. But consider Justice Frankfurter's admonition that "We must not sit like a kadi under a tree dispensing justice according to conditions of individual expediency." *Terminiello v. Chicago*, 337 U.S. 1, 11 (1948). Or Wechsler's (1959) castigation of the Supreme Court for departing from the most fastidiously neutral principles.

133. As Thurman Arnold observed, our law "compels the necessary compromises to be carried on *sub rosa*, while the process is openly condemned. . . . Our process attempts to outlaw the 'unwritten law.'" (1962:162). On the co-existence of stress on uniformity and rulefulness with discretion and irregularity, see Davis (1969).

134. Cf. Black's (1973:142–43) observations on "reactive" mobilization systems as a form of delegation which perpetuates diverse moral subcultures as well as reinforces systems of social stratification (141).

135. Some attempts at delineating and comparing such "local legal cultures" are found in Jacob (1969); Wilson (1968); Goldstein and Ford (1971). It should be emphasized that such variation is not primarily a function of differences at the level of rules. All of these studies show considerable variation among localities and agencies governed by the same body of rules.

136. I employ this term to refer to one distinctive style of accommodating social diversity and normative pluralism by combining universalistic law with variable application, local initiative and tolerated evasion. (Cf. the kindred usage of this term by Rheinstein [1972: chaps. 4, 10] to describe the divorce regime of contemporary western nations characterized by a gap between "the law of the books and the law in action;" and by ten Broek [1964–65] to describe the unacknowledged co-existence of diverse class-specific bodies of law.) This dualistic style might be contrasted to, among others, (a) a "millet" system in which various groups are explicitly delegated broad power to regulate their own internal dealings through their own agencies (cf. Reppetto, 1970); (b) official administration of disparate bodies of "special law" generated by various groups (for example, the application of their respective "personal laws" to adherents of various religions in South Asian countries. See Galanter [1968]). Although a legal system of the kind we have postulated is closest to

dualism, it is not a pure case, but combines all three. For some observations on changes in the relation of government law to other legal orderings, see Weber (1954: 16–20, 140–49).

137. The durability of "dualism" as an adaptation is reinforced by the fact that it is "functional" not only for the larger society, but that each of its "moieties" gives support to the other: the "higher law" masks and legitimates the "operating level"; the accommodation of particularistic interests there shields the "higher law" from demands and pressures which it could not accommodate without sacrificing its universalism and semblance of autonomy. I do not suggest that this explains why some societies generate these "dual" structures.

138. Indeed the response that reforms must wait upon rule-change is one of the standard ploys of targets of reform demands. See, for example, Lipsky's (1970:94–96) housing officials' claim that implementation of rent-strikers' demands required new legislation, when they already had the needed power.

139. Compare Dolbeare and Hammond's (1971:151) observation, based on their research into implementation of the school prayer decisions, that "images of change abound while the status quo, in terms of the reality of people's lives, endures."

140. On litigation as an organizational tool, see the examples given by Gary Bellow in *Yale Law Journal* (1970:1087–88).

141. Cf. Cahn and Cahn's (1970:1016 ff) delineation of the "four principal areas where the investment of . . . resources would yield critically needed changes: the creation (and legitimation) of new justice-dispensing institutions, the expansion of the legal manpower supply . . . the development of a new body of procedural and substantive rights, and the development of forms of group representation as a means of enfranchisement," and the rich catalog of examples under each heading.

142. The reformer who anticipates "legalization" (see text at note 126 above) looks to organization as a fulcrum for expanding legal services, improving institutional facilities and eliciting favorable rules. On the other hand, the reformer who anticipates "de-legalization" and the development of advantageous bargaining relationships/private remedy system may be indifferent or opposed to reforms of the official remedy system that would make it more likely that the official system would impinge on the RP v. RP relationship.

143. It is clear e.g. that what Agnew (1972:930) finds objectionable is the redistributive thrust of the legal services program:

> . . . the legal services program has gone way beyond the idea of a governmentally funded program to make legal remedies available to the indigent. . . . We are dealing, in large part, with a systematic effort to redistribute societal advantages and disadvantages, penalties and rewards, rights and resources.

144. Summed up neatly by the head of OEO programs in California, who, defending Governor Reagan's veto of the California Rural Legal Assistance program, said:

> What we've created in CRLA is an economic leverage equal to that of a large corporation. Clearly that should not be.

Quoted at Stumpf et al. (1971:65).

145. Cf. Note 48 above. It is submitted that legal professions that approximate "Type B" will not only accentuate the "have" advantages, but will also be most capable of producing redistributive change.

References

Abel, Richard L. (1974) "A Comparative Theory of Dispute Institutions in Society," 8 *Law & Society Review* 217.

Abel-Smith, Brian and Robert Stevens (1967) *Lawyers and the Courts: A Sociological Study of the English Legal System, 1750–1965.* Cambridge: Harvard University Press.

Agnew, Spiro (1972) "What's Wrong with the Legal Services Program," 58 *A.B.A. Journal* 930.

Akers, Ronald L. (1968) "The Professional Association and the Legal Regulation of Practice," 2 *Law & Society Review* 463.

Anderson, Stanley (1969) Ombudsman Papers: American Experience and Proposals, With a Comparative Analysis of Ombudsmen Offices by Kent M. Weeks. Berkeley: Univ. of Cal. Inst. of Govt. Studies.

Arnold, Thurman (1962) *The Symbols of Government.* New York: Harcourt Brace and World (First publication, 1935).

Aspin, Leslie (1966) "A Study of Reinstatement Under the National Labor Relations Act." Unpublished dissertation, Mass. Inst. of Tech., Dept. of Economics.

Atleson, James B. (1971) "Disciplinary Discharges, Arbitration and NLRB Deference," 20 *Buffalo Law Review* 355.

——— (1967) "A Union Member's Right of Free Speech and Assembly: Institutional Interests and Individual Rights," 51 *Minnesota Law Review* 403.

Aubert, Vilhelm (1967) "Courts and Conflict Resolution," 11 *Journal of Conflict Resolution* 40.

——— (1963) "Competition and Dissensus: Two Types of Conflict and of Conflict Resolution," 7 *Journal of Conflict Resolution* 26.

Babcock, Richard S. (1969) *The Zoning Game: Municipal Practices and Policies.* Madison: University of Wisconsin Press.

Battle, Jackson B. (1971) "In Search of the Adversary System—The Cooperative Practices of Private Criminal Defense Attorneys," 50 *Texas Law Review* 60.

Berman, Harold J. (1963) *Justice in the U.S.S.R.: An Interpretation of Soviet Law.* Revised Ed. Enlarged. New York: Vintage Books.

Bernstein, Marver H. (1955) *Regulating Business by Independent Commission.* Princeton: Princeton University Press.

Beutel, Frederick K. (1957) *Some Potentialities of Experimental Jurisprudence as a New Branch of Social Science.* Lincoln: University of Nebraska Press.

Black, Donald J. (1973) "The Mobilization of Law," 2 *Journal of Legal Studies* 125.

——— (1971) "The Social Organization of Arrest," 23 *Stanford Law Review* 1087.

——— (1970) "Production of Crime Rates," 35 *American Sociological Review* 733.

Blankenburg, Erhard, Viola Blankenburg and Hellmut Morason (1972) "Der lange Weg in die Berufung," in Rolf Bender (ed.) *Tatsachen Forschung in der Justiz.* Tübingen: C. B. Mohr, 1972.

Blumberg, Abraham S. (1967a) *Criminal Justice*. Chicago: Quadrangle Books.

———— (1967b) "The Practice of Law as a Confidence Game," 1 *Law & Society Review* 15.

Bohannan, Paul (1965) "The Differing Realms of the Law in The Ethnography of Law," in Laura Nader (ed.) *The Ethnography of Law* (= Part 2 of *American Anthropologist*, Vol. 67, No. 6).

Bonn, Robert L. (1972a) "Arbitration: An Alternative System for Handling Contract Related Disputes," 17 *Administrative Sciences Quarterly* 254.

———— (1972b) "The Predictability of Nonlegalistic Adjudication," 6 *Law & Society Review* 563.

Borkin, Joseph (1950) "The Patent Infringement Suit—Ordeal by Trial," 17 *University of Chicago Law Review* 634.

Brill, Harry (1973) "The Uses and Abuses of Legal Assistance," No. 31 (Spring) *The Public Interest* 38.

Bruff, Harold H. (1973) "Arizona's Inferior Courts," 1973 *Law and the Social Order* 1.

Burger, Warren (1970) "The State of the Judiciary—1970," 56 *A.B.A. Journal* 929.

Burghardt, Stephen (ed.) (1972) *Tenants and the Urban Housing Crisis*. Dexter, Mich.: The New Press.

Burnley, James H. IV (1973) "Comment, Solicitation by the Second Oldest Profession: Attorneys and Advertising," 8 *Harvard Civil Rights–Civil Liberties Law Review* 77.

Cahn, Edgar S. and Jean Camper Cahn (1970) "Power to the People or the Profession?—The Public Interest in Public Interest Law," 79 *Yale Law Journal* 1005.

Cameron, Mary Owen (1964) *The Booster and the Snitch: Department Shoplifting*. New York: Free Press of Glencoe.

Carlin, Jerome E. (1966) *Lawyers' Ethics: A Survey of the New York City Bar*. New York: Russell Sage Foundation.

———— (1962) *Lawyers on Their Own: A Study of Individual Practitioners in Chicago*. New Brunswick: Rutgers University Press.

Carlin, Jerome E. and Jan Howard (1965) "Legal Representation and Class Justice," 12 *U.C.L.A. Law Review* 381.

Casper, Jonathan D. (1970) "Lawyers Before the Supreme Court: Civil Liberties and Civil Rights, 1957–66," 22 *Stanford Law Review* 487.

Christianson, Barlow F. (1970) *Lawyers for People of Moderate Means: Some Problems of Availability of Legal Services*. Chicago: American Bar Foundation.

Clark, Peter B. and James Q. Wilson (1961) "Incentive Systems: A Theory of Organizations," 6 *Administrative Services Quarterly* 129.

Cohen, Julius, Reginald A.H. Robson and Alan Bates (1958) *Parental Authority: The Community and the Law*. New Brunswick: Rutgers University Press.

Cohn, Bernard S. (1959) "Some Notes on Law and Change in North India," 8 *Economic Development and Cultural Change* 79.

Columbia Journal of Law and Social Problems (1971) "Roman Catholic Ecclesiastical Courts and the Law of Marriage," 7 *Columbia Journal of Law and Social Problems* 204.

———— (1970) "Rabbinical Courts: Modern Day Solomons," 6 *Columbia Journal of Law and Social Problems* 49.

Community Service Society, Department of Public Affairs, Special Committee on

Consumer Protection (1974) *Large Grievances About Small Causes: New York City's Small Claims Court—Proposals for Improving the Collection of Judgments*. New York: New York City Community Service Society.

Conard, Alfred F., James N. Morgan, Robert W. Pratt, Jr., Charles F. Voltz and Robert L. Bombaugh (1964) *Automobile Accident Costs and Payments: Studies in the Economics of Injury Reparation*. Ann Arbor: University of Michigan Press.

Consumer Council (1970) *Justice Out of Reach: A Case for Small Claims Courts*. London: Her Majesty's Stationery Office.

Coons, John E. (1964) "Approaches to Court-Imposed Compromise—The Uses of Doubt and Reason," 58 *Northwestern University Law Review* 750.

Cressey, Donald R. (1969) Theft of the Nation: The Structure and Operations of Organized Crime in America. New York: Harper and Row.

Dahl, Robert A. (1958) "Decision-making in a Democracy: The Supreme Court as a National Policy-maker," 6 *Journal of Public Law* 279.

Davis, Gordon J. and Michael W. Schwartz (1967) "Tenant Unions: An Experiment in Private Law Making," 2 *Harvard Civil Rights–Civil Liberties Law Review* 237.

Davis, Kenneth Culp (1969) *Discretionary Justice: A Preliminary Inquiry*. Baton Rouge: Louisiana State University Press.

Derrett, J. Duncan M. (1959) "Sir Henry Maine and Law in India," 1959 (Part I) *Juridical Review* 40.

Dibble, Vernon K. (1973) "What Is, and What Ought to Be: A Comparison of Certain Formal Characteristics of the Ideological and Legal Styles of Thought," 79 *American Journal of Sociology* 511.

Dolbeare, Kenneth M. (1969) "The Federal District Courts and Urban Public Policy: An Exploratory Study (1960–1967)," in J. Grossman and J. Tanenhaus (eds.) *Frontiers of Judicial Research*. New York: John Wiley.

———— (1967) *Trial Courts in Urban Politics: State Court Policy Impact and Function in a Local Political System*. New York: John Wiley.

Dolbeare, Kenneth M. and Phillip E. Hammond (1971) *The School Prayer Decisions: From Court Policy to Local Practice*. Chicago: University of Chicago Press.

Doo, Leigh-Wei (1973) "Dispute Settlement in Chinese-American Communities," 21 *American Journal of Comparative Law* 627.

Durkheim, Emile (1964) *The Division of Labor in Society*. New York: Free Press.

Edelman, Murray (1967) *The Symbolic Uses of Politics*. Urbana: University of Illinois Press.

Ehrlich, Eugen (1936) *Fundamental Principles of the Sociology of Law*. New York: Russell and Russell Publishers.

Engle, C. Donald (1971) "Criminal Justice in the City." Unpublished dissertation. Department of Political Science, Temple University.

Ennis, Phillip H. (1967) *Criminal Victimization in the United States: A Report of a National Survey*. (President's Commission on Law Enforcement and Administration of Justice, Field Survey II.) Washington: Government Printing Office.

Felstiner, William L. F. (1974) "Influences of Social Organization on Dispute Processing," 9 *Law & Society Review* 63.

Finklestein, Herman (1954) "The Composer and the Public Interest—Regulation of Performing Rights Societies," 19 *Law and Contemporary Problems* 275.

Foote, Caleb (1956) "Vagrancy-type Law and Its Administration," 104 *University of Pennsylvania Law Review* 603.

Ford, Stephen D. (1970) *The American Legal System.* Minneapolis: West Publishing Co.

Frank, Jerome (1930) *Law and the Modern Mind.* New York: Coward-McCann.

Franklin, Marc, Robert H. Chanin and Irving Mark (1961) "Accidents, Money and the Law. A Study of the Economics of Personal Injury Litigation," 61 *Columbia Law Review* 1.

Friedman, Lawrence M. (1973) *A History of American Law.* New York: Simon and Schuster.

——— (1969) "Legal Culture and Social Development," 4 *Law & Society Review* 29.

——— (1967) "Legal Rules and the Process of Social Change," 19 *Stanford Law Review* 786.

Friedman, Lawrence M. and Jack Ladinsky (1967) "Social Change and the Law of Industrial Accidents," 67 *Columbia Law Review* 50.

Friedman, Lawrence M. and Stewart Macaulay (1967) "Contract Law and Contract Teaching: Past, Present, and Future," 1967 *Wisconsin Law Review* 805.

Fuller, Lon L. (1969) *The Morality of Law.* Revised ed., New Haven: Yale University Press.

Galanter, Marc (1968–69) "Introduction: The Study of the Indian Legal Profession," 3 *Law & Society Review* 201.

——— (1968) "The Displacement of Traditional Law in Modern India," 24 *Journal of Social Issues* 65.

Gellhorn, Walter (1966) *When Americans Complain: Governmental Grievance Procedures.* Cambridge: Harvard University Press.

Gifford, Daniel J. (1971) "Communication of Legal Standards, Policy Development and Effective Conduct Regulation," 56 *Cornell Law Review* 409.

Golding, Martin P. (1969) "Preliminaries to the Study of Procedural Justice," in G. Hughes (ed.) *Law, Reason and Justice.* New York: New York University Press.

Goldstein, Paul, and Robert Ford (1971) "The Management of Air Quality: Legal Structures and Official Behavior," 21 *Buffalo Law Review* 1.

Goldpaper, Sam (1971) "Judge Rules Caldwell Belongs to ABA Club," *New York Times,* Jan. 15, 1971, p. 69.

Gollan, David (1970) "Airline Agency Levies Big Fines," *New York Times,* Nov. 8, 1970, p. 88.

Grace, Roger (1970) "Justice, Chinese Style," 75 *Case and Comment* 50.

Grossman, Joel (1970) "The Supreme Court and Social Change: A Preliminary Inquiry," 13 *American Behavioral Sciences* 535.

Hahm, Pyong-Choon (1969) "The Decision Process in Korea," in G. Schubert and D. Danelski (eds.) *Comparative Judicial Behavior: Cross-Cultural Studies of Political Decision-Making in the East and West.* New York: Oxford University Press.

Hakman, Nathan (1966) "Lobbying the Supreme Court—An Appraisal of Political Science Folklore," 35 *Fordham Law Review* 15.

——— (1969) "The Supreme Court's Political Environment: The Processing of Noncommercial Litigation," in J. Grossman and J. Tanenhaus (eds.) *Frontiers of Judicial Research.* New York: John Wiley and Sons.

Hallauer, Robert Paul (1972) "Low Income Laborers as Legal Clients: Use Patterns and Attitudes Toward Lawyers," 49 *Denver Law Journal* 169.

Hamilton, Walter (1957) *The Politics of Industry*. New York: Alfred A. Knopf.

Handler, Joel (1967) *The Lawyer and his Community: The Practicing Bar in a Middlesized City*. Madison: University of Wisconsin Press.

——— (1966) "Controlling Official Behavior in Welfare Administration," in Jacobus ten Broek et al. (eds.) *The Law of the Poor*. San Francisco: Chandler Publishing Co.

Handler, Milton (1971a) "The Shift from Substantive to Procedural Innovations in Antitrust Suits," 26 *Record of N.Y.C. Bar Association* 124.

——— (1971b) "Twenty-Fourth Annual Antitrust Review," 26 *Record of N.Y.C. Bar Association* 753.

Hart, Henry M., Jr., and Albert M. Sacks (1958) "The Legal Process: Basic Problems in the Making and Application of Law." Cambridge, Mass.: Harvard Law School. Tentative Edition (Mimeographed).

Hazard, Geoffrey C., Jr. (1970) "Law Reforming in the Anti-Poverty Effort," 37 *University of Chicago Law Review* 242.

——— (1965) "After the Trial Court—The Realities of Appellate Review," in Harry Jones (ed.) *The Courts, the Public and the Law Explosion*. Englewood Cliffs: Prentice Hall.

Henderson, Dan Fenno (1968) "Law and Political Modernization in Japan," in Robert E. Ward (ed.) *Political Development in Modern Japan*. Princeton: Princeton University Press.

Hirschman, Albert O. (1970) *Exit, Voice, and Loyalty: Responses to Decline in Firms, Organizations and States*. Cambridge: Harvard University Press.

Hollingsworth, Robert J., William B. Feldman and David C. Clark (1973) "The Ohio Small Claims Court: An Empirical Study," 42 *University of Cincinnati Law Review* 469.

Homberger, Adolf (1974) "Private Suits in the Public Interest in the United States of America," 23 *Buffalo Law Review* 343.

——— (1971) "State Class Actions and the Federal Rule," 71 *Columbia Law Review* 609.

——— (1970) "Functions of Orality in Austrian and American Civil Procedure," 20 *Buffalo Law Review* 9.

Horsky, Charles (1952) *The Washington Lawyer*. Boston: Little, Brown and Co.

Howard, J. Woodford, Jr. (1969) "Adjudication Considered as a Process of Conflict Resolution: A Variation on Separation of Powers," 18 *Journal of Public Law* 339.

Hunting, Roger Bryand and Gloria S. Neuwirth (1962) *Who Sues in New York City? A Study of Automobile Accident Claims*. New York: Columbia University Press.

Hurst, James Willard (1950) *The Growth of American Law: The Law Makers*. Boston: Little, Brown and Co.

Ianni, Francis A. J. (1972) *A Family Business: Kinship and Control in Organized Crime*. New York: Russell Sage Foundation and Basic Books.

International Legal Center (1973) *Newsletter* No. 9, July 1973. New York: International Legal Center.

Jacob, Herbert (1969) *Debtors in Court: The Consumption of Government Services.* Chicago: Rand McNally.

Johnstone, Quintin and Dan Hopson, Jr. (1967) *Lawyers and Their Work: An Analysis of the Legal Profession in the United States and England.* Indianapolis: Bobbs Merrill Co.

Kalven, Harry, Jr. (1958) "The Jury, the Law and the Personal Injury Damage Award," 19 *Ohio State Law Journal* 158.

Kaplan, Benjamin, Arthur T. von Mehren and Rudolf Schaefer (1958) "Phases of German Civil Procedure," 71 *Harvard Law Review* 1193–1268, 1443–72.

Katz, Marvin (1969) "Mr. Lin's Accident Case: A Working Hypothesis on the Oriental Meaning of Face in International Relations on the Grand Scheme," 78 *Yale Law Journal* 1491.

Kawashima, Takeyoshi (1963) "Dispute Resolution in Contemporary Japan," in A.T. von Mehren (ed.) *Law in Japan: The Legal Order in a Changing Society.* Cambridge: Harvard University Press.

Kennedy, Duncan (1973) "Legal Formality," 2 *Journal of Legal Studies* 351.

Kidder, Robert L. (1974) "Formal Litigation and Professional Insecurity: Legal Entrepreneurship in South India," 9 *Law & Society Review* 11.

——— (1973) "Courts and Conflict in an Indian City: A Study in Legal Impact," 11 *Journal of Commonwealth Political Studies* 121.

——— (1971) "The Dynamics of Litigation: A Study of Civil Litigation in South Indian Courts." Unpublished Dissertation, Northwestern University.

Ladinsky, Jack (1963) "Careers of Lawyers, Law Practice and Legal Institutions," 28 *American Sociological Review* 47.

Lafave, Wayne R. (1965) *Arrest: The Decision to Take a Suspect into Custody.* Boston: Little, Brown and Co.

Large, Donald W. (1972) "Is Anybody Listening? The Problem of Access in Environmental Litigation," 1972 *Wisconsin Law Review* 62.

Laufer, Joseph (1970) "Embattled Victims of the Uninsured: In Court with New York's MVAIC, 1959–69," 19 *Buffalo Law Review* 471.

Le Var, C. Jeddy (1973) "The Small Claims Court: A Case Study of Process, Politics, Outputs and Factors Associated with Businessmen Usage." Unpublished Paper.

Leff, Arthur A. (1970a) "Injury, Ignorance, and Spite—The Dynamics of Coercive Collection," 80 *Yale Law Journal* 1.

——— (1970b) "Unconscionability and the Crowd Consumers and the Common-Law Tradition," 31 *University of Pittsburgh Law Review* 349.

Lepaulle, Pierre George (1950) "Law Practice in France," 50 *Columbia Law Review* 945.

Levine, Felice J. and Elizabeth Preston (1970) "Community Resource Orientation Among Low Income Groups," 1970 *Wisconsin Law Review* 80.

Levine, James P. (1970) "Methodological Concerns in Studying Supreme Court Efficacy," 4 *Law & Society Review* 583.

Light, Ivan H. (1972) *Ethnic Enterprise in America: Business and Welfare Among Chinese, Japanese and Blacks.* Berkeley: University of California Press.

Lipsky, Michael (1970) *Protest in City Politics: Rent Strikes, Housing, and the Power of the Poor.* Chicago: Rand McNally and Co.

Lobenthal, Joseph S., Jr. (1970) *Power and Put-On: The Law in America.* New York: Outerbridge and Dienstfrey.

Lockard, Duane (1968) *Toward Equal Opportunity: A Study of State and Local Antidiscrimination Laws.* New York: Macmillan Co.

Loeber, Dietrich A. (1965) "Plan and Contract Performance in Soviet Law," in W. Lafave (ed.) *Law in the Soviet Society.* Urbana: University of Illinois Press.

Lortie, Dan C. (1959) "Laymen to Lawmen: Law School, Careers, and Professional Socialization," 29 *Harvard Educational Review* 352.

Lowry, S. Todd (1973) "Lord Mansfield and the Law Merchant," 7 *Journal of Economic Issues* 605.

Lowy, Michael J. (n.d.) "A Good Name is Worth More than Money: Strategies of Court Use in Urban Ghana." Unpublished paper.

Macaulay, Stewart (1966) *Law and the Balance of Power: The Automobile Manufacturers and Their Dealers.* New York: Russell Sage Foundation.

———— (1963) "Non-Contractual Relations in Business: A Preliminary Study," 28 *American Sociological Review* 55.

MacCallum, Spencer (1967) "Dispute Settlement in an American Supermarket," in Paul Bohannan (ed.) *Law and Warfare.* Garden City, N.Y.: Natural History Press for American Museum of Natural History.

Marshall, Leon C. and Geoffrey May (1932) *The Divorce Court: Volume One-Maryland.* Baltimore: The Johns Hopkins Press.

Matza, David (1964) *Delinquency and Drift.* New York: John Wiley.

Mayhew, Leon H. (1973) "Institutions of Representation." A paper prepared for delivery at the Conference on the Delivery and Distribution of Legal Services, State University of New York at Buffalo, October 12, 1973.

———— (1971) "Stability and Change in Legal Systems," in Alex Inkeles and Bernard Barber (eds.) *Stability and Social Change.* Boston: Little, Brown and Co.

———— (1968) *Law and Equal Opportunity: A Study of the Massachusetts Commission Against Discrimination.* Cambridge: Harvard University Press.

Mayhew, Leon and Albert J. Reiss, Jr. (1969) "The Social Organization of Legal Contacts," 34 *American Sociological Review* 309.

McIntyre, Donald M. (1968) "A Study of Judicial Dominance of the Charging Process," 59 *Journal of Criminal Law, Criminology and Police Science* 463.

McIntyre, Donald M. and David Lippman (1970) "Prosecutors and Early Disposition of Felony Cases," 56 *A.B.A. Journal* 1154.

McPherson, James Alan (1972) "In My Father's House There are Many Mansions, and I'm Going to Get Me Some of Them, Too! The Story of the Contract Buyers League," 229(4) *Atlantic Monthly* 51.

Mentschikoff, Soia (1961) "Commercial Arbitration," 61 *Columbia Law Review* 846.

Merryman, John Henry (1969) *The Civil Law Tradition: An Introduction to the Legal Systems of Western Europe and Latin America.* Stanford, Cal.: Stanford University Press.

Miller, Frank W. (1969) *Prosecution: The Decision to Charge a Suspect with a Crime.* Boston: Little, Brown and Co.

Morgan, Richard S. (1968) *The Politics of Religious Conflict: Church and State in America.* New York: Pegasus.

Morrison, Charles (1974) "Clerks and Clients: Paraprofessional Roles and Cultural Identities in Indian Litigation," 9 *Law & Society Review* 39.

Mosier, Marilyn Miller and Richard A. Soble (1973) "Modern Legislation, Metropolitan Court, Miniscule Results: A Study of Detroit's Landlord-Tenant Court," 7 *University of Michigan Journal of Law Reform* 6.

Moulton, Beatrice A. (1969) "The Persecution and Intimidation of the Low-Income Litigant as Performed by the Small Claims Court in California," 21 *Stanford Law Review* 1657.

Murphy, Walter (1959) "Lower Court Checks on Supreme Court Power," 53 *American Political Science Review* 1017.

Murray, John E., Jr. (1969) "Unconscionability: Unconscionability," 31 *University of Pittsburgh Law Review* 1.

Nader, Laura (1965) "The Anthropological Study of Law," in Laura Nader (ed.), *The Ethnography of Law* (= Part 2 of *American Anthropologist*, volume 67, No. 6).

Nagel, Stuart S. (1973) "Effects of Alternative Types of Counsel on Criminal Procedure Treatment," 48 *Indiana Law Journal* 404.

New York Times, "Arizona Losing Consumer Chief," April 22, 1973, p. 39.

Newman, Donald J. (1966) *Conviction: The Determination of Guilt or Innocence Without Trial*. Boston: Little, Brown and Co.

Nonet, Philippe (1969) *Administrative Justice: Advocacy and Change in a Government Agency*. New York: Russell Sage Foundation.

Northwestern University Law Review (1953) "Settlement of Personal Injury Cases in the Chicago Area," 47 *Northwestern University Law Review* 895.

O'Connell, Jeffrey (1971) *The Injury Industry and the Remedy of No-Fault Insurance*. Chicago: Commerce Clearing House.

O'Gorman, Hubert (1963) *Lawyers and Matrimonial Cases: A Study of Informal Pressures in Private Professional Practice*. New York: Free Press.

Ohlhausen, George C. (1936) "Rich and Poor in Civil Procedure," 11 *Science and Society* 275.

Olson, Mancur, Jr. (1965) *The Logic of Collective Action: Public Goods and the Theory of Groups*. Cambridge: Harvard University Press.

Orbell, John M. and Toro Uno (1972) "A Theory of Neighborhood Problem Solving: Political Action *vs.* Residential Mobility," 66 *American Political Science Review* 471.

Owen, Harold J., Jr. (1971) "The Role of Trial Courts in the Local Political System: A Comparison of Two Georgia Counties." Unpublished dissertation, Department of Political Science, University of Georgia.

Pagter, C.R., R. McCloskey and M. Reinis (1964) "The California Small Claims Court," 52 *California Law Review* 876.

Parsons, Talcott (1954) "A Sociologist Looks at the Legal Profession," in *Essays in Sociological Theory*. New York: Free Press.

Powell, Richard R. and Patrick J. Rohan (1968) *Powell on Real Property*. One Volume Ed. New York: Mathew Bender.

Rabin, Robert L. (1972) "Agency Criminal Referrals in the Federal System: An empirical study of prosecutorial discretion," 24 *Stanford Law Review* 1036.

Rabinowitz, Richard W. (1968) "Law and the Social Process in Japan," in *Transactions of the Asiatic Society of Japan*, Third Series, Volume X. Tokyo.

Randall, Richard S. (1968) *Censorship of the Movies: Social and Political Control of a Mass Medium*. Madison: University of Wisconsin Press.

Rankin, Anne (1964) "The Effect of Pretrial Detention," 39 *N.Y.U. Law Review* 641.

Rawls, John (1971) *A Theory of Justice*. Cambridge: Harvard University Press.

——— (1958) "Justice as Fairness," 68 *The Philosophical Review* 80.

Reich, Charles (1964a) "The New Property," 73 *Yale Law Journal* 733.

——— (1964b) "Individual Rights and Social Welfare: The Emerging Legal Issues," 74 *Yale Law Journal* 1245.

Reichstein, Kenneth J. (1965) "Ambulance Chasing: A Case Study of Deviation Within the Legal Profession," 3 *Social Problems* 3.

Reppetto, Thomas (1970) "The Millet System in the Ottoman and American Empires," 5 *Public Policy* 629.

Republic Research, Inc. (1970) "Claims and Recovery for Product Injury Under the Common Law," in National Commission on Product Safety, Supplemental Studies, Vol. III: *Product Safety Law and Administration: Federal, State, Local and Common Law*. Washington: U.S. Government Printing Office, 237.

Rheinstein, Max (1972) *Marriage Stability, Divorce and the Law*. Chicago: University of Chicago Press.

Rosenthal, Albert J. (1971) "Negotiability—Who Needs It?," 71 *Columbia Law Review* 375.

Rosenthal, Douglas E. (1970) Client Participation in Professional Decision: the Lawyer-Client Relationship in Personal Injury Cases. Unpublished dissertation. Yale University.

Ross, H. Laurence (1970) *Settled Out of Court: The Social Process of Insurance Claims Adjustment*. Chicago: Aldine.

Rothstein, Lawrence E. (1974) "The Myth of Sisyphus: Legal Services Efforts on Behalf of the Poor," 7 *University of Michigan Journal of Law Reform* 493.

Rothwax, Harold J. (1969) "The Law as an Instrument of Social Change," in Harold H. Weissman (ed.) *Justice and the Law in the Mobilization for Youth Experience*. New York: New York Association Press.

Saari, David J. (1967) "Open Doors to Justice—An Overview of Financing Justice in America," 50 *Journal of the American Judicature Society* 296.

Salisbury, Robert H. (1969) "An Exchange Theory of Interest Groups," 13 *Midwest Journal of Political Science* 1.

Schelling, Thomas C. (1963) *The Strategy of Conflict*. New York: Oxford University Press.

Schrag, Philip G. (1969) "Bleak House 1968: A Report on Consumer Test Litigation," 44 *N.Y.U. Law Review* 115.

Schwartz, Richard D. (1954) "Social Factors in the Development of Legal Control: A Case Study of Two Israeli Settlements," 63 *Yale Law Journal* 471.

Scigliano, Robert (1971) *The Supreme Court and the Presidency*. New York: Free Press.

Scott, William G. (1965) *The Management of Conflict: Appeal Systems in Organizations*. Homewood, Ill.: Irwin/Dorsey.

Selznick, Philip with the collaboration of Philippe Nonet and Howard M. Vollmer (1969), *Law, Society and Industrial Justice*. Russell Sage Foundation.

Seymour, Whitney North, Jr. (1974) "Frontier Justice: A Run-In With the Law," *The New York Times*, July 21, 1974, § 10, p. 1.

Shklar, Judith N. (1964) *Legalism*. Cambridge: Harvard University Press.

Shover, John L. (1966) *Cornbelt Rebellion: The Farmers' Holiday Association*. Urbana: University of Illinois Press.

Shriver, George H. (ed.) (1966) *America's Religious Heretics: Formal and Informal Trials in American Protestantism*. Nashville: Abdingdon Press.

Shuchman, Philip (1971) "The Fraud Exception in Consumer Bankruptcy," 23 *Stanford Law Review* 735.

——— (1969) "Profit on Default: an archival study of automobile repossession and resale," 22 *Stanford Law Review* 20.

——— (1968) "Ethics and Legal Ethics: The Propriety of the Canons as a Group Moral Code," 37 *George Washington Law Review* 244.

Simkin, William E. (1971) *Mediation and the Dynamics of Collective Bargaining*. Washington: Bureau of National Affairs.

Simon, William (1972) "Class Actions—Useful Tool or Engine of Destruction," 55 *Federal Rules Decisions* 375.

Skolnick, Jerome (1967) "Social Control in the Adversary Process," 11 *Journal of Conflict Resolution* 52.

——— (1966) *Justice Without Trial: Law Enforcement in a Democratic Society*. New York: John Wiley.

Small Claims Study Group (1972) "Little Injustices: Small Claims Courts and the American Consumer." A preliminary report to The Center for Auto Safety, Cambridge, Mass.

Smigel, Erwin O. (1969) *The Wall Street Lawyer: Professional Organization Man?* Bloomington: Indiana University Press.

Smith, Regan G. (1970) "The Small Claims Court: a Sociological Interpretation." Unpublished dissertation, Department of Sociology, University of Illinois.

Spradley, James P. (1970) *You Owe Yourself a Drunk: An Ethnography of Urban Nomads*. Boston: Little, Brown and Co.

Stumpf, Harry P., Henry P. Schroerluke and Forrest D. Dill (1971) "The Legal Profession and Legal Services: Explorations in Local Bar Politics," 6 *Law & Society Review* 47.

Sudnow, David (1965) "Normal Crimes: Sociological Features of the Penal Code in a Public Defender Office," 12 *Social Problems* 255.

Summers, Clyde (1960) "Individual Rights in Collective Agreements: A Preliminary Analysis," 9 *Buffalo Law Review* 239.

Tanner, Nancy (1970) "Disputing and the Genesis of Legal Principles: Examples from Minangkabau," 26 *Southwestern Journal of Anthropology* 375.

ten Broek, Jacobus (1964–65) "California's Dual System of Family Law: Its Origin, Development and Present Status," 16 *Stanford Law Review* 257–317, 900–81; 17 *Stanford Law Review* 614–82.

Trubek, David M. (1972) "Toward a Social Theory of Law: An Essay on the Study of Law and Development," 81 *Yale Law Journal* 1.

Tullock, Gordon (1971) *Logic of the Law.* New York: Basic Books, Inc.

Vaughan, Ted R. (1968) "The Landlord-Tenant Relationship in a Low-Income Area," 16 *Social Problems* 208.

Virtue, Maxine Boord (1956) *Family Cases in Court: A Group of Four Court Studies Dealing with Judicial Administration.* Durham: Duke University Press.

Vose, Clement E. (1972) Constitutional Change: Amendment Politics and Supreme Court Litigation Since 1900. Lexington, Mass.: D.C. Heath.

——— (1967) *Caucasians Only: The Supreme Court, the NAACP, and the Restrictive Covenant Cases.* Berkeley: University of California Press.

——— (1966) "Interest Groups, Judicial Review, and Local Government," 19 *Western Political Quarterly* 85.

Wald, Patricia (1964) "Foreword: Pretrial Detention and Ultimate Freedom," 39 *N.Y.U. Law Review* 631.

Wanner, Craig (1974) "The Public Ordering of Private Relations: Part I: Initiating Civil Cases in Urban Trial Courts," 8 *Law & Society Review* 421.

——— (1975) "The Public Ordering of Private Relations: Part II: Winning Civil Cases in Urban Trial Courts," 9 *Law & Society Review* 293–306.

——— (1973) "A Harvest of Profits: Exploring the Symbiotic Relationship between Urban Civil Trial Courts and the Business Community." Paper prepared for delivery at the 1973 Annual Meeting of the American Political Science Association.

Wasby, Stephen L. (1970) *The Impact of the United States Supreme Court: Some Perspectives.* Homewood, Ill.: The Dorsey Press.

Weber, Max (1954), Max Rheinstein (ed.) *Max Weber on Law in Economy and Society.* Cambridge: Harvard University Press.

Wechsler, Herbert (1959) "Toward Neutral Principles of Constitutional Law," 73 *Harvard Law Review* 1.

Wexler, Stephen (1970) "Practicing Law for Poor People," 79 *Yale Law Journal* 1049.

Whitford, William C. (1968) "Law and the Consumer Transaction: A case study of the automobile warranty," 1968 *Wisconsin Law Review* 1006.

Wilson, James Q. (1968) *Varieties of Police Behavior: The Management of Law and Order in Eight Communities.* Cambridge: Harvard University Press.

Woll, Peter (1960) "Informal Administrative Adjudication: Summary of Findings," 7 *U.C.L.A. Law Review* 436.

Yale Law Journal (1970) "The New Public Interest Lawyers," 79 *Yale Law Journal* 1069.

Yngvesson, Barbara (1973) "Responses to Grievance Behavior: Extended Cases in a Fishing Community," Forthcoming in Michael Lowy (ed.) *Choice-Making in the Law.*

——— (1965) "The Berkeley-Albany and Oakland-Piedmont Small Claims Court: A Comparison of Role of the Judge and Social Function of the Courts." Unpublished paper.

Zeisel, Hans, Harry Kalven, Jr., and Bernard Buchholz (1959) *Delay in the Court.* Boston: Little, Brown and Co.

PART TWO

Testing the Hypotheses

DONALD R. SONGER, REGINALD S. SHEEHAN, AND SUSAN BRODIE HAIRE

3

Do the "Haves" Come Out Ahead over Time?

Applying Galanter's Framework to Decisions of the U.S. Courts of Appeals, 1925–1988

Introduction

Galanter's watershed analysis (1974) made a compelling case for the proposition that the "haves" tend to come out ahead in litigation. Since the publication of this analysis, Galanter's methods and theoretical insights have spawned numerous studies that have examined the advantages of some litigants in a wide variety of courts. Several studies of trial courts have confirmed Galanter's basic findings (Owen 1971; Wanner 1975). Generally, these findings indicate that classes of litigants with the greatest resources and the lowest relative stakes in litigation have the highest rates of success in trial courts; government has been more successful in litigation than have businesses or other organizations, and organizations have been more successful than individual litigants. Galanter (1974) suggests that these "haves" will win more frequently because they are likely to have favorable law on their side, superior material resources, and better lawyers and because a number of advantages accrue to them as a result of their "repeat player" status. Superior resources allow the "haves" to hire the best available legal representation and to incur legal expenses, such as those associated with extensive discovery and expert witnesses, that may increase the chances of success at trial. In addition, as repeat players, they will reap the benefits of greater litigation experience, including the ability to develop and implement a comprehensive litigation strategy that may involve forum shopping and making informed judgments regarding their prospects of winning at trial or on appeal.

The question of who wins and loses in U.S. courts may be the most important question we seek to answer as judicial scholars. In fact, "Who gets what?" has traditionally been viewed as one of the central questions in the study of politics more generally. In the United States, the courts are widely viewed as key institutions for the legitimate settlement of a wide spectrum of conflicts between individuals and groups that have important implications for the distribution of material and symbolic goods. Therefore, understanding who wins in the courts is an essential component of a full appreciation of "the authoritative allocation of values" in society (Easton 1953). Moreover, because the courts of appeals are the final arbiters for the vast majority of federal litigation, it is important to determine how different types of litigants have been received by these courts. In this article, we assess whether particular types of litigants win, or lose, more frequently in the U.S. Courts of Appeals than other types and whether their success varies over time. Drawing from Galanter's work, our comparison includes examining the success rates of repeat players, the "haves," and one shotters, who are usually "have nots," in the U.S. Courts of Appeals from 1925 to 1988.

Existing Research on the "Haves" in Appellate Courts

At the appellate level, support has been found for Galanter's proposition that the "haves" come out ahead in a wide variety of venues. In a study of 16 state supreme courts from 1870 to 1970, Wheeler et al. (1987) applied the general framework of Galanter's analysis to examine the relative success on appeal of five general classes of litigants. Overall, their findings were consistent with the theoretical expectations derived from Galanter, but the relative advantage of repeat player "haves" was modest. In matchups between stronger and weaker parties, the stronger, repeat player party was consistently more successful, with an advantage averaging 5%. Most notable was the consistent success of governments compared with litigants without organizational resources (ibid.).

The explanation for the higher success rates enjoyed by presumably stronger parties is consistent with that offered by Galanter. According to Wheeler et al. (ibid., p. 441):

The greater resources of the stronger parties presumably confer advantages beyond hiring better lawyers on appeal. Larger organizations may be more experienced and thus better able to conform their behavior to the letter of the law or to build a better trial court record, matters on which we have no evidence. Experience and wealth also imply the capacity to be more selective in deciding which cases to appeal or defend when the lower court loser appeals.

Because Wheeler et al. did not collect any data on judges' attitudes or values, they were unable to systematically determine whether the success of stronger parties was due to attitudinal factors. They speculated, however, that the greater success of large units of government versus small units of government and the greater success of big business against small business made such an interpretation unlikely. Thus, greater litigation resources was the most likely explanation of the empirical results.

More dramatic confirmation of Galanter's insights came in an analysis of the decisions of the U.S. Courts of Appeals. Songer and Sheehan's (1992) examination of both published and unpublished decisions of the courts of appeals discovered that the overall success rate of governments was roughly four times as high as the success rate of individuals and one and a half times the success rate of businesses. Trial court decisions, however, are usually affirmed by the U.S. Courts of Appeals (Howard 1981; Davis & Songer 1988). Therefore, Songer and Sheehan (1992) employed a measure of "net advantage" developed by Wheeler et al. (1987) that takes into account whether parties are able to overcome the tendency to affirm. This index of net advantage is computed for each type of litigant by first taking their success rate when they appear as the appellant and from that figure subtracting their opponents' success rate in those cases in which the litigant of interest participates as respondent. This index of advantage is independent of the relative frequency that different classes of litigants appear as appellants versus respondents. Songer and Sheehan (1992) found that businesses enjoyed an advantage of nearly 20 percentage points over individuals but were disadvantaged compared with the federal government by over 40 percentage points. In a multivariate analysis with controls for the type of issue and judicial ideology, litigant status continued to be strongly related to case outcome. Although the findings were impressive, this study was limited to decisions in a single year (1986) and drawn from only 3 of the 12 circuits.

Several analyses applying Galanter's theoretical perspectives to the decisions of courts in other nations have generated comparable findings. For example, McCormick found that in the Canadian Supreme Court, the federal government enjoyed a net advantage that was approximately five percentage points higher than that of big businesses, 15 points higher than the advantage of other businesses, and approximately 30 points higher than the rate for individuals (1993:532). Similarly, in the English Court of Appeals, Atkins discovered that governments enjoyed a 25% advantage over corporate litigants and corporations enjoyed a 14% advantage over individuals (1991:895). Preliminary studies of the high courts in both South Africa and India have discovered a similar pattern, with the "haves" enjoying higher rates of success than the "have nots" (Haynie et al. 1994). Thus, the general thesis that repeat player "haves" tend to fare well and that one-shot litigants lose frequently appears to have considerable cross-national validity, at least among countries in the English common law tradition.

The major exceptions to the general pattern of success in appellate courts have been observed in the supreme courts of the United States and the

Philippines. Sheehan et al. (1992) examined the success of 10 categories of parties in the U.S. Supreme Court over a 36-year period and concluded that there was little evidence that repeat player status or litigant resources had a major impact on success in that forum. Although the federal government was the most successful litigant and poor individuals had the lowest overall rates of success, other patterns of success were not consistent with predictions derived from Galanter's theory. For example, poor individuals enjoyed a net advantage over state governments, and minorities were more successful than either local governments or businesses when paired against each other. Instead, the success of different classes of litigants was closely related to the changing ideological composition of the Court (e.g., the poor fared substantially better in liberal courts, and business was most successful in conservative courts). A similar failure to find a consistent pattern of success for the most advantaged litigants was observed in an analysis of the decisions of the Philippine Supreme Court. In fact, Haynie (1994) discovered that individuals tended to have higher rates of success than either governments or business litigants. Haynie concluded that in developing societies, there may be pressure for courts to support redistributive policies as a means of enhancing their legitimacy as a political institution. Such a concern for legitimacy may tend to outweigh the advantage that the haves would "normally" receive from superior experience and resources.

Collectively, existing research suggests that Galanter's insights on trial courts are also helpful in understanding case processing and outcomes in appellate courts, particularly state courts of last resort and lower federal appeals courts in the United States. As the summary of existing research in Table 3.1 indicates, in these courts, governmental litigants, with litigation resources and repeat player experience, appear to enjoy more success than any other type of litigant. On the other hand, individual litigants, generally one shotters, are not likely to succeed in lower appellate courts. In this article, we attempt to develop further our understanding of when and why the "haves" come out ahead by analyzing, over time, published decisions from all circuits of the U.S. Courts of Appeals. We apply a framework similar to that employed by Galanter (1974), Songer and Sheehan (1992), and Wheeler et al. (1987) to determine whether earlier findings are time bound. To overcome the limitations of the only previous analysis of the courts of appeals (that examined data from only three circuits and a single year), we focus on decisions from all circuits in the U.S. Courts of Appeals for a 64-year period, 1925 to 1988, and examine the extent to which categories of litigants have prevailed before the appeals courts in different periods. Because the position of the circuit courts within the legal system is closer to that of state supreme courts than it is to either the U.S. Supreme Court or to the trial courts examined by Galanter, the design employed for this analysis parallels the ap-

TABLE 3.1

Applying Galanter's Framework to Decisions of Appellate Courts (Summary of Prior Research)

	Net Advantage				
Type of Litigant	State Supreme Courts (1)	U.S. Courts of Appeals (2)	U.S. Supreme Court (3)	Canadian Supreme Court (4)	Philippine Supreme Court (5)
Federal government	n.a.	+45.1	+35.9	+20.4	-10.8[a]
State/city government	+11.8	+29.9	—	—	—
State government	—	—	+11.2	+3.7[b]	—
Local government	-1.6[c]	—	-6.3	-2.5	—
"Big business"	+6.4	+5.9	-19.3	+15.0	n.a.
Business	+3.1	+1.6	-11.9	-5.9	-9.1
Individuals	-1.5	-18.2	-17.4	-9.6	+13.7

SOURCES: Col. (1): Wheeler et al. 1987; col. (2): Songer and Sheehan 1992 (analysis of 1986 decisions of three circuits); col. (3): Sheehan et al. 1992 (analysis of U.S. Supreme Court decisions, 1953–1988); col. (4): McCormick 1993; col. (5): Haynie 1994 (analysis of decisions of the Philippine Supreme Court, 1961–1986).

[a] Includes all levels of government.
[b] Provincial government net advantage.
[c] "Small" local governments.

proaches taken by Wheeler et al. (ibid.) in their research on state courts of last resort and by Songer and Sheehan (1992) in their earlier study of the federal circuit courts.

Data and Measures

To examine the success of "haves" and "have nots" in cases decided by the U.S. Courts of Appeals, we selected data from the recently released appeals court database. The database includes data on the nature of the appellant and respondent, the issue, the party of the judges on each panel, and the outcome of all cases from a random sample of published decisions from each circuit for each year from 1925 through 1988.

To facilitate the analysis of change over time, the 64 years of data included in the U.S. Courts of Appeals Data Base were divided into five periods. The periods capture significant changes in the legal and political history of the twentieth century that might plausibly affect the relative likelihood of success by certain categories of litigants. In the first period, 1925–1936, the legal system was dominated by conservative, probusiness judges at all levels of the judicial system. Our second period, 1937–1945, begins with the "switch in time that saved nine" that marked the beginning of the Roosevelt Court and its aggressive pro-New Deal policies. Throughout this period, the courts came to be dominated by Roosevelt judges who were selected in large part for their devotion to New Deal economic policies that had a decidedly pro-underdog orientation (Goldman 1997). The third period, 1946–1960, was characterized by economic prosperity and the selection of lower court judges (by Truman and Eisenhower) without much regard for their policy preferences (ibid.). The fourth period, 1961–1969, was most notable for the leadership of the judiciary by the Warren Court (perhaps the most liberal Supreme Court in our history), a pair of Democratic presidents in the White House, dramatic agitation in Congress and on the streets for expansion of civil rights, and strident advocacy for the welfare of poor people that culmi-nated in President Johnson's "War on Poverty." During our final period, 1970–1988, the Supreme Court became steadily more conservative as the appointees of Nixon, Ford, and Reagan ascended to the high bench. These general trends suggest that in two periods (1937–1945 and 1961–1969), the courts should have been staffed by a considerable number of judges who were sympathetic to the interests of one-shot "have not" litigants (especially the poor), whereas in our first and last periods (1925–1936 and 1970–1988), the courts appear to have been dominated by political conservatives who presumably had probusiness proclivities. Our middle period, 1946–1960, would appear to represent a time of moderation. The analysis here examines whether the different political orientations that characterized these five pe-riods were marked by different levels of success in courts for litigants with different status.

As prior attempts to operationalize and apply Galanter's concepts have pointed out (Atkins 1991; McCormick 1993; Songer & Sheehan 1992; Wheeler et al. 1987), specific information about the wealth of particular par-ties in a given case or the relative litigation experience of those parties is of-ten not available in court opinions. Because the data for this study, like the data for these earlier studies, were derived from court opinions, there was rarely enough information to unambiguously classify one of the parties as having greater litigation experience, wealth, or other relevant resources than their adversary. Consequently, we adopted the strategy employed by Mc-Cormick (1993), Songer and Sheehan (1992), and Wheeler et al. (1987) of as-signing litigants to general classes and then making assumptions about which class was usually the stronger party.

Each appellant and each respondent were classified as belonging to one of five major classes: individual litigants, businesses,[1] state and local govern-ments, the U.S. government, or other. "Other" included unions; nonprofit (private) organizations; nonprofit (private) schools; social, charitable, or fra-ternal organizations; political parties; and litigants who could not be unam-biguously categorized. Into this "other" category fell 7.8% of the appellants and 6.3% of the respondents. They were excluded from analysis because they could not be categorized in terms of litigation resources. If the party listed in the case citation was a named individual, but his or her involvement in the suit was due directly to his or her role as an official of a government agency or as an officer, partner, or owner of a business, the code was based on the organizational affiliation and not as an individual. For example, if the chief executive officer of a multinational corporation was appealing a criminal conviction for personal income tax evasion, the appellant was coded as an individual. If the chief of police was the subject of a 1983 suit for damages because of an alleged torture of a prisoner held in that chief's jail, however, the defendant would be classified in the local government category. All government agencies, even those who are "independent" of the chief executive, and government corporations were categorized in the appropriate government class (for example, the National Labor Relations Board and the Tennessee Valley Authority were classified in the federal government class). Like McCormick (1993), Wheeler et al. (1987), and others who have attempted to operationalize and test Galanter's theory, we assume that individuals usually have less experience and fewer resources than either businesses or units of governments.[2] When business and governmental parties oppose one another, we assume that governments will usually be stronger because even when the financial resources of government are no greater than those of the business, the government agency is more likely to be a repeat player (or a more frequent repeat player in the particular issue area involved in the suit).[3]

We defined winners and losers by looking at "who won the appeal in its most immediate sense, without attempting to view the appeal in some larger context" (ibid., p. 415). Thus, for example, if the decision of the district court or the administrative agency was "reversed," "reversed and remanded," "vacated," or "vacated and remanded," the appellant was coded as winning, regardless of whether the opinion announced a doctrine that was broad or narrow and regardless of whether that doctrine might be supposed in general to benefit future haves or have nots. Also, like McCormick (1993) and others, we excluded from analysis all cases with ambiguous results (e.g., those in which the court affirmed in part and reversed in part).

Our focus is on whether or not any relative advantage accrues to those classes of parties with superior litigation experience and resources. In the federal court system, the trial court loser enjoys a constitutional right of appeal. Although rational calculations of the chances of winning may exert a substantial impact on some decisions about whether or not to appeal, it will be rational for many litigants to appeal even if their chances of obtaining a reversal are substantially less than 50%. Appeals are brought by trial court losers after decision-makers (judge and jury) at trial made initial interpretations of the facts and the law. Therefore, even if appellate justice is blind and litigation resources are irrelevant, one would expect that respondents would prevail against the majority of appeals. In the data used in this study, the courts of appeals affirmed 72% of the decisions appealed to them. Therefore, to assess whether the hypothesized relative advantage of repeat players with superior wealth and status exists, it is not enough to know whether or not the "haves" won more frequently in an absolute sense. Instead, we must also explore whether they "were better able than other parties to buck the basic tendency of appellate courts to affirm" (Wheeler et al. 1987:407). Therefore, we used the index of net advantage described earlier because it provides a better measure of litigant success in courts over different time periods than a simple measure of the proportion of decisions won by a given class of litigants would.

Appellant Success and Net Advantage

The beginning point of analysis was to examine the appellant success rate for each of the four basic categories of litigants. The overall data for the 64-year period are presented in Table 3.2.[4] The data roughly parallel the results reported by Songer and Sheehan (1992) for the single year they examined. There were wide disparities in the relative success of different classes of appellants in the courts of appeals, and those differences were quite consistent with the expectations derived from Galanter. Despite the general propensity of the circuit courts to affirm, the federal government was successful on 51.3% of its appeals and had an overall rate of success (from its participation as an appellant and as a respondent) of 70%. At the other end of the spectrum, individuals won only 26.1% of their appeals and had an overall rate of success of only 35.1%. Moreover, the rank order of the success rates was exactly the order that would be predicted from Galanter's theory. Individuals had the lowest rate of success, followed, in order, by business, state and local government, and the federal government. Overall, the United States was twice as successful as individuals and one and a half times as successful as businesses.

As noted earlier, the net advantage index may be a better indicator of litigation success than the raw rate of success because it is unaffected by the relative frequency that a given class of litigant appears as an appellant rather than as a respondent. Thus, if there is a propensity to affirm in the courts of appeals, this propensity will not affect the index of net advantage. This net advantage for each class of litigant, displayed in Table 3.2, reinforces the picture suggested by the raw measures of success. Individuals suffered a sharply negative net advantage, businesses were slightly below zero, and both levels of government enjoyed strong positive numbers for their net advantage. The federal government, which won 51.3% of the cases it appealed, held adversaries to only a 25.7% success rate in the cases they appealed (i.e., the federal government won 74.3% of the cases in which it appeared as respondent),

TABLE 3.2

Combined Success Rates and Net Advantage in Litigation, by Nature of Party in the Courts of Appeals, 1925–1988

Litigant	Success Rate as Appellant		When Respondent, Opponents' Success Rate		Net Advantage	Combined Success Rate	N
Individual	26.1%	–	38.7	=	-12.6	35.1%	9,311
Business	30.8	–	33.6	=	-2.8	48.2	9,313
State or local govern- ment	45.0	–	29.4	=	+15.6	64.5	2,205
U.S. government	51.3	–	25.7	=	+25.6	70.0	7,319

*Significance testing with proportions yielded the following z scores when comparing net advantage figures for these categories of litigants:

Individual-business $z = 8.23, P < .001$.
Business–state/local government $z = 10.27, P < .001$.
State/local government–federal government $z = 6.06, P < .001$.

giving the United States a net advantage of 25.6%. State and local governments had a net advantage of 15.6%, whereas businesses had a slightly negative net advantage of 2.8%. At the bottom were individuals whose net advantage was -12.6%, a finding that reflects that those who filed appeals against individuals won substantially more often than individuals did when they appealed.[5] The data in Table 3.2 suggest that, overall, the fate of individuals and businesses for the entire 64-year period was similar to that noted in Songer and Sheehan's earlier analysis of 1986 appeals court decisions (see Table 3.1). In contrast, governments fared slightly better when analyzing only 1986 decisions rather than decisions from the entire 64 years. Still, the size of the advantage enjoyed by governments over both individuals and businesses displayed in Table 3.2 is substantially greater than the advantage enjoyed by governments in the analysis of state courts and moderately greater than the advantage enjoyed by governments in the Canadian Supreme Court (see Table 3.1 for comparisons).

Turning to the analysis of change over time, it is evident from the data in Table 3.3 that the haves win consistently throughout the 64-year period examined. Looking first at the overall success rates of each category of litigant presented in the top half of Table 3.3, we can see that individuals had the lowest rates of success in all five periods and businesses had lower rates of success than either category of government in every period. Moreover, the success of each category of litigant remains remarkably consistent over time. In every time period, the success of individuals falls within the 31% to 39% range, whereas the success of business litigants varies between 45% and slightly under 49%. Although the gap between individual and business suc-

TABLE 3.3

Combined Success Rates and Net Advantage in Litigation, by Nature of Party in the Courts of Appeals and by Period

A. Combined Success Rates of Litigants by Time Period (No. of Decisions)

Litigant	1925–36	1937–45	1946–60	1961–69	1970–88
Individual	39.2%	39.6%	33.7%	31.0%	33.9%
	(1,020)	(637)	(1,548)	(1,941)	(4,407)
Business	48.4	45.9	48.6	47.9	48.6
	(1,601)	(1,104)	(1,747)	(1,708)	(3,156)
State or local government	59.2	67.4	73.6	68.9	61.9
	(142)	(135)	(227)	(386)	(1,316)
U.S. government	68.8	64.6	67.2	73.6	70.7
	(701)	(625)	(1,267)	(1,578)	(3,205)

B. Net Advantage of Litigants by Time Period (No. of Decisions)

Litigant	1925–36	1937–45	1946–60	1961–69	1970–88
Individual	–11.7	–5.1	–12.9	–7.1	–17.0
	(1,020)	(637)	(1,548)	(1,941)	(4,407)
Business	+0.4	–6.1	–0.6	–4.0	–3.6
	(1,601)	(1,104)	(1,747)	(1,708)	(3,156)
State or local government	+12.9	+19.6	+23.5	+14.9	+14.2
	(142)	(135)	(227)	(386)	(1,316)
U.S. government	+21.8	+15.4	+15.6	+30.6	+33.6
	(701)	(625)	(1,267)	(1,578)	(3,205)

cess varies over time, the highest degree of success achieved by individuals remains 6 percentage points below the lowest level of success achieved by business litigants.

The thesis that the stronger, repeat player litigants should prevail also receives strong support from the data on changes in the net advantage of different classes of litigants displayed in Table 3.3. The net advantage scores, like the overall success rates, show that the "haves" were generally more successful than one shotters presumed to have fewer resources. In all five periods, individuals, presumably most of whom are one shotters whose stakes are large relative to their resources, had sharply negative net advantage rates. Business litigants, a category of litigants that presumably contains nontrivial numbers of both repeat players and one-shot players, had net advantage rates near zero. In contrast, the repeat player government litigants had strongly positive net advantage rates. Predictions derived from Galanter's work appear to be least

TABLE 3.4

Net Advantage of Repeat Player "Haves" for Different Combinations of Opposing Parties, 1925–1988

Repeat Player "Have" Litigant	Relative "Have Not"	Net Advantage
Business	Individual	6.3%
State and local government	Individual	19.5
U.S. government	Individual	34.5
State and local government	Business	21.2
U.S. government	Business	21.9
U.S. government	State and local government	16.9

satisfactory as an explanation of outcomes in the 1937–1945 period. During this period, which includes the height of the New Deal and the ascendancy of the Roosevelt Court, individuals appeared to fare about as well as businesses (slightly lower on overall success rates but with a slightly higher net advantage score). Whereas businesses and individuals fared substantially worse than either level of government, state and local governments were more successful than the federal government on both measures of success.

Both the rates of overall success and the index of net advantage reported in Tables 3.2 and 3.3 include cases in which a litigant faced another party in the same category. To further explore the advantage that the stronger party appears to have in cases before the federal circuit courts, we therefore followed the lead of Wheeler et al. (1987) and selected only those cases in which parties in different categories confronted each other. These comparisons are presented in Table 3.4.

When specific matchups are examined, the findings strongly support Galanter's theory. Individuals have low rates of success against all other categories of respondents, whereas the success rate of the United States as appellant remains high against all other parties. In every matchup, the repeat player party presumed to be stronger enjoyed a substantial net advantage.[6] The matchups involving individuals are particularly revealing. As the presumed strength and litigation experience of the opponent of the individual litigants increase, the size of the net advantage going to the stronger party rises steeply. The 6.3% net advantage that businesses[7] enjoy over individuals rises to 19.5% when individuals faced state governments and increases to a 34.5% advantage for the United States when it faces individuals.

Table 3.5 presents data on these same specific matchups for each of the five periods used in the prior analyses above. Unfortunately, state and local governments were not involved in a sufficient number of cases with opposing litigants in other categories to make comparisons possible in all periods.[8]

TABLE 3.5

Net Advantage of Repeat Player "Haves" for Different Combinations of Opposing Parties, by Period

Repeat Player "Have" Litigant	Relative Underdog	Net Advantage by Period				
		1925–36	1937–45	1946–60	1961–69	1970–88
Business	Individual	8.4%	33.6%	15.6%	–6.4%	8.0%
State and local government	Individual	a	a	a	16.7	16.6
U.S. government	Individual	29.5	33.3	31.5	36.3	43.9
State and local government	Business	31.6	27.5	a	a	22.7
U.S. government	Business	27.6	19.3	9.3	16.1	32.3
U.S. government	State and local government	a	a	a	a	22.8

*a*Matchups with fewer than 10 participations by each party in the indicated pair as both an appellant and a respondent.

An examination of the data reveals that there was only one matchup in which the stronger party did not enjoy a positive net advantage over its opponent. In the 1961–1969 period, individuals enjoyed a 6.4% net advantage over business litigants they faced as appellants and respondents. In all other matchups across time periods, however, the litigant with presumed greater litigation experience and resources enjoyed a strong net advantage (at least 8% in all other cases). For all matchups, the stronger party enjoyed an average net advantage of 22.7%. Most striking is the 33.6% net advantage enjoyed by businesses in their matchups with individuals in the 1937–1945 period. Because it was noted that, overall, individuals had a lower negative net advantage than businesses for this period, the data in Table 3.5 suggest that the apparently weaker showing by businesses in the earlier table was due to the relative strength of the opponents faced by individuals and businesses. Specifically, the data suggest that, on average, businesses were more likely than individuals to face repeat player "have" litigants during this period.

Appellant Strength in a Multivariate Analysis

Although the analysis of bivariate relationships presented above produced results that are consistent with the thesis that litigant status and strength are significantly related to rates of appellant success, the thesis can be only provisionally supported until the effects of potential intervening variables are examined. For example, the apparent success of the presumptively stronger parties may be due in large part to the number of criminal appeals in the sample. Criminal appeals typically match an individual (especially a poor individual) against some level of government. Because many criminal appeals appear to have very little legal merit, the government usually wins. Alternatively, because judicial ideology, as measured by party affiliation or identity of the appointing president, has been found to be related to outcomes in the federal courts (Carp & Rowland 1983; Goldman 1975; Tate 1981), the relative success of the "haves" may be due to the relative number of Democrats and Republicans that were on a court at a particular time.

Wheeler et al. (1987) attempt to account for the effects of a number of variables that might modify the relationship between litigant status and appellant success by introducing control variables (areas of law, nature of legal relationship between parties, and the nature of counsel) one at a time in a series of cross tabulations. In contrast, Songer and Sheehan (1992) argue that a more accurate picture of the effects of a variety of potentially significant variables can be obtained from a multivariate logistic regression model. We adopt the latter position and examine the likelihood of appellant success in a model that assesses the impact of litigant status while controlling for other variables suggested to be related to case outcomes.

The dependent variable in the model is the success of the appellant, coded "1" if the appellant won and "0" if the respondent won.[9] Because least squares regression is inappropriate when the dependent variable is dichotomous (as it is in this analysis), the parameters were estimated by logistic regression, a maximum likelihood estimation technique (Aldrich & Nelson 1984). This method produces estimates for the parameters of a model's independent variables in terms of the contribution each makes to the probability that the dependent variable falls into one of the designated categories (e.g., appellant win or loss). For each independent variable, a maximum-likelihood estimate (*mle*) is calculated along with its standard error (*SE*). The maximum likelihood estimates represent the change in the logistic function that results from a one unit change in the independent variable.

To test whether litigant status affects case outcomes in a multivariate model, we created an ordinal measure that categorizes cases on the basis of appellant strength (1 = individual, 2 = business, 3 = state government, 4 = federal government). Because higher values on this variable identify appellants who are presumed to have greater litigation experience and resources than appellants who fall into the lower categories, it is expected that this variable will be positively related to the dependent variable. The same ordinal measure is used to measure litigant status for respondents. Higher values on this measure would be expected to reduce the likelihood of appellant success.

To distinguish criminal appeals, a dummy variable was created that was

TABLE 3.6

Logistic Regression Estimates for the Likelihood of Appellate Success in Published Decisions, 1925–1988

Independent Variable	mle	SE	Odds Ratio
Intercept	-0.74	0.11	—
Appellant	0.33**	0.03	1.39
Respondent	-0.10**	0.03	0.90
Criminal	-0.28**	0.06	0.75
Political party effect	0.47**	0.05	1.61

Mean dependent variable = 0.31.
Model chi-square = 502.95, df = 4, P < .001.
N = 8,334; % predicted = 63.4%; gamma = .296.
*Significant at .05; **significant at .01.

coded "1" if the case involved criminal law or procedure. Because nearly all these claims are raised by convicted defendants who will appeal even those cases that are without merit, we anticipate that the effect of this variable will be to reduce the likelihood of appellant success. In addition, we created a variable to control for the ideological predisposition of the panel. Previous studies note that judges appointed by Democratic presidents were more likely than judges appointed by Republicans to support liberal decisions (Goldman 1975; Gottschall 1986). Therefore, each panel was identified as having either a Democratic or Republican majority, whereas the decision of the court or administrative agency below was coded as being either liberal or conservative.[10] Previous findings lead to the expectation that panels with Democratic majorities are more likely to support the appellant when the decision below was conservative and that panels with Republican majorities are more likely to support the appellant when the decision below was liberal. Therefore, in both situations, the political party effect variable was coded "1." In the opposite situations (i.e., Democratic panel and liberal decision below or Republican panel and conservative decision below), the party effect variable was coded "0." We anticipate that this variable will be positively related to appellant success.

In Table 3.6,[11] the estimated coefficients assessing the influence of litigant type on case outcomes support our expectations derived from Galanter's theoretical insights. The variable measuring the status of the appellant is positively related to the likelihood of appellant success, and the relationship is significant at the .01 level. Although the magnitude is less, the measure of experience and resources of the respondent was also related to appellant success to a statistically significant degree. The results also indicate that the ideological makeup of the panel will affect case outcomes. Similar to the findings of numerous prior analyses of federal courts, panels with majorities appointed by Democratic presidents are more likely to support appeals from conservative decisions below, whereas panels with a majority of judges appointed by Republican presidents are more likely to support appeals from liberal decisions. More important for this study is that the effects of litigant experience and resources noted in Tables 3.2 through 3.5 remain strong even after controls for partisan preferences are included in the model.

The strong and statistically significant effects of litigant status in this multivariate model of decision-making over 64 years suggest that the nature of the litigant has had an enduring effect on the probability of appellant success that is independent of the policy preferences of the judges and the predisposition to affirm criminal convictions. Moreover, the odds ratios suggest that the impact of resources and experience may vary depending on whether the litigant was an appellant or respondent. Although both make a contribution to the explanatory power of the model, the litigant status measure for appellants appears to be a better predictor of case outcomes.

When the models are run separately for each of the five periods, the results, presented in Table 3.7, are generally consistent with the overall model presented in Table 3.6. In each period, the coefficient for the effect of the appellant's experience and resources is positive, and in all but one of the periods, the coefficient is statistically significant at the .01 level. The measure of litigant strength for respondents reduced the likelihood of appellant success in four of the five periods and is statistically significant at the .05 level for two of the five periods (1946–1960 and 1970–1988).

Conclusion

At its most basic level, the findings of this study reaffirm Galanter's thesis that the "haves come out ahead." The parties that may be presumed to be repeat players with superior resources consistently fared better than their weaker opponents and the disparity in success rates was greatest when the disparity in strength was greatest. Although there was a strong propensity of the federal courts of appeals to affirm, the greater success of stronger parties could not be attributed to the number of times they appeared as respondent rather than as appellant.

The most notable addition of this analysis to the fairly extensive literature that has been built on Galanter's insights is the discovery that this tendency of repeat player "haves" to win more frequently than their less advantaged opponents has been remarkably stable over much of the twentieth century. Since 1925, individuals lost more than 60% of their cases, businesses had success rates slightly under 50%, and governments won a commanding majority (over 68%) of the cases in which they participated.

TABLE 3.7

Logistic Regression Estimates for the Likelihood of Appellate Success in Published Decisions, by Time Period

	Mle (SE)				
Independent Variable	1925–36	1937–45	1946–60	1961–69	1970–88
Intercept	-0.98	-0.85	-0.72	-1.46	-0.39
	(0.34)	(0.47)	(0.26)	(0.25)	(0.16)
Appellant	0.40**	0.20*	0.25**	0.48**	0.33**
	(0.09)	(0.11)	(0.07)	(0.07)	(0.04)
Respondent	-0.14#	-0.14	-0.18**	0.04	-0.14**
	(0.09)	(0.11)	(0.07)	(0.06)	(0.04)
Criminal	-0.12	0.30	-0.03	-0.31*	-0.42**
	(0.22)	(0.25)	(0.16)	(0.13)	(0.07)
Political party	-0.04	0.62**	0.41**	0.63**	0.50**
	(0.16)	(0.22)	(0.13)	(0.11)	(0.07)
Mean dependent variable	.335	.272	.273	.263	.343
Model chi-square	43.43	16.32	58.43	134.30	307.01
df	4	4	4	4	4
$P <$	.001	.01	.001	.001	.001
$N =$	731	489	1,304	1,841	3,969
% predicted	64.5	62.4	63.7	66.3	65.2
Gamma	0.318	0.261	0.289	0.350	0.322

$.10 > P > .05$; *significant at .05; **significant at .01.

Our finding, that the haves come out ahead in appellate litigation in the federal circuit courts of appeals for a 64-year period, parallels the results reported by Wheeler et al. (1987), who noted only modest change over time in state courts of last resort. The persistence of the effects of litigant experience and resources over long periods on lower federal and state appellate courts is impressive particularly when one consider the extensive changes that have occurred in these courts during the same time. Both the federal circuit courts of appeals and state supreme courts have undergone massive changes in their agendas during the periods examined. For example, in the U.S. Courts of Appeals, there have been substantial increases in the proportion of civil liberties and criminal appeals since 1925. Given the common perception that many criminal appeals are frivolous, one might have expected that changes in the proportion of criminal appeals on the docket would affect the relative success rates of advantaged and disadvantaged litigants. The continuity in the effects noted above, however, suggests that the success of the "haves" in court is not primarily a function of the nature of the agenda.

On the courts of appeals (and, presumably, on state supreme courts), there have been significant changes in the partisan and ideological composition of the judiciary over time. The definition of the time periods used in this analysis was determined in large part by a desire to examine whether these changes were related to changes in the influence of repeat player status and litigant resources on outcomes. Our results suggested that there may have been a relatively modest increase in the propensity of the "have nots" to win in the period in which these partisan balances were most favorable to liberal interests (i.e., 1937–1945 period), but even major partisan shifts on the courts do not appear to fundamentally change the patterns predicted from Galanter's theoretical framework. The years since 1925 have also brought several institutional changes that might have been expected to benefit the litigation prospects for the "have nots." Most notable are the advent of a constitutional right of free legal counsel for the poor in some criminal appeals and the dramatic expansion of legal services available to the poor in civil contests. The efforts to provide access to the judicial process for those less fortunate, however, did not appear to significantly diminish the odds of success for governments, and to a lesser degree businesses, in these appellate courts over time.

Although it is thus apparent that the "haves" come out ahead in the U.S. Courts of Appeals to an impressive degree and that they have been coming out ahead throughout most of the twentieth century, we can only suggest, somewhat tentatively, why. Wheeler et al. (1987) considered, but tentatively rejected, the hypothesis that the "haves" came out ahead because of a normative tilt in the law that favored them. It may be that there has always been some normative tilt in the law toward the interests of business and governments, but major changes have affected the tilt since 1925. For example, from the mid 1950s until the early 1970s, the Supreme Court increasingly favored claims made by individuals asserting violations of their rights. Prior to that time, the Court was not sympathetic to individuals raising civil liberties and rights issues. Congress passed numerous statutes in the 1960s establishing Great Society programs and guaranteeing civil rights in employment, housing, and transportation. These changes may have contributed to the success of individuals in appeals involving business litigants during the 1960s. Overall, however, these changes did not appear to significantly affect the relationship between litigant strength and case outcomes in the courts of appeals. The second possibility investigated by Wheeler et al. was that the success of stronger parties might be due to judicial attitudes that favored them. The findings of our multivariate model, however, reinforce the earlier conclusions of Songer and Sheehan (1992) that, on the federal circuit courts, the effect of litigant status is independent of partisan-based influences.

The most probable explanation for the long-term success of the "haves" in the U.S. Courts of Appeals appears to be related to those factors suggested by Galanter (1974); our analysis found that parties presumed to be repeat players with greater resources came out ahead when pitted against presumptively weaker parties even after controlling for other influences affecting case outcomes. Unfortunately, the data are not sufficient to enable us to determine which of the specific characteristics of the stronger parties are the key ingredients of success. As Songer and Sheehan noted:

Each of the categories of litigants we have employed will on average have greater financial resources to invest in litigation, but each is also more likely to reap the benefits of repeat player status and experience. Therefore, comparison of such categories of litigants does not shed much light on whether superior financial resources (with the presumably better lawyers, etc., that result) or the superior case selecting ability and litigation strategy which may accrue to repeat players is more important. The limitations of data derived from court opinions are the root of this problem. Such opinions do not consistently provide much information on the financial resources of the litigants or on whether they are receiving assistance from an interest group or some other outside source of support, nor do they provide much information on the litigation experience of the litigants. (1992:255)

Thus, the limitations of opinion-derived data make it difficult to determine conclusively the basis of the success of the "haves." One piece of data uncovered in the analysis, however, is relevant to the assessment of whether the successes enjoyed by the "haves" are due more to their wealth and status than to the advantages derived from their repeat player status. Whereas the wealth of litigants would reflect on their ability to hire better lawyers and finance more extensive research, repeat player status of litigants would influence their ability to estimate the odds of success on appeal and skill in selecting probable winners. It also might reflect their willingness to absorb trial court losses to avoid the risk of adverse precedent being created on appeal. Such litigants would be more interested in "playing for rules" rather than immediate material gain. If the success of the "haves" was due to wealth alone, one would expect that the effect of litigant status would be the same for appellants and respondents. Our multivariate analysis of appellant success, however, suggested that the status of appellants had a greater impact than the status of respondents. Such a finding may indicate that litigation experience is more important than material resources. The advantages that can be secured by wealth and prestige should benefit both appellants and respondents, but only the potential appellants (i.e., the party that lost in the court below) can take full advantage of a sophisticated litigation strategy that Galanter suggests is characteristic of repeat players.

Although one can presume that governmental litigants, particularly federal agencies, are repeat players, our initial exploratory analysis of previous appearances by litigants before the circuit courts also supports these impressions. Individuals were one shotters; businesses had more litigation expertise but were not repeat players in the same sense as governmental parties. Although we recognize the interrelationship between financial resources and litigation strategy, particularly for private litigants, our findings suggest that the potential causal connection between litigant strength and case outcomes favors an interpretation that emphasizes litigant experience before the courts.

Our findings regarding the overwhelming success of the federal government also support that interpretation. Since 1946, we estimate that the U.S. government has been involved in over half the published decisions by the U.S. Courts of Appeals.[12] Between 1925 and 1945, the federal government also was a repeat player in these courts, participating in over 40% of cases accompanied by published decision. The success rate of the federal government is likely due not to participation alone, however. Since World War II, the administrative state has grown tremendously, leading to litigation involving judicial review of decisions by administrative agencies. These decisions may pit federal agencies against state and local governments, businesses, and individuals. In this type of appellate litigation, principles of case law require that judges generally accord a high level of deference to the expertise of federal agency officials. Finally, the federal government's high success rate, as noted earlier, may also reflect on a substantial number of nonmeritorious claims made by convicted defendants. Our interpretation of these findings, however, must remain somewhat speculative until further research examines this question more directly.

When compared with analyses of other courts (Wheeler et al. 1987; Sheehan et al. 1992), our findings are notable for the magnitude of the advantage enjoyed by the "haves" in the U.S. Courts of Appeals. In state courts of last resort, the "haves" enjoyed a modest advantage in appellate litigation (Wheeler et al. 1987). In the Supreme Court, the "haves" did not enjoy a consistent advantage after controlling for the effects of judicial ideology (Sheehan et al. 1992). These different findings likely reflect on disparities in the types of cases and workload of the U.S. Courts of Appeals. Unlike courts of last resort, the circuit courts must entertain all appeals over which they have jurisdiction. As a result, their docket is not dominated by those "hard" cases where judicial attitudes are more likely to determine case outcomes; instead, their cases include a higher proportion of routine appeals where workload constraints potentially lead judges to rely on the parties to define the issues and arguments to be addressed. As a result, one would expect those litigants, who have greater resources, including experience, to be more likely to put forth arguments that will be more persuasive. Although specifying these underlying causal mechanisms will require future research, the results of this study clearly indicate that Galanter's insights on the relationship between party capability and litigation in the trial courts may be extended to explain patterns of litigants success in the U.S. Courts of Appeals. Moreover, these patterns have been enduring, as the "haves" were more likely to prevail over a half century of appellate litigation in the federal courts.

Notes

Originally published in *Law & Society Review* 33 (4): 811–32 (1999); reprinted by permission. The data analyzed in this work are taken from the United States Courts of Appeals Data Base, Donald R. Songer, principal investigator, supported by the National Science Foundation under grant no. SES-89–12678. The database and its documentation are available to scholars at the Web site of the Program for Law and Judicial Politics, Michigan State University. Although the authors appreciate this support, which made the research reported in this paper possible, all findings and conclusions are those of the authors and do not necessarily reflect the views of the National Science Foundation.

Donald R. Songer is Professor of Political Science at the University of South Carolina. His current research interests focus on decision-making in appellate courts and include an ongoing study of the U.S. Courts of Appeals and an analysis of decisions by the top appellate courts of seven nations with English common-law roots. He was the principal investigator for the creation of the Appeals Court Data Base Project sponsored by the National Science Foundation and is the senior author of *Continuity and Change on the United States Courts of Appeals* (University of Michigan Press, 2000).

Reginald S. Sheehan is Professor of Political Science at Michigan State University. He has published in the leading political science journals, including the *American Political Science Review*, *American Journal of Political Science*, and *Journal of Politics*. He is also coauthor with Donald R. Songer and Susan Brodie Haire of *Continuity and Change on the United States Courts of Appeals* (University of Michigan Press, 2000).

Susan Brodie Haire is Associate Professor of Political Science at the University of Georgia. Her current research projects include an analysis of policy implementation in disability law and a study that explores the linkages between appellate briefs and decisions of the U.S. Courts of Appeals. She has authored articles on decision-making in the federal courts and is a coauthor of *Continuity and Change on the United States Courts of Appeals* (University of Michigan Press, 2000).

1. We did not distinguish "big business" litigants because the conceptualization and operationalization of "big business" varies over this 64-year period.

2. Our impression was supported by closer examination of a 30-case sample decided by the U.S. Courts of Appeals in 1988 in which one of the litigants was categorized as an individual. We searched Westlaw for the number of previous appearances by the named litigant in the 5 years prior to the decision date. We found that none of the litigants who were classified as individuals had previously appeared before these courts.

3. Because governmental agencies may be presumed to be repeat players in the

judicial process, we explored further our expectations that business litigants will be less likely to have litigation experience than governments but more likely to have expertise when compared with individual litigants. We sampled 50 cases decided in 1988 involving business litigants and searched through Westlaw to determine the number of previous appearances by the business litigant in the courts of appeals in the 5 years prior to the decision. We found that 24 of the businesses had previously appeared as a litigant in these courts. Although this test is not conclusive, it does support our conceptualization (and operationalization) of litigant types.

4. In addition to decisions involving "other" parties that did not fall within our categorization of litigants, we also excluded those decisions that could not be unambiguously categorized as a win or a loss for appellants. To take into account differences in sample sizes over time, the data are weighted to reflect on the relationship between the number of sampled decisions and the population of published decisions (see documentation that accompanies the United States Courts of Appeals Data Base SES-89–12678 for information on weighting).

5. Although we did not present the data in Table 3.2, the net advantage figures, when calculated separately for criminal and civil disputes between individuals and governments, support these findings. The net advantage enjoyed by state and local governmental litigants over individuals in civil cases was 11.1%; in criminal cases, the advantage was 34.3%. The net advantage enjoyed by the U.S. government over individuals in civil cases was 26.7%; in criminal cases, it was 43.2%.

6. Admittedly, the broad categorization of litigants can undermine this presumption. In particular, we were concerned that our conceptualization would not apply if matchups between state or local governments and businesses were dominated by appeals in which large corporations with substantial resources were opposing relatively poor local governmental litigants. Further examination of the data, however, suggests that this conceptualization does not undermine our interpretation because only 7% of the matchups in this category pitted big businesses against local governments.

7. Most disputes between businesses and individuals focused on economic issues (82%). Approximately half of these appeals (businesses versus individuals) were torts. Appeals with businesses opposing the U.S. government involved a greater number of labor issues (34%). Still, over half of contests pitting the federal government against businesses involved an economic question. Although they are relatively fewer in number, matchups between businesses and state or local governments raised more diverse issues, with one-third involving an economic regulatory dispute and approximately 18% focusing on a civil rights or liberties question.

8. Net advantage scores were only computed for a matchup in a particular period if there were at least 10 cases in which each litigant appeared as an appellant against the other in the pair.

9. As noted earlier, the sampling procedures used in the United States Courts of Appeals Data Base require weighting the observations in the logit model.

10. We followed the definitions of liberal and conservative described by Goldman (1975). According to this definition, the liberal position is described as for the claims of the defendants or prisoners in criminal and prisoner petition cases, for the claims of minorities in racial discrimination cases, for the claims of plaintiffs in other civil liberties cases, for the government in regulation of business and tax cases, for indi-

vidual workers or unions in disputes with management, for the injured person in tort cases, and for the economic underdog in private economic disputes.

11. As noted elsewhere, only litigants and decisions that could be unambiguously categorized are included in the analysis. In this model, the control variable measuring the effect of the ideological makeup of the panel required the exclusion of observations that could not be unambiguously categorized as liberal or conservative. For example, cases that deal with attorney discipline or boundary disputes between states would be excluded. In addition, we excluded those panels with judges whose political party affiliation could not be determined (generally, judges who were not appointed to the U.S. Courts of Appeals but sit by designation). After deleting these cases, the number of observations analyzed in Table 3.6 fell to 8,334.

12. Estimates are derived from the United States Courts of Appeals Data Base.

References

Aldrich, John H., & Forrest Nelson (1984) *Linear Probability, Logit, and Probit Models.* Beverly Hills, CA: Sage Publications.

Atkins, Burton M. (1991) "Party Capability Theory as an Explanation for Intervention Behavior in the English Court of Appeals," 35 *American J. of Political Science* 881–903.

Carp, Robert A., & C. K. Rowland (1983) *Policymaking and Politics in the Federal Courts.* Knoxville: Univ. of Tennessee Press.

Davis, Sue, & Donald R. Songer (1988) "The Changing Role of the United States Courts of Appeals: The Flow of Litigation Revisited." Presented at annual meeting of the Law and Society Association (6 June).

Easton, David (1953) The Political System: An Inquiry into the State of Political Science. New York: Knopf.

Galanter, Marc (1974) "Why the 'Haves' Come Out Ahead: Speculations on the Limits of Social Change," 9 *Law & Society Rev.* 95–160.

Goldman, Sheldon (1975) "Voting Behavior on the United States Courts of Appeals Revisited," 69 *American Political Science Rev.* 491–506.

——— (1997) *Picking Federal Judges: Lower Court Selection from Roosevelt through Reagan.* New Haven, CT: Yale Univ. Press.

Gottschall, Jon (1986) "Reagan's Appointments to the U.S. Courts of Appeals: The Continuation of a Judicial Revolution," 48 *Judicature* 48–54.

Haynie, Stacia L. (1994) "Resource Inequalities and Litigation Outcomes in the Philippine Supreme Court," 56 *J. of Politics* 752–72.

Haynie, Stacia L., Reginald S. Sheehan, & Donald R. Songer (1994) "A Comparative Investigation of Resource Inequalities and Litigation Outcomes." Presented at the annual meeting of the Midwest Political Science Association, Chicago (2 Sept.).

Howard, J. Woodford (1981) *Courts of Appeals in the Federal Judicial System: A Study of the Second, Fifth, and District of Columbia Circuits.* Princeton, NJ: Princeton Univ. Press.

McCormick, Peter (1993) "Party Capability Theory and Appellate Success in the Supreme Court of Canada, 1949–1992," 26 *Canadian J. of Political Science* 523–40.

Owen, Harold J. (1971) "The Role of Trial Courts in the Local Political System: a Comparison of Two Georgia Counties." Unpublished Ph.D. dissertation, Dept. of Political Science, University of Georgia.

Sheehan, Reginald S., William Mishler, & Donald R. Songer (1992) "Ideology, Status, and the Differential Success of Direct Parties before the Supreme Court," 86 *American Political Science Rev.* 464–71.

Songer, Donald R., & Reginald S. Sheehan (1992) "Who Wins on Appeal? Upperdogs and Underdogs in the United States Courts of Appeals," 36 *American J. of Political Science* 235–58.

Tate, C. Neal (1981) "Personal Attribute Models of the Voting Behavior of U.S. Supreme Court Justices' Liberalism in Civil Liberties and Economics Decisions, 1946–1978," 75 *American Political Science Rev.* 355–67.

Wanner, Craig (1975) "The Public Ordering of Private Relations: Part I: Initiating Civil Cases in Urban Trial Courts," 8 *Law & Society Rev.* 421–40.

Wheeler, Stanton, Bliss Cartwright, Robert Kagan, & Lawrence Friedman (1987) "Do the 'Haves' Come Out Ahead? Winning and Losing in State Supreme Courts, 1870–1970," 21 *Law & Society Rev.* 403–45.

Representing Homeless Families

Repeat Player Implementation Strategies

> The leverage provided by litigation depends on its strategic combination with inputs at other levels. The question then is whether the organization of the profession permits lawyers to develop and employ skills at these other levels. (Galanter 1974:151)

> Without any ability to pose a credible political threat, poverty lawyers have become adept at squeezing resources out of hostile agencies and legislative bodies at all levels of government. (Diller 1995:1427)[1]

> In mounting reform suits, Legal Services lawyers are not properly understood as autonomous, outside agents attempting to impose rationality on the administration of public welfare services over the opposition of a universally hostile state. (Katz 1984:189)

Introduction

In 1974, Marc Galanter examined the strategic role of public interest lawyers in helping the "have nots" come out ahead in the legal system. Galanter argued that, to become agents for social change, lawyers must recognize that their role as advocates extends beyond the courtroom into the implementation process (Galanter 1974:151). This article analyzes the efforts of one group of public interest lawyers—those working in Legal Services agencies dedicated to law reform—to influence the implementation of redistributive programs for a particular group of "have nots": homeless families or those on the brink of losing their housing. Based on my studies, I argue that by skillfully combining adversarial legal tactics with collaboration, poverty lawyers can transform judicial decisions into "symbolic resources" to leverage the implementation of redistributive remedies. When the reform lawyers have the authority to participate in the process of administrative rule-making during the implementation process, they can reshape the norms and organizational infrastructures within state agencies.

Galanter thus was correct when he suggested that public interest lawyers may rely on their own resources to "operate in forums other than the courts" and "form enduring alliances" to influence the implementation process (ibid.). Yet he offered little insight about whether these lawyers can effectively challenge political opposition to reforms when the "have nots" lack clout in political and administrative venues. Under these conditions, judicial oversight can enhance the ability of public interest lawyers to act as "repeat players" during the implementation phase and can expand opportunities for the lawyers to mobilize support for their redistributive reforms. If the implementation of reforms threatens an agency's legitimacy in its own political environment, however, officials are likely to respond with bureaucratic and political countermobilizations against judicial mandates. Galanter also argued that if lawyers identify with their clients, they are more likely to become advocates in nonjudicial arenas and expand their identities as legal professionals (ibid., pp. 114, 115, 118, 151). As lawyers collaborate with administrative actors and become increasingly integral to the implementation process, however, they may also compromise their own capacity to challenge the legality of official policies. Thus, strategic decisions to increase participation in the process of implementation may extend the "temporary advantages" that the lawyers had leveraged through the courts, but they may also narrow future opportunities for the public interest law organizations to pursue reform litigation.

Galanter: Strategic Advantages of Public Interest Lawyers

Galanter's 1974 article portrayed the Legal Services lawyers engaged in law reform activity as the prototype of public interest lawyers who could create strategic advantages for the "have nots." The founders of the federally funded Legal Services Program in the mid-1960s hoped that subsidized legal representation for poor people would not only win favorable decisions for their clients in specific cases, but would also improve the position of the "have nots" for leveraging power in all legal, administrative, and political venues. The creation of the federal Legal Services Program provided a challenge to the undisputed authority of state social welfare agencies to evaluate the best interests of their impoverished clients and administer social policy (Sparer 1965). The poverty lawyers used law reform strategies to (1) expand access to the civil courts, (2) develop new substantive and procedural rights for poor people, (3) challenge abuses by and shape decisions of governmental agencies, and (4) increase opportunities for poor people to influence the political process (ibid., pp. 120–21, 150n. 141; see also Cahn & Cahn 1964; Carlin et al. 1966; Sparer 1965).

According to Galanter (1974:96–97, 138–39), law reforms must "penetrate" the implementing agencies to be meaningful. He argued: "The system has the capacity to change a great deal at the level of rules without corresponding changes in everyday practice or distribution of tangible advantages. Indeed rule-change may become a symbolic substitute for redistribution of advantages" (ibid., p. 149). Galanter considered, however, the strategic advantages of the "haves" in the wake of judicial rule-change neither inherent nor absolute. The ability of the "have nots" to form coherent organizations that become "repeat players" (RPs) is the primary factor that improves their strategic position for using courts to induce redistributive reforms. As RPs, the "have nots" can draw on financial resources to purchase legal expertise. Combining legal and political expertise, RPs can develop long-range goals, pursue additional favorable rule-changes, and mobilize support for the implementation of these new rules (ibid., pp. 141, 150).

When the "have nots" lack coherent organizations that can act as RPs, according to Galanter, public interest law firms that have the capacity to become RPs may provide a substitute (ibid., p. 143). To approximate the strategic position of parties who are RPs, public interest law firms must substantially identify with the goals of their clients so that they do not trade off their clients' best interests for their own long-term professional interests. If lawyers lack a sense of solidarity with their clients, they may structure outcomes to ensure their clients' continued dependence on lawyers rather than create substantive reforms that empower their clients as social groups and individuals (ibid., pp. 118–19). To represent the "have nots" effectively, public interest lawyers must attempt to secure rule-changes that directly alter the strategic position of their clients by facilitating organizing, expanding the resources for legal services, and increasing the costs to their opponents of pursuing counteroffensives. Thus, to provide leverage for the "have nots," the public interest lawyers must have a strategic vision that views litigation as a resource for more long-range strategies to increase the political clout of their clients.

Beyond Galanter: Political and Legal Dynamics of Implementation

Although Galanter's analysis allows that public interest lawyers can enhance the ability of their "have not" clients to achieve redistributive rule-changes, the ability of disadvantaged clients to organize groups with the capacity to influence the implementation process is critical for effective strategies. Yet Galanter leaves open the question of whether the lawyers themselves can extend their temporary leverage from litigation to secure redistributive reforms when the conditions for organizing clients are unfavorable. Other sociolegal scholars have studied the role of poverty lawyers in influencing rule-making processes within the courts (Lawrence 1990; Davis 1995) and Congress (Melnick 1994a), as well as community organizing (Davis 1995; Galanter 1974; Katz 1984; Scheingold 1974; Stumpf 1975). Less attention, however, has been given to the influences of Legal Services litigation on implementing bureaucratic reforms.

Two sociolegal scholars who have addressed the impact of poverty lawyers on bureaucratic processes, Joel Handler and Jack Katz, provide rather negative assessments, for seemingly contradictory reasons. Handler (1966, 1978) argues that judicial mandates won by poverty lawyers are unlikely to influence the microdynamics of administering poverty programs. According to Handler, judicial rule-changes are mediated by "bureaucratic contingencies," which frequently thwart efforts to implement redistributive remedies (1978:18–22). The imbalance between the power of "dependent" clients and state bureaucracies during the implementation process limits the clients' abilities to challenge unjust agency practices (Handler 1966:497–500; 1990:13–34). Furthermore, Handler argues that it is unlikely that poverty lawyers can force the implementation of judicially constructed rules that are perceived by agency workers as conflicting with the existing goals of their state bureaucracies. He suggests that advocates for "dependent" clients would be most effective if they could persuade agency officials that it is in their own best interest to invite their clients into "participatory" relationships (Handler 1996) and concludes that litigation is unlikely to induce any significant bureaucratic reforms because of an inherent capacity for resistance during the implementation process.

In contrast, Katz (1984:179–86) claims that the poverty lawyers can influence agency reform, but only in a way that ultimately deepens the dependency of the poor on the state without providing adequate resources to relieve their poverty. According to Katz, the poverty lawyers' legal reform efforts actually enhance the power of social welfare bureaucracies to pursue their organizational interests in administering policies that segregate the poor and "legalize" poverty. Katz refers to Legal Services lawyers as "external professional rationalizers of state social welfare agencies" (1984:189).

Although Handler offers important insights concerning barriers legal reformers face during implementation and Katz provides a framework for understanding the limitations of using state regulatory regimes as agents for alleviating poverty, neither adequately addresses the independent leverage that public interest lawyers may have during implementation. Both approaches fail to capture the political dynamics of changing administrative rules during implementation and the particular role that lawyers can play in that process.

By applying Galanter's insights concerning the relationship between law and politics in judicial rule-change to our analysis of the implementation process, we can better understand the power RP lawyers can have to influence the practices of state agencies. The implementation process can be seen as a continuing process of conflict and negotiations to create a legal framework for policy reform. Thus, lawyers who are long-term participants in implementation can expand their approach to law reform beyond the negotiation of a particular remedy to the development of long-range strategies to change the architecture of state agencies to be more conducive to redistributive reforms. They can focus their efforts on creating new rules to transform the agency's infrastructure for decision-making and influencing the professional norms that guide agency practices.

This approach to understanding implementation challenges Handler's dichotomy between adversarial legal tactics and opportunities for collaboration with bureaucratic actors. Court orders and judicially constructed remedies can provide the lawyers points of access to implementation decisions. To have an ongoing influence on shaping administrative rules, however, the lawyers must also have the organizational resources to mobilize support for their reform goals inside the targeted agencies. Consequently, when lawyers are RPs, the use of litigation may be an important tactic for gaining opportunities to influence official policies and practices on a microlevel.

Katz's portrayal of poverty lawyers as rationalizers of bureaucratic practices oversimplifies the common interests of poverty lawyers and agency administrators in "legalizing the state's administrative segregation of poverty" (ibid., p. 196). The legalization of reforms involves political conflict and compromise that transform judicial rulings into agency policies and practices. To achieve their reform goals effectively, the legal advocates must both influence the creation of new rules to redefine agency policies and practices and mobilize support within the targeted agencies for those changes. This process of collaboration is most likely when official actors believe that the reforms will enhance their positions within their political environments.

Heimer provides a useful approach for understanding variations in the impact of new reforms on preexisting administrative processes. Although Heimer focuses on the implementation of new legislation, her approach is also useful for analyzing the implementation of judicially induced policy reform. She clarifies the relationship between the political context for implementation and the potential for enduring policy changes. According to Heimer, legislative reforms are most likely to be incorporated into "pre-existing organization routines" when "legal institutions can insinuate themselves into the machinery" of the organization targeted for reform and when legal actors within the organizational setting are "empowered by enforcing law" (1996:30). In addition, the mobilization of support for legal mandates is "intertwined with the question of legitimacy" of the organization within its political environment (ibid., p. 31). Organizations must convince certain actors within this environment to contribute the resources necessary for the organization's continued existence. Thus, the ability of public interest lawyers to transform their symbolic judicial victories into substantive redistributive programs may be directly linked to their abilities to transform their substantive legal frames and agendas into organizational infrastructures that enhance, rather than threaten, the reputations of the targeted organizations, so that they continue to receive financial resources and attract competent staff. This process is likely to be particularly challenging when legislatures are increasingly hostile to redistributive programs. Both Handler and Heimer recognize the important role of agency workers in deciding whether or not changing administrative practices is consistent with their own interests. Heimer, however, offers new insights about both the importance of "legalizing" the implementation process and the conditions under which this process of legalization will be most likely to reform organizational practices. We can see the particular role that "repeat player" lawyers, who are authorized by the court to participate in the implementation process, can have in "legalizing" reforms. The limits of public interest lawyers to defend the interests of the "have nots" during the implementation phase are also apparent. The lawyers must be able not only to influence the development of implementation rules, as suggested by Galanter, but also to convince officials that the new rules will enhance the legitimacy of their agency in its political environment and that compliance with rule-changes will benefit the implementing staff in their work environment.

"Right-to-Home" Cases: Resistance to Disentitlement Strategies

By the time the "right-to-home" class actions were initiated during the 1980s, many broad reform goals of the Legal Services founders had been frustrated. The War on Poverty initiated by the federal government in the 1960s had been abandoned; the National Welfare Rights Organization and many local welfare rights groups had been disbanded; and the U.S. Supreme Court had refused to recognize poor people's constitutional "right to live— a right to sustenance, to food, to decent housing" (Houseman 1991:315). By the 1980s, there was neither sufficient political will nor legal precedent to support policy reforms that would require welfare grants to meet poor people's basic needs for sustenance. It had become standard practice for state public assistance agencies to provide grants that fell far below amounts that government officials had calculated as the poverty threshold. Between 1970 and 1980, the median monthly state public assistance grants for a family of three dropped from $673 to $497, which was 53% of the monthly poverty threshold of $947 (Children's Defense Fund 1994:5). Federal and state administrative reforms implemented to reduce the costs of public assistance created bureaucratic barriers for eligibility that advocates for the poor have characterized as bureaucratic "disentitlements" (Brodkin 1986; Fabricant & Burghardt 1992:73–78). As politicians continued to pressure social welfare administrators to reduce the costs of social welfare programs, a legal environment was being constructed that rationalized the dependence of poor people on a housing market, labor market, and welfare system that left many poor parents unable to provide shelter for their children.

Faced with increasingly adverse political, legal, and administrative environments, Legal Services lawyers in at least eight states initiated class actions with right-to-home legal claims that attempted to expand their states' commitments to providing more generous and accessible assistance programs for their destitute clients. The poverty lawyers argued that existing state policies and practices were contributing to family homelessness and, consequently, violating their clients' rights to take care of their own children.[2] In this sense, the poverty lawyers were challenging the political retreat from providing a safety net for families as violating statutory standards that had established a public responsibility for the protection of children and the right of families to live together in their own homes.

To assess the impact of law reform strategies by the poverty lawyers, I have looked beyond the conventional approaches that focus on the institutional limitations of the courts to force bureaucracies to comply with specific legal mandates. Studies of the judiciary's limited power to enforce its decisions and of the bureaucracies' resistance to legal intervention provide important insights for understanding why litigation "alone" cannot ensure irreversible gains for the "have nots." They provide, however, limited insights about the ways reform litigation can leverage opportunities for the lawyers to influence the policy-making process and reshape regulatory regimes. Galanter (1974, 1983), Garth (1992), and McCann (1992, 1994, 1999) suggest that we shift our attention away from legal judgments as mandates and instead focus on the actors who are interpreting how the courts' decisions affect their future bargaining positions. McCann argues that judicial authorities do not compel a change in behavior with their official legal interpretations. Various actors, however, evaluate how these court decisions "indirectly create important expectations, endowments, incentives, and constraints" for pursuing reform strategies in particular institutional venues (McCann 1999:68).

This article draws on three right-to-home case studies to analyze the strategic responses of poverty lawyers and state agency officials to judicial rule-changes and the consequences of their strategies and counterstrategies to influence the implementation of those rules. For *Hansen v. McMahon* and *Norman v. Johnson*, I examine how four factors influenced the dynamics of implementation: (1) the judicial decisions as symbolic resources, (2) the level of judicial oversight, (3) the organizational resources of Legal Services lawyers available for implementation, and (4) changes in the political environment. An analysis of the third case, *Jiggetts v. Grinker* (also known as *Jiggetts v. Perales* or *Jiggetts v. Dowling*), is incorporated into a concluding discussion about the power of poverty lawyers as repeat players to influence the implementation of remedies.

On a microlevel, this article analyzes the dynamics of conflict and collaboration between the poverty lawyers and state officials during the implementation of redistributive remedies. I evaluate the effectiveness of the poverty lawyers' efforts to influence three aspects of governing new redistributive programs: participation in decision-making concerning agency practices, the transformation of professional norms, and the mobilization of administrative resources to facilitate an economic redistribution to the "have nots." On a macrolevel, I demonstrate how the implementation strategies of the poverty lawyers and state agency officials alter the legitimacy of their own organizations in their political and legal environments. Furthermore, I examine the relationship between the perceptions of organizational legitimacy and the development of long-term commitments to reforms instigated by judicial rule-changes. For the social welfare administrators, I focus on how their implementation strategies are used to mobilize support from legislators and the governor, the actors responsible for their funding, as well as to convince judges of their authority to make administrative decisions. When the poverty lawyers take an active role in bureaucratic reform, on a microlevel, their legitimacy is based on maintaining their authority as legal professionals, who have special skills to evaluate whether the implementers are complying with their legal mandates. In addition, on a macrolevel, the Legal Services organizations must attract funding for their work, develop collaborative relationships with other advocates, and create a work environment that draws and retains skilled lawyers. This analysis of the influence of the poverty lawyers on both the microlevel and macrolevel of implementation provides a basis for assessing the possibilities and limitations of public interest lawyers as repeat players to make the architecture of state agencies more responsive to the interests of the "have nots."

Hansen v. McMahon

FACTORS SHAPING IMPLEMENTATION PROCESS

Judicial Decision as Symbolic Resource

In a right-to-home class action in California, the poverty lawyers claimed that the state's provision of emergency shelter only to children who had been separated from their parents—not to homeless children still living with their parents—violated the intent of state child welfare statutes (Superior Court 1986). Pretrial rulings in *Hansen v. McMahon* required the state child welfare agency to respond to the shelter needs of homeless families (Court of Appeal 1987). The judicial rulings received media coverage that supported the judges' interpretation of law, criticized the child welfare agency's resistance to compliance, praised the poverty lawyers, and offered empathy for the homeless families (Ramos 1986; Murphy 1986). Favorable editorials were published in the *Los Angeles Times* (18 May 1986, Home Edition, sec. 5, p. 4) and the *San Diego Union-Tribune* (9 August 1986, Opinion, Ed. 1, 2, p. C3). The state officials, the poverty lawyers, and child welfare advocates, however, were all opposed to the administration of a homeless assistance program by the state child welfare agency, which primarily served abused and neglected children. Consequently, the substance of these rulings was eliminated during negotiations. The poverty lawyers agreed to the legislative reforms that mooted their suit in exchange for legislation that established a new housing assistance program to be administered through the state agency responsible for distributing economic assistance to poor families (Bird interview). Therefore, the symbolic power that had been provided by judicial decisions quickly dissipated during the implementation of the new Homeless Assistance Program (HAP). The program began to be viewed in the legislature as a bargaining chip that could be cut or substantially reduced for fiscal considerations with little political cost and no threat of judicial intervention.

Furthermore, as a Special Needs program, HAP was particularly vulnerable to political criticism because of the discretion involved in determining whether families were homeless and eligible for assistance. Handler and Sosin (1983:13) argue that for Special Needs programs, "documentation is elusive, and the likelihood exists that a particular decision will be questioned by politicians or journalists on the grounds of waste or fraud." Handler's prediction was borne out during the implementation of HAP. A report by the Auditor General (1990) about fraud in HAP became an important symbolic resource in Governor Pete Wilson's campaign to eliminate the program. He argued that there was no effective way of deciding who was actually homeless and entitled to these benefits (Ellis 1991).

Level of Judicial Oversight

By negotiating the creation of a program outside the purview of the judiciary, the advocates lost more than the symbolic power of the judicial decisions. They also were excluded from participating in decisions concerning implementation. After the poverty lawyers were able to collaborate with state legislators and state officials to create the establishing legislation and to secure federal funding for HAP, the actual administration of the program was limited to the existing actors within the state public assistance agency. The poverty lawyers could not rely on the courts to monitor the process. Furthermore, absent any risk of judicial intervention, funding levels were threatened by waning political commitments.

Poverty Lawyers' Organizational Resources

Lawyers from the Western Center on Law and Poverty, which was a statewide Support Center for Legal Services agencies, had litigated the *Hansen* case. This small staff of seven did not have the personnel capacity to be involved with the details of implementation in any one case. As repeat players in the poverty law field, however, the Western Center did have resources to pursue three kinds of strategies to influence the implementation process. First, the poverty lawyers filed three suits to challenge regulations issued by the Department of Social Services (DSS) that would restrict eligibility and access to the Homeless Assistance Program (Newman interview). Second, the Western Center had a lobbyist in the legislature who collaborated with allies in advocacy groups representing low-income people and sympathetic legislators to prevent legislative cutbacks to homeless assistance (McKeever interview). Finally, in cooperation with networks of providers and advocacy organizations serving homeless families, the poverty lawyers both informed homeless families about gaining access to housing assistance and developed an informational campaign to counter the negative portrayal of the program in the Auditor General's report (Berlin interview; Bird interview; Farber interview; see also California Homeless and Housing Coalition 1991).

Changing Political Environment

Several aspects of the political environment in California created barriers to the implementation of HAP. First, the administrators of county public assistance offices were facing pressures from staff reductions at the same time they were attempting to implement new programs that required immediate, emergency responses to mushrooming caseloads (Auditor General 1990:100–101). Three years after the implementation of HAP began, California faced a $14.3 billion state deficit (Beyle 1992:51–52). The incoming governor, Pete Wilson, targeted welfare programs for deep cuts (Ellis 1991).

IMPLEMENTATION ON A MICROLEVEL

Initially, the rules governing the HAP program created opportunities for social welfare workers to help families who previously had had to rely on the limited resources of volunteer agencies. With the establishing legislation for HAP, the problem of homelessness, which had been largely ignored by official actors, suddenly became an emergency that required an immediate state response. According to the new legislation, if families who had no more than $100 in "liquid assets" could provide evidence that they lacked a "fixed and regular nighttime residence" or that they were living in temporary shelter, they were eligible to receive $30 a day for up to three weeks to cover the costs of temporary shelter. Furthermore, those seeking permanent housing were eligible for permanent housing assistance to cover the last month's rent and security deposits. The county welfare department was required to issue a payment or denial of assistance within one working day after families presented evidence of the availability of permanent housing if they had provided the necessary verification to establish eligibility for the aid.[3]

The HAP program was launched in February 1988, and the new rules were quickly implemented in DSS offices throughout California. During the first 2 years of the program, more than $143 million was distributed to homeless families (Auditor General 1990:68). During the first full year of HAP, more than 90,000 families, including 185,000 children, were served, according to an analysis issued by the Center on Budget and Policy Priorities, which was summarized in a Business Wire Report (14 May 1991).

Although the rules governing HAP initially facilitated the mobilization of existing administrative resources for the widespread implementation of the program, they did not expand participation in the administrative rule-making process to the advocates. Consequently, when county administrators faced cross-pressures to improve the process of verifying the eligibility of HAP applicants and to adjust to staff reductions required by budget cuts, the poverty lawyers were not in a position to help create new rules that could alleviate the stress on county departments. Although the poverty lawyers and advocates for homeless families could establish relationships with the administrators and workers in some local offices to facilitate better treatment of homeless families (Farber interview), they were unable to participate in making decisions concerning the systemwide implementation of the HAP program. Furthermore, when Pete Wilson became governor, he articulated a welfare policy that relied on inadequate benefits as an incentive to force recipients into the low-wage labor market (Ellis 1991). This philosophical approach to social welfare undermined the rationale for providing government funding for housing assistance because the increased threat of homelessness could be considered an incentive for parents to find work.

The lobbyist from the Western Center collaborated with sympathetic legislators and representatives from DSS to create rule-changes for the HAP program that would improve the process of eligibility determination without undermining the redistributive aspects of the program. The Governor's Office, however, ignored these reform proposals because the administration was committed to budget cuts (McKeever interview). Although the poverty lawyers worked in coalitions with other advocates for poor people, they lacked the political clout within the legislature to resist cutbacks in the HAP program (McKeever interview; Berlin interview).

Statutory revisions in 1991 limited eligibility for homeless assistance applicants, linked the process of verifying "family homelessness" to an investigation by the "early fraud prevention and detection unit," and shortened the period for temporary shelter assistance to 16 days.[4] Shelter providers noted that their clients became disturbed by this presumption of fraud in the application process (Berlin interview; Farber interview). By 1995, eligibility for homeless assistance was reduced to once in a lifetime.[5] The director of the California Homeless and Housing Coalition claimed that the new regulations had created a new group of homeless families who were unable even to gain entrance to emergency shelters. The shelters did not want to take in families who had previously received homeless assistance because now they would be ineligible for the resources necessary to leave the shelters and to move into permanent housing (Berlin interview).

IMPLEMENTATION ON A MACROLEVEL

The social service administrators and poverty lawyers had agreed that the judicial mandate to provide a housing assistance program within the child welfare agency was not the most effective way to respond to family homelessness. The child welfare administrators had been very concerned about trying to implement a program to house homeless families within the organizational infrastructure of an agency that was already unable to adequately respond to its legal mandate to protect children who were being abused or neglected by their parents. The poverty lawyers also wanted to prevent homeless families from having to depend on the child welfare agency to get shelter assistance because they feared increased surveillance of homeless families that might lead to unwanted out-of-home placements. Consequently, both parties agreed to make the housing assistance program an add-on to the public assistance program, and the existing infrastructure for determining eligibility and distributing grants could be used. Workers in the public assistance offices and nonprofit agencies serving homeless families would have new resources available for their clients, and the poverty lawyers would not have to devote their scarce resources to developing or monitoring a new bureaucratic structure.

During the implementation process, however, the burden and cost of administering HAP for the DSS administrators outweighed the benefit of providing new resources to clients. When county DSS offices became targets for fraud investigations and public assistance programs targets for budget cutting, the leadership of the department joined the governor's efforts to eliminate the troublesome program. This position was strengthened by a shift in the official social welfare philosophy, which now overtly advocated making benefits inadequate enough to provoke poor people to eschew public assistance grants for low-wage jobs.

SUMMARY

When the poverty lawyers and DSS administrators negotiated a remedy for the Hansen case in the legislature, there was general agreement on the goals for creating a new Homeless Assistance Program. The poverty lawyers thought that clients would easily gain access to housing assistance because it was an add-on to an existing program (Bird interview). In fact, economic resources were distributed fairly quickly throughout California to provide homeless families assistance both for temporary shelter and the transition to permanent housing. All four factors shaping the implementation process, however, significantly impeded the ability of the poverty lawyers to develop a long-range strategy to mobilize a commitment within the agency to the new program. First, the favorable judicial decisions lost their symbolic power when legislative reforms mooted the suit. Second, without judicial oversight, the poverty lawyers had no special authority to participate in the ongoing process of administrative rule-making to legalize the program. Third, as a small organization serving the entire state, the Western Center on Law and Poverty lacked the personnel to be integrally involved in the implementation process. Finally, the governor's response to a burgeoning budget deficit included eliminating and cutting back programs serving poor people. The administrative leadership in the state agency had no political incentive or judicial pressure to try to protect this program that the governor was trying to cut. Consequently, during the first 6 years of the implementation of HAP, revisions to the establishing statutes severely limited the redistributive potential of the program.

Norman v. Johnson

FACTORS SHAPING IMPLEMENTATION PROCESS

Judicial Decision as Symbolic Resource

In a "Memorandum Opinion and Order" delivered in May 1990, a U.S. District Court Judge in Illinois ordered the state child welfare agency to provide sufficient housing and economic assistance to two class plaintiffs in *Norman v. Johnson* (also known as *Fields v. Johnson, Norman v. Suter, Norman v. Ryder,* and *Norman v. McDonald*) (U.S. District Court 1990). The lawyers for the Department of Children and Family Services (DCFS) were discouraged from continuing litigation because the judge had rebuffed all their legal arguments (Tchen interview). When a new DCFS director was hired, he decided to negotiate a consent decree for the *Norman* class action suit as well as for several other class actions against DCFS. The resulting "Consent Order" (U.S. District Court 1991) constructed the legal foundation for child welfare policy reform to provide material assistance to families involved in the child welfare system who were homeless or victims of domestic violence. The inclusion of domestic violence victims in the consent decree expanded the class being served beyond what had been established during litigation. The "Consent Order" set out the requirements for the development of a cash assistance program and housing advocacy program to be operated within the child welfare agency. In addition, the role of the poverty lawyers in the implementation process was established. They would review all new policies, procedures, programs, rules, regulations, training programs, and notices for implementation. During the monitoring process, they would also have opportunities for input.

Level of Judicial Oversight

Judicial oversight was significant during the first 6 years of the implementation of the *Norman* consent decree. The initial "Consent Order" (ibid.) provided that court supervised monitoring would continue for 4 years. The court approved an "Agreed Order" (U.S. District Court 1995) to extend monitoring and judicial supervision for another year. At the end of this period, the court accepted the poverty lawyers' motion to extend monitoring through 1997 (U.S. District Court 1996a, 1996c). Consequently, during the initial period of implementation, court-appointed monitors were submitting regular reports to the district judge concerning compliance with various aspects of the consent decree.[6] The poverty lawyers and attorneys for DCFS also had opportunities to present to the court complaints about the implementation process when they were unable to negotiate satisfactory agreements with each other.

Poverty Lawyers' Organizational Resources

The lead lawyers in the *Norman* case worked in two projects of the Legal Assistance Foundation of Chicago, the Homeless Families Project and Children's Rights Project. They had been involved in previous law reform efforts to improve the quality of legal representation of children in out-of-home care and to expand resources for particular groups of child welfare clients. The "Consent Order" in the *Norman* case provided that the poverty lawyers be reimbursed by DCFS for their participation in the implementation process. Consequently, the poverty lawyers not only had already gained experience and expertise as RPs in child welfare advocacy, but they also established new economic resources through the consent decree to subsidize their role in implementation.

Changing Political Environment

Three kinds of changes in the political environment could have influenced the *Norman* consent decree. First, the child welfare work force was cut by 10% in 1992 (Pearson 1992). Second, in 1993, there was a backlash against "family preservation" policies after intensive media coverage of the grisly hanging of a child who had been returned from foster care to his mentally ill mother. During this period, there was a sharp increase in the foster care caseload as public anxiety about the dangers of child abuse and neglect escalated. The child welfare agency faced cross-pressures to reduce the foster care caseload to make the system more manageable and to prevent child deaths by removing children from parents who were likely to harm them (Vorenberg 1993). The third factor was growing legislative opposition to consent decrees after the *B.H. v. Ryder* settlement contributed to the state child welfare budget increasing from $500 million in 1991 to $1.2 billion in 1995 (Novak 1995).

IMPLEMENTATION ON A MICROLEVEL

The implementation of the *Norman* consent decree was significantly influenced by the role and personalities of the monitors selected. Although the language in the "Consent Order" (1991) called for the appointment of an "impartial monitor" who was agreed upon by the parties, informally the poverty lawyers and lawyers for DCFS negotiated an agreement to hire two comonitors, a former DCFS administrator who was favored by the child welfare agency and an activist in the homeless advocacy community. As social workers, both monitors shared values and a common vision that their role as monitors was to translate the decree into functioning programs. Consequently, they not only evaluated agency progress, but they also facilitated the development of the necessary rules and protocols to guide implementation and mobilized support within the department (Smith interview). The monitors listened to the concerns of those working with various aspects of the developing programs and proposed strategies for addressing their problems. DCFS accepted their recommendations to hire new staff with experience in housing poor people and in advocacy against domestic violence. Community advocates and DCFS staff collaborated in a domestic violence advisory group that both provided policy expertise and mobilized external support for reforms (Smith interview; Shaw interview). Thus, both existing staff and a range of new actors were incorporated in the process for creating new rules and protocols for implementing the *Norman* programs.

Once DCFS officials agreed to negotiate the consent decree, they adopted the philosophy that providing economic and housing assistance to destitute child welfare clients was good child welfare practice (Smith interview; Heybach interview; Redleaf interview). This normative commitment did not waver even though the directorship of the DCFS changed four times during the implementation process, the department faced staff reductions, and the legislature challenged policies within the department that favored keeping families together. The monitor, however, doubted that a financial commitment to *Norman* programs would have been sustained if the judicial oversight had been prematurely ended, because the DCFS faced so many competing demands for resources (Smith interview).

The implementation process involved a number of new actors participating in decisions concerning DCFS policy: the monitors, poverty lawyers, judge, new staff, and community advocates. DCFS attempted to limit the intrusion of outsiders in its policy-making process through the creation of an Office of Litigation Management. The implementation of the *Norman* consent decree as well as other negotiated settlements was administered through this office. In this way, DCFS attempted both to create systems of accountability specific to their legal obligations and to maintain clear definitions of the classes of clients being served so as to limit those mandates. Consequently, although new legal machinery was created to implement the decree, this regulatory regime was not fully integrated into the larger administrative processes (Cheney-Egin interview; Smith interview; Redleaf interview; Heybach interview).

The *Norman* budget grew slowly from $1.8 million for fiscal year 1992–1993 to $2 million for fiscal year 1997–1998 (U.S. District Court 1996d:17). In 1995, nearly 2,500 families who were child welfare clients received some form of cash assistance through the *Norman* program (U.S. District Court 1996b).

IMPLEMENTATION ON A MACROLEVEL

Throughout the implementation process, DCFS administrators considered the *Norman* program a political asset. The costs of the program remained low, and the monitors provided the evidence in their monitoring reports that *Norman* services prevented much greater expenses than would have been required by out-of-home placements. Even when challenging the extension of monitoring in 1996, the department asserted its commitment to the program:

From the day the Consent Decree in this Court was entered, the Department has devoted substantial resources, both monetary and staff, to implementing this systemic reform Decree. These efforts have continued to this day, even in the face of a caseload that has grown from 20,000 to over 52,000 children. As a result of this work, among other things, over $3 million in cash assistance has been distributed to the plaintiff parents to help them keep or be reunited with their children, new Housing Assistance Programs have been established throughout the state, and improvements far beyond this Decree have been made in DCFS's response to domestic violence. These achievements are consistent with the Department's overall reforms to mount programs that will deflect children from entering State custody and returning them safely home more quickly, goals that are consistent with the best interests of these abused and neglected children and with the State's need to efficiently manage scarce public resources by reducing the costs of caring for children in foster care. (U.S. District Court 1996b)

Although the *Norman* program itself was not politically controversial, continued judicial supervision could have become a political liability. After the legislators expressed intense opposition to DCFS's consent decrees in 1995, DCFS administrators unsuccessfully attempted to end the monitoring relationship in the *Norman* case.

SUMMARY

Despite some negative developments in the political environment during the implementation of the *Norman* consent decree, the legislature continued to devote resources to the housing and economic assistance programs in the state child welfare agency. Several factors provided the poverty lawyers leverage to influence the implementation process during the first 6 years. Throughout implementation, the consent decree served as an important symbolic resource for the parties. It provided a structure and resources for the poverty lawyers to influence the administrative rule-making process and established standards for monitoring the agency's reforms. Because the implementation process was under the jurisdiction of the court, the substance of this decree was not subject to legislative revisions for the first 6 years. The comonitors effectively used their positions not only to legalize new programs that could carry out the objectives of the consent decree but also to mobilize support from those responsible for implementing the program and to incorporate new actors into the implementation process. Although DCFS administrators transformed their thinking about the importance of economic support as a component of a child welfare, they still tried to constrain their legal obligations to provide *Norman* resources to child welfare clients.

Discussion: Repeat Players, Rule-Change, and Legitimacy in the Implementation Process

Galanter argued that for public interest lawyers to represent the "have nots" in the legal system effectively, they must develop long-term strategies that would improve the strategic position of their clients in future conflicts. He recognized that the ability of legal reformers to make judicial rule-changes "penetrate" the implementing agencies is critical to achieving redistributive reforms (Galanter 1974:96, 97). He did not, however, elaborate an approach to analyze the dynamics of the implementation process. Conventional approaches to implementation examine the compliance of administering agencies with judicial decisions. In contrast, this study approaches the implementation process in terms of both conflict and collaboration over administrative rule-changes. These right-to-home case studies provide data to evaluate whether public interest lawyers, as repeat players, can develop long-term strategies to restructure the legal architecture of the agencies to facilitate redistributive reforms. Furthermore, we can examine how judicial rule-changes and oversight influence the lawyers' leverage for administrative reforms. Heimer's analysis suggests that critical to the reform process is the ability of the reformers on a microlevel to legalize reforms within the agencies and to establish official actors within the administrative infrastructure who are empowered by enforcing the new rules. Heimer argues that an organizational commitment to new programs is most likely when implementers believe that the reforms will enhance the legitimacy of the organization in its political environment.

Microlevel Implementation: Hansen and Norman Comparison

In both the *Hansen* and the *Norman* right-to-home cases, the poverty lawyers were trying to influence the implementation of redistributive reforms in political environments that were increasingly adverse to expanding resources to poor families. The Legal Services lawyers were able to use judicial decisions to create leverage for constructing redistributive remedies in both cases. These remedies, however, provided different sets of opportunities for the poverty lawyers to influence the ongoing process of legalizing these remedies and mobilizing support for redistributive reforms within the implementing agencies.

Faced with a preliminary injunction, the DSS officials in the *Hansen* case agreed to negotiate the creation of a new Homeless Assistance Program in the state legislature. After collaborating on the writing of the new statutes defining the program, however, the lawyers had no authority to influence the rule-making that would take place during the implementation process. By administering the program within the existing structures of the county public assistance agencies, there was an immediate redistributive impact. The *Sacramento Bee* (9 December 1990) reported that new benefits reached about 10,000 families a month during the second year of implementation (California Homeless and Housing Coalition 1991). Within the first 2 years of implementation, however, the county DSS offices faced increased pressures to prevent "fraud" in the program, and the new governor targeted poverty programs—including HAP—for cuts as a way of controlling a mushrooming state deficit. Despite the poverty lawyers' legislative advocacy and active participation in coalitions with advocates for the homeless, they were unable to mobilize enough political support to protect the program. By 1995, legislation had been enacted that allowed each family to be eligible for homeless assistance only one time.

In contrast, the construction of a consent decree and judicial supervision in the *Norman* case provided the poverty lawyers greater opportunities to influence the rules governing the implementation process and mobilize support for the new redistributive programs than before. In the *Norman* case, the provision in the "Consent Order" for a court-supervised monitor opened negotiations for expanding the position to two monitors. Because these monitors were attuned to both the dynamics of program development in a large bureaucracy and the concerns of the advocacy community, they had the knowledge, skills, and authority to "legalize" the housing and economic assistance programs within the child welfare agency. The system of court-supervised monitoring, which was extended for 2 years beyond the original provision of the consent decree, provided ongoing mechanisms for the poverty lawyers to influence the implementation process. During the first 6 years of implementation, a strong commitment to the program was established within the child welfare department. Despite changes in the political environment for the child welfare agency, there was never any political pressure to cut back the program.

It would be possible to attribute in part the relative stability of the *Norman* programs to their being much less extensive and costly than the program in California. Although the *Norman* programs never topped $2 million, the Homeless Assistance Program in California quickly grew to a $70 million program, with $35 million funded through the state. The low financial cost, however, does not provide a full explanation for the stability of the *Norman* program.

A comparison with the implementation process of a third right-to-home case, *Jiggetts v. Grinker*, provides important insights concerning the importance of judicial oversight for poverty lawyers who are repeat players in the implementation process and concerning the limits of poverty lawyers as guardians of the bureaucratic rule-making process.

LEGAL LEVERAGE AND ADMINISTRATIVE IRRATIONALITY: *Jiggetts*

From March to June 1991, *Jiggetts v. Grinker* was in trial in New York City. The Legal Aid lawyers argued that the existing shelter allowance in the public assistance program was inadequate to cover the costs of rent in New York City (Supreme Court of the State of New York 1991). By the time the judge issued her decision 6 years later, pretrial judicial rulings had already allowed the Legal Aid lawyers enough leverage to create a new supplementary shelter assistance program. About 10% of the families receiving welfare grants in New York City were also receiving *Jiggetts* relief (Wise 1997). The *Jiggetts* program cost at least $72 million annually (Wise 1997), approximately the same cost as the implementation of the Homeless Assistance Program in California. Yet although the California governor was able to significantly reduce HAP, the governors of New York were unable to mobilize political support to change the statutes that had provided the foundation for *Jiggetts*.

In New York City, the poverty lawyers used a preliminary injunction (Supreme Court of the State of New York 1988) as leverage to create a process for intervening new plaintiffs in the *Jiggetts* case. The Legal Aid lawyers became the de facto administrators of a new supplemental shelter program. They codified the rules and supervised the process of eligibility determination. As the number of intervenors grew, city social welfare agencies and landlords became dependent on the housing stability provided by the relief that these clients were receiving. By 1996, between 27,000 and 30,000 welfare recipients were receiving *Jiggetts* payments every month. If these payments were to be stopped, existing emergency housing programs would be completely overwhelmed and landlords would lose an important source of income (Bahn interview; Diller interview; Malin interview; Nortz interview).

Although the *Jiggetts* program enhanced the ability of New York City's Human Resources Administration to create a pressure valve to deal with homelessness, the poverty lawyers and advocates for the homeless never mobilized enough statewide support to legislate increased shelter allowances. Administrators in the New York State Department of Social Services continued to refuse to advocate for grant increases without approval of this strategy by the governor and legislature (Nortz interview). The poverty lawyers used judicial decisions to develop and administer the *Jiggetts* program, which significantly expanded the resources for families threatened with eviction. The poverty lawyers' internal involvement in the *Jiggetts* program, however, also had some unpredicted impacts on the Legal Aid organization itself. Saddled with the bureaucratic task of processing *Jiggetts* claims, lawyers felt that their skills were being underused, and workplace dissatisfaction grew. According to a former Legal Aid lawyer, who had created the legal strategy for *Jiggetts*, the class action had precipitated "a total transformation of Legal Aid practice" (Morawetz interview). She explains:

What happened was these people, for whom in the past you could do nothing, now had to be processed through *Jiggetts* relief, and it is very uninteresting, boring work. At Legal Aid, it has become a very, very difficult issue that people don't want to do these cases. It is debilitating for a Legal Services office to have lots and lots of extremely routine boring cases.

The litigation to establish adequate shelter allowances in the *Jiggetts* case is an example of what Katz referred to as poverty lawyers serving as "outside agents attempting to impose rationality on the administration of public welfare services over the opposition of a universally hostile state" (Katz 1984:189). The ad-hoc negotiations over the rules that created the implementation process for *Jiggetts* relief, however, were the antithesis of administrative rationality.

Macrolevel Implementation: A Comparison

The poverty lawyers and monitors in the *Norman* case seemed most effective in using the implementation process to increase the legitimacy of the child welfare agency in its political environment. They were able to use judicial supervision as pressure to facilitate rule-changes within the bureaucracy and mobilize support within the agency for redistributive reforms. During this process, the child welfare agency in Illinois began to tout the *Norman* programs as fundamental to good child welfare practice and as important resources for preventing the expense of unnecessary out-of-home placements.

In contrast, during the implementation of the Homeless Assistance Program in California, the poverty lawyers lacked the authority to influence the architecture of the state agency. When the beleaguered county welfare offices came under political scrutiny to ferret out "fraud" in the program, the program increasingly became a liability for the state agency. The poverty lawyers collaborated with advocates and state officials to propose rule-changes that would not reduce the redistributive impact of HAP. They were unable, however, to resist the political backlash against welfare programs. Consequently, statutory revisions constrained both eligibility for housing assistance and the amount of aid.

The *Jiggetts* program enhanced the legitimacy of state social welfare agencies in New York City by stabilizing the housing situation of families facing evictions. In addition, as Legal Aid lawyers assumed administrative roles in the *Jiggetts* program, they relieved the state from some of these duties. The integral role of the poverty lawyers in implementing *Jiggetts*, however, also had some negative consequences for the legitimacy of the Legal Aid Society. Staff dissatisfaction increased sharply as lawyers resented being assigned to process *Jiggetts* applications, which felt like clerical work rather than legal advocacy.

Conclusion

In this study, we have seen that poverty lawyers were critical to both the development and defense of new redistributive programs for the "have nots."

Particularly in the two cases where there was judicial oversight, the poverty lawyers and administrative officials negotiated the rule-making processes that would govern the new programs. From their "insider positions" within the implementation process, the poverty lawyers were also able to mobilize support for the judicially induced policy reforms. This analysis of the implementation strategies of the poverty lawyers provides evidence for speculating more broadly about the potential of public interest lawyers, as repeat players, to challenge the "mobilization of bias" in administrative agencies that fail to respond to the concerns of the "have nots." Schattschneider (1983:30) has argued that "organization in itself is a mobilization of bias in preparation for action." Consequently, bureaucratic structures are likely to thwart the implementation of court decisions with redistributive consequences that challenge existing agency goals (Handler 1978, 1996; Kagan 1991; Melnick 1994b; Shapiro 1988). In this implementation study, we are particularly interested in the possibilities and limitations for the legal advocates to reform the organizational infrastructure of the implementing agencies enough to achieve redistributive goals that had seemed untenable under the agency's existing "mobilization of bias."

Galanter has argued that with adequate resources, the litigants or their public interest lawyers could "secure the penetration of rules favorable to them" (Galanter 1974:103). He left unexplained, however, the process of "penetrating" administrative agencies to transform judicial rule-changes into redistributive reforms for the "have nots." Heimer (1996:30) identifies the "legalization" of reforms within agencies as necessary for changing "pre-existing organizational routines." These modifications are most likely when legal actors who are empowered to enforce the new reforms are present. As legal professionals with an expertise in poverty law, the public interest attorneys had special skills to contribute to the process of "legalizing" redistributive reforms. As outsiders to the implementing agencies, however, the poverty lawyers needed the legal authority to participate in ongoing rule-making within the agencies administering the programs. Judicial oversight allowed the poverty lawyers to shape the "legalization" process and influence the microdynamics of reform.

Targets of reform frequently try to appease their constituents with symbolic rewards without actually redistributing new resources (Lipsky 1968:1155; Galanter 1974:149). As repeat players in the implementation process, the lawyers in the *Norman* and *Jiggetts* cases could leverage reforms that would have substantive, not just symbolic consequences. The poverty lawyers negotiated rule-changes to create effective systems for establishing, monitoring, and evaluating the redistributive programs. Furthermore, the lawyers' ongoing involvement allowed them to identify where decisions were being made that impeded the development and administration of new programs.

Court-supervised implementation, however, was not sufficient for integrating new redistributive reforms into the existing bureaucratic structures. In addition, the lawyers had to mobilize intraagency support for reforms by convincing the administrative leadership that the new programs would enhance the reputation of the agency within its political environment and provide the staff with adequate resources to carry out their responsibilities. Thus, effective implementation required not only influencing the microlevel but also the macrolevel of reform. This process was particularly challenging in political environments in which the legislative leadership was retreating from previous commitments to maintaining a safety net for poor people. Under these conditions, even a well-functioning program could be vulnerable to funding cuts. When a diverse set of constituencies were mobilized for a program during the process of implementation, however, the program was more likely to be able to withstand political pressures for elimination.

The integration of the lawyers for the "have nots" into the implementation process had negative consequences when the lawyers not only influenced the rule-making process and mobilized support for reforms, but also assumed administrative roles. At this point, the lawyers not only represented the interests of their class of clients, but also became program constituents with their own set of interests as rule enforcers. Furthermore, the transformation of legal advocacy work to the performance of administrative routines threatened the legitimacy of the Legal Aid Society among its own staff.

Law and society scholars have debated the role of formal rule-making and legal representation in leveraging power for the "have nots." On one hand, some have argued that the attention to the formal "rules of the game" and litigation is misplaced; reform strategies should create collaborative relationships between the various actors in conflicts to shape discretionary decisions. Handler (1966, 1978, 1990, 1996), Melnick (1983), and Kagan (1991) have critiqued the limitations of adversarial legal relationships for achieving administrative reforms. On the other hand, other law and society scholars have argued that when the parties to a conflict have unequal power, formal rules and legal representation for the "have nots" in an adversarial process can be critical for creating leverage (Delgado et al. 1985; Lieberman 1981; McCann 1994).

This study suggests that to create successful implementation strategies, advocates for the "have nots" must combine the leverage created by formal rule-changes with collaborative tactics that mobilize administrative and political support for those changes. Thus, the public interest lawyers can draw on their organizational resources to use the leverage from judicial decisions to "penetrate" administrative agencies. Access to the rule-making process, however, must be complemented with a strategy for developing long-term political and administrative commitments to reform goals. In addition, the involvement of legal advocates for the "have nots" in the implementation process does not ensure the creation of a political environment that will support the concerns of the lawyers' disadvantaged clients. Nonetheless, as repeat players, the public interest lawyers can create spaces in the political and administrative processes for contesting both the existing "mobilization of bias" within official venues and particular egregious administrative policies.

Political commitments in the 1960s to the funding of legal services to represent poor people in criminal and civil courts increased opportunities for the interests of those who were disadvantaged to be addressed in official venues. Although legal representation did not fundamentally transform political and economic relations of power, resources were created for poor people to move from a position of "passive dependence on the system to active assertion of [their] interests" (Feeley 1986:176). In the criminal justice system, the importance of legal representation extended beyond litigation to the plea bargaining process, in which the legal adversarial relationship provided a context for negotiating punishments (ibid., p. 176). The Legal Services lawyers not only represented their clients' interests in judicial arenas, but the threat of increased judicial intervention provided leverage for the lawyers to influence the implementation of redistributive remedies. During the 1990s, the decreased funds for and restrictions on the legal representation of poor people have implications beyond reducing the opportunities for the "have nots" to prevail in courts. In addition, administrative agencies have become more insulated from the grievances of their impoverished clients. Spaces for establishing resources to protect families from the most egregious consequences of poverty have been closed.

Notes

Originally published in *Law & Society Review* 33 (4) 911–39 (1999); reprinted by permission. I am grateful that the Institute of Legal Studies at the University of Wisconsin–Madison Law School invited me to participate in the "Do the 'Haves' Still Come Out Ahead?" Conference (1998), which provided a fertile environment for the development of this article. I thank Michael McCann, Susan Silbey, Herbert Kritzer, and the anonymous readers for their editing guidance. I continue to appreciate those advocates, organizers, and activists who are supporting efforts of the "have nots" to resist the "mobilization of bias" against them in every venue and at each stage of the political process.

Beth Harris is Assistant Professor in the Department of Politics at Ithaca College. She is examining how legal strategies in defense of the "have nots" influence political dynamics in local and international contexts. Current projects include a book, provisionally entitled *The Power of Poverty Lawyers: Defending a Right-to-Home*, and an article about the collaboration among Palestinian, Israeli, and internationalist activists to resist the Israeli demolitions of Palestinian homes in the wake of the Oslo agreements.

1. Matthew Diller worked for the Civil Appeals and Reform Litigation Unit at the Legal Aid Society in New York between 1986 and 1993.

2. The "right-to-home" class actions I have identified are *Connelly v. Carlisle*, Suffolk Civic Act. No. 43–3159 (Mass. Sup. Court 1993); *Consentino v. Perales*, 546 N.Y.S.2d 75 (1st Dept. 1989); *Jiggetts v. Grinker* (N.Y.), 75 N.Y.2d 411 (1990); *Hansen v. McMahon*, 238 Cal. Rptr. 232 (Cal. App. 2 Dist. 1987); *In Re: Petitions for Rulemaking*, N.J.A.C. 10:82–1.2, 117 N.J. 311, 566 A.2d 1154 (1989); *Massachusetts Coalition for the Homeless v. Secretary of Human Services*, 400 Mass. 806, 511 N.E.2d 603 (1987); *Maticka v. City of Atlantic City*, 216 N.J. Super. 434 (App. Div. 1987); *Norman v. Johnson*, 739 F. Supp. 1182 (N.D. Ill. 1990); *Savage v. Aronson*, No. CV-NH-8904–3142 (Conn. Super. Ct., New Haven Housing Sess., 1989); *Washington State Coalition for the Homeless v. Secretary of Department of Social and Health Services*, No. 91–2–15889–4 (Wash. Super. Ct., King Co., 1991); and *Tilden v. Hayward*, Civ. Action No. 1197 (Chancery Ct., New Castle Cnty, Del, 1989). Citations from National Housing Law Project 1992; and Roisman 1991.

3. California State Statutes of 1987, Ch. 1353, Sec. 1, 4895–98.

4. California State Statutes of 1991, Ch. 97, Sec. 6, 518–21.

5. West's California Legislative Service, Vol. 5 (1995), California State Statutes, Ch. 307, Sec. 7, 1441–42.

6. During the implementation process of the *Norman* case, monitoring reports were submitted to the court to Judge William Hart, U.S. District Court for the Northern District of Illinois Eastern Division, on the following dates: the First (1 March 1992), the Second (28 September 1992), the Third (17 March 1993), the Fourth (23 August 1993), the Fifth (15 March 1994), the Sixth (24 May 1995), the Seventh (3 June 1996), and the Eighth (7 May 1997).

References

Auditor General of California (1990) Report by the Auditor General of California: Improvements Are Needed in the State's Program to Provide Assistance to Homeless Families. Sacramento: California State Auditor.

Beyle, Thad (1992) *Governors and Hard Times*. Washington, DC: Congressional Quarterly.

Brodkin, Evelyn Z. (1986) *The False Promise of Administrative Reform: Implementing Quality Control in Welfare*. Philadelphia: Temple Univ. Press.

Cahn, Edgar S., & Jean C. Cahn (1964) "The War on Poverty: A Civilian Perspective," 73 *Yale Law J.* 1316–52.

California Homeless and Housing Coalition (1991) *Facts and Myths about the AFDC Homeless Assistance Program*. Los Angeles: California Homeless and Housing Coalition.

Carlin, Jerome E., Jan Howard, & Sheldon L. Messinger (1966) "Civil Justice and the Poor: Issues for Sociological Research," 1 *Law & Society Rev.* 9–89.

Children's Defense Fund (1994) *The State of America's Children Yearbook.* Washington, DC: Children's Defense Fund.

Davis, Martha (1995) *Brutal Need: Lawyers and the Welfare Rights Movement, 1960–1973.* New Haven: Yale Univ. Press.

Delgado, Richard, Chris Dunn, Pamela Brown, Helena Lee, & David Hubbert (1985) "Fairness and Formality: Minimizing the Risk of Prejudice in Alternative Dispute Resolution," 6 *Wisconsin Law Rev.* 1359–1404.

Diller, Matthew (1995) "Poverty Lawyering in the Golden Age," 93 *Michigan Law Rev.* 1401–32.

Ellis, Virginia (1991) "The Governor's Budget Proposal; Lower Benefits Linked to Shift in Philosophy; Welfare: Governor Says Recipients, Mostly Single Mothers, Don't Have Enough Incentive to Get Off Programs. Critics Believe the Ranks of the Homeless Will Swell," *Los Angeles Times,* 11 Jan., p. A3.

Fabricant, Michael B., & Steve Burghardt (1992) *The Welfare State Crisis and the Transformation of Social Work.* Armonk, NY: M. E. Sharpe, Inc.

Feeley, Malcolm (1986) "Bench Trials, Adversariness, and Plea Bargaining: A Comment on Schulhofer's Plan," 14 *New York Univ. Rev. of Law & Social Change,* 173–78.

Galanter, Mark (1974) "Why the 'Haves' Come Out Ahead: Speculations on the Limits of Legal Change," 9 *Law & Society Rev.* 95–160.

——— (1983) "The Radiating Effects of Courts," in K. O. Boyum and L. Mather, eds., *Empirical Theories about Courts.* New York: Longman.

Garth, Bryant G. (1992) "Power and Legal Artifice: The Federal Class Action," 26 *Law & Society Rev.* 237–71.

Handler, Joel F. (1966) "Controlling Official Behavior in Welfare Administration," 54 *California Law Rev.* 479–510.

——— (1978) *Social Movements and the Legal System: A Theory of Law Reform and Social Change.* New York: Academic Press.

———. (1990) *Law and the Search for Community.* Philadelphia: Univ. of Pennsylvania Press.

——— (1996) *Down from Bureaucracy: The Ambiguity of Privatization and Empowerment.* Princeton, NJ: Princeton Univ. Press.

Handler, Joel F., & Michael Sosin (1983) *Last Resorts: Emergency Assistance and Special Needs Programs in Public Welfare.* New York: Academic Press.

Heimer, Carol A. (1996) "Explaining Variation in the Impact of Law: Organizations, Institutions, and Professions." 15 *Studies in Law, Politics, & Society* 29–59.

Houseman, Alan W. (1991) "Poverty Law: Past and Future," in E. F. Lardent, ed., *Civil Justice: An Agenda for the 1990s.* New Orleans: American Bar Association.

Kagan, Robert A. (1991) "Adversarial Legalism and American Government," 10 *J. of Policy Analysis & Management,* 369–406.

Katz, Jack (1984) *Poor People's Lawyers in Transition.* New Brunswick, NJ: Rutgers Univ. Press.

Lawrence, Susan E. (1990) *The Poor in Court: The Legal Services Program and Supreme Court Decision Making.* Princeton, NJ: Princeton Univ. Press.

Lieberman, Jethro K. (1981) *The Litigious Society.* New York: Basic Books.

Lipsky, Michael (1968) "Protest as a Political Resource," 62 *American Political Science Rev.* 1144–58.

McCann, Michael W. (1992) "Reform Litigation on Trial," 17 *Law & Social Inquiry* 715–45.

———— (1994) *Rights at Work: Pay Equity Reform and the Politics of Legal Mobilization.* Chicago: Univ. of Chicago.

———— (1999) "How the Supreme Court Matters in American Politics: New Institutional Perspectives," in C. Clayton & H. Gillman, eds., *The Supreme Court and American Politics: New Institutionalist Approaches.* Lawrence: Univ. Press of Kansas.

Melnick, R. Shep (1983) *Regulation and the Courts: The Case of the Clean Air Act.* Washington, DC: Brookings Institution.

———— (1994a) "Administrative Law and Bureaucratic Reality," in T. O. Sargentich, ed., *Administrative Law Anthology.* Cincinnati: Anderson Publishing.

———— (1994b) *Between the Lines: Interpreting Welfare Rights.* Washington, DC: Brookings Institution.

Murphy, Kim (1986) "State is Ordered to Revise Welfare Rule," *Los Angeles Times,* 2 Aug., Home Ed., sec. 2, p. 1.

National Housing Law Project (1992) *Annotated Docket of Selected Cases and Other Materials Involving Homelessness.* Working Draft. Washington DC: National Housing Law Project.

Novak, Tim (1995) "DCFS Chief Hits Senate Stall on his Appointment," *Chicago Sun-Times,* 1 June, p. 16.

Pearson, Rick (1992) "State Starts Sending Pink Slips to Public Aid, DCFS Workers," *Chicago Tribune,* 11 Aug., p. Chicagoland 2.

Ramos, George (1986) "State Ordered to Provide Aid to Homeless Families," *Los Angeles Times,* 13 May, sec. 1, p. 1.

Roisman, Florence (1991) *Establishing a Right to Housing: An Advocate's Guide.* Washington, DC: National Support Center for Low Income Housing.

Schattschneider, E. E. (1983) *The Semisovereign People: A Realist's View of Democracy in America.* Fort Worth, TX: Holt, Rinehart and Winston.

Scheingold, Stuart A. (1974) The Politics of Rights: Lawyers, Public Policy, and Political Change. New Haven, CT: Yale Univ. Press.

Shapiro, Martin (1988) *Who Guards the Guardians?* Athens: Univ. of Georgia Press.

Sparer, Edward V. (1965) "Role of the Welfare Client's Lawyer," 12 *UCLA Law Rev.* 361–80.

Stumpf, Harry P. (1975) *Community Politics and Legal Services: The Other Side of the Law.* Beverly Hills, CA: Sage Publications.

Vorenberg, Elizabeth (1993) "Child Services Can Tear Families Apart," *New York Times,* 28 June, p. A16.

Wise, Daniel (1997) "Rent Aid to Welfare Recipients Continued Under Interim Orders," *New York Law J.,* 9 May, pp. 1, 4.

Legal Documents

HANSEN V. MCMAHON, FILE NO. CA 000974

Superior Court of the State of California for the County of Los Angeles (1986) "Class Action Complaint for Declaratory and Injunctive Relief and Petition for Writ of Mandate" (April 17).

Court of Appeal of the State of California, Second Appellate District, Division 6 (1987) "Opinion," by Judge J. Abbe, 1 July.

Jiggetts v. Grinker, File No. 40582/97

Supreme Court of the State of New York, County of New York (1991) "Plaintiffs' Proposed Findings of Fact," 4 Dec.

Supreme Court of the State of New York, County of New York (1988) "Order," by Judge K. Moscowitz, 12 Jan.

Norman v. Johnson, File No. 89 C 1624

U.S. District Court for the Northern District of Illinois Eastern Division (1990) "Memorandum Opinion and Order," by Judge W. T. Hart, 18 May.

U.S. District Court for the Northern District of Illinois Eastern Division (1991) "Consent Order," 28 March.

U.S. District Court for the Northern District of Illinois Eastern Division (1995) "Agreed Order," by Judge W. T. Hart, 27 Feb.

U.S. District Court for the Northern District of Illinois Eastern Division (1996a) "Motion for (1) Continued Monitoring and/or (2) Declaratory and Injunctive Relief Redressing Substantial Non-Compliance with the Consent Decrees and the Court Order of March 10, 1996," 7 Feb.

U.S. District Court for the Northern District of Illinois Eastern Division (1996b) "Defendant's Memorandum in Opposition to Plaintiffs' Motion for Continued Monitoring and/or Declaratory and Injunctive Relief," 26 Feb.

U.S. District Court for the Northern District of Illinois Eastern Division (1996c) "Memorandum Opinion and Order," by Judge W. T. Hart, 11 April.

U.S. District Court for the Northern District of Illinois Eastern Division (1996d) "Seventh Monitoring Report," 3 June.

Interviews with Author

HANSEN V. MCMAHON

Berlin, Nancy (1996) Director of the California Homeless and Housing Coalition. Interview by author. Los Angeles, 14 Oct.

Bird, Melinda (1996) Attorney, formerly with Western Center on Law and Poverty, Los Angeles. Interview by author. Los Angeles, 17 Oct.

Farber, Jeffrey (1996) Social worker, Los Angeles. Family Housing. Interview by author. Los Angeles, 14 Oct.

McKeever, Casey (1996) Legislative advocate with Western Center on Law and Poverty, Sacramento. Phone interview, 7 Oct.

Newman, Robert (1996) Attorney with Western Center on Law and Poverty. Interview by author. Los Angeles, 16 Oct.

JIGGETTS V. GRINKER

Bahn, Susan (1997) Attorney, Legal Aid Society, New York City. Interview by author. New York City, 25 June.

Diller, Matthew (1996) Attorney, formerly with Legal Aid Society, New York City. Interview by author. New York City, 10 July.

Malin, Joan (1997) Former Commissioner for Homeless Administration, New York City. Interview by author. New York City, 25 June.

Morawetz, Nancy (1997) Attorney, formerly with Legal Aid Society, New York City. Interview by author. New York City, 1 July.

Nortz, Shelley (1997) Director for State Policy, Coalition for the Homeless, Albany. Phone interview, 12 June.

NORMAN V. JOHNSON

Cheney-Egin, John (1996) Housing specialist and divisional *Norman* liaison for the Office of Litigation Management, Illinois Department of Children and Family Services. Interview by author. Chicago, 17 July.

Heybach, Laurene (1996) Attorney, Legal Aid Foundation of Chicago. Interview by author. Chicago, 19 July.

Redleaf, Diane (1996) Attorney, formerly with Legal Aid Foundation of Chicago. Phone interview, 18 July.

Shaw, Barbara (1996) Executive Director, Illinois Council for the Prevention of Violence. Interview by author. Chicago, 23 July.

Smith, Jeanine (1996) Monitor, *Norman* Consent Decree. Interview by author. Chicago, 18 July.

Tchen, Christina (1996) Attorney, Partner in Skadden, Arps, Slate, Meagher and Flom, legal counsel for the Department of Children and Family Services. Interview by author. Chicago, 25 July.

KARYL A. KINSEY AND LORETTA J. STALANS 5

Which "Haves" Come Out Ahead and Why?

Cultural Capital and Legal Mobilization in Frontline Law Enforcement

Introduction

Several strands of research in criminology and sociolegal studies argue that higher-status individuals are less subject to law than middle- or lower-status persons (Black 1976; Sutherland 1983). One of the most clearly articulated theories of status differences in law appears in Galanter's seminal 1974 article "Why the 'Haves' Come Out Ahead" (see also Black 1976). We refer to this theory as the legal mobilization hypothesis. Galanter argues that parties with greater resources can mobilize the law more proactively than others to achieve instrumental goals. They can hire more and better-quality legal representation and are more likely to be repeat players knowledgeable about the workings of the legal system. From Galanter's theory, both repeat playership and legal representation provide higher-status parties with an advantage.

Prior research on whether the "haves" come out ahead in the legal system has focused primarily on civil and criminal cases (see, for example, Songer & Sheehan, 1992; Weisburd et al. 1990; Wheeler et al. 1987). As Edwin Sutherland pointed out, though, most allegations of illegal behavior against high-status individuals and organizations are primarily handled through administrative and regulatory law enforcement agencies. Do the "haves" come out ahead in the front lines of civil law enforcement? This article examines this question in the context of state income tax audits. Tax audits are an especially good area for examining questions of relative advantage and equal treatment under the law. Income taxation touches virtually everyone, whatever one's position in society. The enforcement net sweeps broadly, with routine enforcement contacts made with a wide range of peo-

ple of different social statuses, arguably more than any other form of law enforcement in society.

Taxation is also an area of law permeated with claims of victimization and
accusations of privilege, a preoccupation with fundamental questions of distributive justice. The general public tends to perceive economic elites as ex-
ploiters of tax loopholes and recipients of "corporate welfare" while believing the "have nots"—ordinary citizens like themselves—pay more than their
fair share (Kinsey & Grasmick 1993). At the same time, a case can be made
that the "haves" are treated more harshly by tax law than others. For example, higher-income taxpayers face higher marginal tax rates than other taxpayers. Those who try to lower taxes through legal tax avoidance—the
"loopholes" decried by so many others—find in consequence that they have
become even more subject to law in the form of complex rules and regulations, increased record-keeping requirements, greater costs of filing a tax return, and higher risk of audit (Long & Swingen 1988, 1989; Slemrod & Sorum 1984).[1] Business owners also face regulatory burdens through the
withholding system and requirements to submit information reports to tax
agencies. Their compliance burdens are further complicated by the multiple
federal, state, and local tax agencies they have to satisfy.

The first goal of our study was to examine which "haves" do or do not
come out ahead in tax audits. To summarize our results, we find strong and
consistent evidence that taxpayers who own businesses with 10 or more employees are more likely to mobilize legally than other taxpayers. They are
more likely to be repeat players, to engage in legal tax avoidance, and to employ a tax practitioner to represent them during the audit. The key variables
predicting audit outcomes, however, are occupational prestige and whether
the taxpayer runs a "mom and pop" business. This pattern of findings points
to the cultural capital of taxpayers, more than legal mobilization, as a key factor shaping auditor decisions. Further analyses suggest that culturally shared
expectations that people in prestigious occupations are trustworthy and capable of influencing authorities give higher prestige taxpayers an edge in
shaping the auditor's decision-making.

The results point to a somewhat surprising conclusion about the role of
tax practitioners in shaping the relative advantages and disadvantages of different groups of taxpayers. Instead of increasing the advantages of the
"haves," the involvement of tax practitioners *levels the playing field*: status differences in auditors' decisions to assert changes on individual tax issues and
to assess higher taxes appear among unrepresented taxpayers but not among
represented taxpayers. The analysis suggests that practitioner involvement
dampens the influence of status-based normative expectations that otherwise
structure audit interactions when taxpayers represent themselves.

The Case for Legal Mobilization

Galanter (1974) argues that the greater resources and repeat playership of the "haves" make them better able to accomplish instrumental goals by positioning themselves within the requirements of law and couching arguments advancing their viewpoint in the language and format of law. Law in the hands of the "haves," and their legal representatives, is malleable, a tool to be used, not commandments writ in stone.

Several case studies in sociolegal research have described ways in which legal experts create new law and legal forms (see, for example, Powell 1993). Taxation is an area of law that sees an extraordinarily high degree of the mobilization of expertise and creative uses of law in ways not intended by legislators, and often opposed by enforcers. Klepper and Nagin (1989) describe the role of the tax practitioner in the tax system as a two-edged sword: practitioners increase clients' compliance in areas of tax law where the rules and regulations are clear, but also identify and exploit gray areas of the law to their clients' advantage.[2] McBarnet (1992a, 1992b) argues that the crafters of legal tax avoidance schemes use highly legalistic application of the details of tax law to evade the spirit, although not the letter, of the law.

The legal mobilization hypothesis makes specific predictions about the use of law and the role of tax practitioners in tax audits. Any advantage the "haves" might have in tax audits reflects their greater ability to afford legal representation and to use the gray areas of tax law to their own advantage. If true, social status should be related to use and type of tax representation and to indicators of legal tax avoidance. The limited research available on tax practice provides support for the legal mobilization hypothesis in that higher-status taxpayers are more likely than other taxpayers to use the services of highly trained professionals, who in turn are more aggressive in their interpretation of tax law than other types of practitioners (Jackson et al. 1988; Kinsey 1987). Kinsey (1992) also found that people with prior IRS enforcement contacts feel less intimidated by the agency than others, suggesting an advantage for repeat players.

Cultural Capital and Normative Expectancies

One of the earliest and most common findings of small-group research is that higher-status individuals have more influence and receive more deference from others in newly formed groups. For example, one of the first things the 12 strangers in a jury room usually do is to elect a high-status person as foreman (Strodtbeck et al. 1958). Laboratory studies find that high-status persons are among the first to talk and tend to hold the floor for longer periods than other persons. Lower status individuals are usually quieter and tend to get interrupted should they try to talk. Status expectations theory argues that the influence attempts of high-status individuals succeed, and those of lower-status people fail, due to *socially shared* cognitions and expectations that link social status to attributions about personal ability and worth (Berger et al. 1966, 1972; Webster & Driskill 1978); we refer to these socially shared cognitions as normative status-based expectancies. In short, individuals of higher status have more cultural capital due to culturally held beliefs about their character and reputation (see also DiMaggio 1990; Hagan et al. 1991).

The generality of the findings from laboratory studies of small groups to real-life settings is, of course, open to question. As many commentators have noted, laboratory studies are conducted in artificial settings and are potentially subject to a number of demand characteristics that might bias results (Billig 1976; Orne 1962; Rosenthal 1966). The laboratory studies' attention to the microprocesses of interaction, however, suggests some powerful hypotheses for explaining not only the results of the early jury studies—which used real-life jurors—but the status dynamics of interaction in other arenas of law enforcement. Suggestive evidence of generality can be found in various sociolegal settings. Yngvesson (1993), for example, reports that magistrate clerks tend to dismiss the concerns of lower-class complainants as "garbage" cases unworthy of legal intervention.

Some of the laboratory research suggests that status-based expectancies especially influence decisions or judgments about people under conditions of ambiguity or lack of information (Freese & Cohen 1973; Webster & Driskill 1978). The indeterminacy of tax compliance opens the door for status-based normative expectancies to influence the enforcement of tax laws. Determining compliance with tax laws is a highly problematic task; it is often difficult even for officials at the same tax agency to agree on what the correct tax assessment should be in specific cases (Elffers et al. 1989; Long & Swingen 1991). Qualitative studies of practitioners are abundant with signs of influence attempts in practitioners' descriptions of their covert efforts to control the auditor's focus of attention and decision process (Kinsey 1987; McBarnet 1992a).

Status expectations theory points to two ways high-prestige taxpayers may come out ahead in tax audits. The tendency of high-status persons to take the initiative points to a *self-fulfilling prophecy* effect.[3] Because high-status individuals have a greater amount of cultural capital than others, they are more poised and comfortable with the prospect of exercising power. In contrast, a lower-status person will be more nervous and uncertain. Linguistic studies of courtroom interaction (cf. O'Barr & O'Barr, 1995) and legal analyses of Miranda appeals (Ainsworth 1993) find characteristic patterns of "powerless" speech among persons of lower social statuses that suggest uncertainty and hesitation, thus undercutting their ability to convince powerful others of their credibility.

The self-fulfilling prophecy hypothesis argues that, because they enter the audit with greater self-confidence and expectations of good treatment, higher-status taxpayers may end up actually taking a more active role than others in defining audit issues and eliciting cooperation from the auditor. Lower-status persons, on the other hand, might take a more passive role because they feel more insecure and do not believe authorities will respond positively to their influence attempts.

Because our audit data included a panel component, we can test the self-fulfilling prophecy component of the cultural capital hypothesis. If it is true, then higher-status individuals should have greater expectations of future influence over the tax auditor than other individuals. Furthermore, preaudit expectations should affect audit outcomes and reduce the direct effect of social status in statistical analyses.

Status expectations theory also points to a *burden of proof* variant of cultural capital effects. For example, laboratory studies of newly formed groups find that individuals of a higher social status are automatically assumed by others to be knowledgeable and reliable sources of information. Lower-status persons, however, bear an extra burden of proof in establishing their credibility. They are not trusted automatically, but are instead required to prove themselves first (Freese & Cohen 1973; Webster & Driskill 1978). Based on this research, both authorities such as auditors and laypeople may assume that individuals in highly prestigious jobs (such as professors and medical doctors) are trustworthy. This shared assumption leads to differences in the extent to which higher- and lower-status individuals are required to support their statements with additional evidence.

In the burden of proof hypothesis, status effects arise not so much from the initiative and actions of high-status taxpayers, but more from a tendency by people to assume from the onset that high-status taxpayers are more credible and trustworthy people than taxpayers with a lower social status. We have in our data set one variable that directly measures the burden of proof: whether the auditor accepted oral testimony instead of insisting on seeing documentation related to an audit issue. Based on status expectancy theory, we hypothesized that auditors will more often accept the oral testimony of higher-status taxpayers than of lower-status taxpayers.

Data Sources

The data come from a study of state tax audits conducted by researchers at the American Bar Foundation and Oregon State University. A state income tax audit is essentially an audit of the federal return. The Oregon Department of Revenue provided access to information about audit cases in four offices that handle about 70% of the statewide audit caseload.

The study began with individual hour-long semistructured interviews with all auditors about their perceptions of taxpayers and preferred work styles. Over the next couple of years, auditors sent copies of initial audit notice letters to Oregon State University (n = 533).[4] After audits were completed, the auditors also filled out an audit report form describing the issues examined in the audit and their perceptions of the taxpayer and tax practitioners involved. A random sample of taxpayers was selected from the pool of audit notices for a panel study that included both preaudit and postaudit surveys with taxpayers. Another taxpayer sample was selected for postaudit interviews only. Audit case files were also content-coded, and financial information was compiled from departmental records.

This analysis is based on 117 cases for which we have both preaudit and postaudit taxpayer surveys and report forms filled out by auditors. In 92 cases, content codings of specific audit issues recorded in the audit files are also available. In addition, a small sample of the tax practitioners involved were also interviewed ($n = 36$); this information is used to provide descriptive data about practitioner characteristics.

MEASURES OF "HAVE" STATUS

Indicators of Cultural Capital

Occupational prestige is probably the purest measure of general social status employed in this study. Studies find an unusually strong social consensus among all groups in society about the relative rankings of the prestige of individual occupations (Nock & Rossi 1978). Moreover, occupation is highly salient during a tax audit.

Occupation was ascertained by a series of questions asking respondents if they were self-employed or had worked for others as an employee. Follow-up questions for self-employment asked what kind of work was done and whether the work was a respondent's primary job or a sideline. Follow-up questions for employees asked what kinds of jobs they had in the past 3 years. The prestige of the type of work or jobs held by the respondent was coded using the coding categories developed by the National Opinion Research Center for the General Social Surveys (NORC 1991). For those respondents reporting both self-employment and working for others, the primary occupation was determined by the question of whether their self-employment was a sideline or primary work. For those with multiple jobs, the most recent job was used to indicate primary occupation.

The resulting occupational prestige scores were reduced to a three-point scale. Examples of occupations in the high-prestige category are physicians, lawyers, corporate managers, and college professors (33%). The middle-prestige group includes shop owners, real estate agents, restaurant managers, and construction contractors (42%). The low-status group includes occupations such as truck driver, janitorial service providers, food service employee, and general laborers (25%).

Education is another important indicator of cultural capital, but one that is likely confounded with objective knowledge of tax law. It is measured on a four-point scale. About one-fourth (23%) of respondents had a high school education or less, 36% had some college or training school experience, another 16% obtained a bachelor's degree, and 25% had graduate degrees.

A less traditional measure of cultural capital in this study is whether taxpayers run a "mom and pop" business. Family-owned and operated businesses capture a special place in the American imagination; people seem to care more about their fate than more impersonal organizations. Whether the audit involved a family business was operationalized by whether survey respondents reported that they or their spouse were self-employed in the same line of work. About one-fourth (27%) of the sample consisted of family-owned businesses.

Organizational Size

In civil court studies, organizational litigants are hypothesized to be more powerful than individuals and larger organizations to be more powerful than smaller ones. Organizational size was measured with two dummy variables: whether self-employed taxpayers have fewer than 10 full-time equivalent employees (42%) or more than 10 employees (9%). The reference group consists of taxpayers who were employees only (14%) and self-employed taxpayers who work by themselves (35%).[5]

Unfortunately, our data do not include a good measure of income. Because income is an especially sensitive topic in the audit context, it was not asked in the taxpayers' surveys. Data on adjusted gross income (AGI) are available for 101 cases, but AGI systematically underestimates the true income of both tax avoiders and tax cheats. Reflecting its poor reliability as an income measure, AGI is not correlated to either occupational prestige or education. Income is therefore not included in the analysis.

LEGAL MOBILIZATION VARIABLES

Repeat playership is measured as a three-point scale of whether the respondent has never been audited (50%), was audited once before (30%), or has been audited more than once (20%). Consistent with Kinsey (1992), repeat players are less nervous than others about their upcoming audit. A full

67% of those without prior audit experience report feeling nervous, compared with 37% of those with one prior audit, and 23% with two or more (chi square[sub(df 2)] = 5.68, p < .001).

Two objective indicators of legal tax avoidance are available from the data. The number of partnership and S-corporation schedules filed by the taxpayer was computed from information provided on the auditor report form. Partnerships have historically been a primary vehicle for tax shelters, and the decision by small business owners to become an S Corporation is often driven by tax considerations. About three-fourths of audited taxpayers filed neither type of schedule, whereas 17% filed one and 8% filed two or more such schedules.

In the audit report forms, auditors also described up to four types of issues examined during the audit. These issues were classified according to whether they involved complex issues typically reflecting legal tax avoidance, such as timing issues about the year in which something is reported, capitalization and depreciation issues, asset basis and value, and other issues about distributions from partnerships and corporations (see Smith 1995). These types of issues are often implicated in legal tax avoidance schemes. The measure of the legal complexity of audit issues was constructed by first calculating the percent of issues involving legal complexity. This measure was then collapsed into a three-point scale of whether no legally complex issues were involved (61%), up to half the issues were legally complex (23%), or more than half the issues were complex (16%).

Whether a tax practitioner was involved in the audit (48% yes) was measured using information from both the survey forms and the auditor report forms. In 36 cases, we also had interview data from practitioners whose clients had given permission to be interviewed about their audit. Of those, 64% were CPAs, 28% were licensed tax consultants, and 11% were licensed tax preparers. Taxpayers of higher social statuses tended to employ CPAs: 92% of those with college degrees employed CPAs, as did 86% of business owners with 10 or more employees and 92% of high-prestige taxpayers.

TAXPAYER EXPECTATIONS OF INFLUENCE

Research finds that perceptions and attitudes that come to mind most readily tend also to be more important to the person than other attitudes (Krosnick 1989). At the very beginning of their first interview, taxpayers were asked four open-ended questions to assess their expectations of the upcoming audit:

1. "Most people have some idea of what an audit will be like. Take a moment to imagine what you think your audit may be like and describe it to me in your own words."

2. "How do you imagine the auditor will behave during the audit?"
3. "What do you think will go on during the audit—that is, what do you think the procedures will be?"
4. "How do you think things will be decided during the audit?"

All the preaudit interviews were content-coded for major themes. Two researchers developed a coding scheme and used it to code an initial set of interviews. The coding scheme was updated by adding other frequent categories that emerged. Then one of the researchers coded the remaining interviews, while consulting with the other about ambiguous or unusual responses. A third researcher unfamiliar with the purpose of the study coded 50 protocols to check on interrater reliability. They ranged from .90 to 1.00.

Indicators of taxpayers' expectations that they could influence the auditor included codes for statements of whether the outcome would be favorable or unfavorable, whether the taxpayer would be capable of influencing the auditor, and whether the auditor would base decisions on facts and the law or would be biased in favor of the state (and thus resistant to influence attempts). A typical example of an expected lack of influence is the statement, "Someone like them, they have the power/authority, so they'll probably do the deciding." Examples of expected influence were more varied, including statements such as "Auditor will accept my explanations," "The final decision will be a compromise between the auditor and me," and "They can be intimidated."

The resulting measure of taxpayers' expectations of influence consisted of the number of positive comments minus the number of negative comments (mean = -.12, SD = 1.50). Almost half (44%) of taxpayers had more positive than negative expectations; the converse was true for 34%. The remaining 22% either expressed no expectations or had an even mixture of positive and negative expectations.

AUDITOR ACCEPTANCE OF ORAL TESTIMONY

Data were available in 87 cases from the audit files as to whether the auditor accepted oral testimony or estimates of expenses in lieu of documentation. The percent of issues involving oral testimony was first calculated and then collapsed into three categories: no oral testimony (58%), oral testimony accepted up to half the issues (18%), and oral testimony accepted more than half the issues covered in the audit (18%).

AUDIT OUTCOMES

The first audit outcome measure consists of auditors' decisions to accept taxpayer positions on individual issues or to assert changes to the return. Cases where the auditor accepted the taxpayer's position on all issues covered in the audit were assigned a zero (26%), those where every issue was either changed or unresolved (meaning both auditor and taxpayer were holding firm to their respective positions) were assigned a value of 1 (49%), and intermediate cases showing a mixture of acceptance and rejection of taxpayer positions were assigned a value of .5 (25%).

The total amount of taxes, penalties, and interest assessed to the taxpayer was obtained from departmental records. The mean amount assessed was $1,188 (SD $2,530), but the median was considerably lower, with half paying less than $196. A substantial minority of taxpayers (38%) paid no additional taxes, 24% paid less than $500, and 38% paid more than $500 in additional assessments. Due to the skewed nature of the distribution, a log transformation of income was used in multivariate analyses.

AUDITOR PERCEPTIONS OF TAXPAYERS AND TAX PRACTITIONERS

The auditor report form asked auditors to rate on a five-point scale how well they got along interpersonally with the taxpayer and any tax practitioners involved in the audit. In addition, they were asked to rate taxpayers and practitioners on an adjective checklist, also with a five-point scale. Rapport with taxpayers was calculated as the mean rating of how friendly and cooperative the taxpayer was, and how well they got along interpersonally. The mean rating was 3.97 (SD = .80), and the scale had a Cronbach's alpha of .84.

CONTROL VARIABLES

Other factors that might be expected to shape audit outcomes include the quality of taxpayers' records and whether the audit involved such basic compliance issues as math errors, unreported income, and lack of documentation for deductions. The measure of the quality of taxpayer records was based on an average of auditor ratings of the degree to which taxpayers' records were complete and organized (Cronbach's alpha = .91). This measure was trichotomized into equal-size groups of high, medium, and low record quality.

Auditors were also asked to describe the issues covered in the audit, using 14 categories provided by the researchers. These 14 categories fell into three generic groups: the legal avoidance issues used in constructing the complex audit issue measure described above; questions about the taxpayers' eligibility to claim expenses and deductions; and basic compliance issues involving unreported income, undocumented deductions; or math errors. The basic compliance issues are legally quite straightforward, whereas both the legally complex and eligibility issues require some degree of interpretation by the auditor.

Measures of the degree to which audit issues involved basic compliance issues and eligibility issues were constructed using the same procedures as for the measure of complex legal issues. The measure of eligibility issues was eventually dropped from the analysis because it reduced degrees of freedom without yielding any significant findings. We also explored including individual measures for each of the basic compliance issues; doing so yields some marginally significant effects while restricting the degrees of freedom. The combined measure seemed to work best as a control for issue effects that might otherwise confound the status analysis. The resulting measure has a distribution of 35% of cases having no compliance issues (i.e., interpretive issues only), 30% where less than half the issues involved compliance issues, and 35% where most of the issues were basic compliance issues.

Results

WHICH "HAVES" COME OUT AHEAD IN TAX AUDITS?

We begin the data analysis by describing who comes out ahead in tax audits and whether legal mobilization accounts for their success. Table 5.1 investigates this issue using regression analyses that begin by entering the "have" variables in the first equation and then by entering the legal mobilization and control variables in a second equation. Equations are estimated using ordered probit analyses for auditor decisions against the taxpayer, due to the ordinal character of this variable. Because the distribution of amount assessed is truncated, tobit regression is used to estimate equations for the amount owed.

The results for the first equation show significant effects of occupational prestige on both audit outcome measures, with taxpayers of high prestige receiving better outcomes. Bivariate analyses indicate that high-prestige taxpayers are especially less likely than others to have auditors make decisions against them on specific tax issues. Auditors ruled against the taxpayer on every issue in only one-fifth (22%) of cases involving high-prestige taxpayers, compared with almost two-thirds of cases involving lower- (65%) and middle-prestige taxpayers (62%). The median amount of money assessed against high-prestige taxpayers was $0 (only 42% had any additional tax assessments), compared with $287 for medium- and $515 for lower-prestige taxpayers.

The results also indicate that family businesses are assessed less money than other types of taxpayers, but education and organizational size have no effect on either dependent variable. At the bivariate level, less than half (45%) of family businesses paid more taxes (median = 0), compared with 68% of the remaining taxpayers (median = $316).

The results for prestige and family business remain significant even after the legal indicators and control variables are entered into the analysis. Orga-

TABLE 5.1

Effect of Cultural Capital and Legal Mobilization on Auditor Decisions, Unstandardized Coefficients (Standard Errors)

	Decides against Taxpayer[a]				Log Amount of Tax Assessed[b]			
	Equation (1)		Equation (2)		Equation (1)		Equation (2)	
	Coefficient	SE	Coefficient	SE	Coefficient	SE	Coefficient	SE
Cultural capital indicators								
Occupational prestige	-.72***	(.20)	-.86***	(.22)	-2.02*	(.79)	-2.62***	(.71)
Education	.20	(.13)	.25+	(.14)	-.44	(.53)	.29	(.47)
Family business	-.46	(.32)	-.42	(.33)	-3.50**	(1.33)	-3.01*	(1.18)
Organizational size								
1–9 employees	.43	(.28)	.14	(.31)	1.23	(1.18)	.83	(1.03)
10 or more employees	.13	(.45)	.17	(.54)	.93	(2.06)	-.82	(2.16)
Legal mobilization								
Repeat playership	—	—	.06	(.18)	—	—	.20	(.65)
Partnership or S corporation	—	—	.22	(.28)	—	—	1.63+	(.96)
Complex audit issues	—	—	.22	(.23)	—	—	1.48+	(.82)
Use of representation	—	—	-.37	(.28)	—	—	1.68	(1.03)
Controls								
Quality of documentation	—	—	-.31*	(.13)	—	—	-1.61***	(.44)
Basic compliance issues	—	—	.65***	(.20)	—	—	2.06**	(.67)
Intercept(s)								
First	1.67**		1.35*		7.22***		5.86*	
Second	.91***		.44		n.a.		n.a.	
N of cases	92				111			

[a] Ordered probit regressions. The chi-square statistics for the entire equation is 18.41 ($p < .01$) for equation (1) and 37.41 ($p < .001$) for equation (2).

[b] Tobit regression analysis.

+ $p < .10$; * $p < .05$; ** $p < .01$; *** $p < .001$.

nizational size has no effect on audit outcomes, nor do any of the legal mobilization variables affect outcomes in the predicted direction. Two legal mobilization variables—complex audit issues and use of legal representation—reach a borderline significance for amounts owed, but in a direction *opposite* to the predictions of the legal mobilization hypothesis. Both complex audit issues and use of representation tend to be associated with higher, rather than lower, amounts of taxes being assessed.

Not surprisingly, audits involving basic compliance issues of math errors, undocumented deductions, and unreported income are more likely to yield additional assessments than other audits. Likewise, the higher the quality of taxpayer documentation, the less likely auditors are to decide against the taxpayer and to assess new tax dollars.

It could be argued that the findings for the amount of taxes assessed might be distorted by the lack of a control variable for income, because the amount of taxes owed is influenced by the taxpayer's marginal tax rate, which in turn is determined by income. That is, family businesses might have less income and therefore lower tax rates than other taxpayers and thus end up paying less tax. This argument cannot explain the results for prestige, because studies routinely find that occupational prestige is positively correlated with higher income. In fact, this argument suggests that the prestige effect would become even stronger once income were controlled.

We do not have either an income or tax rate variable to test empirically this alternative explanation for the family business effect. Tax rate differences, however, should affect only the amount owed, not the basic question of whether *any* tax was assessed. Logistic regression analysis of a dichotomized version of the amount assessed (0 = none, 1 = some) yielded the same results as the tobit analysis, arguing against an interpretation of an income confound.

WHY DO "HAVES" WITH PRESTIGE COME OUT AHEAD?

Legal Mobilization

Equation (2) in Table 5.1 demonstrates that legal mobilization does not account for the greater success of high-prestige taxpayers in obtaining favorable audit outcomes. The results show no significant effects in the predicted direction for any of the legal mobilization variables on either audit outcome measure.

Table 5.2, which examines which "haves" are more likely to mobilize, further bolsters this finding in that high-prestige taxpayers are no more likely to mobilize legally than lower-prestige individuals. In fact, the only group of "haves" in this sample who are consistently high in legal mobilization are taxpayers who own businesses that employ 10 or more workers. They are sig-

TABLE 5.2

Which "Haves" Mobilize Equally? Unstandardized Probit Coefficients (Standard Errors)

| | Indicator of Legal Mobilization | | | | | | |
| | Repeat Audit Players | | Partnership or S Corporation | | Complex Tax Issues | | Use of Representation | |
	Coefficient	SE	Coefficient	SE	Coefficient	SE	Coefficient	SE
Social capital								
Occupational prestige	-.09	(.16)	-.04	(.49)	-.28	(.17)	.07	(.18)
Education	.16	(.11)	.08	(.13)	.05	(.12)	-.15	(.12)
Family business	.13	(.26)	-.20	(.31)	-.56*	(.29)	.29	(.28)
Organizational size								
1–9 employees	.08	(.24)	.52	(.29)	.28	(.25)	.06	(.26)
10 or more employees	1.16**	(.40)	1.88***	(.43)	1.57***	(.42)	1.05*	(.49)
Intercept(s)								
First	-.38		-1.19**		-1.09**		.00	
Second	-1.28**		-2.10***		-1.93**		n.a.	
Summary statistics								
-2 log-likelihood chi-square	10.93*		21.69***		24.75***		8.58	
Gamma	.28		.48		.46		.27	
N of cases					117			

* $p < .05$; ** $p < .01$; *** $p < .001$.

nificantly more likely than others to be repeat players, to file partnership and S-corporation returns, to have audits involving complex legal issues, and to have a tax practitioner represent them during the audit. This finding is consistent with studies of courts, which argue that organizations are more capable of mobilizing legally than individuals. The puzzle is why legal mobilization does not translate into better outcomes in frontline tax enforcement.

Different Audit Situations and Types of Issues

Another potential explanation for the findings is that family businesses and people in occupations of varying prestige are in fundamentally different tax situations that lead to different types of issues arising in their audits. For example, high-prestige taxpayers may face more questions about their eligibility for deductions, but low-prestige taxpayers may experience math and clerical errors. The inclusion of the control variable of basic compliance issues (and eligibility issues in other analyses), however, rules out this interpretation. Even though compliance issues (but not eligibility issues) increase tax assessments, the inclusion of controls for the types of issues audited does not affect the basic findings for occupational prestige and family businesses.

Cultural Capital and Normative Expectancies

The finding that prestige and family business ownership, but not organizational size or legal mobilization, predict audit outcomes suggests that cultural capital plays a pivotal role in shaping what goes on during an audit. A stronger case could be made for the cultural capital explanation, however, if there were evidence that taxpayers' expectations of influence varied by their social status (the self-fulfilling prophecy effect) or that auditors were more willing to accept oral testimony without substantiating records from higher-status taxpayers than from lower-status taxpayers (the burden of proof effect).

Table 5.3 examines the evidence for and against the self-fulfilling prophecy effect. To begin, the effects of social status on taxpayer expectations before the audit of their ability to influence auditor decisions were examined using ordered probit analysis. Of the cultural capital indicators, only occupational prestige significantly affects taxpayer expectations, with an unstandarized coefficient of .39 ($p < .01$). The coefficient for family businesses is not only nonsignificant, but negative in sign, indicating that self-fulfilling prophecies of greater self-confidence do not play a role in explaining the family business effect.

When analyzed at the bivariate level, the pessimism of low-prestige taxpayers is a quite striking feature of our data. More than half (52%) expressed more negative than positive expectations before the audit, compared with 35% of middle-prestige and 21% of high-prestige taxpayers. A feeling of

TABLE 5.3

Tests of Self-Fulfilling Prophesy Effects, Unstandardized Coefficients (Standard Errors)

| | Taxpayer Expects to Influence Auditor[a] | | Audit Outcomes | | | |
| | | | Decides against Taxpayer[a] | | Log of Amount Owed[b] | |
	Coefficient	SE	Coefficient	SE	Coefficient	SE
Indicators of cultural capital						
Occupational prestige	.39**	(.15)	-.86***	(.23)	-2.23**	(.71)
Education	.05	(.10)	.26+	(.15)	.38	(.47)
Family business	-.27	(.24)	-.42	(.34)	-3.27**	(1.17)
Organizational size						
1-9 employees	.14	(.22)	.14	(.31)	.75	(1.00)
10 or more employees	.26	(.42)	.17	(.54)	-.54	(2.12)
Legal mobilization						
Repeat player	-.18	(.13)	.06	(.19)	-.21	(.64)
Partnership or S corporation	.06	(.19)	.22	(.28)	1.68+	(.94)
Complex audit issues	-.34*	(.16)	.22	(.23)	1.15	(.81)
Use of representation	-.01	(.18)	-.37	(.28)	1.81+	(1.00)
Controls						
Quality of documentation	.13	(.21)	-.31*	(.13)	-1.63***	(.41)
Basic compliance issues	.37	(.22)	.65***	(.20)	1.95**	(.45)
Mediating variable						
Expectations of influence	—		(.01)	(.10)	-.70*	(.22)
Intercept(s)						
First	.92*		1.37+		8.32**	
Second	.49		.46		n.a.	
Third	.03		n.a.		n.a.	
Fourth	-.59		n.a.		n.a.	
Fifth	-1.77***		n.a.		n.a.	
N of cases	117		92		111	

[a] Ordered probit regression. For taxpayer expectations, the chi-square statistics for the equation as a whole is 16.03 (p = n.s.) and for auditor decisions against the taxpayer the chi-square is 34.41 ($p < .01$).

[b] Tobit regression.

$^+p < .10$; $^*p < .05$; $^{**}p < .01$; $^{***}p < .001$.

powerlessness in the face of arbitrary state authority underlies many of these negative feelings: 34% of low-prestige taxpayers report beliefs that they could not influence the auditor or the audit outcome, compared with only 8% to 10% of middle- and high-prestige taxpayers. Middle- and high-prestige taxpayers were more likely to believe auditor decisions would be impartial ones driven by facts and the law (27% to 31% for middle- and high-prestige taxpayers versus 10% for low-prestige taxpayers).

The finding that high-prestige taxpayers have greater expectations of influence entering the audit provides support for one prong of the self-fulfilling prophecy explanation for prestige effects on audit outcomes. The case would be stronger, though, if expectations in turn influenced the outcome of the audit and reduced the size of the effect of prestige on outcomes. The last two columns of Table 5.3 examine this hypothesis and show mixed support. To begin, expectations of influence have no discernible effect on auditor decisions on specific tax issues, ruling out a self-fulfilling prophecy effect for this particular outcome measure. Some support, however, is found for the amount of taxes assessed. The unstandardized coefficient for taxpayer expectations on the amount owed is -.70 ($p < .05$). A comparison of this equation with equation (2) in Table 5.1 also shows a drop in the size of the prestige coefficient, from -2.62 ($p < .001$) when expectations are not included in the analysis to -2.23 ($p < .01$) when taxpayer expectations are included in the analysis. This result indicates that self-fulfilling prophecies mediate to some degree the relationship between prestige and amounts of taxes assessed. They do not completely account for the prestige effect, however, because the coefficient for prestige remains significant.

A similar analysis was conducted to test the burden of proof explanation, using auditor acceptance of oral testimony as the dependent variable. The results suggest some basis in reality for the pessimism of low-prestige taxpayers about their inability to influence auditors in that prestige has a significant negative effect on auditor acceptance of oral testimony ($B = -.58, p < .01$). These results indicate that taxpayers of a low occupational prestige face a higher burden of proof than either middle- or high-prestige taxpayers. At the bivariate level, when a low-prestige taxpayer is involved, auditors accepted oral testimony in 22% of cases, compared with 43% of cases involving middle-prestige taxpayers and 59% involving high-prestige taxpayers.

Evidence for the burden of proof hypothesis, however, is weaker than that for the self-fulfilling prophecy effect. Acceptance of oral testimony has only a borderline effect on auditor decisions for or against the taxpayer on specific issues ($B = -.33, p < .06$) and an even weaker effect on the amount of money owed ($B = -.92, p < .14$).

IN WHAT SITUATIONS DOES "PRESTIGE" MAKE A DIFFERENCE?

Analyses of the overall sample of audit cases provide modest support for self-fulfilling prophecies of expected influence but weaker support for the overall argument of the burden of proof hypothesis in explaining prestige effects on audit outcomes. Cultural capital effects, however, may be contingent in nature, more likely to be triggered in some audit situations than others. Research on small-group processes and qualitative interviews with practitioners suggest that the situational features of task ambiguity and the involvement of a representative may condition the likelihood that normative status expectancies will come into play.

Task Ambiguity and the Burden of Proof

A central feature of the burden of proof hypothesis is that, *absent other evidence*, individuals use status cues to make inferences about the competence and credibility of other people. The laboratory literature reports that people tend to rely less on status to infer credibility when there is more pertinent task-relevant information at hand (Freese & Cohen 1973; Webster & Driskill 1978). If the burden of proof hypothesis is true, then prestige should have stronger effects on auditors' deference in situations that require the auditor to make a credibility judgment in the face of ambiguous information. Moreover, acceptance of oral testimony in turn should in ambiguous situations mediate prestige effects on audit outcomes.

The two control variables provide information useful to constructing a measure of task ambiguity. To begin, the basic compliance issues are legally straightforward: taxpayers are supposed to report all their income, keep adequate records to support claims for documentation, and correctly calculate the amount owed. The remaining two types of issues, eligibility for deductions and the application of complex tax laws, involve some degree of interpretation. Regarding eligibility issues, the auditor must answer questions such as, How much was a car used for business and how much for personal use? Was that trip to Hawaii a business trip or a vacation? Does that loss on a Schedule C reflect a poor year for business or an attempt to deduct the costs of a hobby? These questions all involve instances where the auditor must determine whether the "tax-deductible" label the taxpayer has applied to expenses is legitimate. No matter how complete the documentation, the auditor must still make judgments calls about past situations for which there is no definitive evidence about what really occurred or what the taxpayer's intentions were.

Another element of task ambiguity concerns the quality of taxpayer records. According to qualitative interviews with auditors, the quality of records often serves as an important heuristic for deciding how to approach the audit. Taxpayers who have messy records automatically start off with a low degree of credibility. As several auditors pointed out, how can taxpayers accurately fill out tax returns without organizing their records? Conversely, taxpayers with highly organized records are granted more credibility; the visible signs of diligence and effort convey the impression of a desire on the part of the taxpayer to comply fully with the law. In such cases, there is less incentive for the auditor to spend time going through the records because the auditor knows the numbers are all going to add up.

More difficult are situations where the taxpayer's records are of an intermediate quality. The taxpayer has taken some time and effort to maintain records, but there are gaps and lapses. The auditor is faced with a question: Do the gaps mainly reflect instances where the taxpayer made a reasonable "guesstimate" of legitimate expenses for which they forgot to get receipts, or are they fake or mislabeled expenses invented to lower tax liabilities? In such instances, the burden of proof hypothesis suggests that the auditor would use social status cues to fill in the gaps of knowledge. The auditor might reason that a physician's records are lacking because "doctors are busy people" while thinking that a truck driver's mixed quality of records reflects low compliance norms.[6]

The burden of proof hypothesis predicts that occupational prestige will shape auditors' acceptance of oral testimony primarily in situations requiring interpretation. That is, the social status of the taxpayer will be used as a heuristic for judging the credibility of the taxpayer's position. If correct, then one would expect a significant and positive interaction between prestige and task ambiguity on auditor acceptance of oral testimony.

To test this hypothesis, we defined cases as evidencing task ambiguity if they either involved a mixed quality of records or involved only issues requiring interpretation. By this definition, 54% of audit cases had at least some task ambiguity. Table 5.4 reports results from two ordered probit analyses testing the interaction hypothesis. In the first equation, without the interaction effect, occupational prestige is the only variable significantly predicting auditor acceptance of oral testimony. The interaction term in equation (2), as expected, is positive and significant.

Figure 5.1 provides a visual picture of the observed interaction effect, using raw means of the six combinations of prestige and task ambiguity. The picture shows a strong linear effect of prestige on auditor acceptance of oral testimony under conditions of high task ambiguity, but not under conditions of low ambiguity. Using the results of the multivariate interaction analysis to calculate the slopes of the lines yields an unstandardized prestige coefficient of 1.08 under conditions of high task ambiguity compared with -.26 under conditions of low ambiguity.

Moreover, acceptance of oral testimony mediates the effects of prestige on auditor decisions on individual issues for the subsample of audits involving

TABLE 5.4

Prestige and the Burden of Proof in Tax Audits for Ambiguous Tax Issues, Unstandardized Coefficients from Ordered Probit Analyses (Standard Errors)

	Auditor Accepts Oral Testimony			
	Equation (1)		Equation (2)	
	Coefficient	SE	Coefficient	SE
Social Capital				
Occupational prestige	.58**	(.21)	-.26	(.32)
Education	-.16	(.14)	-.10	(.15)
Family business	-.32	(.34)	-.36	(.35)
Organizational size				
1-9 employees	.16	(.29)	.30	(.31)
10 or more employees	-.42	(.58)	-.23	(.62)
Legal mobilization				
Repeat player	.16	(.19)	.06	(.20)
Partnership or S corporation	-.26	(.29)	-.29	(.31)
Complex audit issues	.16	(.20)	.04	(.21)
Representation	-.13	(.29)	-.05	(.30)
Ambiguity effects				
Main effect of ambiguity	.18	(.27)	-2.68**	(.88)
Prestige ambiguity interaction	—		1.34***	(.40)
Intercepts				
First	-1.29*		.42	
Second	-2.06***		-.43	
Summary statistics				
-2 log-likelihood chi-square	11.41		23.44**	
Gamma	.35		.49	
N of cases	87		87	

$^+p < .10;$ $^*p < .05;$ $^{**}p < .01;$ $^{***}p < .001.$

high task ambiguity. For this group, when oral testimony is not in the equation, the unstandardized coefficient for prestige is -.67 ($p < .01$). Once oral testimony is included in the equation, the coefficient for prestige drops to -.34 and becomes nonsignificant ($p = .26$).

These results indicate considerable support for the burden of proof hypothesis, but only under conditions of task ambiguity. It is worth noting, though, that more than half of the audits in the sample evidenced task am-

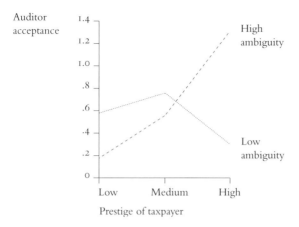

FIGURE 5.1 Accepts oral testimony, by prestige and task ambiguity.

biguity, indicating that the advantages of "haves" in ambiguous conditions is not an isolated phenomenon.

Representation and Audit Outcomes

Prior research also suggests potential interactions between prestige and use of representation. In a qualitative study of Chicago tax practitioners, Kinsey (1987) found that the involvement of a tax practitioner changes interpersonal nature of interaction between taxpayers and auditors. Most practitioners prefer that taxpayers not attend meetings with the auditor. If the taxpayer does attend, practitioners instruct them to sit still and not volunteer any information or express any feelings. The practitioner seeks a situation in which communication occurs mainly between the practitioner and auditor, with the client playing a passive role.

This finding suggests that the involvement of a tax practitioner will dampen the effects of normative status-based expectancies that confer advantages to high-status taxpayers. Figures 5.2 and 5.3 take an initial look at this possibility, using raw scores to map out the mean outcomes for the six possible combinations of taxpayer prestige and use of representation. Both figures show relatively flat lines across the three levels of prestige in the outcomes of taxpayers who employed a tax practitioner to represent them during the audit. In contrast, a downward slope is observed for both types of audit outcomes among taxpayers who represent themselves. Figure 5.2 shows that auditors are especially likely to decide tax issues against lower-prestige taxpayers who represent themselves. Figure 5.3 shows that group with the lowest additional tax liabilities are high-prestige taxpayers who represent themselves.

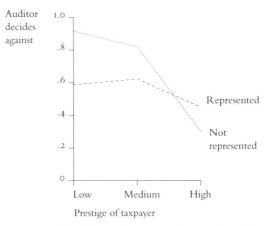

FIGURE 5.2   Decides against taxpayer, by prestige and representation.

Are these results significant? This issue was tested by entering a term for the interaction between prestige and representation to the basic model described in equation (2). The interaction term reached significance for both auditor decisions on specific tax issues ($B = 1.62$, $p < .001$) and the log amount of additional taxes assesssed ($B = 2.77$, $p < .05$). Using the results of the multivariate analyses, predicted means were calculated and plotted for each of the six combinations of prestige and representation. The resulting plots are quite similar to the plots of the raw scores depicted in Figures 5.2 and 5.3.

DOES COMPLIANCE EXPLAIN THE OBSERVED CULTURAL CAPITAL ADVANTAGE?

The analysis so far supports the hypothesis that normative status-based expectancies create an advantage for high-prestige taxpayers that leads to more favorable outcomes than those for other taxpayers. When taxpayers represent themselves, higher-prestige taxpayers are more likely to influence auditors' decision-making and to experience lower standards of proof when making influence attempts than taxpayers in less prestigious occupations. An alternative explanation, though, is that high-status taxpayers who represent themselves are simply more compliant with the law in the first place. Because they know that their tax returns are accurate, they have positive expectations about the audit and thus do not feel any need to hire a representative. In this explanation, it is the compliance with the law, not the status of the individual, that explains both the greater self-confidence and better outcomes of high-prestige taxpayers who represent themselves.

It is not possible to test this alternative interpretation directly. What pieces

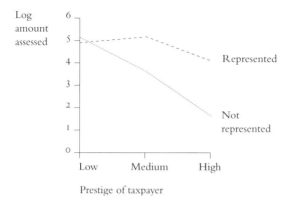

FIGURE 5.3 Log amount assessed, by prestige and representation.

of evidence that do exist, however, fail to support the compliance hypothesis. To begin, high-prestige taxpayers, including those who represent themselves, are not noticeably more compliance-oriented than lower-prestige individuals. Two questions in the survey tapped into attitudes toward compliance. No prestige differences were observed in responses to the statement, "People should comply with tax laws even when they think the laws are wrong." Occupational prestige did affect responses to the other question, but in a direction *opposite* to the compliance hypothesis. Low-prestige taxpayers showed a stronger compliance orientation: 86% disagreed that "A person should comply only with those tax laws that seem reasonable," compared with 75% of middle-prestige taxpayers and 59% of the high-prestige taxpayers (chi square = 6.45, df = 2, p < .05). This pattern is consistent with other research, which finds greater willingness to question authority among higher-status persons (Kohn 1977).

Moreover, one would expect that highly compliant taxpayers would keep excellent documentation. Yet there are no significant differences, either main effects or interaction effects, on auditor ratings of the equality of taxpayer documentation by occupational prestige or use of representation. Visual inspection of a plot of the means shows that what trends exist run in a direction opposite to the compliance hypothesis. That is, auditors give the highest ratings on document quality to low-prestige taxpayers who represent themselves (mean = 2.36, SD = .74), whereas high-prestige taxpayers who represent themselves are given the second-lowest rating (mean = 1.89, SD = .76) among the six groups.

Insufficient documentation is also more likely to be an audit issue among high-prestige taxpayers who represent themselves than among other taxpayers. Over three-fourths (76%) of this group's audits involved documentation of deductions, compared with 29% to 58% for all other types of taxpayers. This group is also the most likely to have oral testimony accepted (77% of cases versus 16% to 50% for the other groups). Although these apparent interaction effects do not reach significance in multivariate analyses, the trends are all in directions that contradict the compliance hypothesis. If high-prestige taxpayers who represent themselves are more compliant than other taxpayers, then they would be going into the audit with impeccable documentation and would not need to have their word taken for it that their deductions and expenses are legitimate.

At the same time, the most convincing evidence for testing the compliance hypothesis is to examine the influence of prestige and representation on an independent, objective measure of compliance. Some researchers, including a National Academy of Science panel on tax compliance research, have argued that the decisions of tax enforcers themselves constitute the most objective measure available (Roth et al. 1989; reviewed by Long & Swingen 1991). We think it is premature, though, to conclude that high-prestige taxpayers who represent themselves are more compliant than others simply because they receive favorable audit outcomes without some prior evidence regarding the reliability and validity of auditor decisions. Only one study, in the Netherlands, has examined this issue, and it found generally low levels of both reliability and validity (kappas in the .30 range). More specifically, an expert team disagreed with 48% of the decisions of frontline auditors, with most of the disagreements (39% of all cases) being in the direction of believing the auditor had been too lenient (Elffers et al. 1989). Our results also point to considerable leniency in the behavior of auditors. Moreover, the findings indicate that leniency is structured by normative status-based processes of social deference and influence that have distributional implications.

LEGAL COMPLEXITY AND ADVERSARIALISM IN TAX AUDITS

The results so far suggest that auditors are especially lenient toward high-prestige taxpayers who represent themselves. Why don't they show the same leniency toward high-prestige taxpayers with representation? As noted earlier, one possible explanation is that tax practitioners disrupt the operation of normative status-based expectancies that lead lower-ranking government officials to show deference toward the high-status individuals with whom they interact. Auditors may find it hard *not* to accept oral testimony in face-to-face encounters with high-prestige taxpayers if refusing to do so implies that they think a "respectable" person is lying. The tendency of practitioners to interpose themselves between the taxpayer and the auditor, however, may make it socially less awkward to deny claims made without proof.

Another possibility is greater adversarialism in audits involving high-prestige taxpayers with representation during the audit. The audits of this group of taxpayers are especially distinctive in terms of the legal complexity of audit issues and the potential for legal conflict. More than three-fourths (86%) of such cases involve at least one complex issue, compared with 14% to 41% of cases in the other five combinations of prestige and representation in the sample. This interaction between high prestige and representation on the complexity of audit issues is statistically significant ($B = 1.01, p < .03$).[7]

If audits involving high-prestige taxpayers who are represented are more likely to involve legal conflict over the meaning and application of complex tax laws, then one might also expect greater interpersonal tension in these audits due to normal social psychological processes of conflict polarization. Such appears to be the case: auditors give the lowest rating of interpersonal rapport (mean = 3.52, $SD = .60$) to this category of taxpayers. In contrast, their highest rating of interpersonal rapport goes to high-prestige taxpayers who represent themselves (mean = 4.14, $SD = .90$). In a multivariate analysis, the interaction between prestige and representation reaches statistical significance ($B = -.16, p < .04$, one-tailed test). These results suggest that any interpersonal status advantages of represented high-prestige taxpayers are offset by greater adversarialism arising from their involvement in the gray areas of tax law.

Discussion And Conclusion

Elite tax practitioners often characterize tax audits as arenas of reverse class conflict in which government bureaucrats—"have nots" with power—exact their revenge on the "haves" of society (Kinsey forthcoming). Do the "haves" come out ahead, or are they victims of overzealous tax enforcers? Our data indicate that some of them do come out ahead in tax audits and shed light on the processes by which that occurs.

Although prior research on status differences in legal settings has focused on the greater ability of people with resources to mobilize legally, we found little evidence of any positive effect of legal mobilization on the outcomes of frontline tax audits. Indeed, the biggest "winners" of tax audits were high-status taxpayers who showed few signs of legal mobilization. Neither use of representation nor involvement in the gray areas of tax law diminished the chances of owing more money.

The negative findings regarding legal mobilization, however, must be put in context: taxpayers active in legal tax avoidance do come out ahead if their tax returns are never selected for an audit in the first place. In fact, the odds are that any given tax return will not be audited; in 1985, for example, the percent of returns reporting more than a $50,000 income audited by the IRS was 3.5%. Even if audited and assessed new taxes, cases involving gray issues have a greater chance of being reversed on appeal due to the necessity of considering the costs of litigation and the likelihood of winning in court at that stage of the enforcement process (Long & Swingen 1991).

Our findings point instead to cultural capital, not legal mobilization, as key predictors of taxpayer success in obtaining favorable audit outcomes. The results for occupational prestige point to normative status-based expectancies as a key factor shaping the outcomes of frontline tax audits. Cultural capital for high-prestige taxpayers takes the form of greater poise and, depending on the circumstances, greater credibility by virtue of their position in social hierarchies. Our data analysis, however, provides little leverage for understanding the specific mechanisms underlying the results for "mom and pop" businesses. Their greater success in obtaining lower tax assessments cannot be attributed to a higher position in normative hierarchies of power and control, but instead may be based on more general sentiments about family businesses.

Regarding the effects for occupational prestige, evidence was found for both the self-fulfilling prophecy and burden of proof variants of interpersonal status processes, albeit in different circumstances and for different audit outcome variables. In general, high-prestige individuals enter the audit with the twin advantages of being used to exercising influence over others and being believed when they make claims without verification.

A tax audit, though, is an anomalous situation for a high-prestige person. It is one of the few settings in modern society where high-prestige persons have to account, sometimes in great detail, for past decisions to a person who typically has a lower occupational prestige than themselves. It is one in which lower-status person can say, "You have to prove it" and declare, "You got it wrong." The unusual status configuration probably accounts for the diminished sense of control expressed by higher-status taxpayers after the audit was over. Despite their greater success in obtaining favorable audit outcomes, high-prestige taxpayers who represented themselves were no more likely than the other taxpayer groups to report that they had actually influenced the auditor's decision-making. They left the audit feeling more powerless than before (see Kinsey forthcoming).

Research on regulatory law enforcement deals with similar status configurations, with corporate officials and business owners being subject to the authority of government inspectors. Much of the regulatory research advocates flexible approaches to enforcement that focus more on educating and securing cooperation than a top-down, legalistic "going by the book" style of enforcement (Bardach & Kagan 1982; Braithwaite 1985; Smith & Kinsey 1985). We suspect that it is precisely because of the status configuration of the regulatory enforcement situation that top-down enforcement does not work well in regulatory settings. Strict adherence to the "letter of the law" by government officials would only exacerbate what is already a tension-producing violation of "normal" status arrangements.

The risk of more flexible forms of law enforcement, though, is the potential for distributional inequities to develop. The greater self-confidence of higher-prestige individuals gives them an important advantage, and their credibility is rarely questioned when they represent themselves or in cases involving some degree of task ambiguity. Although we seriously doubt that tax auditors are consciously biased in favor of high-prestige people, congruent with other research on interpersonal status processes conducted in other settings, they automatically tend to grant more deference to people with high prestige than to others.

The introduction of a tax practitioner into the audit changes things. In contradiction to arguments that practitioners increase inequities in the tax system, our results indicate that they serve to level the playing field. In contrast to the strong prestige effects found among taxpayers who represented themselves, taxpayer prestige had no effect on auditor assertions of change of amounts owed for the clients of tax practitioners.

Why does the involvement of a tax practitioner have a leveling effect? First, practitioners often try to minimize interaction between taxpayers and auditors, thus disrupting normal social processes of influence and deference. Second, and perhaps more important, tax practitioners themselves are repeat players in the tax system. As Galanter (1974) argued, considering and setting precedents are a major concern of repeat players in the legal system. Auditor acceptance of aggressive legal positions might encourage practitioners to persuade their other clients to lower taxes by taking the same position. Similarly, accepting oral testimony on one case could create expectations of future leniency for other clients of the same practitioner. In addition, practitioners might not put as much effort into their procompliance function of training clients to keep good records if they believe that tax auditors will readily waive documentation requirements. For the auditor, giving an unrepresented taxpayer a break here and there does not have the same potential of undermining the overall enforcement of tax laws as being lenient with the clients of practitioners. Auditor motivation to be lenient is further diminished when taxpayers and their representatives stake out aggressive positions in the gray areas of tax law.

The findings of prestige differences among self-represented taxpayers point to a dilemma of tax law enforcement. According to the regulatory literature, shifting to a more legalistic mode of enforcement may antagonize high-prestige taxpayers. Tax auditors may be accepting oral testimony as part of an informal policy of trying to educate the high-prestige taxpayer and secure future cooperation, rather than adopting a punitive approach that would exacerbate status tensions and alienate the taxpayer. If so, then the findings reported here reveal a fundamental conflict between values of organizational effectiveness and the achievement of equity in tax law enforcement.

Notes

Previously published in *Law & Society Review* 33 (4) 993–1023 (1999); reprinted by permission. This research was funded by the American Bar Foundation and the Ford Fund for Dispute Resolution. We are grateful to Bob Mason, Kent Smith, and the Oregon Department of Revenue for making this study possible and especially thank Bryant Garth for his encouragement and support.

Karyl A. Kinsey is a social psychologist whose current research interests include performance measurement in government settings and cognitive biases in citizens' perception of government. Formerly a senior research fellow at the American Bar Foundation, she is currently a senior research analyst with the city of Austin, Texas.

Loretta J. Stalans is Associate Professor of Criminal Justice at Loyola University Chicago. Her research interests are in the area of public opinion about justice and domestic violence. She has coauthored with Julian V. Roberts *Public Opinion, Crime, and Criminal Justice* (Westview Press, 1997).

1. In 1985, for example, tax returns with total positive income greater than $50,000 were 2.7 times more likely to be audited by the Internal Revenue Service (IRS) than the average return (IRS 1985:Table 7). Similarly, 62% of the audited taxpayers in our sample had filed Schedule C for sole proprietors, whereas nationally, only 13% of taxpayers file a Schedule C (IRS 1994).

2. Tax audit representation is the province of a wide array of practitioners with varying levels of credentials. Most are not lawyers yet nonetheless serve as legal representatives in that they have power of attorney to make binding agreements. Certified public accountants (CPAs) and lawyers are automatically certified to practice before the IRS and other tax agencies, as are enrolled agents (practitioners who are either former IRS employees or who have passed a certifying exam administered by the IRS). The state of Oregon, where our study took place, is also one of the few states in the nation to license tax practitioners. Licensed tax consultants are persons who have completed 2 years of formal training and have passed a state exam on taxation, whereas licensed tax preparers have completed 80 hours of training and have passed a tax preparation exam.

3. Earlier usages of the term *self-fulfilling prophecy* referred mainly to instances where expectations of one person elicited behavior by another that otherwise would not have been demonstrated (Merton 1957; Rosenthal & Jacobson 1968). We use it more in accordance with later research, which applies the term more generally to include the effects of expectations about oneself as well as others (Jones 1977).

4. Audit selection processes varied across offices and auditors. All offices begin by selecting a computer-generated pool of potential returns by specifying certain parameters. These were not revealed to the researchers, but were probably weighted to oversample higher-income returns and businesses. Some audit managers select and assign returns from the pool to individual auditors based on current enforcement

priorities and goals for developing auditor expertise. Others allow auditors to select their own returns to examine. In general, the auditor would go to the file cabinet containing the pool of returns, pull out some files, and go through them looking for potential audit issues. Some preferred variety in their caseloads and sought out different types of business or financial situations. Others concentrated on auditing returns reflecting issues in which they had already developed expertise. Others liked to do network audits, where audit of one return would provide leads to other returns worth auditing (e.g., business partners, suppliers).

5. Earlier analyses included a dummy variable for taxpayers who are employees only. It produced no significant results and was dropped to conserve degrees of freedom.

6. Even though research audits conducted by the IRS's Taxpayer Compliance Measurement Program show physicians to be a high-noncompliance group, IRS auditors interviewed by the first author in the 1980s frequently explained doctors' noncompliance in terms of how busy they are, not in terms of motivations to lower taxes. Their attributions regarding truck drivers were less benign.

7. The equation testing the interaction effect omits the compliance issues variable due to a methodological artifact resulting from its being constructed from the same pool of issues as the dependent variable. Because each is expressed as a percentage of total issues, they are by definition negatively correlated. Due to the nature of their construction, it does not make sense to analyze one as "causing" the other.

References

Ainsworth, Janet E. (1993) "In a Different Register: The Pragmatics of Powerlessness in Police Interrogation," 103 *Yale Law J.* 259–322.

Bardach, Eugene, & Robert Kagan (1982) *Going by the Book: The Problem of Regulatory Unreasonableness*. Philadelphia: Temple Univ. Press.

Berger, Joseph, Bernard P. Cohen, & Morris Zelditch Jr. (1966) "Status Characteristics and Expectation States," in J. Berger, M. Zelditch Jr., & B. Anderson, eds., *Sociological Theories in Progress*, vol. 1. Boston: Houghton Mifflin.

Berger, Joseph, Bernard P. Cohen, & Morris Zelditch Jr. (1972) "Status Characteristics and Social Interaction," 37 *American Sociological Rev.* 241–55.

Billig, Michael (1976) *Social Psychology and Intergroup Relations*. New York: Academic Press.

Black, Donald J. (1976) *The Behavior of Law*. New York: Academic Press.

Braithwaite, John (1985) *To Punish or Persuade? The Enforcement of Coal Mine Safety Laws*. Albany: State Univ. of New York Press.

DiMaggio, Paul (1990) "Cultural Aspects of Economic Action and Organization," in R. Friedland & A. F. Robertson, eds., *Beyond the Marketplace: Rethinking Economy and Society*. New York: Aldine de Gruyter.

Elffers, Henk, Henry S. J. Robben, & Dick J. Hessing (1989) "Reliability and Validity of Tax Audits: Can We Have Confidence in the Opinion of the Dutch IRS on Noncompliance?" Presented at the Annual Meeting of the Law & Society Association, Madison, WI (8–11 June).

Freese, Lee, & Bernard P. Cohen (1973) "Eliminating Status Generalization," 36 *Sociometry* 177–93.

Galanter, Marc (1974) "Why the 'Haves' Come Out Ahead: Speculations on the Limits of Legal Change," 9 *Law & Society Rev.* 95–160.

Hagan, John, Marjorie Zatz, Bruce Arnold, & Fiona Key (1991) "Cultural Capital, Gender, and the Structural Transformation of Legal Practice," 25 *Law & Society Rev.* 239–62.

Internal Revenue Service (1985) *Internal Revenue Service Annual Report, 1985.* Washington, DC: Internal Revenue Service.

———— (1994) *Statistics of Income, 1991: Individual Income Tax Returns.* Washington, DC: Internal Revenue Service Publication 1304.

Jackson, Betty R., Valerie C. Milliron, & Daniel R. Toy (1988) "Tax Practitioners and the Government," *Tax Notes,* 17 Oct., pp. 333–41.

Jones, Russell A. (1977) *Self-fulfilling Prophecies: Social, Psychological, and Physiological Effects of Expectancies.* Hillsdale, NJ: Lawrence Erlbaum.

Kinsey, Karyl A. (1987) "Advocacy and Perception: The Structure of Tax Practice." Unpublished manuscript, American Bar Foundation.

———— (1992) "Deterrence and Alienation Effects of IRS Enforcement: An Analysis of Survey Data," in J. Slemrod, ed., *Why People Pay Taxes: Tax Compliance and Tax Enforcement.* Ann Arbor: Univ. of Michigan Press.

———— (forthcoming) "Status Matters: Class, Race, and Perceptions of Bias in Bureaucratic Law Enforcement," in B. D. Garth, R. M. Nelson, and V. S. Woest, eds., *Law's Disciplinary Encounters.*

Kinsey, Karyl A., & Harold Grasmick (1993) "Did the Tax Reform Act of 1986 Improve Compliance? Three Studies of Pre- and Post-Reform Compliance Attitudes," 15 *Law & Policy* 293–325.

Klepper, Steven, & Daniel Nagin (1989) "The Role of Tax Practitioners in Tax Compliance," 22 *Policy Sciences* 167–92.

Kohn, Melvin A. (1977) *Class and Conformity: A Study of Values, with a Reassessment.* 2d ed. Chicago: Univ. of Chicago Press.

Krosnick, Jon (1989) "Attitude Importance and Attitude Accessibility," 15 *Personality & Social Psychology Bulletin* 297–308.

Long, Susan B., & Judyth Swingen (1988) "Complexity, Opportunity, and Compliance." Presented at the Annual Meeting of the Law & Society Association, Vail, CO (10 June).

Long, Susan B., & Judyth Swingen (1989) "The Role of Legal Complexity in Shaping Taxpayer Compliance," in P. Koppen & D. J. Hessing, eds., *Lawyers on Psychology and Psychologists on Law.* Amsterdam: Swets & Seitlinger.

Long, Susan B., & Judyth Swingen (1991) "Taxpayer Compliance: Setting New Agendas for Research," 25 *Law & Society Rev.* 637–84.

McBarnet, Doreen (1992a) "It's Not What You Do but the Way That You Do It: Tax Evasion, Tax Avoidance, and the Boundaries of Deviance," in D. Downes, ed., *Unravelling Criminal Justice: Eleven British Studies.* London: Macmillan.

———— (1992b) "The Construction of Compliance and the Challenge for Control:

the Limits of Noncompliance Research," in J. Slemrod, ed., *Why People Pay Taxes: Tax Compliance and Enforcement*. Ann Arbor: Univ. of Michigan Press.

Merton, Robert K. (1957) *Social Theory and Social Structure*. Rev. ed. New York: Free Press.

National Opinion Research Center (1991) *General Social Surveys, 1972–1991: Cumulative Codebook*. Chicago: National Opinion Research Center.

Nock, Steven L., & Peter H. Rossi (1978) "Ascription versus Achievement in the Attribution of Family Social Status," 84 *American J. of Sociology* 565–90.

O'Barr, William, & Jean O'Barr (1995) Linguistic Evidence: Language, Power, and Strategy in the Courtroom. New York: Academic Press.

Orne, Martin T. (1962) "On the Social Psychology of the Psychological Experiment: With Particular Reference to Demand Characteristics and Their Implications," 17 *American Psychologist* 776–83.

Powell, Michael J. (1993) "Professional Innovation: Corporate Lawyers and Private Lawmaking," 18 *Law & Social Inquiry* 423–52.

Rosenthal, Robert (1966) *Experimenter Effects in Behavioral Research*. New York: Appleton-Century-Crofts.

Rosenthal, Robert, & L. Jacobson (1968) *Pygmalion in the Classroom*. New York: Holt, Rinehart and Winston.

Roth, Jeffrey A., John T. Scholz, & Anne D. Witte, eds. (1989) *Taxpayer Compliance*, volume 1: *An Agenda for Research*. Philadelphia: Univ. of Pennsylvania Press.

Slemrod, Joel, & Nikki Sorum (1984) "The Compliance Cost of the U.S. Individual Income Tax System," 37 *National Tax J.* 461–74.

Smith, Kent W. (1995) "The Cultural Grounding of Tax Issues: Insights from Tax Audits," 29 *Law & Society Rev.* 437–74.

Smith, Kent W., & Karyl A. Kinsey (1985) "Cooperation and Control: Strategies and Tactics for Tax Examination," 2 *Tax Administration Rev.* 13–30.

Songer, David R., & Reginald S. Sheehan (1992) "Who Wins on Appeal? Upperdogs and Underdogs in the United States Courts of Appeals," 36 *American J. of Political Science* 235–58.

Strodtbeck, Fred L., R. M. James, & C. Hawkins (1958) "Social Status in Jury Deliberations," in E. E. Maccoby, T. M. Newcomb, & E. L. Hartley, eds., *Readings in Social Psychology*, 3d ed. New York: Holt, Rinehart and Winston.

Sutherland, Edwin H. (1983) *White Collar Crime: The Uncut Version*. New Haven, CT: Yale Univ. Press.

Webster, Murray, Jr., & James E. Driskill Jr. (1978) "Status Generalization: A Review and Some New Data," 43 *American Sociological Rev.* 220–36.

Weisburd, David, Elin Waring, & Stanton Wheeler (1990) "Class, Status, and the Punishment of White-Collar Criminals," 15 *Law & Social Inquiry* 223–43.

Wheeler, Stanton, Bliss Cartwright, Robert A. Kagan, & Lawrence M. Friedman (1987) "Do the 'Haves' Come Out Ahead? Winning and Losing in State Supreme Courts, 1870–1970," 21 *Law & Society Rev.* 403–45.

Yngvesson, Barbara (1993) *Virtuous Citizens, Disruptive Subjects: Order and Complaint in a New England Court*. New York: Routledge.

The Rule of Law and the Litigation Process

The Paradox of Losing by Winning

Introduction

Law and society scholars increasingly question the capacity of law to produce social change. Despite landmark legal decisions and significant legislation, scholars point out that legal change produced little lasting improvement in the economic and social circumstances of the disadvantaged (Rosenberg 1991). The explanations are myriad and varied. Some argue that relying upon rights reinforces and legitimates an ideological legal system that masks inequality (Kairys 1982). They contend that legal rights not only maintain existing inequality, they also exact psychological costs from those who claim them (Bumiller 1988). Moreover, isolated legal victories can be easily dismantled without an organized and sustained effort toward change (Galanter 1974; Handler 1978). Some fault the structure and nature of courts, concluding that the institutional limitations of courts prevent achievement of lasting social change (Rosenberg 1991). They note the misleading nature of the "myth of rights": that judicially affirmed rights are self-implementing instruments of social justice (Scheingold 1974). For most legal violations, the wronged party must mobilize his or her legal entitlement, which requires resources often unavailable to the intended beneficiaries of remedial statutes (Black 1973; Scheingold 1974). Not all scholars share this pessimism, recognizing the symbolic importance of law and the utility of law for organizing political or social movements (Williams 1991; McCann 1994). Some also recognize how law's subtle influence on the social interactions of everyday life creates the potential for social change (Engel & Munger 1996). Scholars increasingly question, however, whether legal change alone can ensure lasting social consequences.

In his article "Why the 'Haves' Come Out Ahead: Speculations on the

Limits of Legal Change," Marc Galanter suggests that the characteristics of parties also limit law's capacity to bring about social change. He argues that repeat players (RPs) shape the development of law by "playing for the rules": settling cases likely to produce precedent adverse to them and litigating cases likely to produce rules that promote their interests (Galanter 1974). By controlling the cases on which courts create the law, repeat players secure legal interpretations that favor their interests.

Galanter's significant insight suggests how the unequal resources and incentives of parties may allow repeat players to control the content of law and create precedent favorable to their interests. The strategic choices of parties between settlement and litigation, however, do not completely capture the complexity of litigation and how it shapes the development of law. Litigation is a process rather than a choice between two alternatives. Courts intervene in this process not only by encouraging settlement but also through intermediate decisions that may not entirely resolve a case. Indeed, although most cases settle, many do so after some sort of court intervention (Kritzer 1986). These points of intervention, like strategic settlement, also present opportunities to shape the developing law. The ways in which the litigation process and party-driven biases together might affect the evolving law have not been explored, however.

It should also be recognized that not all "law" is created in the same manner. Although Galanter's argument may make sense for judicially created common-law rules, his proposition deserves a closer look in the context of social reform legislation designed to address a social problem or protect the interests of the disadvantaged. Arguably, these remedial statutes strengthen the position of one-shot players (OS) relative to repeat players by transferring the rule advantage to the one-shot player. Thus, through one transaction, legislation may overcome the incremental legal advantages accumulated through strategic settlement behavior. Accordingly, at least in the early actions brought under a social reform statute, one might expect one-shot players to hold their own against repeat players.

On the other hand, legislation granting a new substantive right represents both the end of a long political struggle and the beginning of the battle for meaning in the courts (see Chayes 1976). The ultimate scope and power of these statutes depend not only on their language, but also on opinions generated by the common-law process of the judicial determination of rights in individual disputes. This interpretation process presents another opportunity for repeat players to "play for the rules" and influence the ultimate meaning of a statute.

In this article, I explore the litigation process in the context of employment litigation regarding the rights conferred by a federal employment statute, the Family and Medical Leave Act of 1993 (FMLA). I examine the pattern of adjudicated outcomes in published federal court opinions in the 5 years following the statute's enactment. By taking this recently enacted employment right as a subject, I explore the implications of Galanter's argument for the success or failure of legislated social change. In doing so, I elaborate the process of evolving law that Galanter describes and argue that not only the characteristics of parties but also the institutional features of the litigation process itself systematically influence the judicial determination of statutory civil rights.

I also contend that early published opinions regarding a civil rights statute often set the path of interpretation and the eventual scope and meaning of that statute. As judges review, synthesize, and extend each other's rulings through the system of judicial interpretation and precedent, they perpetuate patterns set early in the interpretation of a new law. Consequently the impact of strategic settlement and the litigation process on the shape of the law may matter most early in the life of social reform legislation.

Because each stage of the litigation process may influence the development of law, I look at the entire process of litigation, rather than focusing on outcomes in only one rule-making opportunity, such as appellate opinions. In addition, I examine the early published opinions regarding a single individual right, nationally recognized, at both the trial and appellate level, rather than comparing appellate opinions regarding disputes in diverse jurisdictions under many different laws (cf. Wheeler et al. 1987). By doing so, I examine Galanter's claims where one would most expect the law to protect the one-shot player: cases arising under a remedial statute granting individual rights.

I conclude that the perceived failure of remedial statutes to bring about social change flows in part from how the litigation process systematically obscures the substantive success of a new law. Although people may experience both success in litigation and significant social change as a result of a new civil right, this progress remains largely invisible in the common-law interpretation of that right. Over time, strategic settlement and the litigation process produce judicial interpretations of rights that favor repeat players' interests, limiting the scope and effectiveness of those rights. In the conclusion, I ask whether unequal access to the lawmaking function of courts undermines the legitimacy of the law.

The Litigation Process and the Evolution of Legal Rules

What forces shape the disputes that become the basis for judicial interpretations of the law? Although the life of the law has been experience (Holmes 1923), that experience is of a highly selective variety. Published judicial opinions in litigated cases capture only a small part of what goes on with regard to a new law. Not every violation of a statute results in a written judicial opinion interpreting that law. Courts do not automatically detect violations of law; they must depend for their caseloads on wronged parties mobilizing the law and bringing disputes to a legal forum (Black 1973). Unrecognized violations never reach a legal forum (Felstiner et al. 1981). Even individuals who recognize a harm sometimes decline to sue, instead "lumping it," or exiting from their relationship with the wrongdoer (Hirschman 1970; Galanter 1974; Miller & Sarat 1981; Bumiller 1988). Some disputants mobilize the law beyond the view of courts by negotiating solutions "in the shadow of the law," with an eye toward the likely adjudicated outcome should the dispute ever reach a legal forum (Mnookin & Kornhauser 1979). Others resolve their legally actionable differences through normative systems other than law (Macaulay 1963; Ellickson 1991). These violations and their resolution do not appear in published judicial interpretations of the law.

What is less obvious is that even violations that reach a legal forum do not necessarily result in a judicial interpretation of the law. It is well known, although often overlooked, that only a small fraction of disputes that reach court are adjudicated (Trubek et al. 1983; Maccoby & Mnookin 1990). It is unlikely that adjudicated disputes are representative of all the disputes that arise under a remedial statute. Understanding how disputes are selected to become the basis of the judicial interpretations of the law provides some insight into whether the law reflects inequalities between the parties, as Galanter argues, as well as any biases present in the litigation process itself. The following sections explore two factors that influence the evolution of judicial interpretations of statutory rights: (1) strategic settlement by repeat players and (2) the nature and distribution of rule-making opportunities in the litigation process.

SETTLEMENT AND SELECTION BIAS

Galanter's argument regarding how repeat players influence the evolution of law suggests that decisions to settle sometimes encompass factors beyond the circumstances of individual disputes. Several factors may influence parties' decisions to settle or litigate, including assessments of the likelihood of success, the costs of going forward, and the resources of the parties. Galanter (1974) argues, however, that repeat players have strategic interests beyond the monetary stakes of a particular dispute. Because repeat players expect to experience similar disputes in the future, generally have low stakes in the outcome of any one case, and often have the resources to pursue long-run interests,[1] they

may be willing to trade off tangible gain in any one case for rule gain (or to minimize rule loss). We assume that the institutional facilities for litigation [are] overloaded and settlements [are] prevalent. We would then expect RPs to "settle" cases where they expected unfavorable rule outcomes. Since they expect to litigate again,

RPs can select to adjudicate (or appeal) those cases which they regard as most likely to produce favorable rules. (Ibid., p. 101)

One-shot players who do not expect to litigate again are more likely to make the opposite trade-off—trading the possibility of making "good law" for tangible gain—because they may not value a favorable legal opinion for future disputes.

This process creates a selection bias in the "sample" of disputes presented for adjudication. Cases that settle drop out of the caseload on which judges interpret the law, shaping the circumstances under which legal questions arise. Strategic settlement influences the "selection" of cases presented for adjudication by tending to select cases in which the repeat player is more likely to win. Consequently, Galanter concludes, "we would expect the body of 'precedent' cases—that is, cases capable of influencing the outcome of future cases—to be relatively skewed toward those favorable to RP" (ibid., p. 102).

Some economic models investigating the effect of selective litigation on the efficiency of rules seem to confirm Galanter's analysis. These models indicate that where parties have asymmetrical future stakes, the choice for litigation over settlement will occur only where the odds for success favor the party with the greater future stakes, that is, the repeat player (Landes & Posner 1979:273–74). Not only is litigation more likely in these circumstances, but the litigant with the greater future stakes will invest more resources into the litigation, and consequently is more likely to win (ibid., p. 279; Cooter & Kornhauser 1980; Cooter 1996:1694). Thus, even if the collective benefit of the opposite rule is greater, rules favoring repeat players will survive because one-shot opponents cannot capture the collective benefit to other one-shot players and thus have no incentive to represent their interests by refusing to settle (Cooter 1996:1693).

Galanter's typology of one-shot and repeat player litigants describes four possible pairings of parties: OS versus RP, OS versus OS, RP versus OS, and RP versus RP (Galanter 1975). Many remedial statutes, however, provide individuals with a private right of action against a larger, more powerful opponent (e.g., consumer rights against businesses or employment rights against employers). Consequently, rights created through remedial statutes typically involve one particular type of pairing, that of one-shot individual litigants suing repeat players, often organizations or institutions, for redress. As Wheeler et al. (1987) point out, in these circumstances, some of the advantages repeat player litigants enjoy come with the status of defendant, the typical position of repeat player litigants in legal actions regarding individual rights.[2]

Employment civil rights litigation can be conceptualized as presenting a classic instance of one-shot player versus repeat player litigation.[3] Employers may consider not only the one-time costs of the outcome of a dispute, but also the future costs of an unfavorable rule. Employers have ongoing relationships with many employees; they must consider the possibility of being sued in the future. Even if they are never sued again, they still must continue to comply with employment laws. Adverse legal developments may increase employers' costs of complying with the law. Consequently, employers have a future stake in the interpretation of substantive provisions of employment laws.

Unlike employers, employees are unlikely to consider the future benefits of favorable rules because these benefits are collective, not individual. Few employees bring more than one employment-related lawsuit. Although they might benefit from a ruling protecting employees in their next job, they are unlikely to turn down an attractive settlement offer for the uncertain chance to preserve this nebulous benefit. Individual employees have little incentive to represent the collective interest of all employees in a favorable ruling because they cannot capture the collective benefit of an employee-friendly ruling to all employees who would be affected by the law. Thus, individual litigants will be likely to forgo rule gain for monetary gain in settlement negotiations.

This point does not mean that categorically, all employers have the characteristics of repeat players. Not all employers are large. Employers also vary in their legal sophistication; those that do business in competitive, high-stakes markets, for example, may have more experience with litigation and may retain more experienced counsel. Similarly, not all employees will necessarily behave as one-shot players. Some litigants may value vindication in court more than the prospect of monetary recovery and thus be less likely to forgo a judicial determination of their dispute for a settlement. In addition, those employees who belong to unions may have more bargaining power than nonunion employees and may receive legal assistance from the union.

In addition, sometimes repeat players appear on both sides of the litigation. Galanter suggests that changing the characteristics of one-shot parties to make them more like repeat players may reduce repeat players' advantage by offsetting the motivational and power imbalances between repeat players and one-shot players. For example, public interest organizations may better represent the collective interests of one-shot employee litigants than individual one-shot players and therefore be less likely to trade rule gain for monetary compensation (Galanter 1974). In addition, public interest organizations sometimes engage in strategic litigation to further social change and occasionally engage in strategic settlement themselves to avoid developing a negative legal precedent.[4] Public interest representation may be more common in disputes arising under remedial statutes. In the employment context, government agencies such as the Equal Employment Opportunity Commission and the Department of Labor undertake litigation on behalf of employees from time to time. Some private, nonprofit organizations also represent employees in employment civil rights actions.

Public interest representation may have limitations, however. Government agencies that undertake civil rights litigation may settle cases for less than they are worth (Handler 1978:142). These "sweetheart" settlements may trade away both rule gain and monetary gain. In addition, even plaintiffs represented by public interest organizations still control their own cases. If a plaintiff wants to trade rule gain for monetary compensation but the public interest organization does not, a conflict of interest arises between the client and the public interest attorney. In these circumstances, repeat players can defeat the social change objectives of the public interest organization by offering the plaintiff a substantial sum for his or her damages while refusing to pay legal fees.[5] This kind of offer induces settlement while simultaneously damaging the public interest organization's ability to undertake future litigation, as public interest organizations often depend on the fees generated from successful litigation to continue their activities.

Despite these qualifications, as a rough approximation an employer is more likely than an individual employee to have the characteristics of a repeat player, particularly in litigation under the FMLA. Only employers with 50 or more employees are covered under the FMLA; smaller employers are not defendants in the data reported here. Employers of this size are organizations; employees generally are not, with the rare exception of union or public interest representation. Only about 16% of workers are covered by collective bargaining agreements, however, and unions do not routinely undertake representation in statutory employment claims, as opposed to disputes arising under collective bargaining agreements.[6] In addition, at least in the data reported here, public interest representation is rare. Accordingly, in employment disputes one would expect that employers generally have the characteristics of repeat players, whereas employees generally do not.

In employment cases, defendants have other incentives, in addition to the incentive to avoid rule loss, to settle cases they are likely to lose. For example, settlement allows employers to control the terms and conditions of the resolution of the dispute, including confidentiality. Employers may settle potential "losers" because a public victory could encourage their other disgruntled employees to sue. Employers who settle cases they expect to lose also avoid the risk of unpredictable damage awards by a jury and in some cases can control dissemination of information about the settlement itself. For example, confidentiality clauses are common in employment settlement agreements. Agreements typically state that the employer denies liability and prohibit disclosing the amount of the settlement, particularly to the employers' current employees. Some also prohibit the plaintiff from publicly announcing the settlement or, in some circumstances, from discussing the factual allegations underlying the dispute. These restrictions sometimes also extend to attorneys representing the plaintiff.

Settlement prior to an adjudicated loss also serves the interests of another repeat player in employment litigation, counsel for the employer. Employers may retain a particular firm to represent them in employment disputes and advise them on compliance matters. Settling a losing case avoids a clear-cut defeat that might damage the firm's relationship with the client and prompt the client to find other representation in the future. Also, the employer may pay more for settlement once the judge rules in the employee's favor on liability, an outcome counsel may want to avoid.[7]

What does this analysis suggest about the development of a remedial employment statute like the FMLA? Although remedial employment statutes give the rule advantage to the employee, repeat player employers may still settle cases they expect to lose and litigate those they expect to win, ensuring that judicial interpretations of the statute occur in cases with the odds in their favor. If repeat players engage in this strategic behavior, Galanter's analysis predicts that judicial opinions will develop a pattern in which repeat players consistently win. Public interest representation of employees may mitigate this pattern, but on balance, one would predict that over time published judicial opinions interpreting the scope and meaning of a remedial employment statute would come to favor employers.

RULE-MAKING OPPORTUNITIES IN THE LITIGATION PROCESS

Although models of legal evolution typically describe the development of law as a result of a binary decision to settle or go to trial (Landes & Posner 1979; Priest & Klein 1984), strategic settlement alone does not capture how the litigation process influences the evolution of law. Very few cases go to trial; many more resolve at some point before trial, often after some kind of court decision or action (Kritzer 1986). Thus, legal evolution depends in part on when in the litigation process a case settles and how it is resolved if it does not. Modeling litigation as the choice between settlement and trial overlooks complexities of the litigation process itself that may create selection bias in the evolution of legal rules.

Litigation is not a one-time choice between trial and settlement. It is a temporally organized process with both rule-making and settlement opportunities along the way. For purposes of this article, by "rule-making opportunities" I mean points in the litigation process that may produce published judicial opinions containing substantive interpretations of a statute. That is, I assume that judges create and shape legal rules through published judicial opinions interpreting the scope of a statute and that both judges and litigants rely on those published opinions in future litigation.

Settlement and rule-making opportunities are not mutually exclusive. Rule-making opportunities occur at different points in the life of a litigated case. Some written judicial opinions set forth interpretations of a remedial statute without resolving all the issues in the case. For example, when deciding summary judgment motions, courts sometimes interpret the legal requirements of a claim without resolving the underlying dispute. Even if the case settles as a result of this ruling, settlement does not remove the judicial interpretation of the law from the public record.[8]

Significantly, choosing to litigate also does not ensure that a rule-making opportunity will occur. Jury verdicts usually do not produce judicial opinions and therefore do not become part of the persuasive or binding judicial authority interpreting the requirements of a statute. Thus, not only settlement behavior but also the litigation process and the rule-making opportunities it presents must be examined to understand how law evolves.

In an employment suit, litigation proceeds in a series of steps, many of which present rule-making opportunities. An employment lawsuit in federal court typically begins with a complaint.[9] Motions to dismiss for failure to state a claim upon which relief may be granted are often the next step in litigation, followed by an answer.[10] After these initial steps, the parties typically engage in a relatively long period of discovery regarding the underlying facts of the case. Toward the end of discovery, one or both parties may bring a motion for summary judgment to narrow the issues for trial or dispose of the case entirely. Should the claim survive summary judgment, the case may proceed to trial, typically a jury trial in employment disputes. During or after trial, the parties may bring a variety of trial-related motions. Once the parties receive a final judgment, the case may, but does not always, proceed to appeal. Figure 6.1 illustrates this process.

Only certain points in the litigation process present opportunities for a substantive interpretation of the statute underlying the employee's cause of action. The most common rule-making opportunities in employment disputes are motions to dismiss for failure to state a claim and motions for summary judgment. These motions may produce written judicial opinions that interpret a statute's substantive legal requirements in a particular factual context. Although courts commonly address a variety of discovery disputes, these disputes rarely involve substantive interpretations of the underlying statute.

Courts sometimes designate their written opinions for publication in official reporters and through electronic databases; other opinions are filed only in the case file at the courthouse. Opinions published in official re-

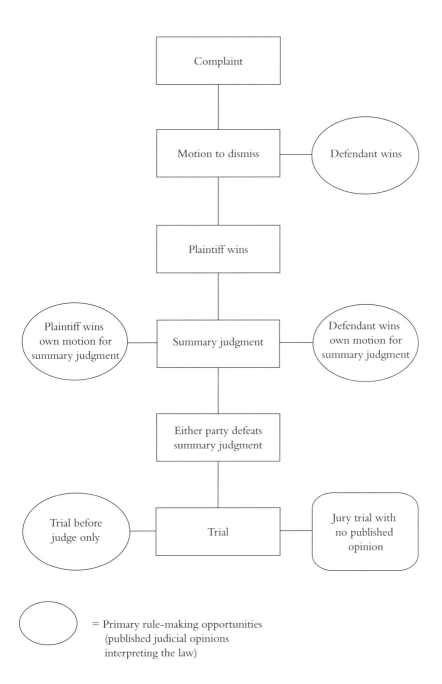

FIGURE 6.1 Rule-making opportunities in the litigation process.

porters generally may be cited to any other federal court, and both parties and courts have access to these opinions through a variety of indexing systems. Online electronic databases such as Westlaw or LEXIS contain all opinions that appear in the official reporters and collect some additional cases not designated for publication in official reporters. These additional cases may come from judges or parties or sometimes are sought out by the database service itself (Olson 1992). Although courts and litigants can access opinions that are published electronically but not in the official reporters, some courts do not allow litigants to cite officially "unpublished" opinions in their legal papers. There is no comprehensive and systematic way for litigants and courts to access opinions that are not published in some manner.

Some points in the litigation process generally do not produce written judicial opinions. For example, the parties may settle at any point in the litigation process, but settlement generally does not produce a judicial opinion interpreting the law and thus is not a rule-making opportunity.[11] Generally, jury trials also are not rule-making opportunities because they do not produce published judicial applications of law. Decisions on some trial-related motions, such as motions for a directed verdict, are the exception.

Appellate decisions are perhaps the most important rule-making opportunities. Published appellate opinions bind trial courts within their jurisdiction, and trial courts in other federal jurisdictions tend to find them authoritative and persuasive. Although appellate courts often issue written opinions, they do not publish every written opinion, and many restrict citation of unpublished opinions in matters before the court.[12]

Because different rule-making opportunities arise at different times in the litigation process, each rule-making opportunity emerges in a distinct procedural posture with a corresponding legal standard. Some rule-making opportunities may be invoked by either party, others by only one. In addition, the frequency of each type of rule-making opportunity varies; appeals are rare compared with more plentiful summary judgment motions. A single case may provide several rule-making opportunities. Not only the outcome of prior similar cases but also the distribution of outcomes and procedural postures among published opinions influence the parties' decisions to settle or go forward, as well as the outcome of future rule-making opportunities. In this way, rule-making opportunities shape the judicial interpretation of a new statutory right.

Below, I discuss the types of rule-making opportunities and their likely influence on the body of published judicial interpretations of remedial statutes such as the FMLA. To simplify the discussion, I assume that the employer will be the defendant and the employee the plaintiff in employment litigation, while recognizing possible exceptions to that assumption.

Motions to Dismiss for Failure to State a Claim

The legal standard for motions to dismiss for failure to state a claim on which relief may be granted favors plaintiffs. These motions test the legal sufficiency of the claim; the court evaluates whether the facts alleged, if true, would entitle the plaintiff to a legal remedy.[13] Courts construe the complaint in the light most favorable to the plaintiff, accept the factual allegations in the complaint as true, and grant the motion only if the plaintiff could prove no set of facts that would support a claim for relief.[14] Courts generally do not consider factual materials outside the pleadings on motions to dismiss for failure to state a claim; if either party includes factual materials, the court may convert the motion to one for summary judgment.[15]

This plaintiff-friendly standard suggests that employees should win most motions to dismiss in employment cases. Defendant employers, however, are unlikely to bring these motions in every case. Bringing an unsuccessful motion to dismiss may simply waste resources and antagonize the court if the court concludes that the employer brought the motion for purposes of harassment or delay. In addition, an employee who survives a motion to dismiss may increase his or her settlement demand. Finally, motions to dismiss on correctable defects seldom result in final judgments, as courts liberally permit amendment of the pleadings.[16] Consequently, a motion to dismiss on a correctable error may simply alert the plaintiff to the need to develop further evidence without disposing of the case. Because motions to dismiss arise early in a dispute, employers may simply wait to dispose of the employee's claim on summary judgment. Thus, rather than routinely filing a motion to dismiss, employers may bring these motions more often in weak cases suffering from legal defects that cannot be cured.

Judges' decisions about publishing opinions also may affect how the law develops. Judges may be more inclined to publish their opinions when they grant motions to dismiss than when they deny them because they believe that granting a motion to dismiss carries more precedential value than a routine denial. This inclination is not because judges are somehow biased against plaintiffs but because granting the motion disposes of the plaintiff's claims, whereas denying the motion does not change the course of the litigation.

Although many federal court opinions are widely available on electronic databases or in official reporters, not every judicial opinion appears in these sources (Songer et al. 1989; Siegelman & Donohue 1990; Olson 1992). Indeed, the Judicial Conference of the United States has suggested that federal appellate and district court judges should only authorize publication of opinions that are of general precedential value (Olson 1992). If judges, publishers, or litigants tend to select for publication those cases in which judges grant motions to dismiss, the law available to litigants and courts will contain more authority for granting employers' motions at this procedural point in the litigation process.

Given these factors, one would predict (1) that rulings on motions to dismiss would be some of the first published opinions regarding a new law, (2) a tendency for defendants to prevail in those published opinions, and (3) fewer motions to dismiss than motions for summary judgment in the published body of case law interpreting a new statute.

Summary Judgment

Summary judgment allows courts to resolve cases without the expense of trial where the undisputed facts show that one party is entitled to judgment. Summary judgment permits piecemeal resolution of the case, such as establishing liability without determining damages, but may also dispose of the case entirely and thus become an appealable final judgment. Parties often bring summary judgment motions in federal employment cases to narrow the issues for trial or avoid trial altogether. Even unsuccessful motions may point out the weaknesses in the opposing party's case and prompt that party to settle rather than risk trial. Summary judgment motions can inform the judge about the facts and issues in the case, and establishing liability through summary judgment may produce settlement by narrowing the dispute to damages. Summary judgment motions typically occur later in the litigation process than motions to dismiss, but before trial.

Unlike motions to dismiss, either party may bring a motion for summary judgment, and the legal standard is weighted against the party who brings the motion. It is much more difficult for a plaintiff than a defendant to obtain summary judgment, however, because the plaintiff generally bears the burden of proof. To prevail on this motion, a defendant must show undisputed facts in its favor on only *one* essential element of the plaintiff's claim, thereby negating the plaintiff's ability to prove his or her case. In contrast, to prevail, a plaintiff must show that the facts establishing *each* element of the claim are undisputed, a difficult burden to carry. Moreover, because summary judgment presents a rule-making opportunity, plaintiffs with undisputed facts supporting every element of their claims are unlikely to reach this stage; as discussed earlier, such clear-cut winners settle.

Simply defeating a defendant's summary judgment motion is a success for a plaintiff because it preserves the case for trial and often produces settlement. Nevertheless, judicial decisions regarding which opinions to publish may limit the availability of this type of precedent for future cases. Judges may be more inclined to publish opinions granting summary judgment, to either party, than opinions denying summary judgment because they believe that a decision that resolves the dispute is a more significant, and thus precedent-worthy, decision. Because it is more difficult to prevail on summary judgment as a plaintiff than as a defendant, however, one would expect the universe of published opinions granting summary judgment to contain many more defendant victories than plaintiff victories.

This discussion suggests that summary judgment will be the most common rule-making opportunity in federal employment cases. In addition, because plaintiffs bear the burden of proof, one would expect to see more defendants than plaintiffs prevail on their own motion for summary judgment. Consequently, it is likely that the early weight of authority addressing a new law will involve summary judgment motions, and most published judicial opinions will be resolution of motions for summary judgment in which the defendant prevails.

Jury Trial and Trial-Related Motions

Jury trials are rare. The Federal Judicial Center estimates that only about 7% of cases brought under federal employment statutes reach trial (Judicial Conference of the United States 1995:Table C4). Some of these cases will settle during trial, leaving an even smaller number of cases on which courts may issue trial-related opinions. Although trial-related opinions such as directed verdicts are possible, those cases resolved by jury verdicts generally do not require a judicial opinion. Some bench trials may result in a published judicial opinion, although in employment cases most plaintiffs prefer a jury trial. Therefore, an employment case resolved by trial may affect the development of law no more than a case that settles.

Even without a published judicial opinion, jury verdicts still may be disseminated, however. Some practitioner publications provide information about jury verdicts. In addition, lawyers may share information through informal networks, unless prevented from doing so by confidential settlements. Also, employees who win at trial may receive media attention. Even when publicized, however, a jury verdict does not change the judicial interpretation of the law or hold precedential value for the cases that follow. Without a published judicial opinion, the results of trials are invisible to the developing body of precedent.

Trials may present rule-making opportunities through trial-related motions, such as motions for directed verdict. Because jury trials themselves are relatively rare, however, opinions addressing both trial-related motions and appeals of jury verdicts will also be relatively rare among judicial interpretations of a statute. Decisions at trial will occur later in the litigation process than motions to dismiss and motions for summary judgment.

Appeal

Of all the rule-making opportunities in the litigation process, appeals are the most important because published appellate decisions bind lower courts within the appellate court's jurisdiction. Because appeals are drawn from final dispositions in the trial courts, the procedural posture of appeals will reflect the distribution of procedural postures of dispositive decisions in the trial courts.[17] Appellate outcomes are affected by the procedural posture of the final judgment that is appealed because that procedural posture determines the legal standard on appeal. Appellate courts review motions for summary judgment de novo, revisiting the question from the same position as the district court.[18] The standard of review for a jury verdict in a civil case, however, requires an appellant to show that the verdict is not supported by substantial evidence, a difficult standard to meet.[19]

Appeals are not automatic. They must be actively "mobilized," and only losing parties may do so. The decision to appeal provides another opportunity for strategic behavior to influence the development of law. Repeat players may choose to appeal only those cases in which they believe they are likely to succeed and forgo less promising appeals that may reinforce unfavorable decisions. Repeat players may also settle a one-shot player's appeal if the appeal appears likely to succeed. In some instances, repeat players may condition settlement of their own appeal on vacating the unfavorable lower court ruling, removing its effect on future litigation (Slavitt 1995; Purcell 1997). Although in employment cases the repeat player is likely to be the employer, public interest organizations engage in this strategic behavior as well, litigating test cases likely to create precedents favorable to their interests.

For the reasons explained above, the largest category of appealable trial court decisions is likely to be orders granting summary judgment. In addition, because summary judgment occurs relatively early in the litigation process, the earliest appeals under a new statute are likely to be appeals of orders granting summary judgment. Appeals take time, and the appeal process alone will delay the appearance of appellate opinions interpreting the new law. Thus, one might predict that appellate opinions will not appear until some time after enactment of a new law and that district court opinions form the primary legal authority in the initial years of a new remedial statute.

The Winnowing Process

One way to think about the winnowing process from initial dispute to lawmaking opportunity is to conceptualize a distribution of possible cases, ranging from "weak" to "strong" and consider how prelitigation processes may screen out particular cases. Determining the quality of a given legal case is necessarily an inexact and subjective process. Most models of the litigation process, however, assume that both lawyer and litigants engage in a rational decision-making process to decide whether to proceed with litigation (see, for example, Priest & Klein 1984).

One might expect that the cases at either end of the distribution would be weeded out fairly early in the process. For example, plaintiffs' lawyers typically screen potential cases before agreeing to represent new clients. Consequently, potential plaintiffs with very weak cases may find it difficult to obtain legal representation and be unwilling or unable to pursue their claims pro se. Cases can be "weak" for a variety of reasons, such as suffering from a fatal defect such as the statute of limitations or because the evidence of wrongdoing is not strong. In addition, a few cases are dropped or dismissed for lack of prosecution even after they reach federal court, suggesting that plaintiffs may abandon weak claims after filing (Siegelman & Donohue 1990:1155).[20]

A similar process screens particularly "strong" cases. Potential plaintiffs with strong cases may be able to negotiate settlement with their employers, even without the assistance of legal counsel. Many attorneys routinely send demand letters to potential defendants before filing an action, and strong cases may settle at this stage. In employment actions, plaintiffs often must pursue administrative remedies as a prerequisite to filing suit, and many disputes may be resolved through this process. As discussed above, plaintiffs with strong cases that proceed to litigation may also, with the aid of preliminary discovery, establish undisputed facts early in the process showing they are likely to prevail. At this point, defendants are likely to settle to avoid additional costs of litigation or future damaging revelations in discovery.

The remaining cases are not as clear. Cases that fall in this middle range may involve disputed questions of fact, or uncertain interpretations of law, such that the outcome is difficult to predict. In those cases closer to the strong end of the spectrum, the facts and the law may slightly favor the plaintiff. In these cases, as discussed above, defendants may be less likely to file a motion to dismiss. Also, Galanter's analysis would predict that defendants would settle these cases to avoid creating a negative ruling at a lawmaking point such as summary judgment, because defendants have a long-term interest in preventing precedent unfavorable to them.

Some cases in the middle of the spectrum will be equally uncertain for plaintiff and defendant. Where that uncertainty results from disputed facts, the case is likely to go to trial or to settle shortly before trial. Disputed facts will preclude summary judgment, regardless of which party brings that motion, and the court is unlikely to publish an opinion on this nondispositive ruling. Where uncertainty results from unsettled law, Galanter's analysis suggests that defendants may settle before reaching a lawmaking point in the process to avoid creating precedent unfavorable to them.

Cases closer to the weak end of the spectrum may be those in which the facts and law slightly favor the defendants. Galanter's theory suggests that defendants will proceed in these cases because these are the cases defendants think they are likely to win. Defendants may win cases suffering from legal defects on a motion to dismiss. In addition, defendants may bring a summary judgment motion before attempting to settle because success on summary judgment is likely and the judge is unlikely to publish an opinion in an unsuccessful motion. Consequently, one might predict that many of the lawmaking opportunities would occur at summary judgment, on relatively weak cases.

The Family and Medical Leave Act

DATA

The Family and Medical Leave Act of 1993 is one of the most recent remedial statutes enacted by Congress. It provides up to 12 weeks of unpaid leave per year for certain employees to care for a seriously ill family member, the employee's own serious illness, or the birth and/or care of a new child.[21] The law requires employers to hold an employee's job, or one like it, open for the employee during his or her leave and to continue to pay the employee's health care premiums during the leave to the same extent the premiums were paid before the leave.[22] An employee's use of leave may not be the basis for any negative employment action, such as demotion, discipline, or termination.[23] Although the FMLA essentially creates an employment benefit, it is structured as an individual right, enforceable through a private right of action or through an action by the secretary of labor.[24] Aggrieved employees may file a complaint with the Department of Labor, or they may proceed directly to court.[25]

The FMLA changes the relationship between employers and employees by carving out a protected area from the norm of at-will employment. It also challenges the traditional line between the public life of employment and the private life of the family. Prior to its enactment, employers had broad discretion to grant or deny leave and to terminate employees who needed time off from work for family responsibilities. Moreover, although many employers voluntarily provided leave to some of their employees before the FMLA, blue-collar, production, and service workers were the least likely to enjoy these benefits.[26] Thus, the FMLA protects individuals who need and use leave against negative employment actions and provides significant new protections to less advantaged workers.

The FMLA provides an opportunity to examine the operation of a remedial statute in the context of litigation involving a repeat player versus a one-shot player. In addition, because the FMLA provides a federal cause of action, FMLA suits can be evaluated nationally through both trial-level and appellate opinions. Unlike state trial court opinions, many federal trial court opinions are published in official reporters or are accessible through electronic databases. The availability of trial court opinions allows closer examination of how the litigation process at the trial level produces law through published opinions, as well as how the distribution of trial-level outcomes and procedural postures influences the nature of appeals.[27] Moreover, the FMLA provides an opportunity to examine who wins in published judicial opinions interpreting an individually mobilized statutory right. Do remedial statutes give the rule advantage to plaintiffs seeking to enforce that right? Does the litigation process affect the outcomes reflected in published judicial opinions in the early life of this new law?

The data presented are drawn from published judicial opinions interpreting the FMLA in the first 5 years after the statute was enacted. An electronic database search for FMLA cases decided by federal courts from 1993 through 1997 produced an initial list of 288 trial-level opinions and 58 appellate opinions.[28] Of these, 64 trial-level opinions and 25 appellate-level opinions involved cases where the plaintiff did not bring a FMLA cause of action; these opinions were excluded from the data set.[29] The remaining 221 trial-level opinions and 36 appellate opinions were coded on a number of factors, including their procedural posture, the gender of the plaintiff, whether the opinion was published in official reporters, the prevailing party, the date of the opinion, amicus curiae participation in the matter, and public interest or government representation of the plaintiff.

It is important to note that the unit of analysis for these data is the published opinion and not the lawsuit itself. One lawsuit could and in a few instances did result in more than one written opinion. Because this article addresses the evolution of judicial interpretations of a remedial statute, however, it is appropriate to include all the published opinions interpreting that statute even where the underlying lawsuit may be included more than once.

Because this study examines published judicial opinions, some cautions are in order here regarding using published opinions in law and society research. It is well known that not all judicial determinations are published, either in electronic databases such as Westlaw and LEXIS or in the official reports such as the Federal Supplement (Songer et al. 1989; Siegelman & Donohue 1990; Olson 1992). For example, Songer et al. found that almost 40% of all cases filed in the Eleventh Circuit in 1986 went unpublished (Songer et al. 1989:969). Siegelman and Donohue found that roughly 80% of the 4,310 employment discrimination cases they studied did not produce a published opinion (1990:1137). Siegelman and Donohue note that the small proportion of cases that produce published opinions renders the representativeness of published opinions suspect, because "other things equal, published cases are more likely to be representative of unpublished cases if the ratio of published to unpublished is 1:2 than if it is 1:10" (ibid., p. 1139).

The research suggests that other, nonrandom factors may also affect the selection of cases that generate published judicial opinions. Songer et al. (1989) classified the litigants in their cases as "upperdogs" (government and corporations) and "underdogs" (labor unions, individuals, minorities, aliens, and convicted criminals). The publication rate for cases in which "upperdogs" were the appellants was higher than for those cases in which the "underdogs" were the appellants, and this difference was statistically significant. Songer et al. also noted that in civil rights cases in particular, only 49% of cases in which the "underdog" was the appellant were published, compared with the 80% publication rate for cases in which the "upperdog" was the appellant. To the extent that "upperdogs" are also repeat players under Galanter's framework, this finding lends some support to the idea that repeat players have greater influence over the development of legal precedent than one-shot players.

Factors unrelated to the nature and identity of the parties may also affect the representativeness of published opinions. For example, Siegelman and Donohue concluded that publication rates varied geographically for employment discrimination cases, indicating that relying solely on cases with published opinions will generally produce a geographically skewed sample of all cases filed in the United States (Siegelman & Donohue 1990:1144).

In addition, as Siegelman and Donohue (ibid., p. 1146) note, it is likely that rulings that dispose of case are more likely to be written and more likely to be published than those that do not. This observation suggests, for example, that even if a plaintiff's case is strong enough to survive summary judgment, an opinion denying summary judgment to the defendant is unlikely to be published. Siegelman and Donohue also point out that judges are more likely to publish opinions with dispositive rulings, and therefore settlement will tend to reduce the likelihood that any given case will generate a published legal opinion. Indeed, they found that settlement in cases without published opinions, 68%, was much more frequent than settlement in cases with published opinions, 35% (ibid., p. 1155).

In the discussion below, I suggest how strategic settlement and the litigation process combine to affect the representativeness of published opinions.

RESULTS AND DISCUSSION

Distribution of Procedural Posture in Early Opinions

Figure 6.2 shows the procedural posture of FMLA cases at the district court level that were published in the first 5 years after the statute was enacted. As expected, the most frequent procedural posture was summary

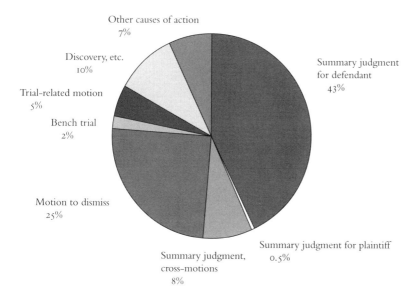

Other causes of action
7%

Discovery, etc.
10%

Trial-related motion
5%

Bench trial
2%

Motion to dismiss
25%

Summary judgment,
cross-motions
8%

Summary judgment for plaintiff
0.5%

Summary judgment
for defendant
43%

FIGURE 6.2   Distribution of procedural posture for District Court FMLA opinions.

judgment, which constituted about half the published opinions. Motions to dismiss were the next most common published opinions. Approximately 21% of the published opinions were motions to dismiss for failure to state a claim under Federal Rule of Civil Procedure 12(b)(6). Another 4.5% were motions to dismiss for other reasons, such as lack of jurisdiction. There were only four bench trials recorded in these published opinions. In addition, 11 opinions were trial related, such as motions to exclude evidence or motions regarding fees. Finally, 22 of these opinions were nondispositive discovery disputes or other types of motions, including motions regarding other legal claims in the lawsuit and motions to compel arbitration.

Figure 6.2 shows that the weight of authority interpreting the FMLA involved motions for summary judgment and motions to dismiss, both of which increased in number over time. The vast majority of early published judicial interpretations of the FMLA were based on these two rule-making opportunities in the litigation process.

Distribution of Outcomes by Procedural Posture in Early Cases

Figure 6.3 shows the distribution of outcomes for trial-level published opinions in the primary rule-making opportunities in the litigation process: motions to dismiss for failure to state a claim, motions for summary judgment, and bench trials. The practical meaning of an outcome clearly de-

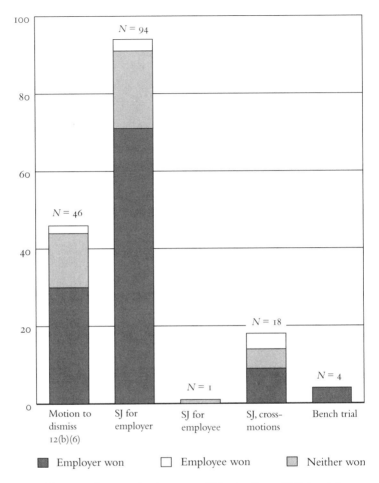

FIGURE 6.3   Outcomes by procedural posture of District Court FMLA opinions.

pends on the procedural posture of the opinion; an employee who survives the employer's summary judgment motion does not win the case, but preserves the claim and may present it to the trier of fact. An employee who prevails on his or her own motion, however, wins at least some of the case outright. Outcomes coded "other" are situations in which neither party prevailed (such as a denial of both motions on cross-motions for summary judgment) or in which the outcome was too mixed to declare one party the victor. Although plaintiffs may have sued under several different but related employment statutes, "wins" and "losses" were coded with regard to only the employee's FMLA cause of action.

As predicted, in the published opinions, employers prevailed much more often than employees when the employer was the only moving party on summary judgment; employers won 76% of their own motions for summary judgment. Where both parties brought motions for summary judgment, however, employers prevailed only 50% of the time. Outcomes on cross-motions may be more balanced because those cases in which employees also brought summary judgment motions were stronger claims. Employees did better in these cases, 28% winning on their own motion, and 22% defeating the employer's motion. Nevertheless, there were many more published opinions in which only the employer moved for summary judgment ($N = 94$) than in which the court addressed cross-motions for summary judgment ($N = 18$). By far the largest category of published opinions were grants of the employer's motions for summary judgment ($N = 80$).

Published opinions on employers' motions to dismiss for failure to state a claim show a similar pattern. Employers prevailed two to one over employees in these opinions. Once again, "prevailing" was coded only on the FMLA cause of action. Despite the dominance of employer success, given the theory that employers would only bring motions to dismiss where they were likely to win, it is somewhat surprising that so many employees defeated motions to dismiss. Closer examination revealed that in many cases, the employer's motion to dismiss encompassed not only the employee's FMLA claim but also other causes of action in the lawsuit. Therefore, employers may have evaluated the chances of success of the motions to dismiss with reference to other causes of action and simply added the FMLA claim because they were bringing the motion anyway.

Employees lost the few bench trials reported, which may simply be a fluke in the small number of bench trials reported ($N = 4$). It may also reflect unequal skill levels in representation of the parties. Generally, plaintiffs' attorneys request a jury trial, believing that a jury will be more sympathetic than a judge and hoping for a large compensatory damage award.

For all opinions, the likelihood of prevailing did not differ significantly by gender of the plaintiff. Also, there was no significant difference in outcome between opinions published in the electronic database and those published in the *Federal Reporter* or *Federal Supplement*.

Appeals

As predicted, appeals were relatively rare and took time to work their way through the courts. Only 36 of these 257 published opinions were appeals. See Table 6.1. Of the 36 reported appellate cases, 30 were decided in 1997, 5 in 1996, and only 1 in 1995. In addition, appeals reflect the influence of the litigation process at the trial level. Sixty-seven percent of published appellate opinions were appeals of a decision granting summary judgment to the em-

TABLE 6.1

Procedural Posture on Appeal in FMLA Actions (N = 36)

Procedural Posture of Decision Appealed	Number	Employer Won	Employee Won
Grant of summary judgment to employer	24	19	5
Grant of motion to dismiss	1	1	—
Judgment for employer following bench trial	2	2	—
Trial-related motion	2	2	—
Non-FMLA cause of action	2	2	—
Other	5	5	—
Total	36	31	5

ployer, reflecting the large number of these types of final judgments. The remaining opinions were scattered among various other types of final judgments, including judgments on claims other than the employee's FMLA cause of action. Only one appeal involved the grant of a motion to dismiss, which is not surprising because a plaintiff generally may amend a complaint after losing a motion to dismiss.

In general, appellate courts tend to uphold trial-level decisions. Data from the Administrative Office of the United States Courts indicate that more than 80% of appeals terminated on the merits in the 12-month period ending September 30, 1995, were affirmed or enforced (Judicial Conference of the United States 1995:Table B5). Published employment opinions in this study followed the pattern reported by the Administrative Office of the United States Courts. Employees were the appellants in every published appellate opinion except two, and employees seldom succeeded on appeal. Employers prevailed in approximately 86% of published appellate opinions.

These data show some trends in the published judicial determination of rights early in the life of this employment statute. First, employers' motions for summary judgment and motions to dismiss were by far the largest categories of published opinions, supporting the hypothesis that motions to dismiss and motions for summary judgment are the most common rule-making opportunities in the litigation process. Appeals reflected the distribution of procedural posture at the trial level and rarely overturned the outcome at the trial level.

Second, in these dominant groups of published opinions, the "haves" come out ahead. Employers prevailed two to one against employees on motions to dismiss, nearly three to one against employees on motions for summary judgment, and four to one on appeal. Consequently, judges reviewing the state of the law and practitioners deciding whether to take on a case will find that the published case law suggests that employees seldom prevail.

These data are consistent with Galanter's argument that repeat players play for the rules; that is, repeat player employers settle cases they are likely to lose, and litigate cases they are likely to win. Indeed, the incentive to engage in this behavior may be greater at the beginning of the life of a statute where almost every dispute raises a question of first impression. These data also reflect, however, the influence of the procedural posture of the rule-making opportunities in the litigation process. The most common rule-making opportunities involved motions for which dispositive outcomes occur primarily when employers win.

In addition, perhaps the most important insight is what is *not* represented in published judicial interpretations of the law: settlement and jury verdicts. That employers win in most published opinions does not necessarily mean that they prevail in most cases despite the protections of the remedial statute. The outcomes in these data may simply reflect the combined influence of strategic settlement and the characteristics of rule-making opportunities in the litigation process. Employers may settle strong cases likely to produce adverse decisions, ensuring that these cases never become the basis for a published judicial opinion. Employers may dispose of weak cases, on the other hand, through motions to dismiss or motions for summary judgment, which often do become part of the judicial interpretation of the law. Cases somewhere in between are likely to involve disputed material facts and consequently proceed to trial. Judges are unlikely to publish denials of motions to dismiss or motions for summary judgment that occur in these cases along the way, however, because these are not dispositive decisions. Many cases that proceed this far settle on the eve of trial. To the extent the rest are decided by jury, they usually do not produce a published judicial opinion that becomes part of the law.

These data only address lawsuits raising FMLA claims, and other types of litigation may produce other patterns.[30] These data are consistent, however, with a recent study regarding another recent remedial statute, the Americans with Disabilities Act (ADA) (ABA Commission on Mental and Physical Disability Law 1998). In a study examining outcomes in trial and appellate cases brought under the ADA, the Commission on Mental and Physical Disability Law found that employers prevailed in 92% of the 760 opinions in which it could be determined which party prevailed. Consistent with the strategic settlement argument, one employee advocate asked to comment on the study noted that "cases that are clearly in our favor usually settle before they are decided" (Flaherty & Heller 1998). Those cases that would have reflected employee wins may have simply never reached a rule-making opportunity in the litigation process. In addition, the study excluded 440 cases in which the final outcome could not be determined. At least some of these cases may have been ones in which plaintiffs survived a motion to dismiss or a motion for summary judgment and then negotiated a settlement, leaving no record of the final outcome of the case. In other words, summary judgment often leaves a clear published record of who won, whereas settlement and trial generally do not.

What do we know about cases that did not produce published opinions, including those that may settle or go to trial? In their study of employment litigation in the federal courts, Siegelman and Donohue found that only about 20% of cases produced a published opinion (1990:1137). Although predicting the outcome of settled cases had they proceeded to adjudication is impossible, indirect evidence may shed some light on the subject. For example, Siegelman and Donohue found that settlement was nearly twice as likely among cases that did not produce published opinions than among those that did (ibid., p. 1155). Although cases may settle for many reasons, the larger proportion of settlements in unpublished cases suggest that these cases may have been more likely to survive a dispositive pretrial motion than those that produced published opinions. Indeed, Siegelman and Donohue report that more cases were resolved by defendants winning 12(b)(6) motions, summary judgment motions, and trial in cases with published opinions than in those without (ibid.). These findings suggest that the common-sense notion that stronger cases settle is not off the mark.

As for trial, few cases proceed that far. Data collected by the United States Administrative Office of the Courts indicate that 77% of employment cases terminate before reaching a pretrial conference, some without any court action (Judicial Conference of the United States 1995:Table C4). These data also indicate that approximately 7% of district court cases brought under federal employment statutes reach jury trial, apparently resolved by verdict or settlement thereafter. Some data collected from different sources suggest that plaintiffs with employment claims who make it to trial may often be successful (Gross & Syverud 1991); other data suggest that these plaintiffs may win at trial only about one-third of the time (Siegelman & Donohue 1990).

What are the implications of these data? The combined effects of strategic settlement and rule-making opportunities in litigation suggest that over time, the published opinions interpreting an employment statute will reflect more adjudicated wins by employers. Advocates seeking authority to support their respective positions will find substantially more published opinions in which courts granted summary judgment for the employer than for the employee. As one court noted in the context of vacatur:

In the normal and traditional operation of the American justice system, each party walks to the courthouse with a compilation of opinions in its favor under one arm and a collection of opposing views under the other. . . . In many instances, particularly in litigation involving institutional litigators, understandably enamored with the majority approach, one or both parties may state that "the weight of authority" supports their view. A string of citations follows. Courts may then, for understandable reasons, accept the majority view as the view tending toward more stability and predictability in the law and toward fewer accusations of renegade activism. (*Benevides v. Jackson Nat'l Life Ins. Co.* 1993:1289)

Because the norms of the rule of law traditionally require law to be generally and consistently applied, rules articulated in case law have implications for the resolution of future disputes. Judges decide cases and generate opinions by synthesizing existing law and applying it to the case at hand. If most published opinions, as opposed to litigation outcomes, favor employers, the synthesized law will come to favor employers' interests. Common-law systems of law are flexible; judges may revise and distinguish rules when faced with counterfactual cases in which the outcomes suggested by the rules seem unjust. Significantly, however, the strategic settlement argument suggests that the counterfactual case will rarely, if ever, appear in the case law because it will settle before reaching a rule-making opportunity.

Public Interest and Government Participation

Galanter suggests that public interest representation or participation of amici curiae representing the interests of one-shot players may ameliorate the advantage repeat players enjoy in shaping the law. Public interest representation was very rare in this group of cases, however. In only seven published opinions did either a public interest organization or the Department of Labor represent the employee. One case in which the Department of Labor represented the plaintiff accounted for three of these seven published opinions, a case the department eventually lost at a bench trial. The Department of Labor also brought actions on behalf of two other plaintiffs in these published opinions, losing on the employer's motion for summary judgment in one and prevailing on the merits in another. The employees represented by other public interest organizations were successful, defeating a motion to dismiss in one instance and winning the plaintiff's own motion for summary judgment in the other.

Amicus curiae participation was rare, and as expected, occurred only at the appellate level where a binding interpretation of the law was at stake. Amici participated in three appellate cases, *Bauer v. Varity Dayton-Walther Corp.* (1997), *Manuel v. Westlake Polymers Corp.* (1995), and *Victorelli v. Shadyside Hosp.* (1997). The Women's Legal Defense Fund (now the National Partnership for Women and Families) led a coalition of public interest organizations in *Bauer* and *Manuel*, and the Department of Labor also participated as amicus curiae in *Manuel*. The Legal Aid Society of San Francisco led a coalition of public interest organizations in *Victorelli*. The employee prevailed in

Manuel and *Victorelli*, but lost in *Bauer*. Although the numbers are too small to draw any meaningful conclusions, on balance, public interest and amicus curiae participation appeared to improve employees' chances of prevailing. Of the eight underlying cases with either public interest representation or amicus curiae participation, plaintiffs definitively lost in only two.

The relative dearth of public interest participation in published judicial opinions may reflect public interest activities outside the judicial forum. For example, the Department of Labor accepts and resolves complaints regarding violations of the FMLA. As of June 1998, the department had received 12,633 complaints from employees and found violations of the FMLA in 7,499, or nearly 60% (Bureau of National Affairs 1998).[31] The department successfully resolved 88% of complaints in which it found a violation of the FMLA, obtaining $11,772,607 in damages from employers.

A few results are striking about the Department of Labor complaint data. First, the figures reported by the Department of Labor suggest that more disputes arise regarding the FMLA than the limited number that reach the federal courts.[32] Indeed, many may not reach court because the department resolves them.[33] Second, the department found violations in 60% of cases, compared with the plaintiff success rate of approximately 22%[34] in the case law, suggesting that employees may mobilize the law and win at least some remedy more often than the case law suggests. Third, the average damage award for the 88% of violations that the department resolved is approximately $1,800, suggesting that administrative complaints address disputes over small damages, although aggregate figures include disputes that vary in value.[35] Thus, the role of the department in resolving violations may be to facilitate settlement of low-damage disputes without resort to the courts. Although this role may help overcome the advantages of repeat player employers over employees with small claims, once again these employee successes will not be reflected in the judicial determination of rights.

A twofold conclusion emerges. First, outcomes in published judicial interpretations of this employment right do indeed tend to favor the repeat player. Employers win far more often than employees in these published opinions. As Galanter would predict, this trend may result in part from the relative power of the parties, as the limited data regarding employees with public interest representation suggest that they do better. The trend, however, may also reflect the influence of the litigation process itself because the most common rule-making opportunities arise when defendant employers prevail on certain motions. The overwhelming trend in favor of employers results not only from victories in individual cases, but also from the concentration of published judicial interpretations of the law in motions to dismiss and motions for summary judgment.

This point leads to a second conclusion, which is that published judicial interpretations of the statute favor repeat player employers because published opinions may not reflect much of what a statutory right accomplishes. For example, unproblematic compliance with the remedial statute is nowhere represented in these judicial opinions because it does not create a dispute (Hadfield 1992). In addition, the common ways to succeed in an employment dispute after surviving dispositive motions—settlement and trial—do not commonly produce published opinions. Also, some cases settle before reaching any rule-making opportunity or even before reaching court. Thus, by "winning"—either by obtaining a settlement or winning a jury trial—employees render their own experiences invisible to the judicial determination of rights, which may eventually erode the power of the remedial statute.

Early Opinions and the Interpretive Path of the Law

Although the data presented here do not directly address this point, it is important to consider how this process of creating early published opinions under a new statute might shape the development of the law. The norms of the rule of law form an institutional coordination structure through which judges examine each other's positions and coordinate the development of law (Rubin & Feeley 1996).[36] Stare decisis and the norm of consistency may amplify the general tenor of early published opinions interpreting a remedial statute if judges seek interpretations that are consistent with the published decisions of their colleagues. Initially, the earliest published opinions may be the only interpretive guidance under a new law. Judges may then rely on these few cases to decide the next wave of disputes arising under that statute. Consequently, early published opinions addressing unsettled areas of law potentially set the direction of the interpretation of a statute. If early published interpretations favor repeat players, later judicial interpretations applying these early authorities may also favor repeat players.

Settlement and the timing of rule-making opportunities in the litigation process suggest that repeat player employers will win in the first rule-making opportunities under a new employment statute. Repeat player employers can avoid early negative rulings by settling cases they are likely to lose. In addition, most early rule-making opportunities are likely to involve motions for which dispositive outcomes occur when employers win—motions to dismiss and motions for summary judgment—because these dispositive rulings occur before trials or appeals in the litigation process. Moreover, because early appeals will be drawn from cases with adjudicated, not settled, outcomes, they are likely to involve these relatively weak cases in which courts granted employers' motions to dismiss or motions for summary judgment.[37]

Parties evaluate the strength of their positions by taking into account published interpretations of the law. Once a sufficient body of authority supporting an employer-friendly interpretation of the law develops, even plaintiffs with strong cases may have difficulty overcoming the weight of author-ity against them. Interpretations unfavorable to employees may cause lawyers to decline to take these cases and cause plaintiffs to settle their cases for less. If these circumstances arise, the scope of rights created by a remedial statute may be slowly narrowed and curtailed.[38]

An empirical exploration of this hypothesis regarding early judicial inter-pretations of a statute is beyond the scope of this article, and I do not claim that the data presented here prove the validity of this argument. There are, however, intuitive reasons to believe that early interpretive paths shape the eventual scope and meaning of a new statutory right. Particularly in federal court, where courts publish many trial-level opinions, early published opin-ions interpreting a new law provide paths of least resistance as well as frames of interpretation for judges grappling with new statutes. Because initially there are few published interpretations of a new law, these interpretations do not compete with as many other authorities for recognition or attention. In the early life of a statute, essentially every issue raises a question of first im-pression. These first published interpretations offer alternatives to starting from scratch for later judges wrestling with similar problems.

Judges mindful that legitimacy of the rule of law rests in part on consis-tency may also be inclined to reach conclusions consistent with those of their colleagues on the bench. Although the earliest published interpreta-tions will be trial-level opinions and therefore not binding on other courts, judges often look to their colleagues, even those in other jurisdictions, for persuasive or at least instructive resolutions of undecided questions (Walsh 1997). Once an interpretive path emerges, a judge may find it hard to reject without contrary authority to support an alternative approach, particularly in federal court where the underlying law often remains the same across ju-risdictions and cannot easily be distinguished. In addition, attorneys may be reluctant to make legal arguments, particularly arguments contrary to exist-ing authority, without some supporting authority.

Judges do not necessarily follow the path set by the first to reach a par-ticular question, however. For example, although many judges interpreting the FMLA have borrowed the burden-shifting analysis applied in antidis-crimination cases, not all have uniformly chosen this interpretive path. A well-respected judge, Judge Easterbrook of the Seventh Circuit, broke ranks with this approach and criticized judges for adopting standards from other employment laws without considering their jurisprudential utility.[39] As this example suggests, however, other judges faced with unsettled issues of law may have concluded that relying on existing authority from any source of-fers some assurance of reaching the right, or at least a defensible, outcome. Judges may be more likely to find a party's arguments persuasive if at least some authority supports them.

The weight of authority among early published opinions also may affect the development of law by affecting the mobilization of a new remedial statute. That is, existing authority affects the parties' estimate of their likely success and accordingly their decisions to settle or proceed. A published opinion is a valuable resource for the party whose position it supports, both in negotiation and in arguing a position before the judge. Although cases can always be factually distinguished, it may be difficult for a party to overcome the weight of negative authority with little contrary authority to cite. Thus, if early authorities favor employers and gain increasing acceptance, employee litigants may confront a less hospitable legal landscape, notwithstanding the terms of the statute.

The Rule of Law and the Paradox of Losing by Winning

These data raise important questions about what it means to win or lose when the resolution of disputes occurs largely beyond the view of the law. They reveal a paradox in the debate among those who believe that law seldom matters for social change and those who believe that law can matter for political movements and the recognition of rights. Studies addressing who wins often treat "winning" as victory in published judicial opinions (Galanter 1975; Burstein & Monaghan 1986; Wheeler et al. 1987; Burstein 1991). As the analysis in this article shows, however, plaintiffs and defendants do not have the same procedural opportunities to win a lawsuit through published adjudication. Many cases eventually settle, and plaintiffs may sometimes negotiate a settlement in the shadow of the law even before their disputes reach court. Indeed, plaintiffs who settle may find a favorable settlement to be as much a victory as a jury verdict after trial. Focusing on disputes alone also overlooks other ways of "winning." Many employees may "win" because their employers comply with the law or because the law subtly changes their everyday social relationships. Workers may even bargain for more than the remedial statute requires, using the legislation as leverage in negotiations (McCann 1994). All reflect tangible benefits enjoyed as a result of statutory rights.

The paradox of losing by winning, however, is that the experiences of individuals who win through settlement, trial, or other legally invisible means are not reflected in the judicial determination of rights. Even if rights *mobilization* creates benefits for some individuals, the coordinating power of rights *adjudication* is not equally available to both parties. Plaintiffs and defendants in employment rights litigation do not have the same procedural opportunities to win in the published judicial determination of rights. Courts, as passive institutions, depend on the private mobilization of rights to create both caseloads and rule-making opportunities (Black 1973). Consequently, when repeat player defendants settle cases they are likely to lose, judicial determinations of rights are based on a selective group of weaker cases. Courts' published opinions do not reflect disputes that eventually settle or result in jury verdicts, nor do they show the benefit of rights in everyday life. At least in employment litigation, the rule-making opportunities in the litigation process magnify this effect by concentrating published judicial determinations of rights in motions where dispositive outcomes occur primarily when employers win: motions to dismiss and summary judgment motions.

Although this point is significant, it is important not to overemphasize the formal law. Courts interpret the law, but what the law will mean flows from the interpretation and transformation of law in ordinary, everyday interactions. Formal legal rules do not predetermine compliance or social behavior. Law's relationship to social practices is not simply instrumental and unidirectional; these practices may inform the formal law as much as the other way around (Erlanger et al. 1987; Yngvesson 1988). Other normative factors may matter more than legal rules in certain social interactions (Macaulay 1963; Ellickson 1991; Erlanger et al. 1987; Maccoby & Mnookin 1990). Organizational culture may translate and transform law's meaning in institutional settings (Edelman et al. 1993). In some instances, organizations may adopt policies to comply with civil rights statutes regardless of the courts' eventual interpretation of those statutes (Kelly & Dobbin 1999). Law's ultimate utility may be as an organizing principle around which to build a social movement; legal defeats may serve this purpose to the same extent as legal victories (McCann 1994). Also, social forces may affect adjudication to counterbalance the process to some extent. Thus, an instrumental, top-down and unidirectional conception of law's relationship to society does not capture its nuances.

Nevertheless formal law remains relevant to social change and everyday life (Engel & Munger 1996). Judicial decisions are important signposts about the meaning of rights; they do more than resolve the disputes of parties. Through adjudication, courts communicate the scope and moral force of remedial statutes.

The relative influence of any legal outcome, however, depends on effective communication of the result and its meaning (Galanter 1983). Not every outcome in the litigation process is communicated equally: grants of summary judgment may become precedential rulings, jury verdicts generally do not. Confidentiality agreements and the dearth of information about settlements limit the influence of settlement compared with a written judicial opinion (Erlanger et al. 1987). By limiting communication of some outcomes, the litigation process may also limit rights' scope and effect.

By deciding disputes, courts specify what constitutes compliance with the law and induce compliance from parties and organizations that may never appear in court (Galanter 1983). For example, employers may evaluate their compliance with the FMLA according to courts' enforcement of employees' rights to leave. If FMLA claims reported in judicial opinions rarely succeed, employers may make fewer efforts to comply with the law. In addition, published opinions in which employers consistently win may create an employer-friendly standard for compliance with the law.[40]

Published judicial opinions also affect private ordering through negotiation. Legal rules establish each party's bargaining endowments in negotiations by indicating the likely outcome should negotiations fail (Mnookin & Kornhauser 1979). If published judicial interpretations of the FMLA favor employers, employers will enjoy an advantage in negotiations by having more legal authority to support their position and arguments. In contrast, little information exists about average settlements or jury awards in similar cases, short of the attorney's own experiences, because these outcomes are difficult to track (Erlanger et al. 1987).[41] Consequently, even employees with strong claims may be forced to lower their settlement demands because they cannot point to any objective authority showing the success of a similar claimant.

The influence of the litigation process on published authority may also affect the future mobilization of rights. Published opinions showing successful claims may encourage wronged individuals to "name" their injury and claim a remedy or may energize a social movement (Black 1973; Felstiner et al. 1981; McCann 1994). Conversely, published opinions documenting unsuccessful claims may cause potential plaintiffs to conclude that success is unlikely and therefore forgo their claims. Published judicial opinions in losing cases may curtail plaintiffs' access to legal representation because attorneys, particularly those who take cases on contingency, decide that those claims are too financially risky to undertake. Thus, the invisibility of successful claims may diminish the mobilization of employment civil rights.

A steady parade of rulings against employees may also undermine the moral authority of the underlying right itself because laws have constitutive as well as instrumental influence in society (Sarat & Kearns 1993). Judicial interpretations enter a dynamic exchange in which law shapes the routines of everyday life and in turn is informed and transformed by everyday categories and routines (Yngvesson 1988; Ewick & Silbey 1992). Without being specifically invoked or even explicitly considered, law may shape everyday thoughts and actions (Engel & Munger 1996). It may change the way social interactions take place and are perceived without any explicit awareness of the legal underpinnings of this change. Finally, legal recognition and validation of rights communicate normative judgments about the underlying rights themselves and those who claim them (Williams 1991).

When the public face of adjudication shows primarily employer wins, judges and citizens may come to believe that the dubious claims reflected in published opinions accurately depict the underlying nature of all rights claims under a statute and that most claims lack merit. Citizens may conclude that the underlying problem the statute addresses no longer exists or never existed to begin with. This erosion of the moral force of the statute may in turn erode individuals' willingness to mobilize its protections and to risk social disapproval by bringing such a claim.

This discussion shows how published judicial opinions can encourage or inhibit social change through feedback effects. If the litigation process systematically excludes information about both violations and successful mobilization of rights from the judicial determination of rights, this information has only limited opportunity to affect future mobilization, compliance, and negotiation. Over time, this dynamic may curtail the capacity of the law to produce social change by inhibiting mobilization, requiring little for compliance, reducing the settlements negotiated in the shadow of the law, and limiting the favorable legal authority available to employees in future disputes and thus curtailing their likelihood of success. Once this process restricts the scope and meaning of statutory rights, the law's capacity to reshape social relations may become similarly confined.

It is important to consider not only courts' dispute resolution function but also their lawmaking role and to theorize the relationship between the two. In his article "Against Settlement," Fiss (1984:1085) argues that the duty of the courts

is not to maximize the ends of private parties, nor simply to secure the peace, but to explicate and give force to the values embodied in authoritative text such as the Constitution and statutes: to interpret those values and bring reality into accord with them. This duty is not discharged when parties settle.

Fiss treats the common law as a public good, socially owned, and with profound social meaning. He takes one position in a larger debate about whether courts are dispute resolution institutions for private disputes or whether their opinions serve wider public and social functions (Chayes 1976). If dispute resolution were the only objective, however, a simple declaration of winner and loser by the courts would suffice. Courts go beyond simply declaring the victor and produce legal opinions because opinions both justify a decision and reinforce the legitimacy and authority of courts (Bourdieu 1987).

Traditional conceptions of the rule of law *presume* that judicial decisions have meaning beyond the resolution of individual disputes. Judicial opinions make the law public, prospective, and clear so that citizens may know and

understand the rules they are meant to obey (Fuller 1964). Opinions in individual cases state rules in general terms in part because universally and
generally applied laws command authority (Unger 1976:69). The doctrine of
stare decisis maintains the generality, stability, and consistency of courts'
opinions, opinions that create rules to be applied in future cases and beyond
the confines of an individual dispute. Thus, the legitimacy of the rule of law
requires that the role of courts be more than just the resolution of individual disputes (Shapiro 1981:25−26). Court-created law enjoys this legitimacy
in part because it possesses the institutional qualities of the rule of law.[42]

Interpreting statutory rights presents an example of courts' public law role
because statutory rights reflect public norms and goals (Silbey & Sarat 1989).
Rights promise to harness the legitimacy and authority of the rule of law to
impose meaningful remedies against the powerful (see Hendley 1996:14). Indeed, social change through statutory rights seems possible because of the
ideal of the rule of law: a society governed not by the arbitrary exercise of
power but by a rational system of rules that claim legitimacy and authority
(Weber 1954). Rights litigation seems to be an attractive avenue for social
change because rights provide democratic access to courts' lawmaking
process as well as the instrumental and constitutive power of law (Zemans
1983).

Scholars have recognized the public significance that the resolution of
landmark cases may carry (Chayes 1976). Even in an ordinary case, however,
more is at stake than resolution of an individual dispute. Individual disputes
form the building blocks of a system of common-law precedent through
which courts explain and interpret the law. Judicial opinions fill gaps in legislation by applying the law to a particular case (Hart 1961), and winning a
legal decision influences the subsequent development of law. Settlement and
trial even in ordinary cases remove a dispute from courts' interpretation of
the law and separate the dispute resolution function of courts from their
lawmaking role.

The influence of adjudication beyond the outcome in an individual dispute may be particularly important for statutory rights with normative objectives. The paradox of losing by winning, however, suggests that the litigation process may hamstring law's capacity for social change by focusing
published adjudication on the weaker claims. The institutional characteristics of the rule of law then extend published judicial opinions through the
system of interpretation and precedent while allowing settlement and unpublished dispositions to drop from sight. The invisibility of at least some attempts to claim the norms expressed in the statute affects the content of the
law and consequently all those who order their relationships according to
that law.

Perceptions of fairness and the ultimate legitimacy of the rule of law flow in part from courts' procedural protections and process (Friedman 1975:112–14; Tyler 1990). The procedural characteristics of the rule of law that seem to constitute a fair and impartial system of justice, however, are safeguards against historical forms of the arbitrary exercise of power, such as the whim of the king, not the more evolutionary influences that may undermine law's impartiality. Procedure may ensure equal access to courts to enforce the laws and to resolve disputes. It does not, however, ensure that all have equal access to courts as institutions of law creation. Even where the courts remain neutral as to outcome, the rule-making opportunities in the litigation process may nevertheless produce interpretations of individual rights that favor repeat players. Procedural protections locate justice and fairness in the equal ability of parties to present their positions and influence the outcomes of their cases, in short, the opportunity to be heard. The paradox of losing by winning suggests that for one-shot players claiming individual rights, success comes at the price of silence in the historical record of the common law. Thus, once again, the "haves" come out ahead.

Notes

Previously published in *Law & Society Review* 33 (4): 869–910 (1999); reprinted by permission. Catherine Albiston is assistant professor of law and sociology at the University of Wisconsin. She holds a Ph.D. in Jurisprudence and Social Policy from the University of California–Berkeley and a J.D. from Boalt Hall School of Law. She practiced employment law at the Legal Aid Society of San Francisco and served as a judicial clerk for United States District Judge Susan Illston. Her dissertation examines how the legal system, the social institution of work, and other normative systems influence the process of mobilizing employment rights created by the Family and Medical Leave Act. Her research interests include law and social change, law and social institutions, legal and scientific conceptions of evidence, public interest lawyers and organizations, and the relationship between law and social inequality.

   I wish to thank Lauren Edelman, Kristin Luker, Marianne Constable, Howard Erlanger, David Lieberman, Gary Gold, Laura Beth Nielsen, Kaaryn Gustafson, Tom Scanlon, Marc Melnick, and the anonymous reviewers for their helpful and insightful comments.

   1. Repeat players are often, but not always, organizations (Galanter 1975).

   2. Indeed, it is difficult to differentiate repeat player status from either employer or defendant status in these circumstances. Employers are almost always organizations, which are likely to have the characteristics of repeat players (Galanter 1975). Remedial statutes are designed to provide rights to employees against their employers, rights that some less powerful employees could not negotiate privately. Accordingly, employers are generally defendants in these actions by definition. Defendant status is not necessarily determinative, however; other researchers have found that

organizations tend to do better than individuals in litigation outcomes, regardless of whether they are the plaintiff or the defendant (ibid.; Songer & Sheehan 1992).

3. Where a public interest organization or the government represents the plaintiff, these types of suits are more like repeat player versus repeat player litigation. Nevertheless, in every employment case there will be an employer, but there will not always be a public interest or government organization. It is also important to note that the FMLA only covers relatively large employers of 50 or more employees (29 U.S.C. 2611 (4)).

4. The November 1997 settlement in *Piscataway Township Bd. of Education v. Taxman*, then before the Supreme Court, is one recent high-profile example of strategic settlement behavior by public interest organizations with long-term interests in protecting affirmative action. Taxman presented a challenge to affirmative action in an exceptional factual context where the decision to lay off a white teacher and retain a black teacher was made solely on the basis of race. The teachers had the same qualifications and had been hired on the same day. See *Taxman v. Board of Education* (1996).

5. See *Evans v. Jeff D.* (1985). In *Jeff D.*, Idaho Legal Aid represented a class of children with emotional and mental handicaps seeking injunctive relief to cure deficiencies in both the educational programs and health care services provided to such children who are under state care. The state offered to settle the case by agreeing to all the injunctive relief requested by the plaintiffs, but refusing to pay any costs or fees associated with bringing the lawsuit. This offer created a conflict of interest between Idaho Legal Aid and its clients. The attorney in question felt ethically bound to protect the interests of the clients by accepting the offer, but made the waiver of costs and fees conditional upon approval by the District Court (ibid., p. 722). The Court of Appeals invalidated the fee waiver and the case came before the Supreme Court, where Idaho Legal Aid argued that this type of settlement offer "exploits the ethical obligation of plaintiffs' counsel to recommend settlement in order to avoid defendant's statutory liability for its opponents' fees and costs" (ibid., p. 729). The Court upheld the fee waiver, noting that "a general proscription against negotiated waiver of attorney's fees in exchange for settlement on the merits would itself impede vindication of civil rights . . . by reducing the attractiveness of settlement" (ibid., p. 732).

6. U.S. Bureau of the Census (1997), Table 688. Approximately 43% of public sector workers are covered by union contracts, but only 11% of private sector workers are covered by union contracts (ibid.).

7. Like most disputes, employment cases typically break down into the issues of liability and damages. Consequently, a judge may establish liability on a plaintiff's motion for summary judgment, for example, while leaving the ultimate question of damages for trial, although most cases settle at this point. Once liability is established, the settlement value of the case increases significantly due to the removal of any uncertainty about recovery.

8. The exception is vacatur or stipulated reversal. Vacatur involves a situation in which the parties settle a case after a court has entered judgment and issued a written opinion, and the settlement is conditioned on the court vacating its judgment. The Supreme Court recently limited this practice (*U.S. Bancorp Mortgage Co. v. Bon-*

ner Mall Partnership 1994). California courts allow the practice of stipulated reversal by which the appellate court reverses the lower court's judgment to accommodate a settlement.

9. Some cases enter federal court through the process of removal. See 28 U.S.C. 1441 et seq.

10. Motions to dismiss also may be brought on other grounds, such as jurisdiction, which are less likely to result in a substantive interpretation of the statute underlying a plaintiff's claims.

11. The rare exception is a consent decree or judicially approved settlement in a class action.

12. At least one commentator has noted the problems associated with this practice (Slavitt 1995).

13. *Conley v. Gibson* (1957:45–46).

14. *Cahill v. Liberty Mutual Insurance Company* (1996:337–38).

15. Fed. R. Civ. P. 12(b).

16. Fed. R. Civ. P. 15; *Foman v. Davis* (1962:182).

17. Although interlocutory appeals of nonfinal decisions are possible, an appellant must meet a high standard to obtain an interlocutory appeal. To certify an interlocutory appeal, a district court must find that the nonfinal order (1) involves a controlling question of law (2) as to which there is substantial ground for difference of opinion and (3) that an immediate appeal from the order may materially advance the ultimate termination of the litigation (28 U.S.C. 1292(b)). Interlocutory appeals are not routinely granted, and are available only in exceptional circumstances (*Coopers & Lybrand v. Livesay* [1978:474]). None of the appeals in this study was an interlocutory appeal, but one case involved an appeal under a related doctrine, the collateral order rule. See *Eastus v. Blue Bell Creameries, L.P.* (1996).

18. *Warren v. City of Carlsbad* (1995:441).

19. *Murphy v. FDIC* (1994:1495).

20. Some plaintiff's attorneys also may be reluctant to bring weak cases that are likely to produce precedent unfavorable to employees. Galanter's analysis suggests, however, that this situation is most likely where plaintiff's counsel has the characteristics of a repeat player, such as a public interest organization or government agency. These organizations may choose their test cases carefully to present the strongest possible facts to argue for a strengthening or extension of the law. Individual practitioners with significant financial pressures may be more likely to evaluate cases on a case-by-case basis for their potential for a successful (and speedy) settlement, without an eye toward the development of the law. Other factors affect screening as well. Cases that are likely to be resolved one way or the other early on with minimal effort may be the most attractive to lawyers. Cases that require a significant investment of resources in depositions and expert witnesses, even those with a high likelihood of success, may be less attractive to lawyers, particularly because many employment cases involve contingency fees.

21. 29 U.S.C. 2612(a).

22. 29 U.S.C. 2614.

23. 29 C.F.R. 825.220(c).

24. 29 U.S.C. 2617.

25. Ibid.

26. U.S. Bureau of the Census (1997:Table 678).

27. Although both state and federal courts have jurisdiction over FMLA claims, even FMLA claims originally brought in state court will likely end up in federal court through the process of removal.

28. These opinions include opinions published only in an electronic database and opinions published in the *Federal Reporter* or *Federal Supplement*. The FMLA was enacted in 1993, and no published opinions were found for that year.

29. Often, judges mentioned the FMLA in passing in circumstances where the plaintiff had taken a leave from the employer but did not include a FMLA cause of action in his or her complaint. Some irrelevant cases came up because the acronym FMLA also refers to the Federal Maritime Lien Act.

30. For example, one study of Title VII cases found that employees were successful to some degree in more than half the reported cases (Burstein & Monaghan 1986; Burstein 1991). Both the measure and the sample in that study, however, are different from my approach here. That study examined only appellate cases and looked only at those cases that were published in *Fair Employment Practice Cases*, a publication compiled by the Bureau of National Affairs. It also used a very broad definition of "winning" and did not include any information about procedural posture or trial-level outcomes.

A different study of state court records indicated that plaintiffs in personal injury suits (the most comparable to civil rights suits) obtained formal settlement or judgments in their favor more than half the time (Wanner 1975). Wanner sampled court records rather than looking at published opinions, however, and therefore his study does not speak to bias in the published interpretations of the law. In addition, "personal injury" actions in that study include actions other than employment civil rights actions.

31. The department found no violation in many instances because either the employer was not covered by the FMLA or the employee was not eligible for leave.

32. Of course, these figures may reflect a lag time between the violation and the appearance of the dispute in court, as the FMLA has a 2-year statute of limitation. In addition, it is unclear how many FMLA lawsuits actually reach court and then settle without any judicial action.

33. It is important to note, however, that Department of Labor administrative proceedings and participation in a federal court action are not mutually exclusive alternatives. In addition, unlike many other federal employment statutes, the FMLA does not require exhaustion of administrative remedies before filing in federal court.

34. This success rate includes success (either winning the plaintiff's own motion or defeating the defendant's motion) on all motions with published opinions, including discovery motions, even if the underlying dispute remained unresolved.

35. There are alternative explanations. The department may resolve disputes before much back pay accrues. The department may also be reluctant to be particularly punitive with employers because the law is new. Alternatively, the department may

cut "sweetheart deals" with the employers, settling cases for much less than they are worth.

36. There is a body of literature regarding judicial decision-making that disputes this proposition (see, e.g., Segal & Spaeth 1996; Spaeth & Segal 1999). Most studies of judicial decision-making that find that judges follow their preferences rather than precedent, however, examine this process at the level of the Supreme Court. There is reason to believe that trial judges will be more likely to follow precedent for fear of being reversed. Some research shows that precedent affects the decisions of appellate judges as well (Songer et al. 1994).

37. That is, appeals are likely to be appeals from grants of summary judgment to the employer in cases that the employer chose not to settle because it believed it could win. Employers are unlikely to appeal grants of summary judgment to an employee because these cases tend to be very strong. Employers are also unlikely to appeal after an employee wins a jury verdict because appellate courts are reluctant to overturn jury verdicts.

38. Negative rulings, however, can sometimes galvanize the opposition, provoke political demands for legislative reversal, and help organize social movements (McCann 1994).

39. See *Diaz v. Fort Wayne Foundry Corp.* (1997). Although looking to existing interpretive paths is common, judges with greater status (or confidence) may be more likely to reject early interpretive paths they find unconvincing.

40. For example, the Seventh Circuit recently ruled that employers with a good faith belief that an employee on leave was not actually sick, even if incorrect, could legally fire that employee for taking leave (*Kariotis v. Navistar Int'l Transp. Corp.* 1997). In this case, the employer hired a private investigator to follow an employee who recently had knee surgery. The investigator recorded her on videotape pushing a grocery cart in the supermarket. When fired, the employee offered additional medical certification of her inability to work, which the employer refused. In addition, the employer refused to arrange an examination by its own doctor, a procedure that the FMLA regulations set forth for these circumstances. The Seventh Circuit ruled that the employer was not obligated to follow those compliance procedures as long as it had a good faith belief that the employee was lying.

41. Lawyers have professional networks and exchange information regarding similar cases so that informal sources of information may help overcome the information deficit faced by plaintiffs. In addition, publications other than the official reporters, such as professional newsletters or jury verdict reports, also provide information about the more "invisible" outcomes. Because these sources generally cannot be cited to the court as authority, however, they may be most useful in negotiating settlements. Moreover, in the context of employment litigation, particularly litigation involving a new remedial statute, there is reason to believe that these factors may not reduce the disadvantage of plaintiffs much. Employment cases are notoriously fact-intensive and often turn on minor differences in the evidence, rendering experiences of other attorneys in all but the most similar cases somewhat irrelevant. In addition, the confidentiality clauses often inserted in settlement agreements may restrict precisely this kind of informal exchange. Finally, because the FMLA is a relatively new law, few attorneys have much experience litigating FMLA

cases, which limits the amount of informal exchange that can take place. My own experience as a practicing attorney also suggests that publication of a favorable opinion in the official reporters is an important factor in facilitating this informal exchange, as attorneys often call the attorney of record in published opinions to request sample pleadings and technical assistance. To the extent that favorable outcomes do not produce published opinions, the informal exchange of information may be dampened.

42. It is appropriate to acknowledge here that the rule of law is a notoriously contested concept and that this description may be useful only for this limited discussion.

References

ABA Commission on Mental and Physical Disability Law (1998) "Study Finds Employers Win Most ADA Title I Judicial and Administrative Complaints," *Mental & Physical Disabilities Law Reporter*, May-June, p. 403.

Black, Donald (1973) "The Mobilization of Law," 2 *J. of Legal Studies* 125–49.

Bourdieu, Pierre (1987) "The Force of Law: Toward a Sociology of the Juridical Field," 38 *Hastings Law J.* 805–53.

Bumiller, Kristin (1988) *The Civil Rights Society*. Baltimore: Johns Hopkins Univ. Press.

Bureau of National Affairs (1998) "Department of Labor Summary of Outreach, Compliance Activity under the 1993 Family and Medical Leave Act," *Daily Labor Report*, p. E1.

Burstein, Paul (1991) "Legal Mobilization as a Social Movement Tactic: The Struggle for Equal Employment Opportunity," 96 *American J. of Sociology* 1201–25.

Burstein, Paul, & Kathleen Monaghan (1986) "Equal Employment Opportunity and the Mobilization of Law," 20 *Law & Society Rev.* 355–88.

Chayes, Abram (1976) "The Role of the Judge in Public Law Litigation," 89 *Harvard Law Rev.* 1281–1316.

Cooter, Robert, & Lewis Kornhauser (1980) "Can Litigation Improve the Law without the Help of Judges?" 9 *J. of Legal Studies* 139–63.

Cooter, Robert D. (1996) "Decentralized Law for a Complex Economy: The Structural Approach to Adjudicating the New Law Merchant," 144 *Univ. of Pennsylvania Law Rev.* 1643–96.

Edelman, Lauren B., Howard S. Erlanger, and John Lande (1993) "Internal Dispute Resolution: The Transformation of Civil Rights in the Workplace," 27 *Law & Society Rev.* 497–534.

Ellickson, Robert C. (1991) *Order without Law: How Neighbors Settle Disputes*. Cambridge: Harvard Univ. Press.

Engel, David M., & Frank W. Munger (1996) "Rights, Remembrance, and the Reconciliation of Difference," 30 *Law & Society Rev.* 7–53.

Erlanger, Howard S., Elizabeth Chambliss, & Marygold S. Melli (1987) "Participation and Flexibility in Informal Processes: Cautions from the Divorce Context," 21 *Law & Society Rev.* 585–604.

Ewick, Patricia, & Susan Silbey (1992) "Conformity, Contestation, and Resistance: An Account of Legal Consciousness," 26 *New England Law Rev.* 731–49.

Felstiner, William L. F., Richard L. Abel, & Austin Sarat (1981) "The Emergence and Transformation of Disputes: Naming, Blaming, Claiming . . . ," 15 *Law & Society Rev.* 631–54.

Fiss, Owen M. (1984) "Against Settlement," 93 *Yale Law J.* 1073–90.

Flaherty, Kelly, & Emily Heller (1998) "Workers Face Tough Odds in Disability Suits, ABA Study Finds," *Fulton County Daily Report*, 30 June. Available on LEXIS LEGNEW library, ALLNWS file.

Friedman, Lawrence M. (1975) *The Legal System: A Social Science Perspective.* New York: Russell Sage Foundation.

Fuller, Lon L. (1964) *The Morality of Law.* New Haven, CT: Yale Univ. Press.

Galanter, Marc (1974). "Why the 'Haves' Come Out Ahead: Speculations on the Limits of Legal Change," 9 *Law & Society Rev.* 95–160.

——— (1975) "Afterword: Explaining Litigation," 9 *Law & Society Rev.* 347–68.

——— (1983) "The Radiating Effects of Courts," in K. Boyum & L. Mather, eds., *Empirical Theories about Courts.* New York: Longman.

Gross, Samuel R., & Kent D. Syverud (1991) "Getting to No: A Study of Settlement Negotiations and the Selection of Cases for Trial," 90 *Michigan Law Rev.* 319–93.

Hadfield, Gillian K. (1992) "Bias in the Evolution of Legal Rules," 80 *Georgetown Law J.* 583–616.

Handler, Joel F. (1978) *Social Movements and the Legal System: A Theory of Law Reform and Social Change.* New York: Academic Press.

Hart, H. L. A. (1961) *The Concept of Law.* Oxford: Clarendon Press.

Hendley, Kathryn (1996) *Trying to Make Law Matter: Legal Reform and Labor Law in the Soviet Union.* Ann Arbor: Univ. of Michigan Press.

Hirschman, Albert O. (1970) *Exit, Voice, and Loyalty: Responses to Decline in Firms, Organizations, and States.* Cambridge: Harvard Univ. Press.

Holmes, Oliver Wendell (1923) *The Common Law.* Boston: Little, Brown.

Judicial Conference of the United States (1995) *Report of the Proceedings of the Judicial Conference of the United States.* Washington, DC: Administrative Office of the United States Courts.

Kairys, David (1982) *The Politics of Law: A Progressive Critique.* New York: Pantheon Books.

Kelly, Erin, & Frank Dobbin (1999) "Civil Rights Law at Work: Sex Discrimination and the Rise of Maternity Leave Policies," 105 *American J. of Sociology* 455–92.

Kritzer, Herbert M. (1986) "Adjudication to Settlement: Shading in the Gray," 70 *Judicature* 161–65.

Landes, William M., & Richard A. Posner (1979) "Adjudication as a Private Good," 8 *J. of Legal Studies* 235–84.

Macaulay, Stewart (1963) "Non-Contractual Relations in Business: A Preliminary Study," 28 *American Sociological Rev.* 55–67.

Maccoby, Eleanor, & Robert Mnookin (1990) *Dividing the Child.* Cambridge: Harvard Univ. Press.

McCann, Michael (1994) *Rights at Work: Pay Equity Reform and the Politics of Legal Mobilization.* Chicago: Univ. of Chicago Press.

Miller, Richard E., & Austin Sarat (1981). "Grievances, Claims, and Disputes: Assessing the Adversary Culture," 15 *Law & Society Rev.* 525–65.

Mnookin, Robert, & L. Kornhauser (1979) "Bargaining in the Shadow of the Law: The Case of Divorce," 88 *Yale Law J.* 950–97.

Olson, Susan M. (1992) "Studying Federal District Courts through Published Cases: A Research Note," 15 *Justice System J.* 782–800.

Priest, George L., & Benjamin Klein (1984) "The Selection of Disputes for Litigation," 13 *J. of Legal Studies* 1–55.

Purcell, Daniel (1997) "The Public Right to Precedent: A Theory and Rejection of Vacatur," 85 *California Law Rev.* 867–917.

Rosenberg, Gerald N. (1991) *The Hollow Hope: Can Courts Bring about Social Change?* Chicago: Univ. of Chicago Press.

Rubin, Edward, & Malcolm Feeley (1996) "Creating Legal Doctrine," 69 *Southern California Law Rev.* 1989–2037.

Sarat, Austin, & Thomas S. Kearns (1993). "Beyond the Great Divide: Forms of Legal Scholarship and Everyday Life," in A. Sarat and T. S. Kearns, eds., *Law in Everyday Life*. Ann Arbor: Univ. of Michigan Press.

Scheingold, Stuart A. (1974) *The Politics of Rights*. New Haven, CT: Yale Univ. Press.

Segal, Jeffrey A., & Harold J. Spaeth (1996) "The Influence of Stare Decisis on the Votes of the United States Supreme Court Justices," 40 *American J. of Political Science* 971–1003.

Shapiro, Martin (1981) *Courts: A Comparative and Political Analysis*. Chicago: Univ. of Chicago Press.

Siegelman, Peter, & John J. Donohue (1990) "Studying the Iceberg from Its Tip: A Comparison of Published and Unpublished Employment Discrimination Cases," 24 *Law & Society Rev.* 1133–70.

Silbey, Susan, & Austin Sarat (1989). "Dispute Processing in Law and Legal Scholarship: From Institutional Critique to the Reconstruction of the Juridical Subject," 66 *Denver Univ. Law Rev.* 437.

Slavitt, Howard (1995) "Selling the Integrity of the System of Precedent: Selective Publication, Depublication, and Vacatur," 30 *Harvard Civil Rights-Civil Liberties Law Rev.* 109–42.

Songer, Donald R., & Reginald S. Sheehan (1992) "Who Wins on Appeal? Upperdogs and Underdogs in the United States Courts of Appeals," 36 *American J. of Political Science* 235–58.

Songer, Donald R., Jeffrey A. Segal, & Charles M. Cameron (1994) "The Hierarchy of Justice: Testing a Principal-Agent Model of Supreme Court–Circuit Court Interactions," 38 *American J. of Political Science* 673–96.

Songer, Donald R., Danna Smith, & Reginald S. Sheehan (1989) "Nonpublication in the Eleventh Circuit: An Empirical Analysis," 16 *Florida State Univ. Law Rev.* 963–84.

Spaeth, Harold J., & Jeffrey A. Segal (1999) *Majority Rule or Minority Will*. Cambridge: Cambridge Univ. Press.

Trubek, David M., Austin Sarat, William L. F. Felstiner, Herbert M. Kritzer, & Joel B. Grossman (1983) "The Costs of Ordinary Litigation," 31 *UCLA Law Rev.* 72–127.

Tyler, Tom (1990) *Why People Obey the Law.* New Haven, CT: Yale Univ. Press.

Unger, Roberto (1976) Law in Modern Society: Toward a Criticism of Social Theory. New York: Free Press.

U.S. Bureau of the Census (1997) *Statistical Abstract of the United States: 1997.* 117th ed. Washington, DC: GPO.

Walsh, David J. (1997) "On the Meaning and Pattern of Legal Citations: Evidence from State Wrongful Discharge Precedent Cases," 31 *Law & Society Rev.* 337–60.

Wanner, Craig (1975) "The Public Ordering of Private Relations, Part Two: Winning Civil Court Cases," 9 *Law & Society Rev.* 293–306.

Weber, Max (1954) *On Law in Economy and Society.* Edited by Max Rheinstein. Cambridge: Harvard Univ. Press.

Wheeler, Stanton, Bliss Cartwright, Robert A. Kagan, & Lawrence M. Friedman (1987) "Do the 'Haves' Come Out Ahead? Winning and Losing in State Supreme Courts, 1870–1970," 21 *Law & Society Rev.* 403–45.

Williams, Patricia (1991) *The Alchemy of Race and Rights.* Cambridge: Harvard Univ. Press.

Yngvesson, Barbara (1988) "Making Law at the Doorway: The Clerk, the Court, and the Construction of Community in a New England Town," 22 *Law & Society Rev.* 409–48.

Zemans, Frances Kahn (1983) "Legal Mobilization: The Neglected Role of the Law in the Political System," 77 *American Political Science Rev.* 690–703.

Cases Cited

Bauer v. Varity Dayton-Walther Corp., 118 F.3d 1109 (6th Cir. 1997).

Benevides v. Jackson Nat'l Life Ins. Co., 820 F. Supp. 1284 (D. Colo. 1993).

Cahill v. Liberty Mutual Ins. Co., 80 F.3d 336 (9th Cir. 1996).

Conley v. Gibson, 355 U.S. 41 (1957).

Coopers & Lybrand v. Livesay, 437 U.S. 463 (1978).

Diaz v. Fort Wayne Foundry Corp., 131 F.3d 711 (7th Cir. 1997).

Eastus v. Blue Bell Creameries, L.P., 97 F.3d 100 (5th Cir. 1996).

Evans v. Jeff D., 475 U.S. 717 (1985).

Foman v. Davis, 371 U.S. 178 (1962).

Kariotis v. Navistar Int'l Transp. Corp., 131 F.3d 672 (7th Cir. 1997).

Manuel v. Westlake Polymers Corp., 66 F.3d 758 (5th Cir. 1995).

Murphy v. FDIC, 38 F.3d 1490 (9th Cir. 1994).

Taxman v. Board of Educ., 91 F.3d 1547 (3rd Cir. 1996).

U.S. Bancorp Mortgage Co. v. Bonner Mall Partnership, 513 U.S. 18 (1994).

Victorelli v. Shadyside Hosp., 128 F. 3d 183 (3rd Cir. 1997).

Warren v. City of Carlsbad, 58 F.3d 439 (9th Cir. 1995).

Statutes Cited

28 U.S.C. 1292(b).

28 U.S.C. 1441 et seq.

29 U.S.C. 2611(4).
29 U.S.C. 2612(a).
29 U.S.C. 2614.
29 U.S.C. 2617.
Fed. R. Civ. P. 12(b).
Fed. R. Civ. P. 15.
29 C.F.R. 825.220(c).

Resource Inequalities in Ideological Courts

The Case of the Israeli High Court of Justice

Introduction

Under what conditions can litigation be distributive? Galanter's influential analysis suggests that the status of litigants before U.S. courts has substantial influence on judicial outcomes. Higher-status parties typically possess superior resources or greater litigation experience (or both). Corporations and government agencies often function as "repeat players" in comparison with one-shot litigants. Therefore, they are presumably better able to "play the rules" in the legal process (Galanter 1974). They are also able to maximize their success rates by forming settlements in cases likely to be lost and by appealing cases they have the best chance of winning. Other explanations for the advantages of the "haves" in litigation refer to their ability to retain better legal counsel, undertake more extensive research, and otherwise invest more in case preparation (Sheehan et al. 1992).

Galanter's party capability theory is based on the assumption that courts are passive institutions that depend on the initiative of the parties who come before them. Accordingly, their decisions reflect the existing disparities in wealth and power in society, while the courts themselves are neutral (if not indifferent) to the inequalities entailed by their institutional passivity and ideological detachment (Galanter 1974:119–20).[1] The theory has been corroborated by studies of the appellate courts in the United States (Songer & Sheehan 1992; Songer et al. 1999) as well as of district courts (Dunworth & Rogers 1996) and, to a lesser degree, in states' supreme courts (Wheeler et al. 1987; Farole 1999). It was also validated by works referring to the Supreme Court of Canada (McCormick 1993) and to litigation before the Court of Appeal in England (Atkins 1991).[2]

Several writers, however, have questioned the assumption of institutional passivity and ideological neutrality of courts that underlies Galanter's argument (e.g., Segal & Cover 1989; Segal & Spaeth 1993; Baum 1998). Accordingly, some studies suggest that the party capability theory fails to provide a sufficient explanation for outcomes of litigation. More specifically, these studies stress that, in some cases, status difference in success rates reflects not only relative resources and experience of litigants but also the values, ideological preferences, and prejudices of the court. Thus, Sheehan et al. (1992) argued that the ideological composition of the U.S. Supreme Court has much greater impact on the success of litigants than the resources the litigants possess. They maintained that cases brought by minorities, the poor, and individuals against businesses or government frequently emphasize claims of individual rights and liberties and therefore are likely to appeal to liberal values and enjoy greater success within courts with liberal majorities (Sheehan et al. 1992; Farole 1999).[3]

Sheehan et al. stressed the importance of judicial preferences in the study of outcomes of litigation. Judicial preferences may, however, relate not only to the ideology of the judges, but also to their will to preserve their institutional autonomy. Thus, Haynie, in a study relating to the Philippine Supreme Court, argued that "have nots" enjoyed higher success rates than other groups due to the institutionalized concerns of social stability and legitimacy of the courts in developing societies (Haynie 1995).

The relations between judicial preferences, institutional concerns, and litigation outcomes are the focus of this study. I checked the relative success of "haves" and "have nots" in litigation before the Israeli High Court of Justice (HCJ). I found that the Israeli HCJ, much like its Philippine counterpart, is heavily influenced in its attitude toward different categories of litigants by ideological and institutional concerns. In contrast to previous research, I included in the current study not only final decisions of the Court, but also litigation that was disposed through out-of-court settlements. In his celebrated article, Galanter hypothesized, "Greater institutional 'activism' might be expected to reduce advantages of party expertise and differences in the quality and quantity of legal services" (Galanter 1974:140). My central argument is that judicial activism may reduce the advantages of the "haves" not only in final judicial dispositions but also in out-of-court settlements. I also argue that attention to variable functions of public agencies in litigation may be essential for the understanding of outcomes in a given field of litigation.

The Research

THE ISRAELI HIGH COURT OF JUSTICE

The High Court of Justice is one of the functions of the Supreme Court of Israel. When a civil or criminal dispute arises in Israel, it normally makes its way to a county court and then—on appeal—to a district court. Only a handful of such cases reach the Supreme Court as a third instance of *cassation*. The Supreme Court also functions as an appellate court for cases involving serious criminal offenses or civil disputes in which the value of the claim is particularly high. If, however, the dispute—no matter how minor or ordinary—concerns a public agency exercising its legal powers, it is brought directly before the Supreme Court and is resolved by this Court with no possibility of appeal. Therefore, the Supreme Court in Israel serves, in fact, in three different capacities: as a court of *cassation*, as a court of appeal, and as a court of first (and last) instance for judicial review cases (HCJ).

That the Supreme Court of Israel functions, in essence, as a trial court for most judicial review cases in the country has wide implications on both the Court's caseload and on its procedures. The Israeli Supreme Court is an extremely busy institution, disposing of over 1,000 applications for judicial review as well as over 3,000 other lawsuits every year.[4] The procedures in the HCJ are characterized by simplicity, brevity, and expediency. A petition to the HCJ can be written by a layperson, and at no stage of the proceedings is representation by a lawyer required. Any person who has reason to believe that a particular public agency denies his or her legal rights may petition the Court and apply for an order nisi. A single judge reviews the petition. The judge may order a preliminary hearing before three justices to take place, requiring the respondent to supply the Court with a concise statement as to the reasons and background for the relevant governmental action. Alternatively, the judge may issue an order nisi, requiring the respondent to appear in Court and show why a particular action should or should not be performed. A full hearing before three judges would then be held before the Court reaches its final decision. Hearings are based on the parties' affidavits and oral arguments. Oral testimony as well as cross-examination are usually not allowed. The Court is able to grant petitioners immediate relief and to issue orders and injunctions, either interim or absolute, at any stage.[5]

All these characteristics seem to make the HCJ a favorable forum from the point of view of "have nots." Gaining access to the Court is easy and inexpensive: fees are remarkably low (approximately the equivalent of $100). The risk of heavy expenses in case of defeat is minimal.[6] In the vast majority of cases, the Court refrains from imposing costs on the losing party, and even when costs are ordered, their amount is usually much lower than in civil cases.[7] Other factors that seem to work for "have nots" are the simplicity of the procedures in the HCJ, the highly informal nature of the process, and the lack of any formal requirement for legal representation.

Although the costs and risks in petitioning the HJC are low, the stakes—from the point of view of "have nots"—are high. The HCJ is the most important and influential judicial forum in the country. The professional expertise of the justices is beyond question. The influence of their rulings on the administrative bureaucracy is immediate, with high effectiveness in mobilizing response from government agencies. The judicial process in the HCJ also enjoys a very high level of visibility. Several journalists cover the Court's activity on a regular basis, which provides a good opportunity for media coverage even for those cases that are not of paramount public importance.

Moreover, the HCJ enjoys a high level of legitimacy within the Israeli public. This public legitimacy is based (among other factors) on the popular belief that the Court functions as the "representative of the common citizen" (Barzilai et al. 1994a:vii).[8] This image of the Court as "the protector of the little person" is promulgated in the rhetoric of the HCJ itself as well as in many other texts (professional and popular) describing the institution.[9] It also serves as the ideological justification for the strong sense of informality and lack of rigidity embedded in the Court's practices (H.C. 2148/94 *Gelbert*). In other words, the "have-not" petitioning the HCJ should expect to meet a judicial forum that is not only devoid of formalistic legal restraints, but also deeply committed to the values of substantive justice and the need to protect the interests of the individual vis-à-vis the government.[10]

The HCJ is also known as an activist court whose policies were directed on many occasions toward the protection of the human rights of minorities and other disadvantaged groups. Although the record of the Court in some areas of human rights, such as the protection of the rights of Palestinian residents of the territories, is controversial,[11] in many other fields the Court did adopt a strong agenda in favor of human rights. Besides the development of a rich jurisprudence concerning political rights in general (such as the freedom of expression, the freedom of procession and association), the Court has intervened in government policies on many occasions for the benefit of members of disadvantaged groups. It struck down governmental decisions in the field of nominations and ordered the government to respect the need to appoint women to senior bureaucratic positions (H.C. 453/94 *Shdulat Ha'-nashim B'Israel*; H.C. 153/87 *Shakdiel*; H.C. 953/87 *Poraz*). It ordered the Israeli Defense Forces to accept female candidates for the posts of combat pilots and commanders of battleships (H.C. 4541/94 *Miller*). The Court acknowledged the rights of homosexuals to equal treatment in the field of labor rights (H.C. 721/94 *El-Al*). Moreover, since 1980, the Court has intervened in some cases in the socioeconomic policies of the government to guarantee equal access to public resources for members of disadvantaged groups. For example, in 1993, the Court ordered a municipal council to rebuild certain public facilities to ensure full accessibility to handicapped persons (H.C. 7081/93 *Botzer*). The Court also ordered the government to appropriate funds for the construction of rehabilitation facilities for juvenile offenders belonging to minority groups (H.C. 3473/92 *The National Council for the Welfare of the Child*). And, recently, the Court ordered the government to take the necessary steps to connect the schools serving pupils belonging to the Bedouin minority in the southern part of the country to the electricity network (H.C. 4671/98 *Awad Abu Fariach*).

Besides its pretensions to values of substantive justice and its political activism, one more factor contributes to the difference between the HCJ and ordinary courts. The Supreme Court of Israel is dominated by justices who come from an academic and bureaucratic background. Unlike many justices serving in lower echelons, they have no prior experience as lawyers in the private sector and no strong social ties to business circles or to political elites.[12] Their social reference group is the bureaucratic elite of the Ministry of Justice, which is composed of bureaucrats serving in the ministry as a life career (unless nominated for the bench).[13] Therefore, it is fair to assume that their ideological commitment as well as their sentiments toward the interests of the business community are minimal. In fact, since 1995, the Israeli polity has seen a series of clashes between two elite groups, the first composed of the Supreme Court justices and the higher functionaries in the attorney general's office (in the Ministry of Justice) and the second composed of a group of businesspersons with strong ties within the party system. These controversies arose when some party leaders and businesspersons associated with them were brought to justice due to their involvement in a series of public scandals. The decisions to charge these top political leaders and businesspersons were taken by the attorney general's office, under the close supervision and the approval of the HCJ.[14] These events, combined with the outright activist tendencies of the Court in general, brought an unprecedented wave of public attacks on the Supreme Court (and the HCJ in particular) from political and party leaders as well as top businesspersons affiliated with political parties.[15] These tensions between the Court and older elite groups do not necessarily prove any preferences of the Court toward "have nots" in society. It does suggest, however, that the common assumption that high court justices tend to identify themselves with socioeconomic elite groups in society (Miliband 1969; Scheingold 1974; Funston 1975; Hase & Ruete 1982; Shamir 1990) may not be completely accurate in the case of the HCJ.

Research Methodology

In this study, I sought to examine the relative success rates of "haves" and "have nots" in litigation before the HCJ between 1986 and 1994.[16] I reviewed a sizable sample of the files of the HCJ during this period by systematically checking all HCJ files in the archives of the Supreme Court for every second year included in the research period (i.e. 1986, 1988, 1990,

1992, and 1994).[17] Although this procedure may seem rather cumbersome and demanding, it was essential to acquire a full and accurate picture on the uses of litigation by "haves" and "have nots." The research could not be based on an inquiry into the Court's registers (rather than on checking the files themselves) because the Court's registers do not always contain full and accurate details of the parties involved in the litigation and of the outcome of the cases. Neither could I limit my research only to *published* decisions of the Court for two main reasons. First, not all the Court's decisions are officially published. The process of generating a published opinion is not random and thus samples of published cases would not be representative of all cases (Siegelman & Donohue 1990; Atkins 1990; Songer & Sheehan 1992:238; Albiston 1999). Second, and more important, is that the vast majority of petitions issued to the HCJ do not reach a final judicial disposition, but are settled out of court. A sample relating only to published decisions, or even one that would refer to all cases *disposed of by the court* (even if not officially published), would nevertheless overlook this important segment of out-of-court settlements.[18]

The study of out-of-court settlements is important to fully understanding the outcomes in litigation for a number of reasons. First, studying settlements is important for understanding the very meaning of the term *success*, or a *favorable* outcome in litigation because the analysis of success in litigation should always refer to all the alternative outcomes for the given controversy (Kritzer 1990:135). Second, it is well known that most cases and controversies are settled rather than disposed by a final judicial decision. Because the relative advantage of the "haves" may result from their ability to use strategic bargaining, their relative advantage in litigation may be reflected in settled cases more intensively than in cases that were fully adjudicated and published. In any case, a sample containing only published cases may well be unrepresentative for the whole population of cases in the relevant research arena (Albiston 1999). Moreover, the study of out-of-court settlements is essential from the point of view of Galanter's argument. According to his hypothesis, some sorts of litigators (such as repeat players) are more likely to develop alternative mechanisms for dispute resolution (such as settlements) than others.[19] Last, the study of out-of-court settlements is particularly important in the context of litigation before the HCJ, not only because the vast majority of petitions to the HCJ are so settled, but also because prior research has shown that the study of out-of-court settlements in the HJC may change profoundly our perception of the relative success rates of certain categories of litigation (Dotan 1999).[20]

To estimate the relative success rates of "haves" and "have nots" in the HCJ, one needs to be able to identify cases in which the petitioners belong to one of these groups. This task is not simple, because the HCJ is a forum addressed by all kinds of petitioners and because this analysis refers to the content of the court files, without any independent knowledge of the socioeconomic state of each of the thousands of petitioners whose court files were examined. To overcome this difficulty, I identified some categories of petitioners that *typically* belong to "haves" and "have nots" in society. For "have nots," I examined files of the following groups: welfare services customers, immigrants, disabled people (attacking administrative decisions related to their disability), people suffering from mental disability (related to the issue of the petition), petitioners challenging decisions of social services (such as adoption agencies), prisoners, and petitioners exempt from the duty to pay court fees. For "haves," I analyzed all petitions that were issued by registered companies and business associations. Following prior research, the "haves" category was also divided to identify a "big corporations" category. This category includes litigants such as banks, oil companies, insurance companies, utilities, and airlines as well as major manufacturing, media, and construction companies that possess both substantial resources and recurrent litigation experience differentiating them from the broader category of business (cf. Songer & Sheehan 1992; Sheehan et al. 1992; McCormick 1993). I am well aware that there is no complete correspondence between these categories and the distinction between "haves" and "have nots." Not all immigrants are necessarily indigent,[21] and not every corporation is necessarily a "have." There may well be indigent petitioners that are not included in our sample, and there are wealthy petitioners that did not address the court as corporations. Nevertheless, because court files do not provide direct measures of financial resources of litigants, previous research has used status as proxy for resources (Wheeler et al. 1987; Atkins 1991:885; Songer & Sheehan 1992:238; McCormick 1993; Haynie 1995:374; Farole 1999). The same strategy was adopted here.

One additional factor that should be mentioned before presenting the outcomes of the survey is that in the HCJ the respondents in court are always public agencies (either governmental or municipal). As I argue later, that public agencies are involved in each and every case of litigation before the HCJ has profound implications on this process at large. For the purpose of this stage, however, this fact is brought only to emphasize that, although the petitioners in the HCJ may be either "haves" (business) or "have nots" (or neither of the two), the respondents are always public agencies defending their administrative decisions. Thus, both "haves" and "have nots" meet the same type of respondents in court and it is therefore relatively easy to compare their success rates.[22]

SUCCESS RATES OF "HAVES" AND "HAVE NOTS" IN THE HCJ

The outcomes of the comparison between success rates of "haves" and "have nots" in the study are presented in Table 7.1. We see that the "haves" enjoy considerable advantage over "have nots" in litigation before the HCJ when one looks at the figures of cases disposed by the Court. Corporations won in court 20 out of 78 cases in the sample that reached final judicial disposition (25.64%: columns A + B divided by the sum of columns A + B + C). "Have nots" won only 19 out of 191 cases (9.9%) disposed by the HCJ.[23] On the other hand, in out-of-court settlements, the success rates of "have nots" are numerically higher than those of the "haves" included in the research population; corporations succeeded fully or in part in 65.5% of the settled cases (97 cases in columns E + F divided by 148 cases in columns D + E + F), whereas "have nots" succeeded fully or in part in 69.5% of the cases that were settled out of court (139 of 200 cases).[24] This difference is not, however, statistically significant.

From Table 7.1, we learn that, by and large, "haves" still enjoy a significant advantage over "have nots" in litigation before the HCJ. The overall gross success rate of corporations in the sample—that is, the number of cases in which they achieved their aims fully or partly in court decisions (columns A + B in Table 7.1) and in out-of-court settlements (columns E + F), divided by the total number of petitions issued by businesses in our sample—is 43.82%. The net success rate of "haves"—that is, after subtracting from the total number of petitions those petitions that cannot be classified as either success or failure (column G)—reaches 51.77%. The net success rate of big corporations is even higher and reaches 56.10%. The overall net success rate of "have nots" is significantly lower: it reaches only about 40% (whereas the overall gross success rate of "have nots" in our sample is 30.5%).

On the face of the matter, these figures seem to say that the special characteristics of the HCJ did not offset the disadvantage of "have nots" in litigation. A more detailed look at the outcomes of the study, however, demonstrates that the situation is much more complex. First, although success rates of "have nots" are lower in comparison with those of the businesses, they are similar to the general (gross) success rates in the HCJ (which is 30%).[25] Second, as Table 7.1 shows, success rates of different categories of "have nots" vary. For example, although the success rates of prisoners (31.65%) and other "have nots" (26.19%) are low, the success rate of immigrants is much higher (60.53%) and, in fact, significantly higher even than the success rate of the "haves."[26]

Third, as already mentioned, although success rates of "haves" are still higher than those of "have nots," the gap between the two groups is significant only when one looks at the outcomes in cases fully disposed by the

TABLE 7.1

Success Rates in HCJ, 1986–1994

| | Outcome | | | | | | | | | Success Rate | |
| | Court Decision | | | Out-of-Court Settlement | | | | | | | |
Petitioner Category	Full Success (A)	Partial Success[a] (B)	Dismissal (C)	With-drawal (D)	Partial Success[b] (E)	Full Success[c] (F)	Other[d] (G)	Total		Gross[e]	Net[f]
Haves	12	10	58	51	71	22	43	267		43.07%	51.34%
Have-nots											
Handicapped	4	5	48	15	27	11	20	130		36.15	42.73
Welfare	1	0	10	4	7	2	5	29		34.48	41.67
Immigrants	5	1	17	13	24	16	4	80		57.50	60.53
Prisoners[g]	1	1	73	22	13	29	87	226		19.47	31.65
Other have-nots[h]	1	0	24	7	6	4	10	52		21.15	26.19
Total for have-nots	12	7	172	61	77	62	126	517		30.56	40.41

There is some dissimilarity between the data presented here and the data included in the paper presented at the conference "Do the 'Haves' Still Come Out Ahead?" at the Institute of Legal Studies, University of Wisconsin Law School, Madison, Wisconsin, May 1–2, 1998. The differences derive from additional verifications made on the files included in the research population that brought me to rule out some files that we initially classified as belonging to have-nots. These changes bear no significant influence on the outcomes of the research.

[a] Included in this category are court decisions in which petitioners achieved anything between more than nothing and less than everything they asked for.

[b] Included in this category are settlements in which petitioners achieved anything between more than nothing and less than everything they asked for in the original petition by an out-of-court settlement. Significant achievements for petitioners by the way of settlement are by no mean rare in our sample. One common outcome classified under this category is when the respondent agency agreed—under the Court's recommendation—to reexamine the petitioner's case. In such a case, according to our experience, the petitioner had significant chances that the renewed administrative process would yield a decision in her favor. In some cases included in this category the settlement was ratified by a court decision after it was

[c] Included in this category are all the cases in which the respondent agreed to allow the petitioner everything that was requested in the original petition.

[d] This category refers to cases that can not be classified as either success or failure, such as cases referred to another tribunal; cases that are still pending; cases in which the outcome can not be discerned from the file, and petitions that became moot or were dismissed for nonprosecution.

[e] The number of cases in which petitioners achieved fully or partly their aims in court decisions (columns A + B) and in out-of-court settlements (columns E + F) divided by the total number of petitions issued (%).

[f] The number of cases in which the petitioners succeeded divided by the total number of cases after subtracting from the total the figure included in column G (%).

[g] Including only Israeli prisoners and excluding Palestinian petitioners (of which the vast majority were arrested due to security reasons).

[h] Including petitioners exempt from Court fees, mentally disabled petitioners (whose petition is related to their disability) and other petitioners attacking decisions of social services agencies.

Court. This gap diminishes in out-of-court settlements. In fact, in out-of-court settlements "have nots" seemed to do better than "haves." Although the higher success rate for "have nots" is not statistically significant, the tendency in direction is at odds with Galanter's assumption that "haves" should be better equipped than "have nots" to reach favored outcomes through settlements due to their higher ability to estimate the chances to win in court as well as their ability to engage in strategic litigation (Galanter 1974:100). This finding suggests that there is something in the out-of-court mechanism of the HCJ that may work to ameliorate the inherent inferiority of "have nots."

THE EFFECTS OF LEGAL REPRESENTATION ON SUCCESS RATES

A second part of the study explored the effects of legal representation on the chances of "have nots" in litigation before the HCJ. I examined success rates of all petitions to the HCJ during the time span of the research in which the petitioners were not represented by lawyers. I also examined success rates of "have nots" who were not represented. The findings are presented in Table 7.2. From the table, we can see that, despite the activist nature of the litigation before the HCJ, representation by lawyer is still a deciding factor when success rates are calculated.[27] Generally, petitioners who were not represented did poorly in the HCJ (net success rate of around 24%). Further analysis of Table 7.2 also enables us to complement our understanding of the practices of the Court toward "have nots." We can see that there is a clear difference between "have nots" with legal representation (net success rate of 58.64%) and nonrepresented "have nots" (net success rate of 27.5%). In fact, the success rates of represented "have nots" in our study were found to be higher than those of "haves" (in Table 7.1). These findings strongly support the assumption that the real reason for "have nots'" relative inferiority in the HCJ is, still, lack of adequate resources for legal representation.[28]

The data in Table 7.2 provide additional perspectives on the Court's attitude toward "have nots." We can see that although, in general, nonrepresented "have nots" had a low rate of success, they did better in comparison with other nonrepresented petitioners (total net success rate of 27.5%, compared with the total net success rate of "other nonrepresented" petitioners, 21.64%). This finding suggests that—the issue of legal representation aside—there is not strong discrimination in the practices of the Court (or its surrounding mechanisms) against "have nots." Therefore, it seems that the practices of the Court contribute to ameliorate, to some extent, the detrimental effects of lack of representation of "have nots" resorting to the Court.[29]

TABLE 7.2

Rate of Success Related to Legal Representation, 1986–1994

| | Outcome | | | | | | | | Success Rate | |
| | Court Decision | | | Out-of-Court Settlement | | | | Total | | |
Petitioner Category	Full Success	Partial Success	Dismissal	With-drawal	Partial Success	Full Success	Other		Gross	Net
All have-nots	12	7	172	61	77	62	126	517	30.56%	40.41%
Have-nots, represented	10	4	39	28	50	31	18	180	52.78	58.64
Have-nots, nonrepresented[a]	2	3	133	33	27	31	108	337	18.69	27.51
Other, nonrepresented[b]	4	4	218	68	31	40	97	462	17.10	21.64
All nonrepresented	6	7	351	101	58	71	205	799	17.77	23.91

[a] The majority of unrepresented have-nots were prisoners. The success rates of unrepresented prisoners and other unrepresented have-nots did not differ remarkably. The overall net success rate of unrepresented have-nots excluding prisoners is 28.35%, i.e., only slightly higher than the success rates of all unrepresented have-nots (27.51%).

[b] All except two of the cases included in this category are petitions by neither have-nots nor haves. All but two of the haves in our sample were represented in court.

DISCUSSION

What can we learn about the validity of Galanter's theory from the comparison of these findings and the findings of previous research? Obviously, any attempt to test the validity of the party capability theory on the ground of a foreign system that differs substantially from that of the United States on legal, institutional, social, and cultural levels, runs the risk of serious distortions and misapprehensions. Nevertheless, the comparison of these findings with those of previous research does seem to offer some interesting insights.

Sheehan et al. suggested that ideological considerations are more likely to influence cases reaching supreme courts that have strong control of their dockets. Correspondingly, they argued that differences in status are less likely to influence cases reaching the U.S. Supreme Court. Cases that are important enough to be granted a certiorari are likely to have a sufficient cachet to attract quality counsel as well as financial support (Sheehan et al. 1992:465). Haynie, on the other hand, showed that ideological considerations that work in favor of "have nots" may be prevalent also in judicial forums that do not employ a strong screening process of cases before they dispose them. The Israeli HCJ conforms to the model of the Supreme Court of the Philippines as described by Haynie in two major respects. First, the Court's docket, unlike its U.S. counterpart, contains many routine decisions (Haynie 1994:756) Second, the Court is heavily influenced in its decisions by institutional considerations, and more particularly, by its wish to preserve its public image and increase its legitimacy (ibid., p. 769; Dotan 1999). Both in the Philippines and in the HCJ ideological and institutional considerations of the court seem to work in favor of "have nots" despite the lack of a strong screening process and agenda control.

Some of our findings seem to conform with Galanter's party capability theory. Big corporations succeeded in litigation more than other businesses. The "haves" in general did better than "have nots," and "have nots" did significantly better when they had legal counsel. On the other hand, when "have nots" were represented by lawyers, there is nothing in the findings to corroborate the claim that the "haves" came out ahead. In fact, the findings suggest that represented "have nots" enjoyed success rates somewhat higher than those of the "haves" (see Tables 7.1 and 7.2). The relative advantage of "have nots" is reflected not only in the comparison between the success rates of represented "have nots" and "haves" discussed above, but also in the comparison between the success rates of nonrepresented "have nots" vis-à-vis the general population of nonrepresented petitioners (Table 7.2). Here again we see that although the success rates of nonrepresented "have nots" are significantly lower than those of represented "have nots," they are still significantly higher than other nonrepresented petitioners. Much in accord with Haynie's argument, I suggest that this advantage of "have nots" over other petitioners to the HCJ may be explained by the ideological propensities of the justices of the HCJ as well as institutional considerations in relation to the issue of the legitimacy of the Court in the eyes of the Israeli public. As in the Philippines, the Israeli HCJ sees its legitimacy tied directly to its decisions. Preserving the image of the Court as "the protector of the little person" is important for preserving the legitimacy in the eyes of the public and for defending its institutional autonomy against threats on behalf of other political forces.[30]

Another issue that our findings raise is the centrality of the role of the government and other public agencies for the understanding of outcomes in litigation. In this study, the respondents in all cases are government agencies. As Table 7.1 shows, the government enjoys extremely high success rates in litigation that reaches final judicial disposition. The finding that public agencies enjoy high success rates in judicial review cases as well as in appellate courts is far from being unique to this study and is corroborated by several other studies (e.g., McCormick 1993; Atkins 1991; Sheehan et al. 1992; Songer & Sheehan 1992). Moreover, as recent research reveals, public agencies are, in fact, the most successful litigant in almost all the surveys that studied outcomes in litigation (Farole 1999; Songer et al. 1999).

There are various possible explanations for this pattern of overall advantage of governments in litigation. Some suggest that governments are successful simply because they are the most capable of all repeat players, possessing the greater resources, expertise, insider knowledge of the judicial process, and other repeat player characteristics (Songer et al. 1999). That government agencies have much higher success rates in litigation than other groups may, however, be explained in terms of resource shortages rather than of the affluence of governments. According to this line of thought, it is resource shortages that lead agencies to litigate only cases where they have high chances of winning, therefore leading to high rates of success (Posner 1972). Yet another explanation relates the strength of public agencies in litigation to substantive legal doctrines that favor their position in litigation, such as the principle that courts should normally defer to the expertise of agency officials (Songer et al. 1999). Finally, it is suggested that governments are successful litigants because they fundamentally differ from other litigants due to their institutional relations with courts, and their key function within the judicial process (Farole 1999).

At this stage, it is impossible, without further research, to rule out any of these explanations for the extraordinary success rates of public agencies in litigation before the HCJ. My findings, however, seem to support the latter explanation that relates the success of the government in litigation to its special status as a party that has an important institutional position in litigation. As this study shows, the full picture of success in litigation cannot be learned by focusing only on the outcomes of court decisions. A fuller picture is revealed by looking into the outcomes of out-of-court settlements. When out-of-court settlements are taken into account, we see that the success rates of petitioners in general are considerably higher than appears from studying cases disposed by judicial decisions exclusively. We also see that the gap between the success rates of "haves" and "have nots" in litigation against the government is considerably narrowed due to the impact of out-of-court settlements. In other words, we see that the government agencies that appear before the HCJ tend to settle many cases to allow petitioners significant achievements in litigation, and this settlement mechanism works to ameliorate considerably the inferiority of "have nots" (vis-à-vis the "haves"). That the inclusion of settlements in the analysis of litigation outcomes results in higher success rates for the petitioners does not rule out any of the above-mentioned explanations for the success of government in litigation. The findings concerning the impact of the settlement mechanism in favor of "have nots," however, can be explained only by regard to the special institutional status of the government, and the government lawyers in litigation before the HCJ.

The explanation for the success rates of "have nots" in settlements has to do with the function of the lawyers representing the government before the HCJ. The State of Israel (including all agencies that are part of the central government) is represented in the HCJ by a small department (normally composed of no more than 10 lawyers) in the office of the attorney general (High Court of Justice Department, or HCJD). Because the lawyers in this department represent the respondents in the HCJ in over 80% of the petitions, they appear before the 14 justices of the HCJ almost daily.[31] Previous study shows that these lawyers tend to internalize the ideological propensities of the Court and serve as its extension rather than as merely representatives of state agencies. Accordingly, these lawyers tend to form settlements in the vast majority of cases that reach the Court, in many cases even before the litigation starts (Dotan 1999).[32] In other words, the settlement mechanism of the HCJD may serve the interests of "have nots," whenever the government lawyers believe that, according to the doctrines and policies set by the Court itself, the petitioner's needs deserve to be met. Correspondingly, although functioning as the extension of the Court, the HCJD enjoys a high degree of trust on behalf of the judges of the HCJ. Their factual statements are taken for granted; their offers for settlements win a high degree of credibility and attention; and when they decide to litigate the case up to a final judicial disposition, they seldom face defeat (Shamir 1990; Kretzmer 1994;

Dotan 1999).[33] This support structure, through the function of the HCJD lawyers, also ensures the effectiveness of the application of the Court's policy in the field of indigents' rights (cf. Epp 1998).[34]

Conclusion

In this study, I found that in litigation before the Israeli High Court of Justice, the "haves" enjoyed only a limited advantage over "have nots" in litigation outcomes. It was also found that when "have nots" were represented by legal counsel, the "haves" did not come out ahead before this forum. Ideological propensities of judges and considerations of institutional autonomy can even out, or at least ameliorate to some extent, the inherent inferiority of "have nots" in litigation. It was also found that those mechanisms that worked in favor of "have nots" operated not only in litigation that reached final judicial disposition but also—and even more forcefully—when the litigation was disposed through out-of-court settlements.

This study also supports the need to focus more closely in research regarding outcomes in litigation on the special status and functions of governments and other public agencies. Governments are not only powerful repeat players; they are also key players in the actual process of litigation. The case of litigation before the HCJ shows that government representatives function as an essential part of the mechanism of the Court itself to carry out judicial policies. Studying the special functions of government in litigation is essential for understanding the litigation process.

Notes

Originally published in *Law & Society Review* 33 (4) 1059–80 (1999); reprinted by permission. An earlier version of this research note was presented at the conference "Do the 'Haves' Still Come Out Ahead?" at the Institute of Legal Studies, University of Wisconsin Law School, Madison, 1–2 May 1998. The research was supported in part by the Israel Science Foundation founded by the Israeli Academy for Science and Humanities. I am indebted to Joya Skappa for her excellent work as a research assistant and to Dorit Rubinstein for her assistance with the empirical survey.

Yoav Dotan is a senior lecturer at the Faculty of Law, Hebrew University, Jerusalem, Israel. His areas of interest are public law, law and politics, and the study of cause lawyers. His current research involves a study of government lawyers and their relationship with cause lawyers and interest groups.

1. Although founding his analysis on the premises of this model, Galanter does not overlook that this model of judicial passivity and neutrality is by no means exclusive. He points out that judicial passivity may be uneven (citing Mosier and Soble 1973:63 at footnote 59 on page 120), and he mentions more "active" courts in non-common-law systems (at footnote 60).

2. For a discussion of the applicability of Galanter's theory to South Africa Appellate Division, see Haynie and Devore 1996.

3. Likewise, Songer et al. (1994) argued that in certain areas of litigation, the judge's gender may have significant influence over his or her attitude toward certain types of claims. They found that female judges tended to be more liberal in employment discrimination cases than male judges.

4. In 1993, for example, the Court dealt with over 1,400 appellate cases, a similar number of *cassation* cases, and over 1,000 other lawsuits apart from the 1,171 HCJ petitions that were disposed by it during that year. The number of cases increases constantly each year, according to the Central Bureau of Statistics of Israel. The question of how (if at all) 14 judges (normally sitting in panels of three) can manage to cope with such a huge caseload and still function both as the Supreme Court and the principal tribunal for judicial review is beyond the scope of this note. The reality of a heavy caseload bears, however, on some of the practices of this court that are described below.

5. The vast majority of cases handled by the HCJ are disposed at the stage of the preliminary hearing without any order nisi being issued. According to the data of the Central Bureau of Statistics of Israel, of 4,266 cases disposed by the HCJ between 1985 and 1993, in only 886 cases was an order nisi issued.

6. The general practice of Israeli courts is to impose costs on the losing party on a "no fault" basis. This practice, which is prevalent in civil law litigation, is less commonly implemented in litigation before the HCJ.

7. We found that out of 172 in our sample of petitions issued by "have nots" dismissed by the HCJ, only in 14 cases (8.1%) did the Court impose costs on the petitioners. The average amount of costs imposed was around the equivalent of $1,100.

8. In a study of a representative sample of the adult Jewish population in Israel about the attitudes of the Israeli public toward the HCJ, over 66% of the respondents said that they agree to the proposition that the HCJ functions as a "representative of the common citizen," whereas less than 15% objected to it. See Barzilai et al. 1994a:211. The HCJ has enjoyed greater public legitimacy than its U.S. counterpart (Epstein et al. 1994; Barzilai et al. 1994b; Barzilai 1996). The level of trust that the Court enjoys among non-Jewish Israelis is, to some extent, lower than the level expressed by Jewish Israelis. Still, a significant portion of Israeli Palestinians expresses trust in the fairness of the Israeli Justice system (Zureik et al. 1993; Rattner 1994:363; Barzilai 1998).

9. See, for example, H.C. 287/69 *Miron*; H.C. 910/86 *Ressler*; H.C. 5364/94 *Volner*; Segal 1988.

10. Some of these sentiments toward "justice" (in its literal and ordinary sense) have to do with the title of this Court: "The High Court of *Justice*." The institution of the HCJ (i.e., a special court for judicial review cases) was first introduced in Palestine during the period of the British Mandate (1917–1948). It was preserved by Israel after the establishment of the State in 1948 (like the rest of the structure of the court system). The name of the Court, in its original (British) sense, means nothing more than a court of law that deals with cases of judicial review. Therefore, its correct translation into Hebrew should have been "The High Court of Law." Due to inaccuracy in translation, "justice" (*tzedek*) was preserved in its Hebrew title. There-

after, the rhetoric of the Court, as well as the public discourse concerning the HCJ, made extensive use of this title to emphasize the special qualities of the institution (see, e.g., Zamir 1970; Zamir 1975:83–84, 102).

11. The Court rendered some important decisions on the protection of the rights of Palestinian residents of the occupied territories (H.C. 2/79 *El Asad*; H.C. 390/79 *Dawikat*; H.C. 320/80 *Kawasme*; H.C. 168/91 *Morkus*). Nevertheless, critics suggest that despite some successes in "landmark" cases, in the vast majority of cases, the Court failed to address Palestinian grievances. The overall impact of Court's decisions in this field remains the subject of much debate. See Shamir 1990; Kretzmer 1994; Dotan 1999.

12. The current President of the Supreme Court, Justice Aharon Barak, who is widely regarded as the leader of the activist revolution, never practiced law. He was a professor of civil law at the Hebrew University and served as attorney general before being nominated to the Supreme Court. The former Chief Justice Meir Shamgar also served as attorney general before his nomination to the Court. Before that, he served as the chief prosecutor of the IDF (the Israeli Army). Two former deputy presidents, Menachem Elon and Miriam Ben-Porat, also came from the same background (the former from the legal academy and the latter from the attorney general's office). Four of the justices currently serving on the Supreme Court (Barak, Zamir, Heshin, and Beinish) served before their nomination in senior positions in the attorney general's office, another Justice (Dorner) served as a senior military judge, and another (Engelard) was a law professor. All these justices have hardly any experience as private attorneys.

13. The appointment of judges in Israel (including Supreme Court Justices) is also based on a process that is chiefly bureaucratic. Judges are not elected or nominated by holders of political positions. Rather, they are nominated by a special committee composed of three justices of the Supreme Court, two representatives of the Government, two Knesset members, and two members of the bar association. Even though the justices have no formal majority in the committee, the process is known to be dominated by them, and no appointment was ever made without their approval.

14. In the 1990s, the HCJ has intervened in a few major cases in prosecutorial decisions. The Court ordered the attorney general to indict leading figures in the Israeli banking community, and it also ordered the prime minister to discharge ministers, deputy ministers, and senior government officials allegedly involved in scandals. The Court also consistently dismissed any attempt to challenge prosecutorial decisions when the attorney general's office decided to issue indictments against top business or political figures (H.C. 6163/92 *Eisenberg*; H.C. 943/89 *Ganor*; H. C. 7074/93 *Swissa*; H.C. 3094/93 *The Movement for the Quality of Government*; H.C. 4267/93 *Amiti*).

15. See, for instance, Adato 1996; Shehori 1996. A recent article in the *Israeli Bar Association Magazine* expressed the concern that the Supreme Court has become "a branch of the Ministry of Justice" (see Kaluf 1998). The private bar is closely related to the political-business group, and its leaders have been known to make public attacks on the Court.

16. This research period was chosen because the tendencies of the Court to ex-

pand its involvement in public issues became increasingly dominant during these years (H.C. 910/86 *Ressler;* Kretzmer 1990).

17. I could not use only a sample of the files in each year because I had no previous information as to the relative size of the relevant groups of files, which would have enabled me to prepare a proportionate representative sample.

18. HCJ decisions are published in two principal ways. An official publication in print, *Piskei Din*, contains only those decisions considered to have a legal precedential value, but a few commercial publications in the form of electrooptical disk (CD-ROM) claim to contain almost all the decisions rendered by the Court. These sources, however, do not contain out-of-court settlements.

19. See Galanter (1974:110–14), discussing "informal bilateral controls" developed by strategic litigators in some cases.

20. According to the data of the Israeli Ministry of Justice (for 1990–1994), only about 40% of the petitions to the HCJ during that period reached the stage of final disposition by the Court. Accordingly, 31% of the cases were withdrawn by the petitioners, whereas 16% were settled with "full success" for the petitioner. Another 10% were settled with "partial success" for the petitioner. Withdrawals may occur at any stage of the litigation, but they most commonly occur after the preliminary hearing, when the remarks of the justices lead the petitioner to believe that his or her case is weak and that he or she had better withdraw than risk a dismissal that is likely to be accompanied by imposition of costs. Settlements with "full success" for the petitioner are, in essence, cases in which the responding agency gives up its original position and allows the petitioner whatever was asked for. These settlements may happen at a very early stage of litigation, even before any court hearing, when the government lawyers decide that the petition has merits. They may also happen at the stage of the preliminary hearing, when the judges "offer" the respondents to "reevaluate" their position. The parties may bring the settlement for the approval of the Court in the form of a consent decree in some cases, whereas in others they only notify the Court that a settlement was reached. It is not always easy to extract from the file of a case whether and to what extent the outcome was successful from the petitioner's point of view, because the formal procedural measures taken by the parties do not necessarily conform with the actual outcomes. For example, the petitioner may inform the Court that he or she "withdraws" his or her petition, whereas, in fact, the reason for the withdrawal is that the government agreed to allow whatever was originally asked for. The outcomes reported by the Ministry of Justice, as well as the outcomes reported in the current research, however, relate to the actual outcomes of the case rather than to the formal procedural format used by the parties to close the file.

21. Israel has long had a strong policy of encouraging immigration and offers immigrants significant economic benefits. Therefore, it may be argued that immigrants petitioning the HCJ to enjoy such special benefits cannot be regarded as "have nots." My sampling brings this point into consideration; see note 26.

22. In some cases, there are additional respondents besides the administrative agency, such as a private party, who may be adversely affected by a decision in favor of the petitioner.

23. In general, the success rates of petitioners to the HCJ are very low in cases

that reach the stage of final judicial disposition (see note 33), whereas most cases in which petitioners achieve all or some of their goals are disposed by out-of-court settlements. The reality that "most cases are settled" is, of course, by no means unique to litigation before the HCJ. For the centrality of settlements (and the process of bargaining toward settlements) in ordinary litigation see, for example, Kritzer 1991.

24. The success rate of petitioners classified as big business in settlements is 73% (38 cases in columns E + F divided by 52).

25. According to the High Court of Justice Department (HCJD) in the Ministry of Justice (data relating to 1990–1994, $N = 3,372$). The department does not have data relating to years before 1990. The figure refers to the gross success rate of all petitions in which the respondents were represented by the HCJD throughout this period (i.e., more than 80% of the petitions that were disposed by the HCJ during the period).

26. It may be argued that not all immigrants to Israel are "have nots" and that some of the immigrants seek the Court to enjoy special benefits related to the policies of the Israeli government to encourage immigration (see note 21). To check the possible influence of this argument on the findings, I went over all the cases initiated by immigrants in the sample. Out of 80 cases of immigrants, I found 44 cases in which the petitioners could *clearly* be classified as "have nots" (such as foreign workers petitioning against deportation decrees, immigrants who were in custody and petitioned for their release). The cases in this group had nothing to do with special benefits allowed to immigrants. In the remaining 36 cases, the issue of the petitions was related to immigrant rights and therefore could involve also demands for immigrant benefits (although it is still quite likely that most petitioners in this group were of low socioeconomic status because most of them immigrated to Israel from the former Soviet Union). I found that the net success rate of the petitioners in the first group (of the "poor immigrants") was still high (54.76%), although it was lower than the success rate of the immigrants belonging to the second group (67.65%).

27. In this respect, the outcomes of the current study correspond with other studies dealing with the issue of legal representation in litigation; see, for example, Genn (1993) and Galanter (1974:114, n. 45). Representation has been proved as a factor that increases the chances of the poor to succeed in litigation; see Adler and Bradley (1975); Lawrence (1990); Monsma and Lempert (1992). Although petitioners to the HCJ are allowed to appear without representation, they are not allowed to be represented by nonlawyers (cf. Kritzer 1997:100).

28. The factor of legal representation can also explain the variance in success rates of different categories of "have nots." For example, although according to Table 7.2 less than 40% of the "have nots" were represented, the rate of representation of immigrants was found to be much higher (around 80%), which can explain their relative high success rate in Table 1. Unlike some other countries, Israel has no legal aid system allowing state support for representation of the poor in courts. Some groups of "have nots" (such as Palestinian residents of the occupied territories) enjoy the services of nongovernmental organizations specializing in HCJ litigation, but there are no such organizations concentrating on providing legal representation for indigents in general.

29. One possible explanation for the low success rates of nonrepresented petitioners is the relative weakness of their cases. The ease of access to the HCJ enables any person to petition to the Court with hardly any mechanism checking the validity of his or her claims. It may be assumed that the lawyers function as a screening mechanism preventing some of the weaker petitions to be issued. This fact can serve as a caveat against drawing direct conclusions from the comparison of success rates of represented and nonrepresented petitioners to the HCJ. This caveat, however, does not apply to the comparison between the success rates of different categories of nonrepresented petitioners, such as "have nots" and other nonrepresented petitioners.

30. Israel has yet to form a complete formal written constitution. Therefore, the Knesset (Parliament) can infringe on the Court's powers by legislation endorsed by a regular majority. The legitimacy of the Court therefore serves as a vital shield against such attempts to curtail the Court's jurisdiction made on behalf of opposing political forces. See Sharfman 1993; Barak-Erez 1995; Hofnung 1996; Dotan 1998.

31. From the Central Bureau of Statistics. The HCJD represents the respondents in all the petitions involving agencies of the government of Israel, excluding only petitions issued solely against local authorities.

32. The mechanism of settlements formed by the HCJD is also necessary, from the Court's point of view, to ease its heavy caseload. See note 4 and Dotan 1999.

33. According to the data of the Central Bureau of Statistics, out of 4,266 petitions against government agencies during the period of 1985 to 1993, only in 190 cases (i.e., 4.45%) did the petitioner win by a final judicial disposition. The bureau has no data concerning the outcomes of out-of-court settlements.

34. Another interesting aspect of this support structure is the ability of the judicial system to create *legal precedents* through settlements. It is normally assumed that settlements are inferior to judicial decisions in the sense that they lack precedential impact on similar cases (Fiss 1984; Albiston 1999). This assumption, however, does not necessarily apply to the case of the HCJ. On many occasions, settlements are made between organized parties (i.e., the HCJD and the pertinent nongovernmental organization that represents the petitioner). In such cases, settlements do create precedents because both parties assume that the same achievement allowed to the individual petitioner will also apply to any other petitioner in a similar situation that will be represented by the same organization (Dotan 1999).

References

Adato, Edna (1996) "Netanyahu Reproves the 'Irresponsible Attacks on the Supreme Court,'" *Yediot Aharonot*, 28 Nov., p. 19 (in Hebrew).

Adler, M., & A. Bradley, eds. (1975) *Justice, Discretion, and Poverty: Supplementary Benefit Appeal Tribunals in Britain*. London: Professional Books.

Albiston, Catherine (1999) "The Rule of Law and the Litigation Process: The Paradox of Losing by Winning," 33 *Law & Society Rev.* 869–910.

Atkins, Burton M. (1990) "Communication of Appellate Decisions: A Multivariable Model for Understanding the Selection of Cases for Publication," 24 *Law & Society Rev.* 1171–96.

Atkins, Burton M. (1991) "Party Capability Theory as an Explanation for Intervention Behavior in the English Court of Appeal," 35 *American J. of Political Science*
881–903.

Barak-Erez, Daphne (1995) "From an Unwritten Constitution to Written Constitution: The Israeli Challenge in American Perspective," 26 *Columbia Human Rights
Law Rev.* 309–55.

Barzilai, Gad (1996) "Courts as Hegemonic Institutions: Bagatz (HCJ) in a Comparative Perspective." Presented at "Israel in a Comparative Perspective: The Dynamics of Change Conference," Univ. of California, Berkeley (2–4 Sept.).

——— (1998) "States against Communities: Communities against States: Minorities
and Law in Israel." Presented at the Annual Meeting of the American Political
Science Association, Boston (3–6 Sept).

Barzilai, Gad, Ephraim Yuchtman-Yaar, & Zeev Segal (1994a) *The Israeli Supreme
Court and the Israeli Public.* Tel Aviv: Papyrus, Tel Aviv Univ. Press (Hebrew with
English abstract).

Barzilai, Gad, Ephraim Yuchtman-Yaar, & Zeev Segal (1994b) "Supreme Court and
Public Opinion: General Paradigms and the Israeli Case," 3 *Law & Courts* (Winter) 3–6.

Baum, Lawrence (1998) *The Supreme Court,* 6th ed. Washington, DC: Congressional
Quarterly.

Dotan, Yoav (1998) "Judicial Review and Political Accountability: The Case of the
High Court of Justice in Israel," 32 *Israel Law Rev.* 448–74.

——— (1999) "Judicial Rhetoric, Government Lawyers, and Human Rights: The
Case of the Israeli High Court of Justice during the *Intifada,*" 33 *Law & Society
Rev.* 319–63.

Dunworth, Terence, & Joel Rogers (1996) "Corporations in Court: Big Business Litigation in U.S. Federal Courts, 1971–1991," 21 *Law & Social Inquiry* 497–592.

Epp, Charles R. (1998) *The Rights Revolution.* Chicago: Chicago Univ. Press.

Epstein, Lee, Jeffrey A. Segal, Harold J. Spaeth, & Walker G. Thomas (1994) *The Supreme Court Compendium: Data, Decisions, and Developments.* Washington, DC:
Congressional Quarterly.

Farole, Donald J., Jr. (1999) "Reexamining Litigant Success in State Supreme
Courts," 33 *Law & Society Rev.* 1043–58.

Fiss, Owen M. (1984) "Against Settlement," 93 *Yale Law J.* 1073–90.

Funston, Richard (1975) "The Supreme Court and Critical Elections," 69 *American
Political Science Rev.* 795–844.

Galanter, Marc (1974) "Why the 'Haves' Come Out Ahead: Speculations on the
Limits of Legal Change," 9 *Law & Society Rev.* 95–160.

Genn, Hazel (1993) "Tribunals and Informal Justice," 56 *Modern Law Rev.* 393–411.

Hase, Friedhelm, & Matthias Ruete (1982) "Constitutional Court and Constitutional
Ideology in West Germany," 10 *International J. of the Sociology of Law* 267–76.

Haynie, Stacia L. (1994) "Resource Inequalities and Litigation Outcomes in the
Philippine Supreme Court," 56 *Journal of Politics* 752–72.

Haynie, Stacia L., & Joseph Devore (1996) "Judging in an Unjust Regime: South
Africa's Appellate Division, 1950–1990," 17 *American Rev. of Politics* 243–63.

Hofnung, Menachem (1996) "The Unintended Consequences of Unplanned Legislative Reform: Constitutional Politics in Israel," 44 *American J. of Comparative Law* 585–604.

Kaluf, Israel (1998) "District Judges as Extras," 3 *Lawyer* (March) 26–29 (in Hebrew).

Kretzmer, David (1990) "Forty Years of Public Law," 23 *Israel Law Rev.* 341–55 (in Hebrew).

——— (1994) "Judicial Review over Demolition and Sealing of Houses in the Occupied Territories," in I. Zamir, ed., *Klinghoffer Book on Public Law.* Jerusalem, Harry Sacher Institute (in Hebrew).

Kritzer, Herbert M. (1990) *The Justice Broker.* New York: Oxford Univ. Press.

——— (1991) *Let's Make a Deal: Understanding the Negotiation Process in Ordinary Litigation.* Madison: Univ. of Wisconsin Press.

——— (1997) "Rethinking Barriers to Legal Practice," 81 *Judicature* (Nov.-Dec.) 100–103.

Lawrence, Susan E. (1990) *The Poor in Court.* Princeton, NJ: Princeton Univ. Press.

McCormick, Peter (1993) "Party Capability Theory and Appellate Success in the Supreme Court of Canada," 26 *Canadian J. of Political Science* 523–40.

Miliband, Ralph (1969) *The State of Capitalist Society.* London: Weidenfeld and Nicolson.

Monsma, Karl, & Richard Lempert (1992) "The Value of Counsel: 20 Years of Representation before a Public Housing Eviction Board," 26 *Law & Society Rev.* 627–67.

Mosier, Marilyn M., & Richard A. Soble (1973) "Modern Legislation, Metropolitan Court, Minuscule Results: A Study of Detroit's Landlord-Tenant Court," 7 *Univ. of Michigan J. of Law Reform* 63.

Posner, Richard A. (1972) "The Behavior of Administrative Agencies," 1 *J. of Legal Studies* 305–47.

Rattner, Arye (1994) "The Margins of Justice: Attitudes towards the Law and Legal System Among Jews and Arabs in Israel," 6 *International J. of Public Opinion Research* 358–70.

Scheingold, Stuart A. (1974) *The Politics of Rights.* New Haven, CT: Yale Univ. Press.

Segal, Jeffery A., & Albert D. Cover (1989) "Ideological Values and Votes of the U.S. Supreme Court Justices," 83 *American Political Science Rev.* 557–65.

Segal, Jeffrey A., & Harold J. Spaeth (1993) *The Supreme Court and the Attitudinal Model.* New York: Cambridge University Press.

Segal, Zeev (1988) *Israeli Democracy.* Tel Aviv: Ministry of Defense.

Shamir, Ronen (1990) "'Landmark Cases' and the Reproduction of Legitimacy: The Case of Israel's High Court of Justice," 24 *Law & Society Rev.* 781–805.

Sharfman, Daphna (1993) *Living without a Constitution: Civil Rights in Israel.* New York: M. E. Sharp.

Sheehan, Reginald S., William Mishler, & Donald S. Songer (1992) "Ideology, Status, and the Differential Success of Direct Parties before the Supreme Court," 86 *American J. of Political Science* 464–71.

Shehori, Dalia (1996) "Rt. Hon. Justice Shamgar: The Attack on HCJ Is Unwarranted," *Ha'aretz* (18 Nov.), p. 12.

Siegelman, Peter, & John J. Donohue (1990) "Studying the Iceberg from Its Tip: A

Comparison of Published and Unpublished Employment Discrimination Cases," 24 *Law & Society Rev.* 1133–69.

Songer, Donald R., Sue Davis, & Susan Haire (1994) "A Reappraisal of Diversification in Federal Courts: Gender Effects in the Courts of Appeal," 56 *J. of Politics* 425–39.

Songer, Donald R., & Reginald S. Sheehan (1992) "Who Wins on Appeal? Upperdogs and Underdogs in the United States Courts of Appeals," 36 *American J. of Political Science* 235–58.

Songer, Donald R., Reginald S. Sheehan, & Susan Brodie Haire (1999) "Do the 'Haves' Come Out Ahead over Time? Applying Galanter's Framework to Decisions of the U.S. Courts of Appeals, 1925–1988," 33 *Law & Society Rev.* 811–32.

Wheeler, Stanton, Bliss Cartwright, Robert A. Kagan, & Lawrence M. Friedman (1987) "Do the 'Haves' Come Out Ahead? Winning and Losing in State Supreme Courts, 1870–1970," 21 *Law & Society Rev.* 403–45.

Zamir, Itzhak (1970) "Justice in the High Court of Justice," 26 *Hapraklit* 212–29 (in Hebrew).

——— (1975) *Adjudication in Administrative Cases.* Jerusalem: Harry Sacher Institute (in Hebrew).

——— (1990) "Public Law—Revolution or Progress?" 19 *Mishpatim* 563–71 (in Hebrew).

Zureik, Elia, Fouad Moughrabi, & Vincent F. Sacco (1993) "Perception of Legal Inequality in Deeply Divided Societies: The Case of Israel," 25 *International J. of Middle East Studies* 423–42.

Cases Cited

H.C. 287/69 Miron v. Minister of Labor, 24(1) P.D. 337.

H.C. 2/79 El Asad v. Minister of Interior, 34(1) P.D. 505.

H.C. 390/79 Dawikat v. Government of Israel, 34(1) P.D. 1.

H.C. 320/80 Kawasme et al. v. Minister of Defense, 35(3) P.D. 113.

H.C. 910/86 Ressler v. Minister of Defense, 42(2) P.D. 441.

H.C. 153/87 Shakdiel v. Minister for Affairs of Religion, 42(2) P.D. 221.

H.C. 953/87 Poraz v. Mayor of Tel-Aviv, 42(2) P.D. 309.

H.C. 943/89 Ganor v. Attorney General, 44(2) P.D. 485.

H.C. 168/91 Morkus v. Minister of Defense, 35(1) P.D. 467.

H.C. 3473/92 The National Council for the Welfare of the Child v. The Minister for Labor and Welfare, 37(1) P.D. 148.

H.C. 6163/92 Eisenberg v. Minister of Housing, 47(2) P.D. 229.

H.C. 3094/93 The Movement for the Quality of Government v. Government of Israel, 47(5) P.D. 404.

H.C. 4267/93 Amiti v. Prime-Minister of Israel, 47(5) P.D. 441.

H.C. 7074/93 Swissa v. Attorney General, 48(2) P.D. 749.

H.C. 7081/93 Botzer v. Municipal Council of Makabim-Reut, 40(1) P.D. 19.

H.C. 453/94 Shdulat Ha'nashim B'Israel v. Minister of Transportation, 38(5) P.D. 542.

H.C. 721/94 El-Al v. Danilovich, 48(5) P.D. 749.
H.C. 2148/94 Gelbert v. President of the Supreme Court, 48(3) P.D. 573.
H.C. 4541/94 Miller v. The Minister of Defense, 39(4) P.D. 103.
H.C. 5364/94 Volner v. The Labor Party, 49(1) P.D. 758.
H.C. 4671/98 Awad Abu Fariach v. The Education Authority for the Bedouins in the Negev (Aug. 23, 1998).

KATHRYN HENDLEY, PETER MURRELL,
AND RANDI RYTERMAN

8

Do Repeat Players Behave Differently in Russia?

Contractual and Litigation Behavior of Russian Enterprises

Adapting the Repeat Player Concept to Russia

In his seminal article, Galanter (1974) argued that repeat players (RPs) are particularly well equipped to use law and the legal system to their advantage. His analysis is based on the U.S. experience, both in terms of the nature of the parties and the institutional environment. This article examines whether Galanter's RP concept smoothly crosses borders, helping to decipher the law-related behavior of enterprises in the new Russian market economy. In doing so, the article offers contributions on two levels. First, it is a case study that examines whether theories and concepts developed in one political, institutional, and social milieu are applicable in another, quite different, context. Second, it provides what is, to our knowledge, the first statistical study examining the determinants of law-related activity in post-Soviet Russia.

For Galanter, the ideal typical RP is an individual or entity that participates or contemplates participating actively in the legal system, "has low stakes in the outcome of any one case, and . . . has the resources to pursue its long-run interests" (ibid., p. 98). He juxtaposes the RP against the one shotter (OS) and outlines the advantages that the RP typically has over the OS. Some of these advantages are related to experience and resources. RPs learn through repeated experiences what works, and they have legal specialists readily available to help in translating experience into improved strategies. They are generally able to exert control over transactions, and they enjoy a reputation within their community for bargaining in good faith that facilitates settlements, when desired by the RP. In contrast to OSs, RPs focus on the long run. Often, their goal is to change the rules—both substantive and procedural—to their benefit. To that end, RPs build and maintain close working relationships with officials at key institutions.

Not surprisingly, Galanter's concept of an RP, which is grounded in U.S. experience, cannot be applied in a whole cloth fashion to Russia. The differences in the institutional landscape and the expectations of the parties have to be taken into account, but the basic components can be replicated. We therefore follow Galanter's RP concept closely in developing and operationalizing the concept of a Russian repeat player (RRP). We do so by breaking down Galanter's RP concept into its four constituent parts: (1) degree of control over the structure and terms of the transaction, (2) access to legal specialists, (3) availability of resources, and (4) strength of relationship with political authorities. Our data on Russian enterprises allow us to construct measures that operationalize each of these four elements separately, leading to the construction of four variables that can be used in statistical tests.

Galanter argues that variations along each of these four dimensions give rise to different types of behavior when parties are confronted with legal disputes. By testing three hypotheses that stem from Galanter's analysis, this article analyzes whether similar relationships are present in Russia. The first hypothesis is that RRPs tend to be more aggressive and innovative in their interactions with trading partners. The second is that RRPs are concerned principally with altering the "rules of the game" to their long-term advantage, rather than focusing on the short-term goal of the outcome of individual cases. The third is that RRPs rarely litigate their disputes with other RRPs.

In all these analyses, the results confound the predictions that would arise by transplanting Galanter's theories to Russia. Being an RRP does not give rise to the same sorts of behavioral patterns as Galanter found among RPs in the U.S. context. Stopping the analysis at this step, however, would obviously be discomfiting because it might leave the reader wondering what factors can explain law-related behavior in Russia and indeed whether our results on RPs reflect some extreme randomness in either the Russian environment or our data, so that no theories would work. Thus, the empirical analyses presented here go a step beyond the parameters of Galanter's original framework examining additional explanatory variables.

For each of the three hypotheses—aggressiveness and innovativeness in interactions, playing for the rules, and intensity of litigation—we examine a series of additional explanatory variables. The choice of variables to examine is driven by common sense and the prevailing assumptions within the scholarly literature. For example, we investigate whether bigger and older enterprises enjoy a comparative advantage in legal matters; whether there is a regional effect, with Moscow showing the first signs of the effect of globalization; and how the nature of the enterprise's transactions affects its later interactions with the legal system. In all instances, we emphasize the approach of Galanter in looking at how the nature of the parties affects the operation of the legal system. Finally, we explore why business litigation has a very different quality in Russia than it does in the United States in that RRPs are suing one another with regularity, whereas Galanter found RP versus RP litigation to be relatively unusual. Our inquiry suggests that this dissimilarity might stem from differences in the structure of the legal profession and the courts.

The analysis draws on the results of a survey of 328 Russian industrial enterprises conducted between May and August of 1997. In each enterprise, Russian surveyors administered different survey instruments to four top managers: the general director and the heads of the sales, purchasing (supply), and legal departments. The sample included enterprises from six regions or oblasts (Moscow, Barnaul, Novosibirsk, Ekaterinburg, Voronezh, Saratov), with each oblast represented roughly equally. The enterprises were concentrated among 10 industrial sectors.[1] Their size ranges from 30 to 17,000 employees, with a median of 300 and a mean of 980. Most of the enterprises were established during the Soviet era, and about three-fourths (77%) are privatized. In virtually all those privatized, some stock is in the hands of insiders, and nearly a third were entirely owned by insiders. Outsiders (nonemployees of the enterprise) held some stock in 60% of the enterprises.

A road map to this article is the following. In the ensuing section, we operationalize the concept of the RRP, making clear how this concept ties to Galanter's notions as well as detailing its implementation using our Russian survey data. This process leads to the construction of four variables, each measuring a separate aspect of RRP-ness. The following section, the principal one in this article, examines in turn the three hypotheses on the law-related behavior of Russian enterprises. For each of these three analyses, we show how the particular hypothesis relates to Galanter's original work, we cast the hypothesis in a framework conducive to statistical testing using our survey data, we consider alternative theories that bear upon the constructs being examined, and we present the results of statistical analyses of both Galanter-type RRP theories and of alternatives. The concluding section of the paper draws together the lessons derived from testing each of the three hypotheses. There are two appendixes. Appendix A provides details on the construction of our four RRP variables and examines which types of enterprises are most likely to be RRPs, and Appendix B details which types of enterprises fall into the RRP category.

Operationalizing the Russian Repeat Player

The basic elements of Galanter's definition of RPs are universal and are applicable in present-day Russia. According to his definition, all our surveyed enterprises would be RPs. They are all actively engaged in business; they regularly conclude contracts with a variety of partners and may expect some of these relationships to sour, leading to conflict and perhaps litigation. Given the serious nature of the nonpayments problem in Russia, disputes are rife. More important is that our enterprises are likely to be "engaged in many similar litigations over time" (ibid., p. 97).

The RP and OS concepts are not absolutes; they are best understood "as a continuum rather than as a dichotomous pair" (ibid., pp. 97–98). This aspect of the analysis is no different when applied to Russia. Our task is to determine the placement of our surveyed enterprises on the spectrum from high-end RP to low-end RP, the latter with characteristics closer to those of Galanter's OSs. We can, for example, categorize enterprises on the basis of their control over the terms of transactions as well as the resources they have available. We can also determine their relative levels of access to legal specialists.

The principal difficulty in applying Galanter's analysis to Russia stems from the importance he places on "playing for the rules." In a common-law system, such as the United States, we would expect RPs to look beyond any single case and to try to change the rules to their advantage. As participants in a civil law system, Russian litigants look to the language of the codes. They would regard efforts to change the law through judicial action as pointless.[2]

Keeping in mind this critical difference between the two legal systems, we define four variables characterizing separate properties of the RRP. To some extent, the definitions of these variables are constrained by the type of information obtainable from surveys, but collectively the four variables capture the essence of Galanter's notion of a repeat player. Breaking down the RRP definition into its component parts allows for greater subtlety in the subsequent analysis of behavioral effects. The following paragraphs describe the four variables, whereas Appendix B provides the details of their construction. Table 8.1 gives summary statistics.

CONTROL OVER TRANSACTIONS

Galanter contends that "it is the RP who writes the form contract" (ibid., p. 98). Our survey asked sales and procurement directors about the source of the documents that served as the foundation for one example transaction.[3] The possible responses were the form contract of the respondent enterprise,

TABLE 8.1

Definitions and Summary Statistics for the Explanatory Variables Used in the Regression Analyses

Name	Definition	Observations available	Mean	Standard Deviation
FORM	See Appendix A	276	5.93	1.93
LAWYER	See Appendix A	328	2.77	1.40
RESOURCE	See Appendix A	325	2.44	1.15
CONTACTS	See Appendix A	328	0.97	0.83
AGE	Age of enterprise in 1997	328	48.45	28.16
SIZE	Number of enterprise employees in thousands	328	0.97	2.15
BARTER	Percentage of enterprise revenues obtained by barter	326	38.79	35.79
NEWCUST	Percentage of customers that are new to the enterprise since 1992	327	48.91	29.53
ARREARS	Index of severity of enterprise arrears on wages, payments to suppliers, and payments to energy companies	327	8.85	7.38
PLAINTIFF	Dummy variable = 1, if enterprise has been to court 6 or more times as plaintiff in the previous year; 0 otherwise	328	0.40	0.49
CONPAY	Contractually stipulated amount of customer prepayment (amount in example enterprise agreement)	325	54.38	42.26
ACTPAY	Actual amount of customer prepayment (amount in example enterprise agreement)	325	47.62	41.88

the form contract of the partner enterprise, a specially created contract, a commercially available form contract, and a form contract provided by the state industrial ministry.[4] On the assumption that behavior on this specific transaction was indicative of enterprise policy in general, the responses can be used to construct a scale indicating the degree of control that the respondent enterprise had over the structure of transactions.

In devising the scale, we were mindful of the historical legacy as well as the obvious indicators of control. In response to persistent shortages in the Soviet period, informal rules developed to govern contractual partners' interactions. Because the customer was usually desperate to obtain goods and had few bargaining tools, the supplier was always able to insist that its form contract be used. Although this power may not have been terribly meaningful during the Soviet era because of the planned nature of the economy, it set a pattern that has outlasted the Soviet system, even though there are no longer shortages in Russia and enterprises now have complete freedom in choosing their trading partners. It remains the suppliers—not the customers—that typically set the structure of the transaction. Our scale incorporates the assumption that a movement away from the old pattern is an important indicator of the relative power of the parties.

For our variable *FORM*, higher scores represent greater control over transactions. Like Galanter, we assume that the use of an enterprise's form contract reflects control. Thus, the enterprise that uses its form for both sales and procurement has the most power. An enterprise that uses its partners' forms for both transactions is the weakest. In between, our ranking of the options is grounded on the assumption that a supplier's loss of control over transactions is a stronger indicator than a customer's continuation of the old pattern of not having control. Also, we assume that using one's own form demonstrates greater power than does compromising on a specially negotiated contract.

ACCESS TO LEGAL SPECIALISTS

The second component of the RRP is access to legal specialists. Commenting on the United States, Galanter notes that repeat players gain expertise and lower their start-up costs through such access. In Russia, the assistance of lawyers does provide an advantage but does not tip the scale as heavily as in the United States, due to differences in the structure of legal institutions. Lawyers are less essential, particularly for litigation among economic entities. Judges in the commercial (or *arbitrazh*) courts that have jurisdiction over disputes between enterprises report that about half the parties who appear before them are unrepresented by counsel.[5] The procedural rules are straightforward, and judges are accustomed to helping nonlawyers through the process (Hendley 1998b). Russia does not have complicated evidentiary rules or prolonged discovery, so the costs associated with litigation are less than in the United States. That does not mean that enterprises necessarily regard the costs as trivial, and lawyers can help in lowering them.[6] Moreover, *arbitrazh* judges freely admit that litigants who have legal representation are better off than others. The lawyers understand both the formal rules and the informal norms and can lessen the confusion and uncertainty that litigation often inspires in laypersons. Thus, although the expertise to be provided by Russian lawyers is of a somewhat lower order than in the United States, access to such expertise is still beneficial.

The survey provided data on whether the enterprise had a legal department and whether it had any kind of relationship with outside counsel. These data are combined to construct the variable *LAWYER*, which has higher scores for enterprises with greater access to legal specialists. Construction of this variable proceeds from the assumption that having lawyers on staff was always better than having outside counsel, because in-house lawyers are inevitably more familiar with the circumstances of the enterprise than outside counsel. Also, an ongoing relationship with outside lawyers is presumed more beneficial than an intermittent relationship.

RESOURCES

The third component of the RRP is the availability of resources. Resources are important because they allow greater flexibility in short-run decisions. Resource-rich enterprises can forgo short-term opportunities to build a reputation as firm bargainers. Resource-rich parties need not pursue every claim, but may wait for the cases that promise to yield long-term benefits. Galanter cautions, however, that although his RPs are often wealthy, the link is far from automatic: those with significant resources are not necessarily RPs and those who are less well-off cannot be assumed to be OSs. Not all resource-rich parties act strategically, and not all impoverished parties are incapable of doing so.

The basic logic of this argument is not geographically specific. It applies to Russia, just as to the United States. Resources can help RRPs advance their interests, but the assumption that possession of resources automatically translates into a strategy for using them to advance legal interests, which Galanter concedes is tenuous, is even more strained in the Russian context. For example, the politicization of the courts and their consequent lack of independence during the Soviet period made most people understandably skeptical of their neutrality. Despite the profound institutional reforms of the past decade (Solomon 1995), this skepticism persists. As a result, some may view going to court as pointless and even dangerous, because it may draw unwanted attention to the petitioner.[7] Thus, we regard availability of resources as a helpful indicator, but perhaps only loosely related to being a RRP.

We constructed the variable RESOURCE to measure this dimension of the RRP. Determining the relative levels of our enterprises' resources is not straightforward; concealing income so as to escape tax obligations and other debts has reached epidemic proportions in Russia, and most enterprises maintain several sets of books. For this reason, we did not rely on the financial data (balance sheet, income statement, etc.), but rather used a set of qualitative indicators: the seriousness of wage arrears, the percentage of the employees on a reduced work week,[8] the general director's response to whether or not the plant had after-tax profits in 1996, and the response to a question on whether the enterprise had recently purchased new production equipment. Each of these four indicators reflects whether the enterprise has any degree of flexibility in the use of current revenues, such flexibility being one characteristic of an entity that can focus on long-term goals in short-term decisions.

Galanter's analysis suggests that there should be a fourth component to our RRP definition. His RPs "have opportunities to develop facilitative informal relations with institutional incumbents" (Galanter 1974:99). As an illustration, he mentions the "routine relationships" that grow up between those who regularly petitioned for garnishment of wages and the clerks for small claims courts (ibid., 99n. 9) In this instance, familiarity breeds credibility. Clerks are more likely to believe the version of the story told by the person they know (the RP) than a stranger's version. The clerks also make a RP's work easier by consolidating all a RP's cases, thereby speeding up the judicial process. Thus, through repeated use of legal institutions, RPs develop and sustain informal networks that they call upon from time to time.

This aspect of Galanter's analysis translates very poorly into Russian reality. One reason is the profound difference in how legal institutions operate. In contrast to the United States, where clerks wield considerable power in docketing cases, *arbitrazh* judges themselves schedule their cases. Cases are channeled to judges through a two-step process. First, the chairman of the court divides the pending cases according to the subject matter, such as bankruptcy, tax, securities, or contracts. Then the presiding judge of the panel that considers a particular type of case assigns the case to a particular judge. At neither stage do the decision-makers take note of the identity of the parties or the specifics of the dispute. In fact, the process has a rote quality, rendering personal contacts ineffective. This conclusion is supported by interviews with enterprise lawyers and observations at *arbitrazh* courts in Moscow, Saratov, and Ekaterinburg. Lawyers occasionally gripe about the bias or corruptibility of individual judges, but have never suggested that ingratiating themselves with court personnel would make much difference, because there is no way to predict or control which judge will be assigned to their case.[9] Most *arbitrazh* courts have many judges, so the chances of encountering the same judge again are minimal.[10]

Despite such doubts about the viability of this element of Galanter's analysis for Russia, we nonetheless constructed a variable, *CONTACTS*, that measured the relative levels of political contacts of our enterprises, with higher scores indicating better contacts. To construct this variable, we use the frequency of meetings between enterprise management and officials, on the assumption that such meetings indicate whether the enterprise has constructed a network of institutional relationships. We also use information on whether enterprises have an expectation that the government will step in to help them if they experience financial difficulties and whether the enterprises have received subsidies from the state, because such assistance is likely to be reflective of close relationships with officials.

Given these four constituent variables describing RRP-ness, a natural question is how they are related to each other. We conducted an analysis of this question and found that the degree of intercorrelatedness is not high. This finding reinforces our decision to examine the effects of each of the four variables rather than combine them in one composite index. Discussion of the relationships between the four variables is presented in Appendix B.

How Do Russian Repeat Players Behave?

The critical question remains, Does it make any difference if an enterprise is an RRP? Galanter's analysis has stood the test of time because it was such a compelling explanation of how the parties' status and experience may affect the operation of the legal system in the United States. We now examine whether his theories are helpful in understanding law-related behavior in Russia.

> *Hypothesis 1.* An increase in an enterprise's RRP-ness leads to more aggressive and innovative relations with their trading partners.

Galanter argues that RPs are likely to be aggressive and innovative in defending and advancing their interests. RPs not only adapt themselves to existing rules (both substantive and procedural), but also are quick to perceive when changed circumstances render existing rules more relevant and quick to take advantage of the new situation. In the U.S. context, RPs are willing to sacrifice victories in the short run to change the rules over the long run.

Although the civil-law tradition makes it almost impossible to modify rules iteratively through case law, we might hypothesize that RRPs exhibit the same underlying qualities of aggression and innovation exhibited by RPs in the United States. Do these qualities manifest themselves in the Russian context? We answer this question by examining the use of two legal tools at the disposal of Russian enterprises in their relations with one another: *protokols* of disagreement (*protokoly raznoglasiia*) and petitions to freeze the assets of defendants in contractual disputes.

WHY DO ENTERPRISES USE PROTOKOLS OF DISAGREEMENT?

As the name suggests, a *protokol* of disagreement is used to indicate disagreement with the terms proposed by a contractual partner. For example, if a seller (S) sends its form contract to a potential buyer (B), then B might respond by sending back a *protokol* of disagreement in which B proposes alternative wording to the sections of the contract it finds objectionable. The *protokol* is not a full-fledged contract, but only a list of sections that are problematic, indicating B's preferences. B sends the signed *protokol* to S, inviting S to sign as well. If they both sign, then the *protokol* operates as an addendum to the contract, modifying its terms. Alternatively, S may respond with its own *protokol*, accepting some of B's suggestions and rejecting others. The process can go on indefinitely, but usually stops after each side has laid out its position. The final terms of the agreement can be determined only by winding through the original contract and the *protokols* to see which terms enjoy the support of both S and B. Sometimes the parties fail to sign the *protokol*, but proceed with the transaction.[11] If problems arise later, determining the substance of the contract is difficult.[12]

Protokols of disagreement were created during the Soviet period as a means of enabling individual enterprises to adapt the form contracts mandated by industrial ministries. Under current Russian law, enterprises have almost complete contractual freedom: a government-approved form is no longer required. Instead, they can develop their own form and adapt it to particular situations. See articles 1 and 5, GK (1994). The increased availability of computers provides the means to tailor contracts. Yet *protokols* of disagreement remain the preferred method of revising contracts.

To an outsider, the continued use of *protokols* might appear to be an indicator of lethargy, rather than of aggressiveness. The use of *protokols* almost invariably gives rise to uncertainty over the substance of contracts. A better approach would seem to be to revise the contract itself. Perhaps Russian legal practice will gradually evolve toward this approach.[13] For now, however, Russian enterprise lawyers seem firmly committed to the use of *protokols*. Our interviews reveal that the lawyers view *protokols* as the best and only means of countering perceived unfairness or lack of balance in the terms of a proposed contract. Thus, the use of *protokols* is a good measure of aggressiveness.

The percentage of contracts of an enterprise that use *protokols* of disagreement is our dependent variable. The mean of this variable is 20.6% of contracts.[14] In examining the enterprise characteristics that are related to the use of *protokols*, we focus on the variables characterizing RRPs.[15]

Because 23% of enterprises reported no use of *protokols*, a value of zero for the dependent variable, we used tobit procedures to implement the regression analysis. The results are presented in Table 8.2. We examined not only the four RRP measures but also other variables that are plausibly related to the use of *protokols*, in line with the view expressed in the introduction that it is important to consider alternative explanations of the dependent variable. Such a procedure also lessens any omitted-variable bias in the estimates for the RRP variables. Column (1) of Table 8.2 contains the basic regression for the RRP variables alone. Column (2) adds four non-RRP explanatory variables. We also tested the importance of regions and of sectors

TABLE 8.2

Tobit Regressions for the Percentage of Enterprise Contracts
Using Protokols

Variable	(1)	(2)
Intercept	17.432*	24.295**
	(1.88)	(2.11)
FORM	-1.172	-0.843
	(-1.06)	(-0.81)
LAWYER	4.758***	3.084**
	(3.15)	(1.98)
RESOURCE	-4.179**	-1.407
	(-2.15)	(-0.69)
CONTACTS	3.126	2.154
	(1.24)	(0.85)
AGE	—	-0.041
		(-0.56)
SIZE	—	0.525
		(0.57)
NEWCUST	—	-0.154**
		(-2.14)
BARTER	—	0.153**
		(2.28)
Sectoral Dummies	—	Yes
Number of Observations	264	262
Log Likelihood	-1054.1	-1025.2

t-statistics are in parentheses.   **Significant at the 5% level.
*Significant at the 10% level.   ***Significant at the 1% level.

in the same manner, using dummy variables, but the details of the results are omitted from the table to economize on space. Definitions of the non-RRP variables are contained in Table 8.1.

Here, we must confront an issue that might trouble some readers as they examine this and the subsequent statistical analyses of this article. Might our results be biased because of the endogeneity of the explanatory variables in our regressions? In the present context, for example, could it not be the case that there is a causal relation from *protokols* to resources, in which the optimal use of *protokols* leads to better economic outcomes and therefore the enterprise has more resources?[16] We cannot dismiss such possibilities, of course, but the context in which our data were collected leads us to downplay the importance of such problems.

We interpret the four RRP variables as indicators of fairly permanent characteristics of enterprises. These characteristics are determined well before decisions on the legal-related behaviors that we are endeavoring to explain. For example, the variable measuring access to legal specialists *(LAWYER)* mostly reflects whether the enterprise inherited a legal department from the Soviet era. Similarly, in the Russian reform context, where the determinants of success have radically changed in a few short years, the variable measuring the availability of resources *(RESOURCE)* mostly reflects fortuitous aspects of the enterprise's characteristics, such as sector, region, and inherited market position, rather than the details of its present legal-related behavior. Thus, we feel justified in treating our four RRP variables as exogenous determinants of the varieties of legal behavior that we examine.[17]

The hypothesis that RRPs tend to use *protokols* more often receives only limited support. The *LAWYER* variable is the only one of the four RRP variables that has a significant positive coefficient. We find no connection between use of *protokols* and the level of control exercised over the transaction *(FORM)* or the extent of contacts with local authorities *(CONTACTS)*. Of course, the results for *FORM* could indicate that powerful enterprises brook no disagreement with their initial contract proposals and therefore exhibit a lower level of *protokols*. If this is a correct interpretation of the results, however, one would expect *RESOURCE* to have a positive coefficient, ceteris paribus, because more powerful enterprises are more likely to challenge the form contracts of partners. The coefficients for *RESOURCE* are, in fact, negative. Therefore, these results indicate that high-end RRPs are not inherently more likely to use *protokols* than low-end RRPs. Consequently, RRPs are not by nature particularly aggressive in pursuing their interests in this first stage of the contractual relationship.

The strong positive correlation between the use of *protokols* of disagreement and the availability of legal expertise *(LAWYER)* is somewhat unexpected in the Russian context. No special legal training is required to draft these *protokols*. Given that *protokols* propose new contractual language, having a lawyer involved might be considered prudent, but many of the issues that commonly arise are straightforward business points and require no legal finesse. During the Soviet period, enterprise lawyers were segregated from the sales and procurement departments and were not usually involved in contract formulation. Our results suggest that this practice might be changing and that Russian lawyers are increasingly becoming part of the contract negotiation process.

If being an RRP is not a compelling explanation for the use of *protokols*, then what factors do emerge as important? Levels of barter *(BARTER)*, the percentage of customers that are new since 1992 *(NEWCUST)*, and the sector of production emerge as significant. Enterprises that engage in high levels of barter are more likely to use *protokols* actively than are other enterprises. This practice makes sense given the inherently idiosyncratic nature of barter transactions. At a minimum, the parties have to revise the payment terms of the form contract, which typically call for some type of monetary transfer.[18] Thus, the strong relationship between barter and *protokols* simply indicates coping with reality.

Less obvious is why enterprises with higher levels of new customers are less likely to use *protokols*. We might expect parties to be wary of one another in their first transaction, which would encourage more *protokols*, yet we found the opposite. An alternative explanation is that new customers have more power to resist the *protokols* than older customers entrenched in specific relationships. This explanation is consistent with our results for sectors: two of the 10 sectors, food processing and textiles/apparel, have significantly lower levels of *protokols*, whereas the heavy machinery sector has significantly higher levels. Certainly, in the current Russian setting, customers of light industrial sectors are less likely to be entrenched in old historical relationships than are the customers of heavy industry.

A number of causal links that are strongly suggested by the literature turn out to be specious. For example, it might be assumed that bigger and older enterprises enjoy a comparative advantage in experience and market power, which could be exercised via these *protokols*. (Alternatively, newer enterprises that are unburdened by long-standing ties with customers or suppliers might be more aggressive in pursuing their interests and therefore more likely to use *protokols*.) Along similar lines, the logic of globalization gives rise to an expectation of regional differences, with enterprises from regions that have been more exposed to Western-style legal adversarial styles (such as Moscow) assuming a more aggressive stance vis-à-vis their contractual partners than do enterprises in more isolated regions. None of these posited relationships is borne out by the data. (See the results for *AGE* and *SIZE* in Table 8.2. The results for the regional dummies are not reported.)

WHY DO ENTERPRISES FILE PETITIONS TO FREEZE ASSETS?

Petitions to freeze a defendant's assets are an obvious indicator of aggressiveness given that they are the first step in seizing property in satisfaction of a judgment.[19] In the Russian context, they may also be considered innovative. During the Soviet period, the law did not allow for this procedure. All industrial enterprises were state-owned and judgments tended to be small and easily collected, making the seizure of assets superfluous. Petitions to freeze a defendants' assets were introduced in the first post-Soviet procedural code for the *arbitrazh* courts in 1992 (Articles 92 and 151, 1992 APK). The law now allows plaintiffs to make such a petition at any point during a case

(Articles 75 and 76, 1995 APK). The law leaves the decision as to whether or not to grant a petition largely to the judge's discretion.[20] Consequently, obtaining such an order requires an understanding of the informal norms of the *arbitrazh* courts and an ability to convince the judge that the defendant is likely to abscond with its assets if the order is not issued. Therefore, taking advantage of this right to petition for a defendant's assets to be frozen is an indicator of both aggressiveness and innovativeness.

At first, litigants were reluctant to make use of this new instrument. Interviews with court and enterprise personnel suggest that such petitions were regarded as somehow rude. As difficulties with implementing court decisions mounted, however, the willingness to file such petitions rose. They are still not routine. Statistics collected by the *arbitrazh* courts for 1997 show that the use ranges from a high of 7.9% of all cases heard in the Moscow City courts to a low of 2% in Voronezh, among the regions included in our survey.[21]

We asked enterprises how often they filed petitions to freeze the assets of defendants in cases of nonpayments of contracted amounts. The enterprises were offered four options: routinely at the beginning of the case, routinely if and when the enterprise received an award of damages, occasionally, and never. Of the 209 enterprises (67% of the sample) who had been involved in nonpayments cases during 1995 to 1996, 12% filed petitions routinely at the beginning of the case, 9% after an award of damages, 36% occasionally, and 43% never. The enterprises that routinely tried to get orders to freeze defendants' assets were generally more successful in having their petitions granted than were other enterprises.

The survey question on the frequency of attempts to freeze assets provides the dependent variable for the present analysis. Because this is an ordered categorical variable, we use ordered probit regressions to obtain our results, which are presented in Table 8.3. As before, we examined not only the four RRP variables but also other variables that are plausibly related to the attempts to freeze assets. Column (1) of Table 8.3 contains the regression that uses only the four RRP variables. Column (2) adds other explanatory variables that are plausibly related to the propensity to petition to freeze assets. We also tested the importance of regions and sectors, using dummy variables, but the results are omitted from the table to economize on space.

We have hypothesized that filing petitions indicates both aggressiveness and innovativeness and that this behavior should be correlated with being an RRP. The propensity to file these petitions is strongly related to the access to legal professionals (*LAWYER*). Although the coefficients on the other three RRP-related variables are all positive, none are significant. The strength of the *LAWYER* variable is to be expected. In contrast to *protokols* of disagreement, legal training or experience is necessary to file and obtain

TABLE 8.3

Ordered Probit Regressions for the Frequency of Petitions to Freeze Assets

Variable	(1)	(2)
FORM	0.007	-0.001
	(0.18)	(-0.02)
LAWYER	0.128*	0.136*
	(2.23)	(2.08)
RESOURCE	0.053	-0.009
	(0.71)	(-0.11)
CONTACTS	0.059	0.141
	(0.62)	(1.34)
AGE	—	-0.007*
		(-2.34)
SIZE	—	-0.0003
		(-0.95)
NEWCUST	—	-0.007
		(-2.31)
BARTER	—	-0.003
		(-0.95)
ARREARS	—	-0.027**
		(-2.07)
PLAINTIFF	—	0.402**
		(2.13)
Regional Dummies		Yes
Log Likelihood	-226.733	-205.980
Number of observations	190	190

Intercept estimates omitted.
t-statistics are in parentheses.
*Significant at the 5% level.

an order to freeze assets. The law sets forth the right to petition, but provides no details on how to exercise it. In view of the nonsignificance of the other RRP-related variables, the strength of this result is best seen as simply reflecting the critical importance of lawyers when filing these petitions. Thus, these findings suggest that RRP status is not a good predictor of whether an enterprise will file a petition to freeze assets and therefore is not associated with this sort of aggressive and innovative behavior in litigation.

If RRP-ness is not a good predictor of aggressiveness and innovativeness among Russian enterprises, then what factors seem to have more explanatory power? We examined the link between litigiousness and the use of these petitions. This hypothesis is suggested by Galanter's analysis, because enterprises that go to court frequently will likely have developed a set routine. Indeed, we found that enterprises that litigated regularly were significantly more likely to file petitions to freeze assets than were other enterprises.[22] Note also that when this variable measuring litigiousness is included in the regression, the significance of *LAWYER* weakens considerably, suggesting that these two variables are partially capturing the same underlying phenomenon. The most plausible common element of these two variables is the presence of skills needed to deal with the courts, suggesting again that our results for *LAWYER* do not reflect the aggressiveness element of being an RRP, but rather the presence of a specific type of human capital in the enterprise.

Common sense suggests that financial desperation stemming from the profound economic depression in Russia might cause enterprises to be more aggressive and, consequently, to file more petitions to freeze assets. To examine this hypothesis, we created a variable (*ARREARS*) that measures the severity of the enterprise's arrears to suppliers, banks, and energy companies. This variable is significantly related to the propensity to petition to freeze assets, but it has the opposite sign to that expected: companies with large arrears are less likely to attempt to freeze assets. Thus, although it may be true that the arrears crisis among enterprises has prompted some enterprises to engage in new types of behavior, a high level of financial desperation does not lead to aggressive litigation behavior.[23]

Finally, we examined the extent to which the basic characteristics of the enterprise affected its tendency to engage in this sort of new-style behavior. Not surprisingly, newer firms are more likely to file petitions to freeze assets than are older enterprises, which seems logical because new firms might be less burdened by historical relationships and more willing to risk rupturing the relationship by moving to seize assets. Also, newer firms might have fewer capital reserves and may be less able to wait for payment. There are no effects of the size of the firm on propensity to file petitions, nor of the firm's sector, nor of the presence of barter. Regional effects are small, with only one region, Barnaul, exhibiting a significant difference from other regions, with a higher propensity for such petitions.[24]

Hypothesis 2. The higher the enterprise's degree of RRP-ness, the more likely that it will establish bilateral "rules of the game" to govern relations with trading partners.

Another key aspect of Galanter's RPs is their willingness to play for the rules, which can manifest itself through efforts to change either formal or informal rules. Depending on the circumstances, RPs may work to effect change in the judicial interpretation of existing laws or they may use their knowledge, skill, and bargaining power to establish informal norms that operate on a bilateral or industrywide basis. In all cases, the goal is to reshape the rules in the interests of the RP.

Given the Romanist legal tradition of Russia, we should not expect parties (whether or not RRPs) to be actively engaged in shaping law through court decisions. For the most part, judicial decisions are binding only on the participants.[25] Although there is a well-established tradition of seeking exemptions to various aspects of the law through executive decree and of lobbying the legislature to change the law to benefit a particular plant or industry, this practice is more common in areas that touch on state regulation (such as tax or environmental law) than in laws that regulate private commercial transactions. Contract law is fixed in federal codes and is not subject to change through executive decree or judicial decision.

In the wake of the end of the planned economy, Russian enterprises now have great leeway in setting the norms that govern their private business transactions. We can hypothesize that RRPs will take advantage of this newfound freedom to impose bilateral norms that work to their advantage. For example, we might expect RRPs routinely to require high levels of prepayment in their sales contracts and to insist that such payment actually be made. In the chaotic world of the post-Soviet market economy, in which nonpayment of contractual debts has become common, payment in advance of shipment might be the only way to ensure that the customer does not default. One might therefore expect that RRPs would be successful in establishing new informal rules in which prepayment was an essential element of a transaction.

Our general hypothesis is that high-end RRPs are able to demand and obtain higher levels of prepayment. We thus analyze two aspects of prepayment, the amount agreed upon in the contract and the amount actually paid. Both aspects are indicators of whether or not RRPs are able to establish bilateral norms that benefit themselves. At the very least, the customers of RRPs ought to be more likely to pay the amount set forth in the contract, indicating that RRPs are able to enforce their contracts. In fact, the correlation between contractual and actual prepayment is so high (the correlation coefficient is 0.89) that there is little difference between the results for these two variables.

For this analysis, the data for the dependent variables are derived from the responses of the sales directors to a series of questions about a specific sales transaction. These questions included detailed queries about the terms of payment, the responses to which reveal that 74% of the enterprises contracted for some form of prepayment and that 41% contracted for full prepayment. The average amount of contracted prepayment was 54% of the total contractual bill. Seventy percent of enterprises actually received prepayment and the average amount of prepayment received was equal to 48% of the total contractual bill.

We analyzed the determinants of the contractual and actual prepayments using standard tobit regression techniques.[26] In the two regressions relating the two prepayment variables (contractual and actual) to the four RRP explanatory variables, there is only one significant coefficient. The variable measuring the strength of the relationship with political authorities (*CONTACTS*) is significantly related to actual prepayment, but not contractual prepayment. Given the loose connection between *CONTACTS* and Galanter's original RP concept (see the discussion above in the section defining this variable), these results strongly indicate that RRP-ness is not related to the amount of prepayment. These results are robust to the inclusion in the equation of the other variables that we discuss below. Thus, we conclude that RRPs are not taking advantage of their position to impose and enforce bilateral norms on their trading partners. (Because the central variables of interest, the RRP variables, are insignificant, and in view of the need to conserve space, we omit a detailed presentation of these results.)

Rather than RRP-ness, the variables that are most strongly related to levels of prepayment, both contractual and actual, are whether the customer is new and whether the transaction involved barter. New customers face higher contractual and actual amounts of prepayment, suggesting that the trust arising from previous interactions can substitute for prepayment. The amount of barter is negatively related to prepayment, because barter transactions do not lend themselves to prepayment. They do not contemplate cash but are "mutually beneficial exchanges" (*vzaimozachety*) of goods. Prepayment is unnecessary: if either party fails to supply the goods as provided in the contract, the transaction will not go forward.

Other explanations for the levels of prepayment that might seem theoretically plausible are not supported by the data. Enterprise size, despite its likely correlation with bargaining power, has no effect on the level of prepayment. Although enterprises with high levels of debt would probably be more desperate for cash and benefit more from prepayment, this does not evidence itself in a relationship between arrears and prepayment.

Hypothesis 3. RRPs are unlikely to litigate against other RRPs.

Galanter argues that OSs and RPs behave differently in the litigation arena. He contends that the "great bulk of litigation" is RP versus OS and that these cases represent "routine processing of claims for parties for whom the making of such claims is a regular business activity" (Galanter 1974:108). These cases are most likely to involve relative strangers, that is, parties without a continuing relationship. By contrast, he sees RP versus RP litigation as

TABLE 8.4

Number of Cases in Arbitrazh *Court During 1996: Frequency Among 328 Russian Enterprises*

Number of Cases as Defendant	Number of Cases as Plaintiff				
	None	1–5	6–19	20–49	50 or more
None	68	49	10	5	4
	(20.7%)	(14.9%)	(3.1%)	(1.5%)	(1.2%)
1–5	20	51	25	10	8
	(6.1%)	(15.6%)	(7.6%)	(3.1%)	(2.4%)
6–19	4	4	21	9	5
	(1.2%)	(1.2%)	(6.4%)	(2.7%)	(1.5%)
20–49	0	1	5	11	4
	(0.0%)	(0.3%)	(1.5%)	(3.4%)	(1.2%)
50 or more	0	1	1	2	10
	(0.0%)	(0.3%)	(0.3%)	(0.6%)	(3.1%)

The percentage of the sample of 328 enterprises is in parentheses.

more likely to involve parties who know one another well. He believes such litigation is considerably rarer, because RPs who deal with one another on a continuing basis will work out mutually beneficial informal norms that obviate the need for litigation.[27] Lawsuits are avoided because they tend to undermine the relationship, making it difficult to pick up the pieces and go on afterward. Under such circumstances, "litigation appears when the relationship loses its future value" (ibid., p. 114).

We asked the surveyed enterprises how many *arbitrazh* court cases they had participated in during the preceding 2 years. Almost 80% of the surveyed enterprises had been to court in some capacity. (See Table 8.4 for detailed information on the number of cases in which the surveyed enterprises participated as plaintiff or defendant.) In addition, a significant proportion of enterprises had been to court a large number of times; over 30% of the enterprises had been to court more than 10 times, either as plaintiff or defendant. This figure in itself is significant evidence against the applicability of Galanter's thesis to Russia. The litigation reported in our survey would mostly be RP versus RP because the typical case in *arbitrazh* court is supplier versus purchaser, a standard RP versus RP pattern (ibid., p. 107). We observe high levels of litigation exactly where Galanter predicts low levels.

By exploiting the differences between the enterprises in our data set, we can further examine Galanter's argument. He predicts that RP versus OS litigation is numerically dominant. Given the absence of the archetypal OSs in our sample, our low-end RRPs can take the place of OSs in this prediction in view of the relative nature of the OS/RP labels. This substitution immediately implies that the frequency of going to court as a plaintiff should be positively related to the RRP variables and that the frequency of going to court as a defendant should be negatively related to the RRP variables, if Galanter's analysis applies to Russia.

To test these predictions, we use the survey responses that are summarized in Table 8.4. In two separate analyses, we examine the factors associated with the frequency of being a plaintiff and the frequency of being a defendant. The dependent variables are ordered categorical (see the categories in Table 8.4), and we therefore use ordered probit regression techniques. The results appear in Tables 8.5 and 8.6. The structure of these tables is the same as that of Tables 8.2 and 8.3: column (1) contains the basic regression for the RRP variables alone, and column (2) adds non-RRP explanatory variables. We also tested the importance of regions and of sectors in the same manner, using dummy variables, but the details of the results are omitted from the table to economize on space. Definitions of the non-RRP variables are contained in Table 8.1.

INITIATING LAWSUITS

Looking first at plaintiff activity, we find that all the RRP variables are positively related to court filings, thus supporting the Galanter hypothesis. Of these, the variable measuring access to legal specialists (*LAWYER*) stands out as being particularly important. A strong relationship between filing lawsuits and access to legal expertise might seem self-evident, but not in Russia. The prerequisites for complaints are clearly spelled out in the law, and the courthouse personnel are accustomed to helping laypersons with procedural questions. Cases need not be argued by lawyers: *arbitrazh* judges estimate that management represents itself in about half of the cases. Our data suggest that the role of lawyers in Russian enterprises should not be underestimated. Although they may not always be on the front lines of litigation, as they are in the U.S. context, their presence matters. Perhaps they play a gadfly role, pushing for the litigation of claims that might have gone uncollected in their absence.

The extent of control over the transaction (*FORM*) is also positively related to plaintiff activity, although only at marginal levels of significance. This linkage is less surprising. Enterprises that were able to exert control over the substance of the contract would be more willing to risk litigation, because the terms of a contract usually favor the drafter. Somewhat more surprising is the unimportance of the level of resources available (*RESOURCE*). Because the *arbitrazh* courts require filing fees equal to about 5% of the value of the claim,[28] we had expected that enterprises with more resources would have a greater capacity to initiate lawsuits. The gatekeeping effect of these rather high filing fees may have been mitigated by the recent willingness of

Ordered Probit Regressions for the Number of Cases in Arbitrazh Court During 1996

	As Plaintiff			As Defendant		
Variable	(1)	(2)	Variable	(1)	(2)
FORM	0.050	0.038	FORM	-0.009	-0.016
	(1.48)	(1.05)		(-0.27)	(-0.43)
LAWYER	0.301***	0.248***	LAWYER	0.390***	0.316***
	(6.36)	(4.65)		(7.67)	(5.57)
RESOURCE	0.042	-0.027	RESOURCE	-0.227***	-0.145*
	(0.71)	(-0.35)		(-3.66)	(-1.79)
CONTACTS	0.216***	0.171*	CONTACTS	0.264***	0.152*
	(2.78)	(1.97)		(3.29)	(1.69)
SIZE	—	0.00006*	SIZE	—	0.000***
		(1.91)			(3.33)
BARTER	—	0.002	BARTER	—	0.005**
		(0.87)			(2.07)
AGE	—	0.006**	AGE	—	0.004
		(2.39)			(1.44)
ARREARS	—	-0.006	ARREARS	—	0.018*
		(-0.55)			(1.69)
NEWCUST	—	-0.002	NEWCUST	—	-0.000
		(-1.10)			(-0.08)
CONPAY	—	0.003	CONPAY	—	0.001
		(0.82)			(0.39)
ACTPAY	—	-0.006	ACTPAY	—	-0.003
		(-0.60)			(-0.94)
Sectoral dummies		Yes	Regional and sectoral dummies		Yes
Log Likelihood	-387.601	-366.994	Log Likelihood	-321.593	-294.950
Number of observations	274	271	Number of observations	274	271

Intercept estimates omitted.
t-statistics are in parentheses.
*Significant at the 10% level.
**Significant at the 5% level.
***Significant at the 1% level.

arbitrazh courts to postpone payment when the plaintiff has no liquid assets. This rule, however, is not statutory. Rather, it has emerged through practice and consequently might not be well-known to enterprises without legal counsel. (See Hendley 1998a, 1998c.)

Looking beyond the variables associated with RRPs, we find that large enterprises are more likely to be plaintiffs. This result might simply reflect the prosaic phenomenon that larger enterprises have more transactions and therefore present more potential for problems and lawsuits. Also, to some extent, we may be observing a legacy from the past being played out in the present, because large enterprises are usually privatized state enterprises, which is certainly backed up by the age of the enterprise (*AGE*) being highly significant. On the other hand, *arbitrazh* courts did not exist in their current form during the Soviet period, so the behavior is new. These large, older enterprises are more likely to have long-standing trading relationships—also inherited—which Galanter suggests should militate against litigation. Thus, the reasons for the strong positive correlation between size and plaintiff activity are not entirely clear from the data we have available.

Some sectoral variations emerge. For example, enterprises in the food processing industry are more likely to initiate litigation. Such enterprises tend to have large numbers of customers and relatively high turnover. They may experience more difficulty in collecting payment and feel more urgency in pursuing customers. Although an analogous argument would seem to apply to the enterprises with high levels of new customers, in fact we find that having high numbers of customers that are new since 1992 (*NEW-CUST*) has no significant effect on plaintiff activity. Similarly, the level of arrears (*ARREARS*) has no effect on the propensity to sue. Financial desperation does not lead enterprises to become more aggressive in their litigation strategy.

Along similar lines, we might hypothesize that enterprises that require (*CONPAY*) and/or receive high levels of prepayment (*ACTPAY*) from their customers would go to court less often than other enterprises. Most inter-enterprise litigation involves nonpayment (Hendley 1998a, 1998c), and prepayment takes that out of the picture. Yet prepayment levels—both contractual and actual—are not significantly related to plaintiff activity.

Although we find that high-end RRPs do tend to be plaintiffs more often than low-end RRPs, the results from the non-RRP variables seem to have little connection to Galanter's theses on relational distance. If these assumptions were correct, plaintiff activity would be higher among enterprises with high levels of new customers, because the level of trust is lower with these newer trading partners, particularly in post-Soviet Russia, where one can never truly be sure of the bona fides of an unknown party. Yet there is not such connection. If Galanter's theses on relational distance held for Russia, it would also have been the case that older enterprises would have less litigation, given that a larger proportion of their relationships would be long-standing ones. The significant relationship between size and plaintiff activity might also undermine the Galanter thesis, because large enterprises are very likely to be embedded in a network of long-term mutually beneficial relationships.

DEFENDING LAWSUITS

If Galanter's argument that RP versus OS litigation is the largest single category applies in the Russian context, then we ought to find higher levels of defendant activity among low-level RRPs than among high-level RRPs. Our data do not support such a proposition. We find that the frequency with which an enterprise is sued is significantly positively related to its access to legal professionals (*LAWYER*) and to its relations with political authorities (*CONTACT*), and there is no significant relation to its control over the transaction (*FORM*). The availability of resources (*RESOURCE*) is the only variable with the significant negative coefficient that is predicted by Galanter's theories. The logic of the use of the resources variable in the U.S. case would be that enterprises with larger amounts of resources are more likely to be RPs and are not likely to be subject to suits from the most common plaintiffs, other RPs. Given the results for the *LAWYER* variable, this logic is probably not the explanation for the sign of the *RESOURCE* variable in Russia. Rather, enterprises that are in trouble in present-day Russia make a practice of not paying their bills and therefore generate constant targets for lawsuits.

The results come into clearer focus when we examine the variables measuring size and arrears. We find that larger enterprises are more likely to end up in court as defendants. The *ARREARS* variable[29] is significantly positively related to defendant activity. When we put together these characteristics—large, resource-poor, indebted enterprises with legal departments—they point to the old heavy industrial enterprises inherited from the Soviet system that have now been mostly privatized.

THE SPECIFIC CHARACTER OF RUSSIAN CONTRACTUAL LITIGATION

In Russia, high-end RRPs sue high-end RRPs with a fair amount of regularity. This fact, of course, contradicts Galanter's thesis that RPs are loathe to sue RPs. How can one explain the high level of RP versus RP litigation?

Although the litigation at issue in our survey is supplier versus purchaser, a classic RP versus RP category, it is qualitatively different from the sort of case typically found in this category in the United States. This is not high-stakes litigation, but rather routine debt collection of the sort Galanter associates with RP versus OS cases. The desired outcome is not to reshape the rules to the plaintiff's advantage, but mere survival. The evidence of the routine nature of the litigation is overwhelming. Over three-fourths of the surveyed enterprises that initiated lawsuits in the *arbitrazh* court had a decision within a month of the first hearing, and 12.5% of these cases were resolved at the initial hearing. Complaints tend to be short and confined to the basic facts (with a detailed accounting of the amount owed). Defendants often do not bother to participate because the outcome is so obvious. (See Hendley 1998a.)

Why has RP versus RP litigation in Russia taken on such a routine character? The explanation stems from the institutional landscape and the crisis mentality that pervades present-day Russian industry. In contrast to the United States, where the barriers to entry are relatively high and the judges are generally passive, it is remarkably easy to file a case in the Russian *arbitrazh* courts. As we have repeatedly noted, no legal assistance is required. Moreover, once filed, cases proceed quickly to decision. The judge usually tells the parties what evidence to present, thereby reducing uncertainties and leveling the playing field between enterprises with highly experienced lawyers and those with lay representatives.

Our data strongly suggest that the most frequent litigants (both as plaintiffs and defendants) are the larger enterprises that have deeply embedded supplier networks dating back to the Soviet era. Why are these long-standing partners suing one another? Part of the answer lies in the debt crisis that has enveloped virtually all Russian industry. In a world in which it has become acceptable not to pay debts and in which enterprises are fighting for their very survival, there might be more willingness to risk the rupture of a relationship with old partners. Moreover, in this heightened crisis atmosphere, litigation does not automatically lead inevitably to the termination of the trading relationship. Interviews reveal that enterprise managers are highly sympathetic to the problems of their trading partners and do not begrudge them any way out.

Conclusions

Our data indicate that RRPs behave differently than do Galanter's RPs. The differences go well beyond what might be expected when comparing common- and civil-law systems. Naturally, the RRPs show little inclination to play for the official rules, because that is a mostly futile pursuit. More interesting is the absence of the qualities that are integral to RP-ness in Galanter's analysis. RRPs are not particularly aggressive or innovative in their use of legal strategies. Nor do they use their advantages—whether reputational or resource based—to impose new informal norms on less well endowed trading partners. Moreover, RRPs use the courts routinely against other RRPs, not sparingly as a means of last resort as do Galanter's RPs.

The failure of RRPs to exhibit the standard RP qualities under current economic conditions is particularly telling given that most Russian enterprises are struggling for their very survival. Because the future payoff of long-run relationships and established business routines is less important when survival is at issue, one might expect to see more aggression and innovation in present-day Russia than would be present under calmer circumstances. Yet even the present exigencies have not led to the patterns of behavior that, according to Galanter, are to be expected in market economies. The RRPs are as conservative as other enterprises in their problem-solving strategies, at least in terms of the legal aspects of contractual relations, preferring to resort to routine use of the courts when negotiations collapse rather than designing transactions that would be self-enforcing.[30]

Why do we not observe the innovation in legal aspects of contractual relations in the very sector where it might be most expected, among the RRPs? Is it simply a lack of innovation in Russian enterprises? This answer is hardly plausible given the extraordinary ingenuity of many Russian enterprises in devising nonmonetary exchanges (using both barter and various forms of commercial paper) as a means of staying in business while avoiding the use of liquid assets.[31] These innovative nonmonetary transactions, however, are based on skills and behaviors acquired under the old system. In contrast, innovation in legal aspects of contractual relations would push many Russian enterprises into truly virgin territory. Because change is constrained by experience (Nelson & Winter 1982) and because the RRPs in our sample, and Russian manufacturing enterprises in general, are of Soviet vintage, the innovation in the legal sphere that is natural for RPs is absent in our results for Russia. In the Russian context, given the history of enterprises and the role of law in the old system, legal innovation is as much to be expected of the new and the weak as the old and the powerful.[32]

Equally intriguing is our finding that access to legal specialists is important in pursuing legal strategies (with the notable exception of prepayment). In contrast to the United States, lawyers have never been anywhere near the center of Russia economic life. The institutional structure reflects this reality. Courts are accessible to laypersons, and cases are resolved expeditiously.[33] Lawyers are typically regarded as technicians. Enterprise management solicits their opinion on whether draft contracts are "legal," but sees little value in including lawyers in broader discussions of the reasons for transaction. Lawyers are not expected to offer general business advice. In interviews, enterprise lawyers are often startled to be asked about the purpose of one or another contract and typically respond that this is not their concern.[34] Galanter suggests that these sorts of legalistic lawyers are less likely to accentuate the advantages of RPs than are lawyers with a more problem-solving approach. The question of how and why the role of lawyers is evolving in post-Soviet Russia deserves further exploration.

Appendix A: Constructing the Variables That Measure an Enterprise's Degree of RRP-ness

The information used to construct the four variables came from a survey whose questions usually asked respondents to choose answers from several categories provided by the questionnaire. The multiple-choice form of response was dictated by the qualitative nature of the information being sought. When creating variables to reflect the different aspects of RRP-ness, however, we combined the information from several questions and constructed quantitative variables. The decision to do so was motivated by simple pragmatic concerns: to simplify the analysis and the presentation of results. Without the use of quantitative variables, our analysis would have required the use of a multiplicity of dummy variables, with accompanying difficulties of interpretation, even in the simplest statistical exercises. Thus, our decision is one to sacrifice some rigor so as to use a simple framework in examining the importance of RRP-ness. In the following paragraphs, we detail the construction of the variables.

FORM

The survey asked about the details of one sales agreement and one purchase agreement for each enterprise. We take these agreements to be indicative of the enterprises' usual relationships with customers and suppliers. The questions on form contracts were not addressed to the small group of enterprises that relied on oral rather than written agreements. Only 11 enterprises used oral agreements for their sales transaction, and 27 did so for their purchasing transaction. We constructed the variable FORM in the following way:

FORM = 8 if the enterprise's form contract is used for both sales and purchases.

FORM = 7 if the enterprise's form contract is used for sales and neither the enterprise's or the supplier's form contract is used for purchases.

FORM = 6 if the enterprise's form contract is used for sales and the supplier's form contract is used for purchases.

FORM = 5 if neither the enterprise's nor the customer's form contract is used for sales and the enterprise's form contract is used for purchases.

FORM = 4 if the enterprise uses contracts that are specially written for individual sales and purchase agreements.

FORM = 3 if neither the enterprise's nor the customer's form contract is used for sales and the supplier's form contract is used for purchases.

FORM = 2 if the customer's form contract is used for sales and neither the enterprise's nor the supplier's form contract is used for purchases.
FORM = 1 if the customer's form contract is used for sales and the supplier's form contract is used for purchases.

RESOURCE

The variable RESOURCE has values in the range of 0 to 4. The base value of RESOURCE is 2, with 1 being added if the enterprise earned positive net profits in the previous year and a further 1 added if the enterprise purchased production equipment in the previous year. Enterprises were asked how serious were their wage arrears, on a scale of 1 to 10, and RESOURCE was reduced by one-tenth of the response to this question. RESOURCE was also reduced by the proportion of the workforce that was working a reduced work week.

LAWYER

LAWYER = 5 if the enterprise has an in-house legal department and uses outside counsel.
LAWYER = 4 if the enterprise has an in-house legal department and does not use outside counsel.
LAWYER = 3 if the enterprise does not have an in-house legal department but has a permanent relationship with outside counsel.
LAWYER = 2 if the enterprise does not have an in-house legal department but has an intermittent relationship with outside counsel.
LAWYER = 1 if the enterprise does not have an in-house legal department and has no relationship with outside counsel.

CONTACTS

The variable CONTACTS has values in the range of 0 to 4. The base value of CONTACTS is 0, with 1 being added if enterprise management meets with federal government representatives once a month or more, 1 being added if enterprise management meets with local government representatives once a week or more, and 1 being added if the enterprises received direct subsidies from the government during the past year. Also, enterprises were asked to indicate on a scale of 0 to 10 how responsive the government would be if the enterprise were in serious financial difficulties, and we added one-tenth of the score on this scale as a final element of CONTACTS. Summary statistics for these variables are presented in Table 8.1.

Appendix B: Who Are the RRPs?

The concept of a RRP (like Galanter's original RP) is a relative one. Thus, RRPs will take on different identities—from high-end to low-end RRP— depending on where they fall on the spectrum. Implicit in Galanter's approach is the notion that an enterprise's degree of RP-ness is captured in the value of a single variable and that other variables measuring specific characteristics of RP-ness are highly correlated with this variable. Therefore, to obtain an unambiguous answer to the question of who the RRPs are, it is necessary to create a single measure of RP-ness. Given the existence of the four constituent variables of RRPs (*FORM, LAWYER, RESOURCE*, and *CONTACTS*) described in the main body of this article, each of which is related to RP-ness, a natural way to construct the single measure is through the use of factor analysis.[35]

The application of factor analysis was not a resounding success. One of the variables, *CONTACTS*, is negatively correlated with two of the other three. Because institutional contacts presented the most conceptual problems in adapting Galanter's approach to the Russian setting, we regard these statistical results as underlining our conceptual misgivings. Hence, we omitted this variable when constructing the one-dimensional RP-ness variable.

Moreover, the three remaining variables (*RESOURCE, FORM*, and *LAWYER*) do not exhibit high intercorrelations. Hence, the constructed variable does not capture a large part of the variation in these individual variables.[36] The correlation coefficients between the composite variable and *RESOURCE, FORM*, and *LAWYER* are .73, .73, and .23, respectively. (Confirming the observations of the previous paragraph, the correlation with *CONTACTS* is negative.)

Thus, in contrast to Galanter, who is able to draw sharply focused pictures of the sorts of individuals and entities likely to be found at the high end and low end of his spectrum, our pictures remain much fuzzier. The reasons are twofold.

First, the rapidly changing economic and political environment in Russia makes reality considerably less coherent than in the stable market economy of the United States. Legal, economic, and political power are likely to be weakly related in a turbulent environment because differences in the speed of change of different economic phenomena imply that the system is far from any long-run equilibrium. This reason is probably why the correlations among our four variables are low, or even negative.

Second, we are looking at a narrower segment of the RP spectrum than Galanter did. Our survey sample includes only industrial enterprises. The classic one shotters, such as parents battling over custody or divorcing spouses, which naturally are present in Russia just as in the United States, are absent from our sample. Our focus is on interaction between purchasers and suppliers, which Galanter clearly categorizes as RP versus RP transactions (Galanter 1974:107). Thus, although some of our enterprises are closer to the archetypal RP than are others, the range of variation across our sample is limited. Such a narrowing of the range of variation will obviously increase the noise-to-signal ratio in the data and reduce the strength of interrelationships between variables.

These reservations aside, in the remainder of this appendix, we examine how various enterprise characteristics and management attitudes are related to RP-ness, that is, to scores on this composite variable. We could, of course, have related the characteristics of enterprises to each of the four variables defining an RP, but that would then leave us with highly ambiguous information when, as is often the case, a characteristic was negatively related to one of the four variables and positively related to others.

Basic Characteristics

Larger enterprises (as measured by number of workers) have higher scores on the RRP composite variable than smaller enterprises, but the relationship is weak. Age of the enterprise is unrelated. These two results indicate that the large, older enterprises that would have been regarded as Soviet RPs do not automatically become present-day RRPs. Location matters. The six oblasts divide naturally into three groups, with enterprises in Novosibirsk and Voronezh scoring highest, those in Moscow and Ekaterinburg in second place, and enterprises in Saratov and Barnaul lagging far behind. The explanation for these groupings is not immediately apparent, because the paired regions share few characteristics.

Ownership Structure

State-owned and privatized companies are equally likely to be RRPs, providing no support for the argument that privatization would spark increased recognition and mobilization of legal rights (see Boycko & Shleifer 1995:78). The identity of the shareholder does seem important. Enterprises with employee owners tend to be higher-end RRPs, whereas those with outside ownership are more likely to be at the low end. Indeed, the bigger the largest outsider-owned ownership block, the lower the score on the RRP composite variable. Once again, these results provide no support for the common wisdom, which is that inside owners tend to be insular, whereas outsiders tend to look to the legal system to protect their rights.[37]

Business

Enterprises in the food processing and paper and printing sectors receive an above average score, whereas those in the electronics and machinery and equipment sectors rank near the bottom. Enterprises in other sectors are scattered across the spectrum.

The type of customers of the enterprise and the nature of competition faced by the enterprise are associated with the RRP composite score. Enterprises that are closer to the high end of the spectrum are less likely to have other industrial enterprises and the government as customers and more likely to have a customer base composed of wholesale and retail enterprises. These high-end RRPs typically import some of their inputs, indicating sustained contact with foreigners. They are also more likely to face import competition, and they have a lower market share in the Russian Federation than do low-end RRPs. Export behavior is not associated with RRP-ness.

High-end RRPs are slightly more likely than low-end RRPs to be members of business associations or financial industrial groups, although they are less likely to rely on old contacts developed during the Soviet period in business dealings. Somewhat incongruously, the nature of the relationship (whether it is regarded as primarily personal or strictly business) between enterprise sales people and their customers does not correlate in any way with the RRP composite variable.

Attitudes Regarding the Use and Value of Law

The portrait of the RRPs comes into clearer focus when we turn from enterprise attributes to management attitudes. For example, when evaluating the importance of different survival strategies, enterprises with high RRP scores had a higher propensity than low RRP scorers to identify the use of laws and legal institutions as important. In contrast, enterprises with low RRP scores viewed delaying payments as a more important strategy.

Management's evaluation of the commercial (or *arbitrazh*) courts takes on a similar character. These courts have jurisdiction over all disputes between legal entities. They are the institutional successor to a Soviet-era administrative agency, known as "state *arbitrazh*" (or *gosarbitrazh*), which used to resolve disputes between state enterprises (Pomorski 1977). Although superficially similar, the work of *gosarbitrazh* pales in comparison to the challenges now facing the *arbitrazh* courts (Hendley 1998b). When asked to compare the *arbitrazh* courts with *gosarbitrazh*, high-end RRPs are more likely than low-end RRPs to rate the current *arbitrazh* courts high. Although the *arbitrazh* courts have been much criticized for delays and an inability to enforce judgments (Black & Kraakman 1996:1914; Vasil'eva 1996), high-end RRPs are considerably less concerned with these problems than are low-end RRPs. We also asked the general directors to compare the *arbitrazh* courts with "private enforcement," which was meant as a polite euphemism for the mafia in Russia. The high-end RRPs are more likely than other enterprises to rate the *arbitrazh* courts as superior to these extralegal alternatives.

Managers in high-end RRPs are more likely than those in low-end RRPs to view contracts principally as a mechanism for clarifying the rights and duties of the parties at the outset of the transaction, rather than as a means of protecting and advancing their interests afterwards. It follows that these same managers are generally uncomfortable about breaching contracts, believing that the enterprise should live up to its obligations, even when reneging might serve the enterprise's interests.

Notes

Originally published in *Law and Society Review* 33 (4): 833–67 (1999); reprinted by permission. Thanks are due to Alla V. Mozgovaya of the Institute of Sociology of the Russian Academy of Sciences, who coordinated the survey throughout Russia, and to James H. Anderson and Berta Heybey for research assistance. We gratefully acknowledge the support of the National Council for Eurasian and East European Research, the World Bank, and the U.S. Agency for International Development under Cooperative Agreement No. DHR-0015-A-00-0031-00 to the Center on Institutional Reform and the Informal Sector (IRIS). The findings, interpretations, and conclusions expressed in this paper are entirely those of the authors. They do not necessarily represent the views of the World Bank, its executive directors, or the countries they represent.

Kathryn Hendley is Professor of Law and Political Science at the University of Wisconsin-Madison. She is the author of *Trying to Make Law Matter: Legal Reform and Labor Law in the Soviet Union*. Her current research focuses on judicial behavior in the Russian courts and the role of law in decision-making in Russian enterprises.

Peter Murrell is Professor of Economics and the Chair of the Academic Council of the IRIS Center at the University of Maryland, College Park. His research interests include the dynamics of economic transition in postsocialist systems, the theory of economic reform, the effects of privatization, and the role of law in the decisions of postsocialist enterprises.

Randi Ryterman is an economist in the World Bank, with responsibility for institutional reforms, including legal and judicial reform, in countries in transition. Her research focuses on the microfoundations of macroeconomic performance in countries in transition.

1. The industrial sectors are (number of enterprises in parentheses) food processing (67); textiles, clothing and leather (60); fabricated metal (34); machinery and transport equipment (23); electronics (34); chemicals and petroleum (33); construction (18); wood products (8); paper and printing (5); and other (46).

2. Judicial decisions (even appellate decisions) are typically short and are geared to the facts of the case, not to interpreting underlying law. Moreover, decisions are not routinely published and, even when published, lack the force of binding law for future cases. Consequently, litigants rely almost completely on the codes (both procedural and substantive). Although it may be possible to observe incremental shifts in how some statutes are used by the courts as a result of practice, that remains very

much the exception. Practice has influenced the interpretation of a statutory rule in the arena of contractual remedies. Russian law allows penalties for nonperformance. During recent years, penalties of 0.5% per day of the amount owed have become common in sales contracts. As a result, penalties often exceed the actual debt. Debtors complained and repeatedly asked the *arbitrazh* (commercial) courts to apply article 333 of the Civil Code, which gives judges the discretion to reduce penalties found to be "disproportional." Beginning in 1997, *arbitrazh* judges began to do so. Russia has a dual court system. The *arbitrazh* courts have jurisdiction over most economic disputes. See, generally, Hendley (1998a) and articles 330–33 (GK).

3. In 15% of cases, the example transaction did not have a written contract and therefore our variable has missing observations for these cases.

4. The latter two options were almost never chosen.

5. The analysis would likely be different if we were discussing the courts of general jurisdiction. In these courts, lawyers are more common. The difference in attitudes toward legal professionals is reflected in the respective procedural codes. Compare article 44, GPK, with article 48, 1995 APK.

6. A prerequisite for initiating a complaint in the *arbitrazh* courts is the payment of a filing fee, calculated as a percentage of the amount demanded. Some enterprises regard this fee as an insurmountable barrier to using the courts. Legal professionals know that an informal procedure now exists for delaying payment until the case is decided. If the plaintiff enterprise prevails, then it is relieved of liability for these fees. If it loses, then it must pay, but at least the payment has been delayed. (See Hendley 1998a.)

7. Close observers of the U.S. legal system identify similar attitudes in the United States and, although the Soviet authorities' manipulation of the courts to achieve their political ends may have been particularly extreme, analogies can be found in virtually every country.

8. Over the past few years, many Russian enterprises have been unable to pay their workers on time. Wage payments are frequently delayed for months. Some enterprises have responded by limiting the work week to two or three days, thereby reducing their wage obligations.

9. Judges who have some personal or material interest in a case can be recused, either by their own motion or by petition of the parties. Articles 16, 19, 1995 APK; Yakovlev and Iukov 1996:38–42.

10. The Moscow City Arbitrazh Court, for example, has over 130 judges.

11. For example, in a review of 21 contracts with *protokols* at a Moscow factory (drawn randomly from contracts over the past 3 years), none of them had been signed by both parties.

12. The parallel with the Western "battle of the forms" is obvious. The difference in Russia is that the parties typically do not exchange entire contracts, but rather *protokols* indicating the points of disagreement.

13. Such embedded patterns of behavior tend to change slowly. The current generation of Russian law students is being trained by professors who take *protokols* to be a matter of course, and these students behave accordingly when they begin to work as lawyers.

14. The standard deviation was 28.21. For most enterprises (46.3%), use has not changed since the Soviet period, with the remainder of the enterprises split roughly equally between increased and decreased use of *protokols*.

15. Despite our misgivings concerning the validity of the variable measuring the enterprises' relationship with political authorities (CONTACTS) as an indicator of RRP-ness, we include it in this article's remaining analyses because there is little cost to including an extra explanatory variable in a regression and some readers might find the results for this variable interesting.

16. There are even better examples of this problem later. See, for example, the later discussion on the relationship between court activities and the presence of lawyers.

17. Testing this assumption would require specifying a theory of how some enterprises come to be RRPs and others do not. Such a theory is beyond the scope of this article, as it is beyond the purview of Galanter (1974). Indeed, Galanter is as susceptible to this same endogeneity-of-RP-ness criticism as we are, given that the empirical regularities he observes are analogous to our regressions.

18. Some enterprises now have separate form contracts for cash and barter transactions, but that is still the exception rather than the rule.

19. A 1996 informational letter from the Presidium of the Higher *Arbitrazh* Court clarifies that such claims are given the same priority as the final judgment. The order of payment is established by article 855 of the Civil Code (see GK), which means that preexisting claims by the state or other private creditors will be paid first (*Vestnik Vysshego Arbitrazhnogo Suda Rossiiskoi Federatsii*, no. 10, pp. 126–28, 1996). A petition to freeze assets represents a low-cost mechanism of preventing the defendant from absconding with the assets in the bank account.

20. Unpublished statistics on the activities of the regional *arbitrazh* court reveal that, among the regions included in our survey, judges were generally sympathetic to petitioners who asked that the defendant's assets be frozen in cases heard during 1997. The success rate ranged from a high of 58% in Novosibirsk and Saratov to a low of 38.5% in the Moscow City court. (See Hendley 1998c.)

21. These data are drawn from the same unpublished statistical forms referred to in note 20, which were made available to us by the Higher *Arbitrazh* Court in Moscow.

22. In carrying out this analysis, we used a dummy variable, *PLAINTIFF*, which equals 1 when the enterprise has been a plaintiff in more than five cases in the previous 2 years and 0 otherwise. This variable is highly significant with the expected sign.

23. Some might argue that high filing fees preclude illiquid enterprises from pursuing contractual remedies through the courts. In reality, however, that is not true. As we discuss elsewhere, *arbitrazh* courts have become increasingly amenable to delays in the payment of filing fees for cash-poor enterprises.

24. The aggregate oblast-level statistics for 1996, which report that 5.6% of contractual disputes in Barnaul involve a petition to freeze assets, do not reflect a higher level of filings for Barnaul, indicating that the enterprises in our sample may be more active in this regard than the typical Barnaul enterprise.

25. As in all civil-law countries, there is some room for maneuver at the margins (Merryman 1985). For example, the top Russian appellate courts issue decrees and instructions that are not tied to specific cases and that are binding on future litigants. See Hazard (1994) and Hendley (1996).

26. The data were censored below at 0 and above at 100.

27. There are certain exceptions to this general rule regarding RP versus RP litigation (Galanter 1974: 111–12).

28. The law establishes a sliding scale with the percentage decreasing as the amount of the complaint increases. For the precise amounts, see "O vnesenii izmenenii" (1996).

29. The variable *ARREARS* measures the severity of the enterprise's arrears to suppliers, banks, and energy companies.

30. The continued use of *protokols* of disagreement, even after their raison d'etre has disappeared, further buttresses this conclusion.

31. See Hendley et al. (1997) for a description of the arcane transactions used by Russian enterprises to avoid the use of liquid assets.

32. See Murrell (1992) for this view of the nature of enterprise behavior during radical reforms.

33. Complaints about delays are legion. The Russian media delights in uncovering Dickensian tales of cases that have dragged through the courts for years with no resolution, but the official statistics indicate that such cases are the exception rather than the rule. More than 95% of 1996 and 1997 contractual disputes were decided by the *arbitrazh* courts within two months of filing, the statutory deadline.

34. In terms of Galanter's model of legal professionals, Russian enterprise lawyers have more characteristics of Type A than Type B (Galanter 1974: 115n. 48).

35. We used the method of principal components.

36. The first principal component accounts for only 37% of the variance of the three variables.

37. These results, however, are only suggestive, because they use only simple correlations.

References

Arbitrazhnyi protsessual'nyi kodeks Rossiiskoi Federatsii [The *Arbitrazh* Procedural Code of the Russian Federation] [1992 APK] (1992) *Vestnik Vysshego Arbitrazhnogo Suda* (no. 1) 5–47.

———— [1995 APK] (1995) *Vestnik Vysshego Arbitrazhnogo Suda Rossiiskoi Federatsii* (no. 6) 25–79.

Black, Bernard, & Reinier Kraakman (1996) "A Self-Enforcing Model of Corporate Law," 109 *Harvard Law Rev.* 1911–81.

Boycko, Maxim, & Andrei Shleifer (1995) "Next Steps in Privatization: Six Major Challenges," in I. W. Lieberman & J. Nellis with E. Karlova, J. Mukherjee, and S. Rahuja, eds., *Russia: Creating Private Enterprises and Efficient Markets*. Washington, DC: World Bank.

Galanter, Marc (1974) "Why the 'Haves' Come Out Ahead: Speculations on the Limits of Legal Change," 9 *Law & Society Rev.* 95–160.

Grazhdanskii kodeks RF (chast' pervaya) [The Civil Code of the RF (first part)] [GK] (1994) *Sobranie zakonodatel'stva Rossiiskoi Federatsii*, no. 32, item 3301.

Grazhdanskii protsessual'nyi kodeks RSFSR (1997) [The Civil Procedure Code of the RSFSR] [GPK]. Moscow: INFRA.

Hazard, John (1994) "Is Russian Case Law Becoming Significant as a Source of Law?" 1 *Parker School J. of East European Law* 23–46.

Hendley, Kathryn (1996) *Trying to Make Law Matter: Legal Reform and Labor Law in the Soviet Union.* Ann Arbor: Univ. of Michigan Press.

—— (1998a) "Growing Pains: Balancing Justice and Efficiency in the Russian Economic Courts," 12 *Temple International and Comparative Law J.*, 302–32.

—— (1998b) "Remaking an Institution: The Transition in Russia from State *Arbitrazh* to *Arbitrazh* Courts," 46 *American J. of Comparative Law* 93–127.

—— (1998c) "Temporal and Regional Patterns of Commercial Litigation in Post-Soviet Russia," 39 *Post-Soviet Geography & Economics* 379–98.

Hendley, Kathryn, Barry Ickes, Peter Murrell, & Randi Ryterman (1997) "Observations on the Use of Law by Russian Enterprises," 13 *Post-Soviet Affairs* 19–41.

Merryman, John Henry (1985) *The Civil Law Tradition.* 2d ed. Stanford, CA: Stanford Univ. Press.

Murrell, Peter (1992) "Evolution in Economics and in the Economic Reform of the Centrally Planned Economies," in C. C. Clague & G. Rausser, eds., *Emerging Market Economies in Eastern Europe.* Cambridge, MA: Basil Blackwell.

Nelson, Richard R., & Sidney G. Winter (1982) *An Evolutionary Theory of Economic Change.* Cambridge: Harvard Univ. Press.

"O vnesenii izmenenii i dopolnenii v Zakon RF 'O gosudarstvennoi poshline' [On the introductions of amendments and additions to the Law of the RF 'On State Fees']" (1996) *Sobranie Zakonodatel'stva RF*, no. 1.

Pomorski, Stanislaw (1977) "State *Arbitrazh* in the U.S.S.R.: Development, Functions, Organization," 9 *Rutgers-Camden Law J.* 61–116.

Solomon, Peter (1995) "The Limits of Legal Order in Post-Soviet Russia," 11 *Post-Soviet Affairs* 89–114.

Vasil'eva, Marina (1996) "Nel'zia zhit' po zakonam dzhunglei [It Is Impossible to Live by the Laws of the Jungle]," *Chelovek i zakon* (no. 7) 54–59.

Yakovlev, V. F., & M. K. Iukov, eds. (1996) *Kommentarii k Arbitrazhnomu protsessual'nomu kodeksu Rossiiskoi Federatsii* [Commentary on the *Arbitrazh* Procedure Code of the Russian Federation]. Moscow: Kontrakt.

PART THREE

Synthesizing and Advancing Theory

9

Common Knowledge and Ideological Critique

The Significance of Knowing that the "Haves" Come Out Ahead

Introduction

In 1974, Marc Galanter published a paper entitled "Why the 'Haves' Come Out Ahead: Speculations on the Limits of Legal Change" in which he analyzed the limits of a legal system, such as that of the United States, to achieve redistributive outcomes. He traced the limits to features of the U.S. legal system's "basic architecture." The specific features to which he referred were a series of structural dualisms or institutional contradictions that permitted symbolic claims to universalism, public authority, and equality to coexist with particularism, private power, and inequality.

Emerging out of these contradictions, Galanter described a complex structure of social action in which repeat players engage in the litigation game very differently from one-shot players, or those "who have only occasional recourse to the courts" (Galanter 1974:97). Repeat players initiate the play, enjoy economies of scale, develop facilitative informal relations, have access to client specialized legal representation, play the odds in their repetitive engagements, and with regard to the rules of the game, play for rule-changes as much, or perhaps more than, for immediate gains.

Although Galanter pointed out that the repeat players are not necessarily the "haves" of the world (nor are the one shotters always the "have nots"), there is considerable overlap among these statuses. Thus, by establishing that the "haves" do come out ahead and specifying wherein lies their legal advantage, Galanter drew a blueprint of the gap between law on the books and law in action, a gap that many have been exploring, mapping, and questioning ever since.

In this piece, we examine a question provoked by Galanter's original paper: To what extent and with what consequence are the contradictions or dualisms characteristic of our legal system perceived and understood by citizens (the repeat players, the one shotters and, we would like to include for this analysis, the no shotters). That Galanter used a vernacular phrase in the title to his paper suggests that he recognized that the perception that "'haves' come out ahead" was common knowledge. Assuming that this perception is common, here we consider the *significance of this knowing for believing*. In other words, what roles do popular understandings of why "the 'haves' come out ahead" play in sustaining or challenging the legitimacy, power, and durability of law?

Scholarly analyses of common understandings and popular consciousness often invoke the notion of ideology as a way of describing the capacity of ideas to effect action, specifically the ways in which ideas contribute to or embed arrangements of power (Silbey 1998). Although the idea of ideology as false consciousness has largely been abandoned by social scientists because such uses seemed to denigrate the lived experience of citizen subjects while valorizing expert or professional accounts, the concept often retains an element of concealment. For instance, understandings of ideology that attribute to it the capacity to naturalize that which is socially constructed exemplify such concealment (sometimes referred to as reification) (Hunt 1985; Cotterrell [1984] 1995; Scott 1990; Thompson 1990; Eagleton, 1991). In studies of legal phenomenon, this conceptualization of ideology emerges out of a constitutive perspective, a theory of law that deftly avoids invoking any foundational truth that can be contrasted with the ideology. From this constitutive perspective, ideology inheres in the *process* of concealment—that is, a claim that "this is the way things are and must be"—rather than in the *content* of that which is concealed, not perceived, nor understood (for example, some scientific truth). Such uses of the concept of ideology imagine, then, the possibility of deception without truth.

Presumably, ideologies lose their ability to define and organize social life when people start to question the inevitability of "the way things are" and come to recognize the interests that operate to construct such a vision of truth and reality. What prompts these ideological penetrations is a source of continuing debate, but essential to all successful challenges is a collective, widespread rejection of the version of reality offered by the ideology such that it no longer holds sway. At this point, an ideology loses its capacity to conceal much of anything.

With this thought in mind, we can now restate the question provoked by Galanter's claim that the "'haves' come out ahead." If it is true that most people (nonprofessional subjects of the law) "know" that the law does not provide equal justice for all, that money and experience advantage some, that the playing field is not level and the game is fixed, can we meaningfully talk about law as ideology anymore? In our discussion, we take up this question and related ones. First, we describe exactly how people think about and act in relation to the law (what we elsewhere call "legal consciousness").[1] Second, we consider the significance of this legal consciousness for the ideology of liberal legalism.

Legal Consciousness of Ordinary Americans

We have been collecting stories of people's experiences of law to track how people think and act in relation to the law. Over a period of 3 years, we interviewed approximately 430 persons randomly selected from four counties in New Jersey, counties that represented the variation in the racial and economic composition of the state. The sample included millionaire venture capitalists, lawyers, real estate brokers, hairdressers, homemakers, and welfare recipients. In the context of a lengthy, largely open-ended interview, we asked about their daily lives, problems or events that they experienced and defined as problematic, and how they reacted to these events.

Because we were interested in how people encountered and constructed legality[2] in their daily lives, the interview was deliberately designed to capture a picture of the legality that might be unmoored from formal legal settings. Consequently, for some of the people with whom we spoke, the law in a formal sense was conspicuously absent. They reported no experience with courts, police, written laws, or regulations. In Galanter's scheme, we might refer to these people as the no shotters. For others, experience in formal legal settings and with authorities and legal agents was a frequent, ongoing feature of their lives and relationships. Most of the people with whom we spoke fell somewhere in between, having had some legal experience.

From the nearly 10,000 pages of transcribed interviews, we were able to identify three overarching stories of law, accounts of law that seemed to reoccur in the individuals' stories and accounts of legality. These metastories of law are more than simply summaries of what individuals said; they are, we argue, the common cultural materials, the interpretive frames that represent and shape how people experience legality. People draw upon these frames in constructing and interpreting their own experiences and accounts of law. Each describes a familiar way of acting and thinking with respect to the law. Each frame or schema draws upon different cultural images to construct a picture of how the law works. Each invokes a different set of normative claims, justifications, and values to express how the law ought to function. Each attributes different capacities and identifies different constraints on legal action. Finally, each story locates legality differently in time and space.

Before the Law

In one story, "before the law" (borrowing from Kafka's parable), legality is imagined and treated as an objective realm of disinterested action, removed and distant from the lives of individuals. In this story, the law is majestic, operating by known and fixed rules in carefully delimited spaces. Here, legality is envisioned and enacted as if it were a separate sphere from ordinary social life: discontinuous and distinctive yet authoritative and predictable. The law is described as a formally ordered, rational, and hierarchical system of known rules and procedures. Respondents conceive of legality as something relatively fixed and impervious to individual action.

This version of legality is, of course, law's own story of its grandeur, something that transcends by its history and processes the persons and conflicts of the moment, offering objective rather than subjective judgment. In this account, the law is defined by its impartiality. Needless to say, in this rendering of law, the "haves" are no more likely to come out ahead than the "have nots."

One of our respondents, a woman we call Rita Michaels, provides several examples of this conception of legality and how it is articulated in thought and action. Rita is a middle-aged, white, divorced woman working as an office manager and supporting two sons in college. She lives in a meticulously neat and well-maintained home in a relatively affluent town. She had been married for 17 years, during which time her husband had been chronically unemployed, eventually refusing to work at all. Her decision to get a divorce, she said, was difficult and painful. According to Rita, none of her friends, neighbors, or family members, who were Roman Catholic, supported her decision to divorce.

The neighborhood was a very nice neighborhood, people knew me from when my kids were little, knew my husband, but no one really, no one knows what goes on inside someone's house. So, when I was divorced, or when I was in the process of doing this, a couple of my neighbors really were very upset. And my husband went and told these people that I was this terrible person and that I was throwing him out. (Rita Michaels)

Later in the interview, Mrs. Michaels said:

the neighbors, their acceptance of the fact that I was going to do this terrible thing, that I was this terrible person, um. . . . And I don't know, I think that maybe was the most painful.

In contrast, she told us:

The divorce was a rather pleasant experience, believe it or not . . . the court experience, what it felt like to go to the courtroom and face the judge or whomever. I don't mean that it was pleasant, I just think that I was pleasantly surprised because the judge had evidently read all the whatever they have, before time, . . . it was evident that he had done his homework. . . . I don't think I was in that court more than, I would say maybe 45 minutes and he awarded me the divorce. He said that there was no reason for me to have to live under these conditions. . . . It left me with a good feeling. That I did do the right thing, and that he thought it was right also. Funny, I remember his exact words because it left a lasting impression.

In contrast to family and neighbors, the judge affirmed her experience and her decision to seek a divorce. She found a validation that she had not expected. Rejected and stigmatized by her family and friends and feeling outside the moral universe they guarded, Mrs. Michaels found that the law offered an alternative moral order in which she was neither wrong, nor morally deviant.

This set of legal values, rights, and expectations, was less particular and partial than the world of her family and neighbors. Her husband had not fulfilled his obligations under these larger, more general set of norms. She was comforted that she could point to these norms as grounding and legitimacy for her action. Here, Mrs. Michaels articulated a very traditional conception and function of legal ordering: protection of the individual against local group norms, a protection that derives from legality residing outside these local norms. Whereas her neighbors lacked information ("one never knows what goes on in someone else's house") and could be swayed by the misrepresentations of her husband that she was "a terrible person," Rita perceived the judge as informed and impartial.

The impartiality that is imputed to law is not just a claim for the objectivity of the law's agents: people believe that the objectivity inheres in what the law should and should not be used for. Many respondents, including Rita Michaels, often police the boundary separating the public world of law from the private worlds of self-interest and individual action by disqualifying their lives from the realm of the legal and refusing to invoke the law.

When asked whether she would call the police in response to a neighborhood conflict, Rita readily rejected the idea, claiming, "I don't use my police that way." At one level, her statement seems contradictory: expressing both identification (my police) and distance (her refusal to call the police). Yet when we unpack her meaning, putting it in the context of her other experiences, it becomes clear that the two meanings expressed are less oppositional than interdependent. In point of fact, Rita Michaels identifies with the police precisely because they do not attend to the messiness of everyday neighborhood conflicts.

Many people expressed the lack of connection between law and ordinary life. For these persons, encountering the law in the course of their lives—whether it involved being stopped by a police officer, being audited by the Internal Revenue Service, or serving on a jury—represented a disruption.

Furthermore, in deciding whether to mobilize the law, people often thought about it as "breaking frame," that is, rupturing normal relationships, practices, and identities. When asked what action he had taken in response to what he described as the deterioration of this neighborhood, Don Lowe disavowed the possibility of doing anything out of the ordinary.

I'm not a person who goes down and pickets or creates a disturbance like that. I'm a normal taxpaying person, I work, come home, pay my bills, pay my taxes, and you know, try to keep a low profile.

For people like Rita Michaels and Don Lowe who understand the law in this way, a decision to mobilize or use legal forms often is preceded by the crucial interpretive move of framing a situation in terms of some public, or at least general set of interests.

Claudia Greer, a black minister and licensed practical nurse living in Camden, New Jersey, explained the conditions under which she would "bother" the police,

I might go to the police, but then again I might not. If they were destructive or fighting, or you know, then I might. I'd call the police . . . if there are gun shots or something like that, then, 'cause everybody's threatened then.

Notably, in this statement, it was not only the severity of the action (the gunshots) that Claudia Greer gave as a reason for bothering the police, but it was the collective nature of the harm it posed that justified her decision to turn to the law.

For some people, refusing to use the law, even if it requires accepting injury or harm, is an indication of moral strength and independence. Sophia Silva criticized a friend of hers, Joanne, for suing a neighbor after that neighbor had run over Joanne's child. Sophia Silva's criticism of Joanne's action is drawn implicitly as she describes her own parents' response to a similar situation years before:

I hope you don't have to interview Joanne, but my friend Joanne, but my friend Joanne's daughter was on a bicycle and a neighbor was coming out of her driveway and the child was knocked down, and they sued the driver. . . . And I myself would not. . . . I remember as a child sitting on the pavement, and I was run over by the car of the people next door. Now you have to remember that my parents had no money, this was Depression time, and my father was bringing home five dollars a week. . . . And the car backed over my leg, and my parents refused any medical help. To this day I have a limp.

Later in her interview, Mrs. Silva told us that she had, in fact, sued a grocery store in her town after she had slipped on a piece of fruit. In explaining her decision to sue, she said, "I did sue, because it would be hard to think of some senior citizen slipping on that." The sincerity of Sophia Silva's altruistic motive is not, of course, the issue. What is important is the perception that such a casting is necessary. Through such a vocabulary of motive, the law is constructed and apprehended as impartial, standing above and outside the truck of everyday life and mundane motive.

With the Law

We also heard a second story of law, a story we call "with the law." Here legality is described and "played" as a game, a bounded arena in which preexisting rules can be deployed and new rules invented to serve the widest range of interests and values.

This account of law represents legality as a terrain for tactical encounters through which people marshal a variety of social resources to achieve strategic goals. Rather than existing outside of everyday life, this version of the law sees it as operating simultaneously with commonplace events and desires. In other words, the boundaries that might be seen to separate law from the everyday (a boundary so meticulously policed by the likes of Rita Michaels, Don Lowe, and Sophia Silva), is here understood to be relatively porous and fragile, as new uses and applications of law emerge. In this second story, respondents expressed less concern about the legitimacy of legal procedures or the universal values that underwrite legality. Instead, they talked about the value of self-interest and the effectiveness of legal rules and forms for achieving their desires.

These accounts of law describe a world of legitimate competition. Less likely to reference the law's power, they often refer to the power of self and other to successfully deploy and engage the law. They explicitly likened the law to a game, a gimmick, like a chess tournament, in short as an arena for marshaling ones' resources and demonstrating one's skill in pursuit of competitive self-interest. In articulating this understanding of the law, people were wise to the "haves" coming out ahead, that resources, experience, and skill matter in who wins this law game.

One man, Ray Johnson, recounted a dispute he had with his landlord about his lease. Mr. Johnson described his landlord as a skilled and experienced player in this game of rights, entitlements, and interests. Yet, despite the landlord's skill and reputation, Ray Johnson was prepared for the engagement, he told us.

This guy was a leading man in the community, and he had ties in City Hall, he used to get people evicted out of here in a week. They didn't know any better. He'd intimidate them. He'd do whatever he did with City Hall, and they'd get the paperwork pushed through, and they'd be gone. So he went into his little song and dance about what he was going to do and so on and so forth. And I said, "Yeah, well, no matter how you look at it, if you want me to persuade you that I have a right to this apartment, we can have that discussion. According to the lease here you cannot cancel the lease. You have to give me the option to renew. Says so right here! You do not have the option not to let me renew." We talked about it. Well, I had no fear that it wasn't [going to work out]. He couldn't evict me!

The right to the apartment to which Raymond Johnson alluded was not a right he saw as grounded in legal principle, natural law, or abstract theories of justice. It was a right that he deduced from the rules of the game, the writing on the lease and the city statutes. Later in the interview, Mr. Johnson declared, somewhat defiantly: "There is no justice. You either win or you lose. As long as you can accomplish your objectives, you win. I'm not concerned about justice."

Mr. Johnson's cynicism was also expressed in the view that not only was the law an arena for pursuing self-interest, but that deceit and manipulation would prevail. Opponents could be expected to lie, bluff, or manufacture a story; smart and wily players should be prepared for that. One respondent stated simply,

I learned you need proper representation because people tend to tell lies when they go to court.

What is significant about this statement and others like it is that it is not a general assessment of human nature and the propensity to lie. The pointed reference to lying "when they go to court" suggests that the tendency to lie is linked to a particular place and time where deceit is expected and permitted.

In this game of skill, resources, manipulation, and deceit, virtually all our respondents agreed that the most crucially consequential resource one can mobilize in a legal encounter is a lawyer. No matter how competent the individual, no matter how much experience or knowledge a citizen might acquire, he or she occupies an amateur status in relation to lawyers. Lawyers represent, then, the professional players in the game of law.

John Collier believed that his failure to hire a lawyer was decisive in his inability to defend himself against charges of illegal dumping. John vehemently denied the charges and appeared in criminal court without a lawyer. At the time of our interview, he admitted that "he should've had a lawyer," but at the time of the incident, he did not think that it was necessary "because I didn't feel I was guilty of a crime." John Collier's original belief that lawyers are necessary only for the guilty was undermined by his experience in court.

They had pictures of my truck with everything in it. When this lawyer [the prosecutor] asked me, "Is that your truck?" I said "Yeah." And they said "OK." And they got me. I should never have admitted that that truck was mine. If I had had a lawyer they would really have no evidence. You know, lawyers are much smarter than the average person. So they sucked me into it.

Another respondent echoed the view that lawyers are skilled at manipulation and trickery. Andrew Eberly reported:

Somebody came by to write a report. They asked me how far was I away from the accident. And, I said, "Well, I don't know how far I was, I wasn't too far from here to there." He said, "I have to have a number." So I said, "Well, twelve feet, if you have to have a number, about twelve feet." Went to court and the attorney asked me how far I was from the accident and I said, "Anywhere from ten to fifteen feet." He says, "Well, under sworn affidavit you said you were twelve feet." I said, "To me that sounds the same. Twelve feet is the same as ten to fifteen." That's the kind of situation that you run up against in trials. The attorneys play games with the minds of people.

In this understanding of the law, it is an open arena for the legitimate pursuit of interest, but it is also one fraught with pitfalls. Lawyers lie in ambush or simply outmaneuver you. Opponents have connections to City Hall and the like. And your own naiveté—a naiveté that simply fails to understand that the law is a game—can undermine one's chances of winning. Still, although some are discouraged from engaging in the play, others find a ludic pleasure in the encounters. Alan Fox, one of the few attorneys we interviewed, grew up in an upper-middle-class community where he still lived. Mr. Fox made numerous references throughout the interview to his friends, some of whom he has known since childhood. He mentioned to us that if any of his friends could benefit from an uncomplicated litigation, he initiates it for them for no fee. In one particular instance, Alan Fox mentioned the property reassessments about to be undertaken by the town.

So I thought what I would do, in a magnanimous gesture, is I would file an appeal for everybody in my poker game. Just do them all at the same time.

Thus, to Alan Fox the law is a gift he can bestow upon others. Deploying the law in this way provides opportunities to achieve personal objectives, not the least of which is displaying his attachment to his friends. I fact, Alan Fox plays law as he plays poker. He said, "Because people who are really my friends, I couldn't do enough for them." Besides, Alan Fox told us, "It's fun."

Up Against the Law

Finally, we heard a third cultural narrative in people's accounts of law, one we call up against the law. In this narrative, law is presented as a product of unequal power. Rather than objective and fair, legality is understood to be arbitrary and capricious. Unwilling to stand before the law, and without the resources to play with the law, people often act against the law, employing ruses, tricks, and subterfuges to evade or appropriate law's power.

People revealed their sense of being up against the law as being unable to either maintain the law's distance from their everyday lives and unable to play by its rules. Bess Sherman is a black, elderly woman who had had difficulty obtaining medical treatment for what turned out to be breast cancer. After months of doctors' appointments and applications she finally obtained Supplemental Security Income (SSI). Recounting the experience, she told us:

I know if I had money or had been familiar, I probably would have gotten on it earlier, like the system is now. That's what they have to do. If people want to get on [SSI], and they know themselves that they are sick, they go to this lawyer, Shelly Silverberg. . . . People say "Well, why don't you go to a lawyer, Bess? Why don't you go to Shelly Silverberg?" Bess can't go, because Bess don't have no money.

Thus, being without resources, Ms. Sherman understood that she had little or no choice but to submit to the round of appointments, forms, diagnoses, and hearings. Finding themselves in such a position of powerlessness, people often described to us their attempts at "making do," using what the situation momentarily and unpredictably makes available—materially and discursively—to fashion solutions they would not be able to achieve within conventionally recognized schema and resources. Footdragging, omissions, ploys, small deceits, humor, and making scenes are typical forms of resistance for those up against the law.

Recognizing themselves as the "have nots" facing some more legally, economically, or socially endowed opponent, people use what they can to get what they need. The feints, tricks, and opportunistic ploys are rarely illegal. Most often, resistance of this sort does not transgress the rules as much as it evades them. It does not challenge power as much as it stuns it.

After repeated calls to the police about problems in his neighborhood were ignored, Jesus Cortez called again pretending to be a woman. He finally succeeded in mobilizing the police. Aida Marks, on the advice of her family doctor, tried unsuccessfully to get her son transferred to another hospital after he had been shot. When the nurse mistakenly handed Mrs. Marks her son's case records, she saw an opportunity. Knowing that neither the transfer nor surgery could not occur without the records, she acted.

I had that big bag from Avon with me and this silly old nurse up there . . . she gave me all of Ronald's records so I pushed them down into my bag. . . . They couldn't find those records, they was having fits!

Refusing to leave retail stores, sitting in guidance counselor's offices, calling the president of a company, and stopping police officers for speeding are all examples of the disturbances and reversals of power that people enacted to escape the law's costs or lighten its burden. Recognizing the futility of demanding a right (to service, protection, attention, or respect), people found other ways of achieving their ends. Notably such efforts to resist the power of law are rarely cynical; more often, people undertake these violations of convention and, sometimes, law with a strong sense of justice and right.

The Ideological Effects of Contradiction

What we found, then, woven through the stories of 430 people were radically different, even contradictory images of law, how it works, and how it ought to work. There was pervasive "ideological penetration" in that people routinely articulated that the law was not about justice, but that it was fixed to advantage the wealthy, big complex organizations, and even quintessential repeat players: the criminal. This penetration, however, was not complete in that it was counterposed by articulations of law as embodying the highest ideals of justice and fairness. In short, the law appears to people as both sacred and profane, god and gimmick, interested and disinterested, here and not here. At times, legality emerged as a formal, fair, impartial, and transcendent arbiter of disputes where "haves" and "have nots" stand equally before the law. Legality was also described as a commonplace, available arena where self-interest prevailed, and having it (money, resources, experience, and determination) made all the difference. Finally, legality was apprehended as a terrain of power, where might makes right; here it is not even a question of losing the game, but of not even being able to play.

If we focus in particular on the first two stories of law ("before" and "with" the law), it appears that we found an opposition in people's consciousness of legality that corresponds to the contradiction Galanter described in terms of the law's structure or architecture: a series of dualisms limiting the achievement of equal justice under law. What complicates this picture is the fact that these different stories of law were expressed by nearly everyone in the sample. The varied images of legality did not, in other words, neatly correspond to persons, with some being "before" the law and others "with" the law. Individuals, almost without exception, expressed more than one of these cultural narratives.

In fact, we found that one person would articulate these contradictory views, not just at different points in the interview, about different matters or experiences, but within a single account or utterance. For example, the statement that the law is "just a gimmick" (and its variants) seems to acknowledge legality as a game (perhaps even one that is "fixed" to benefit the wealthy and powerful). At the same time, through the inclusion of "just" and the tone of disgust and disappointment with which this phrase is typically uttered, the individual expresses an aspiration that law be otherwise.

This finding—commonly expressed alternative and opposing stories of law—brings us back to the question we posed at the beginning of this paper: What is the ideological significance of knowing that the "haves" come out ahead? Is legality rendered imperfect, flawed, and vulnerable because it is understood to be a game as well as transcendent, a realm of power as well as a realm of disinterested decision-making? Does an awareness of the structural contradictions of law—knowing, despite formal assurances of equality before the law, that the "haves" really do come out ahead—lead to critique and disillusionment?

In answering these questions, we suggest precisely the opposite, arguing that the multiple and contradictory meanings of legality protect it from— rather than expose it to—radical critique. For too many years, sociolegal scholars have interpreted the gap between the law on the books and the law in action as a problem, an imperfection in the fabric of legality, something to be repaired. Rather than a flaw, or something to be explained away, we need to think about how the apparent oppositions and contradictions—the so-called gap—might actually operate ideologically to define and sustain legality as a durable and powerful social institution.

As we suggested in the introduction, although there is still much that is contested about the nature and meaning of ideology, there is considerable consensus over what it is not. Few contemporary scholars would claim that ideology is a grand set of ideas that in its seamless coherence precludes all competing ideas. It is not, in other words, a single giant schema that determines how and what people think. In fact, the most promising reformulations of ideology do not posit it as a body of abstracted ideas at all (neither static, nor coherent, nor otherwise). Rather, ideology is a complex process "by which meaning is produced, challenged, reproduced, transformed" (Barrett 1980:97). Construed as a process, ideology shapes social life, not because it prevents thinking (by programming or controlling people's thoughts), but because it actually invites thinking. Ideology derives from and reflects back upon shared experiences, particularly those of power; it is inextricably tied to practical consciousness.

Defined as a form of sense making that embeds power, ideology has to be lived, worked out, and worked on. It has to be invoked and applied and challenged. People have to use it to make sense of their lives. It is only through that sense making that people produce not only those lives but the specific structures and contests for power within which they live. The internal contradictions, oppositions, and gaps are not weaknesses in the ideological cloth. On the contrary, an ideology is sustainable only through such internal contradictions insofar as they become the basis for the invocations, reworkings, applications, and transpositions through which ideologies are enacted in everyday life.

Taken together, these apparent contradictions permit individuals wide latitude in interpreting social phenomena and personal experience in ways that are consistent with prevailing ideologies of legality. Challenges to legality for being only a game, or a gimmick (the realist account "with the law") can be rebutted by invoking legality's reified, transcendent purposes (the idealist account of "before the law"). Similarly, dismissals of law for being irrelevant to ordinary people and mundane matters, housed in leather tomes and marble halls outside the truck of everyday life, can be answered by invoking its gamelike character and routinized availability.

Fitzpatrick (1992) traces what he calls law's mythic power to these same contradictions. Myths create figures that mediate diverse planes or sites in opposition. Heroes and monsters straddle the chaos and order. These mythological heroes and monsters are themselves complex beings with one parent human and the other divine. According to Lévi-Strauss (1968:22):

Thus, Gilgamesh of Mesopotamian myth was two-thirds divine and one-third human. The Church is of this earth but also Christ's mystical body. All mediating figures must retain something of that duality, namely an ambiguous and equivocal character.

To appreciate how legality's power is sustained by its ability to mediate diverse normative aspirations, and how this mediation is achieved through the opposing stories before and with the law, it is useful to consider a hypothetical situation of ideological consistency and purity. An insistence that the law be just, impartial, and objective (an insistence unalloyed by the cynical expectation that it is also a game of manipulation and advantage) would easily be rejected in the face of abundant empirical evidence that law is not entirely fair, just, impartial, or omniscient. To the extent that consent and support were premised on the unfailing enactment and realization of these ideals, they would soon crumble.

In fact, the ideological effect achieved through the images of before and with the law is a rather typical one: a general ahistorical truth is constructed alongside, but as essentially incommensurate to, particular and material practices. Indeed, we suggest that this contradiction may characterize and account for the durability of all social institutions (Ewick & Silbey 1995).

For instance, in his analysis of contests over the meaning and cultural boundaries of science, Gieryn discovered a diverse and contradictory list of qualities and characteristics used to define science and distinguish it from nonscience. The same contestant in a particular battle over what constitutes true science would depict it variously as "practically useful but useless; quantitative and qualitative, . . . finite and infinite (in terms of what can be known scientifically), politically and ethically engaged and detached; driven by theory and data" (Gieryn 1999:21). Although the particular contradictions that characterize science are different from those that we found characterize legality, they similarly juxtapose two very different realms of action: that which is transcendent and detached with that which is mundane and interested.

We are persuaded that these ideological contradictions help sustain institutional authority and power when we further consider institutions that have experienced relative decline, for instance, the role of religion as a central institution in twentieth-century American life. The process known as secularization generally refers to a cultural shift that relegates religion and concern with supernatural matters to fewer and more circumscribed aspects of social life than had been the case in earlier historical periods. Weber traces the roots of twentieth-century secularization to the Protestant reformation and the rise of capitalism. Prior to this shift, daily life was saturated by religious meaning. Saints' days and feasts punctuated the calendar. Religion provided the moral compass for everyone. With modernization, religious observance became temporally and spatially circumscribed. The new spirit of capitalism appropriated the asceticism religion had dictated. The institutional authority religion had possessed shifted to the state. Notably, for the present argument, religion lost its central organizing and defining role not because it became profaned, associated with commerce and politics, but exactly the reverse. Religion and religious observance were increasingly set apart, specifically and contractually in the constitution and foundational documents of the liberal state. By being "set apart" (in time and space and in terms of social interactions), it became merely and wholly sacred. The occasional priest or rabbi joke notwithstanding, religion lost most of its articulation in the routines of daily life, and with that, it lost its institutional and ideological authority.[3]

The apparent incomparability of two of the stories we heard preserves the ideological contradictions by concealing the social organization that connects the general ideal of objective disinterested decision-making in "before the law" to the material practices represented in the story we called "with the law," including the inequality of access, the mediating role of lawyers, and the gamesmanship. The conjunction of the two stories—the contradiction itself—mediates the incomplete, flawed, practical, and mundane world with the normative legitimacy and consent that all social institutions require. Thus, legality becomes a place where processes are fair, decisions are reasoned, and the rules are known beforehand at the same time as it is a place where justice is only partially achieved, if it is at all, where public defenders do not show up, where sick old women cannot get disability benefits, where judges act irrationally and with prejudice, and where the "haves" come out ahead.

By obscuring the connections between the particular and the general, firsthand evidence and lived experience of ordinary people (experiences that might potentially contradict that general truth and the legitimacy it underwrites) are excluded as exceptional, idiosyncratic, or irrelevant. As a consequence, the power and privilege that attach to legal processes are preserved through what appears to be or is asserted to be the irreconcilability or irrelevance of the particular—local and experiential—to the general, universal, or transcendent norm of disinterested, objective judicial decision-making.

Don Lowe, one of our respondents, told us, for instance, that the process of jury selection was manipulated and stacked, as he put it. Jurors were selected according to their demographic characteristics. By carefully selecting jurors on the basis of their gender, race, and social class, according to Mr. Lowe, unscrupulous lawyers could manipulate outcomes, thus subverting justice. Yet after a lengthy and impassioned indictment of this practice, Mr. Lowe concluded by stating that "justice prevails" and "the system works."

In their study of small claims courts, Conley and O'Barr (1990) found the same pattern of critique (of the particular event) and commitment (to the system). The litigants they interviewed reported surprise and frustration with the way their claims were transformed and interpreted in the process of litigation, often rendering them unrecognizable. Despite their frustrations and disappointment, however, litigants rarely blamed the system or condemned the law as unfair. Instead, they tended to blame either themselves for not being prepared or "the particular judge who heard their case" (ibid., p. 96).

How are we to interpret this abiding faith and commitment to a system that is, in people's own experience, unfair or worse? Is it merely an instance of naiveté or illogic? The frequency with which this sort of interpretation is made suggests that it is neither of these. For Don Lowe, as for many of our respondents, the law—the reified, transcendent law—is only partially or incompletely represented in the observable material world. Only partially represented in everyday life, legality cannot be completely assessed or dismissed on the basis of that material or mundane reality. In part, then, the power and durability of law derive from it not being understood as common and observable.

We reiterate, however, that law's power is only in part derived from its status as transcendent and ideal. Were it located only in the rarefied plane of abstraction and ideal, only in leather tomes and marble halls, somewhere other than the everyday life, it would risk irrelevance. A parallel but opposite effect from transcendence must be achieved for legality to become and remain an enduring social form. At the same time that legality is represented and treated as outside of everyday life, as the before the law story suggests, it must also be located securely within the realm of the everyday and the common-place. Thus, it is precisely because law is both god and gimmick, sacred and profane, objective, disinterested, and a terrain of legitimate partiality that it persists and endures. It is precisely because people believe that there is equality under law but also understand that sometimes the "haves" come out ahead that legality is sustained as a powerful structure of social action.

In an important sense, then, we have moved beyond conventional distinctions between ideals and practices, law on the books and law in action. These distinctions enforce false dichotomies. Legality is composed of multiple images and stories, each emplotting a particular relationship between ideals and practices, revealing their mutual interdependence. Because legality has this internal complexity—among and within the schema—it effectively universalizes legality. Any particular experience or account can fit within the diversity of the whole. Rather than simply an idealized set of ambitions and hopes, a fragile bulwark in the face of human variation, agency, and interest, legality is observed as both the ideal (and indeed several different ideals) as well as a space of powerful action. The persistently perceived gap is a space, not a vacuum; it is, in short, one source of the law's hegemonic power.

Notes

Previously published in Law & Society Review 33 (4), 1025–41 (1999); reprinted by permission. This paper was presented to the conference "Do the 'Haves' Still Come Out Ahead?" held at the Institute for Legal Studies at the University of Wisconsin, Madison, 1–2 May 1998. Adapted from Ewick and Silbey (1998), *The Common Place of Law: Stories from Everyday Life* (Chicago: University of Chicago Press).

Patricia Ewick is Associate Professor of Sociology at Clark University. She wrote *The Common Place of Law: Stories from Everyday Life* with Susan Silbey. Currently, she and Silbey are studying legal culture, consciousness, and science.

Susan S. Silbey is Professor of Sociology at Massachusetts Institute of Technology. Her book, *The Common Place of Law: Stories from Everyday Life* (University of Chicago Press) is coauthored with Patricia Ewick. She has conducted research on a variety of topics, including consumer protection enforcement, lower courts, mediation and alternatives to law, and the place of law in popular culture and consciousness. She is past President of the Law and Society Association, and past editor of the *Law & Society Review*.

1. We use the term *consciousness* to denote more than subjective experiences, ideas, or attitudes. We use the term *consciousness* to denote ways of participating in the processes of social construction. Thus, legal consciousness names the fact and forms of "participation in the process of constructing legality" as a structure of social action (Ewick & Silbey 1998:45, 224–26).

2. Legality is understood as an emergent structure of social action that manifests itself in diverse places, including but not limited to formal institutional settings. Legality operates as an interpretive framework and a set of resources with which the social world (including that part known as the law) is constituted.

3. The sacred, according to Emile Durkheim, is not based on a belief in supernatural entities, which others had used as a definition of religion. The central dichotomy in preliterate cultures was to be understood as separating those things, times, places, persons, animals, birds, stones, trees, rivers, mountains, plants, or liquids that were set apart (sacred) from routine (profane) uses in everyday life (Bocock 1996:273).

References

Barrett, Michelle (1980) *Women's Oppression Today: Problems in Marxist Feminist Analysis*. London: Verso.

Bocock, Robert (1996) "The Cultural Formations of Modern Society," in S. Hall, D. Held, D. Hubert & K. Thompson, eds., *Modernity: An Introduction to Modern Societies*. Cambridge, MA: Blackwell.

Conley, John M., & William M. O'Barr (1990) *Rules versus Relationships: The Ethnography of Legal Discourse*. Chicago: Univ. of Chicago Press.

Cotterrell, Roger [1984] (1995) *The Sociology of Law*. Charlottesville, VA: Michie Press.

Eagleton, Terry (1991) *Ideology: An Introduction*. London: Verso.

Ewick, Patricia, & Susan S. Silbey (1995) "Subversive Stories and Hegemonic Tales: Toward a Sociology of Narrative," 29 *Law & Society Rev.* 197–226.

——— (1998) *The Common Place of Law: Stories from Everyday Life*. Chicago and London: Univ. of Chicago Press.

Fitzpatrick, Peter (1992) *The Mythology of Modern Law*. London: Routledge.

Galanter, Marc (1974) "Why the 'Haves' Come Out Ahead: Speculations on the Limits of Legal Change," 9 *Law & Society Rev.* 95–160.

Gieryn, Thomas F. (1999) *Cultural Boundaries of Science: Credibility on the Line*. Chicago: Univ. of Chicago Press.

Hunt, Alan (1985) "The Ideology of Law: Advances and Problems in Recent Applications of the Concept of Ideology to the Analysis of Law," 19 *Law & Society Rev.* 11–37.

Lévi-Strauss, Claude (1968) *Structural Anthropology*. New York: Basic Books.

Scott, James (1990) *Domination and the Arts of Resistance*. New Haven, CT: Yale Univ. Press.

Silbey, Susan S. (1998) "Ideology, Power, and Justice," in B.G. Garth & A. Sarat eds., *Justice and Power in Sociological Studies*, vol. 1, *Fundamental Issues in Law and Society Research*. Evanston, IL: Northwestern Univ. Press.

Thompson, John B. (1990) *Ideology and Modern Culture: Critical Social Theory in the Era of Mass Communications*. Stanford, CA: Stanford Univ. Press.

When the "Haves" Hold Court

Speculations on the Organizational Internalization of Law

Introduction

At the core of Marc Galanter's pathbreaking 1974 article, "Why the 'Haves' Come Out Ahead: Speculations on the Limits of Legal Change," lies the distinction between those litigants who are "one shotters" and those who are "repeat players." Galanter (1974:98–99) argues that repeat players enjoy numerous advantages in the legal system, including (1) advance intelligence and the ability to preplan transactions; (2) ongoing access to specialists, reduced start-up costs, and economies of scale; (3) informal facilitative relationships with institutional incumbents; (4) long-run strategic interests and the ability to "play for rules"; and (5) experience in discerning which rule-changes are likely to "penetrate" into the law in action. Overall, Galanter suggests that these and other repeat player advantages significantly impede the efforts of one shotters to achieve significant social reforms through recourse to the legal system.

Although Galanter draws the dichotomy between one shotters and repeat players primarily in abstract structural terms, his description leaves little doubt that in modern American society, the archetypal repeat player is the large bureaucratic organization (e.g., 1974:97, 113).[1] Consistent with Galanter's definition of a repeat player, the typical large bureaucratic organization generally "has and anticipates repeated litigation, . . . and has the resources to pursue its long-run interests" (1974:98). Organizations take advantage of this repetition by employing all the classic long-term strategies described above. They enlist specialist attorneys to structure future transactions, they routinize their business and legal dealings to exploit economies of scale, and they lobby and litigate to secure favorable statutes and precedents. Moreover, with the rules primarily on their side, organizations also benefit from passive and overburdened judicial institutions, which make it difficult for others to challenge the status quo.

As perceptive as Galanter's 1974 account may have been, however, it omitted several aspects of organizations' law-oriented behavior that, although barely noticeable at the time, have since become significant features of the legal landscape. Galanter's portrait generally depicted organizations merely as ordinary (albeit privileged) parties in the traditional plaintiff-defendant-judge triad—parties who, to a large extent, remained dependent on state-made rules, public dispute resolution, independent lawyers, and governmental law enforcers. Admittedly, Galanter took care to note that organizations also participated in alternative disputing arenas, such as court-appended forums, direct negotiations "in the shadow of the law" (Mnookin & Kornhauser 1979), and private arbitration proceedings. Even here, however, an external legal decision-maker presumably stood above and separate from the disputing parties, either immediately or as a future threat.

In contrast, the following pages offer a somewhat more complex image of how organizational repeat players encounter the law. Specifically, we hypothesize that since 1974, large bureaucratic organizations have increasingly "internalized" important elements of the legal system.[2] This internalization, we argue, has taken at least four forms: (1) legal rule-making has been internalized through the "legalization" of individual firms and of larger organizational fields, (2) legal dispute processing has been internalized through the increasing use of alternative dispute resolution in both intra- and interorganizational conflicts, (3) legal expertise has been internalized through the growing prominence and changing role of in-house counsel, and (4) legal enforcement has been internalized through the reemergence of private organizational security staffs. Together, these shifts carry the potential to transform the large bureaucratic organization from being merely a structurally privileged actor in the public legal order to being a private legal order in its own right. In a very real sense, we suggest, today's organizations *hold court*, incorporating but also subsuming many of the public legal system's central functions. As private legislatures, courthouses, law offices, and police departments, organizations construct within and around themselves a semiautonomous legal regime that simultaneously mimics and absorbs even the most "official" institutions of governmental law.

To date, sociolegal scholarship has rarely examined this internalization of law as a coherent phenomenon, and the available evidence, although suggestive, remains sketchy and disorganized. For this reason, we treat the four components of the internalization process as hypotheses rather than as proven facts. In the spirit of Galanter's "speculations on the limits of legal change," the following pages offer speculations on the extensiveness of organizational change. Like Galanter's original essay, this article seeks to highlight "general features of a legal system like the American by drawing on (and re-arranging) commonplaces and less than systematic gleanings from the literature" (Galanter 1974:95). For each internalization hypothesis, we muster a substantial body of evidence and argumentation; however, we leave conclusive testing of these hypotheses to the future efforts of researchers throughout the law and society community. Our primary objectives here are simply to suggest that several apparently distinct bodies of research may actually fit together into a larger picture, and to consider the implications of that picture for the relationship between society's "haves" and "have nots." Because the composite image has only recently begun to emerge, our arguments are necessarily tentative and conjectural; if true, though, they imply significant changes in the contours of the modern legal order.

To explore these changes, this article examines the nature of organizations as private legal orders. We begin the exploration by presenting the four internalization hypotheses in detail and by surveying the existing evidence on each. We then discuss the ways in which the hypothesized trends, if they are indeed occurring, may carry the potential to transform organizations into private legal orders. Finally, we consider the implications of this transformation for the larger social system:[3] If the "haves" come out ahead as repeat players, how do they come out when they hold court? Although "have not" groups may gain some short-run advantages from the introduction of legal norms into the workplace, we contend that the organizational annexation of law subtly skews the balance between democratic and bureaucratic tendencies in society as a whole, potentially adding to the power and control of dominant elites.

The Internalization of Law

The years since 1974 have brought substantial shifts in the characteristics of large bureaucratic organizations, in the characteristics of the formal legal system, in the relationship between organizations and law, and in our knowledge of all three. This section discusses several of these developments. Specifically, we propose four interrelated hypotheses about the organizational internalization of law, and we draw together various secondary data supporting these hypotheses. Much, but not all, of this evidence comes from the area of employment law, because the employment relation has attracted considerable attention from organizational and sociolegal scholars in recent years. Nonetheless, we believe that our internalization hypotheses pertain to other legal topics as well, and we present data from nonemployment contexts whenever possible. The existing body of theory and research strongly suggests that internalization operates in similar ways across most, if not all, areas of law, and future research would do well to consider the workings of this phenomenon wherever it may occur.

To understand the organizational internalization of law, one must recognize that each hypothesized transformation has occurred at two levels simultaneously: within organizations and throughout organizational fields.[4] This simultaneity is by no means coincidental. Recent work in "neoinstitutional" organizational sociology (see, e.g., Powell & DiMaggio 1991; Scott 1995) suggests that new models and practices spread most rapidly when they become "institutionalized"—that is, "infused with value beyond the technical requirements of the task at hand" (Selznick 1948)—and such institutionalization generally proceeds through interactions between individual organizations and their field-level environments. These interactions have both "top-down" and "bottom-up" components. Some new models and practices emerge from field-level discourses and diffuse downward,[5] gaining legitimacy as individual organizations embrace them, implement them, and translate them into the lived experiences of organizational participants (DiMaggio & Powell 1983; Scott & Meyer 1983); other models and practices emerge from the innovations of individual organizations and migrate upward, gaining legitimacy as field-level discourses theorize them, systematize them and integrate them with the ongoing routines of the interorganizational environment (Suchman 1995a; Edelman et al. 1999). Thus, while changes in environmental conditions reconstruct individual organizations, changes in organizational behavior reciprocally reconstruct fields. Either way, the resulting institutional arrangements reflect both field-level and organization-level dynamics, and it would be a mistake to depict institutional change as solely the product of either isolated organizational decisions or undifferentiated collective rationales.

The four hypotheses that we discuss in this section involve such top-down and bottom-up institutionalization processes. Specifically, recent shifts in the structure of individual organizations and of organizational fields appear to be fostering a legalization of organizational governance, an expansion of alternative dispute resolution, a buildup of corporate in-house counsel staffs, and a proliferation of corporate private security forces. We suggest that each of these internalization dynamics represents an important change in contemporary organizations' legal behaviors and appearances, and we hypothesize that although the extent of these changes varies, all are increasingly acquiring an institutionalized status.

THE LEGALIZATION HYPOTHESIS

In 1974, Galanter argued that repeat players benefit from their capacity to structure transactions in ways that give themselves positional advantages, should disputes subsequently arise. Further, according to Galanter, repeat players augment these positional advantages by playing for rules, that is, by actively pursuing favorable statutes, regulations, and judicial precedents. Today, as in 1974, repeat players continue to invest heavily in shaping public laws. Since the time of Galanter's initial analysis, however, researchers have increasingly suggested that large bureaucratic organizations also structure transactions through a more private process of internal "legalization": by creating and formalizing internal policies that approximate the core principles of legality—due process and substantive justice—large bureaucracies attempt to preempt and displace the interventions of public legal authorities (Selznick 1969; Nonet & Selznick 1978; Edelman 1990). In mimicking the external legal order, organizations may manage, in effect, to construct their own legitimacy, winning the right not only to structure future transactions but also to establish the rules by which those transactions will be judged (Edelman 1992).

Organization theorists since Max Weber have of course noted that bureaucratic organization implies formal rule-making and hierarchical authority (Weber 1947), but the specific homology between organizational and legal rules attracted little attention until the publication of Philip Selznick's *Law, Society, and Industrial Justice* in 1969. Labeling this internalization of law-like rule-making "legalization," Selznick explored how administrative pressures and daily problem-solving challenges lead organizations to develop new workplace practices that draw on the public legal order for models of fairness and objectivity. Over time, these introjections of legality become institutionalized both within organizations as formal rules and procedures, and outside organizations as court rulings and statutes. Selznick argued that such legalization transforms organizations from being hierarchical systems that heed only official power to being normatively constrained polities that provide substantial "citizenship" rights for their members.

In recent years, neoinstitutional organizational sociologists have extended this line of analysis to locate the impetus for legalization not only in internal management challenges but also (and primarily) in the plethora of external strictures that organizations now encounter in the larger legal environment (Sitkin & Bies 1994). New laws create new normative and cognitive preconditions for organizational activity, and organizations respond to these public legal ideals by constructing and displaying formal policies and structures that symbolize key tenets of the new regime (Edelman 1990; Sutton et al. 1994). Empirical work shows how legalization within organizations parallels changes in civil rights law (Baron et al. 1986; Edelman 1992; Schultz 1990; Dobbin et al. 1993; Sitkin & Bies 1994; Sutton et al. 1994; Konrad & Linnehan 1995), antipollution law (Hawkins 1984), disabilities law (Scheid & Suchman 1998), and health and safety law (Bardach & Kagan 1982; Rees 1988). In all these cases, organizational reactions have been both procedural and structural, taking the form of more (and more detailed) written rules, policies, and protections, and new law-related offices, positions, and programs.

Alongside such neoinstitutional analyses linking the legalization of organizational rule-making to developments in the larger legal environment, a variety of competing noninstitutional accounts have generated substantial legalization literatures of their own. Traditional "rational" explanations for legalization have focused on the need for coordination and formalization both within and between firms, thus treating legalization as simply a special case of bureaucratization (Weber 1947; cf. Scott 1987; Sutton et al. 1994). Industrial relations theorists have argued that the threat of organized labor motivates employers to legalize as a way of convincing workers that unionization is unnecessary (Slichter 1919; Jacoby 1985). And critical theorists have pointed to legalization as a mechanism of bourgeois hegemony, a device for obscuring capitalist control by shifting the locus of power from direct coercion to impersonal, universalistic rules (Edwards 1979; Gordon et al. 1982). Despite their divergent explanatory frameworks, however, institutional and noninstitutional analyses largely agree on the contours of the underlying empirical phenomenon: all concur that organizational governance increasingly operates through legalized internal and external polities, with formal rules, rights, and procedures for appeal.

Empirically, the increase in legalization since the publication of Galanter's 1974 essay is especially apparent in the context of employee rights, an area in which the research literature offers several large-scale longitudinal studies. Edelman (1992) reports that in a sample of 346 organizations, only 30 had antidiscrimination guidelines in place in 1969, 118 instituted such rules in the 1970s (mostly between 1975 and 1980), and 75 more followed suit in the 1980s. Edelman's data also reveal a sharp jump in other forms of legalization during the 1970s, including the spread of special offices devoted to civil rights issues and special procedures for processing discrimination complaints. Similarly, in a study of 300 organizations, Sutton et al. (1994) find that the number of organizations granting the right to a formal disciplinary hearing increased steadily from 1955 to 1990, with the steepest rise coming after 1975.

In addition to these organization-level trends, scattered evidence suggests that organizational fields themselves may be becoming more legalized as well. The most obvious source of field-level legalization is the proliferation of industry-specific statutes, regulations, and judicial doctrines (Galanter & Rogers 1991; Blumrosen 1993; Nelson 1994; 349–50). Organizational fields, however, also become more legalized because of increasingly complex private governance regimes (e.g., contracts, associations, joint ventures, holding companies, mergers) among their constituent firms (see generally Nelson

1994:350–52). Equally significantly, changes in both public and private governance open niches for new (and old) professions, each with its own set of rationalized definitional categories and formalized ethical precepts (see, e.g., Edelman et al. 1992; Dezalay & Garth 1996; Suchman & Cahill 1996). Through the interaction of these mechanisms, formal rules increasingly become the accepted way of enforcing or reflecting institutional norms at the field level as well as at the organizational level. This pattern holds true not only for civil rights, but also across a wide range of domains, including workplace safety, employee benefits, pollution control, historical preservation, antitrust, and consumer protection law.

Thus, the "legalization hypothesis" posits that although large bureaucratic organizations still seek to influence public law, they have also come to internalize a substantial amount of lawlike rule-making within their own polity structures and within the polity structures of their surrounding fields. Although the legalization of organizational life was already under way when Galanter first published "Why the 'Haves' Come Out Ahead," this process appears to have accelerated dramatically over the ensuing quarter century as organizations have responded to—and constructed—an ever more complex legal environment. As a result, organizations increasingly manage both internal and external relations through facially neutral universalistic rules and rationalized formal procedures. Internal governance now centers on the establishment of a complex citizenship system of rights, privileges, entitlements, and duties, and external governance now centers on the establishment of an elaborate web of regulations, contracts, norms, and professions. Together, these developments appear to be transforming private lawmaking from an occasional managerial expedient into a core organizational function.

THE ADR HYPOTHESIS

When "Why the 'Haves' Come Out Ahead" first appeared in 1974, the term *alternative dispute resolution* (ADR) was not part of the common lexicon (Galanter 1999; Plapinger 1999). Certainly, many organizations engaged in informal dispute handling of various kinds (consider, for example, the role of the hospital ombudsperson, the church pastor, or even the school principal), but the intentional construction of private disputing forums was a marginal and idiosyncratic activity, embraced by only a few organizational fields. In the years since 1974, however, an "ADR movement"[6] has begun to take shape among legal and other professionals, with proponents advocating a plethora of nonjudicial dispute resolution techniques, including most notably various flavors of mediation and arbitration. Propelled by this movement, systematic private dispute processing appears to be gaining prominence as a way for organizational repeat players to structure their future transactions.[7] Just as legalization allows organizations to internalize lawlike control over their routine activities and operations, ADR—for both inter- and intraorganizational disputes—allows organizations to internalize lawlike control over their "problem cases."

The ADR movement has developed largely as a critique of overly formalistic court adjudication and of the "liberal legal model" of public rights more generally. In place of public lawsuits, ADR allows disputing parties to negotiate their own private solutions to their disagreements, generally with a trained disputere solution professional serving as a "neutral" facilitator. Proponents suggest that such structured informality can resolve disputes more responsively and more durably than traditional litigation, can empower disputants to recognize and assert their needs while simultaneously honoring the needs of others, and can even help to preserve and build community (Fisher & Ury 1981; Menkel-Meadow 1984; Moore 1986; Westin & Feliu 1988; Bush 1989; Rosenberg 1991; Bush & Folger 1994; Lande 1998; cf. Edelman & Cahill 1998). Further, at a more pragmatic level, the ADR movement also promises a relatively inexpensive and efficient alternative to the delay, cost, risk, and bad publicity of litigation (Lande 1998).

Although many of these themes have deep roots in sociolegal thought, the ADR movement itself only emerged in earnest in the mid-1970s, when a series of convocations and experiments began to stir interest and mobilize expertise. Among the most influential of these early events was the Pound Conference, a 1976 meeting of judges, attorneys, and law professors in St. Paul, Minnesota. The conference elicited calls for a new multimethod "dispute resolution center," designed to replace the traditional courthouse (Kaye 1996). The idea of the minitrial followed soon thereafter and was first implemented in 1977 (Plapinger 1999). Two years later, 12 corporate counsel joined together to found the Center for Public Resources (CPR) Institute for Dispute Resolution, a standing body dedicated to promoting ADR both for interorganizational business disputes and also for intraorganizational disputes between employers and their employees (Westin & Feliu 1988).

From these beginnings, the ADR movement has built a solid base of support among practitioners and policy makers alike. Numerous books and articles have touted ADR as the cure for various organizational ills (e.g. Westin & Feliu 1988; Ewing 1989), and professional management journals have brimmed with ADR testimonials (Edelman, Uggen, & Erlanger 1999).[8] Federal law and policy have reinforced such arguments. The Equal Employment Opportunity Commission (EEOC) and many state workers' compensation boards now encourage the use of ADR in employer-employee disputes (Lipsky & Seeber 1998), and both the 1990 Americans with Disabilities Act and the 1991 Civil Rights Act include explicit provisions promoting ADR for a wide range of discrimination claims. The judiciary, for its part, has generally followed suit—as evidenced, for example, by the U.S. Supreme

Court's 1991 *Gilmer* ruling (*Gilmer v. Interstate/Johnson Lane Corp.* 1991), which upheld the validity of mandatory arbitration clauses, even though such clauses may prevent parties from vindicating significant statutory rights (Lipsky & Seeber 1998). Indeed, the use of ADR has even gained substantial currency within the courts themselves. As early as 1980, 10 states and one federal district were experimenting with ADR, and by 1996, nearly half of all state and federal jurisdictions were operating ADR programs of some kind (Reuben 1996, 1997).

In response to these developments, the organizational world has come since 1974 to embrace ADR for a wide variety of both inter- and intraorganizational matters. In a recent survey of 70 outside counsel, 58 inside counsel and 50 senior corporate executives in three states, Lande (1998:15) found that 90% of outside counsel, 84% of inside counsel, and 39% of senior executives reported having participated in an ADR proceeding as a partisan at least once. Over 60% of attorneys (both outside and inside) and 12% of executives reported having participated in ADR four times or more, and in some jurisdictions, the percentages were even higher (Lande 1995:83). Similarly, Lipsky and Seeber (1998:137) report that 88% of the 1,000 largest U.S. corporations use mediation or arbitration on a regular basis, particularly in commercial and employment cases.[9]

For interorganizational disputing, the public court system remains an important forum, but it no longer holds an unquestioned monopoly (Lande 1995). Although rates of traditional business litigation have risen since 1974 (Galanter & Rogers 1991:3−17), ADR appears to have gained substantial legitimacy as well, to the point where many executives reportedly view extralegal dispute processing not only as a viable alternative to formal lawsuits, but actually as a *preferable* alternative, especially when conflicts arise in the context of ongoing business relations (ibid., pp. 18−20; Lande 1995).[10] Thus, for example, Lande reports that almost 80% of senior executives express greater satisfaction with ADR than with litigation (ibid., p. 139), and a similar percentage believe that ADR would be appropriate in half or more of all business lawsuits (ibid., pp. 166−67). Further, over 80% indicate that ADR helps to preserve business relationships (ibid., p. 319), and over 90% believe that ADR is more sensitive than litigation "to the needs and practices of particular business communities" (ibid., p. 321).

Although such attitudes suggest widespread managerial support for ADR, actual shifts in behavior are harder to quantify, because the research literature offers few consistent longitudinal measures of organizational disputing; nonetheless, several indirect indicators suggest that interorganizational ADR has blossomed in recent years. One such indicator is the growing willingness of corporations to sign the Center for Public Resources' (CPR) "ADR pledge,"[11] expressing a commitment to resolve interorganizational disagreements through ADR rather than litigation. From an initial 46 signatories in 1984, the roster of endorsements has expanded dramatically, to almost 500 by 1990 and over 4,000 by 1999 (Galanter & Rogers 1991:19; CPR Institute for Dispute Resolution 1999). A second, somewhat more concrete indicator is the commercial caseload of the American Arbitration Association, which more than doubled between 1975 and 1988 (Galanter & Rogers 1991:Figure 5).[12] During this period, the number of private ADR providers also increased substantially, further adding to the sense that public courthouses are no longer the only "natural" venues for the handling of interorganizational disputes (ibid., p. 19).

A similar pattern seems to be emerging for intraorganizational disputing as well. Here, ADR has served as the model for various types of "internal dispute resolution" (IDR)—informal in-house alternatives to public lawsuits (Edelman et al. 1993).[13] Although longitudinal evidence on intraorganizational disputing remains sparse, several recent studies suggest that IDR in general is on the rise and that ADR-like forms of IDR have become quite common. Perhaps the clearest indicator of the growing prevalence of IDR is the spread of employee grievance procedures beyond traditionally unionized industries. Using two separate samples of firms throughout the economy, both Sutton et al. (1994) and Edelman, Uggen, and Erlanger (1999) report that the proportion of organizations with internal grievance procedures climbed sharply during the 1970s and continued to rise more gradually thereafter. Further, the ADR movement appears to have fostered particular interest in forms of IDR that emphasize active disputant participation, that incorporate mediation or other types of dialogic negotiation, and that focus less on public rights than on private psychological issues (Westin & Feliu 1988; Edelman et al. 1993).[14] In reflection of this, a 1995 General Accounting Office survey of 1,500 businesses found that 88.7% of private-sector companies with 100 or more employees were using some form of ADR for intraorganizational disputes, with mediation (47%) and arbitration (10%) being among the most common choices (General Accounting Office 1995).

Overall, then, the "ADR hypothesis" postulates that although large bureaucratic organizations still make heavy use of the public court system, they have also constructed a growing number of private disputing forums within their own organizational boundaries and within their industries, business communities, and fields. Both intra- and interorganizationally, the spread of ADR promotes informal dispute resolution based on privately negotiated norms and procedures at the same time that it curtails the formal enunciation, vindication, and enforcement of publicly mandated legal rights. Thus, like legalization, the ADR movement allows organizations (and organizational fields) to internalize a core legal function—in this case, dispute processing. To be sure, ADR also rejects some aspects of formal legalism, and in this sense, the legalization hypothesis and the ADR hypothesis may appear to be at odds. In the organizational context, however, the two movements stand for fundamentally similar things: legalization reflects a belief that rule-compliant fairness should be an attribute of private organizations as well as of public institutions, and ADR reflects a belief that rule-compliant fairness should be achieved in private forums, without the intrusion of public authorities.[15] Together, the two outlooks suggest that organizations can become their own courts and can create, embody, and implement rule-compliant fairness on their own behalf.

THE IN-HOUSE COUNSEL HYPOTHESIS

In 1974, Galanter argued that repeat players benefit from low start-up costs and economies of scale, because repeat players can hire lawyers on retainer and can treat legal preparation as a long-run investment. In addition, he noted, repeat players also benefit from greater familiarity with the law, because they can "learn by doing" in the course of their frequent contacts with the legal system. In recent years, several commentators have suggested that these previously distinct advantages of preparedness and expertise may be merging and intensifying as large bureaucratic organizations build increasingly sophisticated internal legal staffs (Chayes & Chayes 1985; Rosen 1989; Galanter & Rogers 1991:22−25; Nelson 1994; Nelson et al. 1997). Thus, a third potentially significant form of legal internalization may be the ascendance—in numbers, in status, and in influence—of the in-house counsel's office.[16]

Rather than simply keeping independent law firms on retainer, large bureaucratic organizations seem increasingly reliant on full-time salaried employees for the provision of general legal services. By some accounts, over two-thirds of the legal budgets of America's largest corporations are now spent on in-house lawyers who work in areas as diverse as real estate, antitrust, employment, intellectual property, and regulatory law (Chayes & Chayes 1985:279; Galanter & Rogers 1991:24).[17] Although commentators disagree over whether the population of in-house lawyers has expanded faster than the legal profession as a whole (see Rosen 1989:482 n. 7; Nelson 1994:370, 391), the absolute number of such attorneys has clearly increased substantially since the early 1970s, with the nationwide total approximately doubling in the 15 years from 1975 to 1990 (estimated from figures reported in Nelson 1994 and Heinz et al. 1998; see also Chayes & Chayes 1985:277 n. 1; Curran 1985; Galanter & Rogers 1991:22−25). In-house legal staffs seem to be growing on a firm-by-firm basis as well. In a replication of Heinz and Laumann's classic 1982 study of the Chicago bar, Heinz et al. (1998) found that the average corporate legal department had ballooned from 17 attorneys in 1975 to 55 attorneys in 1995.[18] Although nationwide evidence is too sketchy to allow unequivocal cross-time comparisons, Galanter and Rogers (1991:22−23) estimate that the proportion of manufacturing companies with in-house legal departments rose from 47% in 1959 to 59% in 1987 and that the total number of in-house lawyers increased across virtually every industrial sector. These trends seem to be particularly marked among Fortune 500 companies, which employ roughly 50% of all attorneys working in private industry (Curran 1985:19).

As these changes unfold, the decision to join a corporate legal staff—to "go in-house"—may be losing its pejorative implications within the legal profession (see, e.g., Chayes & Chayes 1985:277; Rosen 1989:479). Financially, inside counsel have kept roughly abreast of private practice attorneys in the years since 1974, with earnings growth lagging slightly behind large-firm lawyers but easily outpacing solo practitioners.[19] Indeed, even during the economic slowdown of the early 1990s when cost-cutting and downsizing were sweeping corporate America, in-house counsel salaries were rising at close to a 6% annual rate (Becker 1992). Moreover, with many young lawyers perceiving that workloads are lighter and autonomy greater in corporate legal departments than in independent "megalaw" firms (cf. American Bar Association 1991; Heinz et al. 1998:744), in-house counsel offices are no longer seen merely as refuges for attorneys who lack the acumen to earn partnership outside (Chayes & Chayes 1985:277, 293; Gilson & Mnookin 1985:382). Consequently, although reliable data on hiring trends are hard to find, most observers agree that the ability of large bureaucratic organizations to recruit and retain highly credentialed, experienced legal talent has risen substantially in recent years (Strasser 1985; Rosen 1989:504; Becker 1992).

Along with their increased size and status, corporate legal staffs appear to have gained new responsibilities as well. Although few studies have gathered detailed historical evidence on the activities of this segment of the bar, most observers agree that, in the past, the bulk of in-house work amounted to little more than routine ministerial housekeeping (Slovak 1979; Chayes & Chayes 1985; Spangler 1986). In contrast, today's in-house lawyers increasingly style themselves as active "law managers," buffering the corporation from external legal demands and bridging to outside service providers (Chayes & Chayes 1985:289 ff.; Rosen 1989:545; cf. Scott 1992:194). During pretrial discovery, for example, inside attorneys now play an assertive, autonomous role in screening corporate documents and in negotiating with outside counsel over the scope of the company's disclosures (see, generally, *Fordham Law Review* 1998).

In such interactions with outside attorneys, in-house counsel draw strength not only from their coequal claims to legal expertise but also from their extensive discretion over the selection of outside law firms for future business (Chayes & Chayes 1985:292; Nelson 1994:355). Legal work is increasingly put out to bids, with the inside counsel's office presiding over the "beauty pageants" that choose among potential representatives. At the extreme, a number of large corporations have even moved toward a subcontractor model in which the inside counsel's office "unbundles" legal services by, for example, assigning paralegal tasks to one outside firm and drafting tasks to another (Suchman 1998:857). For obvious reasons, these new approaches to the procurement and supervision of legal services substantially expand the role and influence of staff attorneys, especially with respect to their colleagues in private practice.

Relatively little systematic research has explored the forces driving this emerging "in-house counsel movement" (Rosen 1989), but most observers attribute the apparent shifts to at least three factors. First, the growth of in-house counsel offices responds, in part, to an increase in the cost of outside legal representation. As legal fees rise (both on a per-case basis and as a share of overall corporate budgets), expanded internal legal staffs can (1) absorb and routinize some tasks that might otherwise be performed at premium prices outside and (2) manage and rationalize the purchase of any legal services that the organization continues to seek externally (Chayes & Chayes 1985:297; Strasser 1985; Becker 1992; Nelson 1994:355). Second, in-house counsel offices may also be expanding in response to the increasing complexity and intrusiveness of the general legal environment. Organizations theory teaches that organizational structures tend to mirror environmental variety (Pondy & Mitroff 1979:7), and as legal regulations and liabilities proliferate in areas such as employment, labor relations, health and safety, antitrust, pollution abatement, intellectual property, and international trade, organizations are likely to respond by creating internal structures—staffed by lawyers—to manage these new external contingencies (Chayes & Chayes 1985:284–85; Nelson 1994:349–50). Finally, the expansion of in-house legal staffs may both reflect and reinforce the larger legalization trends described above. As organizations construct internal lawlike polities, inside counsel often play central roles in staffing the positions and drafting the rules that constitute these "corporate citizenship" regimes (Chayes & Chayes 1985:285–86; Cronin-Harris 1997).[20]

Whatever the origins of the in-house counsel transition, the attendant internalization of professional expertise holds the potential to subtly alter the character of corporations as legal actors. Instead of being lay consumers of legal services—who, as Galanter notes, know the legal system primarily through their pragmatic contacts with it—organizations are increasingly becoming "corporate legal professionals" in their own right. Where inside attorneys once served merely as glorified notaries or as passive conduits between the corporation and its outside law firm (Slovak 1979; Spangler 1986), the modern in-house counsel's office now stands as the highly professionalized face that the corporation shows to the legal world (Nelson et al. 1997; Chayes & Chayes 1985). In some areas, in-house counsel supplant outside law firms entirely, while in others, they merely supervise outside services. In either mode, however, expanded legal staffs allow corporations to confront the external legal system with more information, more authority, and more initiative than ever before.

Thus, the "in-house counsel hypothesis" posits that although large bureaucratic organizations still seek external legal representation when the economics (or occasionally the politics) of the situation demands, they no longer encounter their outside lawyers from the position of lay clients. Rather, many if not most large organizations now operate as fully empowered legal experts, negotiating over the scope and terms of any outside representation and often dictating the strategies that their legal subcontractors will pursue. Further, this internalization of expertise meshes with the two internalization hypotheses offered above: in-house counsel generally play a central role in drafting the formalized regulatory compliance policies that promote legalization (Rosen 1989), and they often make the initial determination of which disputes the organization will litigate and which it will submit to ADR (Chayes & Chayes 1985:297; Cronin-Harris 1997). As Nelson et al. (1997:27–28) note, the rise of in-house counsel blurs the distinction between doing business and doing law (see also Chayes & Chayes 1985:298). For the members of this ascendant segment of the bar, and for the organizations that employ them, it is sometimes hard to say exactly where legal rationality leaves off and bureaucratic rationality begins.

THE PRIVATE SECURITY HYPOTHESIS

The fourth apparent form of internalization of law since 1974 is the rise—or, more correctly, the reemergence—of corporate private security.[21] Theory and research on this development remain sparse (Marx 1987:188; but see Shearing & Stenning 1981, 1983, 1987; Cunningham et al. 1990; Davis et al. 1991); there are, however, sound grounds for believing that just as large bureaucratic organizations may be internalizing legal governance, dispute resolution, and expertise, they may also be internalizing enforcement.

Private policing is not a new phenomenon, of course. Historically, private or entrepreneurial security forces were the norm and not the exception throughout much of the industrial revolution (Traub 1996; cf. Spitzer & Scull 1977a). U.S. labor history, for example, offers numerous instances in which private enforcers, such as the Pinkerton Agency and the Ford Service, imposed industrial "order" at the behest of large corporations (Morn 1982; Weiss 1987). In the early 1900s, however, the emergence of modern, bureaucratized public law enforcement agencies pushed private policing into abeyance. Although many organizations continued to maintain modest security forces, most such forces engaged primarily in routine guard duty, with only limited surveillance, investigative, or punitive responsibilities. For active policing, public law enforcers were generally seen as both more capable and more legitimate than their private counterparts.

The available research on private security suggests that this situation may now be changing. As budget constraints and political agendas channel the efforts of public law enforcers away from corporate settings, private security forces have begun to reemerge as active agents of social control (Spitzer & Scull 1977b:265; Cunningham et al. 1990:236). Few hard statistics are available, but recent reports suggest that private police may outnumber public police in the United States by as much as 3:1, up from a ratio of 0.7:1 in 1970 and 1.7:1 in 1980 (Economist 1997; Cunningham et al. 1990:229; Chaiken & Chaiken 1987:5; Marx 1987:174). If accurate, these figures imply a total private force of roughly two million individuals, double the force size of 1980 (Bureau of Justice Statistics 1999; Cunningham et al. 1990:229; see also Davis et al. 1991:396). Expenditure measures show a similar pattern of growth. According to most estimates, private security spending has risen by an order of magnitude in the past 25 years, from $6 billion in 1974 to somewhere between $35 and $90 billion in the late 1990s (Cunningham et al. 1990:238; Traub 1996; Economist 1997); by comparison, public law enforcement spending has risen relatively modestly, from $11 billion in 1975 to roughly $40 billion in 1997 (Cunningham et al. 1990:238; Economist 1997).[22] Further, private security efforts appear to extend broadly across a variety of economic sectors: One 1990 study estimated private protection expenditures of $13.4 billion in manufacturing, $9.5 billion in retail, $4.2 billion in finance, and $2.8 billion apiece in health care and education; even government has participated in the private security boom, with state agencies supplementing the $30 billion public police budget with an additional $10 billion of spending on "private" protection of their own (Cunningham et al. 1990:198, 238; cf. Cunningham 1980).

Alongside their traditional guard and patrol responsibilities, corporate security personnel have increasingly assumed surveillance, detective, and undercover duties as well (Traub 1996), and private law enforcement now plays a significant role in arenas as diverse as shoplifting, embezzlement, industrial espionage, and substance abuse. Since the early 1980s, drug testing programs have become a major focus of expansion. The proportion of Fortune 500 companies maintaining such programs reportedly climbed from 18% in 1985 (Ackerman 1985) to 40% in 1991 (Hartwell et al. 1996) and 78% in 1995 (May 1999). Electronic surveillance is also common: A recent American Management Association study found that 63% of surveyed organizations practice some form of electronic monitoring, including 34% that videotape workspaces to counter theft and sabotage, 16% that videotape employee performance, 15% that store and review electronic mail, 14% that store and review computer files, 10% that tape and review telephone conversations, and 5% that tape and review voice mail (American Management Association 1997). In addition, as concerns about personal safety have risen, private security forces have assumed a leading role in designing "safe spaces," such as parking lots configured to minimize the risk of sexual assault (Joh 1999).

To a remarkable extent, as in the case of ADR, legislatures and courts have endorsed and abetted these developments. The retail sector provides a particularly clear example. Under the laws of most states, private security officers enjoy extensive authority to monitor, hold, search, and interrogate suspected shoplifters, with few if any due process constraints (Davis et al. 1991; cf. Traub 1996). "Merchant privilege" statutes have traditionally immunized store police from liability for claims of false arrest, false imprisonment, or unlawful detention (Bishop 1988:68), and courts have generally followed suit, ruling, among other things, that private persons acting without government supervision fall outside the search-and-seizure restrictions of *Mapp v. Ohio* (1961) and beyond the interrogation restraints of *Miranda v. Arizona* (1966) (Davis et al. 1991:399).[23] Furthermore, in recent years, many jurisdictions have augmented these private arrest powers with "civil recovery" provisions, which give store police the option of recovering monetary damages in lieu of handing the accused over to public authorities for arrest. Although the resulting penalties are civil rather than criminal in character, their dollar value can be quite substantial. Many statutes allow merchants to recover not only the cost of any pilfered merchandise, but also "exemplary" fines or treble damages, legal fees, and even the cost of maintaining store surveillance (ibid., p. 396). Taken as a whole, this legal regime not only gives private organizations the capacity to monitor, investigate, arrest, and indict, but also (in the absence of a right-to-counsel for civil defendants) the effective capacity to try and sentence.

Presumably, the other aspects of legal internalization described above have, if anything, buttressed and accelerated the resurgence of corporate private security. At the turn of the twentieth century, public bureaucratized law enforcement played a crucial role in legitimizing corporate capital. Operating under the banner of the rule of law, public police departments offered a legitimate, ostensibly neutral way for corporate interests to maintain order without appearing excessively instrumental or dictatorial (Traub 1996). At the twentieth century's end, however, the legalization of the workplace has created a quite different situation. As corporate policies and structures become increasingly formal, impersonal, and lawlike, the legitimating mantle of legality is almost as readily available to private security forces as to their public counterparts. Insulated against charges of thuggery, corporations are publicly applauded when they "help the police" by patrolling their own domains.

The private security hypothesis suggests that this shift in climate has combined with a perceived scarcity of public policing capacity to foster the widespread incorporation of active private law enforcement functions into the emerging polities of many large bureaucratic organizations. Although less often noted than the three internalization trends described above, this fourth change is cut from much the same cloth. Admittedly, the movement toward private security is still in its youth; nonetheless, if current patterns continue, the potential impact could be substantial indeed.

The Organization as Court (and Lawmaker, Judge, Counsel, and Cop)

To the extent that the legalization hypothesis, the ADR hypothesis, the in-house counsel hypothesis, and the private security hypothesis are correct, the internalization of law may subtly transform large bureaucratic organizations from being well-endowed players in the legal game (Galanter's repeat players) to being nothing less than the playing field itself. In this section, we consider how these hypothesized changes, to the extent that they are indeed occurring, might transform the relationship between organizations and law. As organizations internalize law, they move beyond the repeat player's traditional role as a disputing party, to act, at varying times and to varying extents, as a legislator, adjudicator, lawyer, and constable.

THE ORGANIZATION AS LEGISLATOR

Whereas traditional repeat players must use their strategic advantages to wring favorable rules from public lawmaking authorities, the legalization hypothesis suggests that organizations often act as private legislatures in their own rights, promulgating their own sets of rules and constructing their own internal legal regimes to implement those rules. To a striking extent, the organization as legislature replicates many central features of traditional public legislation; at the same time, however, legalization shifts the locus of lawmaking activity inside the corporate hierarchy, often with substantial consequences.

The similarities between public and organizational legislation are many. Like legislators in the public realm, organizational legislators attempt to read the social environment—including the needs and wishes of their constituents—and to write rules that implement a particular vision of what that environment and those constituents require. At the same time, again like legislators in the public realm, organizational legislators may also pursue less lofty ends, writing rules that are cynically calculated to enhance the author's visibility and to bolster the author's career. For organizational legislatures as for public legislatures (which, of course, are themselves organizations), a common route toward both these ends is to write rules that restate, reinstitutionalize, or in other ways incorporate prevailing public norms (cf. Bohannon 1965). At times, the organization as legislature may consciously pursue social and economic benefits by promulgating rules that symbolize compliance with the norms of public authorities. At other times, the organization as legislature may incorporate public norms less consciously, by adopting "prefabricated" rules that have acquired an institutionalized status within the larger environment—that is, rules that the surrounding organizational field has come to take for granted as the rational, proper, and obvious way to conduct a particular activity. In either case, by mirroring and re-presenting elements of the public legal order, legalization allows organizations to borrow from the legitimacy of established legal principles. For example, organizations routinely adopt grievance procedures as a rational, proper, and obvious response to a legal environment that favors fair treatment of employees; they routinely adopt hazardous materials precautions as a rational, proper, and obvious response to laws addressing occupational safety and health; and so on, down the line.

As with public legislatures, some organizations are "pioneers," others are "tinkerers," and still others are "followers" in this rule-making game. Such heterogeneity is likely to be reflected in organizations' motivations for rule adoption, although perhaps in complex ways. Often the earliest adopters of a particular rule are those firms whose cultures feature strong value commitments to the rule's underlying normative agenda. In these "progressive" polities, organizational legislators will have much to gain, both in personal satisfaction and in public prestige, from the enactment of rules that symbolically declare the sanctity of locally prevailing customs (cf. Gusfield 1963). Thus, for example, a firm that prides itself on being "disability friendly" might proclaim this corporate identity by proactively legislating certain workplace accommodations, even in the absence of any external pressures to do so (Scheid & Suchman 1998). Although such principled pioneers are generally few in number, they often generate the patterns and premises from which other organizations subsequently proceed. Typically, if the ethics of these pioneers win favor in the larger environment, a second wave of more cautious tinkering will follow, as less committed organizations strategically assemble limited subsets of the new rules, in an effort to preserve the legitimating symbolism of the pioneering enactments while facilitating a substantial degree of decoupling between formal structure and informal practice (Edelman 1992). For example, in an effort to insulate themselves from employment discrimination lawsuits, firms may legislate extensive formal evaluation and grievance procedures, while doing little to challenge informal managerial biases and prerogatives (ibid.; Scheid & Suchman 1998). Finally, as standardized models of acceptable compliance begin to emerge, a third wave of more reactive followers may simply mimic the behavior of other organizations in the field, accepting (and implicitly reinforcing) the presumed rationality of the prevailing regime.

Whether pioneering, strategic, or merely imitative, legalization can be a mixed blessing, both restricting and enhancing organizational power, simultaneously. As several commentators have noted, legalization tends to constrain traditional managerial prerogatives by infusing external legal values into internal organizational practices (see e.g., Selznick 1969; Sitkin & Bies 1994). Irrespective of the reasons for legalization or the intentions of top administrators, lawlike rules and structures often subtly shift the organizational agenda. Practices designed to promote (or merely to symbolize) workplace safety, or equal employment opportunity, or environmental protection tend to expand the "rights consciousness" of organizational stakeholders, encouraging demands for ever more substantive reforms; moreover, the officials who implement these practices tend to become internal advocates for the values that the practices symbolize, giving the law an indirect voice in organizational decision-making (Edelman et al. 1991; Edelman & Petterson 1999). Thus, organizational rulemaking can create important new political claims and allegiances that skillful players can deploy in subsequent debates (cf. Scheingold 1974). Despite the rhetorical appeal of calls to subject organizations to the rule of law, at a practical level these internal political resources may matter far more than external legal mandates. Because the vast majority of organizational problems do not result in lawsuits, legalized bureaucratic routines may provide society's best hope for protecting the rights and interests of otherwise disempowered organizational citizens (cf. Heimer & Staffen 1998).

Nonetheless, attention to legalization as restraint should not obscure the fact that internalized lawlike rulemaking also significantly alters the locus of the legal game, often to the organization's great advantage. In 1974, Galanter argued that repeat players can often "play for rules" by using lobbying and strategic litigation to shape the legal principles that govern future transactions (1974:100–103). Although such tactics continue to dominate many organizations' playbooks, the rise of organizations as legislatures raises a second potent possibility. Sometimes, rather than playing for rules alone, organizations can "play for literary license" by incorporating legal standards and rewriting them internally.

The resulting advantages can take several forms. In some cases, organizations can actually legislate legislation away—as they do, for example, when they adopt standard-form contracts that contain mandatory arbitration provisions. By substituting private dispute resolution for the traditional right to sue and by requiring employees and customers to agree to these provisions, organizations explicitly remove certain matters from the purview of the public courts. Even when private legislation cannot formally eliminate public legislation from the picture, however, "house law" may nonetheless effectively trump "state law" in many contexts. This situation is particularly true for employee relations, an area in which house law's more immediate impact on organizational legal culture makes private legislation the primary legal force shaping the emergence and transformation of workplace disputes (Fuller et al. 2000; cf. Felstiner et al. 1980). Finally, and most profoundly, when standardized internal legislation is aggregated across entire organizational fields, it can actually colonize state law itself by effectively redefining what is seen as "normal," "reasonable," "rational," and "compliant." Far from being mere private perturbations, which aggressive public enforcement could readily correct, internal rephrasings of legal rules often profoundly reconstitute external legality itself, as courts look to the organizational world for viable models of social responsibility and sound management practice. Edelman, Uggen, and Erlanger (1999) report, for example, that internal grievance procedures have become such effective symbols of attention to due process that public courts, which once saw internal reviews as legally irrelevant prologues to litigation, now increasingly treat the existence of such in-house proceedings as a central consideration in determining whether to hold an employer liable for workplace discrimination.

Taken as a whole, then, the legalization of large bureaucracies converts organizational decision-makers into private legislators. This shift, in turn, substantially enhances the ability of organizational repeat players to structure future transactions and to establish the rules under which breakdowns in those transactions will be resolved. Although organizational legislation often responds to public norms, it does so through the filters of organizational culture, organizational politics, and organizational interests. Not only can the resulting private laws displace public laws from organizations' internal polities, but also these private laws can occasionally reconstruct *external* polities in the organizational world's own image. These advantages go beyond simply playing for individual rules; they make organizations the authors, editors, and publishers of the rulebook itself.

THE ORGANIZATION AS ADJUDICATOR

If the legalization hypothesis implies that organizations are increasingly becoming lawmakers, the ADR hypothesis implies that organizations are increasingly becoming judges and courts—or, more broadly, dispute processors. Whereas an organization might once have simply referred problem cases to public legal institutions for resolution, ADR procedures instead allow it to resolve many matters in situ, in private forums that are, themselves, organizational subunits.[24] Of course, the organization as court is a rather strange adjudicatory arena, in that some organizational employees (usually line managers and workers) appear as first-party disputants, while others (usually personnel officers) appear as third-party "neutrals," and still others (usually members of the legal staff) appear as system designers and administrators. Thus, the best intentions of individual officials notwithstanding, organizational dispute processing forums are rarely level ground.

Because different organizational forums serve different organizational purposes, dispute processing structures vary widely, from formalized, court-like regimes to much more informal, flexible alternatives. At the courtlike end of the continuum, some formal grievance structures resemble entire judicial systems, with explicit fact-finding procedures, decision standards, and opportunities to appeal up the managerial hierarchy.[25] Although disputants generally retain the right to remove their claims to the public legal system, external courts will, in practice, often defer to the results of internal hearings and will dismiss the claims of any plaintiffs who have failed to exhaust their in-house remedies (Edelman, Uggen, & Erlanger 1999). At the opposite, informal end of the continuum lie "open-door policies," in which a senior official makes himself or herself available to address disputes at any level of the organization. Holding plenary power to act as investigator, advocate, and adjudicator all in one, the open-door officer usually serves as the sole arbiter, with no explicit provision for appeal. External legal authorities may be somewhat less likely to defer to such informal decisions, if any grievances actually make it to court; when coupled with mandatory arbitration provisions in disputants' contracts, however, open-door systems can maintain much of the binding authority of formal grievance regimes while eliminating many of the procedural safeguards and constraints. Finally, between these two poles, some organizational forums resemble mediation, with a third-party facilitator easing negotiations without directly imposing any particular resolution. Although ostensibly neutral, such facilitators generally either maintain ongoing business ties with the organization or are themselves members of management, and as a result, both the impartiality and the nondirectiveness of their interventions are open to question. Thus, although mediation-like forums may provide excellent therapeutic devices for ventilating and defusing frustrations (cf. Lind & Tyler 1988), they rarely pose any greater threat to managerial authority than do formal grievance procedures or informal open-door policies. As a general proposition, the more closely an internal proceeding resembles the public courts, the more thoroughly it will insulate organizational rulings from external scrutiny; even the least formal and least legalistic versions of IDR, however, have the potential to make in-house forums the first and last venues for a large number of disputes.

There are, of course, many ways in which ADR can benefit "have nots," both within and around organizations. If ADR proponents are correct, informal dispute resolution allows organizations to handle a much broader set of problems, and to do so more quickly and economically, than traditional litigation (Westin & Feliu 1988). Such efficiencies have particular value for "have not" disputants, who can rarely afford or endure protracted lawsuits. Further, Edelman et al. (1993) report that internal complaint handlers generally want to resolve all complaints—even those complaints with little legal basis—so as to maintain good morale and smooth working relations. Thus, aggrieved parties who lack legally cognizable claims may find solutions in IDR where they would find none in law. ADR forums such as mediation or arbitration may help "have nots" outside organizations as well, when those claimants possess too little clout to prevail in court. Environmental groups who enter into mediation with a large polluter, for example, may be able to achieve a negotiated resolution that exceeds their strict legal entitlements (Edelman & Cahill 1998). Perhaps most important, internal adjudication may also benefit "have nots" indirectly by providing a channel for legal values to enter organizational culture. Thus, similar to internal rule-making, internal adjudication may help to institutionalize legal ideals within organizations and organizational fields by raising the legal consciousness of employers and employees alike (cf. Selznick 1969).

At the same time, however, internalized adjudication also has an opposite potential to increase the power of organizational "haves" vis-à-vis the "have nots." In particular, when lawlike disputing moves in-house, the meaning of a "neutral" forum becomes muddy, indeed. In theory, legalization may reframe the organization as a liberal polity, complete with well-institutionalized citizenship rights and formal due process protections; but in practice, the organization nonetheless remains a bureaucratic hierarchy, and the power and authority patterns of that hierarchy inevitably define the relationships between the parties and the court. Not infrequently, a worker complainant will face a manager respondent before a "judge" who is also a member of the organization's management team. Thus, irrespective of their formal roles within the disputing arena, the judge and the respondent share a structural bond that creates a substantial potential for perceptual bias, if not conscious favoritism.

The structural situation becomes even murkier when one considers that, if IDR fails, intraorganizational disputes can potentially progress into the extraorganizational forums of the public legal system. Viewed in this light, the respondent in most intraorganizational cases is really the organization itself, because upon removal to the public legal system, the organization would often be vicariously liable for the acts of its agents (*Miller v. Bank of America* 1975). Moreover, were the internal dispute to proceed to a public lawsuit, the internal "judge" would quite likely transmogrify into a key witness for the organization, if not into one of the organization's own lawyers. Thus, the presiding figure in the in-house hearing is an employee and agent of the respondent, whose livelihood and future career depend on other (and higher) employees and agents of the respondent, and who must act in anticipation of potentially becoming a witness for, or a representative of, the respondent. To suggest that such a third party might have structural incentives for protecting the organization's (external) legal position would be to engage in heroic understatement. The informal linkages and mixed motives in organizational IDR "courts" make Blumberg's (1967) criminal courts look like the very picture of impartiality.

Internalized adjudication may also put "have nots" at a disadvantage by depoliticizing and delegalizing conflict, divorcing grievances from principles of law. ADR in general and mediation-like dispute processing in particular tend to emphasize consensus and compromise in place of legal rights, and this tendency is, if anything, accentuated in organizational settings. Organizational complaint handlers, after all, are usually managers, not judges, and their outlooks reflect their training, background, and social milieu. The limited empirical evidence on IDR suggests, for example, that organizational forums tend to recast grievances in ways that downplay legal issues and that focus instead on more typically managerial concerns, such as communication, problem solving, teamwork, and leadership; disputes that originate as rights violations (e.g., safety hazards, discrimination, environmental degradation) are likely to be handled as interpersonal difficulties, administrative problems, or psychological pathologies (Edelman et al. 1993). The "managerialization of law" (Edelman, Fuller, & Mara-Drita 2001) is, therefore, a natural consequence of processing claims in a setting where managerial problems are the most familiar and the easiest to remedy. Because the underlying bias is fundamentally a structural one, it seems unlikely that organizational courts could be made into more rights-conscious forums simply by staffing them with more judicious personnel.[26]

To further complicate matters, one must recognize that organizations as courts experience few constraining institutional commitments to substantive or procedural precedent. As noted in the previous section, the organization itself constructs the substantive rules that guide adjudication, and, hence, the organization acts as legislator and adjudicator together. Equally important, the organization as court also acts as institutional architect, constructing the *procedural* as well as the substantive rules for hearing disputes.[27] Thus, managers enjoy broad leeway to tailor particular dispute resolution procedures to particular organizational objectives, drawing on the full range of formal and informal proceedings outlined above.

To be sure, there are some noteworthy limits to this architectural flexibility. In particular, many of the legitimacy benefits that accompany internal due process will disappear if the forum looks too unfair or if the invitation to express grievances seems to be merely a sham. Thus, to some degree, organizational courts reproduce the "problem of legal autonomy" in microcosm: to serve the long-term interests of the elites who support them, organizational courts, like public courts, must maintain at least an appearance of detachment from the short-term interests of those elites in specific cases (cf. Thompson 1975; Balbus 1977).[28] Also like public courts, organizational courts are constrained by their larger institutional environments. For the public legal system, this environment consists primarily of diffuse social principles and ideals, along with the institutionalized rules of other social sectors; for in-house legal systems, the institutional environment encompasses all these elements, plus, most centrally, the principles, ideals, and institutionalized rules of the public legal system itself. At its core, the entire internalization enterprise rests on the public legal system's willingness to cede jurisdiction to those organizational forums that persuasively mimic their public counterparts. Thus, despite the formal authority that accompanies organizations' newfound legislative, judicial, and administrative powers, most firms strive for (at least the appearance of) fairness, so as to retain their legitimacy as surrogate legal regimes.

Nonetheless, organizational courts enjoy a considerable degree of insulation from outside observation and, hence, a considerable degree of leeway in institutional design. Internal hearings rarely involve public audiences, reporters, or even lawyers, who could act as external monitors; consequently, the larger society is unlikely to take proactive notice of organizational dispute handling practices. Although disputants generally retain the right to remove their claims to the public legal system, organizations often seek to curtail this right by, for example, requiring that prospective employees (and other contractual partners) agree in advance to forgo future lawsuits and to rely solely on private ADR/IDR should a dispute arise. In theory, procedural shortcomings might still expose organizational decisions to external review, but in practice few one shot disputants will have the inclination or the resources to pursue such outside litigation, especially as long as the disputant's relationship to the organization remains intact. Thus, although internal legal proceedings are not entirely free from external constraint, there is considerable room for slippage, before an internal forum's legitimacy is likely to be put to the test. In this gap, organizations hold court.

THE ORGANIZATION AS LAWYER

Just as organizations appear to have absorbed legal norms through legalization, and legal procedures through ADR, they also appear to have absorbed legal expertise through their in-house counsel offices. If the in-house counsel hypothesis holds true, then in a very real sense the large bureaucratic organization is no longer a lay actor in the legal arena, any more than it is a passenger on its own vehicle fleet, a licensee of its own research and development efforts, or a bailor in its own warehouses. Rather, organizations are themselves now legal experts, and outside attorneys are merely hired help. On issues where a lay organization might defer to outside counsel, the organization as lawyer will often adopt a more autonomous stance, with inside attorneys relying on their independent legal judgment to filter recommendations to their executive "clients." And on ordinary business issues, where a lay organization might act without prior advice of counsel, the organization as lawyer is much more likely to vet and preengineer its activities, so as to minimize the chances of encountering future legal obstacles. As a result, when the organization as lawyer engages in law-oriented behavior—whether in external forums or internal ones—it displays a much more coherent and self-conscious legal persona than its lay counterparts. If the prevalence and capacity of in-house counsel are indeed increasing, this change promises to transform the role of the legal profession in the external governance of organizational activity, both for better and for worse.

On one hand, several commentators have noted that the internalization of legal expertise could give the bar an unprecedented level of input into day-to-day organizational decision-making (e.g., Chayes & Chayes 1985; Rosen 1989). Rather than simply rubber-stamping or vetoing nearly final decisions—or, worse yet, defending the organization from liability for decisions long since taken—in-house lawyers could, potentially, insert legal considerations into the earliest stages of the decision process, setting the premises for organizational action in a particularly profound yet subtle way (Chayes & Chayes 1985:280). The archetype of such in-house legal activity is the practice of "preventive law," whereby staff lawyers construct proactive training, compliance, and monitoring programs, to minimize the organization's potential exposure to lawsuits and regulatory enforcement actions (ibid., p. 284 ff). A similar, albeit less formalized, sort of preemptive framing can occur when staff lawyers participate in routine meetings among executives or when lawyers themselves ascend to positions of direct executive authority. Finally, and most obtrusively, in-house counsel can occasionally embrace a "cop" role (Nelson et al. 1997), setting themselves up as internal guardians of corporate legality and then erecting checkpoints at which they can monitor and, if necessary, quash potentially unethical or illegal initiatives. In all these capacities, the staff lawyer's familiarity, immediacy, and continuity within the organizational hierarchy allow him or her to introduce legal ethics and professional standards into routine decision-making, thereby reinforcing and furthering the most "prosocial" aspects of workplace legalization.

On the other hand, however, an increase in internal legal talent may serve not to make organizations more compliant, but rather to make them more skillfully evasive. Compared with the traditional lay organization, the organization as lawyer sees more legal barriers, but it also sees the loopholes through those barriers. It knows more about the constraints of the law, but it also knows more about which black-letter constraints are actually printed in gray. It can better understand the arguments of its outside lawyers, but it can also better dispute or resist any unwelcome advice. The purported social benefits of the in-house counsel movement center on legal professionals gaining access to the corporate decision-making process, but giving lawyers more access does not necessarily guarantee that they will use that access to promote external legal values.[29] Thus, even the apparently legalizing effects of in-house counsel offices may prove to be illusory: preventive programs may produce compliance with the letter of the law while largely vitiating the law's spirit (Rosen 1989:501, 520); lawyers may participate in business meetings as sources of strategic, rather than cautionary, advice (Nelson et al. 1997:23 ff); and attorneys who embrace the role of "cop" may find themselves marginalized and displaced by those of their colleagues who adopt a more "entrepreneurial," can-do attitude (ibid., p. 11). Indeed, the very decentralization of in-house legal activity that optimists often extol as a source of grassroots influence can also expose attorneys to intense cooptation pressures (Chayes & Chayes 1985:289; Nelson et al. 1997) and can undercut the structural capacity of the in-house counsel office to act as a coherent, independent voice in organizational politics (Rosen 1989). The more deeply lawyers are embedded in the organization, the more likely they become to use their expertise to serve, rather than to question, prevailing managerial objectives.

In short, professionalism is not an indivisible whole, and there is no particular reason to think that the internalization of legal expertise will bring with it an equivalent internalization of legal ethics. Despite its newfound access to legal knowledge, the organization as lawyer differs from a traditional lawyer in at least one significant respect: private organizations are generally better able to absorb the bar's *technical* training than to absorb its *normative* socialization. Although, as described above, an in-house counsel office may inject certain legal sensibilities into organizational decision-making, the reverse influence is often at least as strong. Organizations are themselves powerful engines of socialization, and inside lawyers are as likely to adopt managerial values of profitability, efficiency, and hierarchical authority as to impart legal values of equity, due process, and collegiality. Research suggests, for example, that in their attitudes toward both ADR and litigation ethics, inside attorneys stand midway between their law firm colleagues and their executive superiors (Lande 1995; Suchman 1998). Moreover, the trend among in-house lawyers appears to be toward an increasingly managerial orientation, accompanied by efforts to "market" the legal function to executives as a source of "value added" (Nelson et al. 1997:18–23). In this regard, the organization as lawyer might better be termed the organization as legal expert; through the alchemy of cultural indoctrination and structural constraint, it splits professional skills from professional values, concentrating the former while diluting the latter. Thus, when conflicts arise, the organization as lawyer seems far more likely to use its legal capacity to pursue traditional corporate goals like market dominance and regulatory freedom than to uphold professional norms like civility, fair play, and reasoned deliberation.[30]

It is here that the in-house counsel hypothesis becomes most troubling for the public governance of organizational activity. Given the already substantial advantages of organizations as repeat players in the legal system, one of the few remaining levers of external social control has traditionally resided in the ability of independent attorneys to identify issues and to frame alternatives, unobtrusively inserting legal standards into nonlegal decision-making (cf. Chayes & Chayes 1985:298). Sociologists have long recognized that the lay/professional interface can be a source of substantial professional discretion and agenda-setting power, and in the traditional configuration of lay organizations and outside attorneys, the position of this interface allowed the Bar to promote and defend its own systemic commitments (such as a commitment to the institutional legitimacy of the formal legal order) in ways that were hard for most managers to second guess. When organizations subsume the lay/professional interface into their own hierarchies, however, the situation changes substantially. Able to assess legal risks and evaluate legal services on its own, the organization as lawyer can filter out professional punctiliousness and can treat outside attorneys as contract laborers, rather than as respected advisors (ibid., p. 298; Rosen 1989:485). Thus, although the in-house counsel movement promises to elevate individual lawyers to pivotal positions in organizational decision-making, it represents something of a Faustian bargain for the legal profession as a whole. If in-house counsel come to espouse essentially managerial values (either as a matter of expedience or as a matter of belief), then the internalization of legal expertise may, ironically, *reduce* the impact of the profession as an agent for the larger legal order. When legal capacity moves to inside the organization, society risks losing whatever leverage an autonomous outside counsel system might otherwise provide.[31]

THE ORGANIZATION AS CONSTABLE

Given the relative scarcity of systematic empirical research on private security enforcement, any claims about the character of the organization as constable must remain tentative at best. Nonetheless, the existing evidence suggests that if the private security hypothesis holds true, the internalization of policing may change the law enforcement landscape in several significant ways. In particular, the work of private security forces appears to differ from the work of their public counterparts in at least three regards, which can be designated "visibility/accountability," "intensity/pervasiveness," and "hierarchy/directionality." We examine each of these in turn.

Perhaps the most obvious distinction between private and public policing involves the degree of scrutiny that the two systems typically receive from scholars, the media, elected officials, and the general public. Although public policing is widely studied and intensely debated, private policing goes largely unobserved.[32] At present, we do not even know the exact *number* of security officers in the private sector, let alone their demographics, attitudes, or practices (Davis et al. 1991:396). Although a substantial portion of the public criminal caseload originates from private arrests (ibid., p. 407), public agencies rarely gather systematic data on this phenomenon, and no central repository monitors the overall disposition of cases by private security forces. Indeed, the general trend in relations between the private and public systems seems to run in the opposite direction, toward allowing private police to conclude ever more cases without involving public authorities at all. As a result, private security occurs largely outside of the public eye, and its coercive potential rarely attracts the notice of civil libertarian watchdogs.

Along with this difference in visibility, private and public policing also differ in accountability. Not only do private enforcers generally escape the attention of elected officials and public interest groups, but also they largely escape the supervision of the public judiciary. As noted earlier, many of the constitutional safeguards against abusive policing do not apply to the actions of private parties, especially if those parties are operating on their own property. Thus, aided by protective legislation such as the "merchant privilege" statutes described above, private police can usually go quite far in monitoring, detaining, interrogating, and searching suspected wrongdoers, without even incurring civil tort liability, let alone endangering any subsequent criminal prosecutions. Of course, this lack of public accountability hardly implies that private security forces are entirely masterless. Freed from public supervision, these agencies nevertheless remain tightly linked to their organizational supervisors, and it seems safe to assume that few private police officers could long pursue a line of action that did not serve the organization's larger managerial objectives (Shearing & Stenning 1983). As Traub (1996:253) puts it, "[For private police,] crime is defined in instrumental terms, and the interests of the corporate client take precedence over the demands of the law." Although it is certainly true that public police, too, often work in secrecy and often serve powerful special interests, private police clearly stand near the top of the continuum in their insulation from public scrutiny and in their responsiveness to exclusively private purposes.

If in-house security departments were simply a sleepy backwater on the map of social control, the absence of public accountability might prove to be of little consequence. If anything, however, private law enforcement is actually *more* intensive and pervasive than the public alternative. Indeed, in the current literature, this omnipresence is perhaps the private regime's most widely noted attribute (e.g., Shearing & Stenning 1981; Marx 1987; Reichman 1987; Davis et al. 1991; Traub 1996). As discussed above, recent estimates suggest that private security officers outnumber public police by a factor of roughly 3:1, and the intensity and pervasiveness of private security goes beyond numbers alone. Compared with public law enforcement agencies, police in the private sector are far more proactive, intrusive, and persistent as well.

Mass surveillance provides a telling case in point. For the most part, budgetary and constitutional constraints prevent public law enforcement agencies from engaging in large-scale preventive observation; in contrast, however, the routine monitoring of customers and employees forms a central weapon in the private security arsenal. Moreover, as detailed above, private surveillance goes well beyond traditional "beat patrols" and guardposts, to include both such overtly intrusive techniques as blood and urine testing and also such covertly intrusive techniques as electronic monitoring and computerized background checks. Frequently (albeit perhaps inadvertently), these activities extend the organization's gaze beyond the boundaries of the workplace, into private homes and after-business hours. Although such enforcement efforts again are not unique to the private sector, they occur here with an unusual level of intensity and systematicity. The upshot is that organizational security holds the potential to transform the workplace (and the adjacent precincts of private life) into an expanded version of Bentham's Panopticon, a world in which individuals are deterred and disciplined as much by the internalized fear of observation as by the actual experience of detection and punishment (Bentham 1791; cf. Foucault 1979).

This is not to say, however, that private enforcement systems are in any way lax in detection and punishment. In one study of shoplifting, for example, Davis et al. (1991:400, 407) found that private store police showed much less leniency than even the most aggressive public police forces, releasing only six of 555 detainees over a 3-year period while seeking civil recovery (essentially a stiff fine) from 40% and passing the remainder along to the criminal justice system for arrest and prosecution. Presumably, a similar pattern holds in other contexts as well, especially in those settings in which the organization can avail itself of internal administrative remedies, such as repossession, firing, or demotion, that do not require any public intervention. Admittedly, the internal equivalent of "prosecutorial discretion" might still prevail if the apprehended individual were a well-connected executive or if the preferred punitive response would trigger a formal grievance proceeding or attract adverse publicity; in the typical case, however, organizational enforcement agents seem far more likely than overburdened public prosecutors to persist to the final punishment. Thus, taken to its logical extreme, organizational policing is not only panoptical but also totalitarian, offering few gaps and interstices to shelter oppositional activity (Marx 1987; cf. Goffmann 1961).

The relentlessness of private policing becomes particularly significant by virtue of its interaction with bureaucratic hierarchy. Because in-house security forces are accountable primarily to management, their legitimacy does not depend on their ability to appear neutral with respect to the organization's stratification system.[33] Indeed, unlike public police, private police may actually *strengthen* their political position by being overtly "directional" in their enforcement efforts. Although this does not generally mean that private police can discard objectivity and take partisan positions in organizational turf battles, it does mean that they can systematically adopt different postures toward the top and the bottom of the bureaucratic hierarchy.

This directional bias may appear in many guises, but perhaps the most consequential is the role that private security forces play in focusing the organizational gaze "downward," that is, in exposing the activities of lower-level participants to panoptical surveillance while shrouding the activities of upper-level participants behind a veil of secrecy. Thus, for example, at the same time that they subject employees and customers to routine videotaping, eavesdropping, and background checks, private security personnel also operate the perimeter patrols, telephone scramblers, document shredders, and computer firewalls that protect the executive suites from prying eyes. In short, private security acts as a sort of one-way mirror, revealing the activities of subordinates to superiors while obscuring the activities of superiors from subordinates. Beyond simply mobilizing public law on behalf of private interests, the internalization of law enforcement therefore plays an active part in the construction of a new organizational regime, one that is uniquely responsive to the control of elites and uniquely fortified against the critiques of the public.

Implications for the Legal Process

When organizations act as entire private legal systems, rather than simply as repeat players in the traditional public system, they gain increased control over the construction, implementation, and impact of law, not only within their own boundaries, but also throughout their organizational fields. The internalization of each legal role—legislator, adjudicator, lawyer, and constable—adds to the organization's ability to manage, transform, and even supplant external societal rules. It is the *merging* of these roles, however, that truly cements organizational power, both to regulate social behavior and to constitute social reality (cf. Edelman & Suchman 1997). Although the consequences of legal internalization are often complex, and although internalization may involve considerable benefits for the "have nots," nonetheless when organizations hold court, the "haves" tend to come out still further ahead.

INTERNALIZATION AS COLONIZATION

As students of civil litigation have long noted, the stock of potentially adjudicable grievances in society stand in a so-called disputing pyramid, tapering (through a mixture of resolution and attrition) from a broad base of injurious experiences to a narrow crown of formal court decisions (Felstiner et al. 1980). Although public law may remain ensconced at the apex of this pyramid, the internalization of legal roles and processes effectively allows private organizations to colonize the pyramid's lower tiers.[34] This places such organizations squarely athwart the portals of justice—a strategic position both because it establishes these private bureaucracies as de facto legal gatekeepers and also because, given the geometry of the pyramid, it grants them custody of the only formal disputing arenas that most parties are ever likely to see.

The organizational colonization of disputing begins at the pyramid's base, with organizations' capacity to help shape, in the first place, *what constitutes a dispute* and *what the nature of that dispute is*. Superficially, it might seem that organizations play a more limited role in this framing process than does the public legal order: although the public courts use explicit rules about causes of action, mootness, standing, and so on to circumscribe the range of justiciable claims, organizational forums generally purport to hear any complaints that come before them. Selectivity, however, is only one way that a legal system can shape the recognition and definition of disputes, and even without elaborate screening rules, organizations subtly influence the course of dispute construction through the substantive rules they create in their capacity as legislators, the hearings they conduct in their capacity as adjudicators, the advice they dispense in their capacity as lawyers, and the enforcement mechanisms they deploy in their capacity as police. Organizational legal systems may be more reluctant than their public counterparts to proclaim that some grievances are none of their business (Edelman et al. 1993), but this hardly means that the contours of the organizational system will not influence the emergence of disputes. Indeed, by treating *all* disputes as organizationally adjudicable, the private regime may simply exchange selection and preemption for expanded jurisdiction.

The impact of internalization on the disputing pyramid is not limited, of course, to the anticipatory framing of disputes as they emerge from inchoate injuries into explicit complaints. Once disputes enter the organizational legal system, that system directly influences their elaboration, their progression, their outcomes, and their consequences. Galanter's repeat players enjoyed certain positional advantages in acquiring legal representation, lobbying for rule-changes, and persuading courts. Presumably, those advantages continue to accrue to repeat players in the external legal system. In addition, though, today's large bureaucratic organizations—acting as internal legislators, judges, lawyers, and cops—also enjoy the benefits of extensive in-house dispute processing, long before their problem cases might ever come before external authorities. Whereas Galanter's repeat players could hire specialist lawyers to represent them in encounters with the external legal system, today's large bureaucratic organizations *are* their own lawyers, and they can act in a legal capacity in all phases of their internal and external activities. Whereas Galanter's repeat players could petition public legislatures for favorable legal rules, today's large bureaucratic organizations *are* their own legislatures, and they can arrange their polities in ways that fundamentally constrain and reconstitute the terms of debate with their employees and the wider environment, alike. And whereas Galanter's repeat players could develop facilitative relations with court personnel, today's large bureaucratic organizations *are* their own courts and *supply* their own court personnel, and they can resolve internal disputes in ways that not only maximize internal organizational peace but also shape the case should it move to the external courts. Perhaps these changes could all be subsumed under Galanter's rubric of using "advance intelligence" to structure transactions, but the emerging pattern goes far beyond the simple negotiation of favorable contractual terms with arm's-length exchange partners. As the sphere of advance planning has widened to include the internalization of law, organizations have moved from holding a position of power within the external legal field to holding, within their own boundaries, a private simulacrum of the field itself (cf. Baudrillard 1994).

To be sure, a number of factors place limits on the organization's ability to colonize the disputing pyramid. Perhaps the most important of these limiting factors is the culture of the organization itself. Internal legal systems, like all legal systems, depend on a supportive cultural context for much of their power, especially their power to frame and transform disputes. Yet, because organizational culture (including organizational legal culture) emerges out of both organizational gestures and participant interpretations, it is never entirely under managerial control. Once created, organizational rules and disputing arenas take on a symbolic status; that is, independent of their official purposes or technical functions, they convey cultural meanings to various audiences. How particular observers interpret such symbolism depends on their social backgrounds, their general views of law and of the organization, their specific past experiences with the symbols in question, and their perceptions of the consistency or inconsistency of symbols and actions (Fuller et al. 2000). Over time, certain interpretations become shared among similarly situated participants, become institutionalized in collective expectations and accounts, and, hence, become part of the organization's legal culture. In predicting the workings of organizational legality, this emergent culture (and the legal consciousness that it implies) may be at least as important as the formal dispute-processing structures erected by managerial fiat (cf. Ewick & Silbey 1998).

The precise contours of organizational legal culture—including its degree of coherence or fragmentation and the presence or absence of oppositional subcultures (cf. Martin 1992)—may vary from one site to the next. In all cases, however, cultural meanings will play a significant role in determining whether participants welcome and embrace the organizational colonization of disputing, or whether instead they oppose it as a tool of oppression, or even appropriate it as a vehicle for resistance (Fuller et al. 2000; cf. Merry 1988). Organizational legal culture influences participants' rights consciousness, their attitude toward compliance efforts, their definition of wrongful behavior, and their likelihood of mobilizing the law when perceived violations occur. Organizational culture also influences who employees see as parties to a dispute: In an environment where workplace harassment is common, for example, cultural accounts of rights and responsibilities might influence whether the targets of that harassment blame themselves, their individual harassers, the harassers as a group, the harassers' supervisors, or the organization as a whole (cf. Felstiner et al. 1980). Further, organizational culture interacts with the procedural rules of internal legal forums to affect the nature and timing of dispute resolutions, the perceived justice of those resolutions, and the conditions (if any) under which unsatisfied disputants will take their claims outside the organization to the formal legal realm. In all these ways, organizational culture can play a substantial role in shaping participants' conceptions of what constitutes a dispute and of what (if anything) to do about it. Thus, to a degree, emergent cultural understandings can limit management's ability to control disputing through structural adjustments alone.

As significant as this limitation may be, however, it offers only partial reassurance at best. Although the emergence (or fear) of oppositional cultural accounts may constrain an organization's efforts to internalize legal roles and to supplant public constructions of legality, this countervailing force is itself limited by the interorganizational environment. As suggested above, the internalization of law evolves not only within individual organizations but also within larger organizational fields. If internal rule-making, dispute resolution, legal counseling, and policing were merely idiosyncratic attributes of a single firm, any participants who were inclined toward resistance would find plenty of models and allies beyond that firm's boundaries. However, when the internalization of law is occurring simultaneously in many firms throughout an organizational field—and, indeed, is buttressed by supportive intraorganizational structures at the level of the field itself—even the most disgruntled participants may have trouble enunciating persuasive counterarguments or describing plausible alternatives. Thus, for example, as in-house counsel gain prevalence and prestige, and as bodies such as the American Corporate Counsel Association emerge to carry forward this "professional project" (Abbott 1988), the leadership of the bar becomes ever less likely to voice opposition to the mixing of organizational and legal values (cf. Rosen 1989:490 ff.; Nelson et al. 1997). Similarly, as ADR takes on an increasingly institutionalized status and as bodies such as the Society of Professionals in Dispute Resolution emerge to give it substance and publicity, employers, employees, and society in general become ever less likely to question the claim that private organizational proceedings are simply the most *rational* way of handling disputes in the context of employment or business relations (Edelman, Uggen, & Erlanger 1999).[35] As a general matter, organizational culture comes from the interplay of direct experiences in the organization and vicarious exemplars in the organizational environment. Consequently, although opposition to the internalization of law remains a possibility, the simultaneous legalization of organizations and organizational fields tends to promote, not inhibit, the view that legal problems are best addressed by private personnel in private arenas.

DO THE "HAVES" STILL COME OUT AHEAD?

Before concluding, it is perhaps worthwhile to revisit, explicitly, the larger question of whether the organizational internalization of law accentuates or moderates the advantages that society's "haves" experience in legal life. On one hand, the previous discussion outlines numerous ways in which recent internalization dynamics have extended organizational authority into ever widening provinces of legal activity, replacing public regulation *of* organizations with private regulation *by* organizations. Because the large bureaucracies that are pursuing this annexation generally represent society's "haves,"[36] the organizational internalization of law would seem to strengthen the position of social elites and narrow the limits of legal change. On the other hand, however, recent trends include other, more progressive, aspects as well. To the extent that internalization implies the absorption of legal standards, values, and outlooks into organizational decision-making, it is possible that the private organizational world is being domesticated by public law and not vice versa.

On the optimistic side, there is good reason to believe that organizations cannot internalize law without, in the process, transforming their own orientations (Selznick 1949). Neoinstitutional sociology, in particular, has demonstrated that legal pronouncements (and organizational responses to those pronouncements) can generate a symbolic feedback loop, in which legality comes to be seen as inseparable from efficiency, rationality, and modernity. Not only may law coerce conformity from those organizations that are most vulnerable to direct sanctions (see, e.g., Scott 1987; Fligstein 1991), but also, and more important, the search for acceptable models of compliance may lead organizations to embrace new policies, new outlooks, new structures, and new personnel in ways that permanently alter the basic standards of practice throughout entire organizational fields (Suchman & Edelman 1996; Edelman & Suchman 1997). Thus, rather than simply displacing public law, legalization brings public normative commitments and public cognitive frameworks into the decision-making dynamics of even those organizations that are not covered by formal legal sanctions (e.g., Edelman 1990). Indeed, even "merely symbolic" compliance can exert lasting substantive effects as it redirects organizational attention, alters the organization's public identity, and draws new sets of participants into the organization's dominant coalition (Edelman & Petterson 1999).

In light of these findings, one might take internalization as a sign that organizations are, in effect, being "resocialized" by law. In the past, organizations have often adopted a recalcitrant stance toward external regulation—acting arbitrarily, exploitatively, and even dictatorially and then using their advantages as repeat players to prevent aggrieved "have nots" from obtaining meaningful redress through the public courts. In comparison to this bleak alternative, the internalization of law arguably represents a significant (although limited) victory for the forces of reform. As disadvantaged groups have secured increasingly protective rules from the public legal system, managers have attempted to control the resulting legal uncertainty by progressively removing organizational operations from public jurisdiction, but this strategy has proven to be a two-edged sword. To legitimate their jurisdictional claims, organizations have had to legalize their internal polities, often creating at least as many citizenship rights as most underfunded one shotters would have been able to wrest from a passive and overburdened public court system. Organizational rules have become more rational and more clearly linked to valid, publicly articulable goals; organizational dispute resolution procedures have become more accessible, more balanced, and less arbitrary; organizational decisions have become more responsive to the views of legal professionals; and organizational policing efforts have become more objective, more scientific, and less brutal. Taken as a whole, legalization may have profoundly altered the basic character of organizational authority, perhaps to the point where the paradigmatic large bureaucracy is no more an instrument of the "haves" than is the public legal system itself.

Unfortunately, this account, although not necessarily inaccurate, remains only partial. Internalization may indeed moderate some of the most exploitative features of organizational life, but it does little to make bureaucracy more democratic. To the contrary, when the legal game moves onto an organizational playing field, organizational ground rules tend to prevail. Although liberal legal systems and bureaucratic organizations share a common legal-rational commitment to systematic, objective decision-making, they embody largely divergent ideological orientations toward the trade-offs between bottom-up participation and top-down authority, and between individual autonomy and hierarchical control. To date, organizations have been quicker to internalize the public legal system's formalization and systematicity than to embrace its legitimating myths of democratic sovereignty and personal freedom;[37] despite extensive legalization, the rationality of organizations remains fundamentally authoritarian and instrumental. Legal pressures may make organizations more rule bound and more paternalistic, but short of redefining corporate personhood, the law is unlikely to make organizations substantially more responsive to voices from below.

This pattern holds true across all four domains of internalization: rule-making, dispute processing, legal counseling, and policing. Although the legalization of organizational rules may transform many firms into private polities with extensive "citizenship" rights, these rights seldom include the right to vote, the right to assemble, or even the right to speak. Similarly, although organizational dispute resolution may create new forums for airing employee grievances, these forums tend to embody a managerial logic, allowing little publicity, creating few binding precedents, and favoring largely "therapeutic" restorative remedies, over the vindication of formal rights. In-house attorneys, too, tend to adopt distinctly managerial orientations, entrepreneurially seeking to "add value" to the organization's bottom line (Nelson et al. 1997), but rarely offering pro bono services to aggrieved employees, or engaging in the internal equivalent of "cause lawyering" (cf. Sarat & Scheingold 1998). Finally, although private security forces increasingly employ the rationalized methods of the public police, they do so with virtually no equivalent constraints on their powers of search, seizure, surveillance and secrecy.

In the end, then, internalization benefits the "haves" not so much because it undercuts legal neutrality or formality, as because it undercuts democratic governance. After all, private legal systems are not distinguished by being housed within large organizations; states, too, are large organizations, and states, too, hold legislatures, courts, lawyers, and police. The difference is that, to the extent that states embrace an ethic of participatory democracy (and, admittedly, this is often sadly limited), they tend to build structural safeguards for popular sovereignty and normative commitments to distributional equity. In contrast, most private organizations are constructed to be ruled from the top and are normatively committed to enhancing the welfare of their chiefs. Whereas the archetypal democracy fosters communication and control from the populace to the leadership, the archetypal bureaucracy fosters communication and control from the leadership to the populace. And whereas the archetypal democracy exposes official decision-making to publicity and shields individual decision-making in privacy, the archetypal bureaucracy shrouds official decision-making in secrecy and exposes individual behavior to panoptical surveillance.[38] If one believes that the welfare of the "have nots" ultimately depends on their effective political mobilization and not on the judiciousness and charity of the "haves" above them, then one should find little to celebrate in the movement of rule-making, dispute processing, legal counseling, and policing out of the public legal system and into private organizations.[39]

Future Research

By their nature, "speculations" open rather than close lines of inquiry. In this article, we have offered hypotheses about the internalization of law; we have gathered a sampling of existing evidence that points, we believe, toward the validity of these hypotheses; and we have explored the possible implications of these hypotheses for the fortunes of society's "haves" and "have nots." Our analysis, however, has suggested, not tested; illustrated, not demonstrated; proposed, not concluded. The possible directions for future study are many, and we highlight only a few here.

At the most basic level, more research is needed simply to determine whether, and to what extent, legal internalization has in fact occurred. In particular, because our hypotheses inherently imply change over time, future studies should seek to develop more systematic longitudinal data both on the development of in-house legal systems and on the consequences of those systems for various participant groups. Equally importantly, to move beyond counterfactual hypotheticals ("If law had not been internalized . . . "), researchers should search out relevant comparison cases, looking across organizational fields, legal jurisdictions, or nation-states. Internalization probably has not proceeded at an equal pace in all social settings, but to put this variation to good empirical use, we will need far more fine-grained observations than the current literature provides.

Assuming that our basic hypotheses withstand such testing, future investigations should extend the inquiry to consider the extent to which the four internalization dynamics work in concert. If in-house counsel draft lawlike policies to govern the workings of internal dispute resolution systems, or if private police bring suspects before internal disciplinary panels for violating organizational rules, resonances among the four trends may dramatically intensify the internalization effect. Conversely, if the four trends all operate at different times, in different settings and upon different subjects, their weave may be too porous to block the gaze of public law.

Finally, and most importantly, scholars should carefully examine how the internalization of law affects the standing of society's "haves" and "have nots." Although our theoretical account suggests that, on balance, the internalization of law expands corporate power vis-à-vis individuals, this thesis deserves thorough testing. Each of our four movements carries with it a justificatory account that promises benefits to "haves" and "have nots" alike; although many aspects of these accounts may be mere puffery, only detailed empirical study can determine whether any important kernels of truth lurk within. In the end, a theory of why the "haves" come out ahead is only as good as the remedies that it suggests. To find appropriate remedies, we must know both the best and the worst that current trends hold in store.

Conclusion

In the years since Galanter wrote "Why the 'Haves' Come Out Ahead," the legalization of organizational governance, the expansion of private dispute resolution, the rise of in-house counsel, and the reemergence of private policing appear to have interacted to transform the large bureaucratic organization from being merely a repeat player in the public legal system to being an entire private legal system in its own right. By merging the roles of legislator, administrator, forum, judge, lawyer, and cop, such organizations have colonized the base of the disputing pyramid and have infused it with a distinctly managerial logic. As this colonization has proceeded, the new private legal order has annexed increasingly large segments of territory from the traditional public legal order, subtly shifting the balance between democratic and bureaucratic tendencies in society as a whole. Although "have not" groups may gain some short-run advantages from the introduction of citizenship norms into the workplace, the long-term prognosis seems much less optimistic. The power of repeat players to win disputes and to structure transactions, which Galanter discussed in 1974, simply pales by comparison to the new power that arises when the "haves" hold court.

Notes

Previously published in *Law & Society Review* 33 (4) 941–91 (1999); reprinted by permission. Authorship of this paper was fully collaborative. The authors would like to express their appreciation to the Institute for Legal Studies at the University of Wisconsin for organizing the conference that inspired this essay. Thanks also go to Richard Lempert, Elizabeth Joh, Deborah Carr, and four anonymous *Law & Society Review* referees for their insightful commentary on earlier drafts and to Iona Mara-Drita and Dan Steward for their able research assistance.

Lauren B. Edelman is Professor of Law and Sociology at the University of California–Berkeley. Her work addresses the relationship of organizations to their legal environments, organizational dispute resolution, and the internal legal cultures of organizations.

Mark C. Suchman is Associate Professor of Sociology and Law at the University of Wisconsin–Madison. His primary research interests center on the legal environments of organizational activity in general and on the role of law firms in the development of Silicon Valley in particular. He has also written on organizational legitimacy, on the relationship between institutional and ecological models of organizational communities, and on the impact of changing professional structures on corporate litigation ethics.

1. Although some of the arguments discussed below apply with equal force to all organizations regardless of size and structure, our analysis focuses primarily on the large bureaucratic organizations that form the core of the modern economy and polity. Only this subset of the organizational world enjoys the material and cultural capacity to implement fully the strategies described here. Smaller organizations, although still often among society's "haves," generally face a more restricted set of legal options.

2. The organizational internalization of law may represent a special case of Perrow's (1991:726) more sweeping assertion that "large organizations have absorbed society. They have . . . made organizations, once a part of society, into a surrogate of society."

3. Our analysis focuses primarily on the likely *effects* of internalization, rather than on its causes. Although both topics merit scholarly attention, we follow Galanter in choosing to emphasize the impact of particular institutional arrangements on the societal balance of power while remaining largely agnostic about the processes that brought those arrangements into existence in the first place. Others (including ourselves, elsewhere) have devoted substantial attention to delineating the social forces that drive organizations to internalize central elements of public law; here, however, our attention turns instead to sketching the ways in which such internalization may, reciprocally, reshape the workings of the sociolegal order itself.

4. Organization theorists use the concept of an "organizational field" to describe a system of social relations that makes up a relatively discrete and immediate chunk of the organizational environment, larger than an individual firm but smaller than an entire society. The field around any particular focal organization includes "key suppliers, resource and product consumers, regulatory agencies, and other organizations that produce similar services or products" as well as the webs of information and in-

fluence that link these entities into a coherent enterprise (DiMaggio & Powell 1983:148). By applying this definition to legal matters, one could, for example, discuss the role of law in the health care field, in the field of steelmaking, in investment banking, or in the performing arts.

5. The organizations literature supplies several explanations for this diffusion process. Some theorists emphasize the social construction of cognitive frames and behavioral scripts, suggesting that dominant models often become so ritualized and taken for granted that they serve as preconscious templates for action, literally "constituting" organizational behavior, independent of intentional agency by individual firms or their managers. Other theorists adopt a more eclectic stance, attributing the diffusion of institutionalized models not only to cognitive framing mechanisms, but also to an array of more conscious rational and normative motivations, coupled with internal and external structural pressures (cf. Suchman 1997). Thus, organizations might adopt institutionalized models to secure public resources, to obtain legitimacy, to pursue shared value commitments, or to ease communications with other actors in their field (Suchman & Edelman 1996; Scott 1995; cf. Suchman 1995b).

6. Here and below, we use the term *movement* loosely, to identify a suggestive preliminary trend or tendency coupled with a set of justificatory rational myths and a significant constituency. A movement in this sense is partly an empirical pattern, partly an ideological program, and partly a political mobilization.

7. Even in 1974, Galanter noted that when repeat players engage in ongoing dealings with one another, they frequently set up private governance structures to handle disputes (1974:110–11). At the time, however, Galanter attributed such private dispute handling to rational calculations of the expense and disruptiveness of litigation; ADR was, in a sense, organic to the community of repeat players. Today, the tendency toward private dispute resolution is perhaps as much a function of a general social climate that favors and institutionalizes ADR per se as it is a function of calculated efforts by individual actors to circumvent litigation. Carried forward by a substantial social movement, the privatization of interfirm conflict has become an organizing principle of the broader institutional order, promoted evangelically even where it may not be supported indigenously.

8. ADR has also attracted growing attention among academics and business journalists. A search for the term *alternative dispute resolution* in the ABI/INFORM database (a comprehensive online database of business periodicals) yields only two references in the decade from 1970 to 1980, compared with 316 in the 1994–1995 biennium alone.

9. These authors report that ADR is also fairly widely used in personal injury and product liability disputes but is less popular in matters of corporate finance.

10. There is good reason to believe that businesses with ongoing relationships have long favored extralegal dispute resolution (see, e.g., Macaulay 1963); in the past, however, such resolution has generally taken the form of direct negotiation or informal community pressure rather than organized ADR.

11. The CPR pledge reads, in part, "In the event of a business dispute between our corporation and another corporation which has made or will then make a similar statement, we are prepared to explore with that other party, resolution of the dis-

pute through negotiation or ADR techniques, before resorting to full-scale litigation" (quoted in Galanter & Rogers 1991:19).

12. The caseload of the federal courts also rose substantially during this time (Galanter & Rogers 1991:5 ff), suggesting that the growth of ADR measured in proportion to all business disputing may not be quite as great as the growth measured in absolute numbers. The available data, however, are not comprehensive enough to allow a calculation of precise ratios, and in any case, absolute numbers may actually be a more appropriate indicator of the degree to which ADR has become a familiar, if not predominant, feature of the disputing landscape.

13. In many ways, IDR actually preceded (and to some degree presaged) the ADR movement of the 1970s. Disputes involving union workers have been resolved through grievance arbitration ever since the labor movement of the 1930s (Slichter 1941), and even in nonunion settings, personnel professionals have long promoted internal mediation and arbitration as ways of forestalling unionization and encouraging smooth employment relations (Jacoby 1985). Moreover, from the 1960s onward, the civil rights movement, like the labor movement, motivated significant interest in IDR, as employers sought both to incorporate publicly legitimated models of just treatment and also to discourage discrimination-related lawsuits (Edelman 1990; Sutton et al. 1994). This history notwithstanding, however, the ADR movement appears to have engendered significant changes in both the prevalence and the character of IDR in recent years, as discussed in the following pages.

14. Even "formal" internal grievance systems, which often mimic aspects of the public courts, are nonetheless considerably more flexible and ADR-like than true litigation. Most such systems operate with minimal rules of evidence, no prehearing discovery, no right to counsel, and no principle of stare decisis.

15. The key to this reconciliation of legalization and ADR is that the ADR movement does not attack the "rule of law" as much as it attacks the *linkage* between the rule of law and a particular set of public adjudicatory institutions. Whether correctly or not, the ADR movement asserts that, with the help of a third-party facilitator, lay actors can construct their own interpretations of law, and the law thus constructed will be more fair than the formalistic rulings of a passive court reacting to a stilted confrontation between professional adversaries. Thus, ADR embraces the principle of rule-compliant fairness at the same time that it rejects the specific rules of traditional litigation.

16. In this essay, we use the terms *in-house counsel's office, corporate legal department*, and *corporate legal staff* to refer generically to all attorneys who practice law as salaried employees of nonlegal organizations. Although recent research suggests that there may be important differences between lawyers who work in a centralized legal department and those who hold positions elsewhere in the organizational hierarchy (Rosen 1989; Nelson et al. 1997), few statistical analyses differentiate between these two categories, and for the most part, this distinction lies beyond the scope of our analysis. Our general argument, we believe, applies to centralized and decentralized legal staffs alike, although in practice a few of the particulars may vary.

17. Litigation is the one area of practice that continues to be dominated by outside law firms, but even here, the role of inside counsel has grown substantially (see below).

18. Government legal staffs experienced an even larger increase, rising from an average of 64 attorneys per office in 1975 to 399 per office in 1995.

19. Nelson (1994:394–95) reports that in 1975, the average starting in-house lawyer earned 98% as much as the average starting law firm associate, 32% as much as the average large firm partner, and 97% as much as the average solo practitioner. In 1990, the comparable percentages were 82%, 32%, and 111%, respectively. According to a recent American Bar Association survey, 77% of in-house counsel reported 1990 income in excess of $55,000, compared with only 58% of private practitioners; 36% of in-house counsel topped $100,000, whereas only 28% of private practitioners reached this level (American Bar Association 1991).

20. Of course, these three dynamics are often related. Outside legal expenses may have risen, in part, due to the increasing scope, complexity, and criticality of organizations' legal exposure. Similarly, legalization tends to proceed fastest where external regulatory efforts are most salient (cf. Edelman 1990). And legalization, in turn, may spur the proliferation of in-house attorneys precisely because rising legal fees militate against the hiring of outside specialists to preside over increasingly routinized internal legal orders.

21. In this article, we use the terms *private security* and *private policing* interchangeably to refer to the provision of in-house security and enforcement services by an organization's employees or subcontractors. Elsewhere in the literature, private policing often denotes a broader phenomenon, encompassing not only in-house police services but also such nongovernmental law enforcement activities as volunteer block watches and vigilante justice; these additional aspects of private policing, however, lie well beyond the scope of our analysis here.

22. In inflation-adjusted 1998 dollars, private policing expenditures in 1974 totaled approximately $20 billion, whereas public policing expenditures totaled slightly over $36 billion.

23. As Marx (1987) notes, when public law enforcement agencies work alongside corporate private security forces, these exemptions create the possibility that the government may acquire secondhand information obtained through techniques that it would have been enjoined from using itself.

24. Interorganizational ADR rarely takes place entirely within a subunit of either disputant organization; rather, it generally occurs in a free-standing entity within the larger organizational field or in a subunit of a field-level institution such as an industry association or a leadership council. For the sake of brevity, our discussion focuses primarily on the intraorganizational context (that is, on IDR), because this form of dispute processing most clearly illustrates the implications of the organization as court. Nonetheless, because field-level interorganizational disputing forums are private organizational creations too, much of our analysis should apply to them as well.

25. Even the most formal organizational grievance systems are far less formal than the public courts, with organizations generally offering few if any rules about evidence, representation, or other aspects of due process. Indeed, because organizational adjudicators frequently conduct their own investigations, many in-house grievance procedures ultimately look more like arbitration than like adversary litigation.

26. The delegalization of dispute resolution is not a purely organizational phe-

nomenon. As the logic of ADR diffuses across an ever wider range of forums, public judges, too, become more likely to consider the psychodynamic underpinnings of disputes and to pursue therapeutic compromise solutions (Merry 1990). Still, however, legal rights remain a centerpiece of the public court system's institutional identity, whereas such rights occupy a distinctly subordinate position in most organizational forums (Edelman & Cahill 1998).

27. Admittedly, joint responsibility for these legislative, judicial, and architectural functions rarely falls to any one individual (or even to any one organizational subunit), and the claim that "the organization" acts in all these capacities may obscure the potential for intraorganizational segmentation and even confrontation. Nonetheless, although it is important to avoid an excessive personification of large bureaucratic organizations, it is also important to recognize that incentive structures, career ladders, and social networks make it unlikely that internalized legal functions will remain truly distinct from one another over the long run.

28. The problem of legal autonomy implies that legal institutions must *appear* neutral, even while buttressing prevailing patterns of social inequality. Thus, as Galanter's original arguments suggest, to understand the relationship between law and stratification, one must trace the subtle structural biases that allow the "haves" to come out ahead even in the absence of overt, instrumental manipulation. Presumably, this injunction holds for internal legal structures as well as for their more frequently studied external counterparts.

29. Nelson et al. note that the converse is true as well: "The autonomy of corporate lawyers does not, by itself, guarantee corporate legality. If lawyers are autonomous but isolated from key information and decisions, they may have little impact on corporate behavior" (1997:4; cf. Stone 1975).

30. One might, of course, question whether even the private corporate bar upholds these professional norms in anything but the most hollowly symbolic ways (see *Fordham Law Review* 1998). Nonetheless, it seems unlikely that in-house practice would be *more* conducive to legal professionalism than practice in an independent law firm.

31. One would not, of course, want to overstate this portrayal, because even nominally independent law firms are often beholden to their largest corporate clients and because, in any case, the legal standards nearest outside lawyers' hearts often have more to do with professional prestige than with societal justice (Nelson 1988; Rosen 1989). Nonetheless, research suggests that the ideological and institutional commitments of inside and outside counsel do differ along a number of dimensions and that, of the two groups, outside counsel are generally somewhat more receptive to the messages of the public legal order (see, e.g., Rosen 1989:506; Lande 1995; Nelson et al. 1997).

32. We do not intend here to disparage the small group of scholars who have labored valiantly in recent years to shed light on private policing activity. Indeed, this article owes much to their efforts. Nonetheless, in quantity if not in quality, a huge disparity remains between these scattered investigations and the surfeit of research, data, and media coverage surrounding public law enforcement. This imbalance, we argue, represents a sociologically interesting phenomenon in its own right.

33. Anecdotal evidence suggests that a substantial proportion of private policing is conducted not by large bureaucratic organizations on their own behalf, but rather by smaller security firms, working, in essence, as independent contractors. Although the contrast between these two models may have important consequences for the economic contours of this emerging sector, the distinction seems unlikely to dramatically affect the central questions under consideration here. Presumably, private security officers remain strongly beholden to managerial interests, even when an organization buys their services in "prepackaged" form through a subcontractor. Nonetheless, subtle differences between the two structural arrangements may exist, and future research would do well to consider whether outside security agencies, like outside law firms, display greater responsiveness to nonmanagerial professional norms (and other external legitimacy concerns) than do in-house departments.

34. Technically, of course, the lowest tiers of the disputing pyramid—the "naming" of injuries, the "blaming" of culprits, and the "claiming" of redress (Felstiner et al. 1980)—remain outside even the organizational legal system; internalization, however, serves to insert several additional layers of organizational processing between the emergence of disputes in daily life and the entrance of those disputes into public legal arenas. Thus, as internalization progresses, the first formal institutions that disputants encounter are increasingly likely to be private, not public, in character.

35. This shift is evident, for example, in the internalization of civil rights claims. Although public legal authorities may once have seen themselves as the primary guardians of minority rights, by the early 1990s both legislatures and courts had begun to endorse organizational handling of employment-related discrimination claims. This new attitude can be seen in legislation like the 1991 Civil Rights Act and the 1990 Americans with Disabilities Act, which both endorse ADR, as well as in court decisions like *Meritor Savings Bank v. Vinson* (1986), which suggest that grievance procedures, if proper in form, may protect employers from liability in external legal actions.

36. The identity between large bureaucratic organizations and society's "haves" is, of course, not a perfect one. Some organizations forward the agendas of the poor and downtrodden, and some elites operate through primarily nonorganizational devices. Nonetheless, just as Galanter's one shotter-repeat player typology "define[s] a position of advantage . . . and indicate[s] how those with other advantages tend to occupy this position" (1974:103), so too does formal organization correlate with and augment other advantages in the contemporary stratification regime.

37. Many observers dispute whether such legitimating myths make much practical difference (see, e.g., Tushnet 1984; cf. Sarat 1998), and our argument here should not be read as a full, substantive defense of the liberal legal model. Nonetheless, at the margins, the democratic and libertarian pretensions of the public legal order at least provide symbolic resources that "have not" groups can invoke to mobilize support in various political debates (Scheingold 1974). Few equivalent symbolic resources exist within the more authoritarian and instrumentalist ideology of bureaucracy.

38. We do not intend to argue here that top-down communication, authoritative leadership, official secrecy, and mass surveillance could never have a place in a democratic polity. Nor do we intend to argue that any particular real-world public order

334 LAUREN B. EDELMAN AND MARK C. SUCHMAN

fully embodies the democratic ideal (or, for that matter, that any real-world private order fully embodies the bureaucratic alternative). We offer these archetypes simply to highlight the underlying differences between the democratic and bureaucratic logics and to suggest that the distinction between the two may carry substantial implications for the fate of society's "have nots."

39. As an aside, it is perhaps worth noting that the internalization of law by large bureaucracies may represent a sort of "unhappy medium" in the tug of war between public law and indigenous law (see Galanter 1981; Macaulay 1986). When authority resides in the state, the legal order may suffer from excessive artificiality and formalism, but it is also likely to offer substantial protections for democratic access and minority interests. When authority resides in indigenous communities, the legal order may reproduce customary prejudices, exclusions, and favoritisms, but it is also likely to offer grassroots involvement, common-sense familiarity, and a pragmatic foundation in "living law" (Ehrlich [1936] 1962). When, however, authority resides in large bureaucratic organizations, the legal order is likely to be formalized without being democratic, and privatized without being grounded in the grassroots. To that extent, the organizational internalization of law represents the worst of both worlds.

References

Abbott, Andrew (1988) *The System of Professions: An Essay on the Expert Division of Labor.* Chicago: Univ. of Chicago Press.

Ackerman, Deborah L. (1985) "A History of Drug Testing," in R. H. Coombs & L. J. West, eds., *Drug Testing: Issues and Options.* New York: Oxford Univ. Press.

American Bar Association (1991) *The State of the Legal Profession.* Chicago: American Bar Association, Young Lawyers Division.

American Management Association (1997) Electronic Monitoring and Surveillance [online]. Available: *http://www.amanet.org/survey/elec97.htm.*

Balbus, Isaac (1977) "Commodity Form and Legal Form: An Essay on the 'Relative Autonomy' of Law," 11 *Law & Society Rev.* 571–88.

Bardach, Eugene, & Robert A. Kagan (1982) *Going by the Book: The Problem of Regulatory Unreasonableness.* Philadelphia: Temple Univ. Press.

Baron, James N., Frank R. Dobbin, & P. Devereaux Jennings (1986) "War and Peace: The Evolution of Modern Personnel Administration in U.S. Industry," 92 *American J. of Sociology* 350–83.

Baudrillard, Jean (1994) *Simulacra and Simulation.* Ann Arbor: Univ. of Michigan Press.

Becker, Allison (1992) "Survey Shows In-House Pay Up in 1991," *The Recorder,* 29 Jan., p. 1.

Bentham, Jeremy (1791) *Panopticon; or, The Inspection House.* London: T. Payne.

Bishop, Thomas B. (1988) "The Law of Shoplifting: A Guide for Lawyers and Merchants," 19 *Cumberland Law Rev.* 43–74.

Blumberg, Abraham (1967) "The Practice of Law as a Confidence Game: Organizational Cooptation of a Profession," 1 *Law & Society Rev.* 15–39.

Blumrosen, Alfred W. (1993) *Modern Law: The Law Transmission System and Equal Employment Opportunity*. Madison: Univ. of Wisconsin Press.

Bohannon, Paul (1965) "The Differing Realms of Law," 67 (Suppl.) *The American Anthropologist* 33–42.

Bureau of Justice Statistics (1999) Law Enforcement Statistics: Summary Findings [online]. Available: *http://www.ojp.usdoj.gov/bjs/lawenf.htm*.

Bush, Robert A. Baruch (1989) "Mediation and Adjudication, Dispute Resolution and Ideology: An Imaginary Conversation," 3 *J. of Contemporary Legal Issues* 1–33.

Bush, Robert A. Baruch, & Joseph P. Folger (1994) *The Promise of Mediation: Responding to Conflict through Empowerment and Recognition*. San Francisco: Jossey-Bass.

Chaiken, Marcia, & Jan Chaiken (1987) *Public Policing—Privately Provided*. Washington, DC: National Institute of Justice.

Chayes, Abram, & Antonia H. Chayes (1985) "Corporate Counsel and the Elite Law Firm," 37 *Stanford Law Rev.* 277–300.

CPR Institute for Dispute Resolution (1999) "Focus, Education, and Legitimacy: CPR Celebrates 20 Years of ADR," 17 *Alternatives to the High Costs of Litigation* 1–2.

Cronin-Harris, Catherine (1997) *Building ADR into the Corporate Law Department: ADR Systems Design*. New York: CPR Institute for Dispute Resolution.

Cunningham, William C. (1980) *Crime and Protection in America: A Study of Private Security and Law Enforcement Resources and Relationships*, Executive Summary. Washington, DC: National Institute of Justice, U.S. Department of Justice.

Cunningham, William C., John J. Strauchs, & Clifford W. Van Meter (1990) *Private Security Trends 1970–2000: The Hallcrest Report II*. Boston: Butterworth-Heinemann.

Curran, B. (1985) *The Lawyer Statistical Report: A Statistical Profile of the U.S. Legal Profession in the 1980s*. Chicago: American Bar Foundation.

Davis, Melissa G., Richard J. Lundman, & Ramiro Martinez Jr. (1991) "Private Corporate Justice: Store Police, Shoplifters, and Civil Recovery," 38 *Social Problems* 395–411.

Dezalay, Yves, & Bryant Garth (1996) Dealing in Virtue: International Commercial Arbitration and the Construction of a Transnational Legal Order. Chicago: Univ. of Chicago Press.

DiMaggio, Paul J., & Walter W. Powell (1983) "The Iron Cage Revisited: Institutional Isomorphism and Collective Rationality in Organizational Fields," 48 *American Sociological Rev.* 147–60.

Dobbin, Frank, John R. Sutton, John W. Meyer, & W. Richard Scott (1993) "Equal Employment Opportunity Law and the Construction of Internal Labor Markets," 99 *American J. of Sociology* 396–427.

Economist (1997) "Welcome to the New World of Private Security," 342 (8013) *Economist* 21–24.

Edelman, Lauren B. (1990) "Legal Environments and Organizational Governance: The Expansion of Due Process in the American Workplace," 95 *American J. of Sociology* 1401–40.

——— (1992) "Legal Ambiguity and Symbolic Structures: Organizational Mediation of Civil Rights Law," 97 *American J. of Sociology* 1531–76.

——— (forthcoming) "Constructed Legalities: Socio-Legal Fields and the Endogeneity of Law," in W. Powell & D. Jones, eds., *Bending the Bars of the Iron Cage: Institutional Dynamics and Processes*. Chicago: Univ. of Chicago Press.

Edelman, Lauren B., Steven E. Abraham, & Howard S. Erlanger (1992) "Professional Construction of the Legal Environment: The Inflated Threat of Wrongful Discharge Doctrine," 26 *Law & Society Rev.* 47–83.

Edelman, Lauren B., & Mia Cahill (1998) "How Law Matters in Disputing and Dispute Processing (Or, the Contingency of Legal Matter in Alternative Dispute Resolution)," in B. Garth & A. Sarat, eds., *How Law Matters*. Evanston, IL: Northwestern Univ. Press.

Edelman Lauren B., Howard S. Erlanger, & John Lande (1993) "Employers' Handling of Discrimination Complaints: The Transformation of Rights in the Workplace," 27 *Law & Society Rev.* 497–534.

Edelman, Lauren B., Sally Riggs Fuller, & Iona Mara-Drita (2001) "I Live for Golf While You Prefer Tennis: Diversity Rhetoric and the Managerialization of Law," 106 *American J. of Sociology* 1589–641.

Edelman, Lauren B., & Mark C. Suchman (1997) "Legal Environments of Organizations," 23 *Annual Rev. of Sociology* 479–515.

Edelman, Lauren B., & Stephen Petterson (1999) "Symbols and Substance in Organizational Response to Civil Rights Law," in K. Leicht, ed., *Research in Social Stratification and Mobility*, vol. 17. Greenwich, CT: JAI Press.

Edelman, Lauren B., Stephen Petterson, Elizabeth Chambliss, & Howard S. Erlanger (1991) "Legal Ambiguity and the Politics of Compliance: Affirmative Action Officers' Dilemma," 13 *Law & Policy* 73–97.

Edelman, Lauren B., Christopher Uggen, & Howard S. Erlanger (1999) "The Endogeneity of Legal Regulation: Grievance Procedures as Rational Myth," 105 *American J. of Sociology* 406–54.

Edwards, Richard (1979) *Contested Terrain: The Transformation of the Workplace in the Twentieth Century*. New York: Basic Books.

Ehrlich, Eugen [1936] (1962) *Fundamental Principles of the Sociology of Law*. Translated by W. Moll. New York: Russel and Russel.

Ewick, Patricia C., & Susan S. Silbey (1998) *The Common Place of Law: Stories from Everyday Life*. Chicago: Univ. of Chicago Press.

Ewing, David W. (1989) *Justice on the Job: Resolving Grievances in the Nonunion Workplace*. Cambridge: Harvard Business School Press.

Felstiner, William L. F., Richard L. Abel, & Austin Sarat (1980) "The Emergence and Transformation of Disputes: Naming, Blaming, Claiming . . . ," 15 *Law & Society Rev.* 631–54.

Fisher, Roger, & William Ury (1981) *Getting to Yes: Negotiating Agreement without Giving In*. Boston: Houghton Mifflin.

Fligstein, Neil (1991) "The Structural Transformation of American Industry: An Institutional Account of the Causes of Diversification in the Largest Firms, 1919–1979," in Powell & DiMaggio, eds., *The New Institutionalism*.

Fordham Law Review (1998) "Symposium on Ethics: Beyond the Rules," 67 *Fordham Law Rev.* 691–883.

Foucault, Michel (1979) *Discipline and Punish: The Birth of the Prison.* New York: Vintage Books.

Fuller, Sally R., Lauren B. Edelman, & Sharon Matusik (2000) "Legal Readings: Employees' Interpretation and Enactment of Law," 25 *Academy of Management Rev.* 200–216.

Galanter, Marc (1974) "Why the 'Haves' Come Out Ahead: Speculations on the Limits of Legal Change," 9 *Law & Society Rev.* 95–160.

——— (1981) "Justice in Many Rooms: Courts, Private Ordering, and Indigenous Law," 19 *J. of Legal Pluralism* 1–47.

——— (1999) Personal communication, Univ. of Wisconsin Law School, Madison, 21 June.

Galanter, Marc, & Joel Rogers (1991) "A Transformation of American Business Disputing? Some Preliminary Observations." Institute for Legal Studies Working Paper DPRP #10–3, Madison, WI.

General Accounting Office (1995) "Employment Discrimination: Most Private-Sector Employers Use Alternative Dispute Resolution" (Letter Report, 5 July) GAO/HEHS-95–150. Available: *http://frwebgate.access.gpo.gov.*

Gilson, Ronald J., & Robert H. Mnookin (1985) "Sharing among the Human Capitalists: An Economic Inquiry into the Corporate Law Firm and How Partners Split Profits," 37 *Stanford Law Rev.* 313–92.

Goffmann, Erving (1961) *Asylums: Essays on the Social Situation of Mental Patients and Other Inmates.* New York: Doubleday/Anchor.

Gordon, David M., Richard Edwards, & Michael Reich (1982) *Segmented Work, Divided Workers.* Cambridge: Cambridge Univ. Press.

Gusfield, Joseph (1963) *Symbolic Crusade: Status Politics and the American Temperance Movement.* Urbana: Univ. of Illinois Press.

Hartwell, Tyler D., Paul D. Steele, Michael T. French, & Nathaniel F. Rodman (1996) "Prevalence of Drug Testing in the Workplace," 119 (11) *Monthly Labor Rev.* 35–42.

Hawkins, Keith (1984) *Environment and Enforcement: Regulation and the Social Definition of Pollution.* Oxford: Clarendon Press.

Heimer, Carol A., & Lisa R. Staffen (1998) *For the Sake of the Children: The Social Organization of Responsibility in the Hospital and the Home.* Chicago: Univ. of Chicago Press.

Heinz, John P., & Edward O. Laumann (1982) *Chicago Lawyers: The Social Structure of the Bar.* New York: Russell Sage Foundation.

Heinz, John P., Robert L. Nelson, Edward O. Laumann, & Ethan Michelson (1998) "The Changing Character of Lawyer's Work: Chicago in 1975 and 1995," 32 *Law & Society Rev.* 751–75.

Jacoby, Sanford M. (1985) *Employing Bureaucracy: Managers, Unions, and the Transformation of Work in American Industry, 1900–1945.* New York: Columbia Univ. Press.

Joh, Elizabeth (1999) Personal communication, New York University, New York City, 18 June.

Kaye, Judith S. (1996) "Symposium on Business Dispute Resolution: ADR and Beyond: An Opening Statement," 59 *Albany Law Rev.* 835.

Konrad, Alison M., & Frank Linnehan (1995) "Formalized HRM Structures: Coordinating Equal Employment Opportunity or Concealing Organizational Practices?" 38 *Academy of Management J.* 787–820.

Lande, John (1995) "The Diffusion of a Process Pluralist Ideology of Disputing: Factors Affecting Opinions of Business Lawyers and Executives." Ph.D. diss., Department of Sociology, University of Wisconsin-Madison.

——— (1998) "Failing Faith in Litigation? A Survey of Business Lawyers' and Executives' Opinions," 3 *Harvard Negotiation Law Rev.* 1–70.

Lind, E. Allan, & Tom R. Tyler (1988) *The Social Psychology of Procedural Justice.* New York: Plenum Press.

Lipsky, David B., & Ronald L. Seeber (1998) "In Search of Control: The Corporate Embrace of ADR," 1 *Univ. of Pennsylvania J. of Labor & Employment Law* 133–57.

Macaulay, Stewart (1963) "Non-Contractual Relations in Business: A Preliminary Study," 28 *American Sociological Rev.* 55–66.

——— (1986) "Private Government," in L. Lipson and S. Wheeler, eds., *Law and the Social Sciences.* New York: Russell Sage Foundation.

Martin, Joanne (1992) *Cultures in Organizations: Three Perspectives.* New York: Oxford Univ. Press.

Marx, Gary T. (1987) "The Interweaving of Public and Private Police in Undercover Work," in C. Shearing & P. Stenning, eds., *Private Policing.* Beverly Hills, CA: Sage Publications.

May, David (1999) "Testing by Necessity," 68 (4) *Occupational Health and Safety* 48–51.

Menkel-Meadow, Carrie (1984) "Toward Another View of Legal Negotiation: The Structure of Problem-Solving," 31 *UCLA Law Rev.* 754–842.

Merry, Sally E. (1988) "Legal Pluralism," 22 *Law & Society Rev.* 869–96.

——— (1990) *Getting Justice and Getting Even: Legal Consciousness among Working-Class Americans.* Chicago: Univ. of Chicago Press.

Mnookin, Robert H., & Lewis Kornhauser (1979) "Bargaining in the Shadow of the Law: The Case of Divorce," 88 *Yale Law J.* 950–97.

Moore, Christopher W. (1986) *The Mediation Process: Practical Strategies for Resolving Conflict.* San Francisco: Jossey-Bass.

Morn, Frank (1982) *The Eye That Never Sleeps: A History of the Pinkerton National Detective Agency.* Bloomington: Univ. of Indiana Press.

Nelson, Robert L. (1988) *Partners with Power: Social Transformation of the Large Law Firm.* Berkeley: Univ. of California Press.

——— (1994) "The Futures of American Lawyers: A Demographic Profile of a Changing Profession in a Changing Society," 44 *Case Western Reserve Law Rev.* 345–406.

Nelson, Robert L., Laura Beth Nielsen, & Lisa E. Douglass (1997) "Cops, Counsel, or Entrepreneurs: The Shifting Roles of Lawyers in Large Business Corporations." Presented at the Law & Society Association Annual Meeting, St. Louis, MO (29 May-1 June).

Nonet, Philippe, & Philip Selznick (1978) *Law and Society in Transition: Toward Responsive Law.* New York: Harper and Row.

Perrow, Charles (1991) "A Society of Organizations," 20 *Theory & Society* 725–62.

Plapinger, Elizabeth (1999) Personal communication, CPR Institute for Dispute Resolution, New York City, 23 June.

Pondy, Louis R., & Ian I. Mitroff (1979) "Beyond Open System Models of Organization," in B. Staw, ed., *Research in Organizational Behavior*, vol. 1. Greenwich, CT: JAI Press

Powell, Walter W., & Paul J. DiMaggio, eds. (1991) *The New Institutionalism in Organizational Analysis*. Chicago: Univ. of Chicago Press.

Rees, Joseph (1988) *Reforming the Workplace: A Study of Self-Regulation in Occupational Safety*. Philadelphia: Univ. of Pennsylvania Press.

Reichman, Nancy (1987) "The Widening Webs of Surveillance: Private Police Unraveling Deceptive Claims," in C. Shearing & P. Stenning, eds., 1987.

Reuben, Richard C. (1996) "The Lawyer Turns Peacemaker," 82 *ABA J.* 54–62.

——— (1997) "Public Justice: Toward a State Action Theory of Alternative Dispute Resolution," 85 *California Law Rev.* 577–641.

Rosen, Robert E. (1989) "The Inside Counsel Movement, Professional Judgement, and Organizational Representation," 64 *Indiana Law J.* 479–553.

Rosenberg, Gerald N. (1991) *The Hollow Hope: Can Courts Bring about Social Change?* Chicago: Univ. of Chicago Press.

Sarat, Austin (1998) "Going to Court: Access, Autonomy, and the Contradictions of Liberal Legality," in D. Kairys, ed., *The Politics of Law: A Progressive Critique*, 3d ed. New York: Basic Books.

Sarat, Austin, & Stuart Scheingold (1998) *Cause Lawyering: Political Commitments and Professional Responsibilities*. New York: Oxford Univ. Press.

Scheid, Teresa L., & Mark C. Suchman (1998) "Ritual Conformity to the Americans with Disabilities Act: Coercive and Normative Isomorphism." Unpublished manuscript, Univ. of North Carolina-Charlotte.

Scheingold, Stuart (1974) The Politics of Rights: Lawyers, Public Policy, and Political Change. New Haven, CT: Yale Univ. Press.

Schultz, Vicki (1990) "Telling Stories about Women and Work: Judicial Interpretations of Sex Segregation in the Workplace in Title VII Cases Raising the Lack of Interest Argument," 103 *Harvard Law Rev.* 1749–1943.

Scott, W. Richard (1987) "The Adolescence of Institutional Theory," 32 *Administrative Science Q.* 493–511.

——— (1992) *Organizations: Rational, Natural, and Open Systems*. 3d ed. Englewood Cliffs, NJ: Prentice Hall.

——— (1995) *Institutions and Organizations*. Thousand Oaks, CA: Sage Publications.

Scott, W. Richard, & John W. Meyer (1983) "The Organization of Societal Sectors," in J. Meyer & W. Scott, eds., *Organizational Environments: Ritual and Rationality*. Beverly Hills, CA: Sage Publications.

Selznick, Philip (1948) "Foundations of the Theory of Organization," 13 *American Sociological Rev.* 25–35.

——— (1949) *TVA and the Grass Roots*. Berkeley: Univ. of California Press.

——— (1969) *Law, Society, and Industrial Justice*. New York: Russell Sage Foundation.

Shearing, Clifford D., & Philip C. Stenning (1981) "Modern Private Security: Its

Growth and Implications," in M. Tonry & N. Morris, eds., *Crime and Justice: An Annual Review of Research*. Chicago: Univ. of Chicago Press.

Shearing, Clifford D., & Philip C. Stenning (1983) "Private Security: Implications for Social Control," 30 *Social Problems* 493–506.

Shearing, Clifford D., & Philip C. Stenning, eds. (1987) *Private Policing*. Beverly Hills, CA: Sage Publications.

Sitkin, Sim B., & Robert J. Bies, eds. (1994) *The Legalistic Organization*. Thousand Oaks, CA: Sage Publications.

Slichter, Sumner (1919) *The Turnover of Factory Labor*. New York: Appleton.

——— (1941) "Union Policies and Industrial Management," Brookings Institution Institute of Economics Publication No. 85, Washington, DC.

Slovak, Jeffrey S. (1979) "Working for Corporate Actors: Social Change and Elite Attorneys in Chicago," *American Bar Foundation Research J.*, 465–500.

Spangler, Eve (1986) *Lawyers for Hire: Salaried Professionals at Work*. New Haven, CT: Yale Univ. Press.

Spitzer, Steven, & Andrew T. Scull (1977a) "Privatization and Capitalist Development: The Case of the Private Police," 25 *Social Problems* 18–29.

Spitzer, Steven, & Andrew T. Scull (1977b) "Social Control in Historical Perspective: From Private to Public Responses to Crime," in D. Greenberg, ed., *Correction and Punishment*. Beverly Hills, CA: Sage Publications.

Stone, Christopher D. (1975) *Where the Law Ends: The Social Control of Corporate Behavior*. New York: Harper and Row.

Strasser, Fred (1985) "The In-House Lure Gets Stronger," *National Law J.*, 22 July, p. 1.

Suchman, Mark C. (1995a) "Localism and Globalism in Institutional Analysis: The Emergence of Contractual Norms in Venture Finance," in W. R. Scott and S. Christensen, eds., *The Institutional Construction of Organizations*. Thousand Oaks, CA: Sage Publications.

——— (1995b) "Managing Legitimacy: Strategic and Institutional Approaches," 20 *Academy of Management Rev.* 571–610.

——— (1997) "On Beyond Interest: Rational, Normative and Cognitive Perspectives in the Social Scientific Study of Law," 3 *Wisconsin Law Rev.* 475–501.

——— (1998) "Working without a Net: The Sociology of Legal Ethics in Corporate Litigation," 67 *Fordham Law Rev.* 837–74.

Suchman, Mark C., & Mia L. Cahill (1996) "The Hired-Gun as Facilitator: The Case of Lawyers in Silicon Valley," 21 *Law & Social Inquiry* 679–712.

Suchman, Mark C., & Lauren B. Edelman (1996) "Legal Rational Myths: The New Institutionalism and the Law and Society Tradition," 21 *Law & Social Inquiry* 903–41.

Sutton, John R., Frank Dobbin, John W. Meyer, & W. Richard Scott (1994) "Legalization of the Workplace," 99 *American J. of Sociology* 944–71.

Thompson, E. P. (1975) *Whigs and Hunters: The Origin of the Black Act*. New York: Pantheon Books.

Traub, Stuart H. (1996) "Battling Employee Crime: A Review of Corporate Strategies and Programs," 42 *Crime & Delinquency* 244–57.

Tushnet, Mark V. (1984) "An Essay on Rights," 62 *Texas Law Rev.* 1363–1403.

Weber, Max (1947) *The Theory of Social and Economic Organization*. New York: Oxford Univ. Press.

Weiss, Robert P. (1987) "From 'Slugging Detectives' to 'Labor Relations': Policing Labor at Ford, 1930–1947," in C. Shearing & P. Stenning, eds., 1987.

Westin, Alan F., & Alfred G. Feliu (1988) *Resolving Employment Disputes without Litigation*. Washington, DC: Bureau of National Affairs.

Cases Cited

Gilmer v. Interstate/Johnson Lane Corp., 111 S. Ct. 1647 (1991).

Mapp v. Ohio, 367 U.S. 643 (1961).

Meritor Savings Bank v. Vinson, 106 S. Ct. 2399 (1986).

Miller v. Bank of America, 600 F.Supp. 161 (1975).

Miranda v. Arizona, 384 U.S. 436 (1966).

The Government Gorilla

Why Does Government Come Out Ahead in Appellate Courts?

Introduction

One strand of research inspired by Marc Galanter's "Why the 'Haves' Come Out Ahead" has involved statistical analyses of winners and losers in appellate court cases. Going under the rubric of "party capability theory," these studies have examined outcomes in a variety of courts:

- The U.S. Courts of Appeals (Songer and Sheehan 1992; Songer et al. 1999, reprinted in this volume)
- The U.S. Supreme Court (Sheehan et al. 1992)
- State supreme courts in the United States (Farole 1999; Wheeler et al. 1987)
- The Supreme Court of Canada (Haynie et al. 2001; McCormick 1993)
- The Philippine Supreme Court (Haynie 1994; see also Haynie 1995; Haynie et al. 2001)
- The High Court of Australia (Smyth 2000; Willis and Sheehan 1999; Haynie et al. 2001)
- The Court of Appeal of England and Wales (Atkins 1991)
- The House of Lords (Great Britain) (Haynie et al. 2001)
- The Indian Supreme Court (Haynie et al. 2001)[1]
- The South African Supreme Court (Haynie et al. 2001)
- The Tanzanian Court of Appeal (Haynie et al. 2001)

With some exceptions, these studies have reported support for the proposition that, in the context of appellate litigation, parties likely to have more resources and experience have an advantage over opponents with less in the way of resources and experience. The general interpretation of these findings is to provide broad, but not universal, support for the argument that the "haves" come out ahead because they have tangible and intangible resources that advantage them against weaker parties.

In this chapter, I revisit the analyses testing party capability theory in the appellate court context and suggest that the dominant pattern is not advantageous to "haves" but advantageous to government. While there may be evidence that parties with more resources have an advantage, I will argue that the big advantage comes to government parties rather than to business parties. Moreover, this advantage is not simply one of greater resources. Government is different, and these differences, rather than simple party capability, account for government's advantage.

I posit that there are two key components to government's advantage that go beyond the usual resource and experience associated with repeat players. First, the government makes the rules, which the courts in turn enforce. In some ways, this is almost so obvious that it gets overlooked. I will lay out a variety of ways in which government "stacks the deck" to its advantage. Second, despite norms of judicial independence, courts and judges are not independent of government; they are part of government. Courts are agencies of the state (Shapiro 1964, 1968). One possible impact of this is that judges feel some loyalty toward the government or regime of which they are a part (see Derthick 2002, 83, 218). This does not mean that judges blindly back the actions of the other branches but rather that there may be a tendency in relatively close cases to give the edge to a governmental party or to give the government a more sympathetic hearing (Rosenberg 1991, 14–15).

I conclude with a discussion of what my analysis of this body of research focused on the appellate courts may mean for litigation in first instance or trial courts. This is an important question because the cases that get to the appeals level are a highly selective subset of an already selected subset of an already selected subset. That is, using the pyramid metaphor that has been applied to understanding the dispute resolution and litigation hierarchy (see in particular Miller and Sarat 1980–81), appellate litigation cannot be deemed to be typical of disputes that arise, that lead to demands for redress, or that become formal court actions. However, despite the atypicality of appellate cases, understanding the sources of advantage in those cases has implications for cases throughout the dispute pyramid.

The Evidence Concerning Government's Appellate Advantage

Table 11.1 brings together summary information from eleven different studies that considered sets of cases in appellate courts involving government

TABLE 11.1

Net Advantage for Different Types of Parties

	Source	Federal or National Government	State and City/Local Government	State Government	Local Government	Government	"Big Business"	Business or Corporations or "Other Business"	Other Groups or "Other"	Individuals
United States										
State Supreme Courts	(1)		+11.8		-1.6[a]		+6.4	+3.1		-1.5
State Supreme Courts	(2)			+32.3	+11.0		+11.1[b]	-2.4	-6.7	-12.5
Federal Courts of Appeals	(3)	+45.1	+29.9				+5.9	+1.6		-18.2
Federal Courts of Appeals	(4)	+25.6	+15.6					-2.8		-12.6
U.S. Supreme Court	(5)	+35.9		+11.2	-6.3		-19.3	-11.9		-17.4
Canada										
Supreme Court	(6)	+20.4		+3.7[c]	-2.5		+15.0	-5.9		-9.6
Supreme Court	(10)					+28.7		-27.8		-16.2
England and Wales / Great Britain										
Court of Appeal[d]	(7)	+27.0						+6.0		-14.0
House of Lords	(10)					+34.1		-8.4		-26.3
Australia										
High Court	(8)	-0.1	-3.6					+1.2		-1.0
High Court	(10)					-12.4		+10.7		+4.8
High Court	(11)	11.8[e]		-2.5	-16.5		+1.3	-3.5	+7.6	+0.5
Philippines										
Supreme Court	(9)	-10.8[f]						-9.1		+13.7
Supreme Court	(10)					+16.7		-10.5		-7.5
India										
Supreme Court	(10)					+1.0		-6.4		-2.7
South Africa										
Supreme Court	(10)					+2.0		-4.9		+2.7
						+1.8				
Tanzania						+25.0		+14.3		-18.7

SOURCES

(1) Wheeler et al. 1987 (analysis of samples of cases from sixteen state supreme courts, 1870–1970)

(2) Farole 1999 (analysis of sample of 1975, 1980, 1985, and 1990 cases from six state supreme courts)

(3) Songer and Sheehan 1992 (analysis of 1986 decisions of three circuits)

(4) Songer et al. 1999 (reprinted in this volume) (1925–1988)

(5) Sheehan et al. 1992 (analysis of U.S. Supreme Court decisions, 1953–1988)

(6) McCormick 1993 (1949–1992 decisions of the Supreme Court of Canada)

(7) Atkins 1991 (analysis of Court of Appeal cases, 1983–1985)

(8) Willis and Sheehan 1999 (High Court decisions, 1988–1998)

(9) Haynie 1994 (analysis of decisions of the Philippine Supreme Court, 1961–1986)

(10) Computed from table 2 in Haynie et al. 2001 (data from the Comparative Judicial Database Project; varying number of recent years for each court)

(11) Smyth 2000 (High Court appellate decisions, 1948–August 1999)

[a] "Small" local governments.

[b] Almost all cases against individuals or small businesses.

[c] Provincial government net advantage.

[d] Net advantage scores are author's estimates based upon tabular data in original article.

[e] "Crown" has a net advantage of −2.0.

[f] Includes all levels of government.

while examining whether the "haves" come out ahead. These studies involve eleven different courts in eight different countries, with five of the courts considered in two different studies. Ten of the eleven studies reported the relative advantage of various types of parties using a measure commonly referred to as "net advantage." For the remaining study, that of the English Court of Appeal, I derived estimates of net advantage from the original author's tables.

The net advantage measure was introduced by Wheeler et al. (1987, 418) in the first of the studies in this series. Net advantage is computed as follows:

Net Advantage = Success Rate as Appellant - (1 - Success Rate as Respondent)

The latter element of this formula can alternately be read as the success rate of the opponent when the opponent is the appellant. This formula takes into account a common pattern that a given court's decisions may tend to advantage one side or the other and that some types of parties are more likely to appear as appellants while others are more likely to appear as respondents. In most appellate courts, the U.S. Courts of Appeals (see Howard 1981), for example, the respondent tends to prevail. An exception to this is the U.S. Supreme Court, which has a well-recognized tendency to reverse lower courts (Sheehan et al. 1992, 467), in part reflecting the discretionary nature of its docket whereby the justices can pick and choose which cases to hear (Brenner and Krol 1989; Perry 1991). Appellate courts that have mandatory dockets (that is, where the court is required to decide appeals brought to it) are more likely to uphold the lower court's decision. For example, in one of the studies of the U.S. Courts of Appeals (Songer et al. 1999, 819), the authors determined that the federal government prevailed in 51.3 percent of appeals when it was the appellant; when the federal government was the respondent, it prevailed in 74.3 percent of appeals (that is, the appellant prevailed in 25.7 percent of appeals); the federal government's net advantage was then computed as 51.3 - (1 - 74.3) = +25.6. In contrast, individuals as appellants prevailed in 26.1 percent of appeals and in 61.3 percent of appeals as respondents (that is, the appellant prevailed in 38.7 percent of appeals); thus, the net advantage of individuals is 26.1 - (1 - 61.3) = -12.6.

My interest is not in the general question of how parties do relative to their resources but in the relative success specifically of governmental parties. For some of the studies, there are two levels of governmental parties involved; when those two parties are pitted against one another, the case will normally be dealt with in the courts of the higher entity and will be decided according to the law and procedure of the higher entity (that is, cases involving a state and the federal government in the United States are handled in federal court using federal procedural rules and are decided according to federal law).

Table 11.1 shows a very clear pattern for governmental parties to have an advantage.[2] When there are two levels of government, the higher level has an advantage over the lower level. The average net advantage to governments shown in Table 11.1 is 11.08, while the average net advantage to business is -1.42 and to individuals is -8.03. With the exception of Australia and the Philippines (for the earlier of two periods only), the only negative net advantages for government were for local government; probably a significant proportion of cases involving such litigants were with higher units of government, so it is not necessarily surprising that they would have a low net advantage. The two settings showing a net disadvantage for government merit some additional discussion.

The studies of the Australian High Court report both overall net advantage patterns and patterns for specific pairings of parties. Table 11.2 shows specific pairings. For my purposes, the key anomaly here is the net advantage of individuals in cases with the federal government of Australia. This appears to reflect one peculiarity of High Court cases: a large proportion of cases pitting an individual against the federal government are criminal cases, and the High Court has taken on a role as a watchdog vis-à-vis the protection of defendants' rights. Smyth (2000) categorized these as "Crown" cases, and hence these are separated out in his study. Specifically, most cases involving government are categorized as criminal or public law cases. According to one study (Haynie et al. 2001, table 4), the government has a net advantage of -43 in criminal cases, virtually all of which involve individuals. In public law cases, the government's net advantage is +19. Interestingly, Smyth's study shows a similar advantage in "federal government" (presumably, mostly public law) cases but a much smaller gap in "Crown" (presumably, criminal law) cases involving individuals; this may reflect the time period covered by the studies, with Smyth's going back much farther (1948) than do the other studies. (See Table 11.2.)

The pattern for the Philippines differs radically depending on the period examined. In her analysis of the earlier period, Haynie concluded that the absence of apparent party capability effects might reflect that country's status as part of the Third World and a concern for legitimacy and stability among developing countries. In such countries, she argued, it may be that the courts recognize their unique status within the society, and in order to maintain the court's integrity and legitimacy, the judges take care to not allow the "haves" to take advantage of their resources and capabilities in cases before the court (Haynie 1994, 769; see also Tate and Haynie 1994). While this may be the case, a careful examination of the patterns in the Philippines

TABLE II.2

Party Pairings for Australia

	Willis and Sheehan 1999	Haynie et al. 2001	Smyth 2000
Crown			
vs. "other" business			-42.1
vs. individuals			+5.4
Federal government			
vs. state and local	+41.7		
vs. business	+14.2		
vs. big business			+20.3
vs. "other" business			+15.5
vs. individual	-8.7		+3.2
State and local government			
vs. business	-8.0		
vs. individuals	+16.7		
State government			
vs. big business			-7.0
vs. "other" business			-9.8
vs. individuals			+2.9
Local government			
vs. "other" business			-14.5
vs. individuals			-8.4
Government			
v.s business		-4	
vs. individuals		-17	
Business			
vs. individuals	22	+17	
Big business			
vs. "other" business			+24.7
vs. individuals			-7.4
Other business			
vs. individuals			-0.5

suggests that the government as litigant may in fact have greater success than the simple results indicate. Breaking down the results by specific party configurations shows the following (Haynie 1994, 764):

Government

      vs. business   +32.57

      vs. individuals   -19.36

Business

      vs. individuals   -20.26

These results are in a sense quite consistent with Haynie's argument: it appears that the court is looking out for the interests of individuals. However, Haynie shows some additional results that serve to qualify this conclusion. She provides breakdowns by type of party for six different categories of cases (torts, creditor/debtor, landlord/tenant, labor/management, workers' compensation, and contempt). The net advantage of individuals is strongest in workers' compensation cases, +57.94, and these constitute a very significant proportion of cases, particularly those between individuals and government (in fact, 43 percent of all cases involving government are workers' compensation cases). I suspect that if one were to eliminate workers' compensation cases, government would show a clear net advantage vis-à-vis individuals. This would leave the question of why the Philippine Supreme Court was particularly pro-individual in workers' compensation cases, but one could imagine an explanation that turned on such cases serving a calming effect on a potentially restive population. In thinking about this issue, one also needs to keep in mind that the Philippine Supreme Court's docket differs from that of the other appellate courts shown in Table 11.1; specifically, it "contains many routine decisions generally associated with the lower courts, such as landlord-tenant disputes, property ownership disputes, and debtor/creditor disputes" (Haynie 1994, 756). Thus, there may be differences in the relative success of differing types of parties depending on the level of the court and the general approaches to litigation by various types of parties; for example, if Government A has a policy of stonewalling at the trial level, it may be that government loses a large proportion of cases compared to Government B, which tries to resolve cases before they get into litigation if there is a basis for the opposing party's claim.

The more recent data from the Philippines does not show individuals having any advantage. Part of the reason for this may be a shift in the docket of the Philippine Supreme Court. While in the early period a large proportion of the cases involving individuals were workers' compensation matters in which the Court seemed to favor individuals, by the later period the bulk of cases involving individuals were criminal cases in which the Court favored government (Haynie et al. 2001, table 4). Moreover, while into the mid to late 1980s, the Philippine Supreme Court was held in relatively high esteem, by the 1990s the Court had slid from favor due to a series of corruption scandals (see Coronel 1997, 2000, 196–231) and the politicization of the court (Haynie 1998).

There is one final issue that I need to consider before turning to possible explanations of government's relative success: the authors of the study of the U.S. Supreme Court conducted a series of multivariate analyses that led them to the conclusion that party resources are relatively unimportant despite the net advantages they reported for different types of litigants. However, the authors make the following crucial observation (Sheehan et al. 1992, 467):

> Further weakening the resource argument is the evidence that the effects of resources in the business and state and local model stem almost entirely from the tendency of these parties to lose consistently to the federal government. In analyses in which cases involving the federal government are removed, resources cease to be statistically significant in the business model and are reduced to borderline significance in the state and local government model.

In other words, in U.S. Supreme Court cases that involve the federal government, the federal government has a strong advantage, and the degree of advantage is not linked to the presumed resources of the opposing party. In cases involving state and local governments, there is a small but discernible linkage, which would indicate that state and local governments maintain at least some advantage over nongovernmental parties. Thus, even though the authors conclude that party capability theory, as they have operationalized it, does not account for the relative success of different types of parties before the U.S. Supreme Court, their analysis is consistent with a conclusion that government, particularly the federal government, is advantaged in this forum.

Some authors who focus specifically on the federal government's success do attribute that success to repeat player/party capability factors (McGuire 1998; Salokar 1995, 66–67), while others attribute it, at least in part, to factors such as "special relationships" and the like (Cohen and Spitzer 2000, 405–406; Puro 1981, 221).[3] The most persuasive of these analyses is that of McGuire (1998), which predicts the likelihood of winning before the Supreme Court as a function of party status (appellant or respondent) and the relative litigation experience of the advocates before the Court for the two sides. He finds that the Solicitor General gains no advantage over the opposing side beyond that of being the more experienced advocate.[4]

Explaining Government's Advantage

Looking across the range of studies considering party capability theory in the appellate court context, the strongest pattern is the advantage that accrues to government litigants. While there are some specific types of exceptions, the advantage to government greatly exceeds that of the other set of "haves," business or corporations. Moreover, in cases pitting one level of government against another level of government, the higher level of government, in whose courts the case is typically decided, has an advantage.

The standard explanation for the success of government is that it is a have with more resources than virtually any possible opponent. At one level, this is undoubtedly true: a government litigant has a potential resource base (that is, taxes) that is not subject to the limits of the marketplace. However, in the context of democratic systems, the ability to draw on this resource base is highly constrained by political forces. Government legal offices routinely deal with resource constraints that would be unlikely to concern a large corporation. While in principle government legal offices have extensive experience, many or most government legal offices experience high turnover and often have relatively inexperienced staffs of attorneys who receive little in the way of training and mentoring. Of course, there are exceptions to this: some specific government legal offices, such as the office of the Solicitor General of the United States (see Salokar 1992), have exceptionally competent staffs; as discussed above, McGuire (1998) argues that the federal government's advantage before the Supreme Court can be fully explained by the experience of the advocates from the Solicitor General's office.

Still, it seems too facile to accept the simple assertion that government comes out ahead because the government has greater economic and experiential resources. Undoubtedly, resources have something to do with government success in litigation, but government has other advantages as well:

- Government makes the rules by which litigation is conducted.
- Government often has extensive structures for filtering out cases where its position is weak.
- Government litigates in its own courts before judges that are part of the larger governmental regime.

Let me examine each of these sources of advantage in turn.

MAKING THE RULES TO SECURE ADVANTAGE

Immunity

It some ways, it seems almost too obvious to say that government makes rules for its own advantage, but it is probably a central aspect of government's advantage. Under the concept of sovereignty, government itself decides whether it can be taken to court (Fox 1997, 423–24). Many contemporary governments may choose to allow suits to be brought against them, but this need not be the case and sometimes is not the case. In the United States, most states have invoked sovereign immunity to limit or eliminate liability for common torts arising from actions of the states, their subunits, and employees of states and subunits (see Eaton and Talarico 1993; Gellis 1990; Shepard's Editorial Staff 1992).

In the United States, the Eleventh Amendment has recently become the subject of significant litigation. Under this amendment as interpreted by the U.S. Supreme Court, states may not be sued without their consent by individuals and corporations except where the issue affords strong protections under the Fourteenth Amendment (or earlier amendments within the Bill of Rights that have been deemed incorporated by the Fourteenth Amendment). In recent decisions, the U.S. Supreme Court has disallowed federal suits brought against states by individuals on the grounds of age discrimination (*Kimel v. Florida Board of Regents*, 528 U.S. 62 [2000]) and disability (e.g., *Board of Trustees of the University of Alabama v. Garrett*, 531 U.S. 356, 148 L.Ed.2d 866 [2001]), and on other grounds as well (*Seminole Tribe of Florida v. Florida*, 517 U.S. 44 [1996]; *College Savings Bank v. Florida Prepaid*, 627 U.S. 666 [1999]). In 2002, the Court extended state immunity to cases before federal agencies (*Federal Maritime Commission v. South Carolina Ports Authority*, 535 U.S. 743 [2002]). Cases can still be brought by the federal government against state or local governments on behalf of individuals; that is, the *federal* Supreme Court did not limit the *federal* government's power to use the *federal* courts against lower levels of government.

Federal Tort Claims Act

While restrictions on the right to bring government to court constitute the most extreme form of stacking the deck, one can find many other examples of government creating rules that work to its benefit even when it does allow itself to be sued. In the United States, claims concerning some torts caused by federal employees can be brought against the federal government under the Federal Tort Claims Act, 28 U.S.C. § 1346(b) (see Fox 1997, 429–33; Weaver and Longoria 2002). This law specifically abrogates the federal government's immunity from suit for injuries caused by the government or government personnel in certain situations (that is, the employee must have acted within the scope of his or her duties). This act limits the government's liability to compensatory damages only (that is, no punitive damages are available) and requires that cases be decided by judges rather than by juries (all cases must of course be handled in the federal courts).[5] It also requires that claimants must first try to reach a settlement with the agency before filing suit.[6]

Federal Employees Compensation Act

Another example of government control of the rules is the Federal Employees Compensation Act (5 U.S.C. §§ 8101–8193), which governs workers' compensation cases for federal employees injured in the course of their employment. This statute is administered by the Office of Workers' Compensation Programs (OWCP), which in turn has established a set of administrative regulations.[7] A number of years ago, I spent a month observing a lawyer who handles contingency fee cases, a significant proportion of which are workers' compensation cases. He will not touch federal workers' compensation cases. Sometime later, I contacted him to ask him for specifics as to why he did not take federal workers' compensation cases; he said they were just a quagmire and gave me the names of several other lawyers who might handle them. The second lawyer also said she didn't handle such cases because they were so difficult, and she gave me the name of another lawyer my first contact gave me. That lawyer said he tried handling such cases at one time (about ten years earlier) but found he could not do so in a way that was financially viable. He attributed the problems to two factors.

First, under federal workers' compensation, there is no procedure to "protect" the attorney's fee. The attorney has to collect the fee directly from the client rather than there being some provision such as having the workers' compensation insurer send separate checks to the lawyer and to the claimant or having the insurer pay the settlement or award jointly to the lawyer and client so that the lawyer could deduct the fee due before forwarding the balance to the client (the latter is the common practice in most other types of contingency fee cases). Furthermore, all fees must be approved by the OWCP before the lawyer can collect any fee from the client, and there is no simple formula, such as a standard percentage of any disputed compensation (in Wisconsin, the standard fee for nonfederal workers' compensation cases is 20 percent of disputed compensation other than medical expenses). While in some, perhaps many or all, states there is a requirement of administrative approval of attorneys' fees in workers' compensation cases, these approvals typically turn only on the question of whether there was any genuine dispute that required attorney assistance; the result is that the fee approval process is generally pro forma. Finally, by the time OWCP approves the fee, the client has long since received any lump sum payment that was due, and collecting from the client is very difficult because clients tend to be in fairly dire straits and may have spent any money they received.

Second, the bureaucratic structure of OWCP forces the lawyer to spend unproductive time. The lawyer I spoke with reported that he or his parale-gal often was put on hold for extended periods of time. (I suspect that sim-ply asking to be called back was not a viable option.) There is no mecha-nism to force OWCP to be more responsive. In contrast, in a private workers' compensation case, the state hearing officer has some power to force the workers' compensation insurer to deal with contested claims in a reasonably timely and responsive manner.[8]

Limitations on Attorney Fees

One way in which government creates advantages for itself is by impos-ing special limits on attorney fees applicable in proceedings against govern-ment. One of the most notorious examples of this was a statutory limit of $10 on any legal fees that existed for many years in cases brought to secure benefits for veterans. The impact of this limitation was to make it extremely difficult for veterans who believed that they had incorrectly been denied government benefits to obtain recourse through the courts (Kochman 1979). In Social Security cases, attorneys typically charge on a no win, no pay basis, collecting 25 percent of back due benefits as a fee if the appeal is suc-cessful, a system that was challenged unsuccessfully in a case decided by the Supreme Court in 2002 (*Gisbrecht v. Barnhart*, 535 U.S. 789). If the challenge had been successful, attorney fees would have been limited to a maximum of $125 per hour. In defending the current system attorneys asserted that the proposed limits would have discouraged attorneys from taking many Social Security cases (see Coyle 2001). Finally, in those situations where the gov-ernment makes provisions whereby it will compensate counsel who bring successful cases against it, the government may turn around and impose lim-its on those fees, which effectively discourages attorneys from bringing the cases.

Notice Requirements and Reduced Statutes of Limitation Periods

Because governments make the rules by which claims can be brought against them, they can impose requirements that do not apply to other types of defendants or respondents (see Eaton and Talarico 1993; Shepard's Edito-rial Staff 1992). For example, as with the Federal Tort Claims Act, there may be a requirement that the potential claimant notify (and negotiate with) the potential defendant before initiating any formal court action. There may also be a relatively short time period within which a claim or court case can be filed; that is, where for ordinary defendants the statute of limitations might be three years, all claims against a governmental unit might have to be filed within twelve months of the injury. Moreover, rules related to statutes of limitations, such as their not starting to run for minors until the minor reaches age eighteen, do not necessarily apply to the statutory filing period for claims against a governmental entity. It might also be the case in some situations that rules requiring notice interact with shortened time horizons in a way that serves to bar a suit. For example, there might be a twelve-month time horizon, and a government might have three months to respond to a claim before any suit can be filed; if notice is not given until after nine months have elapsed, the governmental unit can effectively time-bar the claim by simply not responding to the notice until after the twelve-month period has elapsed.

Wisconsin is an example of a governmental entity that applies special notice and time limit rules to claims against it and its subunits. Before filing suit in a Wisconsin state court against the state, a local government, or a governmental officer, the claimant must give notice of the alleged injury within 120 days of the injury's occurrence (180 days for injuries due to medical malpractice). The defendant then has 120 days to grant or disallow the relief that the claimant requests. If the defendant disallows the relief, the claimant must file suit within six months of receiving notice of the disallowance.[9]

Damage Limitations

Another way that government sets rules for its own benefit is by imposing limitations on the damages that can be collected (see Eaton and Talarico 1993; Shepard's Editorial Staff 1992). While tort reform proponents in the United States have for some years advocated caps on damages, particularly caps on noneconomic and punitive damages, such caps are fairly common in cases against state and local governments in the United States. A number of states specifically preclude any punitive damages being awarded against them.[10] Many states place limits on all categories of damages, including economic (medical expenses, property loss, and lost income) and noneconomic damages (pain and suffering, loss of consortium, and so forth). For some types of cases, such as medical malpractice cases against governmental health care facilities, the limits are sufficiently low that bringing cases can be too costly to merit the potential attorney's fee that might be earned on a percentage basis. Even if the limit does not absolutely deter bringing a case, it may limit the investment that a percentage-fee lawyer can afford to make in the case and hence advantage the governmental defendant in any settlement negotiations.

SECURITY FOR COSTS

One final rules advantage that governments may have can arise in legal systems employing a "loser pays" rule. Under such systems, in use in some form in most countries of the world other than the United States, the loser in a court case is obligated to pay some or all of the winner's legal fees. One feature that is sometimes associated with a loser-pays rule is a provision allowing a defendant to request that the plaintiff be ordered to give "security for costs," whereby the plaintiff must provide some type of guarantee that it will pay the defendant's costs if the requesting party wins the case. In Ontario, for example, security for costs is allowed when (Ontario Rules of Civil Procedure, Rule 56.01 [1]):

(a) the plaintiff or applicant is ordinarily resident outside Ontario;

(b) the plaintiff or applicant has another proceeding for the same relief pending in Ontario or elsewhere;

(c) the defendant or respondent has an order against the plaintiff or applicant for costs in the same or another proceeding that remain unpaid in whole or in part;

(d) the plaintiff or applicant is a corporation or a nominal plaintiff or applicant, and there is good reason to believe that the plaintiff or applicant has insufficient assets in Ontario to pay the costs of the defendant or respondent;

(e) there is good reason to believe that the action or application is frivolous and vexatious and that the plaintiff or applicant has insufficient assets in Ontario to pay the costs of the defendant or respondent; or

(f) a statute entitles the defendant or respondent to security for costs.

These rules apply to all cases, but in cases where the Crown (that is, the government) is the defendant, the Public Authorities Protection Act (1980) allows government to apply for security for costs if the "plaintiff is not possessed of *property sufficient* to answer the costs of the action in case a judgment is given in favour of the defendant, and the defendant has a good defence upon the merits, or that the grounds of action are trivial or frivolous" (Watson et al. 1991, 442; emphasis added).

CREATING STRUCTURES TO AVOID TAKING LOSING CASES TO COURT

Governments have extensive control over how disputes in which they are involved are processed. They can create fairly elaborate structures to deal with routine errors in administration whereby the cases that ultimately make it to court have gone through very extensive screening. At the very top of the U.S. federal hierarchy of legal representation sits the office of the Solicitor General (see Salokar 1992). This office oversees most of the federal government's appellate litigation and all of the litigation before the U.S. Supreme Court. The office has a well-deserved reputation for rigorous screening of cases that federal agencies bring to it for appeal. Of course, this does not necessarily help when the government is appealed against, unless the office takes a position that the lower court's decision was incorrect, which does happen on occasion (see Salokar 1995, 69–70); in the latter case, the Solicitor General's office may let the agency defend the appeal, or it could conceivably insist that the agency settle or drop the case to the appellant's benefit.

At the other end of the governmental case review process one finds administrative tribunals that rigorously review the initial decisions of agencies. A good example of this is found within the Social Security Administration (SSA). While the SSA is best known for the Old Age and Survivors Program, it also administers several disability-related programs that involve a high degree of discretionary determination of whether a claimant meets the legal definition of disability. In two of the programs, Disability Insurance (DI) and Supplemental Security Income (SSI), the majority of applicants are initially denied (60 percent for DI and 76 percent for SSI for claims filed in 1996, the most recent year for which I could find complete data). Of those appealed for reconsideration (62 percent of the initial DI denials and 43 percent of the initial SSI denials), 15 percent (DI) and 12 percent (SSI) are allowed. Of those denied at reconsideration, 81 percent of DI and 68 percent of SSI denials are appealed to the Office of Hearings and Appeals; 80 percent of DI and 56 percent of SSI denials are allowed by the administrative law judges.[11] If the decision of the administrative law judge is to deny the claim, that decision is then appealed to the Appeals Council, and only after the Appeals Council denies the claim can a claimant initiate a suit in federal district court. In one sense, this many-layered process might serve to discourage claimants who did not achieve a quick positive response. Generally, however, the rate by which unsuccessful claimants move on is quite high, particularly those who are unsuccessful at the first reconsideration. More important for my argument is that the multi-layered review process at the agency level means that a number of people have examined the case before it gets to court, and it is likely that a large proportion of the incorrect denials have been filtered out. By the time the case gets to court, the judge has good reason to presume that there is a strong basis to the denial. Thus, except in unusual situations, the cases that make it to court are likely to be those where the agency has a strong basis for its decision. Situations can arise where the courts and the agency come into conflict if the agency adopts a stance that the courts find inconsistent with the governing statute; this happened in the early 1980s when the Reagan administration sought to discontinue disability payments to large numbers of recipients.

REGIME LOYALTY

Close to forty years ago Martin Shapiro advanced the construct of political jurisprudence. His argument was that we had to understand courts by combining ideas of law and ideas of politics. As applied to the Supreme Court, Shapiro saw political jurisprudence as "an attempt to treat the Supreme Court as one government agency among many—as part of the American political process, rather than as a unique body of impervious legal technicians above and beyond the political struggle" (1964, 15). While today this may seem almost trite, one aspect of his argument has been largely lost: courts are part of the larger government and function within the context of that government.

But what exactly does this mean? In his own work, Shapiro approached the Supreme Court and courts more generally as agencies of government. As an institutionalist, he was concerned with the politics of institutions and institutional relationships. In carrying out their primary function, deciding disputed cases, courts determine their roles vis-à-vis the other institutions of government, and this is particularly true when one of the parties to the case being decided is an agency of government. Contingent on the nature of an issue, courts may take a primary or subordinate role in establishing policy. This may depend upon either the nature of the substantive issues being decided or the history and role of the agency involved, and courts may be more or less successful in their interventions into the policy process (see particularly Shapiro 1968).

Norms of Deference

While the courts compete with other government agencies in the process of creating and administering policy, judges must engage in this competition in a way that is sensitive to the ongoing nature of the relationship the courts have with other agencies. In most countries, courts are highly, if not entirely, dependent on those other agencies to enforce the decisions the courts hand down. As a result, one might expect judges to be hesitant about "slapping down" agencies in the other branches upon which the courts depend. It is important here to distinguish between administrative tribunals, specialist administrative courts, and specialist constitutional tribunals, which exist solely to review the administrative decisions of government bureaucracies or the constitutionality of legislative enactments. Specialized tribunals such as these have less dependence on governmental agencies because the range of cases they are dealing with is limited. My argument is that the generalist courts are particularly dependent on other parts of government and have to be wary of being perceived as being overly inclined to put roadblocks in the paths those other parts of government are seeking to travel.

One good example of a tendency for deference can be found in the practice of judicial review in England. In the English setting, "judicial review" refers not to "constitutional review" as the term is customarily used in the United States but to the judicial review of administrative decision-making. The practice of such review, which is handled by a part of the High Court known as the Divisional Court, has become much more common in the last several decades; in 1962 there were only 190 cases, but by 1993 the caseload had grown to 3,636 (Jacob et al. 1996, 157), and in 2000 the number of applications for judicial review was 4,247, actually down slightly from a peak of 4,539 in 1998 (Sunkin 2001, table 1).[12] Parties seeking to challenge the actions of administrators must first obtain leave to apply for judicial review, and only then will the Divisional Court consider the merits of the case. As of the mid-1990s, the Divisional Court granted only about half of the applications for leave, and then found for the applicant on the merits in only about half of the cases where leave was granted (ibid.); thus, the government prevailed in about three-quarters of the cases where judicial review was sought. In 1999, the Court granted a smaller proportion of applications for permission (28 percent), but the proportion of those granted that were "allowed" by the Court remained about the same, at 47 percent (Lord Chancellor's Department 2000, 17).

A second example can be found in American administrative law. One of the leading Supreme Court cases in this area is *Chevron v. National Resources Defense Council* (467 U.S. 837 [1984]), which enunciated a principle of judicial deference to agency expertise in the absence of explicit standards established by the authorizing legislation. Specifically, if Congress has not spoken "to the precise question at issue"—that is, if Congress is either silent or ambiguous—courts are to defer to the agency's position if that position is a "reasonable" interpretation of the statute. While there can be much debate over the question of when Congress has spoken, the decisions of both federal appellate courts (Schuck and Elliott 1990) and the U.S. Supreme Court since *Chevron* (Canon and Giles 1972; Chae 2000; Crowley 1987; Handberg 1979; Kilwein and Brisbin 1996; Sheehan 1990, 1992) have shown evidence of this deference, and at least in the case of appellate courts, deference appears to have increased in the wake of *Chevron*.[13]

More broadly, there is evidence that the Supreme Court is more deferential to acts of the federal government than to those of lower levels of the states. Even while arguing that justices' decisions are dominated by their attitudes, Segal and Spaeth (1993, 305–13) provide evidence that justices more likely tend to uphold acts and actions of the federal government and its agencies than acts and actions of state governments. Marshall (1988, 302) shows that justices were more likely to defer to the federal government than to state governments after controlling for whether the policy or statute being challenged was consistent with nationwide opinion. Research has repeatedly shown that even in cases not involving the federal government as a direct party, having the support of the Solicitor General (as an amicus) increases a party's likelihood of success (George and Epstein 1992, 329–33; Puro 1981; Scigliano 1971, 179; Segal 1988; Segal and Reedy 1988).

Another example of deference in the U.S. context directly involves challenges to the President before the courts. A recent study examined challenges of presidential executive orders (Howell 2003, 136–74). Such orders can reflect either authority delegated to the President by statute or inherent authority under the Constitution itself. Since the 1940s, there have been thousands of executive orders (see Mayer 1999), but only forty-four have actually been challenged in the courts; these challenges have involved eighty-two separate cases (because some orders have been challenged multiple times). The challenges were successful in only fourteen (17 percent) of the cases (Howell 2003, 154–55). Equally interesting as the high level of deference by courts to the President when an executive order is challenged are the factors that predict deference. First, courts are more likely to uphold executive orders when the President is in a situation of political strength (that is, no divided government, high public approval, and lack of interest group opposition to the President in court). Second, and even more interesting, variations among individual judges link clearly to loyalty to the person who appointed the judge. Specifically, judges appointed by the President who is defending the executive order are more likely to vote to uphold the President than are judges appointed by a different President of the same party as the defending President or by a President of the other party. This is clearly a regime loyalty effect rather than a simple effect of ideology because if it were the latter, one might expect that those appointed by the President would be most supportive, but one would also expect that judges appointed by a different President of the same party would be more supportive than would judges appointed by an opposing-party President; in fact, there is no difference in support between these latter two groups (Howell 2003, 163–68).

One final indicator of regime loyalty comes from a study that predates Galanter's seminal article. In 1967, Kenneth Dolbeare published a study entitled *Trial Courts in Urban Politics*. Part of his analysis examined 388 cases reported in *New York Miscellaneous Reports* involving decisions by state trial courts in one urban county (population about 1,000,000) in New York during a sixteen-year period (Dolbeare 1967, x). Dolbeare divided the cases into those involving a zoning issue and those involving other types of issues. He found that government won 51 percent of the former and 67 percent of the latter cases; when he split the cases into a finer set of categories, government won 60 percent or more in eight of thirteen categories and lost a majority of cases in only three categories (ibid., 72). Furthermore, Dolbeare observes:

Some subject areas are seen to be largely controlled by State statutes and hence to have more precedents applicable to them, whereas other areas depend upon local ordinances or the fairness of a local procedure. In the former areas, judicial support for government is decidedly high, whereas in the latter it is distinctly low; in other words, when the judges are presented with cases hinging upon locally created law or action, having fewer controlling precedents, they are much more likely to act in behalf of the private claim and against governments (ibid., 70).

Another way of interpreting this pattern is that state court judges give greater deference to the primary regime that their court is a part of, which in this case is the state rather than the local government.

Verdicts For and Against the Government

Another way we can examine government success in court is to look at cases that involve a trial. A study of civil verdicts in state courts located in forty-five large counties (selected to represent the seventy-five largest counties in the United States) in 1996 (DeFrances and Litras 1999) includes 1,223 cases involving government either as plaintiff or as defendant;[15] for 1,214 of these cases, there is usable information on outcome.[16] Government is strikingly unsuccessful in cases that come to trial: as plaintiffs, they win 23 percent of their cases, while losing 43 percent as defendants, for a net advantage of -20. Government has a negative net advantage even if one controls for whether the case is tried to judge or jury; however, government does less poorly before a judge (net advantage -12) than before a jury (net advantage -19).[17]

If one controls for type of opponent, individual or business, government has a negative net advantage in every comparison. Ignoring type of decision-maker, the net advantage is -14 against individuals and -21 against business. However, against both business and individuals, the government's disadvantage is less when a judge is making the decision: -4 versus -15 against individuals and -36 versus -15 against business.

While it is possible that some of the difference before juries and judges reflects case differences, the alternate explanation is that judges are more inclined to give governmental parties a bit of an edge in a close case. Certainly this pattern does not support the proposition that government is the more powerful party, otherwise one would ask why government has such a consistent net disadvantage.

Conclusion

In this chapter, I have argued that "party capability theory" is not adequate to explain the strong pattern of government success in appellate litigation around the world. Government is not just "more capable" in terms of resources and experience, but it has a fundamental advantage that flows from the fact that it sets the rules by which cases are brought and decisions are made, and it is government officials, judges, who make the decisions. While norms of judicial independence are supposed to insulate judges from other parts of government, this separation only goes so far. Ultimately, judges are part of the regime, and when the regime comes under challenge, the government will tend to receive any breaks or benefits at the margin that might accrue.

In the beginning of this chapter, I suggested that I was not necessarily calling into question the broad thrust of party capability theory, only asking whether it can fully account for the advantage possessed by government. Let me now briefly consider the larger question: how much does party capability really matter in appellate courts, at least in terms of what decisions those courts make on the merits of cases? I returned to the same studies cited at the beginning of this essay and compiled the specific net advantage scores for all comparisons of individuals versus business (or, in one case, unions). I found a total of twenty-four such comparisons in the various studies. While in sixteen of the twenty-four comparisons business had a net advantage over individuals, the average net advantage to business was only 0.98. If I make the obviously incorrect assumption that I have a random sample of measures of business advantage and test the statistical hypothesis that business has an advantage (that is, the average net advantage is nonzero and in business's favor), I obtain a t-test value of 0.34, which does not support in any way a hypothesis of advantage.[18]

One problem with this analysis, and any analysis of cases decided by courts, is that of selection bias. Actually, this problem extends to well before the filing of court cases because, as suggested by the dispute pyramid metaphor (Miller and Sarat 1980–81), cases get selected out continuously along the litigation process. Parties may decide not to bring a case because of the perceived resource advantage of an opponent, or a well-resourced defendant may decide immediately to settle a claim to avoid creating a precedent or letting it be known that there is some larger problem. If one limits the question to the advantage of parties *given the entrance of a case into a particular stage of the litigation process*, then the analysis here is quite revealing because of the absence of any statistically discernible advantage to business. If one accepts the argument that one advantage that a repeat player has is the ability and resources to "play for rules," one would expect that would enhance the advantage of non-governmental "haves" because such litigants would be more selective in proceeding with appeals, trying to settle weaker cases to avoid any court decision, and if that is unsuccessful and they lose at trial, not appealing to avoid establishing a citable precedent.

While my focus has been on appellate litigation, the evidence I present raises some intriguing questions about government advantage, or lack of advantage, at the trial level. One striking pattern from the study of verdicts in forty-five large counties around the United States (DeFrances and Litras

1999) was the overall low win rate for government parties: government won only 23 percent of verdicts as plaintiffs and only 43 percent as defendants. Why is government so unsuccessful at trial? I do not have a good answer to that question.

One possible explanation is that government "loses" a large proportion of cases because it is less willing to settle cases that a nongovernmental party would settle when the dispute is largely over the amount of damages. This might explain government's low success rate as a defendant, but it does not explain the low success rate as a plaintiff. That is, in plaintiff verdict cases, it is hard to know who actually benefited from the trial, and hence who *really* won, without knowing what the pretrial settlement offers looked like (Kritzer 1990, 146–49). Thus, when the government lost as a defendant, it may have actually "won" if the award was substantially below what it would have had to be paid to settle a case.

Perhaps the apparent weakness of government in the forty-five-county study reflects that most government cases may involve a local government litigating in a state court of general jurisdiction. Local government has little control over the rules of the game (these are set at the state level), and it may well be that local government is actually relatively resource poor. If this is the case, one would expect government to bring relatively few cases as a plaintiff; in fact, in only 19 percent of the cases involving government did the government appear as the plaintiff, and in 65 percent of these cases, government had brought suit against a business rather than an individual. This pattern would be consistent with the argument that some governmental litigants are more advantaged than others.

The argument that government is less willing to settle cases than other litigants would be consistent with an analysis of tort cases terminated in 1980–81 in three federal districts (Schwab and Eisenberg 1988, 775–76). The authors of this study found that the U.S. government as a defendant was more likely to win than were other types of defendants. Looking at all cases, including those where it was not possible to determine which side won, they found plaintiffs' verdicts in 8.1 percent and defendants' verdicts in 14.9 percent of cases when the U.S. government was the defendant compared to 7.1 percent and 9.1 percent for plaintiffs' and defendants' verdicts, respectively, when some other type of party was defending the case. Thus, the odds of a defendant's verdict was 1.84 for the U.S. government as defendant compared to 1.28 for other types of defendants (that is, almost 50 percent higher). Moreover, when the U.S. government was defending a case, a settlement appeared to be less likely. Some of the advantage of the U.S. government might reflect that tort cases involving the U.S. government must be brought under the Federal Tort Claims Act, which mandates a bench trial, while other types of torts are covered by the Seventh Amendment's guarantee of a right to a jury trial.[19] There is no easy way to determine whether the government's advantage in these cases reflects what might be labeled "regime effects" (that is, the case is decided by a judge who is him or herself part of the regime) or resource/experience effects. However, if one assumes that the other defendants in these cases were largely insurance companies, then one might presume that they bring to the cases expertise equal to that of the federal government (perhaps greater, given that the lawyers representing the insurance companies are likely to have greater expertise in tort cases than the typical Assistant U.S. Attorney who would try a Federal Tort Claims Act case).[20]

Finally, what does my analysis say about the broad issue of whether the "haves" come out ahead at the trial level of litigation? The key question suggested by my discussion is the crucial importance of considering, at the trial level, settlements as well as verdicts. In a recent review of what we know about contract cases, Galanter (2001, 599–604) surveyed studies of outcomes in contract cases and found that "haves" did seem to come out ahead, even taking into account settlements. In contrast, in my study of "ordinary litigation," which in that study was predominantly tort litigation, I found evidence that both plaintiffs (typically "have nots") and defendants (typically "haves") can be seen as coming out ahead, but this presumes very different baselines for the two sides (Kritzer 1990, 143–55).[21] In his study in this volume of cases brought to the Israeli High Court, Dotan concludes that "have nots" do quite well once settlement is considered. In contrast, Albiston, also in this volume, argues that in the new area of litigation created by the Family Medical Leave Act, the "haves" were able to "play for rules" by settling weak cases or cases that might lead to bad precedents and litigating cases that looked to produce long-term favorable results. The conclusion to be drawn from this is that it is too simple to just assert that the "'haves' come out ahead"; the "haves" can come out ahead in some, and perhaps a majority, of contexts, but this depends on complex factors and how one defines coming out ahead.

Notes

The author would like to thank Charles Epp, Marc Galanter, and Susan Silbey for helpful suggestions on an earlier draft of this chapter. Stacia Haynie kindly replied to a number of inquiries about her work, as did Kevin McGuire.

1. According to the senior author of this study, 10 percent or less of the cases included are on the Indian Supreme Court's original jurisdiction docket (Stacia Haynie, personal communication, November 26, 2001).

2. One simple speculation might be that government's advantage at the appellate

level comes largely through criminal cases. However, the studies that have controlled for type of case show that the advantage is by no means limited to criminal cases or is even at its maximum in such cases (Farole 1999, 1049; Haynie et al. 2001, table 4; Wheeler et al. 1987, 426).

3. Given the discretionary nature of the Supreme Court's docket and the ability of the Solicitor General's office to select with care the cases it brings to the Court, some of the federal government's advantage may reflect this selectivity (see Cohen and Spitzer 2000, 408–9) and hence the government's ability to "play for rules." The federal government may be particularly selective given the practice of "administrative nonacquiescence," whereby the decisions of lower courts in administrative law matters do not bind administrative action in other cases, a practice upheld by the Supreme Court (see *United States v. Mendoza*, 464 U.S. 154 [1984]). There is at least one analysis of cases that applies a selection model to consider both the certiorari stage and the merits stage, and it finds that the federal government's advantage at the merits stage disappears after taking into account the selection stage (Schmeling 2000); later, more refined analyses by this author suggest that there may be some advantage at the merits stage for cases in which the federal government is a respondent but not in cases in which the government is a petitioner (Thomas Schmeling, personal communication, June 16, 2002).

4. In personal correspondence, Kevin McGuire provided me with additional results from his data set that enhance his argument that the Solicitor General's advantage can be explained in terms of experience. First, in the 321 cases in which the Solicitor General's office appeared, the advocate from that office was less experienced in only 5 cases and was equally experienced by McGuire's measure in only 7. Second, at my request, McGuire ran a logistic regression eliminating all cases in which the experience of the advocate from the Solicitor General's office had equal or less experience than the other side and all cases not involving the Solicitor General's office where the experience of the two advocates was equal (leaving 645 observations); the model included two parameters: for cases with the Solicitor General appearing, which side the Solicitor General represented (1 petitioner, -1 respondent, 0 not appearing); for cases without the Solicitor General, which side had more experience (1 petitioner, 0 neither, -1 respondent). The values of the estimates of the two parameters were virtually identical, indicating that the Solicitor General has no greater advantage than that of a side with a more experienced advocate.

5. While it is a common assumption that judges are less plaintiff-oriented than are juries, recent statistical evidence raises some doubts about that (see Clermont and Eisenberg 1992; DeFrances and Litras 1999; Eisenberg et al. 2002).

6. The Tucker Act (28 U.S.C §1481) provides for contract-related claims against the federal government; those claims must be brought in a special court, the U.S. Claims Court (see Fox 1997, 433–34).

7. CFR Parts 10 and 25 (http://www.federallaw.com/20CFR10-25.htm).

8. Interestingly, while one might expect federal employee unions to support improvements in the system, that does not seem to be the case. Most workers' compensation cases involve claims that lawyers would not handle (because nothing is in dispute). Unions provide a benefit to their members in assisting the members in

dealing with workers' compensation claims, a benefit that can be a strong incentive to pay union dues. From the union's perspective, there is more to be gained from the incentives provided by union assistance with workers' compensation than by making a system simpler in a way that makes it viable for a lawyer to handle the kinds of disputed and difficult cases that may be problematic for the union representatives. Thus, the unions' interest in creating incentives to join works in concert with the government's interest of minimizing complex, high-value claims of the type lawyers would want to handle.

9. Wis. Stat. Chapter 893.80

10. Ariz. Stat. § 12-820.04 (no punitive damages against public entity or employee); Fl. Stat. Ann. § 768.28(5) (government immune from punitive damages); Hi. Rev. St. § 622-2 (no punitive damages against government); Ind. Code Ann. § 34-4-16.5-4 (no punitive damages against government entity); Minn. Stat Ann. §§ 3.736 (state will not pay punitive damages), 466.04(b) (no punitive damages against municipalities); Vernon's Ann. Mo. Stat. § 537.610(3) (no punitive damages against governments); Wis. Stat. § 893.80(3) (no punitive damages against governments).

11. The statistics are from reports found at the Social Security website (visited October 29, 2001):

http://www.ssa.gov/OACT/NOTES/AS114/as114Tbl_2.html

http://www/sssa/gpvOACT/SSIR/SS101/AllowanceData.html

12. The Lord Chancellor's Department's *Judicial Statistics Annual Report 1999* actually shows a total of 4,959 applications for permission to apply for judicial review being received in 1999 (Lord Chancellor's Department 2000, 17).

13. In a 2001 case, *United States v. Mead*, 533 U. S. 218 (2001), the justices appear to have pulled back somewhat from *Chevron*. However, while this may affect the level of deference courts show to administrative decision-makers, it does not mean that deference will disappear.

14. This is not simply a matter of lack of statistical significance. In a logistic regression analysis including a number of control variables, judicial partisanship was included as a pair of dummy variables: appointed by defending President and appointed by a different President of the same party; appointed by a President of the opposing party is the omitted category. The regression coefficient for appointed by the defending President was .922, while the coefficient for appointed by a different President of the same party was .094, which is essentially zero.

15. I obtained the data for reanalysis from the website of the Interuniversity Consortium for Political and Social Research (http://www.icpsr.umich.edu/), ICPSR Study No. 2883, "Civil Justice Survey of State Courts, 1996."

16. This is the number of cases included in my analysis. The original coding of the party type variable separated out "hospital" as a different category; because I did not know whether the hospital was government owned or private, I threw out cases involving a hospital. This actually involved deleting only three cases.

17. One obvious question here is why is government so unsuccessful at the trial stage. I discuss that question in the conclusion.

18. The test is a one-tailed, single-sample t-test against a null hypothesis of a mean advantage of 0; the standard error of the mean is 2.93.

19. Lest the reader jump to the conclusion that bench trials are more favorable to

defendants than are jury trials, at least two different studies, one of federal cases (Clermont and Eisenberg 1992) and one of state cases (DeFrances and Litras 1999), do not show this to be the case

20. The only other type of likely defendant is a large corporation with the resources to mount a substantial defense; individuals are not going to be sued in tort cases if they are uninsured, and state and local governments cannot typically be sued in federal court for tort cases other than certain types of constitutional torts that are excluded from Schwab and Eisenberg's computations.

21. A study of jury verdicts in Cook County from 1959 to 1979 found that in tort cases where the plaintiff had suffered serious injuries, juries awarded higher damages depending on the defendant; for one comparison, the median award in 1979 dollars against corporate defendants was $161,000, $98,000 against governmental defendants, and $37,000 against individual defendants (Chin and Peterson 1985, 43). This certainly does not suggest an advantage to "haves."

References

Atkins, Burton M. (1991) "Party Capability Theory as an Explanation for Intervention Behavior in the English Court of Appeal," 35 *American Journal of Political Science* 881–903.

Brenner, Saul and John F. Krol (1989) "Strategies in Certiorari Voting on the United States Supreme Court," 51 *Journal of Politics* 828–40.

Canon, Bradley C. and Michael Giles (1972) "Recurring Litigants: Federal Agencies before the Supreme Court," 25 *Western Political Quarterly* 183–91.

Chae, Young-Geun (2000) "The U.S. Supreme Court's Policy Preference and Institutional Restraint in Environmental Law," 7 *Wisconsin Environmental Law Journal* 41–92.

Chin, Audrey and Mark Peterson (1985) *Deep Pockets, Empty Pockets: Who Wins in Cook County Jury Trials*. Santa Monica, Calif.: Rand.

Clermont, Kevin M. and Theodore Eisenberg (1992) "Trial by Jury or Judge: Transcending Empiricism," 77 *Cornell Law Review* 1124–77.

Cohen, Linda R. and Matthew L. Spitzer (2000) "The Government Litigant Advantage: Implications for the Law," 28 *Florida State Law Review* 391–425.

Coronel, Sheila S. (1997) "Justice to the Highest Bidder," *Manila Times*, May 21–23.

———, ed. (2000) *Betrayals of the Public Trust: Investigative Reports on Corruption*. Quezon City: Philippine Center for Investigative Journalism.

Coyle, Marcia (2001) "U.S. Supreme Court Rulings," *National Law Journal*, December 10, B6.

Crowley, Donald W. (1987) "Judicial Review of Administrative Agencies: Does the Type of Agency Matter?" 40 *Western Political Quarterly* 265–83.

DeFrances, Carol J. and Marika F. X. Litras (1999) "Civil Trial Cases and Verdicts in Large Counties, 1996," Washington, D.C.: Bureau of Justice Statistics, U.S. Department of Justice [http://www.ojp.usdoj.gov/bjs/pub/pdf/ctcvlc96.pdf].

Derthick, Martha A. (2002) *Up in Smoke: From Legislation to Litigation in Tobacco Politics*. Washington, D.C.: CQ Press.

Dolbeare, Kenneth M. (1967) *Trial Courts in Urban Politics: State Court Policy Impact and Functions in a Local Political System.* New York: John Wiley & Sons.

Eaton, Thomas A. and Susette Talarico (1993) "Toward Informed Policy Making: Tort Reform, Social Science, and Data Collection: A Proposal for Georgia. Appendix A: Alphabetical Summaries of Tort Reform Statutes for the Fifty States and the District of Columbia [A Report Issued to the Georgia Civil Justice Foundation, Atlanta, Georgia]." Athens: University of Georgia.

Eisenberg, Theodore, Neil LaFountain, Brian Ostrom, David Rottman, and Martin T. Wells (2002) "Juries, Judges, and Punitive Damages: An Empirical Study," 87 *Cornell Law Review* 743–82.

Farole, Donald J., Jr. (1999) "Reexamining Litigant Success in State Supreme Courts," 33 *Law & Society Review* 1043–58.

Fox, William F., Jr. (1997) *Understanding Administrative Law.* New York: Matthew Bender.

Galanter, Marc (2001) "Contract in Court; or Almost Everything You May or May Not Want to Know about Contract Litigation," 2001 *Wisconsin Law Review* 577–627.

Gellis, Ann Judith (1990) "Legislative Reforms of Governmental Tort Liability: Overreacting to Minimal Evidence," 21 *Rutgers Law Journal* 375–417.

George, Tracy E. and Lee Epstein (1992) "On the Nature of Supreme Court Decision Making," 86 *American Political Science Review* 323–37.

Handberg, Roger (1979) "The Supreme Court and Administrative Agencies: 1965–1978," 6 *Journal of Contemporary Law* 161–76.

Haynie, Stacia L. (1994) "Resource Inequalities and Litigation Outcomes in the Philippine Supreme Court," 56 *Journal of Politics* 752–72.

——— (1995) "Resource Inequalities and Regional Variation in Litigation Outcomes in the Philippine Supreme Court, 1961–1986," 48 *Political Research Quarterly* 371–80.

——— (1998) "Paradise Lost: Politicisation of the Philippine Supreme Court in the Post Marcos Era," 22 *Asian Studies Review* 459–73.

Haynie, Stacia L., C. Neal Tate, Reginald S. Sheehan, and Donald R. Songer (2001) "Winners and Losers: A Comparative Analysis of Appellate Courts and Litigation Outcomes." Paper presented at the annual meeting of the American Political Science Association, San Francisco, August 30–September 2.

Howard, J. Woodford, Jr. (1981) *Courts of Appeals in the Federal Judicial System: A Study of the Second, Fifth, and District of Columbia Circuits.* Princeton, N.J.: Princeton University Press.

Howell, William G. (2003) *Power without Persuasion: The Politics of Direct Presidential Action.* Princeton, N.J.: Princeton University Press.

Jacob, Herbert, Erhard Blankenburg, Herbert M. Kritzer, Doris Marie Provine, and Joseph Sanders (1996) *Courts, Law and Politics in Comparative Perspective.* New Haven, Conn.: Yale University Press.

Kilwein, John C. and Richard A. Brisbin Jr. (1996) "Supreme Court Review of Federal Administrative Agencies," 80 *Judicature* 130–37.

Kochman, Frank (1979) "Investigation into the Present State of Special Legal Representation of Veterans." In *Special Legal Problems and Problems of Access to Legal Services of Veterans, Migrant and Seasonal Farm Workers, Native Americans, People with Limited English-Speaking Abilities, Individuals in Sparsely Populated Areas.* Washington, D.C.: Legal Services Corporation.

Kritzer, Herbert M. (1990) *The Justice Broker: Lawyers and Ordinary Litigation.* New York: Oxford University Press.

Lord Chancellor's Department (2000) *Judicial Statistics Annual Report 1999* [CM4786]. London: HMSO.

Marshall, Thomas R. (1988) "Public Opinion, Representation, and the Modern Supreme Court," 16 *American Politics Quarterly* 296–317.

Mayer, Kenneth R. (1999) "Executive Orders and Presidential Power," 61 *Journal of Politics* 445–66.

McCormick, Peter (1993) "Party Capability Theory and Appellate Success in the Supreme Court of Canada, 1949–1992," 26 *Canadian Journal of Political Science* 521–40.

McGuire, Kevin T. (1998) "Explaining Executive Success in the U.S. Supreme Court," 51 *Political Research Quarterly* 505–526.

Miller, Richard E. and Austin Sarat (1980–81) "Grievances, Claims, and Disputes: Assessing the Adversary Culture," 15 *Law & Society Review* 525–65.

Perry, H. W. (1991) *Deciding to Decide: Agenda Setting in the United States Supreme Court.* Cambridge: Harvard University Press.

Puro, Steven (1981) "The United States as Amicus Curiae." In S. Sidney Ulmer, ed., *Courts, Law and Judicial Processes.* New York: Free Press.

Rosenberg, Gerald N. (1991) *The Hollow Hope: Can Courts Bring about Social Change?* Chicago: University of Chicago Press.

Salokar, Rebecca Mae (1992) *The Solicitor General: The Politics of Law.* Philadelphia: Temple University Press.

———— (1995) "Politics, Law, and the Office of the Solicitor General." In Cornell W. Clayton, ed., *Government Lawyers: The Federal Legal Bureaucracy and Presidential Politics.* Lawrence: University Press of Kansas.

Schmeling, Thomas A. (2000) "Sample Selection Effects and the Success of the Federal Government before the U.S. Supreme Court." Paper presented at the annual meeting of the Law and Society Association, Miami Beach, Florida, May 26–30.

Schuck, Peter H. and E. Donald Elliott (1990) "To the *Chevron* Station: An Empirical Study of Federal Administrative Law," *Duke Law Journal* 984–1077.

Schwab, Stewart J. and Theodore Eisenberg (1988) "Explaining Constitutional Tort Litigation: The Influence of the Attorney Fees Statute and the Government as Defendant," 73 *Cornell Law Review* 719–84.

Scigliano, Robert (1971) *The Supreme Court and the Presidency.* New York: Free Press.

Segal, Jeffrey A. (1988) "Amicus Curiae Briefs by the Solicitor General during the Warren and Burger Courts," 41 *Western Political Quarterly* 135–44.

Segal, Jeffrey A. and Cheryl D. Reedy (1988) "The Supreme Court and Sex Discrimination: The Role of the Solicitor General," 41 *Western Political Quarterly* 553–68.

Segal, Jeffrey A. and Harold J. Spaeth (1993) *The Supreme Court and the Attitudinal Model*. New York: Cambridge University Press.

Shapiro, Martin (1964) *Law and Politics in the Supreme Court*. London: Free Press of Glencoe.

——— (1968) *The Supreme Court and Administrative Agencies*. New York: Free Press.

Sheehan, Reginald S. (1990) "Administrative Agencies and the Court: A Reexamination of the Impact of Agency Type on Decisional Outcomes," 43 *Western Political Quarterly* 875–85.

——— (1992) "Federal Agencies and the Supreme Court: An Analysis of Litigation Outcomes, 1953–1988," 20 *American Politics Quarterly* 478–500.

Sheehan, Reginald S., William Mishler, and Donald R. Songer (1992) "Ideology, Status, and the Differential Success of Direct Parties before the Supreme Court," 86 *American Political Science Review* 464–71.

Shepard's Editorial Staff (1992) *Civil Actions against State and Local Government, Its Divisions, Agencies, and Officers*. Colorado Springs, Colo.: Shepard's/McGraw Hill.

Smyth, Russell (2000) "The 'Haves' and the 'Have Nots': An Empirical Study of the Rational Actor and Party Capability Hypothesis in the High Court 1948–99," 35 *Australian Journal of Political Science* 255–74.

Songer, Donald R. and Reginald S. Sheehan (1992) "Who Wins on Appeal? Upperdogs and Underdogs in the United States Courts of Appeals," 36 *American Journal of Political Science* 235–58.

Songer, Donald R., Reginald S. Sheehan, and Susan Brodie Haire (1999) "Do the 'Haves' Come Out Ahead over Time? Applying Galanter's Framework to the Decisions of the U.S. Courts of Appeals, 1925–1988," 33 *Law & Society Review* 811–32 [reprinted as chapter 3 of this volume].

Sunkin, Maurice (2001) "Trends in Judicial Review and the Human Rights Act," 21 *Public Money & Management* 9–12.

Tate, C. Neal and Stacia L. Haynie (1994) "The Philippine Supreme Court under Authoritarian and Democratic Rule," 22 *Asian Profile* 209–26.

Watson, Garry D., W. A. Bogart, Allan C. Hutchinson, Janet Mosher, and Kent Roach (1991) *Civil Litigation: Cases and Materials*. Toronto: Emond Montgomery.

Weaver, William G. and Thomas Longoria (2002) "Bureaucracy that Kills: Federal Sovereign Immunity and the Discretionary Function Exception," 96 *American Political Science Review* 335–49.

Wheeler, Stanton, Bliss Cartwright, Robert A. Kagan, and Lawrence M. Friedman (1987) "Do the 'Haves' Come Out Ahead? Winning and Losing in State Supreme Courts, 1870–1970," 21 *Law & Society Review* 403–46.

Willis, Joy and Reginald S. Sheehan (1999) "Success in the Australian High Court: Resource Inequality and Outcome." Paper presented at the annual meeting of the Southern Political Science Association, Savannah, Georgia, November 6–9.

BRIAN J. GLENN 12

The Varied and Abundant Progeny

MARC GALANTER'S 1974 article, "Why the 'Haves' Come Out Ahead: Speculations on the Limits of Legal Reform," (1974) is one of the most cited articles ever to appear in a legal journal. Its breadth of analysis and fresh perspective on dispute resolution provided the groundwork for a wide range of research agendas and, just as important, offered scholars in law and the social sciences a common analytical framework and terminology for discussing the actors and issues involved in redistribution through the court system. These two contributions—generating new questions and shaping the language of discourse—are perhaps the greatest contributions a piece of scholarship can make.

This chapter reviews the varied and abundant progeny of Galanter's article. The tables included at the end of the chapter reveal the breadth of its reach into the world of academic scholarship. "Why the 'Haves' Come Out Ahead" has sparked inquiry by legal scholars, anthropologists, political scientists, business and management scholars, and sociologists, with work ranging the spectrum from normative argumentation to comparative large-N analyses of court outcomes. Galanter's article has even been cited in court opinions (*Russell v. Acme-Evans Co.*; *Coleman v. Gulf Ins. Group*; *Covenant Mutual Insurance Co. v. Young*; *In re RHONE-POULENC RORER Inc.*), making it one of the rare few to move beyond the world of academe and into the practice of law itself.

The idea that the "haves" would come out ahead in a legal and political system such as America's is not new, of course. Indeed, it is as old as the U.S. Constitution itself, where the issue arose in the ratification debates of the late 1780s between the Federalists and the Anti-Federalists. The most famous work in favor of constitutional ratification was the *Federalist Papers*, written by Alexander Hamilton, James Madison and John Jay under the common pseudonym of "Publius." For them, the secret of the new constitution was found primarily in institutional design. The Founding Fathers, according to Publius, constructed a system predicated on the idea that "men were not angels" and hence needed a system of rules that pitted interest against interest in a manner that promoted democratically determined results that were both representative of the entire people and just (Federalist #51). The Federalists understood America's proposed constitutional system as one whose sovereignty sprang from the people themselves, and the judiciary's independence assured that interpretations would remain in their interests even in times of passion when unjust, irrational opinions prevailed (Federalist #78).

The idea of judicial independence from day-to-day politics was important for Publius. The authors (in this case, Hamilton) argued that with lifetime tenure, the learned members of the bench would protect the rights of all citizens against the passions of the majority. Under the proposed new federal system, judges would not be beholden to anyone once they were appointed and thus could administer justice with impartiality. Publius also forwarded the idea that the court system would be the least dangerous branch because it possessed, "neither FORCE nor WILL but merely judgment; and must ultimately depend on the aid of the executive arm even for the efficacy of its judgments" (ibid., 433). In other words, the courts could not control the implementation of the decisions they produced.

The Anti-Federalists argued against ratifying the proposed constitution, fearing a return to a system of tyranny by the "haves" such as that which they had experienced under British rule. Tyranny was understood by these individuals as naturally arising whenever government was extended beyond local, direct rule, where average citizens could keep an eye on their leaders. The Anti-Federalists understood the Constitution as a document created by a small wealthy elite ("the natural aristocracy"), with the goal of creating a permanent aristocracy that would use the institutions of government to serve their own purposes rather than those of the common people ("the natural democracy"). Anti-Federalists also viewed law as inherently political. For them, the judicial branch was part of the political system, not separated from it.

One of the most articulate and important Anti-Federalist authors, who wrote under the pseudonym "Brutus," understood the legal system as being not one of the most important but in fact the *primary* institution for bringing a system where the "haves" would come out ahead. He warned the American people "to examine with care the nature and extent of the judicial power, because those who are to be vested with it, are to be placed in a situation altogether unprecedented in a free country" (Brutus 1985a, 163). Brutus saw the judicial system as threatening the "have nots" for four reasons. First, the natural aristocracy were better able to organize themselves and represent their own interests through association than were the natural democracy. They would be something similar to Galanter's repeat players. Over time, the "haves" would be able to shape legal precedent in a manner that protected their interests over those of the "have nots," regardless of attempts by the popularly elected legislature to define the law otherwise (ibid., 167). Second, the proposed system favored the "haves" through the expense and delay involved in protracted litigation, often taking place far from home (Brutus 1985b, 177–78). Third, the Supreme Court would have the final say over interpreting both the letter and the spirit of the law, leading not only to favorable precedent being set on behalf of the "haves" but also to favorable implementation (Brutus 1985a, 134–38). Finally, judges were neither elected nor accountable to the people, and those judges not already fortunate enough to come from the class of "haves" would quickly join their ranks and represent their interests from behind the bench (Brutus 1985c, 187).

We see many elements of Galanter's argument found in these debates. The Anti-Federalists understood the American judicial system as one reliant on the rule of precedent that could be shaped over time by "haves" who were favored by the expense, delay, and mobilization demands that successful litigation entailed. The Federalists understood the courts as being incapable of tyranny because the courts relied on the other branches for implementation—which later came to be understood as a system that allowed for symbolic victories for the "have nots" while actual implementation favored the "haves." Thus, we can understand that even from the beginning, the Founding Fathers had created a system that indeed was not neutral but rather favored those whose experience, knowledge, and resources allowed them to take a long-term strategy toward litigation—and, importantly, toward the broader system of governance in general. As Galanter clearly explains, the "haves" come out ahead not only because they win in court but also because they win outside of it as well.

Building a New Vocabulary

The most famous concept Galanter's article contributed to academic discourse is that of the "repeat player."[1] Since the definition has significant implications and is frequently misused, the term needs to be understood clearly: A repeat player is an actor, be it an individual, organization, or corporation, who litigates over the same issues enough times to benefit from a strategy of shaping precedent over the long term, even if that entails taking losses in the short term. In other words, a repeat player is a litigant who has the incentive to act strategically over a large time horizon when deciding upon a litigation strategy. Unlike a "one shotter" who must win the case at hand, a repeat player is both willing and able to take short-term losses in order to receive long-term gains.

The concepts of repeat players and one shotters have done more than merely provide academics with a common vocabulary, and this is important because they are loaded terms in the sense of having empirical implications behind them. Repeat players and one shotters should *think* differently about the nature of any given case, and they should *act* differently based upon those conceptions. This has led Frank Cross (2000), for example, to argue for public policies that provide support for "irrational" have not plaintiffs seeking to litigate against repeat player "haves" on the basis of values and emotions such as fairness, vengeance, or vindication. Classical economic analysis predicts that one shotters will conduct a risk analysis of potential costs and benefits of litigating or settling, and that, over time (for the reasons Galanter explains), the "haves" will routinely begin to come out on top. One shotters who predicate their actions on reasons other than the economics of litigation—that is, those who are "irrational"—might, over time, actually have a leveling effect on rules. So for normative reasons of fairness, Cross suggests that irrational one shotters might be what is necessary to prevent the outcomes Galanter predicts. Beginning his analysis with Galanter's terms, Cross generates new theoretical perspectives which themselves are open to modeling and empirical tests.

Galanter has facilitated communication across a wide range of academic disciplines that otherwise are separated by the lack of a common vocabulary, and the fact that he has facilitated research across academic boundaries should not be downplayed. His framework has allowed for academics from different disciplines to apply the most powerful analytical tools and perspectives of their respective fields to a common set of questions in a manner that allows them to build on each other's work, to replicate tests, and to search for further implications over a broad range of venues, such as court systems, for example, both within countries and across them. Few other modern works have been so influential as to shape research agendas across such a wide range of disciplines as has "Why the 'Haves' Come Out Ahead," and this can be seen by the fact that it is cited in articles in journals such as *Political Research Quarterly* (Palmer 1999; Ringquist and Emmert 1999; Songer et al. 2000; Tauber 1998), *Criminology* (Philips 1982), the *Australian & New Zealand Journal of Sociology* (Tomasic 1983), *Yale Law Review* (Ackerman 1983; Mnookin and Kornhauser 1979; Nader 1979; Yale Law Journal 1979, 1981, 1983), and *Academy of Management Review* (Matusik et al. 2000), to name but a few.

The Varied and Abundant Progeny of "Why the 'Haves'"

Recall that in the debate over the ratification of the Constitution, Brutus predicted that the "haves" would come out ahead for four main reasons. First, repeat players would litigate strategically, giving them the advantage over time and shaping precedent to their favor. Second, their ability to delay and bear the burden of legal expenses would advantage them over "have nots," thus preserving the status quo. Third, implementation of decisions would favor the "haves," who would enjoy great success in having their interests protected by the other branches. Finally, judges themselves would join the ranks of the "haves" in their socio-economic status and outlook and thus act to protect their own interests. These four categories form a convenient way of classifying much of the research that has stemmed from Galanter's 1974 article.

WHO WINS IN COURT AND WHY?

The question of whether the "haves" really do come out ahead in court has generated a wide range of empirical research. More than any other work, Galanter's article has shaped the nature of large-N empirical studies of the U.S. court system and beyond.[2] As one can see from Table 11.1, Galanter's article has launched a wide spectrum of inquiry over who wins in court.[3] Researchers have sought to see if one-shot criminals are winning more or fewer appeals since 1870 (Meeker 1984); who wins in the U.S. Supreme Court (McGuire 1995; Sheehan et al. 1992; Ulmer 1985), in federal appeals courts (Haire et al. 1999; Songer and Sheehan 1992; see also the chapter by Songer et al. in this volume), and federal district courts (Trubek et al. 1983; Yarnold 1995); and who wins in environmental litigation (Wenner 1983) and in federal nuisance cases (Wahlbeck 1998). Studies of the court system have also been used to test for other implications, such as why those who win do prevail and whether repeat players litigate against one another or, as Galanter predicts, whether they avoid litigation whenever possible to protect their ongoing relationships with one another.

Research on who wins in court has largely been shaped by the methodology used in a 1987 article entitled "Do the 'Haves' Come Out Ahead? Winning and Losing in State Supreme Courts, 1870–1970," by Stanton Wheeler, Bliss Cartwright, Robert Kagan, and Lawrence Friedman. The authors examined 5,904 state supreme court cases drawn from sixteen states, sampled in roughly equal numbers every five years from 1870 to 1970. The goal was to test the hypothesis that "financially and organizationally stronger parties tend to prevail in litigation against weaker parties, either because the normative structure of the American legal system has favored 'the haves,' or because judges' attitudes do, or because stronger parties have strategic and representational advantages in litigation" (Wheeler et al. 1987, 403).

The authors created a typology that could be used by examining court records. They divided actors into four categories: individual litigants, individual business proprietors, business corporations, and government parties (which was further subdivided on occasion into city and state governments and small-town governments). Acknowledging that not all corporations had equal resources or litigation experience, they speculated that if any businesses truly are repeat players, they would be railroads, banks, manufacturers, and insurance companies, which were singled out for testing. Finally, the data set was able to draw out cases where the litigants used a law firm versus those who made use of an independent attorney on the assumption that law firms would have greater resources and in general would be able to provide better representation.

Armed with a large, over-time data set, Wheeler et al. tested for implications through a wide variety of methods. Aggregate outcomes of actors as appellants versus respondents, head-to-head comparisons of each specific category versus each other, and comparisons over time were made, along with testing for the effects of using the two different types of counsel. Along a wide range of tests, the "haves" usually do appear to come out ahead by roughly a 5 percent margin—although the authors themselves warn against reading too much into this:

> Putting aside the tendency of respondents to win and looking instead at the combined success rates, individuals, small businesses, small governments, and business organizations all won in state supreme courts just about as often as they lost. Taking lower court outcomes as the baseline, the courts did not systematically redistribute resources toward any of these interests. (Wheeler et al. 1987, 443)

From a normative standpoint, this is reassuring, since all types of actors appear to come out roughly equal. The "haves" (especially state and large city governments) do still have a marginally higher success rate, and the authors caution that data in the aggregate can mask a wider variability among different subcategories, noting, "the more sharply party [distinctions] can be delineated, the larger the net advantage of the stronger parties [appears to be], and some of those advantages are really substantial" (ibid.). This study provided a methodology that has been used over and over to study different levels of courts, and notably, most studies find much clearer and more significant evidence that the "haves" come out ahead.

Studies of the varied American court systems have allowed scholars to ask why those who seem consistently to win do so. One finding that virtually all authors discovered is that government attorneys tend to do better when paired against other litigants, and this is especially true for attorneys representing the federal government (but see Ulmer 1985). Federal prosecutors litigate case after case using the same federal laws, often with certain individuals highly specializing in narrow fields of litigation. Speculation as to why government litigators find such high levels of success routinely points to their ability to choose which cases to litigate and which to ignore or settle. Government lawyers seem to win primarily because they are repeat players capable of choosing which cases to litigate strategically, just as Galanter predicted (see Hellman 1985; Mather 1998; Meeker 1984; Shapiro 1980; Wenner 1983).

Research on who wins in court has not been limited to the United States. Often referred to as party capability theory, testing of repeat player versus one shotter victories has been extended to the English Court of Appeal (Atkins 1991), the European Court of Justice (Mattli and Slaughter 1998), the Israeli High Court of Justice (Dotan, this volume), the supreme courts of Canada (McCormick 1993) and Australia (Willis and Sheehan 1999), and the judicial system of the Philippines (Haynie 1994). Haynie et al. (2001) comparatively examine who wins in the supreme courts of Canada, the Philippines, India, South Africa, Tanzania, and in the British House of Lords. The comparative works have generated useful insights into causation both in the countries under study and also for the United States. Haynie (1994), for example, discovered that in the Philippines, the "have nots" win cases more often when matched against either the government or a corporation, and she speculated that this is because judges feel the need to protect the legitimacy of the court system in the eyes of the vast majority of the population, who are the "have nots."

In Third World nations where disparities between the "haves" and the "have nots" are generally more extreme, one might expect an even greater advantage to those with greater resources, but I argue that concerns for stability, legitimacy, and development in nonindustrialized systems lead to biases for those within society who have less. Systemic biases affect outcomes in both industrialized and nonindustrialized countries, but in less developed nations these biases can lead to outcomes favoring those with fewer resources. Courts in Third World nations can use their policy-making function to redistribute resources, at least within some components of their docket, thus potentially increasing their own legitimacy and stability within the political system. (ibid., 753)

As Haynie's case reveals, looking across legal systems has the additional advantage of not only being an additional large-N study but also facilitates comparisons between systems as whole entities, allowing for the testing of cultural forces whose impact might not otherwise have been understood.

Finally, studying court systems has resulted in testing of Galanter's prediction that repeat players would litigate against each other as little as possible, preferring instead to settle their differences in a non-confrontational manner outside of the court system in order to protect their ongoing relationship. Ross Cheit and Jacob E. Gersen tested for evidence of this by examining lit-

igation between corporations in the state courts of Rhode Island. Their results supported Galanter's theory strongly. "We conclude that contextual economic conditions favoring the creation of long-term business relationships
help prevent litigation between firms" (Cheit and Gersen 2000, 789). Donald Landon's (1985) study of small-town attorneys reached much the same
conclusion, finding that repeat players attempt to avoid litigation against
those with whom they must interact in the future in order to protect relationships from which they might expect to benefit (see also McIntosh 1980).

In summary, party capability theory has tested Galanter's article for a
range of implications. Scholars have asked who wins in court and have
largely discovered it is the "haves." Moreover, the "haves" largely win, it
seems, because of their ability to act strategically in their litigation decisions,
which include deciding which cases to bring to court and when to settle.

DO THE EXPENSES OF LITIGATION WORK AGAINST THE "HAVE NOTS"?

The idea that the American court system is biased against the "have nots"
has been examined by members of the Civil Litigation Research Project. In
a series of articles, William L. F. Felstiner, Herbert M. Kritzer, Austin Sarat,
David M. Trubek, and others studied an array of issues surrounding fee
arrangements, differences in activities between hourly-fee lawyers and those
who work on contingency, fee shifting, and the costs of litigation (Kritzer
1984, 1990, 1991; Kritzer, Felstiner, et al. 1985; Kritzer, Sarat, et al. 1984;
Trubek et al. 1983). They found that litigation does "pay off" in the sense
that those whose cases actually lead to litigation usually believe that the outcome was worth the effort. However, they also discovered that few actionable harms result in a claim being made.

In their classic article, "Adjudication as a Private Good," William M. Landes and Richard A. Posner (1979) use a law and economics rational choice
approach to model litigation expenditures by different types of actors. They
concluded that, over time, the "haves" should come out ahead because their
potential economic gains are dramatically larger than those of any particular
one shotter, and thus they will devote more resources toward successful litigation. While the most expensive attorney does not always win the case,
having an attorney who has been able to conduct adequate research and discovery before entering the courtroom certainly does not hurt (see also
Molot 1998).

Many scholars have taken it for granted that the "have nots" suffer because of their inability to afford sufficient representation—if they can afford
any at all—and thus many authors turn their attention to the role played by
attorneys from the Legal Services Corporation (LSC). For normative reasons, several scholars have argued in favor of the LSC precisely because it has

the ability to act as a repeat player in protecting the interests of the "have nots" (Gerwin 1977; Lawrence 1990; Yale Law Journal 1981). When conservative politicians attempted both to defund and prevent the attorneys from the LSC from acting as repeat players, the attorneys responded in innovative ways to protect their repeat player status (see Mentor and Schwartz 2000).

DOES IMPLEMENTATION FAVOR THE "HAVES"?

Galanter suggested that implementation issues would plague the "have nots," making their rare victories in court symbolic rather than substantive, since, as Publius noted, the courts may define the law but they do not implement it (see Ackerman 1983). Van Koppen and Malsch (1991) tested to see how the "haves" and "have nots" fared once their cases had been settled in court. Drawing from three years' worth of civil court cases in the Netherlands, they interviewed close to a thousand attorneys to see if their clients (who had all won their cases) received the awards the courts had granted them. Their study revealed that full implementation was rarely enjoyed, with only about half of the victorious litigants receiving as much as half of the amount they were awarded by the court. Moreover, while repeat players were more likely to win than one shotters were when they were plaintiffs, one shotters were more likely to recover a larger percentage of their awards. The exact opposite has proven to be the case in the United States, where a study conducted by Austin Sarat (1976) revealed that repeat players recover almost twice as much of their awards as one shotters do (see also Boyer 1981 and, broadly, Galanter 1975).

Whether the members of the executive branch implement decisions according to the spirit of the judge's opinion is contingent upon a number of factors, largely centered around the incentive for them to do so. The chapter in this volume by Beth Harris, for example, explores the nature of those contingencies. While authors have used Galanter's framework to argue that the courts must ensure that their decisions are implemented not only to the letter of the law but also to the spirit of it (see Bell 1976; Bellow and Kettleson 1978), the provocative chapter by Lauren B. Edelman and Mark C. Suchman in this volume suggests even that may not be enough to provide equal justice to the "have nots," since many large corporations have internalized the law and modified it to serve their interests.

ARE JUDGES BIASED?

More than two hundred years ago, Brutus warned that if they did not start off that way, judges would quickly join the ranks of the "haves" and side with their interests when making decisions from the bench. Along similar lines, the final major vein of research informed by "Why the 'Haves' Come Out Ahead" is concerned with the role judges play in deciding conflicts between the "haves" and the "have nots." Wolf Heydebrand (1979) speculated that the "have nots" might come out behind not so much because the judges were biased toward the "haves" per se but rather because judges were biased toward hearing their *issues*, as opposed to those of the poor and the weak. Thus, the "haves" came out ahead because the issues they decided to litigate made it before the bench, while those the "have nots" wanted to litigate did not (see also Bellow and Kettleson 1978).

Studies factoring in the ideological makeup of the bench have greatly forwarded empirical research on whether the "haves" come out ahead in court. In their 1992 analysis of cases heard by the U.S. Supreme Court, for example, Reginald S. Sheehan, William Mishler, and Donald R. Songer found that the primary independent variable in determining outcomes of cases was the ideological leanings of the nine justices. In bringing the Wheeler et al. (1987) study up to date, Donald J. Farole (1999) obtained robust, statistically significant results revealing that the "haves" come out ahead more frequently both as appellants and respondents when the ideological composition of the courts are factored into the calculations (but see Kritzer in this volume). The leanings of judges do in fact appear to matter quite a bit, and it does appear that Brutus was correct; judges do seem to favor the "haves" more than the "have nots" in deciding cases.

Conclusion

Marc Galanter provided scholars with a fresh perspective on a question that has existed since America's founders debated over the ratification of the Constitution. By basing his answer to why the "haves" might come ahead on the nature of the actors rather than on the rules of the game, he provided a generation of scholars with a wide range of opportunities for empirical testing, along with a common set of terms to discuss the issues. The impact of this article on the academic community rivals the greatest works of the era in terms of the research it has generated.

In a pattern that can conveniently be mapped onto the very debates held by the Founding Fathers, research into questions brought to light by Galanter can be placed into four categories. First, there is the question of who wins in court, often referred to as "party capability theory." This field usually involves large-*N* studies of a court system in order to see who comes out ahead and why. Second, academics have focused on a variety of questions revolving around the expenses of litigation and the implications of this on a system that is supposed to treat all parties equally. Questions regarding litigation costs, differences between hourly-fee lawyers versus contingency-fee lawyers, rational choice modeling of expenditures according to payoffs to different parties, and the role played by LSC attorneys fall under this category. Third, scholars have looked at numerous aspects of implementation to see if the "haves" come out ahead and, if so, why. Studying implementation has allowed a wide range of methods to be employed, and studies have spanned the spectrum from institutionalist perspectives on the capacities of various actors to shape the system to their advantage to empirical studies of whether "winning parties" actually receive the money and protection awarded to them in court. Finally, there has been a focus on judges themselves to see if justice is blind or whether judges bring biases of one sort or another with them when deciding cases.

Appendix

The following three lists reveal a representative cross-section of the work Galanter's article has informed. In order to be useful to researchers seeking to learn what types of questions have been asked, the lists have been sorted by area of inquiry. The first list contains research whose primary focus has been outcomes in court cases, although many articles on closely related aspects are also included. The second list consists of works whose primary area of interest involves the nature of the actors themselves. The third list includes works whose primary focus is on how institutions other than courts affect who comes out ahead. Obviously, there is a great deal of overlap, and many articles could just as easily have found their way into a different list. However, listing them in this manner seemed to be the most useful way for scholars who perhaps are not widely familiar with the field quickly and easily to find work that is relevant to their own.

I. THE COURT AS THE VENUE OF ACTION

Atkins 1991
Tests party capability theory by examining circumstances in which the Court of Appeals reverses and remands lower courts.
Treats it as a "tough case" of Galanter, since the British court system is not assumed to "participate in the process by which resources and values are allocated."

Baar 1979
Uses administrative perspective to compare court reform with executive and legislative reform to specify limits inherent in the system.
"What court reform lacks is a non-governmental clientele outside the organized bar. At this stage, the courts' major non-professional clientele, the litigants, do not engage in concerted action. Their common interests have not been identified, and the divergent interests of OSs and RPs may make litigant organization impossible."

Baker 2001

Do lawyers go after personal assets ("blood money") of defendants in addition to insurance assets?

There is a moral economy of litigators who typically refuse to go after "blood money." This benefits the "have nots," who will not be pursued to the extent that "haves" are.

Baum 1977

Study of Court of Customs and Patent Appeals, with the goal of understanding impact of specialization of judicial behavior.

Given what can be frequent appearances before the same bench, RPs enjoy wide ability to construct a favorable position for themselves over OSs.

Blankenburg 1981

What effect does legal insurance covering legal fees and court costs have on litigant behavior?

A "breakdown of the data by type of party showed that, in all cases of appeal found in the insurance files, the insurance holders were small firms, landlords, or employers. As they are more likely to be repeat players in legal conflicts, their decision to appeal may be related to considerations beyond the single case at issue."

Brace and Gann Hall 2001

Study every case decided by a state court in 1996 to answer two questions. First, what determines whether courts will take cases involving "haves" v. "have nots"? Second, which forces determine the extent to which courts favor the "have nots"?

For civil-private conflicts where amici were filed, the supply of lawyers, more than any other variable, emerges as critical in accounting for "have nots" getting to court and succeeding once there. Although court ideology did not appear significant, the funding of the court system did.

Bradley and Gardner 1985

Study the filing of amicus briefs by interest groups to the U.S. Supreme Court 1954–1980 to see if there are patterns between groups with differing resources.

By 1985, Galanter's framework had become so pervasive that in this article, a portion of the very first footnote was dedicated to explaining how the authors' classification system differed from his and should not be confused with it.

Cartwright 1975

Methodological pitfalls of studying just reported cases.

Notes the importance of studying litigant characteristics and questioning whether both enter the arena (if they do at all) as equals.

Cheit and Gersen 2000

Study business litigation in Rhode Island 1987 and 1988 to test empirically a number of hypotheses, including whether RPs litigate against one another.

"We conclude that contextual economic conditions favoring the creation of long-term business relationships help prevent litigation between firms."

Dotan 1999

Final decisions of the Israeli High Court of Justice and also those disposed by out-of-court settlements.

Both in the Court and in settlements the "haves" do better, but "have nots" with representation do better than any category of "haves." Whether because they are seeking legitimacy as an institution or for ideological purposes, courts can protect "have nots."

Farole 1999

Five state supreme courts at five-year intervals 1975–1990 (follow-up to Wheeler et al. 1987 but also includes partisan makeup of bench).

"haves" were generally more successful both as appellant and respondent. Takes into account partisan majorities of justices.

Flemming 1998

Focuses on understanding change in trial courts by viewing them as contested terrains made up of various sites over which disputes occur.

"Reform is nothing more than an effort by mobilized interests to alter what they perceive as inappropriate patterns of 'who wins what, when, and how' in trial courts." The "haves" and RPs attempt to shape the rules, and even the "have nots" and OSs do on occasion.

Friedman and Percival 1976

Study of civil load of two trial courts in California 1890–1970 (see also Lempert 1978).

Many cases (such as divorces) have already been resolved and are looking for a legal rubber stamp. Example of Galanter's "appended" settlement system which, though unofficial, is "normatively and institutionally appended to the official system."

Galanter 1975

Review of studies that test success of RPs v. OSs in court.

Presents strong evidence that RPs come out ahead in court.

Goldberg 1985

Empirical study of "what actually happens to duty of fair representation cases in the courts."

What explains why unions differ in their involvement in duty of fair representation litigation? Notes that one must distinguish between unions that can act like RPs and individuals who cannot.

Gross and Syverud 1996

Sampled civil jury verdicts reported by two state courts along with interviews from 735 lawyers to consider the trials in the context of the pretrial bargaining through which most cases are resolved.

Authors note the potential for conflict of interest between attorneys of RPs. Plaintiff attorneys may want to go to trial to build a reputation, even when settling might help the OS litigant. Authors' data reveal that RPs win the majority of cases over OSs.

Hagan 1982

If we conceive of corporations as "juristic persons," how do they fare in litigation as victims when compared to individual victims?

Empirical analysis includes a RP variable, defined as whether the actor had been the victim of a similar crime previously. Corporate entities were far more likely to be RPs, and the authors suggest this improved their chance of success in court.

Harvard Law Review 1981

Issues involved in allowing parties to settle dispute in private, for-hire courts.

Under market conditions, for-hire courts might eventually come to favor their RPs with the goal of receiving more business from them in the future.

Haynie 1994

Decisions of the Philippine Supreme Court.

Finds the "have nots" have a significant advantage in head-to-head matchups due to Court striving to maintain its legitimacy among all sectors of the polity.

Hellman 1985

How do justices decide which cases to hear? Studies opinions and orders against the background of the parties' submissions, the holdings of the lower courts, and developments elsewhere in the legal system and in society generally.

State prosecutors' petitions are far more likely to receive a hearing than those filed by defendants. One reason is the RP nature of prosecutors, who have the ability to choose their petitions selectively.

Hurst 1980

Continuation of his book, The Growth of American Law, *in which he studied*

*the organization and functions of the federal judicial branch from 1790 to 1940. Brings
the study up to 1980.*

Substantively integrates multiple aspects of Galanter into his study.

Kagan et al. 1977
*Empirical study of how caseload size affected the structure and business of American
state supreme courts from 1880 to 1970.*

Methodological point that if proportion of lower court appeals remained
constant over time, the number of appeals would rise naturally; however, one
key variable is the proportion of RPs who have full-time specialists in appeals.

Kastenmeier and Remington 1979
The three basic themes of time, economy, and quality of justice are beset with difficulties. Analysis of prospects for reform.

"The lawmaker should recognize that there are enormous social costs if
people are obliged, either because of high legal costs or extended court delays, to solve many disputes by avoidance or self help."

Lempert 1999
Methodological concerns of studying judicial outcomes.

Norms must be factored into accounts, otherwise it is difficult to understand who comes out ahead, e.g., what does it mean if "haves" win 90% of
cases when 95% of claims they bring are valid? Have they come out ahead?

Lempert 1978
Reanalysis of Friedman and Percival 1976 (see this table).

Methodological point that quantitative analyses must be aware of pitfalls
that RPs and OSs may not litigate in equal quantities, and this must be factored into the analyses.

Lizotte 1978
Uses data from Chicago trial courts to test for prejudice against minorities.

Thoroughly integrate Galanter into modeling bail amounts requested by
district attorneys, among other aspects.

Mather 1998
*What role do litigation and trial courts play in shaping policy? In a study of tobacco
litigation, the author suggests such litigation contributed to agenda setting, new ways of
defining the problem of tobacco and the policy alternatives, political mobilization, new legal norms, and new political and legal resources for opponents of tobacco.*

Beginning in 1993, the attorneys general of several states filed claims against tobacco companies to recoup costs for Medicaid related to smoking, with a conscious effort to aggregate plaintiffs in a manner to overcome the numerous hurdles facing "have nots."

McCormick 1993
Tests party capability theory in Supreme Court of Canada.
Litigant categories are explicitly based on Galanter. Finds strong support that "haves" come out ahead.

McGuire 1995
How important are lawyers to U.S. Supreme Court decision-making?
Finds experienced RP lawyers are more efficacious, regardless of the parties they represent.

McIntosh 1980
Studies rate of litigation (cases filed per capita) and case disposition patterns among five categories of torts in a state trial court from 1820 to 1970 at fifteen-year intervals.
Compares tort cases, where author suggests litigants are typically OSs with no ongoing relationship to each other, with contract disputes between litigants with long-term relationships to each other.

Meeker 1984
Examines state courts 1870–1970 to determine if criminal defendants are winning more appeals, given the increase in due process rights of the 1980s and 1990s.
Finds defendants are far more likely to lose an appeal than they were a century ago and largely credits Galanter's model of states as RPs and criminals as OSs for the cause.

Palmer 1999
How much fluidity is there in the issues on which Supreme Court justices choose to make rules? How often do justices make rules for issues other than those presented by the attorneys?
Models the Solicitor General's office as an RP in her analysis of whether the Warren Court was more or less likely to base its decisions on issues other than those raised by the attorneys.

Philips and Ekland-Olson 1982
Do the clients of RPs enjoy special benefits or bear special burdens when punishments are distributed? Examine 300,000 cases in one year of a state felony court.
Compares clients of public defenders against those of private attorneys at many stages of litigation.

Ringquist and Emmert 1999
Study published and unpublished decisions in federal district courts regarding environmental litigation to see if their model predicts severity.
Using Galanter, authors model defendants as "haves" or "have nots" on the basis of whether they were a Fortune 500 company.

Rubenstein 2001
Introduces transaction model of adjudication.
In terms of litigation, one of the best methods for leveling the playing field between the "haves" and the "have nots" is the class action lawsuit.

Sarat 1978
Methodological considerations in studying the question of rationally allocating court resources and improving the internal operation of the courts.
Methodological point that not every dispute becomes a lawsuit, and research should try to identify how disputes that do enter the system find their way to court.

Sarat 1976
Maps alternative path to dispute resolution once a claim has been filed in small claims court. Focuses on two modes: do parties appear, and do they opt to settle out of court?
Characteristics of the litigants are the primary consideration. RPs are more effective in using litigation either to facilitate ongoing settlement activity or to initiate settlement efforts where none had occurred. In cases that are litigated, RPs recover almost twice the percentage of their request that OSs do.

Schacter 1998
Surveys U.S. Supreme Court's October 1996 term and finds 50% of opinions drew from legislative history, then discusses implications for controversies about statutory interpretation.
Notes that concerns about staff and lobbyist influence on shaping legislative history is a valid concern but warns that if these individuals represent the "haves," these same groups will also have a hand in shaping judicial interpretation through litigation.

Shapiro 1980
Survey article on appeal, emphasizing its significance for political regimes rather than for individual litigants.
Is the government so successful in litigation because it is capable of shap-

ing favorable precedent or because it has great leeway in selecting the cases it appeals?

Sheehan et al. 1992
U.S. Supreme Court 1953–1980.
The ideological makeup of the bench is the primary factor determining who comes out ahead in head-to-head matchups between various categories of litigants.

Sheskin 1982
Perspectives on the functions of trial courts.
"The demographic characteristics of defendants processed in trial courts are an important indicator of the court's mission." Instructs readers to classify actors as RPs or OSs.

Siegelman and Waldfogel 1999
Use Priest/Klein (1984) model with a structural model to predict trial rates and plaintiff win rates.
Use Galanter to model litigants.

Songer et al. 2000
Use state supreme courts "to explore how the normal advantages of the RPs are modified by the entry of amicus curiae in support of OS disadvantaged litigants."
An explicit test of RPs v. OSs in courts and how amicus briefs can alter the relationship.

Songer and Sheehan 1992
Study three federal appeals courts, examining both published and unpublished decisions.
Clear and significant evidence that the "haves" come out ahead.

Tauber 1998
Does the NAACP's involvement in a federal death penalty case alter the outcome at the appellate level?
Since the NAACP can pick and choose its cases to build a precedent, it can in effect function as a repeat player. This article tests the effects of having one of the group's lawyers on the final sentencing decision.

Trubek et al. 1983
Survey sample populations in five federal judicial districts and 1,600 cases to analyze direct expenditures of time and money on processing disputes through litigation.
Use Galanter as basis of categorizing litigants as individuals or organizations in order to capture whether they were OSs or RPs.

Ulmer 1985

Examines civil liberties cases involving "underdogs" at the U.S. Supreme Court level to test whether governmental litigants were more successful than non-governmental ones.

Finds that governmental litigants do worse as time progresses and that Galanter's theory is not supported.

Van Koppen and Malsch 1991

Interviewed 970 attorneys to study compliance with civil court decisions.

"On average, only a little more than half the award is collected after three years. RPs continue to prevail if they are plaintiffs, but are worse off than one-shotters if they are defendants."

Wahlbeck 1998

Studies federal nuisance law at the appellate level to examine how laws develop.

The independent variables operationalizing the litigants use Galanter.

Wenner 1983

Study of 2,178 federal court cases (at different levels) involving environmental litigation.

The government won over 50% of the cases in which it was involved, more when as plaintiff than as defendant. The RP nature allows it to pick and choose its litigation carefully when plaintiff.

Wheeler et al. 1987

Sixteen state supreme court outcomes studied every five years from 1870 to 1970.

The "haves" do appear to come out ahead, but their advantage is slight.

Yarnold 1995

Uses federal district court abortion cases to test success of litigants along the lines of resources (specifically RP status), political clout, and more general organizational resources.

Finds resources and RP status are not significant predictors of litigation success but that political factors are.

Yngvesson and Hennessey 1975

Dispute resolution in small claims courts.

Proposed reforms of small claims courts to offer a true alternative to the adversary model are hampered by lawyers' collective desire to preserve the complexity and mystique of the system.

2. ACTORS AS THE CAUSAL VARIABLE

Albiston 1999

Subject is the Family and Medical Leave Act. Carefully maps out incentive structure of RPs and ODs at each node of the litigation route.

OSs have incentives to settle or to litigate before juries, both of which are invisible to setting precedent. The most likely cases to be published are motions to dismiss and motions for summary judgment, also favoring RPs.

Best and Andreasen 1977

Based on a 1975 survey of consumer responses to problems with products and services.

"The fundamental unfairness of contemporary complaint processing is simple to state: it appears to favor people who have relatively high status and who are able to articulate judgmental problems, a group of consumer 'haves' over 'have-nots.'"

Cain 1979

How can one tell whether a lawyer had done a good job? The concept of lawyering as a "profession" obscures the work lawyers do.

Empirical data reveal that when RPs approach the lawyers studied, they were more likely to have their objective retained than OSs were.

Cross 2000

Argues for policies that encourage irrational plaintiffs to pursue litigation against the "haves."

Predicates his article on Galanter, exploring the conditions under which the long-term effects of the "haves" can be prevented.

Davies 1981

Organizational analysis used to model incentives facing appellate judges to allocate scarce resources toward civil appeals and away from criminal appeals.

In criminal appeals, state lawyers themselves may have moderate to low status, but the attorney general's office has a supportive "public" in state legislators, and as a RP, its lawyers can develop a working relationship with members of the court.

Edelman and Suchman 1999

Hypothesis-creating piece examining four changes in the nature of have organizations that lead to their success.

Large, RP organizations play different roles, on occasion being either lawmaker, judge and court, lawyer, or constable, allowing them not only to win in front of the law but to effectively become the law.

Engler 1999

Given the number of unrepresented poor in the court system, what is the role of judges, mediators, and clerks in maintaining justice?

Notes that the mere alteration of rules in favor of the "have nots" may not bring about change, but such changes at least are the first step in the process and thus deserve great attention.

Fitzgerald 1975

Explores aspects of litigation by poor and minority groups. Subject is the Contract Buyers League, a group of black homebuyers in Chicago claiming disparate treatment, 1967–1974.

Test cases were difficult given the importance of any particular case to the family (OS), while cases that went well often resulted in a settlement offer by the RP landlord to avoid later court precedent.

Flanders 1984

A critique of Resnik's 1982 article (see this table) about the effects of judges taking on managerial responsibilities.

Resnik "draws upon Professor Galanter's interesting but irrelevant work on repeat *litigants*." Resnik is concerned with "repeat" experience in one case, Galanter with the very different matter of repeat, cumulative experience over many cases.

Flemming 1986

Interviewed 155 defense attorneys from nine felony trial courts to understand how these lawyers understand their relationships to their clients.

As RP attorneys with OS clients, defense lawyers can be modeled as easily becoming co-opted by the legal system in order to protect their careers. Many defense attorneys readily acknowledged that their clients often did not trust them and believed they were not litigating aggressively enough.

Galanter and Rogers 1991

Study the nature of business disputing in America.

Economic disruptions can lead to litigation between repeat actors because they cast expectations of long-term relationships into doubt.

Guthrie 1999

Proposes the Regret Aversion Theory, which posits individual litigants as both calculating and emotional actors who make decisions that minimize postdecision regret.

Corporations are not only RPs, they also lack emotion, while OS individuals are more prone to understand litigation as serving both economic and emotional purposes.

Harris 1999
Role of cause lawyers and bureaucrats in implementing court successes.
For court victories to move beyond mere symbolism, they must have the support of those who will have to implement them.

Heck and Stewart 1982
Focus on the day-to-day work of southern civil rights lawyers in the 1960s, which was not on constitutional litigation so much as on defending both civil rights workers and ordinary black citizens against assorted litigation meant to hamper their cause.

"Civil rights lawyers had to face the tension between short-term needs of single clients and the long-term goals of the movement.

"Likewise, the establishment of a staff, however meager, helped overcome the problems of volunteer lawyers who were only briefly on the scene. Staff attorneys focusing on civil rights became, in Galanter's term, 'repeat players' able to take advantage of experience, thus enhancing their chances of victory."

Hendley et al. 1999
Focus on "Russian Repeat Players" (large businesses) in their use of protocols of disagreement, petitioning to freeze assets, contractual prepayment, and litigation activity.
Businesses that should act as repeat players do not often do so. One possibility is that there is little confidence that the rules will even be around in the future, so there is little incentive to invest in shaping them.

Houseman 1976
Director of Washington, D.C., legal aid society speaks on issues surrounding equal justice for poor people.
Access to a lawyer simply isn't enough if resource disparities with "haves" exist.

Jensen and Griffin 1984
Study appellate court decisions in California to support their argument that increasing amounts of educational policy-making is developed through litigation.
"Policy" cases are more likely to be brought by RP advocacy groups than by individuals and hence serve as test cases rather than as developing in some organic manner.

Kidder and Miyazawa 1993
Study how litigation can be used in the pursuit of a social movement's wider objectives despite the paucity of resources within the Japanese legal system.
Use Galanter's definition of "rule development" to discuss high-impact litigation, whose goal is to enact substantive changes leading to judicial precedents with the potential for changing practices.

Kinsey and Stalans 1999

Empirical study of who comes out ahead in tax audits.
"haves" can come out ahead when they interact directly with auditors, since there is a norm of deference, but when lawyers are employed, the advantage "haves" enjoy disappears.

Kritzer 1990

Empirical examination of the functions played by lawyers in American civil courts.
Kritzer's outlook on the nature of actors is substantively informed by Galanter, and the book thoroughly integrates this understanding into the analysis.

Landon 1985

Examines the effects of being in a small-town environment on zealous advocacy by attorneys.
Galanter notes that RPs are unlikely to want to litigate against each other, fearing damage to ongoing relations. The same may be true in small communities where members have no choice but to interact with one another repeatedly.

Landes and Posner 1979

Economic modeling of litigation expenditures by parties.
When one party has larger future stakes, the system may become inefficient because that party invests more in litigation, increasing the probability not only of winning that case but future cases on precedent.

Laumann et al. 1985

Focus on Washington, D.C., lawyers and others who represent clients in Washington who are concerned with initiating or preventing change in federal government policy.
Structured their inquiry so as to be able to detect RP clients. "We suspect that the RPs are oriented towards certain agencies more than others and that they may be concentrated among the clients of particular types of Washington representatives."

Levine and Mellema 2001

Study of how women involved in the street-level drug economy experience and interact with the law.
Drug dealers and prostitutes are RPs in the legal system, and these women know how to interact strategically, often taking short-term setbacks to avoid longer sentences, for example.

Lipartito 1990

Historical article focusing on the role of large law firms in the development of U.S. business.

Large firms formed relatively early in America and specialized to the extent that they could replace inside counsel for companies, allowing the "haves" to enjoy loyalty in ongoing representation.

Macaulay 1985
Studies the social function of law by examining the gaps between contract doctrine and the daily functioning of the business and commercial world.
Even when contract law offers remedies to harmed OS parties, the legal system promotes giving up or settling rather than adjudicating against RPs to vindicate rights.

Macaulay 1982
Notes the gap between what is taught in law school and the actual practice of law.
Anecdotes about small-town lawyers beating large corporations in litigation usually fail to mention the support of a trade association or other RP providing support to the attorney.

Macneil 1985
Argues that relational thinking is a necessary element for understanding the development of contract law.
RPs do not mind general equitable standards because they know that OSs still have great difficulty in making use of them. Most welcome of all are points of law that allow for delay.

McCann 1994
Legal strategies in the pay equity movement.
Strategic organizing can turn OSs into RPs, leading to success in shaping meaning and application of policy.

Menkel-Meadow 1999
"In this article, I will explore theoretically and address empirically (by reporting on the little but evocative currently available data) the question of whether the 'Haves' come out ahead in ADR too, as they do in the more official arena of litigation."
Reviews the literature and finds it inconclusive. The author then speculates that the "haves" probably do still come out ahead in ADR but perhaps for different reasons. Concludes with a list of potential research topics that could provide some answers to questions regarding who comes out ahead in ADR.

Mentor and Schwartz 2000
Study of how two branches of the Legal Services Corp. reacted to restrictions from Congress designed to prevent cause lawyering.
Congress specifically created restrictions to prevent the LSC from acting as a RP.

Miller and Sarat 1980

Survey data used to explore the origins of disputes in grievances and claims. Studies events that could have resulted in litigation, and models probabilities for different households initiating claims for redress.

"Just as the configuration of parties has been found to be significant in explaining how disputes are handled and the existence of differential patterns of success in dispute processing, one might expect similar patterns in the pre-dispute phase."

Nardulli 1986

Studies the nature of defense attorney ties to the local court community to see if this impacts how defendants are treated at trial.

Focuses on "insiders" who see themselves as having a relationship to the court system as well as to their clients and suggests that these individuals have a function of creating norms. The insider role is adopted because of the RP nature of appearing before the same bench in combination with the OS nature of many client interactions.

Nelson 1988

Galanter's 1983 article on whether there was a litigation explosion garnered wide support from academics and generated great interest in the public media, yet its effect on policy has been largely non-existent. The author explores why this is so and what the debate over the litigation crisis teaches about the relationship between ideology, sociolegal scholarship, and legal change.

Claims that a 1986 report on insurance availability utilized poor social science and was a tool used by RPs in the insurance industry to further their own litigation interests; in effect, they were RPs acting precisely as Galanter suggested they would.

Nelson 1985

How values influence client relationships in large law firms.

Substantive integration of Galanter into the analysis. Notes that lawyers can use their autonomy to moderate the advantages corporate RPs possess over "have nots."

O'Connor 1983

Studies amicus curiae participation of three U.S. Solicitors General during the Burger Court across three issue areas for differences in litigation activities.

The three Solicitors General screened carefully for cases they could win and should be understood as classic RPs in their litigation activities.

O'Connor 1980

Studies how women's groups have used the courts to further their goals.

Notes that business or labor groups are so well entrenched and have so many political friends that they can act like RPs, carefully selecting what to litigate and when. States that women's groups have not had that luxury.

Resnik 1982

Treatise on managerial judges, arguing that new managerial responsibilities have led many judges to abandon the disinterested stance that is the essence of the judicial role.

"As 'repeat adjudicators,' judges are generally confined to the record. They rely upon traditional adversarial exchanges, publicly explain their decisions, and know that their work may be reviewed on appeal. In contrast, as pretrial managers, judges operate in the freewheeling arena of informal dispute resolution."

Salokar 1992

Empirical study of the U.S. Solicitor General, the major conclusion being that the Solicitor General is ideologically tied to the administration but institutionally constrained from advancing purely partisan views.

Attributes success of Solicitor General to being a RP who possesses "advance intelligence, access to specialists, a wide range of resources, expertise, opportunities to build informal relations with the Supreme Court, and a high degree of credibility."

Sanders et al. 1982

Why lawyers use social scientists as experts in school desegregation cases.

In their study of school desegregation cases, they discovered most of the plaintiff attorneys were RPs who had developed a network of experts who could testify on their behalf, while most defendant school districts had no such network.

Simon 1978

Discussion of "ideology of advocacy," whose purpose is "to rationalize the most salient aspect of the lawyer's peculiar ethical orientation: his explicit refusal to be bound by personal and social norms which he considers binding on others."

Substantively integrates Galanter into the discussion of issues surrounding advocacy.

Tomasic 1983

Categorizes Australian lawyers and studies ideology of each, noting that contrary to the ideal of service, "cynical-realism" was prevalent.

Studies how OSs and RPs are served by each category of attorney.

Vidmar 1982

Psychological dynamics involved in the development, continuance, and resolution of disputes between private citizens.

Substantive integration of multiple aspect of Galanter, from RP v. OS, to a focus on alternative venues for dispute resolution, to cultural attitudes toward the use of the legal system.

Wasby 1984

Studies litigation initiated by the NAACP and its Legal Defense and Educational Fund from the late 1960s to early 1980s in order to see how litigation arises. Is it carefully planned based on pre-existing criteria, and if not, why?

Finds that the lawyers for the various organizations do not in fact act much like RPs, carefully choosing their fights in order to develop strong precedent, but rather are buffeted by political considerations and concern for individuals who need representation.

Yale Law Review 1981

A defense of the Legal Services Corp. against proposed defunding by President Reagan.

Substantively integrates Galanter into why the "haves" need organizations that serve as RPs to protect them.

Yarnold 1992

What makes for a successful attorney?

Successful attorneys are those who understand the politics of the courts and in the work are modeled as RPs who not only know the system but can shape it.

3. INSTITUTIONS AS THE CAUSAL VARIABLES

Abel 1985

How adequate are the prevailing accounts of legal aid? What criteria do they use to assess legal aid programs? What are the interests of the various actors involved? What has legal aid achieved in terms of quantity and quality of service and reach of those being served? What can legal aid achieve, and what are its limits?

Acknowledges the weakness of the RP v. OS dichotomy: after defining the categories in terms of the relationship of members to the system, it assumes they are similar on all other relevant traits. Author still finds the concept useful and bases much of his defense of legal aid lawyers as a method of turning OS litigants into RPs, garnering at least some of the advantages that follow.

Abel 1982

Argues that informal institutions do not necessarily benefit the "have nots"; in fact, it may be just the opposite.

Moving from formal to informal processes will not function to equalize relations between "haves" and "have nots" if the nature of the adversaries does not also change, since all of Galanter's factors will still come into play—perhaps more so, since the "have nots" have less opportunity to be represented by RP organizations on their behalf.

Abel 1981

Focuses on informal dispute resolution institutions to understand if they are conservative (favoring status quo, i.e., "haves") or liberating (favoring "have nots").

Thoroughly integrates Galanter into the analysis, attempting to understand which actors are favored by which systems.

Abel 1974

Conceptualizes dispute institutions both through how norms enter into the process and how structural elements shape outcomes.

Institutional stratification can lead to the "haves" coming out ahead since they have greater control over economic resources and are socially and culturally closer to the institution's practices.

Ackerman 1983

Place of law in an "activist state," defined as "an awareness that our society's existence depends upon a continuing flow of decisions by politically accountable state officials."

"Given the high costs of litigation and legislative lobbying, many systemic 'inconveniences' may never appear in a way that is 'visible' to reaction decision-makers, because the injured parties may lack the money, energy, and organizational incentives to force their grievances onto the reactive agenda."

Anderson and Hayden 1980

Methodological article describing the issues that must be taken into account when conducting simulation research on court systems.

In simulating a scenario, "it becomes necessary to consider who uses the institution and to what end; what resources (money, knowledge, political influence) actors possess; whether some people are regular participants (e.g. 'repeat players' cf. Galanter, 1974), and similar factors."

Baruch Bush 1986

Addresses the emerging shift in tort law from individual to group responsibility and its legal, political, and philosophical implications.

When individuals accept the liberal conception of the self, they lose conception of group ties, making them highly vulnerable to RPs who actively seek to structure the legal system to their own benefit.

Baruch Bush 1984

Identifies goals of the civil justice system and the costs of not achieving them, then models which forum is most appropriate for obtaining the goal at the least cost.

"Part of the goal of this article is . . . to relate heretofore unrelated insights of different commentators on the subject of dispute resolution alternatives and civil justice reform." Galanter is a significant influence on his models.

Bell 1976
Legal aspects and opportunity for racial remediation.
The problem for minorities seeking social change via the court system is that legal success will be nothing more than symbolic unless it is implemented, which often requires support from majorities.

Bellow and Kettleson 1978
Issues facing legal services lawyers.
"It is not client demand, but program defined, non-economic criteria that generally determine the content and character of representation," and the nature of RPs v. OSs creates a bias in favor of the former.

Bovens 1990
Review article on the social steering of complex organizations.
"What is striking about the modern asymmetry [of power relations] is that the parties involved are completely different classes of entities, natural persons [later described as OSs] and complex organizations [later described as RPs]."

Boyer 1981
Examines effects of agency funding of public participation in administrative proceedings at the FTC.
"To a considerable extent, the statistics support the contention that compensation awards have been relatively concentrated in a few repeat applicants."

Braithwaithe 1980
Do laws aimed at controlling corporate RPs actually have the intended effect?
Reminds readers that laws still need to be interpreted and implemented, and RPs (often the targets of the laws) have the upper hand in shaping both of these, creating the paradox that the more they are targeted for control, the more RPs can shape the law for their own ends.

Buffalo Law Review 1975
Warranty of habitability in residential leases on NY state housing stock.
The fact that a law is worded in a certain manner does not automatically mean it will be advantageous to the "have nots" it was designed to protect.

Cappelletti and Garth 1978
Introductory article to a four-volume series comparing worldwide access to justice.

Thoroughly integrate numerous elements of Galanter into their framework for accessing justice and assessing the potential to enact social change.

Carroll 1981
Game theory modeling to examine anomalies in the expectancy remedy for breach of contract.

"Proponents of [a class conspiracy] theory would conclude that the breach-encouraging expectancy remedy was intentionally made part of the law in order to benefit the strong, smart, and economically powerful."

Cross 1999
Critiques public choice claims that the judiciary branch serves the "have nots" better than the democratic branches do.

Notes that public choice critiques about special interests being able to buy legislation in Congress largely holds for the judiciary as well, where the system is stacked against the "have nots."

Ellis 2000
Argument against mandatory arbitration provisions.

Many union members are forced into arbitration, being represented by unions which they did not choose and which they would not join if given the choice. Companies often are allowed to select the arbitrators and, as RPs, will select ones favorable to their side.

Engel 1983
Examines the emergence of legal conflicts from the fabric of social relationships in the community and compares cases and parties in the court with those that gravitate toward nonjudicial settings, then compares processes and outcomes available in the court with those that may be obtained nonjudicially.

Studies an unnamed civil trial court. Two RPs, a collection company and a phone company, accounted for almost 3.4% of all collection cases brought in 1975 and 1976.

Epp 1998
Argues that the rights revolution was not primarily due to activist judges or to a rights consciousness or a written Bill of Rights in the U.S. but rather because of "deliberate, strategic organizing by rights advocates."

Draws from Galanter in the project of proving that support structures are essential for mobilizing rights.

Felstiner 1974
Relationship between social organizations and the forms of dispute resolution adopted.

Litigation as a form of dispute resolution may be tilted against the "have nots" due to their lack of resources.

Felstiner et al. 1981
Mechanisms by which disputes emerge and are transformed.
"The grievant's choice of an audience to whom to voice a complaint and the disputant's choice of an institution to which to take a controversy are primarily functions of the person's objectives and will change as objectives change," much of which is contingent upon whether actors involved are OSs or RPs.

Fiss 1979
Argues that the need to give the values found in the Constitution a meaning must involve all members and institutions in the polity.
Criticizes Rehnquist for denying cert on grounds that institutional advocates such as the NAACP or ACLU (RPs) should not be allowed to speak on behalf of victim groups.

Genn 1987
Studies out-of-court settlements in personal injury actions in Great Britain.
Uses Galanter substantively in her analysis, which frequently involves insurance companies, one of the classic RPs.

Gerwin 1977
Over 70% of the defendants involved in civil litigation in the District of Columbia Superior Court have their cases assigned to the Landlord and Tenant Branch. How are cases resolved, and what are the systemic biases in this process?
Calls for greater support for legal services while acknowledging that victories in court are not automatically implemented in practice.

Goodpaster 1992
"Since most lawsuits settle before trial, it is useful to view litigation not solely as a way to reach an adjudicated result, but also as a highly structured negotiation game, a refined and constrained version of competitive bargaining."
In the author's model of strategic bargaining, RPs and claim discounting form two of the significant variables.

Heimer 1999
Studies competition between legal, medical, and familial institutions in shaping the practices of neonatal intensive care facilities.
Categorizes state agents and medical personnel as RPs and families as OSs for her analysis.

Hendley et al. 2001

Comparative study of economic actors who suffer different penalties for breach of contract under different legal systems.

Model propositions of how RPs should behave when the legal system provides for punitive damages v. when it does not. Uses Galanter to create and test new propositions.

Hendley et al. 2000

Overview of the mechanisms that Russian enterprises use to enforce agreements and to solve problems that arise in their relations with other enterprises.

Russian RP enterprises use the law but not litigation. They develop long-term relationships and protect them through the use of contracts.

Heydebrand 1979

Argues the American judicial system is responding to its crisis in capacity by gradually moving toward a technocratic form of administration with functions more closely integrated with executive branch.

"By selectively responding to corporate and governmental actors at the expense of individual or 'minor' cases, courts inadvertently increase their relative accessibility in favor of politically and economically powerful actors."

Heydebrand 1977

Effort to construct a Marxian theory of organizational theory.

Largely informed by Galanter's distinction between OSs and RPs in shaping his discussion of litigation surrounding productive forces attempting to shape the social relations of production.

Hickerson 1982

Economic perspective on the power of the corporate enterprise system.

Corporations have great influence over shaping the legal order due to their being RPs.

Hoffmann 2001

Compares dispute resolution at a British coal mine when it was run by a conventional hierarchy and afterward when turned into a worker cooperative.

Draws upon Galanter for the concept of "lumping it," i.e., putting up with harms because nothing can be done about it.

Kennedy 1976

Relationship between rhetoric of individualism and altruism, on the one hand, and the use of clearly defined general rules versus equitable standards producing ad hoc decisions with relatively little precedential value.

Formal rules developed in part through precedent may lead to systemic biases in favor of those with the resources to shape them over time.

Kritzer 1991
Study of negotiation in ordinary litigation.
RPs have a degree of power over OSs because they believe they have less to lose in any negotiation and hence are not as willing to compromise

Kritzer 1984
Comparative study of the use of inside lawyers and fee shifting. Theorizes that in settings where there are formal controls on what lawyers can charge, there will be less use of internal counsel or close monitoring of outside law firms.
Creates a four-part table of individual v. corporation (to reflect OSs v. RPs), and small cases v. large ones. "The impact of fee shifting would seem likely to depend upon which of the four cells one is thinking about."

Kritzer et al. 1984
What does it mean to talk about the "cost of civil justice"? What can be done to bring that cost down? Authors examine the components of cost and analyze the dominant element, which is legal services, then discuss how the analysis speaks to the issue of lowering costs.
Code litigants as individuals or organizations based on Galanter's theorizing that the former are OSs and the latter are RPs.

Kritzer et al. 1985
Examine the impact of fee arrangement on the amount of time lawyers are likely to devote to civil cases.
The authors employ the same coding system as in 1984, giving emphasis to the nature of the litigants.

Leubsdorf 1982
Places changes to the legal profession into three models and discusses strengths and drawbacks of each.
If the "have nots" are to be given a fair chance in the legal system, there must be a holistic attempt to remedy the problems raised by Galanter.

Macaulay 2001
Comment on Galanter (2001).
Uses the comment to fit Galanter's 2001 article on uphill vs. downhill litigation into the perspective on "haves" vs. "have nots."

Marcus 1979

Studies the increase in litigation and possible "buffers" to an eventual implosion of the judicial system.

Uses Galanter to suggest that the high rate of settlements runs contrary to what one would expect in a rights-conscious society

Mather and Yngvesson 1980

Develop an analytic framework for comparing dispute processing within a single institution and across different cultures by focusing on the transformation of disputes.

The dispute process involves more than just the attributes of individual participants, since RPs may, over time, develop significant advantages.

Mattli and Slaughter 1998

Review essay on political science research on the European Court of Justice.

Use the OS-RP dichotomy to classify litigants before the court.

McCaffrey 1982

Why politically and legally strong corporations face significant regulatory pressure.

Argues that public interest groups and law firms, along with unions, are powerful RPs.

McKie and Reed 1981

Canadian women are represented to a lesser extent than their proportion of the population would suggest. Authors point to credit-granting practices of large financial institutions and to the types of litigable rights and interests that Canadian women habitually seek to protect.

Use Galanter's model to frame actors involved.

Menkel-Meadow 1985

Discusses the uses and abuses of mandatory settlement.

Noting that Galanter's model leaves little cause for hope that the "have nots" will fair well under litigation, the author suggests that settlement is the best option.

Menkel-Meadow 1984

Suggests that negotiators might serve as better dispute resolution devices if they sought out all the goals of parties, beyond mere profit maximization.

Substantively grapples with Galanter's concern over resource disparities between "haves" and "have nots."

Mnookin and Kornhauser 1979

"We see the primary function of contemporary divorce law not as imposing order

from above, but rather as providing a framework within which divorcing couples can themselves determine their postdissolution rights and responsibilities."

Divorcing couples have no incentive to take their cases to court for precedential purposes, since this is not the mind-set of OSs.

Molot 1998

Argues that changes to the Federal Rules of Civil Procedure since 1938 have diminished the importance of judicial evaluation of lawsuits in important ways.

The "haves" can stack the deck against the "have nots" by bringing what previously would have been considered frivolous points with the goal of delay, which usually works in their favor.

Nader 1979

Anthropological perspective on why Americans lack recourse to law for certain types of problems.

Many programs obstruct complainants' paths with complex procedures and repeated delays, with the result that many OSs fail to persist in their pursuits of justice.

Neal and Kirp 1985

Use the 1975 Education for All Handicapped Children Act as a case study in how legalization shapes education policy.

Parents of children with disabilities often require the most help from a school district, but the RP nature of the relationship can make these parents hesitant to litigate for their rights out of fear of future retribution.

Olson and Batjer 1999

Study a hotly contested judicial re-election campaign to understand questions about legal consciousness and resistance.

Subversive stories tend to originate with the marginalized "have nots," who are more likely to have had a negative experience with the judiciary.

Priest 1984

Examination test of a model of how rules structure the relationship between litigated disputes and those that are settled.

An important factor is the nature of the parties. Are they OSs or RPs for whom precedent will affect future outcomes?

Purcell 1997

Argues against permitting discretionary vacatur of judgments.

"Allowing discretionary vacatur will allow wealthy, RP litigants to shape the law according to their interests by eliminating rules of law that affect their interests adversely."

Resnik 2000

Discussion of judicial interventions creating subsidies and awarding costs and fees in litigation.

Judges should insist on revelation of lawyers' financial arrangements in order to prevent RP attorneys using unethical arrangements in mass torts.

Rhode 2001

What does "access to justice" mean, and why is it so hard to attain?

Equal justice under law is ambiguous. Does it mean substantive or procedural fairness? Having one's day in court is not all that satisfying; the "haves" always seem to come out ahead.

Rosenberg 1984

Mass exposure accidents pose unique problems under traditional rules of litigation. Argues that courts should determine causation under a proportionality rule, and that courts should allow mass exposure cases to proceed as class actions that could use damage scheduling and insurance fund judgments.

RP defendants also have an upper hand because they alone may know the terms of agreements they settled earlier and about discovery materials from previous cases that might not have been made public.

Rosenberg 1991

In-depth case studies of several "seminal" U.S. Supreme Court cases, with the claim that the court system cannot bring about social change.

To say that the "haves" come out ahead implies that court cases have the capacity to structure society. Yet on occasions when the courts do come out ahead of the legislature (which is more representative of the polity), cases are often ineffective. If the "haves" do come out ahead in court cases, they must still be placed in the larger picture.

Ross and Littlefield 1978

Study of dispute resolution at an appliance and TV store.

Many customers were treated as RPs on the assumption that they would return for future purchases if treated well and hence received more generous concessions than required by law.

Rowe 1984

Attempts to create a comprehensive and detailed effort at identifying and analyzing the major likely effects of fee shifting. Also provides a plain language introduction to many law and economics terms and theories.

RP v. OS nature of litigants is modeled as one of the three main situation factors affecting outcomes.

Rutgers Law Review 1984
Issues involved in resolving "minor" disputes in prisons.
In an environment where inmates are often depersonalized through multiple methods, inmates' so-called nuisance suits can be understood as attempts to obtain justice, regardless of outcomes. Thus, one should not expect these suits to be settled, since the goal is symbolic gratification. Over time, however, these suits may hurt the cause of the following generations of inmates.

Sarat and Grossman 1975
Study of the nature of social relationships and the method of adjudication that is most likely to be used. Examine impacts and implications for use of one method versus another.
Social development leads to more formalistic relations, leading to formal adjudication over informal methods, which can lead to systemic biases.

Simon 1980
Defense of the doctrinal tradition of legal theory from the critiques of the "Psychological Vision."
"Talking and thinking about the lawyer-client relationship as a community-of-two tends to direct attention away from the relation between lawyering and political action," i.e., assisting disadvantaged clients by acting as RPs.

Southern California Law Review 1978
Magnuson-Moss Warranty—Federal Trade Commission Improvement Act of 1975, which was the first federal effort to legislate in the area of warranty law, requiring suppliers of consumer products offering a warranty to disclose clearly and conspicuously the contents of the warranty.
Applies Galanter in noting that under traditional methods of dispute resolution, warrantors (RPs) are significantly advantaged in that the consumer must bear the initial costs of dispute resolution procedures, while transaction costs to the warrantor may be near zero for most of the process.

Stewart 1985
Argues that the current federal regulatory structure promotes costly litigation because it decreases the opportunity for the development of long-term continuing relationships between regulator and regulated.
Substantively integrates Galanter throughout the article. Public interest groups in particular are understood as being an obstacle to developing relationships between regulators and industries. Suggests that market incentives should replace regulatory legalism whenever possible.

Thornburg 1999
Reviews potential effects of 1998 Standing Committee on Rules of Practice amendment proposals to discovery rules.
The amendments will allow for delay, which is a powerful tool of the "haves."

Thornburg 1991
Argues against work product immunity.
Product immunity suppresses information to the trial, and its costs benefit frequent litigants at the expense of OSs.

Tomasic 1985
Review of sociology of law relating to legal services and society.
Is seeking legal services the best response to a particular problem? Extensive discussion of Galanter as to why it might not be.

Trubek 1999
Examines relationship between innovations in family law practiced by Legal Services attorneys and how the practices influence professional autonomy.
Notes that simplification of the legal process would aid the "have nots" in their pursuit of justice, yet this goal runs counter to the interests of the very attorneys who serve their needs.

Trubek and Galanter 1974
Study of how changes in understanding of scholarly activity are affected by moral attitudes of scholars toward their professional work.
Questions centrality of courts as a neutral arbiter when structural biases lead to systemic biases against specific groups.

Whitford 1982
Issues in designing consumer protection legislation.
In understanding the effects of unconscionability legislation, modeling merchants as RPs and consumers as OSs yields insight into long-term effects (or lack thereof).

Whitford 1979
Consumer Credit Collection System.
Creditors are far more willing to litigate than debtors because their victories may be long-term via signaling to debtors that if they do not pay, creditors will forced to litigate regardless of costs.

Yale Law Journal 1979
Use of special masters to implement decrees for prison reform stemming from Eighth Amendment appeals from prisoners.

"Inmates and their attorneys also have resisted the use of the implementation process to confront internal problems. Inmates often appear more concerned with the court's implicit recognition of their having possession of inalienable rights than with the outcome of a particular legal issue." Galanter noted how "have nots" often seek symbolic success while failing to achieve tangible gains.

Yale Law Journal 1983

Economic model of common law rules arguing the system is inefficient. The focus is on accident rules and how unforeseen losses are produced and allocated.

The OS nature of most injured actors results in a focus on the current stakes, while the RP nature of industrial injurers allows them to focus on precedent, which over time will lead to inefficient outcomes.

Yarnold 1990

"This analysis is concerned with factors which impact the United States refugee and asylum policy, post-1980."

Involvement of organizations led to high levels of litigation success because they had superior litigation resources with which to argue the merits of a case (Galanter) and also because of their political clout.

Yngvesson 1978

Outlines anthropological approaches to the study of law in preindustrial societies and suggests areas of future research.

Notes that victory can take many forms and that RPs may be willing to take a short-term loss to enjoy long-term gains.

Notes

The author wishes to thank Marc Galanter and the editors for their numerous comments and suggestions. I am greatly indebted to the reference librarians at Harvard University's Law School Library for their patience and assistance with my frequent and often complicated requests for help.

1. Whether the term was used prior to Galanter has been difficult to assess. Galanter himself notes that if it had been used previously, he was not aware of it. (Marc Galanter, personal communication, November 8, 2001)

3. In their discussion of empirical research on the U.S. court system, Tracey George and Reginald S. Sheehan (2000, 244) note that the majority of the studies using the U.S. Courts of Appeals Data Base, for example, are studies testing for efficacy of repeat players.

4. This is also the subject of Herbert Kritzer's chapter in this volume.

References

Abel, Richard (1985) "Law without Politics: Legal Aid Under Advanced Capitalism," 32 *UCLA Law Rev.* 474–42.

——— (1982)"The Contradictions of Informal Justice," In *The Politics of Formal Justice.* Vol. 1. New York: Academic Press.

——— (1981) "Conservative Conflict and the Reproduction of Capitalism: The Role of Informal Justice," 9 *Int'l J. of the Sociology of Law* 245–67.

——— (1974) "A Comparative Theory of Dispute Institutions in Society," 8 *Law & Society Rev.* 217–347.

Ackerman, Bruce A. (1983) "Forward: Law in an Activist State," 92 *Yale Law J.* 1083–28.

Albiston, Catherine (1999) "The Rule of Law and the Litigation Process: The Paradox of Losing by Winning," 33 *Law & Society Rev.* 869–10.

Anderson, Jill K. and Robert M. Hayden (1980) "Questions of Validity and Drawing Conclusions from Simulation Studies in Procedural Justice," 15 *Law & Society Rev.* 293–303.

Atkins, Burton M. (1991) "Party Capability Theory as an Explanation for Intervention Behavior in the English Court of Appeals," 35 *American J. of Political Science* 881–903.

Baar, Carl (1979) "The Scope and Limits of Court Reform," 5 *Justice System J.* 274–90.

Baker, Tom (2001) "Blood Money, New Money, and the Moral Economy of Tort Law in Action," 35 *Law & Society Rev.* 275–319.

Baruch Bush, Robert A. (1986) "Between Two Worlds: The Shift from Individual to Group Responsibility in the Law of Causation of Injury," 33 *UCLA Law Rev.* 1473–1563.

——— (1984) "Dispute Resolution Alternatives and the Goals of Civil Justice: Jurisdictional Principles for Process Choice," *Wisconsin Law Rev.* 893–1034.

Baum, Lawrence (1977) "Judicial Specialization, Litigant Influence, and Substantive Policy: The Court of Customs and Patent Appeals," 11 *Law & Society Rev.* 823–50.

Bell, Derrick A., Jr. (1976) "Racial Remediation: An Historical Perspective on Current Conditions," 52 *Notre Dame Law Rev.* 5–29.

Bellow, Gary and Jeanne Kettleson (1978) "From Ethics to Politics: Confronting Scarcity and Fairness in Interest Practice," 58 *Boston Univ. Law Rev.* 337–90.

Best, Arthur and Alan R. Andreasen (1977) "Consumer Response to Unsatisfactory Purchases: A Survey of Perceiving Defects, Voicing Complaints, and Obtaining Redress," 11 *Law & Society Rev.* 701–42.

Blankenburg, Erhard (1981) "Legal Insurance, Litigant Decisions, and the Rising Caseloads of Courts: A West German Study," 16 *Law & Society Rev.* 601–24.

Bovens, Mark A. P. (1990) "The Social Steering of Complex Organizations," 20 *British J. of Political Science* 91–117.

Boyer, Barry B. (1981) "Funding Public Participation in Agency Proceedings: The Federal Trade Commission Experience," 70 *Georgetown Law J.* 51–172.

Brace, Paul and Melinda Gann Hall (2001) "'Haves' Versus 'Have Nots' in State Supreme Courts: Allocating Docket Space and Wins in Power Asymmetric Cases," 35 *Law & Society Rev.* 393–417.

Bradley, Robert C. and Paul Gardner (1985) "Underdogs, Upperdogs and the Use of the Amicus Brief: Trends and Explanations," 10 *Justice System J.* 78–96.

Braithwaite, John (1980) "Inegalitarian Consequences of Egalitarian Reforms to Control Corporate Crime," 53 *Temple Law Q.* 1127.

Brutus (1985a [1788]) "Essay XI." In Herbert J. Storing, ed., *The Anti-Federalist Papers*. Chicago: University of Chicago Press.

——— (1985b [1788]) "Essay XIV." In Herbert J. Storing, ed., *The Anti-Federalist Papers*. Chicago: University of Chicago Press.

——— (1985c [1788]) "Essay XV." In Herbert J. Storing, ed., *The Anti-Federalist Papers*. Chicago: University of Chicago Press.

Buffalo Law Review (1975) "Comment: An Assessment of the Impact of an Implied Warranty of Habitability of New York State," *Buffalo Law Rev.* 189–210.

Cain, Maureen (1979) "The General Practice Lawyer and the Client: Towards a Radical Conception," 7 *International J. of the Sociology of Law* 331–54.

Cappelletti, Mauro, and Bryant Garth (1978) "Access to Justice: The Newest Wave in the Worldwide Movement to Make Rights Effective," 27 *Buffalo Law Rev.* 181–292.

Carroll, David W. (1981) "Four Games and the Expectancy Theory," 54 *Southern California Law Rev.* 503–26.

Cartwright, Bliss (1975) "Conclusion: Disputes and Reported Cases," 9 *Law & Society Rev.* 369–84.

Cheit, Ross and Jacob E. Gersen (2000) "When Businesses Sue Each Other: An Empirical Study of State Court Litigation," 25 *Law & Social Inquiry* 789–816.

Cross, Frank B. (2000) "In Praise of Irrational Plaintiffs," 86 *Cornell Law Rev.* 1–32.

——— (1999) "The Judiciary and Public Choice," 50 *Hastings Law J.* 355–82.

Davies, Thomas Y. (1981) "Expedited Processing Techniques and the Allocation of Appellate Resources," 6 *Justice System J.* 372–404.

Dotan, Yoav (1999) "Do the 'Haves' Still Come Out Ahead? Resource Inequalities in Ideological Courts: The Case of the Israeli Court of Justice," 33 *Law & Society Rev.* 1059–80.

Edelman, Lauren B. and Mark C. Suchman (1999) "When the 'Haves' Hold Court: Speculations on the Organizational Internalization of Law," 9 *Law & Society Rev.* 941–91.

Ellis, Rosetta E. (2000) "Mandatory Arbitration Provisions in Collective Bargaining Agreements: The Case against Barring Statutory Discrimination Claims from Federal Court Jurisdiction," 86 *Virginia Law Rev.* 307–48.

Engel, David M. (1983) "Cases, Conflict, and Accommodation: Patterns of Legal Interaction in an American Community," *American Bar Foundation Research J.* 803–74.

Engler, Russell (1999) "And Justice For All—Including the Unrepresented Poor: Revisiting the Roles of the Judges, Mediators, and Clerks," 67 *Fordham Law Rev.* 1987–2070.

Epp, Charles R. (1998) *The Rights Revolution: Lawyers, Activists, and Supreme Courts in Comparative Perspective*. Chicago: University of Chicago Press.

Farole, Donald J. (1999) "Reexamining Litigant Success in State Supreme Courts," 33 *Law & Society Rev.* 1043–58.

Federalist. Alexander Hamilton, James Madison, and John Jay (1999 [1787/1788]) *The Federalist Papers*. New York: Mentor Books.

Felstiner, William L. F. (1974) "Influences of Social Organization on Dispute Processing," 9 *Law & Society Rev.* 63.

Felstiner, William L. F., Richard Able, and Austin Sarat (1981) "The Emergence of Transformation of Disputes: Naming, Blaming, Claiming," 15 *Law & Society Rev.* 631–53.

Fiss, Owen (1979) "The Supreme Court 1978 Term. Forward: The Forms of Justice," 93 *Harvard Law Rev.* 1–58.

Fitzgerald, Jeffrey M. (1975) "The Contract Buyers League and the Courts: A Case Study of Poverty Litigation," 9 *Law & Society Rev.* 165–93.

Flanders, Steven (1984) "Commentary: Blind Umpires—A Response to Professor Resnik," 35 *Hastings Law J.* 505–22.

Flemming, Roy B. (1986) "Client Games: Defense Attorney Perspectives on Their Relations with Criminal Clients," *American Bar Foundation Research J.* 253–77.

——— (1998) "Contested Terrains and Regime Politics: Thinking about America's Trial Courts and Institutional Change," 23 *Law & Social Inquiry* 941–65.

Friedman, Lawrence M. and Robert V. Percival (1976) "A Tale of Two Courts: Litigation in Alameda and San Benito Counties," 10 *Law & Society Rev.* 267–301.

Galanter, Marc (2001) "Contract in Court; or Almost Everything You May or May Not Want to Know about Contract Litigation," *Wisconsin Law Rev.* 577–627.

——— (1975) "Afterword: Explaining Litigation," 9 *Law & Society Rev.* 347–68.

——— (1974) "Why the 'Haves' Comes Out Ahead: Speculations on the Limits of Social Change," 9 *Law & Society Rev.* 95–160.

Galanter, Marc and Joel Rogers (1991) "The Transformation of American Business Disputing? Some Preliminary Observations." Dispute Processing Research Paper 10–3, Institute for Legal Studies, University of Wisconsin School of Law.

Genn, Hazel (1987) *Hard Bargaining: Out of Court Settlement in Personal Injury Claims*. Oxford: Clarendon Press.

George, Tracey E. and Reginald S. Sheehan (2000) "Circuit Breaker: Deciphering Courts of Appeals Decisions Using the U.S. Courts of Appeals Data Base," 83 *Judicature* 240–47.

Gerwin, Leslie E. (1977) "A Study of the Evolution and Potential of Landlord Tenant Law and Judicial Dispute Settlement Mechanism in the District of Columbia. Part II: A Critical Examination and Proposal for Reform," 26 *Catholic Univ. Law Rev.* 641–755.

Goldberg, Michael J. (1985) "The Duty of Fair Representation: What the Courts Do in Fact," 34 *Buffalo Law Rev.* 89–171.

Goodpaster, Gary (1992) "Lawsuits as Negotiations," 8 *Negotiation J.* 221–39.

Gross, Samuel R. and Kent D. Syverud (1996) "Don't Try Civil Jury Verdicts in a System Geared to Settlement," 44 *UCLA Law Rev.* 1–64.

Guthrie, Chris (1999) "Better Settle Than Sorry: The Regret Aversion Theory of Litigant Behavior," *Univ. of Illinois Law Rev.* 43–90.

Hagan, John (1982) "The Corporate Advantage: A Study of the Involvement of Corporate and Individual Victims in a Criminal Justice System," 60 *Social Forces* 993–1022.

Haire, Susan Brodie, Roger Hartley, and Stefanie A. Lindquist (1999) "Attorney Expertise, Litigant Success, and Judicial Decision-making in the U.S. Courts of Appeals," 33 *Law & Society Rev.* 667–85.

Harris, Beth (1999) "Representing Homeless Families: Repeat Player Implementation Strategies," 33 *Law & Society Rev.* 911–39.

Harvard Law Review (1981) "Notes: The California Rent-a-Judge Experiment: Constitutional and Policy Considerations of Pay-As-You-Go Courts," 94 *Harvard Law Rev.* 1592–1615.

Haynie, Stacia L. (1994) "Resource Inequalities and Litigation Outcomes in the Philippine Supreme Court," 56 *J. of Politics* 752–72.

Haynie, Stacia L., C. Neal Tate, Reginald S. Sheehan, and Donald R. Songer (2001) "Winners and Losers: A Comparative Analysis of Appellate Courts and Litigation Outcomes." Paper presented at the annual meeting of the American Political Science Association, San Francisco, August 30–September 2.

Heck, Edward V. and Joseph Stewart Jr. (1982) "Ensuring Access to Justice: The Role of Interest Group Lawyers in the 60s Campaign for Civil Rights," 66 *Judicature* 84–95.

Heimer, Carol (1999) "Competing Institutions: Law, Medicine, and Family in Neonatal Intensive Care," 33 *Law & Society Rev.* 17–66.

Hellman, Arthur D. (1985) "Case Selection in the Burger Court: A Preliminary Inquiry," 60 *Notre Dame Law Rev.* 947–1055.

Hendley, Kathryn, Peter Murrell, and Randi Ryterman (2001) "Punitive Damages for Contractual Breaches in Comparative Perspective: The Use of Penalties by Russian Enterprises," *Wisconsin Law Rev.* 639–79.

——— (2000) "Law, Relationships and Private Enforcement: Transactional Strategies of Russian Enterprises," 52 *Europe-Asia Studies* 627–56.

——— (1999) "Do Repeat Players Behave Differently in Russia? Contractual and Litigation Behavior of Russian Enterprises," 33 *Law & Society Rev.* 833–67.

Heydebrand, Wolf (1979) "The Technocratic Administration of Justice," 2 *Research in Law and Sociology* 29–64.

——— (1977) "Organizational Contradictions in Public Bureaucracies: Toward a Marxian Theory of Organizations," 18 *Sociological Quarterly* 83–107.

Hickerson, Steven R. (1982) "Legal Counsel, Power, and Institutional Hegemony," 16 *J. of Economic Issues* 191.

Hoffmann, Elizabeth A. (2001) "Confrontations and Compromise: Dispute Resolution at a Worker Cooperative Coal Mine," 26 *Law & Social Inquiry* 555–96.

Houseman, Alan W. (1976) "Equal Protection and the Poor," 30 *Rutgers Law Rev.* 887–906.

Hurst, James Willard (1980) "The Functions of the Courts in the United States, 1950–1980," 15 *Law & Society Rev.* 401–71.

Jensen, Donald N. and Thomas M. Griffin (1984) "The Legalization of State Educational Policymaking in California," 13 *J. of Law & Education* 19–33.

Kagan, Robert A., Bliss Cartwright, Lawrence M. Friedman, and Stanton Wheeler (1977) "The Evolution of State Supreme Courts," 76 *Michigan Law Rev.* 961–1005.

Kastenmeier, Robert W. and Michael J Remington (1979) "Court Reform and Access to Justice: A Legislative Perspective," 16 *Harvard J. on Legislation* 301–42.

Kennedy, Duncan (1976) "Form and Substance in Private Law Adjudication," 89 *Harvard Law Rev.* 1685–1778.

Kidder, Robert L. and Setsuo Miyazawa (1993) "Long-Term Strategies in Japanese Environmental Litigation," 18 *Law & Social Inquiry* 605–27.

Kinsey, Karyl A. and Loretta J. Stalans (1999) "Which 'Haves' Come Out Ahead and Why? Cultural Capital and Legal Mobilization in Frontline Law Enforcement," 33 *Law & Society Rev.* 993–1023.

Kritzer, Herbert M., William L. F. Felstiner, Austin Sarat, and David M. Trubek (1985) "The Impact of Fee Arrangement on Lawyer Effort," 19 *Law & Society Rev.* 251–78.

Kritzer, Herbert M., Austin Sarat, David M. Trubek, Kristin Bumiller, and Elizabeth McNichol (1984) "Understanding the Costs of Litigation: The Case of the Hourly-Fee Lawyer," *American Bar Foundation Research J.* 559–604.

Kritzer, Herbert M. (1991) *Let's Make a Deal: Understanding the Negotiation Process in Ordinary Litigation*. Madison: University of Wisconsin Press.

——— (1990) *Justice Brokers: Lawyers and Ordinary Litigation*. New York: Oxford University Press.

——— (1984) "Fee Arrangements and Fee Shifting: Lessons from the Experience in Ontario," 47 *Law & Contemporary Problems* 125–38.

Landes, William M. and Richard A. Posner (1979) "Adjudication as a Private Good," 8 *J. of Legal Studies* 235–84.

Landon, Donald D. (1985) "Clients, Colleagues, and Community: The Shaping of Zealous Advocacy in Country Law Practice," *American Bar Foundation Research J.* 81–111.

Laumann, Edward O., John P. Heinz, with Robert L. Nelson, and Robert H. Salisbury (1985) "Washington Lawyers and Others: The Structure of Washington Representation," 37 *Stanford Law Rev.* 465–502.

Lawrence, Susan E. (1990) *The Poor in Court: The Legal Services Program and Supreme Court Decision Making*. Princeton, NJ: Princeton University Press.

Lempert, Richard (1999) "A Classic at 25: Reflections on Galanter's 'Haves' Article and Work It Has Inspired," 33 *Law & Society Rev.* 1099–1112.

——— (1978) "More Tales of Two Courts: Exploring Changes in the 'Dispute Settlement Function' of Trial Courts," 13 *Law & Society Rev.* 91–138.

Leubsdorf, John (1982) "Three Models of Professional Reform," 67 *Cornell Law Rev.* 1021–54.

Levine, Kay and Virginia Mellema (2001) "Strategizing the Street: How Law Matters in the Lives of Women in the Street-Level Drug Economy," 26 *Law & Social Inquiry* 169–207.

Lipartito, K. (1990) "What Have Lawyers Done for American Business? The Case of Baker and Botts of Houston," 64 *Business History Rev.* 489–526.

Lizotte, Alan J. (1978) "Extra-Legal Factors in Chicago's Criminal Courts: Testing the Conflict Model of Criminal Justice," 25 *Social Problems* 564.

Macaulay, Stewart (2001) "Almost Everything That I Did Want to Know about Contract Litigation: A Comment on Galanter," *Wisconsin Law Rev.* 629–38.

——— (1985) "An Empirical View of Contract," *Wisconsin Law Rev.* 465–82.

——— (1982) "Law Schools and the World Outside Their Doors II: Notes on Two Recent Studies of the Chicago Bar," 32 *J. of Legal Education* 506–42.

Macneil, Ian R. (1985) "Relational Contract: What We Do and Do Not Know," *Wisconsin Law Rev.* 483–525.

Marcus, Maria (1979) "Judicial Overload: The Reasons and the Remedies," 28 *Buffalo Law Rev.* 111–41.

Mather, Lynn (1998) "Theorizing about Trial Courts: Lawyers, Policymaking, and Tobacco Litigation," 23 *Law & Social Inquiry* 897–940.

Mather, Lynn and Barbara Yngvesson (1980) "Language, Audience, and the Transformation of Disputes," 15 *Law & Society Rev.* 775–821.

Mattli, Walter and Ann-Marie Slaughter (1998) "Revisiting the European Court of Justice," 52 *International Organization* 177–209.

Matusik, Sharon F., Sharon R. Fuller, and Lauren B. Edelman (2000) "Legal Readings: Employee Interpretation and Mobilization of Law," 25 *Academy of Management Review* 200–216.

McCaffrey, David P. (1982) "Corporate Resources and Regulatory Pressures: Toward Explaining a Discrepancy," 27 *Administrative Science Q.* 398–419.

McCann, Michael (1994) *Rights at Work: Pay Equity Reform and the Politics of Legal Mobilization.* Chicago: University of Chicago Press.

McCormick, Peter (1993) "Party Capability Theory and Appellate Success in the Supreme Court of Canada, 1949–1992," 26 *Canadian J. of Political Science* 523–40.

McGuire, Kevin T. (1995) "Repeat Players in the Supreme Court: The Role of Experienced Lawyers in Litigation Success," 57 *J. of Politics* 187–96.

McIntosh, Wayne (1980) "150 Years of Litigation and Dispute Settlement: A Court Tale," 15 *Law & Society Rev.* 823–48.

McKie, Craig and Paul Reed (1981) "Women in Canadian Civil Courts," 6 *Canadian J. of Sociology* 485.

Meeker, James W. (1984) "Criminal Appeals Over the Last 100 Years," 22 *Criminology* 551–71.

Menkel-Meadow, Carrie (1999) "Do the 'Haves' Come Out Ahead in Alternative Judicial Systems? Repeat Players in ADR," 15 *Ohio State J. on Dispute Resolution* 19–61.

——— (1985) "For and Against Settlement: Uses and Abuses of the Mandatory Settlement Conference," 33 *UCLA Law Rev.* 485–514.

——— (1984) "Toward Another View of Legal Negotiation: The Structure of Problem Solving," 31 *UCLA Law Rev.* 754–842.

Mentor, Kenneth W. and Richard D. Schwartz (2000) "A Tale of Two Strategies: Adaptation Strategies of Selected LSC Agencies," 21 *Justice System J.* 143–69.

Miller, Richard E. and Austin Sarat (1980) "Grievances, Claims, and Disputes: Assessing the Adversary Culture," 15 *Law & Society Rev.* 525–66.

Mnookin, Robert H. and Lewis Kornhauser (1979) "Bargaining in the Shadow of the Law: The Case of Divorce," 88 *Yale Law J.* 950–97.

Molot, Jonathan T. (1998) "How Changes in the Legal Profession Reflect Changes in Civil Procedure," 84 *Virginia Law Rev.* 955–1051.

Nader, Laura (1979) "Disputing without the Force of Law," 88 *Yale Law J.* 998–1027.

Nardulli, Peter F. (1986) "'Insider' Justice: Defense Attorneys and the Handling of Felony Cases," 77 *J. of Criminal Law & Criminology* 379–417.

Neal, David and David L. Kirp (1985) "The Allure of Legalization Reconsidered: The Case of Special Education," 48 *Law & Contemporary Problems* 63–87.

Nelson, Robert L. (1988) "Ideology, Scholarship, and Sociolegal Change: Lessons from Galanter and the 'Litigation Crisis,'" 21 *Law & Society Rev.* 677–93.

——— (1985) "Ideology, Practice and Professional Autonomy: Social Values and Client Relationships," 37 *Stanford Law Rev.* 503–51.

O'Connor, Karen (1983) "The Amicus Curiae Role of the U.S. Solicitor General in Supreme Court Litigation," 66 *Judicature* 256–64.

——— (1980) *Women's Organizations Use of the Courts* Lexington, Mass.: Lexington Books.

Olson, Susan M. and Christina Batjer (1999) "Competing Narratives in a Judicial Retention Election: Feminism versus Judicial Independence," 33 *Law & Society Rev.* 123–60.

Palmer, Barbara (1999) "Issue Fluidity and Agenda Setting on the Warren Court," 52 *Political Research Q.* 39–65.

Philips, Charles David and Sheldon Ekland-Olson (1982) "'Repeat Players' in a Criminal Court," 19 *Criminology* 530–45.

Priest, George L. and Benjamin Klein (1984) "The Selection of Disputes for Litigation," 13 *J. of Legal Studies* 1–55.

Purcell, Daniel (1997) "The Public Right to Precedent: A Theory and Rejection of Vacatur," 85 *California Law Rev.* 867–917.

Resnik, Judith (2000) "Money Matters: Judicial Market Interventions Creating Subsidies and Awarding Fees and Costs in Individual and Aggregate Litigation," 148 *U. of Pennsylvania Law Rev.* 2119–2195.

——— (1982) "Managerial Judges," 96 *Harvard Law Rev.* 374–448.

Rhode, Deborah L. (2001) "Access to Justice," 69 *Fordham Law Rev.* 1785–1819.

Ringquist, Evan J. and Craig E. Emmert (1999) "Judicial Policymaking in Published and Unpublished Decisions: The Case of Environmental Civil Litigation," 52 *Political Research Q.* 7–37.

Rosenberg, David (1984) "The Causal Connection in Mass Exposure Cases: A 'Public Law' Vision of the Tort System," 97 *Harvard Law Rev.* 851–929.

Rosenberg, Gerald N. (1991) *The Hollow Hope: Can the Courts Bring about Social Change?* Chicago: University of Chicago Press.

Ross, H. Laurence and Neil O. Littlefield (1978) "Complaint as a Problem-Solving Device," 12 *Law & Society Rev.* 199–216.

Rowe, Thomas D., Jr. (1984) "Predicting the Effects of Attorney Fee Shifting," 47 *Law & Contemporary Problems* 139–171.

Rubenstein, William B. (2001) "A Transaction Model of Adjudication," 89 *Georgetown Law J.* 371–438.

Rutgers Law Review (1984) "Comment: Dispute Resolution in Prisons: An Overview and Assessment," 36 *Rutgers Law Rev.* 145–78.

Salokar, Rebecca M. (1992) *The Solicitor General: The Politics of Law.* Philadelphia: Temple University Press.

Sanders, Joseph, Betty Rankin-Widgon, Debra Kalmuss, and Mark Chesler (1982) "The Relevance of 'Irrelevant' Testimony: Why Lawyers Use Social Science Experts in School Desegregation Cases," 16 *Law & Society Rev.* 403–28.

Sarat, Austin (1978) "Understanding Trial Courts: A Critique of Social Science Approaches," 61 *Judicature* 318–26.

——— (1976) "Alternatives in Dispute Processing: Litigation in a Small Claims Court," 10 *Law & Society Rev.* 339–75.

Sarat, Austin and Joel B. Grossman (1975) "Courts and Conflict Resolution: Problems in the Mobilization of Adjudication," 69 *American Political ScienceRev.* 1200–1217.

Schacter, Jane S. (1998) "The Confounding Common Law Originalism in Recent Supreme Court Statutory Interpretation: Implications for the Legislative History Debate and Beyond," 51 *Stanford Law Rev.* 1–71.

Shapiro, Martin (1980) "Appeal," 14 *Law & Society Rev.* 629–61.

Sheehan, Reginald S., William Mishler, and Donald R. Songer (1992) "Ideology, Status, and the Differential Success of Direct Parties before the Supreme Court," 86 *American Political Science Rev.* 464–71.

Sheskin, Arlene (1982) "Trial Courts on Trial: Examining Dominant Assumptions." In James A. Cramer ed., *Courts and Judges.* Beverly Hills, Calif.: Sage.

Siegelman, Peter and Joel Waldfogel (1999) "Toward a Taxonomy of Disputes: New Evidence through the Prism of the Priest/Klein Model," 28 *J. of Legal Studies* 101–936.

Simon, William H. (1980) "Homo Psychologicus: Notes on a New Legal Formalism," 32 *Stanford Law Rev.* 487–559.

——— (1978) "The Ideology of Advocacy: Procedural Justice and Professional Ethics," *Wisconsin Law Rev.* 29–144.

Smyth, R. (2000) "The 'Haves' and the 'Have Nots': An Empirical Study of the Rational Actor Party Capability Hypothesis in the High Court 1948–99," 35 *Australian J. of Political Science* 255–74.

Songer, Donald R., A. Kuersten, and E. Kaheny (2000) "Why the Haves Don't Always Come Out Ahead: Repeat Players Meet Amici Curiae for the Disadvantaged," 53 *Political Research Q.* 537–56.

Songer, Donald R. and Reginald S. Sheehan (1992) "Who Wins on Appeal? Upperdogs and Underdogs in the United States Courts of Appeals," 36 *American J. of Political Science* 235–58.

Southern California Law Review (1978) "Comment: Incentives for Warrantor Formation of Informal Dispute Settlement Mechanisms," 52 *Southern California Law Rev.* 235–57.

Stewart, Richard B. (1985) "The Discontents of Legalism: Interest Group Relations in Administrative Regulations," *Wisconsin Law Rev.* 655–86.

Tauber, Steven C. (1998) "On Behalf of the Condemned? The Impact of the

NAACP Legal Defense Fund on Capital Punishment Decision Making in the U.S. Courts of Appeals," 51 *Political Research Q.* 191–219.

Thornburg, Elizabeth G. (1999) "Giving the 'Haves' a Little More: Considering the 1998 Discovery Proposal," 52 *SMU Law Rev.* 229–65.

——— (1991) "Rethinking Work Product," 77 *Virginia Law Rev.* 1515–83.

Tomasic, Roman (1985) "Trend Report: The Sociology of Law," 33 *Current Sociology* 1–267.

——— (1983) "Social Organisation amongst Australian Lawyers," 19 *Australian & New Zealand J. of Sociology* 447–75.

Trubek, David M. and Marc Galanter (1974) "Scholars in Self-Estrangement: Some Reflections on the Crisis of Law and Development Studies in the United States," *Wisconsin Law Rev.* 1062–1102.

Trubek, David M., Austin Sarat, William L. F. Felstiner, Herbert M. Kritzer, and Joel B. Grossman (1983) "The Costs of Ordinary Litigation," 31 *UCLA Law Rev.* 72–127.

Trubek, Louise G. (1999) "Context and Collaboration: Family Law Innovation and Professional Autonomy," 67 *Fordham Law Rev.* 2533–52.

Ulmer, S. Sidney (1985) "Governmental Litigants, Underdogs, and Civil Liberties in the Supreme Court: 1903–1968 Terms," 47 *J. of Politics* 899–909.

Van Koppen, Peter J. and Marijke Malsch (1991) "Defendants and One-Shotters Win After All: Compliance with Court Decisions in Civil Cases," 25 *Law & Society Rev.* 803–20.

Vidmar, Neil (1982) "Justice Motives and Other Psychological Factors in the Development and Resolution of Disputes." In Melvin J. Lerner and Sally C. Lerner, eds., *The Justice Motive in Social Behavior.* New York: Plenum.

Wahlbeck, Paul (1998) "The Development of a Legal Rule: The Federal Common Law of Public Nuisance," 32 *Law & Society Rev.* 613–37.

Wasby, Stephen L. (1984) "How Planned Is 'Planned Litigation'?" *American Bar Foundation Research J.* 83–138.

Wenner, Leslie McSpadden (1983) "Interest Group Litigation and Environmental Policy," 11 *Policy Studies J.* 671–83.

Wheeler, Stanton, Bliss Cartwright, Robert A. Kagan, and Lawrence M. Friedman (1987) "Do the 'Haves' Come Out Ahead? Winning and Losing in State Supreme Courts, 1870–1970," 21 *Law & Society Rev.* 403–45.

Whitford, William C. (1982) "Structuring Consumer Protection: Legislation to Maximize Effectiveness," *Wisconsin Law Rev.* 1018–43.

——— (1979) "A Critique of the Consumer Credit Collection System," *Wisconsin Law Rev.* 1047–1143.

Willis, Joy and Reginald S. Sheehan (1999) "Success in the Australian High Court: Resource Inequality and Outcome." Paper presented at the annual meeting of the Southern Political Science Association, Savannah, Georgia, November 6–9.

Yale Law Journal (1983) "Notes: The Inefficient Common Law," 92 *Yale Law J.* 862–87.

——— (1981) "Notes: In Defense of an Embattled Mode of Advocacy: An Analysis and Justification of Pubic Interest Practice," 90 *Yale Law J.* 1436–57.

——— (1979) "Notes:'Mastering' Intervention in Prisons," 88 *Yale Law J*. 1062–91.
Yarnold, Barbara M. (1995) "Do Courts Respond to the Political Clout of Groups or to Their Superior Litigation Resources/'Repeat Player' Status?" 18 *Justice System J*. 29–42.
——— (1992) *Politics and the Courts: Toward a General Theory of Public Law*. New York: Praeger.
——— (1990) *Refugees without Refuge: Formation and Failed Implementation of U.S. Political Asylum Policy in the 1980s*. Lanham, Md.: University Press of America.
Yngvesson, Barbara (1978) "Law in Preindustrial Societies." In Harry Johnson, ed., *Social System and Legal Process*. San Francisco: Jossey-Bass.
Yngvesson, Barbara and Patricia Hennessey (1975) "Small Claims, Complex Disputes: A Review of the Small Claims Literature," 9 *Law & Society Rev*. 219–74.

Cases Cited

Coleman v. Gulf Ins. Group (41 Cal. 3d 782).
Covenant Mutual Insurance Co. v. Young (179 Cal. App. 3d 318).
In re RHONE-POULENC RORER Inc. (51 F.3d 1293).
Russell v. Acme-Evans Co. (51 F.3d 64).

About the Authors

CATHERINE ALBISTON is an assistant professor at the University of Wisconsin-Madison, having earned a Ph.D. in jurisprudence and social policy at the University of California-Berkeley and a J.D. from Boalt Hall School of Law. She practiced employment law at the Legal Aid Society of San Francisco and served as a judicial clerk for U.S. District Judge Susan Illston. Her research has examined how the legal system, the social institution of work, and other normative systems influence the process of mobilizing employment rights created by the Family and Medical Leave Act. Other research interests include law and social change, law and social institutions, legal and scientific conceptions of evidence, public interest lawyers and organizations, and the relationship between law and social inequality.

YOAV DOTAN is a senior lecturer at the Faculty of Law, Hebrew University, Jerusalem, Israel. His areas of interest are public law, law and politics, and the study of cause lawyers. His current research involves a study of government lawyers and their relationship with cause lawyers and interest groups.

LAUREN B. EDELMAN is professor of law and sociology at the University of California–Berkeley. Her work addresses the relationship of organizations to their legal environments, organizational dispute resolution, and the internal legal cultures of organizations. She is currently a Guggenheim Fellow working on the formation of law in the workplace.

PATRICIA EWICK is associate professor of sociology at Clark University. With Susan Silbey, she wrote *The Common Place of Law: Stories from Everyday Life*. Currently, she studies legal culture and consciousness.

DONALD J. FAROLE JR. was assistant professor in the Department of Political Science at the University of North Carolina at Greensboro from 1996 to 1999. He is the author of *Interest Groups and Judicial Federalism: Orga-*

nizational Litigation in State Judiciaries (1998). His research interests include state judiciaries, judicial federalism, and rights litigation.

MARC GALANTER, formerly editor of the *Law & Society Review* and president of the Law and Society Association, is the John and Rylla Bosshard Professor of Law and South Asian Studies at the University of Wisconsin–Madison and Centennial Professor at the London School of Economics. He has written extensively about lawyers, litigation, and legal culture in the United States and India.

BRIAN J. GLENN earned his doctorate in Politics from Oxford University in January 2003. His research focuses on issues of risk, insurance, and the role of private insurers in the development of the U.S. welfare state. His article, "The Shifting Rhetoric of Insurance Denial" (*Law & Society Review* [2000]) won prizes from the Law & Society Association and the New England Political Science Association.

SUSAN BRODIE HAIRE is associate professor of political science at the University of Georgia. Her current research projects include an analysis of policy implementation in disability law and a study that explores the linkages between appellate briefs and decisions of the U.S. Courts of Appeals. She has authored articles on decision-making in the federal courts and is a coauthor of *Continuity and Change on the United States Courts of Appeals*.

BETH HARRIS is assistant professor in the Department of Politics at Ithaca College. She is examining how legal strategies in defense of the "have nots" influence political dynamics in local and international contexts. Current projects include a book, provisionally entitled *The Power of Poverty Lawyers: Defending a Right-To-Home*, and an article about the collaboration among Palestinian, Israeli, and internationalist activists to resist the Israeli demolition of Palestinian homes in the wake of the Oslo agreements.

KATHRYN HENDLEY is professor of law and political science and director of the Center for Russia, East Europe, and Central Asia at the University of Wisconsin–Madison. She is the author of *Trying to Make Law Matter: Legal Reform and Labor Law in the Soviet Union*. Her current research focuses on judicial behavior in the Russian economic courts and the role of law in managerial decision-making in Russian enterprises.

KARYL A. KINSEY is a social psychologist whose current research interests include performance measurement in government settings and the cognitive biases in citizens' perception of government. Formerly a senior research fellow at the American Bar Foundation, she is currently a senior research analyst with the city of Austin, Texas.

HERBERT M. KRITZER is professor of political science and law at the University of Wisconsin–Madison. He is the author of numerous articles and books on the public perception of law and courts, as well as the organization and practice of law, including *Legal Advocacy: Lawyers and Non-lawyers at Work*; *Let's Make a Deal: Understanding the Negotiation Process in Ordinary Litigation*; and *Justice Brokers: Lawyers and Ordinary Litigation*. He is currently editing *Legal Systems of the World*.

PETER MURRELL is professor of economics and chair of the Academic Council of the IRIS Center at the University of Maryland, College Park. His research interests include the dynamics of economic transition in post-socialist systems, the theory of the economic reform, the effects of privatization, and the role of law in the decisions of the postsocialist enterprise.

RANDI RYTERMAN is an economist with the World Bank, with responsibility for institutional reforms, including legal and judicial reform, in countries in transition. Her research focuses on the microfoundations of macro-economics performance in countries in transition.

REGINALD S. SHEEHAN is professor of political science at Michigan State University. He has published in the leading political science journals, including the *American Political Science Review, American Journal of Political Science*, and *Journal of Politics*. He is also coauthor with Donald R. Songer and Susan Brodie Haire of a book examining decision-making in the U.S. Courts of Appeals entitled *Continuity and Change on the United States Courts of Appeals*.

SUSAN S. SILBEY is professor of sociology and anthropology at the Massachusetts Institute of Technology. Her recent book, *The Common Place of Law: Stories from Everyday Life*, is coauthored with Patricia Ewick. She has conducted research on consumer protection enforcement, lower courts, mediation alternatives to law, and the place of law in popular culture and consciousness. She is past president of the Law and Society Association, former editor of the *Law & Society Review*, and currently at work on a new project on the legal regulation of laboratory science.

DONALD R. SONGER is professor of political science at the University of South Carolina. His current research interests focus on decision-making in appellate courts and include an ongoing study of the U.S. Courts of Appeals and an analysis of decisions by the top appellate courts of seven nations with English common-law roots. He was the principal investigator for the creation of the Appeals Court Data Base Project sponsored by the National Science Foundation and is the senior author of *Continuity and Change on the United States Courts of Appeals*.

LORETTA J. STALANS is associate professor of criminal justice at Loyola University Chicago. Her research interests are in the area of public opinion about justice and domestic violence. She has coauthored with Julian V. Roberts *Public Opinion, Crime and Criminal Justice* and is currently a coauthor with Roberts, Mike Hough, and Dave Indermaur of *Penal Populism and Public Opinion*. For the last four years, she and her colleagues, Magnus Seng and Paul Yarnold, have been evaluating sex offender probation programs in Illinois, examining compliance with treatment and probation.

MARK C. SUCHMAN is associate professor of sociology and law at the University of Wisconsin–Madison. His primary research interests center on the legal environments of organizational activity in general and on the role of law firms in the development of Silicon Valley in particular. He has also written on organizational legitimacy, on the relationship between institutional and ecological models of organizational communities, and on the impact of changing professional structures on corporate litigation ethics. From September 1999 through July 2001, he was on leave from the University of Wisconsin, serving as a Robert Wood Johnson Foundation Scholar in Health Policy Research at Yale University.

Index